BABYLON'S
BURNING

BABYLON'S BURNING

From Punk to Grunge

Clinton Heylin

CONONGATE

Edinburgh • New York • Melbourne

First published in Great Britain in 2007 by
Penguin Books Ltd., London, England.

Printed in the United States of America

FIRST AMERICAN EDITION

ISBN-10: 1-84195-879-4
ISBN-13: 978-1-84195-879-8

Canongate
841 Broadway
New York, NY 10003

Distributed by Publishers Group West

www.groveatlantic.com

07 08 09 10 11 12   10 9 8 7 6 5 4 3 2 1

To Stuart Pearce, a true punk

Contents

Illustrations

The Punk Pandemic 1974–94

Birdman deliver a dark surprise, 1976
Courtesy of Tim Pittman

Television turn on, 1974
Courtesy of Richard Hell

Rocket from the Tombs ponder whether to get haircuts, 1975
Courtesy of Jim Clinefelter

Pere Ubu in the heart of darkness, 1976
Courtesy of Tim Wright

Palm Olive and Ari Up at the Royal Variety Performance, 1977
Courtesy of Palm Olive

Wire reflect on future glory, 1978
Courtesy of Colin Newman

The Minutemen wave a pink flag
© Naomi Peterson

Henry Rollins uncages the beast inside: Black Flag live
© Naomi Peterson

The Meat Puppets as they appear in their high school yearbook
© Naomi Peterson

Hüsker Dü awaiting the AAA
© Naomi Peterson

New York no noise in its Youth
© Naomi Peterson

Mudhoney take on some fluid
© Naomi Peterson

Kurt Cobain, fellow band members, and assorted dummies
© Naomi Peterson

Every effort has been made to contact copyright holders. The publishers are grateful for permission to use the photographs listed above, and will be glad to rectify any errors or omissions brought to their attention.

PROLOGUE:
IN THE BEGINNING
WAS THE WORD . . .

My personal candidate for the 'original punk' was born with the unfortunate Christian names Leslie Conway, at a hospital on the outskirts of San Diego, Ca., in December 1948, a baby boomer if ever. His mother was a zealot of the Witness program – Jehovah, that is; his father a drunk, who disappeared from his son's life before he was ten. As disenfranchised from opportunity as they come, Lester Bangs – for it is he – spent most of his life wanting to go back home, spiritually speaking, and running away from home, in mind and body.

Lester was a searching-for-something shoe-clerk when he realized he had as much to say as the Greil Marcuses and Paul Williamses then defining rock scribedom. After a typically amphetaminized crash course in all things Beat, locked and loaded by paint-stripping, nightly replays of the first two Velvets albums, Bangs decided to send a review of the latter noisefest to that bastion of underground rock-writing, *Rolling Stone*, then based 750 miles away up Highway One to San Francisco. Though his firebrand evangelism was not what owner Jann Wenner believed to be required, Bangs was not dissuaded, and followed up with a review of the MC5's *Kick Out The Jams* that they did run in the 6 April 1969 issue. Perhaps surprisingly, Bangs poured scorn on the Five for coming on like a 'bunch of sixteen-year-old punks on a meth power trip'.

For the next year and a half, Bangs became the *Stone*'s token punk, without ever being given anything feature-length, or let near one of their Holy Cows. Not until he reviewed a Fugs album in the summer of 1970, for fledgling fanzine *Creem*, based near the Michigan home of the Five and The Stooges, did Bangs feel a kinship for the contents surrounding his screeds. When this monthly broadsheet, ostensibly edited by Dave Marsh, not only published a 10,000-word essay purporting to review The Stooges' quintessential *Fun House* at year's end, but ran it *uncut*, Bangs thought to himself, 'This is where I belong.'

Moving to Detroit, Bangs began to write a series of articles that took up where his *Fun House* review left off. Between that two-parter, an 8,000-word obituary for The Velvet Underground and a fictitious 'history' of the Count Fives – all published in a seven-month period ending June 1971 – he articulated an entire aesthetic that was, in all but name, punk-rock.

Even this early, it seemed like the term had always been there, like the background static on a rock & roll radio station. As Lenny Kaye opines, 'Even in the liner-notes to *Nuggets*, I talked about how the word [punk] was in the air. I think it referred to more than attitude, always – Iggy would be a classic example of a punk. [But] all the garagebands had aspects of it.'

By the end of this fruitful period it was also punk-rock in *name*. Dave Marsh used the term to describe a reformed ? & the Mysterians in a May 1971 article (their comeback apparently being 'a landmark exposition of punk-rock'); and in the following issue, Bangs himself referred to how 'punk bands started cropping up who were . . . taking The Yardbirds' sound and reducing it to this kind of goony fuzztone clatter.'

Marsh, even then, seems to have picked up on a word that 'was in the air', and applied it to the kind of Loud Rock he liked. Bangs had a much clearer idea of what it meant to him. That aesthetic – and in Bangs' hands it certainly deserves such a high-falutin' term – was laid out in a coherent if rambling form in Part Two of the *Fun House* piece; or to give it its almost-full title, 'A Program for Mass Liberation in the Form of a Stooges Review'. The section begins with Bangs considering the possibility that some band out there could take all 'the possibilities for controlling the distortions of Who/Yardbirds feedback and fuzz' and make 'a new free music that would combine the rambling adventurousness of the new free jazz with the steady, compelling heartbeat of rock.'

In Part Three, 'The Outline of Cure', he sees The Stooges as the most likely exponents for this free rock because they 'are probably the first name group to actually form before they even knew how to play . . . [and] rock is mainly about . . . asserting yourself way before you know what the fuck you're doing.' For Bangs, the eternal adolescent, rock 'can't grow up – when it does, it turns into something else which may be just as valid but is still very different from the original'. Stumbling around for an archetype on to which he could attach said aesthetic, he had found his beloved Stooges, now a saxed-up quintet.

With this out of his system, Bangs decided to take his schtick and run with it. As he put it some years later, in a memorable piece on the roots of punk in a short-lived rock zine called *New Wave*, 'Over the five years I worked at *Creem* we used our basic love for it to exploit the punk aesthetic and stance in just about every way humanly possible . . . Dave Marsh . . . me, Robot Hull, we all thought we were punks, that having rejected the counterculture as a lot of horseshit now we and Iggy and even Alice Cooper for a while, along with all the other depravo fuckyou rock musicians and fans, had a scene going which was the only possible alternative to all the mainstream garbage going on around us.'

The kind of rock that Bangs sought to eulogize was a rare beast indeed. His kinda punk-rock had all the intuitive innocence of Joe Schmoe's garageband but was capable of stretching out like the Velvets, *Fun House*-era Stooges, Albert Ayler or John Coltrane. It was both a return to the down-to-the-bone simplicity of a 'Woolly Bully' or a 'Louie Louie' *and* a mandate for extemporization along the lines of 'Black To Comm', 'Sister Ray' or Yardbirds-era 'Dazed And Confused'. Natch.

Creem's punk-rock always put punk before rock. Even as an early hybrid of the infant form (and, lest we forget, rock was itself barely a bairn when *Sgt Pepper* capitalized it), punk rock began on the page not in the clubs, only picking up its Fender and going in search of those elusive three chords afterwards. Those who defined it initially – i.e. between 1970 and 1975 – did so with a pen, not a guitar. Folk-rock (which, ironically, predates rock as a journalistic term), country-rock, jazz-rock and even frat-rock had recognizable exponents on to which they could latch, becoming a convenient catch-all. Punk-rock – in the period before it was defined as the Ramones, the Sex Pistols, The Clash, and/or anyone directly inspired by one or more of them – was an attitude of mind, not tied to a specific sound (or tempo).

Of course, as long as punk-rock remained at the behest of this small band of critics, ideologues and preservers of a 'purer' rock & roll heritage, it was no more real than Ireland's fabled communitarian past, for which members of the Gaelic League, and later on, Sinn Fein, were prepared to lay down their lives in the first quarter of the twentieth century. Like most revolutionaries, what Bangs and his *Creem* brethren were attempting to restore was an idealized state – a prelapsarian era in rock & roll when the rules of commerce did not apply.

Not surprisingly, the result was an extraordinarily eclectic set of keepers of the flame championed in the pages of *Creem* (and, by the mid-seventies, *NME* as well). Beefheart and The Fugs were as much a part of the credo as the Kingsmen and the Sonics. And the writers in *Creem* in the first half of the seventies, when rock seemed to be sinking 'neath its own weightiness, provided the only real alternative. As Charlotte Pressler, wife to Peter Laughner, wrote in her seminal essay, 'Those Were Different Times', '[Writers in] *Creem* . . . then . . . were fresh and exciting. They were writing about music the other magazines ignored; printing articles on the Velvets and The Stooges; blowing away in a deliberately snotty-adolescent way the solemn jive of the counterculture; pushing for the new, the experimental, the obscure.'

Unlike many a garageband 45, *Creem* also had distribution. In the early seventies, transporting records around the world was a chore. A rock magazine was altogether easier to get airborne and, like as not, usually contained something worthwhile. Pre-internet, pre-cheap international calls, pre-worldwide networks of like-minded souls; the currency on which the likes of *Creem* traded was the kudos it applied to something potentially rare and exotic – *real* rock music, the way it was.

And their quest for the most atonal, cacophonous, plain-incompetent exponents of the form was allowed to interact with a certain experimentalism. That they were pushing an agenda – even when articles weren't called 'A Program for Mass Liberation' – was never in doubt. Aspirational, in the best sense of the word, Bangs and the likes of Ben Edmonds, Robert Hull and Richard Meltzer were advocates for a kind of rock music that they hoped – by sheer exercise of will – might yet (re)form.

Though they found unwitting converts in places as far-flung as Sydney, Brisbane, Cleveland and Manchester, the first real sign that they were getting through to some folks was when an English would-be rock critic turned up at the *Creem* office in the spring of 1973, hoping to catch some of the sparks that still flew from Bangs. Nick Kent had already started writing for the *New Musical Express*, an English music weekly that was already closing in on its more successful rival, *Melody Maker*. He hoped he might find a kind of inspiration from this unkempt guru.

Having already met the likes of Beefheart and Iggy Pop in a hectic year as cub reporter for the failing English underground paper, *Frendz*, by 1973 Kent was becoming jaded. As he says, 'Everything . . . was a bit lesser in my eyes.' After the MC5, The Stooges, Roxy Music, *Ziggy*-era Bowie and *Transformer*-era Lou had made London a fulcrum for fab folk through 1972, they had unceremoniously decamped to Max's Kansas, New York. Kent thought Bangs might be the cure-all.

Nick Kent: I went over [to Detroit] basically to hang out with [Lester] and talk to him and find out how he did what he did, 'cause that's what you do . . . What I wanted to do was find out [about] the *Creem* environment, 'cause *Creem* was happening. The *NME* [had] Charlie Murray, [and] Ian MacDonald was already there, so there was already talent in place but I felt we needed that kind of *Creem* irreverence and the sharpness. Bangs' thing was great – he was really on his top form then. So I spent two months on and off at the *Creem* 'home'. Dave Marsh was living there as well ... It was Bangs, Marsh and Ben Edmonds. Bangs really liked to overindulge in alcohol and Quaaludes, and lived in a complete pigsty. The worst thing was the smell of stale beer. But he had the best hi-fi. It was intense. [When he was writing] the door was locked. You could hear him pounding away on his typewriter, and several hours later he'd open the door very dramatically, smoke would pour out and he'd look completely burnt out and rattled ... [Whereas] Marsh was like an old woman, 'Oh Lester, that's your second beer of the day.' ... As a youth I had read avidly Jack Kerouac's *On The Road*; and now I was in America with an ersatz Neal Cassady in Bangs. We'd go over to Canada because he had a girlfriend in Canada, and he was so drunk most of the time, he always needed a passenger and poor old Ben was fed up constantly having to drive from Birmingham, Michigan to Canada – it was a three hours' drive – but ... when Bangs was in a good mood and he'd start talking, you were in this Kerouac thing. I was living it.

At the time, Kent confined himself to pills 'n' Pils. The other guy who sought Bangs out as mentor/guru in 1973–4 was further down the road. Peter Laughner was already something Kent and Bangs longed to be, a hugely talented musician, but knew way too much about death-wish aspects of the rock & roll nightmare. As Bangs typified their relationship in those years, they had 'met ... via what was to be the first of many three a.m. phone calls. I had been listening to *White Light/White Heat* at the time; he told me he was listening to *Berlin*. It was the kind of thing on which long friendships were born.'

Also writing for *Creem* by now was published poetess, Patti Smith, who had already co-written a play with Sam Shepard, in which she admitted that, 'Any great motherfucker rock 'n' roll song can raise me higher than all of Revelations.' Her scribblings became ever more lyrical, as the magazine became part training-ground for her emergence as a real-deal rock & roller. When she wrote her 'final' piece for the magazine in July 1975, she had decided to 'refuse to believe Hendrix had the last possessed hand / that Joplin had the last drunken throat / that Morrison had the last enlightened mind.'

It seemed like the line separating scribe from songwriter was fast disappearing. Indeed, before Bangs reached his Darvon-induced death in 1982 both he and Kent would attempt to make records of their own, which simply served to reinforce the axiom: to each his own. Even though the pair played out their musical apprenticeship in the course of punk, formulating ideas in scrappy jams and rehearsals with members of Pere Ubu and the Voidoids (in the former's case), and the Sex Pistols and The Damned (in the latter's), it was their critical contributions that provided a punk aesthetic in instalments. Others would have to run with it.

As of September 1975, both Bangs and Kent were regular contributors to the new-look *NME*, the Bible for all English (and certain important non-English) would-be punks. The weekly had suffered a destructive, prolonged strike in the winter of 1974, but had returned all the stronger for it. As Banshee Steve Severin points out, 'When [the *NME*] came back, it seemed to have this new critique that I'd never read before. It wasn't like *Disc* or *Record Mirror*, which was press releases tarted up. This was actually people saying what they liked and what they didn't, and the writing had an intelligence I hadn't read before about rock music.'

With hindsight, 'this new critique' was along lines laid down by Bangs and his *Creem* cohorts back in 1970–71. But *Creem* remained an underground documenter of Rock, even as it went for glossy full-colour covers, abandoning its newspaper origins, while the *New Musical Express* was an (increasingly) mainstream magazine, read by a generation of music fans, not merely the already informed. And so while *Creem* championed the New York CBGB's scene – even as it remained underground – the *NME* (and the equally influential, if less-read *Sounds*) championed English punk, and ensured it stood a chance in the mainstream it despised and denigrated.

By the time England was ripe for this revolution, *Creem* had long ceased to expound the aesthetic. Bangs, like Karl Marx before him, had gone where he thought the revolution might catalyze. In his case, this was New York; for Marx, it was London. Both got the conditions for revolution right, but the location of its arch-exponents wrong. Bangs found the free-form exponents he craved in New York, but minus that all-important ramalam rubicon, while Marx envisioned a Britain swept along on a socialist tide.

It took finger-on-pulse punk John Lydon to recognize the right political system for a country so disaffected. Anarchy in the UK was his vision, and for a while it seemed like he might yet succeed where Marx failed – making the disaffected rise up alongside a wave of one-chord wonders. Rotten's own Program for Mass Liberation went something like this: 'Right, here we go now, a sociology lecture, with a bit of psychology, a bit of neurology. A bit of fuckology. No fun . . .'

Clinton Heylin
November 2006

PART ONE

1.1
FUCK ROCK & ROLL
(I'D RATHER SUMMARIZE
A BOOK)
1971-75

Each of the bands at CBGB was like a little idea. It wasn't that kind of style of punk rock that happened when England took over. Here it was all like little art projects . . . There was no one dominant thing.

— Lenny Kaye, quoted by Roman Kozak in *This Ain't No Disco: The Story of CBGB*, Faber, 1988

In the winter of 1974, there was precious little sign that Bangs' program was taking hold, even in the havens of alternative rock that had served the likes of the Velvets and The Stooges so well – Detroit, Cleveland, Boston and New York. As of 9 February 1974, even those great white hopes Iggy and The Stooges were no more. Their final, homecoming gig – captured on *Metallic K.O.* – ended in the usual hail of feedback, broken bottles and heckling of the audience.

By this juncture, The Stooges had reverted to type. Ever since the commercial failure of *Raw Power*, the band's musicianship had become largely secondary. Iggy's dementia had become what people came to see; much as they had in the pre-Elektra days. Yet because that final show was recorded, and would be released into the world at the tipping point of punk – thanks to Nick Kent passing a cassette of the show to Marc Zermati at Skydog Records – *Metallic K.O.* would become an important addition to the small canon of protopunk 'classics', even though Giovanni Dadomo's *Sounds* review pointed out that 'by any normal criteria [it] is one hell of a long way from being a good rock 'n' roll record'.

Iggy had perhaps achieved an ambition of sorts; though only if, as Bangs once suggested, he 'wanted to have the most fucked-up band in history so as to externalize his own inner turmoil'. It might have made more sense for Skydog to have called the album *The Art Of Confrontation*. But no one had had the wit to record The Stooges live when Iggy was the consummate tightrope walker, riding the crowd through every facet of performance, from comedy to confrontation.

There had been a time when his performances spanned that gamut. But that had been a hundred years ago. The Stooges' first New York concert, at the Brooklyn Academy of Music [sic], in 1969, made a convert of Alan Vega, who tends to remember it in prismatic shards: 'This . . . was the real deal. Iggy was jumping into the audience, flying into them. The artist/audience relationship was broken down, as you were now part of the whole act . . . Iggy was bleeding, cut up to shit. Coupla times he was comin' right at me, y'know? He never got to me, he stopped somewhere else. But he puts you in a position of "Oh shit – whatamigonna do now?" Somebody who was running the sound system had the genius to put on a Bach Brandenburg Concerto . . . right after Iggy and the band walked off to broken instruments, broken bodies, and just feedback.'

Vega was one of the chosen few that found such performances transformative; and alone in taking the elements of The Stooges (and the Velvets) that did not involve rock and casting them anew, to make 'a new free music that . . . combine[d] the rambling adventurousness of the new free jazz'. The sonic duo he formed with Martin Rev would stretch this gossamer-thin strand of performance-art far enough to carry over to punk-proper. These guys actually called themselves punks back then.

Alan Vega: [Our first gig] was at the end of 1970, at a thing called the Punk Best, this was before the word punk was ever used . . . in a loft in a place in Broadway, and we had a riot. At that gig Marty Rev . . . actually played drums. I had a trumpet and a guitar and we had a guitar player and we just played noise, we didn't have songs.

Five months later they were calling one of their art-performances a 'punk-rock masque', pre-Marsh, pre-*Nuggets*. To Rev and Vega, though, punk-rock meant anti-rock, not Loud Rock. Theirs was a deconstruction of the music of their youth, and a deliberate one. As Vega says, 'The sixties thing after a while was so ridiculous and monotonous . . . so Marty and I [decided] the first thing that has to go is the drums, and the next thing was the lead guitar. Enough of these guitar solos and drum solos!' What was left in – at least initially – was just what the name Suicide suggested, noise sans songs.

Martin Rev: [In the early days] we had no space between songs, we would run one into another. There would be a wall of sound, the riff would be in there, but there was so much feedback that only we could hear the riff.

The essential difference between early Suicide and latterday Stooges was that Alan and Martin performed their caco-symphonies in the art spaces – lofts and the like – that peppered New York's downtown. As

Alan Vega pointed out to an English journalist in 1978, '[When] we used to come out ... there was nothin' around. There wasn't any Ramones and there wasn't any, uh, Sex Pistols. There wasn't any kinda sound that had any kinda theatricality [or] drama about it. We came outta nowhere and people were *lost*, man.' Suicide were so far underground at this juncture that it is perhaps not surprising that their anti-rock ideas should be adopted on the other side of the world first.

For now, Suicide found the *expectation* of the rock spectacle was missing from these early performances. As long as they played New York art spaces, their audience was destined to remain thoroughly jaded. And so began a series of memorable appearances at the Mercers Arts Center, culminating in a coming-out ball on New Year's Eve 1972, across the hall from The New York Dolls and the Modern Lovers, where they embraced a new circle of constant confrontation. That, after all, is what Suicide was all about. As Chris Stein states, 'Alan really used to get people stirred up. Suicide were one of the first components of a punk sensibility – the antagonism with the audience.'

By 1973, they had got as far as the upstairs room at Max's. Record producer Craig Leon saw them there when 'there were six people in the audience. Here was this guy doing James Brown ... beating himself with chains and everybody was walking out. And I said, "Well, this is definitely where it's at."' The regular habitués of the 'old' Max's were used to seeing Iggy roll in some broken glass, but Suicide were *something else*.

When Mercers collapsed – quite literally – and Max's changed hands (and its booking policy) in the winter of 1974, Suicide found themselves outside again. Their solution was to find a nice, comfortable little space – and make it a most uncomfortable place to be. They seemed to have lucked out when they stumbled on the Townhouse Theatre. Essentially a screening room that housed a hundred souls at best, they made their debut there in January 1974. But even in this controlled environment, few folk were prepared to come see Vega beat himself up in the name of art.

Among the brave, though, were two struggling poets looking for a venue to unveil their own art-statement, a four-piece rock band who could not play, but felt they had something to say. Richard Meyers and Tom Miller had already reinvented themselves in print as Theresa Stern, a feminine alter-ego. Now they became Richard Hell and Tom Verlaine. The band they were preparing to take out of storage went by the name of Television.

Hell and Verlaine had been confidants since before coming to New York, having run away together from a Kentucky 'country-club reform school' in 1969. Caught and sent home, they still both made it to New York, albeit separately, their plan to become poets intact. Unfortunately, New York had other plans. Verlaine found that New York's multi-tiered art scene was full of 'so-called painters and so-called poets [that were] so snotty . . . Their whole writing is like, "I woke up and I had a cup of coffee," which is an attitude . . . [that] gets boring very quick.' Hell just wanted to make a difference.

Richard Hell: I was twenty at the time and it felt very futile. I wanted to shake up the world. I wanted to make noise, but nobody reads. I could identify with that. I wanted to be true to my heroes, but I could see reading could be very boring if you weren't conditioned to enjoy it . . . and I got to feel that was a dead end. About 1972–3 [Tom and I] decided we were going to make a band. I was real inspired by the attitude of The New York Dolls and The Stooges. We were both big fans of The Velvet Underground . . . The [essential] idea was 'I don't care'. That was one of the first songs we wrote, and that was really the root of the idea of the blank generation. [1988]

Verlaine's own epiphany came not through listening to the Dolls or The Stooges, but from the source of *their* wellspring: 'A Hare Krishna kid came up to me in the street and . . . he had this little box of 45s, and he said, "You wanna buy these?" . . . And this box was "All of the Day and All of the Night", "For Your Love", five Beatles [singles] and a bunch of other singles . . . The energy of these records was great. They were [all] rhythm-guitar orientated songs . . . The rhythm guitar was way out front . . . I thought, "That's where the excitement comes from."'

Hell and Verlaine's first attempt to make a difference was forestalled by an insuperable lack of anyone else willing to play 'way out front' rhythm guitar (the unmusical Hell having elected to play bass). The Neon Boys, as they were called at this time, never got beyond the rehearsal stage, though in the winter of 1973 they recorded a set of six demos. Even these vacuum-sealed songs were an attempt at something edgy, with pithy song titles like 'Love Comes In Spurts' and 'If I Hadn't Lost My Head, I Wouldn't Have Lost My Hat' (aka 'Poor Circulation') and trebly, ringing guitars. But they hadn't quite dug to 'the root of the idea of the blank generation'. When their drumming buddy Billy Ficca took off for Boston in the early spring of 1973, the poetical pair put their experiment on the back burner.

By the time Ficca returned from his Boston blues-band experience, at the end of 1973, Hell and Verlaine had made little progress. Verlaine had been mostly trying to make a small-time name for himself as a Village 'folkie', playing the likes of 'Venus De Milo' and a much-abbreviated 'Marquee Moon' to bemused punters at Reno Sweeney's. After one such solo performance, Verlaine was introduced to a blond boyfriend of Terry Ork, whose loft had provided the Neon Boys with a place to rehearse in.

Richard Lloyd knew almost no one in New York, being fresh from the west, and so had little context in which to judge the band they now reassembled. Verlaine himself states, 'I had a lot of reservations about it actually.' Richard Hell, though, felt that they were working along the right lines, which to him meant 'short, hard, compelling and driving music.'

Richard Hell: They were frantic songs . . . Real unlike what Television became after I left . . . As great as the guitar playing is on *Marquee Moon*, the original band was more to the point . . . It was a return to the values of the Kingsmen and the Sonics and Them and The Velvet Underground. It still had this really . . . ecstatic, explosive guitar . . . but it was more driving and crazed.

Hell and Verlaine probably qualified as the most erudite pair of punks ever. One of the songs they worked up in those early rehearsals was called simply 'Fuck Rock & Roll (I'd Rather Read A Book)', by which – Hell patiently explains – 'I meant fuck the mythology [of rock & roll].' It was, quite simply, the first rock song (sic) to challenge the notion that rock & roll's capacity to communicate had a greater validity than any other means of communication; and as such was one of a number of songs in the nascent Television set which made a statement at odds with rock's own autocratic message.

Likewise, 'Blank Generation' was no mere up-date to 'My Generation', but a clarion-call to 'every hung-up person in the whole wide universe' to fill in the blank/s to their own satisfaction, to reinvent one's self afresh. 'I Don't Care', in its original guise, led Hell to suggest that all three frontmen sing a verse each; expressing some of the things that didn't matter to them. These were radical ideas to introduce into rock's slipstream in 1974. If early Verlaine songs like 'One On Top Of Another', '(You're So) Hard On Love', '(Looking At You)(I Get A)

Double Exposure', and '(The Arms Of) Venus De Milo' were not as didactic as Hell's, they bore equally unexpected titles (and themes).

But Television remained little more than a sketchbook of ideas from Tom and Dick before they made their debut at the Townhouse Theatre on 2 March 1974. Backed by a bank of television screens, they clung to their instruments like life rafts, debuting some of the most untogether rock NY had seen since the Dolls learnt to tune their instruments. Verlaine recalls thinking to himself, 'We've got to rehearse a lot more. This sounds horrible.'

And yet Television played their second show before the month was out, at a bikers' bar on the Bowery, incongruously named CBGB's (Country, Blue Grass & Blues). Verlaine and Lloyd had come across the owner of the bar, Hilly Kristal, putting up a sign proclaiming its new name, and promptly assured him that they played just those types of music. A sceptical Kristal was finally persuaded to book them. After pasting up some DIY handbills around the neighbourhood and putting a small ad in the *Village Voice*, Lloyd remembers, 'We started playing at CBGB. By God, we drew enough people and Terry Ork bought enough drinks by himself to set the place up. Hilly was making money.' Kristal didn't quite know what to make of it, but he got a charge from the sheer enthusiasm of the band and their still-tiny audience.

Hilly Kristal: I thought it was very crude music. It was not that it was strange, but it was hard to take. It was very loud and abrasive. It was not what I liked in music. But what I liked was that these people were really into it. They were very sincere and they really believed in themselves. They had a real desire to express themselves. In fact, I think of that as the beginning of new wave . . . because they were not musicians . . . and that's why it started getting into a different area from what was happening in other places.

The fact that Television 'were not musicians' was a statement in itself. As Hell avers, 'The immediate publicity around Television always mentioned, and we encouraged it, that I'd just picked up a bass six months before.' By the time they made their first, shatteringly dexterous album, two and a half years later, Television were the most musical band America had produced in a decade. But that would be a lifetime away. This bunch of brats knew they were ragged but right; and their demeanour alone demanded the audience went along with them. Even those who *could* play guitar were impressed.

Bob Quine: [Terry] Ork said, 'Come see this band Television.' . . . And I was fairly well stunned by it. When I saw them I said, 'There's definitely a place for me.' They were completely unprofessional. They were out of tune at all times. They were breaking strings tuning up, [with] about four minutes between each song. An amp would blow up! . . . [Yet] the thing that surprised me most was [not] how unprofessional they were, [but] how well accepted by everybody in the club.

One thing that immediately set Television apart – aside from their quirky songs and patent nerve – was their unique look. As Verlaine notes, 'There was a deliberate thing about having short hair. I remember thinking before we do a gig, we gotta get haircuts' – and the effect was profound – 'I guess we looked real different. Everyone else had real glamorous clothes on, and we had torn shirts and safety pins.' Later on, Verlaine would become uncomfortable with any suggestion that the look was as important as the sound, insisting, 'We weren't out to make a point, [or] to represent anything.' Early photos of the band, though, suggest it was carefully choreographed. And Hell certainly exuded an air of individuality.

Richard Hell: One thing I wanted to bring back to rock & roll was the knowledge that you invent yourself. That's why I changed my name, why I did all the clothing style things, haircut, everything.

Hell would subsequently suggest that there *was* always some kinda master plan, telling *Sounds* in 1977, 'I consciously set out to make it possible for there to be a trend . . . It was designed to get a particular message across . . . but I felt so apart from everything I didn't think it was too likely.' Those who saw the band in that first year, when they were still crossing *Nuggets* with *Five Live Yardbirds*, opening with 13th Floor Elevators' 'Fire Engine' and closing with Count Five's 'Psychotic Reaction', talk animatedly about their early aesthetic, which was so different from what it (and they) became.

Roy Trakin, later editor of *New York Rocker*, enthused, 'They looked so cool onstage, the juxtaposition between Richard Hell's sort of chaos and Verlaine's neurotic uptightness, and the interchanges between Lloyd and Verlaine on guitar, just their styles and the way they meshed.' Chris Stein also describes the Hell-Verlaine version of the band as 'really exciting. Even Richard's own performance was different from what he was known for in later years. He really used to do this Townshend thing, a whole series of leaps and bounds across the stage. It was more dynamic. Verlaine was on the end and Lloyd was in the middle . . . It was a subtle [visual] thing.'

Stein's own band, Blondie, regularly supported Television throughout this initial era, so he had ample opportunity to observe. Indeed, the prototype Blondie, still called the Stillettoes, made their first appearance at CBGB's barely a month after Television's debut. In the era of personal contacts, all it took was a personal referral.

Chris Stein: With the Stillettoes and Television, Hell was going out with Elda – one of the Stillettoes – and she said [to us], 'Oh, I heard this bunch of guys, and they dress like old men, and they're very funny, and they play in this weird bar downtown.' We asked them where they were playing, and they said CBGB's.

The first Television/Stillettoes CBGB's bills occupied a series of Sundays in May 1974 (advertised on further handbills, with positive endorsements from the likes of David Bowie, Patti Smith and Danny Fields). The Stillettoes at this point were a throwback to the days of Mercers, three girls fronting a ragged garageband, blending covers of rock classics with demi-monde pastiches thereof.

Stein and his girlfriend, Debbie Harry, though, quickly realized the way the wind was blowing. Within a month or two they had dumped those elements that suggested a trash-Supremes, i.e. Elda Gentile and her coloured friend Amanda, and enlisted two other eye-candyish ladies, Tish and Snooky (who later formed the Sic Fucks). The new pair were strictly backing singers, albeit striking ones. Chris and Debbie redubbed themselves Angel and the Snakes (for a single gig), and then Blondie, putting Debbie centre stage. They debuted in this new guise at the now-buzzing Bowery bar in August '74.

In these early days, what Blondie had most in common with Television was an equally intrinsic ineptitude and an unexpectedly orthodox cover of 'Venus De Milo'. Alan Betrock, a collector of rock ephemera and publisher of sorts, who would record their first demos, recalled how they 'just couldn't play live. They'd stop in the middle of a song and start over again, the amps would go out, the guitar would go out, strings would break and they wouldn't have extra ones.' Tish and Snooky put a kinder spin on it, suggesting that the early Blondie 'had a completely different sound [from later on]. There wasn't really anything wild, but it was raw. It wasn't fast and loud like the Ramones. It was kind of funny the way we fit in, but didn't fit in, at the time.'

In this hierarchy of hopelessness, the early Ramones trashed all comers. A three-piece Ramones had made their live debut the night before Television's CBGB debut, at a loft/rehearsal studio owned by band manager Thomas Erdelyi. Erdelyi had invited the band – fronted by Dee Dee Ramone (aka Douglas Colvin) on bass/vocals, with Johnny Ramone (né Cummings) on guitar, and the gangly Joey (né Jeffrey Hyman) on drums – to the studio sometime that winter, having shared a previous musical association with Johnny. Erdelyi remembers that, 'They were terrible. It was the worst thing I've ever heard. But . . . they had something.'

The trio were unfazed by Tommy's blunt assessment, and convinced him to give them rehearsal space to work up a twenty-minute set of originals before inviting thirty or so wary souls to his Performance Studio. Things had not greatly improved. By Johnny's own admission, they were still 'terrible. Dee Dee was so nervous he stepped on his bass guitar and broke its neck.'

Whatever they had, it was not something which seemed to work in a live situation. The decision was made to demote Dee Dee to bass, put Joey upfront and recruit a new drummer. But Tommy recalls that every drummer they auditioned was 'from the Carmine Appice School of drumming . . . It just didn't mesh. Y'know, "Give me a $\frac{4}{4}$." "A what?"' In the end, Tommy resolved to show auditionees what they wanted – and found himself recruited instead, giving the Ramones a whole new rear suspension.

Tommy Ramone: Actually, as soon as I started playing drums, it really clicked. The combination of John's guitar playing and the drumming I was doing really did click right away. Within a month we were playing CBGB, and the sound developed from there. [PSF]

In fact, five long months separate the only 'trio' gig from their CBGB debut. In that time, the boys in the band decided to check out the competition, and found a base and a basis for proceeding. Dee Dee gave the credit to Tom Verlaine, for being 'the person who changed everything . . . At CBGB Television were really special and created a real atmosphere of freedom. [But] you couldn't imagine anyone else doing what they were doing.' They proved that something this left-field was possible, and could attract an audience. The Ramones had found a necessary alternative to the fading glam scene, even if at least one band member begrudged wearing the dressed-down uniform Johnny imposed almost immediately.

Dee Dee Ramone: We were glamorous when we started, almost like a glitter group. A lot of times, Joey would wear rubber clothes, and John would wear vinyl clothes or silver pants. We used to look great, but then we fell into the leather-jacket-and-ripped-up-jeans thing. I felt like a slob.

Tommy had the wit to get the scoop on the club from Chris Stein, whom he knew from Mercers: 'I hear you're playing at this weird bar. What's that [about]?' He also took as much from Television as his fellow Ramone: 'When I saw Television, who weren't that much more proficient musically but . . . had interesting ideas, it gelled that this was exciting and something new.'

The Ramones, though, weren't about to start doing their own version of 'Venus De Milo'. Actually, they couldn't. Back in 1973, Dee Dee had auditioned for Television as bassist, and had shown an ignorance of the basics that made even Hell appear proficient. In the Ramones, he was no longer alone. As he once recalled, 'We started trying to figure out songs from records – and we couldn't.' The radical simplicity of the Ramones stemmed from an underlying ineptitude.

Tommy Ramone: Right from the start there were no solos and it had a unique sound, basically because the roots of it weren't from the current music scene . . . It was absurd. It was [also] original. Especially in those days. It was so raw. Television . . . were also breaking away from the rock & roll look . . . but musically they were totally different.

Early eyewitnesses were generally nonplussed by the peculiar dynamic of a band where everybody played their own rhythm track, middle-eights were for pussies, and guitar solos were beyond the pale. But some got it straightaway. Richard Hell sees them as, 'A great combination of stripping rock & roll to its essence – in a cartoon-like way, which was really calculated to succeed, like Andy Warhol or something – [and at the same time] pure real street emotion and narrative.' They were also fast. Thirty years of bands who think rock is some kind of race have made them sound less so, but back then the Ramones sounded a mile a minute, and their sets a twenty–six–minute marathon. This happy accident was bound to acquire a grand design.

Tommy Ramone: The actual speed of the songs came from Johnny. The brevity of the songs – we were looking for short songs, because we wanted to bring back the original feel of rock & roll, which by the seventies had disappeared . . . We wanted to bring back that 'whomp bop-a-lua' . . . And of course short songs played fast become very short. [PSF]

As the conceptualist and spokesman for the group, Tommy was later obliged to play down the fortuitous nature of the collision of styles. As he told the *NME*, 'People thought *everything* [my italics] was an accident. [Like] these four morons are really cute and they're doing something really *neat*, but obviously it's all an accident. First of all, it wasn't four morons; second of all, none of it was an accident; and third of all, it's four talented people who know what they like and who know what they're doing.' Yet it took some time for the band to iron out the glitches, even with these 'short songs played fast'. Gary Valentine, a member of Blondie, the Ramones' perennial gig-partners, gave a condensed version of those early shows in his recent memoir of those times:

Most of their songs clocked in at under two minutes, and they invariably started with Dee Dee chanting '1–2–3–4' before the wash of distorted guitar, thudding bass and clockwork drums came on. I never figured out if Dee Dee's mantra was just part of the act or if they really needed it to start in time. If they did, it didn't always work. Half of the time they'd start, stop, and then Dee Dee would shout 'One, two, three, four' again, only to stop again. Johnny's guitar was so loud that it would feed back as soon as they stopped playing. Most of the time Dee Dee's bass was out of tune. He played it like a jackhammer, drilling 'duh-duh-duh-duh-duh-duh-duh-duh' about half a step sharp or flat of Johnny's wall of sound. Joey['s] . . . terse staccato vocals barely [broke] through the waterfall of Johnny's guitar. Tommy's drums were the most stable thing about the act.

Tommy readily admits that, 'in the early days Dee Dee would shout 1–2–3–4 and *everybody* would start playing a different song. Then we'd throw the instruments around and walk off.' But the Ramones found their lack of chops no more of a hindrance than their fellow biker-bar bands. When they first attracted a little local publicity, it was as much to celebrate their incongruity as to champion such a pared-down aesthetic. Alan Betrock wrote one of the first accounts in the *Soho Weekly News* in the summer of 1975:

Each tune is built on a few chopping, grinding chords, heavily churned out by Johnny Ramone, [while] Dee Dee and Tommy Ramone form this unified rhythm section which seems devoted to capturing the three best riffs in rock and utilizing them over and over again. [And] Joey Ramone . . . tries to get the lyrics out over the surge, while at the same time pushing his specs back on to his face.

By the winter of 1975, the Ramones, Television and Blondie were dividing up weekend residencies at CBGB's, while venturing as far afield as Club 82, the notorious transvestite bar that the Dolls had once played in full drag (for the one and only time). For the marginally more proficient Television there was also Max's, where they had shared a six-day residency with New York's one rock-poetess of note, Patti Smith, at the end of August, less than six months after their shaky debut.

A tape exists of one of those shows, and it would be fair to say that however much Television had come on as a combo, their sets still teetered on the verge of collapse every minute spent onstage. Island A&R man Richard Williams caught a show at around this time, and in his *Melody Maker* column recollected, 'four musicians diffident but defiant in the face of a tiny audience and troublesome electronics. That defiance impressed me immediately, particularly when the equipment failed utterly in the middle of an already shaky ballad . . . and Verlaine fought through the song as though his life depended on it. Otherwise the playing was awfully rickety, almost amateurish.'

Patti Smith's act was only marginally less rickety, and not a lot more structured, having evolved from a year's worth* of augmented poetry readings. In 1973 she started bringing out guitarist Lenny Kaye for the second half. According to Chris Stein, she 'just sorta made fun of him . . . He was just bashing these chords out and drowning her out and she abused him. It was almost a comedy routine that they did. She was just poking fun at the whole rock & roll syndrome.' But the pair had a game plan, and when they added the classically trained Richard Sohl on piano,

---

* Though Smith and Kaye first played together in February 1971, they did not resume their partnership until the fall of 1973. In the interim, Smith tried out other accompanists, including the blues-guitarist and rock critic, Tony Glover.

the 'comedy routine' crawled out the window, as the lyrical ramblings began to resemble songs.

Lenny Kaye: I remember Artie or Happy [Traum] seemed really mad at us one day, talking about, 'What do you know about your three chords?' But we just did our thing, and I'm not sure people really understood what we were doing but we were having a good time doing it . . . We'd just get on these rhythmic moves – we called them fields – where we just kinda like rode around in them. And a lot of our early songs, that's all they were. 'Free Money' was just those chords repeated over and over again; and over the course of playing them for six months you start hitting moves at the same time in each song. 'Land Of A Thousand Dances', 'Gloria' certainly, they weren't really songs, but over the course of performing them we would get into things that . . . were [then] incorporated into the song [itself].

At Max's that August, Patti Smith brought her little performance-art/poetry act into the rock arena. Just playing Max's was indication of an intent. But she also now had songs like 'Kubla Khan' and 'Land'. Bringing along her favourite local band to share the stage was not mere altruism either. Television's Tom Verlaine, described by Patti in a contemporary article as 'a languid boy with the confused grace of a child in paradise', was her new paramour and – or so she hoped – musical collaborator. Playing lead guitar on one side of her new, independently financed single, 'Hey Joe', he was also helping her write the likes of 'Break It Up', 'Space Monkey' and 'We Three', a triad of tonal poems born of their tryst.

One unexpected by-product of their relationship was that Smith's pull as a personality and lighter-of-the-way began to take Television in a less urgent direction. Having rhapsodized about their 'lyrics . . . as suggestive as a horny boy at the drive-in' and the fact that 'they play undulating rhythm like ocean . . . [and] pissed-off psychotic reaction' in pieces for *Soho Weekly* and *Rock Scene*, the lady organized for the Patti Smith Group and Television to share a two-month residency at CBGB's in the winter of 1975 that resulted in Hell quitting Television.

Television now began taking off in a more improvisatory direction akin to the long, lyrical journeys through 'Land' and 'Birdland' which the PSG were now traversing; with Verlaine's guitar providing its own wordless lyricism. Indeed, an eleven-minute rendition of the previously terse 'Hard On Love' and the increasingly elastic 'Marquee Moon', which had been debuted at Max's in its original five-minute frame, provided fair notice of where they were going – 'the rambling adventurousness of the new free jazz'.

Hell, on the other hand, had now got the scene he had long wanted, and was determined to talk it up as much as he could. Ostensibly plugging the Ramones in *Hit Parader*, he described them as 'among the original five or six groups drawn to CBGB in New York by Television's "success" there'; before describing the scene itself as 'the most exciting thing happening in rock music today and probably for the next few years. The ambition level is staggering.' What Hell did not realize was that Television's evolution would ensure that the pivotal role of these scene-forgers would soon be overlooked.

Lenny Kaye: [Of] all the CBGB's bands, which were referred to as punk bands, I would say that . . . the Ramones came to embody the template, but previous to that it was such a broad description; [one that] applied [first] to Television, [but also] to a certain idea of trash-culture, a certain sense of outsiderness, a certain sense of the bizarro universe where everything is somewhat opposite from what is previously considered laudable . . . [The New York bands] were all kinda weird takes on life, slightly intellectual and artistically conscious of the moves they were placing themselves along the rock spectrum.

The long gestation period – a fate common to punk's pioneers – did have some attendant perks. As Stein observes, the 'two years when nobody showed up and everybody just did it for fun . . . added to the whole impetus of the thing. That's what doesn't happen any more. Nothing gets to cook.' In the case of Blondie, it meant at times painful rebirth-pangs, as they went through a number of stillborn styles before settling on the garagey pop that would make them millions of fans and dollars. For the Ramones, it gave them an opportunity to file the whole thing down to its nub, amassing a repertoire of songs that would suffice for three albums chock-full of anthems during a blitzkrieg eighteen months.

Television, meanwhile, was breaking in its heart. Verlaine insists that he was just 'trying to concentrate on keeping the band focused. I was already getting bored with that . . . kinda riff thing . . . [with] the rhythm guitar way out front . . . and got more into the improvisational stuff . . . [But] my whole orientation was towards music and performance, rather than getting the photographs right.'

Hell started to realize that 'Tom resented my preoccupation with this imagery stuff . . . [but] I wanted it all to be consistent. I wanted our clothes to say something before we even opened our mouths and the same thing for the graphics and the way we behaved in interviews . . . I wanted us to stand for something that showed in everything we did.' He suspected that the end might be nigh when Verlaine 'told me to stop moving onstage . . . I used to go really wild onstage . . . He said he didn't want people to be distracted when he was singing.'

However, it was only when the prospect of a record deal entered the equation that a split became inevitable. As Verlaine told *Sounds* in 1977, there came a point when 'you hear tapes of yourself and you find it's very hard to defend your performance, other than it being just a sort of vibe . . . If you want to sound better to your own ear, then you've got to work at it. And if you're around people that don't give a fuck . . .' This is clearly an allusion to hearing the band in a proper studio environment for the first time. In late February 1975 Television were taken into a midtown studio usually used by Latin American bands, to record a set of demos that may well have resulted in a deal with a real label, the UK's leading independent, Island Records.

Richard Williams: I saw Television and Blondie at the Truck & Warehouse Theater. Blondie could barely function at that point. Television were very, very rough but you could hear something really good. I came back, [and told the label] I'd like to do some demos with this lot, and Island said OK. They had a salsa studio on Broadway . . . called Good Vibrations, so we used the salsa engineer. He couldn't get the hang of the group at all. [I brought along Brian Eno] I suppose [because] I was not confident of my own ability to produce the demo properly, and I also thought if Eno was attached to the project then that would give it some clout, but when we came back with the demos you could tell Island were just not interested, and I was beginning to lose heart with the company. I'd signed Cale, I'd signed Nico, but I sensed that there wasn't a real willingness to do what Elektra [later] did with Television. Tom was very keen to sign with Island. I [guess] Television would have done a Hendrix and come to England. [And] I thought the demos were great – we only had three days in the studio. I think [Eno] was surprised, as I was, [that] Tom was [so] fastidious about what he wanted. Tom knew exactly how he wanted to sound. So he was pleased to have me and Brian there, but he wasn't interested in us telling him how his band should sound. We didn't produce it in the interventionist kind of way. Tom worked with the engineer to get the guitars to sound the way he wanted, and we were just supervising.

To Verlaine's ears, though, 'It sounded so bad. I kept on saying, "Why does it sound like this?" And [Eno]'d say, "Whaddya mean, it sounds pretty good to me . . ."' Though Tom had declined to record any of Hell's songs – even the ever-popular 'Blank Generation' – he still suspected Hell was holding the band back. In truth, Verlaine was going someplace – already evident on the 'Marquee Moon' they recorded at Good Vibrations – Hell didn't feel compelled to follow. As Hell now says, 'When I was in the group, it was a rock & roll band.' After a weekend of shows with the also-imploding Dolls at the beginning of March, Hell felt he'd had enough heartbreak, and left Verlaine to it.

It was a brave move. The scene had at last started to attract some attention from the media and the medallion men, and Television, as its self-proclaimed instigators, were in pole position. Indeed, the word had spread as far as London – hence Williams' interest, closely followed by the likes of Steve Lake and Chris Charlesworth at *Melody Maker*. Unbeknownst to these Bowery bands, other so-inclined American souls were producing results, working from almost the same template of influences. Their home address was The Plaza, Cleveland, Oh.

– – –

A number of young Clevelanders were fully aware of the scene in New York. Even in the early days of CBGB's two regular visitors made the hop, skip and long jump to the island city – Miriam Linna and Peter Laughner. Miriam was in fact collared by *NME*'s Charles Shaar Murray one night at CBGB's in 1975, there researching a piece on the New York scene, and admitted flying east to see Hell and his Heartbreakers play. She duly informed the amazed journalist that, 'There is a group of people [in Cleveland] who get *NME* sent over to them from England, [and they] all have the first [Dr] Feelgood album on import.'

Peter Laughner, more circumspect, was no less interested in checking out the downtown scene. By 1976 he would be using his mentor Lester Bangs' Manhattan apartment as a crash-pad, having finally got his musical act together, even as his personal life was spiralling rapidly downward to death. His tortured relationship with Bangs – mostly late-night phone calls of epic length, paid for by his parents – undoubtedly shaped his way of thinking.

An accomplished guitarist by the time he left school, Laughner would take the longest time to find a band who thought his way *and* could play – the latter proving just as hard as the former. As his then wife, Charlotte Pressler, later wrote, there was no shortage of opportunities to 'sit around and elaborate the aesthetic. We'd just sit there and go, "What's cool? How do you figure out how to live in the world?" This endless discussion about how can you possibly take an attitude to things that will let you live. We would go on for hours. It did have something to do with the Dexamyl.'

For Laughner, music was everything. It was something he'd discovered young, sneaking into Velvet Underground shows at La Cave when he wasn't even sixteen. At the same time, he had begun making music with a high school band, Mr Charlie, drawing on a range of influences that was not always electric, but was always eclectic. In the five years before he fired up Rocket from the Tombs, most of his music-making was solo, acoustic; or one-off projects like the Finns, where the Velvets and Beefheart collided with Eno in somebody's backyard one summer day. The only one of Laughner's bands that had some kind of basis in fact, Cinderella Backstreet (later Cinderella's Revenge), played barely a handful of gigs in the two years 1972–3 before she took her revenge. The sense of isolation from the mainstream, the local scene, indeed any scene, was palpable.

Charlotte Pressler: There were no stars, in Cleveland, then. Nobody cared what these people were doing. If they did anything at all, they did it for themselves . . . Most of the people [in that scene] were not natural musicians . . . John Morton and David Thomas and Allen Ravenstine and Jamie Klimek would probably have done something else, if there had been anything else for them to do.

Such was the shape of things in the moribund state of Ohio circa '73. David Thomas, who dubbed himself Crocus Behemoth while writing reviews for the same local rag as Laughner, tried to describe Cleveland to an uninformed *NME* journalist half a decade later, and came up with: 'A giant, blown-out factory town. There's the Flats with all this incredible industry, steel mills going flat out all day and all night, and it's just a half-mile away from where all the people live. This gives them the feeling that there's no future for somebody here, and all the musicians seem to be in love with that fact. In Cleveland nobody's going to pay any attention to you. The bands all know there's no future in a commercial sense for them, so they all say we're going to do what we goddamn want.'

Devo spokesman Mark Mothersbaugh was asked by an equally bemused English journo if the place they came from 'affect[ed] the outcome of the music'. He assured the man it did – because 'when you're in Ohio, nothing else is happening. You're in a wilderness. You kinda feel that you have no direct connection with what's happening in the world apart from through the TV.'

Any local scene was buried deep underground. One could walk around so-called music clubs in Cleveland as late as 1976 and meet no one who'd heard of Pere Ubu or Devo, let alone the Mirrors and the Electric Eels. To them, the Raspberries were the first and last band to break out of the place. In this pre-Ubu era, even the few hardy souls who were naturally inclined to experimentation had a hard time finding each other. Devo, who were holed up in Akron, barely an hour away, gave their first performance in April 1973, yet were strangers to their fellow suburban weirdos throughout the period that spawned the likes of Mirrors, the Electric Eels, Tin Huey and Rocket from the Tombs.

All of which makes it a minor miracle that, by the summer of 1974, Cleveland had a handful of bands within its city boundaries prepared to expound some kind of confrontational, Velvets/Stooges-based aesthetic. Of these, the Mirrors were perhaps the most orthodox, being essentially Cleveland's answer to British art-rock (as Laughner wrote in an early local piece, 'Their sound is a composite of all that was promising in the sixties . . . Floyd, the Velvet[s], the raunchiness of The Troggs and The Stooges'). They still had the temerity to play original material, making it difficult for them to find any regular gig in Bar-band Land until the fall of 1973, when Clockwork Eddie gave them a weekly slot at his Clockwork Orange bar.

Mirrors' sister band, the Electric Eels, were a whole other proposition. As Mirror man Michael Weldon duly notes, 'Mirrors was unusual enough to not get bookings, but were civil enough to get bookings if they tried. The Electric Eels looked stranger, played stranger and either didn't care or purposely wanted to antagonize people – or a combination of the two.'

In the period before they were allowed to participate in the occasional bout at the Viking Saloon, the Eels were more of a rumour than a rock & roll band. As Pressler later wrote, 'It is hard to say whether they were even a band in those [early] days. "The Electric Eels" seemed more to be the name of a concept, or perhaps a private club, with John [Morton], Brian McMahon and Dave E as members. The Eels may have practised, but never tried to play out.'

When they eventually did play out, the results were mayhem. Their debut was as support to local optimist Jamie Lyons at a downtown bar, where they emerged onstage with an anvil, a gas-powered lawnmower and a large sheet of metal. While the locals wondered what the hell was going on, Morton appeared wearing a coat apparently held together with safety pins, while Dave E had used rat traps to achieve the same effect. Morton duly began hitting the sheet of metal with a sledge-hammer.

The Eels coined the term Art Terrorism to convey their intent. Morton, who saw himself as both artist *and* terrorist, was determined to erect his own bridge between performance-art and rock performance. As he says, 'I liked the excitement of being a "rock star" but I also liked doing artwork and I wanted to combine the two, because doing artwork didn't have the excitement of performing . . . [But] we were a dichotomy, to have that fragile and explosive a thing made it exciting but it also made it doomed.' When *MM*'s Ian Birch later called it 'degenerate flash', he perhaps had a point.

Of course, the Eel-Art of Confrontation contained a certain parodic element, exemplified by their cover of National Lampoon's 'Pull The Triggers On The Niggers'. But they remained serious about what they were trying to do. David Thomas, on the other hand, felt his entire Crocus Behemoth persona lent itself to satire. When he debuted Rocket from the Tombs at the Viking on 16 June 1974 – billed as The World's Only Dumb-Metal Mind-Death Rock & Roll Band – they were intended as an extension of his previous spoof-rock band, the Great Bow Wah Death Band. Peter Laughner, though, saw some real potential, and according to his wife 'convinced [David] that something serious could be done out of the Rocket from the Tombs joke atmosphere . . . [Because] when David started writing the songs that the Dead Boys later took over he was writing them consciously punky.'

By October 1974, Laughner had rebuilt the band from its chassis up. Two inner-city delinquents, Gene O'Connor and Johnny Madansky, had answered an ad placed by Laughner in Cleveland's *Plain Dealer*, asking for 'real punks'. They fit the bill, O'Connor (aka Cheetah Chrome) had enough chops as a guitarist to play off Laughner's licks, while Madansky had a drum kit of his own. Welcome to the Tombs.

With O'Connor adding his own songwriting to the equation, RFTT had 'something serious' to say when they participated in the Viking's first Special Extermination Night in December '74. It was to be the only time that the Electric Eels, Rocket from the Tombs and Mirrors would share a stage; and the Eels headlined, presumably on the grounds that they were impossible to follow. But it was the Rockets who made a real musical mark that night, introducing the likes of 'Thirty Seconds Over Tokyo', 'Down In Flames' and 'Life Stinks' to the real world.

Laughner at last had a band that was neither art-project nor time-filler. Thomas, too, began to take his role as frontman and main lyricist seriously, even if a lot of the material remained 'consciously punky'. By February 1975, they had an album's worth of material to demo. So they set about recording on a reel-to-reel at their rehearsal loft on West 4th Street. The results suggested that they were as ready for recognition as Television, who recorded their own set of demos a week later at Island's behest. The RFTT renditions of 'Thirty Seconds Over Tokyo' and 'Ain't It Fun' in particular – both about suicide, one quick, one slow – were as edgy and psychodramatic as anything emerging from New York's east side.

Though still stuck in Boondock, USA, Laughner used his connections at WMMS, the radio station that was a beacon of hope to all local musos, to get the demo tape played over the air the following Sunday. Every song was given audio annotation by Laughner, who ended up telling everyone listening not to care what anyone else might think, but to 'do it for yourself'. His rock & roll evangelism was entirely sincere. Interviewed for the *Plain Dealer* in July 1975, he told Jane Scott, 'What we really want to do with our music is to change the audience's way of looking at things. If people leave a Rocket from the Tombs concert somehow changed in any small way, then we've succeeded . . . Rock & roll used to be able to get you to do things. It used to get you to think about what you were doing.'

By July, O'Connor, Laughner and Thomas had come up with two more songs that would help define the band's nine-month apotheosis of atonal energy, 'Final Solution' and 'Sonic Reducer'. The former was debuted at a 'Heavy Metal Showcase' at the Agora in May (broadcast in part on WMMS), its sludgy riff ripped clean off Blue Cheer's 'Summertime Blues'. As for Thomas's claim in the lyric that his 'parents threw me out till I get some pants that fit', there was perhaps more to it than that:

Charlotte Pressler: [Thomas]'s parents were rather actively rejecting him. What got him thrown out [of the house] was the RFTT gig at the Berea Community Centre . . . He did the dance where you wallow along on your belly over the floor, and he had a box of dog biscuits and he was doing 'I Wanna Be Your Dog' and he started throwing the dog biscuits . . . It wasn't happening fast enough, so he threw the whole box, and it hit his father on the head.

Thomas's home arrangements were not the only volatile aspect of the exercise. RFTT was (equally) divided between those who felt Thomas could sing, and those who did not. Strangely enough, Thomas fell into the latter camp, so before the band played a 'prestigious' two-nighter at the Piccadilly Penthouse – as support to Television – they drafted in Steve Bators as a(nother) vocalist. Bators had been at the Berea gig that had got Thomas expelled from house and home, and was impressed by their rendition of 'I Wanna Be Your Dog', even though he had seen the real thing (Bators had been the person who handed Iggy the peanut butter he famously smeared himself with at the Cincinatti Pop Festival in 1970).

Bators, though, was not such a good idea. The precarious equilibrium between the band's art-rockettes and fuck-art rockers was fatally undermined at precisely the time when things were starting to change for the better. Laughner's New York connections, and his powers of persuasion, had ensured that the first time Television left the big city they would come to Cleveland for two shows. Scheduled for 24–25 July, Television arrived to find neither gig sold out, and the support band in a bad way. Indeed, Verlaine recalls someone from the Tombs sitting on the stairs at the end of the first night, in tears, apparently the result of some particularly powerful downers. Actually, the whole band was down. As Chrome says, 'Everything came to a head that night.'

The Television that arrived in Cleveland town was no longer the band that had first endeared itself to New York. Richard Hell was no longer a focal point. They had a new bassist, ex-Blondie Fred Smith, to keep things tethered while Verlaine and Lloyd took the likes of 'Little Johnny Jewel', 'Breakin' In My Heart' and 'Kingdom Come' spiralling off into the stratosphere. Verlaine even tipped a hat to Hendrix's famous 'Star-spangled Banner' at the start of a recast 'Foxhole'. This was no garageband.

Rocket from the Tombs attempted to show that they could stretch out too, impressing Verlaine with 'Thirty Seconds Over Tokyo' and the Laughner-original 'Amphetamine'; but the lack of cohesion was obvious to all, as was an essential incompatibility at the heart of this band's particular darkness. As Thomas says, 'It was a brave attempt, a brave experiment to fuse two incompatible forms.' Like the Electric Eels, who also drilled their last that summer, the Tombs discovered that 'to have that fragile and explosive a thing made it exciting but it also made it doomed.'

The two American punk precursors whose ambition extended beyond three chords in three minutes had both imploded in the past five months. As such, neither would be part of the two most creative (and important) homegrown scenes when the A&R men came around. Yet many of the songs they left behind – 'Blank Generation', 'I Don't Care', 'Friction', 'Venus De Milo', 'Prove It', 'Thirty Seconds Over Tokyo', 'Final Solution', 'Sonic Reducer' – would become punk anthems in the fullness of time, albeit recorded by bands at least one step removed from its original aesthetic.

1.2
ESKIMO PIE COMES
TO OZ
1973-76

There's gonna be a new race
Kids are gonna start it up.   — 'New Race', Radio Birdman

If a number of New York neophytes had direct experience of the likes of The Velvet Underground, The Stooges and The New York Dolls, further-flung fans were required to decode their vinyl testimonies. Their one other recourse was the writings (and images) contained within *Creem* and *Crawdaddy*, shipped from the States, or *ZigZag* and *Frendz*, from ol' Blighty.

Australia in the early seventies was as removed from any happening hub as any part of the English-speaking world. And yet, even here could be found the odd disciple of discord; and in a single instance, someone who came with his own eyewitness accounts of the Creed of the Ig. Deniz Tek arrived in Sydney, for the second time, in February 1972. Brought up in Ann Arbor, twin city to Detroit, he had enjoyed an antipodean year already – half a decade earlier – when he returned in 1972 to a quite different musical climate.

Deniz Tek: My dad was a professor at the University of Michigan. Right at the beginning of 1967 we went to Australia, because my dad did a sabbatical year in Sydney. I was fourteen when we took off, and then we got back to America in the spring of '68. That meant I completely missed the summer of love, 'cause it happened in Australia a year later . . . Australia had had a very active, thriving rock scene in the late sixties. When I was there in 1967 I had heard some really good bands on the radio – the Easybeats, the Master's Apprentices, the Loved Ones, the Zoot, guys like that. But by the time I got back there in the early seventies there were a few boogie bands and some stoned-out electric blues bands, but nothing that was exciting. Everybody was interested in [whoever was] the last international band that had come to Sydney – which when I got there was Deep Purple and Led Zeppelin. So whenever I met some musicians, it would be, 'Let's play "Smoke on the Water".'

Tek had a more subterranean grounding as a guitarist, having spent most Sundays in his teens going to the free concerts they held in the park in Ann Arbor, at which he caught just about all of the Grande Ballroom bands who made Detroit such a happening scene from 1966 through 1969. If the MC5 were already moving on to greater things,

The (Psychedelic) Stooges, SRC and Bob Seger were all grateful for the exposure; and Tek drank his fill. He had already formed his first high school band, The Inducers (which also contained Roger Miller, later guitarist in Boston post-punkers, Mission of Burma); and shortly before setting out for Australia again, he acquired his own talisman, a white Epiphone Crestwood from none other than the MC5's Fred 'Sonic' Smith. It also made the journey to Oz, the pair going by a rather circuitous route, via Africa, Europe and England, where Tek visited one of London's most famous musical breeding grounds, the Marquee Club in Wardour Street.

Deniz Tek: I went to . . . see the place where the Stones and The Who played, and it was The Pink Fairies [playing], and it just blew me away because it was so hardcore and raw and edgy and loud. It was easily the equal of anything going on in Detroit . . . It really opened my mind, because I realized that this stuff's happening all over the world.

Arriving in Australia, he began to rethink that view. 'Smoke On The Water' he could certainly play, but it was not his cup of Assam. Ditto 'Stairway To Heaven'. Finally, after six to eight months there, he formed a band with some fellow misfits, brothers Gerry and Chris Jones and Giles van der Werf. Starting out as the Screaming White Hot Razorblades, they quickly passed through the questionable moniker Cunning Stunts, to arrive at TV Jones. As with most nascent noisemakers, TV Jones began as a covers band – with a difference.

Deniz Tek: We were covering Velvets, The Stooges, MC5, 'Just Like An Aborigine' by the Up, and a lot of early Alice Cooper songs. We were semi-into that glam/Alice Cooper thing – wearing clear plastic raincoats and make-up, and blowing stuff up on stage. I sort of borrowed that look from Alice Cooper and the early Stooges, who [had been] a performance-art band rather than a rock band. Iggy used to spray-paint his body silver, and had aluminium foil in his hair . . . We just started playing at functions and parties, then we landed a residency gig at a pub. So we're playing every Friday and Saturday night at the Charles Hotel in Wollongong. That's where the band really cut its teeth.

Aspects of the TV Jones set-list were as avant-garde to the average Aussie as Albert Ayler would have been to an Ann Arborite. Stooges slamfests '1969' and 'Search And Destroy' vied with Chuck Berry and John Mayall songs; while the Velvets played tag with Detroit-era Alice Cooper. Despite sugar-coating their set with familiar fare from the Stones and The Doors, TV Jones found few friends within Sydney's supposed bohemia. The rest of TV Jones were becoming less convinced about Tek's ideas.

Deniz Tek: The stuff I wanted to do went over pretty good at the Charles Hotel, but when we tried to move it into the big clubs in Sydney it didn't go over well at all – we kept getting thrown out of places. We would get booked for a week in a big club and we would last half of the first night. The other guys in TV Jones got sick of it, 'cause they wanted to be successful. I didn't really care about being successful, I just wanted to do something with integrity.

Like it or not, TV Jones were never going to be more than a stepping stone for Tek. And sometime in the spring of 1974 he found out he was not so alone. One of the live beats with whom Tek was sharing a dilapidated shack played drums in another local band, the Rats. At a Rats rehearsal said drummer had informed the band's singer, Rob Younger, that he knew this guy who played the same sort of stuff the Rats did, even sharing some of the same songs. Younger's response was definite, and to the point, 'Bullshit! No one's doing this sort of stuff. No one's heard of it out here!' The Rats were, if anything, more outré than TV Jones. If the latter attempted to cross the Stones with The Stooges, the Rats preferred the ramshackle to the Rolling. Taking their template from New York's own cracked-sidewalk Stones, The New York Dolls, the Rats infused everything with a dose of The Stooges' raw power.

Thanks to one of those anomalies seemingly designed to yield a vinyl oddity, both of The Stooges' Elektra albums (*The Stooges* and *Fun House*) had been given a domestic release in Australia. Rats singer Younger came upon *Creem* before The Stooges, but there was little to choose between these respective epiphanies. In the spring of 1972, he had discovered the February issue of *Creem*. The magazine, in Younger's words, 'tipped me off to a lot of things', beginning that spring day with a lengthy exposition by Richard Meltzer on Blue Oyster Cult.

What Younger liked about the zine was the fact that it was 'extremely opinionated'. One band in particular came with the *Creem* stamp of approval: 'I just kept hearing references to . . . The Stooges, and [sometime in] '72, I saw a copy of *Fun House* – an Australian copy, [which] didn't have the foldout cover. It was only two bucks . . . So I took it home and got loaded up on hash, lay on the sofa and cranked it up really loud, and I was completely taken by it. It cast quite a spell.' Within a year, Younger would have the first New York Dolls album to go with worn copies of the Stooges and Velvets long-players. He also had some money to spend, and a yen to do the pop himself.

Rob Younger: I'd inherited some money. [So I decided] to buy a PA . . . I thought, 'Maybe we should have a wack at this,' because it didn't seem too untoward to knock out David Johansen-style vocals. I got a band to-gether doing that. It was all Dolls, the look and the sound of the Dolls is what I was really interested in. We'd wear tight crushed velvet pants with brocade jackets – it was definitely a glam look. Our guitar player, Mick Lyne, was an English guy. [He had] this Telecaster Thinline with the treble really jacked up, and thrashed away at it more like a banjo. It was really insistent, but [also] really piercing. Then we had [Warwick Gilbert] on lead guitar, flay[ing] away, and I just tried to shout through the middle of it. It was all covers – six or seven Dolls songs, a couple of MC5, the ones we could play, [and] we did stuff like 'Waiting for the Man'. Our first gig was out on the lawn of the Royal Women's Hospital in Paddington . . . I can't believe they tolerated it. We played the Oxford [Tavern, when] it was the Oxford Hotel . . . on the first floor – it was really dingy, had a small stage and a hole in the wall for a bar. A lot of bikers used to hang out there. We lasted about a year and from memory we did about seventeen gigs. [But] the Australian rock scene was dominated by bands that dressed like Free and Deep Purple . . . No one sought us out, that's for sure.

Not surprisingly, when Tek and Younger finally compared notes and found that they had both been playing from the same chart for a year or more, oblivious to the other's existence, they became firm friends. Oddly enough, though, it was Younger who seemed more *au fait* with US underground sounds and scribblings. Tek freely admits he was introduced to the Detroit-based *Creem* by Younger, 'We [both] just got into the writing style of guys like Meltzer and Lester Bangs. We didn't care what they wrote about, we just loved the journalistic style that they had.' He also discovered that Rob 'knew things about American music that I never ever dreamed, at that stage. Somehow he had the sources to know about this stuff.'

ever more incendiary music. As Tek told Johnson, 'In the early days, [the Oxford] was like an exclusive club, because the only people that went there were the people that knew about the band already, and it was sort of like a clique. We could do anything – experimental-wise – because it was always the same crowd . . . So we were always looking for new things to do and [ways to] explore new ideas . . . When it's the same crowd you've got to keep moving on.'

With a capacity of maybe 300 hungry souls, the Oxford contained that clique who needed a regular Birdman fix, while still leaving enough room at the back and sides for the nominally curious. As a film of four songs shot at the Oxford for ABC documentary, *Where The Action Is*, serves to illustrate, the one drawback tended to be a stage where the band – recently expanded to a sextet by the return of Pip Hoyle, but retention of Chris Masuak – were cheek to jowl.

By the time ABC turned up, the Oxford had been recast in Birdman's image. Between Tek and new manager, George Kringas, they had decided to run the place themselves, even booking all the other bands. In keeping with its new status, the Oxford Tavern was rechristened the Oxford Funhouse, as Tek and the band instituted a policy of booking 'bands that couldn't get gigs anywhere else. Anyone who was trendy or mainstream we wouldn't allow them to play there, even if they wanted to – [which they did] because it was a burgeoning scene . . . But we excluded them. We'd say, "No, this is for outcasts. This is for under-dogs." We used [the Funhouse] to get revenge on what we perceived as all the powers that had prevented us from working in the past.' The ad they placed for the 'new' venue was as elitist as it gets:

BANDS WANTED FOR GIGS AT
THE OXFORD FUNHOUSE!

The Funhouse is Sydney's only genuine rock 'n' roll venue. We are having trouble finding good bands to book. To us, a good band is energetic, exciting, innovative (or unashamedly derivative) playing rock 'n' roll with real manic fervour.

WHAT IS NOT WANTED

Bands who play shit like Quo, Purple, Queen, Zeppelin, ZZ Top, Bad Co., Ted Nugent (post '72), Bowie. In short, any of the crap anyone can hear anywhere in this boring burg.

> Dumb clothing – stage gear consisting of fashion jeans and overalls, platforms, hippie gear (beads, baggy overalls, shoulder bags, etc.)
>
> The Equipment Obsession Syndrome – the popular notion that a new expensive brand amp and guitar and monster PA will automatically make the group 'insane', 'incredible', 'good', 'rock 'n' roll'. Equipment freaks rarely cut it when it comes to actually playing rock 'n' roll.
>
> We've made a few mistakes through booking groups who said they played certain good material and, when hired, played these songs in a thoroughly gutless fashion. Bands who play original material only (or mostly) would be asked to bring tapes or lay down so crazed a testimony of their fervent commitment that they would persuade the management to forget about the tapes.

Lines weren't merely being drawn, they were being scored in indelible ink. This was a manifesto. Make no mistake, Birdman were placing themselves at the heart of something, even if no one was quite sure what they should call it. Wayne Elmer, though championing the band in Australian *Rolling Stone* as early as March 1976, refused to call it punk though that term was assuredly in the air – insisting that 'Birdman play, and are influenced by, a particular brand of music that is covered neither by the term heavy metal nor punk-rock. Their music is more cerebral than the former and tougher than the latter.'

Actually the most cursory scan of the songs Birdman covered – and they always gave audiences a smattering of the standard-bearers they marched to – read like a lexicon of punk influences: MC5, The Stooges, Velvet Underground, New York Dolls, Alice Cooper, The Kingsmen, Trashmen, The Outsiders, The Remains, Thirteenth Floor Elevators, the Rivieras, Garland Jeffreys, to name a dozen. In fact, the Jeffreys song that was a bulwark of Birdman shows, 'Wild In The Streets', was the same obscure garage classic that Laughner had wanted to make Rocket from the Tombs' debut single.

Nor were Birdman unaware of the first sparks flying from America's new proto-punk scene. Younger was already buying *Rock Scene*, '[Be]cause you'd see "candid" shots of David Johansen and Cyrinda Fox, and the Ramones coming out of the Metro with their guitars in brown paper shopping bags. I used to read that sort of thing avidly. I just *saw* the emergence of these acts.' His interest piqued, Younger was one of the few folk in town to pick up Television's first single, 'Little Johnny Jewel'. Likewise, he snagged copies of early Pere Ubu singles at Sydney's hippest record store, White Light, run by Mark Taylor, Birdman disciple and later founder of the Lipstick Killers.

And then suddenly, in the summer, there was the Ramones' debut album . . .

Thankfully, by the time that austere long-player made its way across the Pacific, Birdman had their own sound, and the assurance to stick with their own schtick. Indeed, they had already begun recording their own contribution to the revolution prophesied by Bangs. By the time the *Burn My Eye* EP made it into the world, in the last few weeks of 1976, it was already viewed as merely the first instalment in a series rich with promise. Birdman had been recording in every moment of down time Trafalgar Studio made available.

The four songs picked for the EP – 'I-94', 'Burn My Eye', 'Snake' and 'Smith And Wesson Blues' – certainly packed a punch. On the title-track, Younger even decided to have 'people standing around a microphone in a circle smashing beer cans against their head to the beat . . . We thought that the good feeling that's caused by doing that would somehow get through the wiring into the record.' All part of the Birdman vibe, this was as confident, assured and original as anything coming from the East Coast – all points of reference being somehow both implicit and explicit in one Birdmanesque blur of sound.

— — —

And yet, *Burn My Eye* was not destined to be the first Australian punk 45. Those months waiting for slots at Trafalgar – and the failure of the *RAM* single to happen – had allowed that honour to pass to a band from beyond the boonest dock. Brisbane, for pity's sake! Going under the name The Saints (as in 'better a saint, than a sap'), these cave dwellers still had the foresight to send their privately pressed single not only to White Light, Sydney's one hideout for musos, but to the English music papers. 'I'm Stranded' certainly stunned the guys from Birdman, when it appeared in September 1976. Taken in tandem with the Ramones' debut album, it seemed to Tek and co. 'like something was about to happen in the world again'.

Rob Younger: There was no word on these guys [beforehand], that I can recall . . . There was no underground where the word of mouth seemed to filter down about them, or anything else. They seemed quite isolated. [I guess] the nature of their music would have precluded people being interested . . . [But] I thought, 'This is fantastic.' . . . I was a bit jealous actually. I was [also] quite surprised there was a band this accomplished, that I might never have even heard of, if they hadn't put out a record.

What made the appearance out of the Queensland mists of these hellraisers truly astonishing was the shared antecedents, and similar aesthetic, they brought to the party. When the Birdman boys discovered that The Saints had been together as long as themselves, they realized this had to be a band who had remained in some kinda self-imposed incubation. Whereas Birdman had gotten radioplay, write-ups in *RAM* and *Rolling Stone*, a residency in Sydney, as well as venturing as far afield as Melbourne and Adelaide, The Saints had stayed put, listening to loud rock & roll, and playing almost entirely for the neighbours' benefit.

Because of this curious strategy – being the garageband that stayed in the garage – The Saints' origins remain shrouded by a subsequent mythology designed to fill in a lot of blank pages. The Saints began as the bedroom band of Ed Kuepper, a guitarist in love with primal sound, and Chris Bailey, his belligerent buddy, probably around 1973. Kuepper's points of reference included The Stooges and the Velvets, having picked up those domestic versions of the first two Stooges albums, along with a weird German double-album that had one side devoted to The Velvet Underground. Kuepper, like Younger, was especially blown away by *Fun House*.

Bailey's tastes were more conventional, but no less rooted in rock & roll. Indeed, the pair shared an abiding appreciation of the likes of Bo Diddley, Eddie Cochran, Chuck Berry and Elvis. As Kuepper later told *Australian Guitar*, 'That sort of music I thought had never been really surpassed' – hence their original name, Kid Galahad and the Eternals. The band stayed in that bedroom for a year and a half or more, before venturing out. At this point, they found it all but impossible to slow down the tempo of the songs they'd written.

Ed Kuepper: When we actually had to play in front of people we got incredibly nervous and that's how we started getting faster and faster [laughs]. But the earlier stuff has a slightly more narcotic feel . . . By the time we started playing live . . . I couldn't move back from it, it was like a necessary hit to get on stage. It was like, just slam into it.

As Bailey stridently informed the *NME* on landing in Britain at the height of punk, 'We was like this long before we even *heard* the Ramones.' A recent CD of early rehearsals by the band, dating from 1974–5, including a rough and ready rendition of 'I'm Stranded', appears to confirm Kuepper's contention that the speed came with gigging (as it did with the Ramones).

The Saints' mutating sound reflected their isolation; for they were, in Bailey's words, 'on our own down there in a way you couldn't imagine'. Their attempts to break down even outer layers of resistance were fraught with problems. As Chris Bailey told *Mojo* magazine, 'We tried to be a part of the circuit, but were consistently rejected. But we [still] thought we were going to make it. We probably had delusions of grandeur.' The more practical Kuepper adopted a DIY approach similar to Birdman, in order to take those first faltering steps.

Ed Kuepper: We'd hire an RSL [Returned Serviceman's League] hall in the suburbs, a function hall, they had a bar, or Country Women's Association halls. So we'd hire a hall for like forty bucks a night and you'd sweep up at the end of the night.

However, it was only when the four-piece at last found a dependable bassist in Kym Bradshaw, and moved to a delapidated house on the notorious Petrie Terrace in the winter of 1975 that the band became a more serious proposition. Throughout 1975, progress remained slow, with shows at RSL clubs, the local college and even a Communist Party bash hardly suggesting some great breakthrough. Kuepper and Bailey, though, remained fixated on making something happen. They finally decided that they would have to form their own club, prophetically named the 76 Club.

The 76 Club was hardly the Oxford. Chris Bailey began a little mischievous myth-making during his first UK interview, for *Sounds* in May 1977, describing how, 'We played Brisbane's famous Club 76 [and] neighbours complained unjustifiably about the noise, and the police started raiding the place on the grounds they were looking for underage drinking.' He refrained from mentioning that the 76 Club was actually the band's own semi-derelict abode. That they got away with playing at their own late-night parties was down to Petrie Terrace itself, described by Andrew MacMillan, in the first national article on the band, in a December 1976 *RAM*, as 'a notorious piece of turf in the midst of condemned buildings, railway yards and permanently shadowy streets. It is home to winos, derelict aborigines and vicious brawls.'

As Saints bassist Bradshaw has observed, when the quartet played at Petrie on a Sunday afternoon, 'You could hear us half a mile away.' Their idea of baffling for each performance was to place a curtain across the big plate-glass window that had once been its shopfront. Not surprisingly, neighbours took matters into their own hands, and one night someone threw a brick through the window. According to drummer Ivor Hay, 'We just boarded up the window and wrote Club 76 on the boards.'

If ever a band was unfazed by the antipathy of others, it was The Saints. In time, this intractability would signpost their own road to ruin. But for now, those elements that needed confronting were more apathetic than antipathetic. Kuepper informed *RAM*'s MacMillan, 'We don't use volume as a substitute for excitement, though we probably play twice as loud as most other local bands. It all boils down to realism. We haven't got the attitude of, "Who gives a damn, man." '

In order to overcome the twin banes of isolation and apathy, The Saints finally decided to make a vinyl memento – a document of a band with no time to spare. Bailey later claimed that 'a few punk bands [had] started up . . . in Brisbane, doing songs like "Hitler Wasn't Bad", and we decided we'd better get something on record.' (This joke song-title was undoubtedly a dig at Birdman, whose 'New Race' would induce Bailey to assume some right-wing agenda on their part.) In reality, there were no like-minded bands within a thousand miles of Petrie Terrace. The means of production, though, had been there all along.

Ed Kuepper: [Even though] I'd been working at a record distributor, Astor Records . . . I just didn't know what was involved [in making a record]. It was only after I quit my job and had been away for a while [that] I called them up and said, 'If I send you a tape, will you actually press a record?' And they said, 'Yes, we do it all the time.' . . . It was . . . necessary. It had gotten to the point where I didn't think it was a consummated marriage until we had a record out.

They could have been galvanized into getting something pressed by the appearance of something surprisingly similar in the shops of Brisbane – *The Ramones* album. Certainly the divide between the release of *The Ramones* and the recording of 'I'm Stranded' can be measured in weeks. Bailey recalls getting a call from his guitarist, bemoaning the fact that, 'The Ramones have stolen our sound.'

The process of laying claim to some kind of antipodean precedence began shortly after the Saints single spun off the presses in August 1976. A couple of copies were promptly despatched to music papers in England – though not as legend has suggested to *Sounds*, the weekly then most attuned to the embryonic punk aesthetic. Instead, they reached the singles desks at *NME* and *Melody Maker*, accompanied by the world's first handwritten press release. It was mere good fortune that the singles reviewer at *MM* was Caroline Coon, who immediately phoned kindred spirit (and Aussie) Jonh Ingham at *Sounds* to inform him that a bunch of blokes from Brisbane had sent along this astonishing call from the wild.

Jonh Ingham: She'd received ['I'm Stranded'] in the mail, and she said, 'I've just got this amazing record, and they're from Queensland!' And she plays it to me on the phone. I lived in Ealing, and she's in Chelsea. So it took like forty-five minutes [to get to her place]. But I must have listened to it six or seven times in a row.

Suitably stunned, Ingham made 'I'm Stranded' *Sounds*' Single Of This And Every Week, along with a quarter-page review in the 16 October 1976 issue, illustrated with a barely recognizable shot of the band behind bars. The opening line of Ingham's rave ran: 'There's a tendency to blabber mindlessly about this single, it's so bloody incredible.' He went on to suggest that, 'Australian record companies think the band lack commercial potential. What a bunch of idiots!' In fact, the Australian record industry – such as it was – knew nothing of the band, which was not entirely surprising given that they had yet to make it beyond the confines of Brisbane.

Ingham, though, hadn't finished hyping this single to the heavens. The following *Sounds*, the single of the week was even more to the point – The Damned's 'New Rose'. But beneath that important review, and Still Single Of This Week And Any Week, was another plug for The Saints, promising anyone smart enough to order a copy from Eternal Productions in Queensland, 'It will change your life.' Suddenly, The Saints found all those Australian companies who lacked A&R departments in Brisbane clamouring for their signature. In fact, some prescient soul at EMI in the UK promptly instructed the Sydney office to send for The Saints, and sign 'em up.

So it was that The Saints arrived in Sydney during December 1976, to meet with the folk at EMI and record some demos. To The Saints, though, there was no such thing. Their last set of demos had become their debut single. This set of demos, recorded over a weekend, made up the remaining eight songs on what became the debut album, *(I'm) Stranded*. For The Saints, things now began to happen very quickly. The single had been re-pressed by Australian distributor Power Exchange, who began exporting copies by the pallet (it eventually sold around 16,000 copies in the UK alone). And with EMI-Australia's backing, they could finally spread the word in places like Melbourne and Sydney.

The Saints even found themselves invited to play the Oxford Funhouse in early April 1977 as headliners in their own right, to be followed by a potentially portentous gig at Paddington Town Hall, where they would support Radio Birdman at the first gathering of the clan. Plans were also afoot to film the event for possible promotional material as and when The Saints headed for the mother country, where they were now booked to play at the beginning of June, on the back of the UK release of their long-player.

Rather than some great unifying moment, the Paddington concert would pass into legend as a confrontation-charged collision between two entirely different takes on the Stooges/Velvets legacy. Radio Birdman and The Saints would never share a stage again. Indeed, The Saints would leave for Blighty barely six weeks later, never to return. Their reception in Sydney would provide a presentiment of the one accorded in London two months later, as they went out of their way to alienate the few advocates they had.

Deniz Tek: We welcomed The Saints when they came to Sydney with open arms. We did everything to make them feel welcome – introduced them to people, had them over to our house, got them gigs, just did all this stuff [to help them]. And yet, immediately when they got there, they were hostile. Some of them were quietly hostile . . . [but] the singer was like a drunken Irishman, [who] would get drunk and want to fight us because we were 'rivals'.

Though Tek avoided fighting The Saints, he did end up in a brawl with a biker at the Saints' Funhouse gig the night before Paddington, which resulted in him playing Birdman's biggest gig to date with his guitar hand taped up and in a splint. His mood took a further dip when, prior to The Saints' set, Chris Bailey's sister 'went berserk, ran on to the stage and started tearing our flag down'. She had decided that the band's symbol – which, as Tek says, 'was meant to be a confronting gesture to the music press, [who] had made a big deal of [our approach] being like a military campaign' – was some covert endorsement of fascism.

Amazingly, she didn't get her lights punched out and the banner stayed down for the duration of The Saints' performance. This, however, did not seem to sate the Bailey clan and after debuting their brand-new composition, 'This Perfect Day', Chris announced his thanks to 'the local chapter of the Hitler Youth for putting up such fine props'. It showed Bailey to be fearless, even when vastly outnumbered by Birdman's band of disciples. The comment was certainly intended to get a rise out of the audience; and as Rob Younger says, 'The whole situation got a bit revved up.' But the reaction to the set, from all save a few band friends bouncing away at the front, seemed more one of studied indifference.

Part of the problem was that The Saints' sound was swamped by the large hall. And for all their hammer-and-tongs pacing, they were clearly out of their depth, Bailey's stagecraft at this point extending to leaning on the mike with a lit cigarette in his hand. When even their grand finale, the usual 'Nights In Venice' freak-out, failed to galvanize the alienated audience, Bailey jumped into the crowd and slumped down against the stage. As the feedback rang out at set's end, he interjected, 'What a waste of fucking time!' throwing the mike down and leaving through the crowd, another gesture seemingly intended for the film crew.

If Birdman weren't amused, they did what they had always done, feeding their anger into the music. With their fanatical fans out front, and the cameras set to capture their set too, the band walked on in their new uniforms – dyed army shirts and arm-patches sporting the Birdman symbol (now restored as a backdrop) – indicating not so much membership of the Hitler Youth as New Youth. The half-empty hall suddenly became a maelstromic mass of heaving bodies, punching the air in time to the music.

Greg Foster captured the dichotomy that night in his *RAM* review, which suggested that: 'If The Saints were a pneumatic drill, Radio Birdman were a lightning rod . . . [as] their banner rose and they hit the stage with the impact of a cocaine charge.' The final song, 'New Race', would become both a video for the band's first single, and cast-iron evidence of Birdman's credentials as keepers of the flame. Unlike the band, though, the clip never made it out of Australia, and they were destined to remain an almost Masonic secret among discerning rock fans.

Bailey, though, was not prepared to lay this 'rivalry' to rest. In the interviews he gave in the next few months, as The Saints rode a fleeting wave of interest in Britain, he made a number of digs at Birdman and Sydney's music scene, claiming that he'd 'played Sydney for a week. But that [scene]'s more camp.' He insisted he felt more at home in Melbourne, which apparently had 'a whole pub scene' sprouting up just as the Brisbane boys were leaving for the island-home of punk. If they had made almost no converts in Sydney, they certainly made their mark in Melbourne. With performances not dissimilar to the one with which they had crashed and burned at Paddington, they inspired at least one disenchanted soul to take his equally perverse musical ideas and run with them.

Nick Cave: [The Saints] would come down to Melbourne and play these concerts which were the most alarming things you've ever seen, just such anti-rock kind of shows, where the singer wouldn't come on stage. When he did, he was this fat alcoholic. It was so misanthropic, it was unbelievable, and the whole band was like that. They were so loud!

1.3
SOMETHING BETTER
CHANGE
1973-75

It's a fruitless business looking for the origins of the Sex Pistols in the Ramones [or] in The New York Dolls, as them CBGB wallies would like you to believe. It's like saying Mort Sahl was Lenny Bruce's predecessor, innit?

— David Dalton, *Gadfly*, 2/98

It is often overlooked that England had a handful of 'proto-punk' outfits contemporary with the CBGB's scene; and that the leading exponent of *this* scene — given the slighting soubriquet, pub-rock — had a number-one album the same month The Damned issued 'New Rose', thus taking their rough 'n' ready aesthetic full square into the mainstream. Just like Television in New York, Dr Feelgood had been in a kind of self-imposed isolation from their peers in the eighteen months before assaulting the country's capital. What they found there was little in the way of obvious competition, and just one serious claimant to originality — Ian Dury's Kilburn & The High Roads.

Dr Feelgood weren't content to be from Southend, a rundown re-sort propped up by coaches of Cockney OAPs bent on a bingo bender. They preferred Canvey Island — a pillar-post detour from the joys of Southend-on-Sea. Appropriately, the sound they came up with was as out-of-time as the town, itself hankering for a return to its holiday-ing heyday. Formed in 1972 by ex-hippy John 'Wilko' Wilkinson, a guitarist from the 'no frills' carousel of R&B, the Feelgoods were the offspring of two local blues bands, the Pigboy Charlie Band and The Fix.

With the dynamic tension that spumed from its two sweaty frontmen, singer Lee Brilleaux and Wilko the wind-up guitarist, the Feelgoods kicked life into the cadaver of British R&B, which had once spawned everyone from the Stones to Led Zeppelin. By 1973, though, as Wilko recently told *Mojo*, 'We were the only people doing R&B — everybody else was doing Wishbone Ash or David Bowie stuff, and they poured scorn on us.' As so often, it was the reactionary nature of the Feelgoods that made them seem so revolutionary.

Wilko Johnson: [Dr Feelgood] are only original in that, for all that's been said of us, I don't think you could find another band like us . . . It's all derived from here, there and everywhere, but it's our sound. [1977]

In the beginning, the Feelgoods' ambitions extended no further than the town boundaries, and a good time had. Initially, they failed to keep tabs on any scene that might have been happening in London, though it was little more than an hour away. By the time they actually took their sound (and Energy) to the Ol' Smoke, what they had was no longer rough cut, but a polished gem bound to shine alongside the costume jewellers making up most of London's formulaic pub-rock scene. As Andrew Lauder, the A&R man who took them to United Artists, points out, 'The Feelgoods were [just] so different to what else was going on at the time.'

It was fellow Canvey musician, Will Birch, who told the boys in the band to check out the pubs of London, 'Do you realize there's a circuit . . . where this sort of thing is happening?' Singer Brilleaux spoke for the band when he told Birch, 'Don't be ridiculous.' But Birch persevered, even getting them a gig at the Tally Ho pub to prove it. The Feelgoods descended on London for the first time on 13 July 1973, and almost immediately found themselves in the eye of a storm of interest. Evidently, they weren't alone in their desire to return rock to its $\frac{4}{4}$ formalities.

Wilko Johnson: Dr Feelgood came quite late to that [pub-rock] scene. It was already up and going . . . We were gonna get these gigs up in London, and we went to check out some of the bands, which filled me with confidence . . . They were making out [that] there was this scene up here, playing a certain type of music, but when you actually got up there, what you found was musos doing a bit of country, a bit of funk . . . and Dr Feelgood took off really fast there because we were doing something a bit unusual, a bit twisted . . . [We were] quite shocking really. You'd never quite seen this before! A lot of these bands were jamming away – we were very *urgent* about it. A lot of these other bands were known [quantities] . . . [but] we'd come up from Canvey Island, and we'd got our thing together by then. We'd had a couple of years bashing around Southend. So suddenly there's these people that no one's ever seen before coming along with this 'thing'. It attracted a lot of attention.

For a generation of jaundiced rock scribes, the Feelgoods immediately provided something to get excited about again. Wilko recalls the time when *NME* journalist Tony Tyler literally 'burst into The Lord Nelson one evening, told us who he was and that he wanted to write about us. Unfortunately, the *NME* was not being published at the time due to a publisher's strike. [But] he started telling the other guys [at *NME*], people like Mick Farren and Charles Shaar Murray, who were [also] very positive.'

In fact it was Farren, already a known quantity in counterculture circles, who wrote the first major *NME* feature on the Feelgoods, in the 29 June 1974 issue of the revamped weekly, now back from the brink. He was also probably the first writer to apply the words 'Feelgoods' and 'punk' in the same context:

[Dr Feelgood] are far from being a rock-revival band. They are somewhat recherché, their choice of songs comes mainly from the period 1960–65, but they're a long way from the sparking, pop-art doo-wop that has become the trademark of a lot of musicians who try to use it in order to cover up a paucity of ideas . . . [In fact] they're covering similar ground to Them, [though] they have a long way to go before they produce their own 'Mystic Eyes' . . . They seem to have attained the elusive thing that bands like Flamin' Groovies have been looking for for years. It's that kind of butch coarseness that the glitter punks seem to have lost.

The so-called pub-rock bands (not that the term was in common use at the time, only gaining currency as the antithesis to the equally pub-based punk-rock, circa '76) had been filling drinkers' haunts like the Lord Nelson, the Kensington and the Tally Ho for eighteen months or more. Those like Bees Make Honey, Brinsley Schwarz and Eggs Over Easy had been playing a regular circuit, and making a steady living. But there was something more insistent about the Feelgoods and the handful of bands that came in their immediate wake, such as fellow Canvey-combo Eddie & the Hot Rods, Graham Parker & the Rumour, and the 101ers – proto-punks all. Wilko would talk dispassionately about the Feelgoods' influence in *Sounds* at the end of 1976, when the course of punk was by no means set. His comments apply as much to these second-generation pub rockers as the advance guard of punk itself:

There are certain elements in what we did when we were in the clubs . . . which meant that others could organize punk-styled bands . . . Where we differ is that we've always had a lot of respect for the music we're playing, and have always been pretty knowledgeable about it . . . The essence of punk music, on the other hand, is to be naive about what you're doing . . . What I think we laid down – as a path – are certain aspects of image . . . like short hair, and minimal equipment, and most of all the whole atmosphere of aggressive excitement. [*Sounds*, 1/1/77]

If the New York bands were only names in a music paper at this point, the Feelgoods were flesh and blood; and those thirsting for authenticity checked them out. John Wardle recalls how he and his friends John Gray and John Lydon 'went to see them out in Essex, Canvey Island maybe, a couple of times . . . Great performers, though it was very sixties style.' By August of the following year, the young John Lydon would be Rotten to the core; but at the time Lydon had zero musical ambition.

The Feelgoods galvanized aspirants looking to cut loose as early as 1974. One such soul was Joe Strummer, né John Mellor, son of a low-level diplomat, who had been trying on aliases for size ever since his brother's suicide in 1970. He had been thinking of stepping out from the squat he shared with two Spanish sisters and friend Richard Dudanski to play something with a feelgood factor. Dudanski, who was appointed drummer, clearly recalls seeing, 'Wilko Johnson in the pub up the road, [which] was a big inspiration to start the band.' Strummer went further in an interview with *Uncut* shortly before his death in 2002, describing Dr Feelgood as 'the first group to strip down the music in a punk way'.

The 101ers – originally the 101 All Stars, after the address of their squat, 101 Walterton Road – made their live debut in September 1974, and had a residency at The Elgin in Ladbroke Grove by spring 1975. One of the first London bands to not only feel but also fan the Feelgoods' flame, theirs was an equally amped-up R&B. In their case, though, frontman Strummer attempted to *be* both Lee Brilleaux *and* Wilko Johnson.

Back on Canvey, the Feelgoods had long stopped being a secret. Their success in both rocking London to the core and capturing a contract (with UA) gave renewed impetus to a number of local musicians who had previously swopped band line-ups with Feelgoods' frontmen. Dave 'Eddie' Higgs had been in bands with both Brilleaux and Wilko. As he told Will Birch, 'Seeing the Feelgoods doing so well gave me the confidence and inspiration to have a go myself [again]. I put an ad in Chris Stevens Music Centre [in Southend] and met Steve Nichols and Barrie Masters . . . and started playing around Southend.' Eddie & the Hot Rods would make their London debut at the Kensington in May 1975, prompting a handful of music journalists to start talking about a Canvey Sound, something Higgs rejects: 'We got accused of sounding like the Feelgoods, but we were all listening [more] to the J. Geils Band.'

The Canvey energy, though, was proving contagious. The Kensington, in Russell Gardens, had played host to the Brinsleys, the Bees, the Kilburns *and* the Feelgoods. The previous July it also put on another Canvey combo, the Kursaal Flyers. The Feelgoods were returning a favour, Will Birch now being the Kursaals' drummer. However, the Kursaals stuck to a more poppy sensibility, and were not so patently the bastard offspring of Brilleaux and co.

Equally immersed in sixties pop – and a lot more embittered about the musical status quo – was the frontman to Flip City, who also debuted at the Kensington in July 1974. Singer-songwriter Declan MacManus would make almost no impact as a pub rocker, before acquiring a new pair of specs, a tight suit and a new name, Elvis Costello.

At the end of 1974 the Feelgoods were preparing to take their winning ways beyond the home counties, as part of a pub-rock package tour reflecting the tunnel vision of one man, Andrew Jakeman, later to reinvent himself as Jake Rivera, co-founder of Stiff Records. Jakeman was ostensibly manager of Chilli Willi and the Red Hot Peppers, whose debut album, *Bongos Over Balham*, had appeared in the shops in October 1974, after almost two years of hard slog on the pub circuit.

In a gesture of solidarity, Jakeman devised a 'Big Xmas Beat Extravaganza' at London's Roundhouse on 15 December 1974, featuring the likes of Brinsley Schwarz, Ace (a spin-off from cult rockers, Mighty Baby), Kursaal Flyers and – top of the bill – Chilli Willi. The success of this single gig convinced Jakeman that a similar package tour would work. The Naughty Rhythms Tour, starting in mid-January, featured Chilli Willi, Kokomo and Dr Feelgood. Jakeman knew that none of these bands were successful enough to fill provincial theatres but, together, they just might.

If the Feelgoods stood on the verge of greatness with *Down By The Jetty*, their back-to-mono long-player, due out mid-tour, the Chillis had shot their bolt. As the Chillis' Paul Bailey says, 'Dr Feelgood . . . were working the audiences and we weren't. [And] Jake had definitely seen an opportunity.' Sure enough, Jakeman positioned himself to take over the Feelgood management when the tour was over, as the Chillis imploded in real time.

The Feelgoods' performances on the Naughty Rhythms Tour, and their attendant album, would inspire a number of folk looking to translate their own vision into something visceral enough to matter. In Guildford, lightning struck twice, once with the seventeen-year-old

Paul Weller. His own band, The Jam, would be rehearsing by year's end, working on a more Mod-ish kind of sixties revivalism. Equally poleaxed was 26-year-old Graham Parker, who still remembers the shock he got.

Graham Parker: [They] were really something – short hair, straight trousers. Wham! In the face! I pulled out my old pinstriped suit from when I was seventeen and I was still able to wear it, but the arms were up to the elbow. Straight-leg jeans – it was definitely a reaction versus the hippy thing.

Parker almost immediately placed an ad in *Melody Maker*, hoping to put together a band that would help him make a similar kind of statement. Cutting demos which made their way to Hope 'n' Anchor landlord Dave Robinson, Parker then managed to co-opt remnants of two first-generation pub-rock bands destined to remain legends in their own lunchtime, Brinsley Schwarz and Ducks Deluxe. With his own pub-rock supergroup, Parker was ready to confirm the rumours by October 1975. Graham Parker & the Rumour were to be the last band to benefit from the pub-rock A&R goldrush, signing to Vertigo at year's end.

Also impressed by the Feelgoods was a New York musician on a spring sabbatical from his band, Blondie, and the Bowery in general. Guitarist Chris Stein gathered up vinyl evidence of the Feelgoods to take back to Manhattan with him, playing *Down By The Jetty* to the CBGB's throng at the first loft party he could make. He still maintains that, 'Dr Feelgood catalyzed the scene here in a way that a lot of people don't realize.'

Throughout 1975, the Feelgoods continued to find favour with other disaffected souls. 'Wreckless' Eric Goulden, then at college in Hull, caught them there and describes the experience as 'life changing . . . because of the manic energy and drama'. Andy Gill, who would later front Gang of Four, felt a similar kinship stemming from 'that minimal, stripped-down nature, [and] the barely suppressed violence of the dramatic presentation of their personas onstage . . . they were incredibly powerful.' At Belfast City Hall, playing to fans starved of British bands who'd brave the barricades, Brian Young of Rudi remembers they 'tore the place apart – [it was] a *very* influential gig locally.'

The Feelgoods – and those tarred with the same vibrating brush – had noisily moved in to help clear away the remnants of a self-satisfied pub-rock scene. But along with the bad and the plain ugly, they took out the good. One of the casualties of the Canvey clear-out was Kilburn & the High Roads, whose brand of music hardly fit the 'pub-rock' tag, no matter how many bills they shared with fellow imbibers. By June 1975, the Feelgoods had done for the Kilburns – after five years of highs and lows, two record deals, two singles, one nationwide tour with The Who, but no actual hits. Mr Kilburn himself, aka Ian Dury, realized: 'We were still doing Cleopatra's Club in Derby . . . We knew we were on a sticky wicket. Also, I'd seen the Feelgoods go screaming past us like a rocket ship, and I started worrying that we were doing it wrong.' He decided a rethink was in order, returning at year's end as Ian Dury and the Kilburns and then, after a full-year sabbatical, fronting the Blockheads.

A gigging entity since November 1971, the Kilburns were in intent *and* execution edgier than the competition. As Dury told Will Birch for his pub-rock chronicle, 'The other bands I saw in the pubs were a bit samey. We wanted to be a little more brittle. Plus, most of us had been to art school and we considered ourselves a bit snappy. It was always important to us that it was funny.'

The humour never left Dury's songwriting, but the Kilburns were not just a prototype Blockheads – the band with whom he would finally find his audience. Aside from their knockabout ribaldry, they had a frontman who could put you in stitches, in both senses of the word. As Rough Trade impresario Geoff Travis recalls, 'Dury had a threatening presence . . . mixing rock & roll and music hall.' Charlie Gillett, journalist, DJ and Kilburns Konvert, believes that it was the Kilburns' very originality that explains their exclusion from much of the press pub-rock enjoyed.

Charlie Gillett: The people that were writing about pub-rock liked the kind of rehashed R&B thing. Dr Feelgood, Eddie & the Hot Rods, Ducks Deluxe – they just got a lot more coverage than [the Kilburns] did. [They] were seen as far too musical and diverse and inexplicable by any of the criteria that people had.

Dury's art-school rock was not lost on everyone. Eric Goulden, who caught the latterday Kilburns, enjoyed the fact that, 'They sounded and looked as though they might fall to bits in front of you, but somehow . . . never did . . . the Englishness of it all . . . was [also] so inspiring.' Bassist and sometime shop assistant at Let It Rock, Glen Matlock was another hopeful musician who considered 'pride of place in the pub-rock pantheon [should go] to Wilko Johnson's Dr Feelgood and the wonderfully esoteric Kilburn & the High Roads.'

Matlock evidently attended some of the same Kilburns shows as those Feelgood followers, 'the three Johns' – Wardle, Gray and Lydon. He also remained part of London's most enduring rehearsal-only combo, still caught between being Swankers and Sex Pistols. Lydon just liked the music. A year later, though, after the reformulated Kilburns were headlining above the now-functioning Sex Pistols, their manager B. P. Fallon remembered that he 'had seen this geezer hanging around at a lot of Kilburns gigs . . . down the front, watching Ian. [He] turned out to be Johnny Rotten.'

Even at this early juncture Lydon was clearly taken by Dury's notion of sartorial elegance, which included razor blades that doubled as earrings and safety pins strategically pinned to his jacket. When Matlock next saw Lydon, he had already co-opted elements of Dury's look, and seemed prepared to join the gang.

Meantime, the English music press decided they had already stumbled on a thing called punk-rock, applying it to bands like The Count Bishops, the 101ers, and Eddie & the Hot Rods. A few voices, like Giovanni Dadomo in a November 1975 *Sounds* article, challenged such an attribution on the grounds that 'the implication is that they don't play too well, and that they have more guts than talent. And while that's occasionally true, it's a bit unfair to lump them all together in a heap as their aims and effects are pretty easy to tell apart.'

Already punk rock was seen as synonymous with crude ineptitude. Dudanski, drumming for the 101ers, remembers thinking, 'What does that [term] mean?' His room-mate Joe Strummer, though, must have been delighted with the *Sounds* write-up, which described him as coming on 'like vintage Rory Gallagher [!] crossed with the familiar Wilko' until he 'generates enough energy to light [up] a small supermarket'. Since their debut at the Brixton Telegraph on 6 September 1974 (billed as El Huavo and the 101 All Stars), the 101ers had shed a number of less committed members, including El Huavo himself and Richard Dudanski's brother. They were now making the kind of racket they wanted, which *NME* described at the time as 'some very fine rock & roll with no pretence at all towards music, let alone art'.

The 101ers' set-list had precious few originals, concentrating instead on Chuck Berry, early Elvis and the best of earlier British garagebands.

The fact that these revivalists attracted rave reviews from the likes of *Melody Maker*'s Allan Jones and *NME*'s Chas de Whalley incensed other aspirants. Tony James recalls going down the Nashville with his guitarist friend Mick Jones specifically to heckle the band: 'We never really liked them, although we thought the singer was really good.' After a while, Jones stopped heckling and started listening.

Press interest in the 101ers, though, was as nothing to that meted out to Eddie & the Hot Rods, who were attracting major-label interest, something to which the 101ers couldn't aspire without overhauling their wholly reactionary repertoire, even if it stemmed from a genuine disenchantment with (the current state of) Rock itself. As Strummer told Allan Jones in July 1975, just as Rotten was 'auditioning' for his new band: 'If you go and see a rock group, you want to see some-one tearing their soul apart at thirty-six bars a second, not listen to some instrumental slush. Since '67, music has been chasing itself up a blind alley with all that shit.' If Strummer was still a reformer, Rotten was a revolutionary. As he admitted the following summer, he 'would listen to rock & roll, but I had no respect for it. It was crawling up its own arse.'

— — —

Strummer and Rotten were reflecting a disenchantment with What Rock Had Become that was already being articulated by the likes of Nick Kent, Charles Shaar Murray and Jonh Ingham in the music weeklies. Sharing a general distaste for the political arena – after both main parties took a turn at running the country (down) the previous year – theirs was a generation instructed to believe they had never had it so good, all sensory evidence notwithstanding.

The one thing these wild youths had previously clung to was the seeming renewal of rock by successive generations of British art students. But even that now began to feel a little artificial. It would take someone with that fundamental *distaste* for the form itself to shatter the picture and remake it in their own image. Rotten would later tell *NME* about when he began to have doubts: 'I liked Roxy Music. They were good . . . And then *he* took *his* image seriously . . . The same with Bowie doing his Ziggy bit and then changing and thinking, "Oh, I am like that."'

For other überpunks, Bryan Ferry's Roxy Music and Bowie were the only two British art-rockers to retain any vestige of credibility (after all, even as late as 1975, they managed *Siren* and *Young Americans*). Most of those calling out names to be damned for all eternity considered the so-called dinosaur bands topped it. As Mick Jones told one documentary maker, 'The[se] bands left you as they found you . . . You were the same after you'd seen them, except they were richer.' There was no greater example of this than the shows Led Zeppelin gave at Earl's Court in May 1975, where each night's three-hour-plus show was punctuated by interminable piano, drum and guitar solos, each of which was like water torture for anyone conversant with that band in its pomp.

Mark Perry: I remember seeing the Earl's Court shows that Led Zeppelin did . . . It lasted too long, the venue was too big. John Bonham's drum solo was about thirty minutes long, and he was playing with his elbows. [I thought,] 'What's all this about?' Another pivotal thing was Yes at Reading [F. C. on] the *Tales of Topographic Oceans* [tour]. It was a nightmare, sitting in the pouring rain . . . thinking, 'What the fuck is this about?' . . . The rock scene seemed kind of distant – it didn't have anything to do with what was happening. [PSF]

Just as real as their disenchantment was the disinclination to get a job. Contrary to what students of PopCul at Misinformed, Ma. may have been taught, the Britain of the mid-seventies offered extraordinary opportunities for the work-shy and the plain indolent. The 'dole' – as unemployment benefit was called by one and all (erroneously, as it happens – you had to have worked to get the dole. Squatters and/or punks were on 'sup. ben.', i.e. supplementary benefit) – was a godsend to the aspiring artist/musician. There were precious few checks to the system, and they even paid your rent – if you weren't in a squat, that is.

As then-art-student Sebastian Conran told Pat Gilbert, debunking at least one punk myth, 'The life of a musician on the dole, and the life of someone who's genuinely looking for a job and on the dole, well, you couldn't get further apart. Most of the [punks] who used to talk about being on the dole would not have *dreamed* of getting a job. And times were nowhere near as hard then as they became later.'

Johnny Rotten put it best back in 1976 – 'You won't see me working nine to five / Too much fun being alive ['Problems'] – and, more prosaically, in '77: '[Music] shouldn't be about some cunt on a stage yapping about how terrible it is to be on the dole. 'Cause when I was on the dole it was *not terrible*. I was being *paid* for *not* working.' In fact, a beneficent, if impersonal, welfare state provided precisely the conditions required to create a musical revolution among its rapscallions, scallywags and slubberdegullions. As journalist John Orme, writing about the punk scene in the north east in 1977, observed:

The state has [previously] assumed the role of sponsoring the arts, pouring millions into opera, ballet and classical music, if not rock music. But in an area of extreme unemployment like Newcastle, a strange form of state subsidy has emerged. Kids with the stirrings of a musician inside them save up their dole and buy some gear. The dole then keeps them while they rehearse and take the odd gigs that come up. The social security has become patron of the arts because most of the kids reckon there is not much danger of them getting jobs in Newcastle. [*MM*, 29/10/77]

Another by-product of Britain's post-imperial malaise conducive to itinerant musos taking time out to learn about life was the preponderance of squats in the bigger cities of the UK, especially London. Though the term itself might suggest houses and flats on the verge of collapse, this was not always the case. Ruts drummer Dave Ruffy remembers 'there were squats everywhere. When I left my ex-missus, she went with a bloke who lived in a squat. Some of the best people and some of the best houses I ever saw. They weren't student hell-holes, they were really sorted . . . and it was cool – away from the normal. Away from society.'

The collapse of a number of public-housing schemes, and the Labour-controlled urban councils' unwillingness to either repair or replace said housing, made for whole rows of so-called squats, most of which enjoyed communal lifestyles and a *laissez faire* attitude to possessions. Joe Strummer, in the official Clash documentary, *Westway to the World*, drew a picture of 'hordes of people in London who couldn't afford to pay rent . . . The only thing to do was to kick in these abandoned buildings and then live in them.' In fact, the dole would have paid his rent. Those who squatted in London in the mid-seventies were making a statement about the way they wanted to live their life. Indeed, when the Greater London Council threatened to clear the Chippenham Road/ Elgin Avenue area – where Strummer had holed up – in September 1974, the Maida Hill Squatters and Tenants Association organized a large demo in Notting Hill. For Strummer's then-girlfriend, Paloma, those years at 101 were a low-maintenance idyll.

Palm Olive: It was like a cultural revolution . . . Because of the squats, there was all these people . . . that could think about ideas and ways of living without having to work. We were supported by the government . . . When I came from Spain, I was very political because of the situation with Franco. [But] the Spanish young people were really on edge, and pushing for a Socialist type of government. So when I went to London, the idea [there] was that the revolution had to come from the heart. It wasn't political, so much as a change of perspective. All the time we would talk. We would all eat together and drink tea and talk. So there was a real exchange of ideas. And there was dope too. The 101ers were [an integral] part of that.

Where Strummer is spot-on, and not just right-on, is in his claim that, 'If we hadn't had the squats . . . we could [never] have set up a rock & roll group.' Squats like the one at 101 were convenient – one could walk to the West End or jump on and off an open-backed bus – and the neighbours were more likely to compete with than complain about the noise. Some even found ways of getting free electricity, to power those power-chords.

The lack of landlords was just a bonus, more appealing to 'students' like Sid Vicious (né John Beverley) than benefit claimants like Joe Strummer, the student grant being designed to include rent. According to Strummer, he first encountered his fellow Clash city rockers, Mick Jones and Paul Simonon, while standing in line at the Lisson Grove 'Dole' Office. Having spotted two leather-clad lads giving him the eye, he was deciding whether to throw the first punch or run when the pair asked him if he wanted to join their as-yet-unnamed band.

Strummer's distaste for even the most basic educational framework, presumably inculcated at the boarding school he attended but tried so hard to disown, meant that even the art school he briefly attended had too many rules for him. For a whole underclass of 'underachievers', though, there remained an entire sub-structure of educational establishments designed to keep the would-be student from the dole (and therefore the unemployment statistics). The most appealing, for its Britpop associations, its modernistic connotations, its lackadaisical regime and minimal attendance requirements, was the art college.

Jerry Dammers, later Svengali to The Specials, told *NME* how he 'ended up at Nottingham Art School for a year, and then I went to Lanchester [Polytechnic] in Coventry. [But] the actual degree was pretty irrelevant, really – that was just a by-product of what I was *really* doing, which was just using the college's facilities to do what I wanted.' Eric Goulden ended up at Hull Art School, but 'nobody seemed to care what you did or where you did it.' Tim, later TV, Smith also found art school provided an adequate front (and the finance) for him to form a band in 'the English Riviera', somewhere that he later claimed was 'great for learning to get bored. You've got to have something like a band or you go insane.'

TV Smith: [Torquay Art College] was not even a proper art college. I only went there 'cause I didn't know what to do. I tried to get into university, but I didn't get accepted, so I went to art college to carry on with my bands and get a grant, basically . . . I put a band together straightaway, called Sleaze. [We] did our own stuff, which was kinda unpopular at the time 'cause bands were supposed to do [like] Free covers. If you didn't play 'All Right Now' in the set, you didn't stand a chance.

Some art schools had a better class of social misfit, especially when it came to acquiring the 'many radical ideas, extreme political and philosophical points of view and . . . archly opinionated notions of what was and was not cool', which Pete Townshend considers their greatest legacy. Hornsey Art College, because of its (Not Quite) London location, cheap rents in its environs, and an active music scene, drew every delinquent who could paint with a stick.

Graham Lewis managed to make himself social secretary during Hornsey's mid-seventies heyday, and used his position to book his two favourite pub-rock bands, the Kilburns and the Feelgoods, on a regular basis. The Feelgoods got their first booking after Lewis had seen them 'at the Lord Nelson [in Islington]. We turned up and basically it was empty – apart from [these] Teds . . . By the time it was over the whole place was just broken glass. These guys were just slamming glasses on the table. I booked them for sixty quid and paid their petrol from Canvey.'

Leaving aside his own later wiring for sound, Lewis also interacted with future members of The Slits, The Vibrators and the Ants at Hornsey. In fact, the college had its own proto-punk combo at the time, Lipstick. Fronted by Knox in pre-Vibrator mode, Lipstick was a three-piece with obvious influences – Dolls, Velvets etc. – who 'used to do "Whips And Furs", and "Sweet Sweet Heart" in 1975 in The Elgin . . . [But] I didn't think we were pub-rock.'

Lipstick were in that classic English tradition 'of art-school students who get together, and . . . learn their instrument just well enough to play the songs that one of them's written, [so] they're more eccentric, therefore more original, [as] technique [often] flattens out the eccentricities.' Such was the view of American producer, Joe Boyd. The annals of punk support his thesis.

For those to whom the art-college route proved too demanding, there were always technical colleges. Also in north London was Kingsway College, which had its own punk credentials. It was here that John Lydon and John Beverley, aka Rotten and Vicious, did a course in 'boozography' as that other John (Gray) put it. Rotten admitted to Pistols chroniclers the Vermorels, 'It's easy money, isn't it? [You] get your grant.'

For the fortunate few, these courses sometimes led to a place at a polytechnic or university, and three more years of grants. Pick the right course and it was even possible to rehearse a band as often as attend lectures. Such was the case with Tony James, co-founder of English punk's 'great lost band', London SS. This Brunel student and Mick Jones had met at a Heavy Metal Kids gig at the Fulham Greyhound, signalling the end of Jones's previous ensemble, the Mott-inspired Violent Luck (who included the luckless Barry Jones, later co-owner of The Roxy, who remembers his namesake at this time as 'like this Tiny Tim on guitar, in this tiny girl's shirt that didn't fit him. He couldn't play guitar').

Tony James, an equal novice on bass, was just as in love with the rock & roll world. But their search for other like-minded souls proved almost hopeless. Perhaps they were looking for the wrong type. Their first ad for musicians in a March 1975 *Melody Maker* asked for a: 'DECADENT MALE VOCALIST. Must be exciting, pretty and passionately committed to the rock & roll lifestyle.'

The ad generated little response, save an enquiry from a fellow NY Dolls fanatic in Manchester named Steve Morrissey (James admits that 'our [main] reference point would have been New York Dolls'). There was evidently a shortage of folk 'passionately committed to the rock & roll lifestyle', at least among readers of *Melody Maker*. No matter how they phrased their aesthetic, replies were few and far between. It is perhaps necessary to put the problem in context.

Tony James: When we were advertising for a guitarist into New York Dolls and MC5, it was as if it was an alien world that people didn't seem to know about

– you couldn't buy the records. You had to search them out in record bins in Portobello Road.

Finally, they got a call 'from a payphone outside Mick's little flat in Archway'. It was another namesake recently returned from Belgium, where he'd fronted a band with the punkiest name, Bastard. And Brian James concurs with Tony's view, 'No one that you'd run into had ever heard of The Stooges or the MC5 . . . and then I get back [from Brussels], and I saw this ad [in *MM*] and it mentions like Stooges – there's somebody else out there! So I phoned up and it was Mick and Tony, looking for a guitar player and drummer; so I went up and played them a tape of [my band] Bastard. They liked it. I was with the drummer from Bastard, but [they felt] he didn't look rock & roll [enough].'

Despite his drummer friend receiving the cold shoulder, James joined Tony and Mick's gang. Older and more experienced than either, Brian had an altogether wider palate of influences (in a 1977 *MM* Fact File he would list his main ones as James Williamson, Syd Barrett, John Coltrane and Cecil Taylor). But he was also impressed by one song Mick Jones had already written, 'I'm So Bored With You' – 'I thought it was a cool, ironic little love song' – and felt that 'Mick was a talent'. But he also 'always felt London SS was a transitory thing'. What bolstered that sense of passing through was the presence from day one of a balding 'band advisor' called Bernie Rhodes.

Brian James: I thought [Bernie] was a creepy little guy . . . I had been around a little bit longer than Mick and Tony, and I could see they were taken in by him – particularly Tony. To me, he was just another bullshitter – 'Go away!'

After years of painstakingly covering his tracks, Rhodes liked to present himself as a mysterious man-about-town, with all the contacts but no past. In truth, he was concerned that Opportunity had passed him by. He had been looking for a band to compete with – and/or complement – the one his sometime boss Malcolm McLaren was coaxing along. Hence his interest in London SS. It was probably at a Deaf School gig at the Nashville in West Kensington that Bernie first came across this pair of Dolls devotees, one of whom was wearing a t-shirt from McLaren's King's Road shop – the selfsame t-shirt the short, stocky Rhodes had on. When the more forward of the two, Tony James, told him, 'Don't wear the same t-shirt as us – go and stand over there,'

Rhodes memorably replied, 'I designed it, you cunt.' (Still a matter of dispute, as it happens.)

On such pithy retorts are many great friendships founded. When Rhodes discovered that the duo had a band, he arranged to meet the boys the following day at the café on Praed Street they had made their base – conveniently located next to Bizarre Records, their other favourite hang-out, where Jones says he 'used to get all the imports . . . all those [MC5 and Stooges] records'. Rhodes could see it was high time they stopped jamming to get their kicks, and got back to the UK.

Tony James: We both had this fantasy of this café as our base. We decided we'll meet anyone we audition in the café, and [try and] see if we can sort the jukebox out. [Then] Bernie said, 'I've found your rehearsal space,' and we followed him out of the café, into the mews behind the café and it was in a basement, underneath the café – our own rehearsal space. Bernie rented it for us. We would audition the people in the café and if they passed the first audition we would walk them round the corner to the rehearsal place . . . We used to sit in the café for hours and hours while Bernie would talk about all this stuff. We never knew what he was talking about. [But] I remember coming in one day saying, 'I've got this idea for a song called "Rockets For Sale" about selling nuclear weapons in Selfridges,' and Bernie's eyes lit up, 'Now you're talking. Now you're on to something.' . . . Bernie absolutely changed our attitudes and got us to understand what it took to be great. We thought you were in a band, wrote a bunch of songs, and looked great – like the Dolls and MC5. Even though we didn't go to art school, what we did have was the idea the group had to be about something. [But] Bernie would never tell us [anything straight]. We call[ed] it the Riddle. [It was like,] when you understand the answer to the riddle then you'll be ready, but I can't tell you the answer to the riddle. Bernie would always say to us – 'What are you about? You haven't told me anything interesting. What have you got to say?' We didn't know what he was talking about – 'We're a rock band.' 'That's not good enough.' 'Well, we've got songs.' 'That's not good enough. What are you about?' I used to live with my parents. He'd phone me up and be on the phone for two hours, bending my ear – 'You're not about anything. You don't understand. Have you read Jean-Paul Sartre? No, well you better fucking do. I'll send you a reading list.' And he did. He made us go to art galleries. [One] classic [conversation] was, 'You're too staid. Tell your parents you're going to spend Christmas with hookers. You need to go to your local newsagent's and buy Gay News so that you broaden your horizons, because you don't know what's going on.'

The acquisition of a manager of sorts and its first real musician, in fairly rapid succession, changed the band's approach. Even the wording of the ads they continued to place in *MM* altered. One November week they were looking for someone into 'Loud Punk Rock', the next they were looking for a 'wild young drummer . . . must be aware of current NY scene and MC5 thru to The Stooges . . . be dedicated, and look great.' The latter phrase was The Bernie Creed Writ Large.

They had already attempted to recruit at least one bloke based solely on the look he had. Paul Simonon may have been a walking *objet d'art*, but he was as undedicated as they come. Though the band tried to persuade him to sing Jonathan Richman's 'Roadrunner', while they banged out its A and D chords, he couldn't even pull this off. If the ensuing cacophony wasn't bad enough, he turned to Bernie afterwards and said, 'Are you the manager?' Rhodes snapped back, 'Why, what's it to you?' Rhodes was already showing a truly rare capacity for alienating just about everyone that crossed his path. Indeed, when the band got its first and only reply to its 22 November 1975 ad for a 'wild young drummer', Rhodes did his darnedest to dissuade this one madcap drummer from taking it any further:

Rat Scabies: There was an advert in *Melody Maker*, which had run for several weeks . . . [and] I finally rang it up, realizing they wanted something different. It said 'Must be aware of MC5, New York Dolls and The Stooges, and the current New York scene', or something like that. So I rang up Bernie, and he was really quite snotty, 'Why do you think you should be given this great opportunity? What do you know about New York?' And I said, 'I live in Caterham. How on earth do you expect me to know about New York? But I do know who the MC5 are. You either want the greatest drummer in the country to come down, or you don't.'

Chris Miller, aka Rat Scabies – so christened because at his audition in the rat-infested basement he was continually scratching from that unfortunate condition – was perfectly entitled to challenge Rhodes re any supposed awareness of 'the current New York scene'. At this point in time there had been exactly one 45 rpm bulletin from that esoteric enclave, Television's 'Little Johnny Jewel (Parts 1 & 2)'. And Miller knew all about it.

Rat Scabies: I was incredibly relieved when I heard 'Little Johnny Jewel' ['cause] I kinda thought, 'Well, we're not all that good either.' [But] they actually pissed all over [the more pretentious] free-form performers. They [just] did it in a much cooler way.

Across the river, the also-attuned Vic Goddard felt vindicated: 'When I heard "Little Johnny Jewel", I thought it was a modern jazz quartet. I was totally blown away – it was one of the best things I ever heard.' But the release of this left-field *leitmotif* for NY punk perplexed as many as it fulfilled. Banshee Steve Severin recalls buying it at Bonaparte Records in Bromley and thinking, 'I really liked his voice, and the lyrics, and the guitar sound but the drums were too jazzy. I remember one of the reviews said [Verlaine] used a Fender Duosonic. You got this weird juxtaposition where something was obviously changing, but it wasn't changing fast enough.' Another proto-punk was finding it equally impenetrable on a single spin at Penny Lane Records in Liverpool.

Julian Cope: I . . . couldn't believe that they had the nerve to record it. It made The New York Dolls sound like Yes – the bass had no bass, the guitars had no power at all and the singing was awful. In fact the whole record was awful. And epic.

Those who had expected something a little more garagey, more sardonic, wackier, were confused. Some, like Goddard, had spent the past six months staring at a pair of Television posters that illuminated the walls of the Sex boutique – brought back by McLaren as a souvenir of his abortive attempt to save The New York Dolls from themselves in the spring of 1975 – and imagining how weird songs like 'I Fell Into The Arms Of Venus De Milo' and '(I Get A) Double Exposure' might really sound. In Vic Goddard's fevered brain he thought the former would be 'a bit like electric medieval music, [but] instead of lutes, having guitars strum. [I] was uncannily close.'

Shopworker/songwriter Glen Matlock was intrigued by another title on those posters, 'Blank Generation'. As he admitted in his autobiography, 'As soon as I saw that I thought – that's the kind of feeling that we want to get across in our songs.' Without anything more than the germ planted by this poster, he came up with 'Pretty Vacant', which may have lacked the underlying sophistication of Hell's three-minute manifesto ('blank is a line where you can fill in anything') but would have a whole lot more impact.

As it is, much has been made of the connection between the early

Television and the Sex Pistols, based upon McLaren's time in New York, and his interest in Hell. Verlaine told me about how 'Malcolm came backstage [at the Little Hippodrome in March 1975]. Him and Hell were gabbing a mile a minute . . . And he loved the look. I remember him being really taken with the torn-shirt look.' Their discussion actually focused on Hell's disenchantment with Television and his old friend, Tom Verlaine. In fact, Hell quit the following week. As he told one punk documentary, McLaren 'wanted me to go back to England and start a band with me as the singer'.

So far, so good. But Hell also baldly states that, after he decided to take his chances with the equally disillusioned Johnny Thunders to form the Heartbreakers, McLaren appropriated 'everything that was transportable — the haircut, the clothing style and the mode of the material.' Apparently McLaren was the undisclosed singer of the Sex Pistols. Yet, as is well documented elsewhere, those elements as utilized in the Pistols originated with Rotten, who brought them along when recruited to the band some four months after McLaren abandoned the Dolls *and* New York.

Unbeknownst to those few aware souls in London Town who frequented the likes of Bizarre, Beggar's Banquet and Rough Trade, the choice of 'Little Johnny Jewel' as Television's debut single had been contentious enough for the *other* Richard, guitarist Richard Lloyd, to follow Hell's lead. They had in fact recorded a number of their more punky paeans at the single session, including 'Hard On Love', 'Friction', 'I Don't Care' and 'Prove It', all of which might have suggested a justified precedence over the Ramones when it came to brevity *and* wit. But to band leader Tom Verlaine, 'It seemed much more [the point] to put out something like what the band did live'; and anyway this felt 'more like an album track in miniature.' The tension that had already impelled one Richard to walk the plank again threatened their hard-won position on the scene.

'Little Johnny Jewel' was the message *Verlaine* wanted to convey. Indeed, he would later impertinently claim that 'this particular kind of energy that started out with a couple of bands that came out of New York . . . had a big impact on a community in England . . . [but] it seemed that all these people in England went out and got guitars with some big fantasy in their heads . . . [yet] no ability to communicate beyond pounding out some really confused message.' Unlike Television then, Tom?

That 'fantasy' might no longer have been Verlaine's, but it was a carefully cultivated one, those on the CBGB's scene hoping to suggest a greater cohesion than was the case. Lenny Kaye, Patti Smith's guitarist and the conceptualist behind the seminal *Nuggets* anthology, admits, 'A lot of it was encouraged by *Rock Scene*, which I was associate editor of. [We] were publishing pictures and providing a camaraderie for all these [folk] to become bands . . . [They were] like-minded mutants, who we called space monkeys.' Mick Jones was one such mutant, receiving *Rock Scene* and *Creem* from his expatriate mother, who had married an American. Indeed, the fact that Jones 'was the only guy I'd ever met in London who bought *Creem* magazine and understood the humour of it' was an important factor in Tony James's decision to befriend the guitarist.

What these media-savvy New Yorkers had not quite realized was that in the hands of these Brits their precious aesthetic might mutate. As Caroline Coon articulated in one of her early proselytizing pieces, 'Like Cliff Richard, John Lennon, Pete Townshend, Mick Jagger and Roger Waters before them, Johnny Rotten, Dave Vanian, Mick Jones and Pete Shelley were excited by their idea of what was happening in New York. [So] they amplified that idea into an image more potent than the reality.'

Glen Matlock: There's this whole debate, who copied who? . . . Well, nobody copied anybody else. We'd heard of 'em 'cause of Malcolm, who'd brought back flyers for gigs and told us about Richard Hell, but nobody had heard the other band's music, 'cause nobody had made a record. The one thing we heard [early], 'cause we were mates with Nick Kent, [was] the Modern Lovers album. A year and a half before it came out, we were doing 'Roadrunner'.

In fact, Nick Kent was a key figure in the London/New York axis, for a number of interrelated reasons. First and foremost was his position at *NME*, which was exalted enough for him to be welcomed with open arms by the CBGB's cognoscenti when he visited New York in the winter of 1976. Indeed, it was Hell who personally welcomed Kent to New York, a contact facilitated by their mutual friend, Malcolm McLaren. Though the likes of Steve Lake at *Melody Maker* and Charles Shaar Murray at *NME* had been there already, *NME* editor Nick Logan had now decided to send his fastest gunslinger.

Murray had been converted by Patti Smith's debut platter, *Horses*, which he had given a rhapsodic review in *NME*, following it up with a trip to the Bowery. What he had not expected to find was 'that New

York [just] has a thriving local band scene, and they get coverage in their local rags just as . . . a pub band with promise might get a little space in *NME*, even though they're only playing to a hundred people a night.' He also felt that most of the bands he encountered still lacked the kind of chops a medallioned A&R man might demand. His description of the Ramones was certainly precise and prophetic: '[They] are pocket punks, a perfect razor-edged bubblegum band. They should never make an album. They should make a single every week.' When Kent arrived two months later, he was less taken with the Ramones, but revelled in a scene containing (as it did) a perfect combination of sex, drugs and rock & roll.

Nick Kent: I went to CBGB's and saw the Ramones and was impressed, but at the same time there was a Mickey Mouse quality to it. 'Cause I was used to The Stooges. Whereas with the Ramones, you just stood there and watched these guys, and it was fast and it was a gimmick – 'I got it, yeah, yeah'. [I mean,] I liked it. I could see there were good songs there, and I liked the image . . . but I didn't feel that it was groundbreaking.

Howard Trafford (aka Devoto), then at technical college in Bolton, was just one of many young Brits who read Kent religiously in those days. He recalls how Kent made New York seem like 'a very interesting scene'. Wire-man Graham Lewis remembers reading Nick Kent's report on CBGB's in the February 1976 *NME* while in a London launderette and just going, 'Oh fuck. That's it.' Meanwhile, temporary Scouse student Julian Cope was scanning all the music papers 'for sightings of all these weird sceneheads who had beamed down from another planet: Patti Smith and Lenny Kaye, Richard Hell, Tom Verlaine, the Ramones'. Geordie lass Pauline Murray and boyfriend Robert remained desperate 'to go to New York – that's where we thought it was happening. We knew the Ramones were *it* . . . as soon as we saw the pics.'

None of these prescient souls thought there was time for 'it' to happen 'here' before it happened 'there'. Kent also failed to see 'it' coming, even as he pushed 'it' along. In the eighteen months after *NME*'s return Kent wrote a series of seminal pieces, a critic's hall of fame for forgotten heroes like Captain Beefheart, Syd Barrett and Iggy Stooge. These articles provided vital reference points for figures like Johnny Rotten, Howard Devoto, Brian James and Mick Jones. Kent, though, was becoming increasingly frustrated by the strictures of pop journalism, no matter how much lattitude Logan allowed him. When he wrote a three-part serial on Brian Wilson's fall from grace in the early summer of 1975, he was already searching for another gospel plow.

Nick Kent: A real slump set in with that [Brian] Wilson piece. I remember starting it and it was going really well. I felt really inspired, really up. On the last part of it, though, I spent literally hours between sentences just staring at the paper. Something had snapped, and I just couldn't write any more. And it *freaked* me. I just wouldn't write. That . . . was when I started messing around with the Sex Pistols. [1981]

Kent was so freaked – and so frequently out of it – that one time when he was nodding away on the Tube, coming home on the Piccadilly Line, he 'didn't even notice all the other people in the compartment staring at [him]'. One voyeur, no longer fronting Flip City, 'was just amazed that one person could draw that much reaction from others', and returned home to Whitton to write the memorable opening lines of 'Waiting For The End Of The World': 'The man from the television crawled into the train / I wonder who he's gonna stick it in this time . . .' It wouldn't be the last song Kent inspired from the pen of a would-be punk.

— — —

Kent's own dreams of a rock & roll future would ultimately come to naught. However, in a nine-month period spanning the summer of '75 through early spring '76, he would play his part in pushing the Sex Pistols and The Damned out of those rehearsal rooms where they'd settled in semi-permanent hibernation. In the case of the Pistols, he had been enjoined by Malcolm McLaren to act as a possible catalyst for the trio of shopworkers who had been rehearsing together since the summer of 1974. Steve Jones, Paul Cook and Glen Matlock needed *someone* to start pushing and shoving.

Nick Kent: When Malcolm McLaren took me into their rehearsal room, they were [already] very good . . . Just that song 'Did You No Wrong' – you could see that a band playing a set of eight or nine songs as strong as that was going to win, whoever the singer was . . . They played well. This whole story that these guys couldn't play at all was crap. The deal there was [for me] to weed out all this retro sixties stuff. My job there was to bring them into the seventies. I sat around with Matlock and Steve Jones for hours and hours and hours playing the Modern Lovers' 'Roadrunner' – John Cale had given me a tape [of that]. And The Stooges – endlessly . . . There was too much reverence – the music we were coming up with eventually was still gonna be a respectful nod to rock . . . but what they needed was someone who had a total irreverence for rock history. I [also] realized it wasn't going to work with me in it, simply because of who I was. The whole focus would have been on me if the group had started out with me in it. Also I was four years older than them, and a different class . . . Things were happening very fast for me at the *NME*. I became a kinda celebrity writer, and it cast a long shadow, whether I wanted it to or not.

If the band appreciated the push, they never acknowledged it, even giving Kent a hearty shove when he showed signs of sticking around. The likes of 'No Fun' may have entered their repertoire, but the rest of the set stayed bedded in Britrock. Indeed, the bands that pulled their trigger played much the same kind of 'rhythm-guitar orientated songs . . . [with] the rhythm guitar . . . way out front', which had inspired Tom Verlaine to turn on Television.

Glen Matlock: My whole thing was pirate radio in the sixties, really – Luxembourg, Caroline and [Radio] London. Hearing the Kinks, Small Faces and Yardbirds going hammer and tongs; and it's got this whole atmosphere. That's where the Pistols' construction of songs came from . . . I remember on Malcolm's jukebox there was [the Stones'] 'Have You Seen Your Mother' and it's just the sound of it, everything's in the red, and it was on this big old jukebox. When it was recorded, it was all valves, there's one riff, and everybody in the whole band . . . plays everything together always, all the time. It's just like this incessant row, but it's a glorious racket – I like things like that.

McLaren clearly shared a love of that era. After all, it was he who suggested the band learn Dave Berry's 'Don't Give Me No Lip, Child', a song that was on the Sex shop jukebox, because, in Jonh Ingham's words, 'He loved the sound of it – coming back to Gene Vincent. There was this sense that, "This is English."' Here was another one who wanted to turn back the clock. The source of McLaren's master plan was only revealed when interviewed by fanzine writer Sandy Robertson in June 1977, and he admitted that, 'What you want is [the band] playing the Gaumont in Blackpool at six in the evening for every thirteen-year-old kid for 75p . . . That's the way you're gonna open the scene and get it outside of the rock press.'

This has the authentic ring of youthful experience. It also betrays a deep distrust of the very medium Kent represented, which perhaps explains why he ultimately turned on Kent in such a brutal fashion. For McLaren, rock critics became redundant once he had successfully 'incite[d] those kids to create more adventure in their lives and give them confidence to say what they think'. At the same time he spoke of 'hat[ing] the idea . . . of playing to a university audience'. Evidently, the Pistols' distaste for students and distrust of rock critics was something they shared with their manager, if indeed it didn't originate there. McLaren brought a certain evangelism to the process of 'making it' that his three shopworkers lacked.

Tony James: I remember going for a meal with Malcolm and Bernie, and Malcolm telling me the story of what he was going to do with the Pistols. And it unfolded just like he told it – he said, 'We're going to have this group. It's going to be the hottest thing in England – it's going to shake up music.'

McLaren's input may have been real, but it could never be musical. Helen Wellington-Lloyd, with whom he lived at this time, suggests he was 'actually tone-deaf, but that didn't matter. He was always trying different types of music.' What he did drive into his prodigies was the importance of ideas. 'To get across the *idea* of the band in the *songs* of the band' was a mantra that filtered down at least as far as Matlock. At the same time Bernie Rhodes, occasional chauffeur, gofer and sounding board to the Pistols, was pushing the band to find a content to match its chops, though this usually manifested itself as just asking, 'What are you *about*?'

Glen Matlock: Bernie did one very important thing for the Pistols. He made us focus our thoughts. In the early days of the band, before John arrived, he'd beaver away at us in the pub, making us think through our attitudes.

Rhodes also apparently made a better talent scout than his erstwhile boss. According to John Lydon, it was Rhodes who 'spotted me wearing my "I Hate Pink Floyd" t-shirt on King's Road and asked me to come back that night to meet Malcolm, Steve Jones and Paul Cook in The Roebuck pub on the King's Road . . . I was emaciated – very thin with spiky hair. I was wearing what later became full punk garb – ripped shirts and safety pins . . . [which] was me rehashing all those awful pop-star images.'

The three-piece was close to the end of its tether, rehearsing the same old stale repertoire of covers and a couple of faltering originals night after night. They needed more than a singer, they needed a town crier. As drummer Paul Cook told *MM* the following July, 'We [had] played for three years . . . rehears[ing] every night, just shutting ourselves away from everything.' Their one contact with other young musicians came as a shock. Bernie had brought his 'own' band to a meeting with McLaren at Denmark Place. It was the only time the Pistols crossed paths with London SS and they were not impressed. As Matlock says, 'I couldn't believe it – they just looked like Mott the Hoople meets The New York Dolls, hair down here, Mick had leopard-skin trousers on and stack-heel boots and a woman's blouse.'

At least this Johnny guy looked the part. And that capital-A attitude he assuredly had was no act. This was one seriously alienated dude. Steve Jones remembers thinking he 'was a bit of an arsehole, because he had an attitude. [It] was a cool attitude really, but I didn't dig it at the time. I just wanted to be in a band and play rock and this guy was kind of threatening that with his attitude. He weren't, "OK let's go and do it." It was like, "Uhhhhh."' Lydon/Rotten was prepared to push it as far as was necessary just to shake this endemic torpor.

John Lydon: [I was] doing nothing that anyone else wouldn't do. Except that my hair was . . . hacked all over the place and my clothes were torn to shit . . . I was only doing it to be *spiteful*. It was almost like, 'GRRRHHH! I'M SICK OF BEING BORING!!!' [1978]

The fact that Rotten had been spotted walking down the King's Road – not in McLaren's shop itself – is a significant departure from the legend. McLaren's partner, Vivienne Westwood, subsequently suggested, 'It was a big occasion for John to come into my shop, apparently. Later on, when he began to get a bit known, he made out that he'd always been down the clubs and he was the one who'd started it all.' According to Westwood, it was his friend John Wardle (aka Jah Wobble) who was responsible for bringing him into the shop that first time.

Wobble subsequently typified their friendship as Lydon 'just started crawling around after me, and I let him be my mate. He used to buy me drinks . . .'cause no one liked him then. He used to wind everyone up.' Certainly some deep-rooted insecurities lay behind Johnny's need to be constantly chaperoned by two or more of the other Johns – Gray, Beverley and Wardle (the latter two soon adopted less confusing soubriquets – Sid Vicious and Jah Wobble).

At his audition, though, miming along to Alice Cooper's 'Eighteen' on the Sex jukebox, Johnny was out there on his own. As Jones trenchantly recalls, 'Rotten looked the part, with his green hair, but he couldn't sing. Then again, we couldn't play, so it was okay.' They may have been recruiting a man who 'couldn't sing', but Rotten knew his music, even if his tastes had no great rock bias. As he told Vivien Goldman at the time, 'I listen to everything. I love my music, and I make very sure I know all about it.'

Shopkeeper Vivienne was not so sure he was the answer; and though, 'We all went along with John . . . in the beginning,' she quickly realized, 'He'd been a very strange little boy – he used to collect records with his friends and . . . all they ever did was sit around playing them.' Her business partner and ex-lover Malcolm McLaren, however, was thoroughly taken with 'his' discovery, and couldn't wait to tell the one man who might just understand.

Nick Kent: Rotten had a profoundly *middle-class* love of music. [He] liked Van Der Graaf Generator, for Christ's sake. You don't get more Prog or cerebral than that. [But] the guy had something. The first time Lydon's presence was made known to me was when McLaren and I were walking down Denmark Street, and he turned to me and said, 'We've found a singer. He's the best thing in the group. He looks like a spastic, and he's just written this song, "You're only twenty-nine / You got a lot to learn."' . . . Just hearing that, it was like, 'OK, they've found someone.' They needed some kinda teenage Ian Dury, another working-class misfit, that would create an explosion. If they'd found just another good singer, they would have been successful. But they wouldn't have been a phenomenon.

Sure enough, the song-lyric Rotten had written – then called simply 'Lazy Sod', but known to the world as 'Seventeen' (as in, one less than 'Eighteen') – was unlike anything already out there. And with a cluster of new originals like 'Seventeen', 'Submission' and a rejigged 'Pretty Vacant' came an overhaul of the set. As Matlock recalls, 'We used to play covers, just to learn . . .'em, most of which, when we started

rehearsing with John, he didn't like, so [they] had to go.' This lurch
into forward gear still didn't convince one of the original trio that they
were on the right track.

Steve Jones: Cook . . . said it was just a fuckin' noise. We thought it was rock,
just not very good, but John liked it just because it wasn't [rock], because it
was noise.

As McLaren told Jon Savage, 'Rotten wanted it like the sixties –
Captain Beefheart, all weird,' but he was still just a callow youth with
no stagecraft to his name. Not surprisingly, he took from those sources
close to hand. There was one consummate performer on whom both
Rotten and McLaren could and did agree – Ian Dury. Rotten may have
seen Dury's band, the Kilburns, a number of times, but Kursaal Flyer
Will Birch believes it was McLaren who 'held Ian up to Lydon: "See
how good he is – see how he draws the audience in – he stands behind
the mike – one hand on the mike – he hangs on it – Gene Vincent
style, looking up, because he's short." . . . Lydon took quite a bit from
Ian visually.'

Dury, a regular at Sex, certainly thought so. When he finally got to
see the Pistols for himself, he saw someone wearing safety pins, 'the
sartorial elegance that I had inspired myself with', and 'leaning forwards
and growling and holding the microphone just like I did. And Malcolm
[was] on one side and [I'm] going, "What's all that about then, Malcolm?
He's copying me, isn't he?"'

Rotten, with a nod to Dury, was the catalyst Kent failed to be. In
little more than three months the Pistols were ready to gig, if still not
exactly rock. As Lydon later told *MM*'s Allan Jones, 'We just went out
and we done it in front of the public. We didn't stay in a rehearsal studio
until we were so perfect we were boring.' To the others, the opportunity
came as an enormous relief, even though Jones admits, 'We'd start[ed]
playing live shows before we could play, really. I mean, we could make
noise and some sort of construction of the songs . . . but it was madness,
it was total madness.'

The first Sex Pistols gig was at St Martin's School of Art, on Charing
Cross Road, across from the band's Denmark Place rehearsal loft, on
5 November 1975. Matlock, ostensibly enrolled at the school, approached 'social sec' Sebastian Conran, requesting the opportunity to
play without any pecuniary obligation. Conran asked what they were

called and, when told, replied, 'Oh, with a name like that we really must have you.' They were still only the support act, to an outfit called Bazooka Joe – but the Pistols were determined to blow away the rehearsal blues.

Paul Cook: We were really pumped up! . . . They pulled the plug on us . . . So, yeah, we were running on high energy. Malcolm was there, and I think he made a decision [then] to get more involved. I don't know what he thought about the music. I don't think he knew much about music, myself. But he did know we were able to shock.

Eddie Edwards, Bazooka Joe's roadie (and later drummer for The Vibrators), does not think the plug was pulled. He recalls that, 'They had a rehearsal place across the road in Denmark Street (sic) [but] they didn't want to bring all their gear up. [So] they said, "Oh, can we share gear?" Steve, [though,] didn't want to use the amps [Bazooka Joe] had. He wanted to use [his] Fender Twin. And then Rotten got up and sang in his torn woolly, and everyone said, "Oh they're not much good, are they?" and went and sat in the bar. They did a few covers, [but] they were a bit untogether.'

Hardly the apocalyptic entrée into the entertainment industry McLaren had imagined. Yet Bazooka Joe lead singer, Stuart Goddard, later told Savage, 'The rest of my band . . . thought they couldn't play; in fact somebody said as much to Glen, and he said, "So what?" But I thought they were very tight . . . [and] I left Bazooka Joe the next day; I came out of that gig thinking, "I'm tired of Teddy Boys," and it seemed to me that the Sex Pistols were playing simple songs that I could play. I just wanted to go away and form my own band.'

If it really happened this way, then Goddard was the first of a legion of converts over the next twelve months who took a simple ethos away from a Sex Pistols gig: 'Do It Yourself'. It would also suggest he was one of their less galvanized converts, since it would be another eighteen months before he reinvented himself as Adam, of the Ants.

Throughout the next two months the Pistols continued to assault the art-school circuit, their gigging opportunities circumscribed by McLaren's determination to bypass the pub-rock venues of London. Instead, McLaren stoked a legend that from the outset 'we used to . . . turn up at the college, never tell them, said we had a gig, and [I] blagged my way through to the social sec, saying that we're a support group.'

It's a terrific story, but no such gig has ever come to light. On the other hand, there is evidence galore to support Matlock's contention that, in the early days, 'They always used to take us off halfway through . . . and [the MC] would say, "Thank you very much the Sex Pistols and their wall of sound," in a very piss-taking kind of way.'

Lydon, though, was loving it, not just the attention − though that played its part − but what he liked to call 'the cluttering of it all. Complete breakdown of music . . . Rubbish Rock it should've been called.' And yet the Pistols were attracting interest, and press, almost immediately. Their fifth gig − and third at a London art school − was at 'the Chelsea', a month to the day after St Martin's, and it brought a mention in *NME* from reviewer Kate Phillips, who reported McLaren's claim that 'they're going to be the Next Big Thing', before adding her own suspicion, 'Or maybe the Next Big Thing After That.'

It seems McLaren was at last taking a hands-on role with the band. Yet fetish business beckoned, and according to guitarist Keith Levene, who now enters the McLaren-Rhodes sphere of influence, 'Malcolm went away for two weeks [at this time] and had Bernard look after the Pistols. Bernard did this thing where he'd spoken to John and questioned his motives and questioned Steve Jones. The band really improved a lot in these two weeks Malcolm was away. This *really* pissed Malcolm off.' Lydon also suggests Rhodes played a mentor role in his 1993 autobiography: 'Bernie would often take me aside and tell me, "Go with it. Honest, it will be good. You'll get there." . . . He would sow a seed and then wait to see if I would pick up on it.'

At the Chelsea School of Art gig, Rhodes brought along London SS bassist Tony James, who remembers that 'it was all quite chaotic. [But] they had a frontman. And we still hadn't found a frontman.' It dawned on the pair that 'their' band was being left behind. The Pistols were not merely more developed than London SS. They were a real band. London SS were not. Rhodes' solution was a radical one − he broke up the band.

James and Jones had already decided that new drummer Rat Scabies, like the poor Bastard drummer, was not right, that he didn't look rock & roll enough. As it happens, Scabies thought the same about them: 'Brian was the real deal − [he] had a short, spiky barnet. Whereas the other two looked like something off the King's Road − fashionable gentlemen. Brian was also very sussed on The Stooges, the Dolls and the Five. And he was into avant-garde jazz.'

The (de)merits of Miller became the wedge that drove Brian James out of the band, and damned him for eternity. Already disenchanted, he decided enough was enough, and confided in Miller that they should form a band of their own.

Brian James: [Bernie] started hanging around . . . That's one of the things that really put me off. Plus Mick and Tony's conception of everything had to be so rock & roll . . . When Rat came down, it was, 'Like, wow, this guy is great,' but they were like, 'He doesn't look so good.' 'Who cares what he looks like, man. Listen to him!'

If Bernie Rhodes alienated Brian, he also had his doubts about the 'other' James in his gang. And Tony began to realize he did not fit into the Rhodes master plan: 'Bernie's thing was you had to be working class to be credible. That was always the problem with me and Bernie all the way through. I was clearly someone who went to university and read a book! Wasn't dangerous enough.'

The first clue that Tony James did not figure in future plans came when Rhodes brought along a pretty, mouthy American, Chrissie Hynde, to play some Iggy Pop songs with the guys. Hynde was the sister of Cleveland musician Terry Hynde (from 15–60–75), and had been at school with some of the key figures in Cleveland's music underground, before electing to make London home in 1973.

With little save her brazen charms going for her, she managed to befriend enough mavericks to meet and ensnare Nick Kent, and secure a gig of sorts as token female rock scribe at the *NME*, thanks to Kent and Ian MacDonald; before then befriending the McLaren-Westwood team. Supplementing her *NME* earnings by working part-time at Sex, she became friendly with Rhodes, who took turns with McLaren finding possible projects for her. In the last days of London SS, Brian James recalls, 'Mick and Chrissie started working on this project . . . I was really surprised when that didn't happen.'

Meanwhile, Brian and 'Rat' continued scouting around for like-minded folk, hoping to get their own musical ambitions off the ground. Their method was much the same one used by Rhodes to recruit Rotten.

Rat Scabies: There weren't many people around that looked good . . . Anybody that looked interesting, you struck up a conversation. So we spent our time looking round . . . Brian [had been told by] Bernie [that he] and Malcolm were gonna come up with three bands and start a movement. They were pretty tight then . . . [So] one night I went to Dingwall's, and met Malcolm there. He knew who I was, and he just took my details. Then the next night he turned up with Nick Kent and Chrissie Hynde, and asked me if I wanted to form a band with them. At this point Chrissie was gonna play guitar.

According to Hynde, she and McLaren had been 'sitting in this café in Soho . . . and we were talking about how to form the ideal rock band. What we need, said Malcolm, is someone who's young, intelligent, looks great, and is totally dedicated to rock & roll. And we both looked at each other at exactly the same moment, Nick Kent!' There was just one insurmountable problem – Kent and Hynde were no longer an item, and there were clearly some unresolved 'issues'.

Kent says that the day after meeting Miller at 'this shabby rented room in Croydon . . . Chrissie came round and we had this huge row, so that was out the window.' Kent, though, was still interested in working with 'Rat'. In fact, he needed a band to play a weird little gig in Cardiff that his new girlfriend, Hermione, had arranged. 'Rat' suggested they enlist Brian James and his old friend Ray Burns, aka Captain Sensible.

According to Kent, the gig in question, at 'this female liberation festival', prompted them 'to be obnoxious; [so] we did songs like "Under My Thumb", "He Hit Me And It Felt Like A Kiss" by The Crystals. We also played "New Rose" and "Fish", which Brian sang.' Both songs were penned by James, and according to the man himself, 'We did Nick's set, then the rest of the band walked off, and there'd be just the three of us, and we did three numbers which became Damned numbers, turned the amps up and let rip.' They were finally on their way to damnation. For Kent, though, 'it was too fast . . . I prefer a slower groove,' and the so-called Subterraneans returned underground.

The Subterraneans were not the only band utilizing Rat and the Captain as a rhythm section in the weeks before that solitary gig. Rat's induction into the McLaren circle had made him a cohort in another project McLaren was hoping to make an adjunct to his musical movement, the fabled Master of the Backside.

Rat Scabies: Malcolm introduced me to Dave Vanian, at Helen the dwarf's flat which was just round the corner from the dole office [at Lisson Grove]. We [also] had another Dave, who was also a singer, who was the complete antithesis of Vanian . . . a blonde, effeminate hairdresser from Essex, brilliantly funny. Malcolm asked me if I knew anyone with a bass, and we were at Jamie Reid's house, which was just round the corner from where Sensible lived. [So] we had the two Daves as singers, Captain played bass, [Chrissie Hynde on guitar]. She was just a gobby Yank who couldn't play guitar. And Malcolm was gonna be the manager. We tried to put a few things together, but I really missed Brian's playing . . . I just ended up getting really frustrated with the whole thing.

Brian and Rat continued to be frustrated by the lack of prospective punk musos. In this, they were not alone. Mick Jones – having cut free from London SS – was equally adrift. As Kent recalls, 'There was always this threat that Mick Jones would get this group together. At this time they were known as the Mirrors.' Jones, too, was now a man on a mission, after some kind of epiphany: 'I was [just] going up the stairs one day and God hit me on the head with a mallet and said, "You be in a group, you cunt." . . . It's the way you get ideas across *faster* than anything else. You don't wanna waste ten hours doing a painting – which may flop . . . You just go out and do it.'

In the winter of 1976, the one place where contacts were made – and notes compared – was down Portobello Road market on a Saturday afternoon. As Scabies suggests, 'There were [now] a few more leather jackets. Mick and Tony had got their hair cut by this point. We'd meet up at Portobello Road . . . for these lunchtime sessions, and you'd always get a couple of bands there. The guys from The Boys were always there – and they were mates – but weren't really on the same wavelength.' Sid Vicious, now sharing a squat with Mick Jones, sometimes tagged along, as did sometime-girlfriend Viv Albertine. Also a fixture at these lunchtime sessions was Keith Levene, who was Mick Jones's sidekick in the Mirrors. Levene was careful not to let slip that he was fresh from a stint as underage roadie for his favourite band, Yes.

Keith Levene: [Mick] really dug me and we became really fast friends. He thought I was fucking great on guitar. [One] week, he invited me down to Portobello Road, and . . . introduced me to this guy called Paul [Simonon]. He told me, 'This guy comes across as a bit thick but he's a really great artist. I think he could be the bass player, but he can't play.' I was cool with that. We were looking for something. We didn't know what it was . . . [but] we had a bit of a manifesto. We were trying to tear things down . . . We just knew that a lot of things were fucked. [PSF]

While the Subterraneans came and went – and Master of the Backside too – Jones cajoled the evergreen Simonon into picking up the bass. Finding a drummer, though, preoccupied him for some months, despite discarding an ideal one in Scabies. So while Scabies' new band prepared to make some demos, at a tiny four-track studio run by The Boys' Matt Dangerfield with Barry Jones in Maida Vale, Bernie and Mick were still auditioning timekeepers, with occasionally hilarious results.

Barry Jones: The audition I particularly remember was [Filthy Animal from Motorhead] coming down into my basement. He had this huge kit and he auditioned for The Clash. We were like, 'Oh my God', 'cause we were into stripped kits – bare minimum – it was punk.

This sense that the sands of opportunity were running out – felt by Tony James at the Chelsea School of Art back in December – now struck Mick Jones. In the second week of February 1976, he finally caught the Sex Pistols at a party held by the 'arteest' Andrew Logan at Butler's Wharf. As he recently revealed, 'As soon as I saw the Sex Pistols, you just knew this was it – it had happened.' Jones had gone there with Tony and Brian James; and like Mick, Brian was impressed, though for wholly non-musical reasons.

Brian James: I thought, 'Oh, they're not very good players, but they ain't half got a lot of attitude.' It was between the numbers when John used to come into his own, when he'd be talking. It was just like a stand-up comic. He'd be taking the piss like one of your mates, but he was onstage. He did put over this air of [just] not giving a fuck.

This aspect of the early Pistols is often overlooked by those unable to explain their cathartic impact – Lydon always knew how to push buttons. As he states in Pistols biopic *The Filth And The Fury*, 'We managed to offend all the people we were fed up with. We [just] went into full attack format. This band wasn't about making people happy, it was about attack. Attack, attack, attack.' Student filmmaker Julian Temple recognized as much: 'The idea of the Sex Pistols . . . didn't just have to do with being in a band. It was about throwing a spanner in the works.'

As an example of what Lydon later typified as 'go[ing] where you're not wanted first – there's more to achieve', the Logan party and its fey debauchery clashing with the sheer vitality of the Pistols and their followers was as apposite as one could get. Jordan, the full-figured Amazon that put the Sex in McLaren's Pistols, remembers how after 'the Sex Pistols started up . . . Andrew [Logan] was freaking out, because it was like anarchy had been transported into his little paradise . . . [Then] someone from *NME* arrived . . . and Malcolm came rushing up to me and said . . . "Jords, the enemy is here! They've actually turned up! We've got to do something that will create a scuffle, a story . . . Why don't you go up there and take your clothes off."'

Jordan duly obliged, jumping onstage, coaxing a suddenly self-conscious Rotten into ripping off her top, but the gesture proved unnecessary. Unbeknownst to McLaren, the *NME* were already preparing to run a review of their Soho debut – at the Marquee four nights earlier – setting the tone, and much of the vocabulary, for press coverage to come.

While Logan's party for his wharf rats represented some kind of camp citadel, a place like the Marquee was the real enemy encampment in McLaren's eyes. Built upon a notion of the club as the centre of sixties Britpop, the place's musical heritage was largely appropriated (i.e. almost no important band *established* its reputation there). And it had now become a belated bastion for up-and-coming pub-rockers, such as the headliners on that fateful night in February 1976, Eddie & the Hot Rods.

The Pistols were already looking to spoil this party, attendant upon the Hot Rods signing to Island Records. To Rotten, they were 'everything that was wrong with live music . . . playing in pubs. It was all about denim and plaid shirts!' McLaren was also anxious to stoke up any rivalry. Indeed, Will Birch firmly believes he was 'trying to orchestrate a sort of a conflict – you know, dividing this thing off by saying Eddie & the Hot Rods were old hat,' though they had actually been part of the London music scene for less than nine months.

For the first time, there were even some folk there egging the Pistols on. Simon Barker and Steve Bailey (aka Severin) had made the trip into London specifically to see the spiky-topped quartet. Barker had caught the last song of an earlier show at the Ravensbourne Art College, and informed [Severin] that he had just seen 'The English Stooges'. Recognizing 'Malcolm and Vivienne a little bit from going up to the shop', Steve began talking to the band, who informed him that they were playing the Marquee the following week.* By the time Severin

---

* The only documented gig at Ravensbourne was 9 December 1975, some two months before the Marquee; so it seems that the band returned to the college in the new year.

and Barker had got their overpriced drinks, Rotten was already throwing 'a few chairs around. Jordan got on stage and wiggled about, and they upset everybody, including the Hot Rods. [So it] became the first schism between the old and new. We watched about two songs [of the Hot Rods] and walked out. The lines were [already] drawn at that point.'

The Bromley boys promptly decided to catch the band again, and to bring along more satellite kids. And they weren't the only witnesses bowled over by the sheer aggression and attitude evident that night. The set was also partially caught by a pair from Barnes, Vic Goddard and Rob Symmons; who, as Goddard says, made a habit of 'go[ing] down the West End on our bikes, and look[ing] for the best gig'.

Vic Goddard: We were just going down Wardour Street, and you could hear this right racket going on, and you could tell something good was going on. The [Pistols'] set was nearly over when we went in – [but] they were having a big row with the management, and chairs were flying through the air. We just had to find out when the next gig was after that.

If the Pistols made a handful of converts at the gig itself, the spark that ignited a movement came from one bemused journalist in attendance. *NME*'s Neil Spencer was there ostensibly to see the Hot Rods, who were media darlings of sorts. As he now admits, he was slightly surprised to witness people shouting abuse at the Pistols but 'what was [truly] novel was that the band screamed right back'. The review that ran in the following week's *NME* failed to mention the Hot Rods, while the Pistols were described as 'sixties-styled white punk rock'. And it bore a prophetic headline, 'The Sex Pistols are coming'. Never was a truer word written. Time to lock up one's children.

PART TWO

LIGHT THE BLUE
TOUCHPAPER
2/76 – 4/76

Page 10 SOUNDS April 24, 1976

The Sex Pistols are four months old, so tuned in to the present that it's hard to find a place to play. Yet they already have a large, fanatical following. So their manager, who runs a rubber and leather shop called Sex, hired a strip club where the two sides could meet...

By Jonh Ingham

THE SMALL, sleazoid El Paradise Club in Soho is not one of the more obvious places for English rock to finally get to grips with the Seventies, but when you're trying to create the atmosphere of anarchy, rebellion and exclusiveness that's necessary as a breeding ground, what better place? Name a kid who will tell their parents they'll be home really late this Sunday because they're going to a strip club to see the Sex Pistols.

The front is the customary facade of garish, flourescent lit plastic and enticing lit pix, gold flecked wallpaper and a life-size gold framed lovely beckoning you within.

Conditioning expects me to go down a hall or some stairs, but the minute you turn the corner you're there. A small room 20 to 30 feet long, bare concrete floor, a bar at one end, three and a half rows of broken down cinema seats. (The other half seems to have been bodily ripped out.) It's an unexpected shocking sight at first, but after it gets comfortable the thought occurs that perhaps it's not sleazy enough. It needs more black paint peeling from the revealing walls, a stickier floor...

With luck, the second gathering occurred there last Sunday (the Maltese landlords can be a little difficult to unearth). The first such gathering accumulated entirely by word of mouth, and by midnight the joint was jumping.

Flared jeans were out. Leather helped. All black was better. Folks in their late twenties, chopped and channelled teenagers, people who frequent Sex, King's Road avant leather, rubber and bondage clothing shop. People sick of nostalgia. People wanting forward motion. People wanting rock and roll that is relevant to 1976.

At the moment, that groups is best embodied in the Sex Pistol. They fill the minuscule mirror backed stage, barely able to move in front of their amps. They are loud, they are fast, they are energetic. They are great.

Coming on like a Lockheed Starfighter is more important to them than virtuosity and sounding immaculate. This quarter has no time for a pretty song with a nice melody.

Guitarist Steve Jones doesn't bother much with solos, preferring to just pick another chord and power on through. ("There's two reasons for that — I can't play solos, and I hate them anyway.' As he said that 'I'm Mandy, Fly Me' came on the juke box and everyone agreed the jukebox was playing good thing in it was the solo.)

But imitating the roar of the Industrial Age doesn't mean they're sloppy. Although earlier reports reckoned their time-keeping somewhat off, to the point of cultivating an ethic of them being so bad they were good, Glen Matlock (bass) and Paul Cook (drums) seem to have the beat on the rails, and in this stripped down item the beat is where it's at. One also has to remember that the Sex Pistols has only existed professionally since Christmas and that Steve has only played guitar for five months.

With inaudible lyrics the music is very similar from song to song, but a crucial trigger says that song is great (applause), but that one is just okay (don't applaud). Everyone else seems to think similarly. Which annoys singer John Rotten endlessly. "Clap, you fuckers. Because I'm wasting my time and hearing myself," he begins a slow handclap, about three people join in.

John is a man who likes to confront his audience, not to mention the rest of the band. It's this Stooges like aura of complete unpredictability and violence that gives the Sex Pistols that extra edge. Paul reckons the broken glass attitude will only disappear when they get as old as Pete Townsend and just do it for the money.

The Pistols' roots lie with Paul and Steve, who left school with a healthy desire to avoid work. The obvious alternative was rock, even though neither could play an instrument. Their musical models were the Stooges and the Who and the early Small Faces, which doesn't say much for Seventies rock, and was a reason for starting a band.

Out of the last six years Steve rates the Stooges. Paul admits to being fueled by Roxy Music for three albums. Later he

[The Pistols are] a quartet of spiky teenage misfits from the wrong end of various London roads, playing sixties-styled white punk rock as unself-consciously as it's possible to play these days, i.e. self-consciously . . . I'm told the Pistols repertoire includes lesser-known Dave Berry and Small Faces numbers, besides an Iggy and The Stooges item and several self-penned numbers, like the moronic 'I'm So Pretty Vacant'. — Neil Spencer, *NME*, 21/2/76.

There is a legend that almost nobody saw The Velvet Underground play, but those that did went and formed bands. In fact, the tally of bands *directly* inspired by the Velvets is surprisingly unimpressive (the Modern Lovers, Mirrors, Cinderella Backstreet, and Eric Emerson and the Magic Tramps is my top-of-head list). The Sex Pistols, on the other hand, were the lightning conductor for a generation of bands. And what bands! In the thirteen months that they were a gigging, breathing entity – as opposed to mere tabloid whipping boys – they inspired battalions of musos to get out of their bedrooms and start gigging.

Almost all of these disciples were waiting for something that – like Godot – never looked like arriving. Yet when the Pistols burst upon the scene, every attuned anarchist knew this was IT. Just reading the above review, and seeing the insolent expression across Rotten's face, set pulses racing in yon valleys and dales. In the provinces *NME* held particular sway, and in February 1976 it was at the cusp of its influence, a weekly Bible to all and sundry, the views of its 'star' journalists mentioned in revered tones in school playgrounds around the land.

Prefect Robert Lloyd, stuck in Shropshire, speaks for many when he says, 'As soon as I read the review of the Sex Pistols in *NME* I knew I wanted to see them. Somehow you knew. I can't begin to describe it.' Gaye Black (aka Advert) and her boyfriend Tim, both at Torquay Art College, who read the *NME* 'from cover to cover', were also struck by that famous Marquee review, and resolved to check out this band. For Martin Bramah, in Prestwich, north Manchester, not yet heading for The Fall, it was the juxtaposition of Spencer's description against its accompanying photo that struck a chord.

Martin Bramah: There was a little article in *NME* . . . a review of a London gig that the Sex Pistols had done, in which they described this band doing a couple of Stooges songs and there was a little picture of Johnny Rotten. Now to us, seeing a kid with short hair doing Stooges songs didn't add up.

The Undertones' John O'Neill accurately describes the *NME* at this time as 'influential in emphasizing this Highly Critical [attitude to] the self-indulgence of the lumbering progressive rock acts, [and] hark[ing] back to an earlier time when you could equate rock & roll with rebellion and excitement and fun'. He, too, felt the pull of the Pistols just by reading about them. Howard Trafford and Peter McNeish, two friends who had found each other at Bolton Institute of Technology, after Trafford had presciently placed an ad on the bulletin board looking for 'musicians . . . both sexes, to do version of Sister Ray', formed the habit of reading their communal *NME* at college on a Thursday lunchtime.

Howard Devoto: I was reading [the *NME*], but I completely missed [the review], and Pete handed it back to me, and said, 'Did you read this?' It was that 'we're not into music, we're into chaos' line, and the fact that they played a Stooges song. And it was like, 'Who the fuck in Britain plays Stooges songs?' I didn't know anybody else who had a single Stooges record. And it was obviously confrontational.

For Devoto (né Trafford), The Stooges had become an obsession. He later claimed to *NME* that in 'the pre-Pistols sterility period', as he then described it, his 'rock listening was pared down to the three Stooges albums, because they were the only records that made sense to me'. For Shelley (né McNeish), too, The Stooges were the archetype whenever the pair talked about a band of their own: 'We had in our mind what music we wanted to do. It was The Stooges . . . We wanted people to say it was rubbish and walk away – all that sort of stuff.'

Progress to date had been slow, almost tortoise-like. Devoto recalls that they had 'been trying things with a drummer . . . some Stooges songs, some Eno songs . . . But it was really not happening. By February 1976, I don't think we really knew where any of this was going, except that we were vaguely still trying to get a band together . . . One was reading about all that happening in New York, but you couldn't hear any of it.' For some reason, though, they felt galvanized enough by Spencer's review to consider driving the two hundred miles to London to see this band who were 'into chaos'. And happenstance decided to work its wonders this time. Though Devoto didn't have a car, he shared a house with someone who did, and she was going away for the weekend, leaving Devoto in charge of the keys to the Renault. The M1 beckoned.

First off, they needed to establish whether the Pistols were actually playing anywhere. Devoto, who in his spare time was unpaid pub-rock correspondent for the *New Manchester Review*, a right-on *Time Out* clone on a shoestring budget, knew enough to phone Neil Spencer at the *NME*, who wasn't sure of the band's whereabouts but put him on to McLaren. Spencer's exact words were, 'They're managed by this guy called Malcolm. He runs the Sex shop on the King's Road. It's at the World's End,' leaving Devoto to conjure up an image of 'this guy [who] runs a sex shop at the end of the world'. Another necessary piece of the jigsaw was having a place to stay. As it happens, Devoto's friend, Richard Boon, was doing Fine Arts at Reading University, and close enough to London for punk.

Richard Boon: I got a phone call from my oldest friend, Howard Trafford, 'Did you see that [review]? I've rung the *NME*, got the phone number of the [Pistols'] manager, who seems to run a sex shop, and me and my friend Pete McNeish are coming down [this weekend]. You can put us up.' So they drove down, went to Sex – which was not a sex shop at all – and the Pistols were playing High Wycombe that night and Welwyn Garden City the following night. The first night they were opening for Mr Big, and it was a horrible student-union venue. All these horrible students didn't like [the Pistols] at all. [In fact, they] sat at the front of the stage with their back to the band, making mocking gestures to the back [of the hall]. So when they started 'No Fun', Johnny ran along the front of the stage and tousled all these guys' hair . . . [who then] picked Johnny up, threw him on the floor and there was a big mêlée. People who were a bit more sympathetic piled in. The band kept playing, [as] Johnny crawled out from this scrum, got back on the stage, and said, 'Well, that was no fun.' We talked to them afterwards, and they were very tickled that people from Manchester had come to see them.

All three northerners were gobsmacked. For Shelley, they had 'the basis of [any] exciting music – fast, loud, no kowtowing to the audience . . . We felt an immediate affinity . . . There was [also] this sense that it could fall apart at any minute . . . [another] very attractive quality.' For Devoto, it was beyond affinity. The following year he told Paul Morley, 'I'm not very good at envisaging finished musical product. I knew *what*

I wanted to say but I couldn't see *how*. The Pistols made me realize how I could express what I was trying to say.' More recently he observed that it wasn't just 'the aggro, the look, Lydon's charisma', it was something less definite; this sense of, 'We'll go back and do something like this in Manchester.'

That sense of impetus would be replicated by audience members in places as far-flung as Hastings, Scarborough, Birmingham, Manchester, Caerphilly, Hendon and Leeds over the next ten months; but Devoto and Shelley were the first, and most fleet-footed. They even had the foresight to tape the Welwyn Garden City gig, from which they quickly worked up their own arrangement of '(I'm Not Your) Steppin' Stone' for their first public performance, propitiously booked for 1 April at the college they attended. The band even had a name, Buzzcocks – a cryptic sentence in a review of TV's *Rock Follies* ('It's a buzz, cock') which caught their eye in that week's *Time Out*.

For their debut gig – organized by the Textile Students' Association – the boys had worked up a dozen-song set, including two originals ('The True Wheel', aka 'No Reply', and 'Get On Our Own'), two Stooges covers ('Raw Power' and 'Loose'), one Bowie song ('Diamond Dogs') and a smattering of garageband standards by the Kinks, Beatles and Stones; culminating in the Troggs' cult classic, 'I Can't Control Myself' (also part of the early Clash repertoire).

However, the actual show seems to have collapsed as soon as they began playing their own material. As Devoto wrote to Boon, the day after the show, 'Buzzcocks played their first gig last night. We were great. The music was pretty awful. A third of the way through the set, they, the management, switched off the PA and started up the disco. It was only after our last number that the audience clapped . . . It was our first rehearsal, live.' The hastily assembled rhythm section, though, was not long for the band. Drummer Denis, who played everything like it was 'All Right Now', went back to playing 'All Right Now'; while bassist Garth Davies went back to drinking full-time; and Devoto and Shelley felt they were back in Notlob Gaol, having not passed go, having not collected two hundred pounds.

If the Buzzcock boys took their inspiration from the Marquee review, two other souls started their infatuation with the Pistols by attending that fabled affair. Rob Symmons and Vic Goddard had met at sixth-form college in Sheen, south west London, back in 1973. Symmons was a Feelgood fan – 'Not pub rock. Only Dr Feelgood' – while Goddard was into soul music, David Bowie and the Velvets, both of whom he introduced to Symmons. On Wednesday afternoons, Symmons says, they had a ritual that involved skipping 'games' and going into town 'to buy the *NME*, because in Barnes it came out on Thursday. We'd go to Kensington Market and get some bootleg albums, and Vic would go to Johnsons in Ken Market. Vic bought suits there.'

Later on, they began to venture down the King's Road, where another branch of Johnson's lay, and where they came upon Sex, so to speak. Symmons recalls that, 'Sex was very intimidating. [But] Vic had some shirts [from there], that his sister had bought him.' They also sometimes crossed the Wandsworth Bridge in search of secondhand clothes. One time in 1975, they were wandering past the Rose and Crown on Wandsworth High Street when some lads who rehearsed there noticed how they looked – 'because we wore straight, bleached Levis' – and shouted to them. It was their first introduction to the Sex Pistols.

The next time they came across the quartet was at the Marquee. After that, Symmons and his friend just 'looked in *NME* to see when they were playing, and went to see them . . . [at the] Nashville, 100 Club, everywhere . . . We used to tape them and everything. We'd take photographs of them. We'd just find them. [But] it didn't last long – [till the] summer.' Meanwhile, they had begun to plunk out the odd cacophonic chord progression on an acoustic guitar which Symmons had got for Christmas, and which by his own admission, 'we couldn't [even] tune up'. Despite crippling limitations, the pair had ambition – if nothing else – and some influences far removed from the Stooges school of garage rock.

Vic Goddard: [We liked] the way [the Feelgoods] mingled with their fans in the pubs – a lot of it came from their attitude. On the other hand, they were doing rock & roll. The idea of putting things that were nothing to do with rock & roll into the mix [was ours]. [When] we started out as a band . . . we were really into Debussy, Satie; but we were [also] really into Television. I don't think we were into the Ramones – we went to see them live, and could enjoy them, but it was the opposite of what we wanted to do as a group.

Starting from somewhere short of scratch, the Subway Sect took a tad longer than Buzzcocks to find their sound, or summon up the nerve to gig. The closest London got to another garageband in the immediate aftershock of the Pistols were successors to Lipstick, and were calling themselves The Vibrators. Formed in February 1976 by Knox, John Ellis, Pat Collier and Eddie Edwards, they had no intention of sounding, 'like that band that we saw supporting Bazooka Joe. They were gone and forgotten by then . . . We just wanted to play fast and loud. All the bands playing on the club circuit were all trying to be like The Band, [with] this half-assed country & western music at nought miles an hour, and it was absolutely not what [we] considered rock & roll.'

The Vibrators represented the culmination of a certain reactionary streak in frontman Knox traceable all the way back to skiffle, and that now became Britrock sifted through The Stooges and Lou Reed. After missing the boat with previous formulations like Despair and Lipstick, they were finally taking something from the general *gestalt*. The name itself seemed indicative of a change of tack, even if Knox says it came after going through 'other [band] names like Terry Lene and the Trousers. We were [all] going to have funny names like Poly Ester and Brian Nylons – so that was in the air.'

After a history of off-centre bands, Knox whipped The Vibrators into some kind of shape in less than six weeks and by the middle of March they were ready to make their debut at north London's answer to St Martin's, Hornsey College of Art, supporting those other proto-punks, The Stranglers. Rehearsals, though, had not quite ironed out all the chinks – possibly because they had been rehearsing in the freezing cold garage of John Ellis's parents, with their gloves on most of the time. As Knox recalls, in his memoir, 'At the end of one song [at Hornsey], which Pat thought was out of tune, he asked the audience, "Hands up who liked that in A, and hands up who liked it in B?"'

Certain youth-obsessed latecomers would seek to disown The Vibrators after September's Punk Festival, but in the spring of 1976 they were bouncing off the same wall of incomprehension as the Pistols. Lacking a frontman with Rotten's 'front', they had come up with an alternative strategy for subduing the inevitable hecklers. Knox suggests, 'Our way of dealing with [those early] support slots was to come on and play really fast with almost no gaps between songs . . . One time at the Nashville we came on and just strummed our open guitars making a terrible noise, with Eddie making a racket on the drums. Over this we shouted "Fuck off! Fuck off! Fuck off!" This was so people would notice we were about to play.'

Most of the time they preferred to start with Pink Floyd's 'Interstellar

Overdrive', going into The Beatles' 'Day Tripper'. Syd Barrett-era Floyd was just about acceptable, but The Beatles were a no-no association until The Damned rendered 'Help' with full punk thrust. Though The Vibrators did their own Stooges cover, '1969' (with part of 'No Fun' inserted as a middle-eight), and already had punky originals like 'We Vibrate' and 'Whips And Furs', covers of 'Route 66' and 'Let's Twist Again' hardly screamed cutting edge. When the time came to draw lines they would be on the outside, looking in. For now, though, they were associate members of this no-name movement.

Through the late winter and spring 1976, the Pistols still felt they were out on their own, even if this was not quite the case. Their galvanized garment-trader manager already had irons in the furnace. Steve Severin, a Marquee convert, recalls how 'right from the start, Malcolm was keen to build an entourage around the band and the shop. He would ring to tell us when the Pistols were playing "secret" gigs.' McLaren also had in mind to create sister- and brother-bands from the flotilla surrounding Sex. As Chrissie Hynde, a potential star from the throng, states, 'Malcolm would . . . put people in motion. He tried to do it with me and a couple of different bands.'

Most of McLaren's game plan, though, remained in that maniac brain much of the time. Guitarist Steve Jones was certainly oblivious to any sociological subtexts as the Pistols went from strength to strength: '[McLaren] didn't tell us [his] every move . . . It was [always] in his head . . . He knew he couldn't make us do what we didn't want to; what we didn't realize was how all these things was pleasing him. We just wanted to play music, really. For us it was a laugh causing a big fuckin' stir, but everyone had to hate it, before he liked anything.'

What McLaren *really* liked was 'causing [that] big fuckin' stir'; and – tone-deaf or not – he knew that there was something about his charges that seemed to be stirring things up, in both a positive and a negative sense (every action having an equal and opposite reaction). Howard Devoto, talking to *New York Rocker* in 1979, tried to explain to an American audience what one got from an early Pistols performance, how 'there was a certain identification, because it did *provoke* [my italics] . . . People would go see the Sex Pistols and say, "They were awful," as if it really did disturb them. We wanted to share that.' Devoto's friend, Richard Boon, experienced that sense almost immediately after putting the Pistols on at the university.

Richard Boon: The art department at Reading had a club called Art Exchange, which had a little budget from the student union, and I persuaded the woman who held the purse strings that this band would be really fantastic to put on in this studio. They had, as a support act, a performance act called the Kipper Kids, who . . . [would] sit and work their way through a bottle of whisky each, and tell . . . stories and then punch each other up. Good opening. Johnny comes on and does the classic, 'We've seen your paintings – we pay our taxes for this rubbish.' Then they were just blistering.

That quintessential element of provocation was not merely one extended 'fuck you', like the Kipper Kids. It danced the light spastic between confrontation and comedy. Wire's Colin Newman caught them at Hendon Polytechnic one time in 1976, and recalls, 'It was Us and Them. There were all these rugby types who hated them. They were hilariously funny, shouting at you from the stage, and they had a whole batch of audience who looked a bit like them . . . [I thought,] "Why are those people getting so pissed off at them?" They were a comedy act.'

Newman was not the only one to recognize that comedic element – and discerning how integral it was to the Pistolean live experience. Guitarist John Perry thought 'they were funny in the best sense – they were genuinely entertaining, and there were bits where you laughed out loud.' Joe Strummer, in one of his last interviews, also emphasized how 'there was a comedy in what they did – and it wasn't inadvertent, it was something they used.' Pete Shelley, who saw it too, lamented the fact that 'the comedy part of punk always got lost in the translation. It was Theatre of the Absurd in some respects, making a God-awful noise to get a reaction.' And in this the Pistols were its arch-exponents.

Rotten had quickly refined his stagecraft to the point where he could upend any audience's preconceptions at a moment's notice. Nils Stevenson, McLaren's assistant and sometime road-manager for the band, remembered one instance at the infamous Logan party where Rotten actually went and sat in the audience, with a really long microphone lead, saying, 'I've always wanted to watch my band play.' The contrast between the band's intense, lurching ur-rock and Rotten's comedy routines was starkness standing tall. Tracie, secretary to the band when one was required, told the Vermorels how she and her friends liked to 'just stand around and dance, [but] when he started doing all the verbal bits, [you] sort of wondered what had hit you really'.

It was in High Wycombe that promoter Ron Watts saw them for the first time. What he witnessed was a frontman who 'insulted the audience well enough, [but] pulled back just in time to let me know they were in control of what they were doing. They did have a definite idea of presentation.' He was impressed enough to offer them an opening slot at the R&B club he ran at 100 Oxford Street, a hundred yards from Centre Point.

The Pistols made their debut at the 100 Club, as support to Plummet Airlines, on 30 March 1976, in what very nearly turned out to be their last gig. Chrissie Hynde had brought guitarist/producer Chris Spedding along for the ride. Having heard about this band that 'couldn't play', but was managed by McLaren, Spedding wanted to check them out for himself.

Chris Spedding: There was hardly anybody there. They'd frighten audiences away in those days. There'd be twenty people in the club at the beginning and about two by the time they finished playing. They used to have fights on stage and Rotten [would be constantly] running off stage.

That night the Pistols were in usual taunting mode, but were too busy winding each other up to notice the audience. According to Matlock, 'John was really out of it . . . I think he'd shot himself up with speed or something. He sang all the words perfectly, but to all the wrong songs.' It was Matlock who bore the brunt of Rotten's antipathy. Hynde recalls, 'Johnny kept picking up his mike stand, over his shoulder, trying to spear Glen Matlock. There was always this tension, [as if] he was trying to do grievous bodily harm to Matlock onstage. He not only left the stage, he left the club. And Malcolm McLaren went running out into the street to try and retrieve him.' Apparently, McLaren delivered an ultimatum to Rotten, 'Get back on stage or you're out.' It did the trick, but Rotten was firing daggers with his eyes for the remainder of the set, and on into the night as he went off with his circle of Johns.

No one knew if he would turn up when the band resumed live operations the following Wednesday, at the Nashville Rooms, West Kensington. He turned up all right, but in no better state of mind. According to his autobiographical self, 'When the Nashville curtain went down, I went over to Malcolm and said, "I quit. I've had enough."' He did not, however, carry out his threat. This was fortunate, given that this was the show when punk finally came to town, setting in motion a series of events that had The Damned and The Clash surfing the same wave by summer's end.

Playing the Nashville seemed like a surprising concession from McLaren, who had spent the past five months bypassing every pub-rock venue in town. Indeed, little more than a week later, he would be telling *Sounds*, 'If you want to change things you can't play pubs. You don't have the freedom.' He would be even blunter to *Rolling Stone* the following year, insisting, 'I didn't want them playing to 25-year-old beer-drinkers who wouldn't give them the time of day unless they were playing Chuck Berry songs. I wanted a fresh, untainted audience.' Yer average Nashville audience was pretty 'tainted'. As for Chuck Berry songs, the headliners that night – the 101ers – usually belted out no less than five Berry R&B ballads, every one of 'em a crowd-pleaser ('Route 66', 'Johnny B Goode', 'Carol', 'Too Much Monkey Business' and 'Roll Over Beethoven' hardly requiring to raid the Chess vaults).

But it was a matter of necessity. It was high time the Pistols played a high-profile gig to which the (other) music papers might come. Unfortunately, the one scribe who did – Allan Jones at *Melody Maker* – was something of a press-champion for the 101ers. He also liked to mix beer and music, hence the appeal of pub-rock. And the Nashville served it by the pint. His embittered view of the Pistols that night would come back to haunt him:

Their dreadfully inept attempts to zero in on the kind of viciously blank intensity previously epitomised by The Stooges was rather endearing at first . . . [but] the novelty of this retarded spectacle was . . . soon erased by their tiresome repetition of punk clichés. They do as much for music as World War II did for the cause of peace.

Great copy, mile-wide of the mark. Yet other, regular attendees also felt something was wrong. Rotten's later view – that 'both Nashville gigs were horrid' – may have been coloured by the two Johns, Wardle and Beverley. For the former, 'The Pistols' gigs were just a good place to go and listen to some raucous, out-of-tune music . . . [and] watch Rotten take the piss out of everyone.' The latter liked it when his friend 'just did robot dancing and fucked around and took the piss out of everybody'. A support slot at the Nashville provided Rotten with little opportunity to do the piss take, save when the band screwed up 'Pretty Vacant', and he was at last in his element, muttering over Paul Cook's attempts to pick up the beat and resurrect the song, 'Rock & roll, ahhh rock & roll, the way it should be.' The rest of the time he was required to get on with it. The extant tape suggests he did.

Despite sound problems – and Allan Jones's partisan view – 101ers vocalist Joe Strummer was impressed enough to tell his girlfriend, Paloma, then in Scotland, all about the Pistols when next they spoke on the phone. When he heard them again, three weeks later, the scales really would fall from his eyes.

Also in the audience at that first Nashville show were all four of the soon-to-be-Damned. James and Scabies (who brought Ray Burns, aka Captain Sensible, along) were there because of the entertainment value the Pistols invariably provided. As Scabies says, 'They were fun gigs, people would boo and throw things at them, they'd never get an encore, but there'd always be half a dozen spiky-headed oiks.' Meanwhile, Dave Vanian, part of McLaren's short-lived Master of the Backside and one of his standbys for the next Sex band, was there at the manager's behest.

Brian James had yet to meet Vanian, who still looked the same as when Scabies first met him, i.e. 'oddly pale . . . his eyes were sunken black hollows, hair black as coal. This guy was spooky.' Scabies forgot to mention to James that, 'He was also the biggest pain in the ass I'd ever met.' As it happens, the lads were starting to despair of ever finding a frontman. When James said, of Vanian, 'He looks fuckin' great,' Scabies did the introductions, and they invited Vanian to their local, Lisson Grove church for an audition. Unbeknownst to Vanian, they also invited Sid Vicious down that Nashville night. Sid, though, failed to show. So Vanian got the gig, and Vicious had to wait in the wings.

At last James and Scabies had their band and could begin rehearsals. They also had a name – The Damned – after two of their favourite movies. As Scabies explains: 'I was a big *Midwich Cuckoos* fan [filmed as *The Village of the Damned*], and we really liked the idea of being the band that came from Midwich . . . There was also Visconti's movie, *The Damned*, [which] was on TV . . . Brian was quite into the Nazi decadence thing.'

In double-quick time, The Damned also had a manager. Having already discounted Rhodes and McLaren, they fleetingly considered John Crevene, whose Acme Attractions was the main King's Road rival to Sex when it came to outlandish attire at fashionable prices. In the end, though, they turned to the man who did McLaren's and Crevene's books, Andy Czekowski. Czekowski had already noticed Vanian in

Acme, where, 'He stood out in that he had very black dyed hair, very pale face, very skinny and [had a] very intense air about him . . . slightly different to your local shopper who bought fifties clothing.' Andy had keys to the warehouse in Bermondsey where Acme stored its stuff – enabling the band to rehearse there. As Brian James recalls, he 'let us get away with murder. The things we used to nick from the Bermondsey warehouse!'

Rehearsing was always something of a chore for The Damned. Indeed, they told journalist Jonh Ingham in July that they never rehearsed – 'because they figured that was gonna spoil the excitement'. But the quartet now needed to get up to speed – in their case, literally – so in the three months before their first gig, James instituted an unrelenting regime, until he felt they were ready to challenge the Pistols' punk hegemony.

— — —

If James and Scabies left the pub that April night buoyantly believing they were on their way, John Lydon was down in the dumps until he met Don Letts. Letts worked at Acme along with his china-doll girlfriend Jeannette Lee, and they 'went back to Forest Hill and spent the whole night rapping on about reggae . . . Don didn't know, but it was the night I was frustrated and getting ready to quit the Pistols.'

Rotten had always felt like an outsider in the band he had made his own. After rehearsals he would invariably 'go home on the Tube. I always felt alienated inside the Pistols . . . They never really allowed me to be a mate . . . I would never be invited to parties. I found out years later that was because Malcolm would say, "Don't talk to John. He's a mystery."' Not the most convincing explanation. Actually, the antipathy Rotten inspired in audiences had already seeped a little into the band itself.

Vivienne Westwood: We had to put up with terrific aggravation from [Rotten], especially Steve Jones . . . To have this little bloke who'd led such a safe existence turning round and telling him where it was at was a bit much . . . to take.

The night after the Nashville, Rotten dutifully turned up at a Soho strip club, El Paradise, that McLaren had hired hoping to create a residency of sorts for the band, but the place was ultimately too seedy even for this self-styled shyster. This time there was a sympathetic music journalist there, jotting down notes. *Sounds'* Jonh Ingham had been trying to find out about the Pistols since he'd read Spencer's review of the Marquee show in its main rival, but to no avail.

As Ingham observes, 'It wasn't so much what he wrote, it was the name itself. I was very bored at that time by all that was going on musically. I really wanted to find out more about [them]. I was well into hatred by that time.' It would be Ingham, followed by Caroline Coon at *Melody Maker*, who would first run with the punk pack; not Spencer, nor the *NME*. Ingham believes it was prompted by McLaren calling 'a *Sounds* writer called Vivien Goldman while we were at our weekly meetings. I just told her, "You're not gonna like this band," and commandeered the phone. So McLaren put my name on the door.'

Ingham's review, which *Sounds* ran the following Wednesday, could almost have been written as a riposte to Allan Jones (it wasn't): 'If you hate Patti Smith for all that noise and rock & roll energy at the expense of technique and sounding pretty, then you'll hate the Sex Pistols. Their aesthetic is Shepherd's Bush Who and speed-era Small Faces – they play it fast and they play it loud.' In fact, then-editor Alan Lewis called Ingham into his office the day after the gig to ask him for some details. As a result of what he heard, Jones instructed Ingham 'to write a story about them'.

Jonh Ingham: I said, 'It's way too early for that. Why?' He just looked at me, 'How long have you been standing here telling me about them?' I'd been there, like ten minutes. So I had to go and meet Malcolm, [to] pass some [kinda] test . . . and he gave me the Malcolm Manifesto. His music was Gene Vincent, Jerry Lee and Eddie Cochran, but he kept coming back to Gene Vincent as the stuff that excited him. I understood exactly where he was coming from. [He] was wanting to start something new, and how do you start something new – you do the opposite of what's going on. If everyone's got long hair, you have short hair; if everyone has flared trousers, you have straight trousers. He went on and on, for like forty-five minutes.

McLaren proved articulate and perceptive, even in preacher mode – unlike his old ally, Bernie Rhodes. At one point he informed Ingham that 'pretty soon Richard Hell is going to leave the Heartbreakers, and Sire Records will dangle a contract in front of him and he knows it won't help and won't do any good, but he'll sign it because that's what's expected of him.' This was one smart cookie-cutter – Hell left the band a matter of weeks later, and had signed to Sire by the end of the year.

McLaren had something far more radical in mind for the Pistols, who he constantly referenced against the Stones: 'No one came to sign [them] up . . . no one wanted to know. But when they saw a lot of bands sounding like that, with a huge following, they had to sign them. Create a scene and a lot of bands . . . and they'll have to sign them, even though they don't understand it.' An impressed Ingham found 'his overall philosophy of trying to break down these walls of complacency . . . just really refreshing.' Having passed the test, they arranged to meet the band a week later, at the rehearsal studio in Denmark Place. However, when Ingham turned up, someone was missing. The writer looked for Johnny in vain.

Unperturbed, Ingham adjourned to the Blue Post with Malcolm and the original trio. As he remembers it, 'Steve was doing all the talking. They're talking about John in the third person, and it's clear that they're not sure about him at all. Somewhere in the conversation, he walks in. There's two girls with him. He sits about ten, fifteen feet away and he's talking to the two girls. And they're still talking about him in the third person.' Invisible wounds remained from a week of gigs that had tested their resolve like never before but Ingham was unaware of the cause of this mutual animosity. Finally, Rotten's curiosity got the better of him and he joined the others. Ingham asked him what he thought and, as he says, 'It was like a searchlight suddenly clicked on. Later on, he became media savvy and he slowed down the vitriol, but this was just like a machine gun.'

I hate hippies. I hate what they stand for. I hate long hair. I hate pub bands. I want to change it so there are rock bands like us . . . I want people to go out and start something, to see us and start something. [*Sounds*, 24/4/76]

Richard Hell may still believe that, 'The Sex Pistols . . . didn't have any of that baggage of thinking about it in advance – they were just restless, loud-mouthed, obnoxious kids who behaved that way in public,' but the Rotten that let rip that April afternoon had been 'thinking about it' long and hard. Nor was every American taken in by the anti-intellectual facade he constructed (and which he maintained long after the Pistols expired). *Bomp* editor Greg Shaw, then in London with The Flamin' Groovies, recalled 'having long talks with Rotten . . . From the beginning, his agenda was that he hated rock stars, he hated the whole rock culture.'

Not surprisingly, McLaren insists that the Pistols' lyric-man was inspired to write (and say) all that he did because of 'the circle he was involved with. You know . . . when you've got a buzz going and you have a drink and a critique, it's inspiration.' Certainly the songs Rotten was now writing – and the likes of 'Satellite', 'Problems' and 'No Feelings' had all appeared in the set in the last six weeks – were riddled with anxiety about the welfare of the state, intercut with accounts of the dehumanizing nature of modern life, infused by rage:

'Bet you're all so happy in suburbia dream
But I'm only laughing, I ain't in your scheme'

'I kick you in the head when you get down and pray
Do you pray to your God?'

'The problem is you
Whatcha gonna do?'

Ingham's media interest not only gave Rotten another medium where he might vent his splenetic fury, it also probably saved the band. As Ingham observed at the end of the journey, reviewing the final show at Winterland, 'One of the first things that impressed me . . . was how much this singing misfit was enjoying the attention, feeding off of it with a hunger that was not going to allow that attention to ever slip away.' Ingham's first article in *Sounds*, which appeared on news-stands on 21 April, was enough to convince Rotten he wasn't actually wasting his time. In fact, for a national weekly like *Sounds* to give a two-page spread to an unsigned, unknown band – who, as the headline said, had been gigging less than six months – was more than just a push, it was a hard shove in the right direction.

Not surprisingly, that Friday's show at the Nashville, again supporting the 101ers, was jammed to its rickety rafters. And this time the Pistols were determined to get it right, even hiring a proper PA from a local sound company. The result, according to 101er Richard Dudanski, was that, whereas 'the first night the sound was awful, the second time it was really good and you could [finally] hear Steve Jones's guitar'. If soundman Dave Goodman arrived to find McLaren had pulled a familiar fast one, he left the pub a confirmed convert.

Dave Goodman: We did it real cheap for the Albion Agency, and we felt we were conned into doing a cheap PA for the support band, [because then] the 101ers got full use of it. Indeed Strummer kicked in one of the monitors, after he sat there gobsmacked, watching the Pistols . . . Anyway, after the gig I said to the band, 'You got any more gigs? We like what you're doing.' . . . And Malcolm was like, 'Fucking hell, someone's offering us some help.'

Second time around, the 101ers were the support act in all but name. No question who most punters came to see, and the Pistols responded with bilious surges of sound; attacking every song with pent-up fury after nineteen days off. If some of the curious became antagonistic, it only served to drive Rotten on. As Jordan has said, 'The thing about the Pistols is they did, to some extent, feed off other people's aggression . . . In a way [Rotten] didn't really like people liking him, because it meant that he wasn't doing it right.' Unfortunately, this time that negative energy spilled off the stage and into the audience, where a full-blown ruckus ensued.

To the band, this was nothing new. As Paul Cook once said, 'There were fights at all of the gigs. John used to instigate them. He'd get that attitude from the crowd; an aggressive attitude that worked both ways.' This time, though, it was not Rotten who incited the problem, but Vivienne Westwood who took a swing at some unfortunate; providing the perfect excuse for a mêlée to accompany the music. Westwood would later claim that she was bored and decided to liven things up. Photos of the gig suggest she was simply drunk, belligerent and confident of aid if things got out of hand. In fact, according to Matlock, Sid Vicious 'hated Vivienne, so used this as an excuse to lay into her'. Nor did the band just play on, they joined in, much to the delight of photographer Barry Plummer, who stepped forward and snapped the moment. Less impressed was rock manager Bryan Morrison, standing at the back with Jonh Ingham and wife.

Jonh Ingham: We're standing there . . . All of a sudden there's this guy flying sideways from stage-left and Malcolm is just coming right behind the guy, and then John is leering, and Steve is leaning forward, trying to pull people apart. At which point, Bryan Morrison turns to me and says, 'You got to drop this band. You're gonna ruin your career.'

Neil Tennant, the later Pet Shop Boy, also believed that this outburst of laddishness was not a smart career move, rhetorically asking in a letter to the *NME*, 'How do the Pistols create their atmosphere when their music has failed? By beating up a member of the audience, how else?' But the fracas – and subsequent chest-beating in the media – only served to heighten the band's profile, even prompting *Melody Maker* editor Ray Coleman to let Coon have her say on the phenomenon, albeit with a counter-argument from the pen of Allan Jones running underneath.

The quotient of new converts was also maintained at the Nashville. Graham Lewis thought the whole thing 'hilarious. [And] they were playing loads of my favourite tunes by the Small Faces and Stooges.' Music fan Colin Keinch told Marcus Gray that he thought, 'The Pistols were totally challenging and the 101ers weren't.' All four members of the singer-less Clash – Mick Jones, Paul Simonon, Bernie Rhodes and Keith Levene – were there calibrating just how far off the pace they already were. Levene was particularly struck by Rotten, 'I just liked the look of him.'

Bernie and Mick were primarily there to see the 101ers frontman. Richard Boon, who sat at the table behind, well remembers them 'checking Joe out . . . in his Eddie Cochran suit, *being* Eddie Cochran.' Strummer was feeling the pressure that night. This time the Pistols had been firing on all cylinders, and the PA had served them right. According to Pete Silverton, a friend of Strummer's with music-journalist ambitions, the singer already knew it was over before he took to the stage:

As [the Pistols] played, Joe stood in the crowd, eyes locked on the stage, staring into his future. He told me he'd seen them before and that they'd changed his life, or some such phrase which barely made sense at the time but seems surprisingly rational now. I stared with him, listening to a gleeful racket, feeling a bit lost and unsure, till they played a Small Faces song which helped me start to make sense of it . . . Later, when Joe had finished his own show and was recovering, sweatily, in the cubbyhole of a dressing room, he told me that he'd broken up his band.

If so, Strummer told Silverton of his decision some time before he told the rest of the band, though he consistently insisted he was instantly converted. He told Caroline Coon, less than a year later: '[When] I saw the Pistols . . . it just knocked my head right off . . . There were these four guys and I felt just like them. I mean, they couldn't play great . . . but they were just going, "So what!" And that hadn't ever occurred to me at all . . . The other guys in the [101ers] . . . played good . . . but they were just too old. What I really wanted was to get in with some young yobbos who I was more in tune with.'

As the years rolled on, Strummer became ever more dismissive of his roots as an erstwhile pub-rocker, claiming in a press release he penned for The Clash's first full US tour that he had been 'singing with a London pub band, which he had formed in order to pass the time and pay the rent [sic]. Upon being asked, he quit his group immediately and joined the prototype Clash.' According to Levene, it required a little more persuasion.

Keith Levene: We had this singer who was this real Mick Jagger imitation. Me and Bernard [Rhodes] went off to a 101ers gig one night and talked Joe [Strummer] into coming over to my squat in Shepherd's Bush. I was playing guitar with him and playing some 101ers tunes . . . I said, 'Will you do it?' He [finally] said yeah.

Richard Dudanski does not remember it this way, and contemporary diaries back him up. Always the closest to Strummer in the 101ers, Dudanski remembers them both articulating this feeling 'that we wanted something to be happening — it was in the air, something was gonna change, not that we were necessarily part of it. It wasn't quite like a Damascus experience [for Joe].' In fact, there were already problems with the band. Strummer had autocratically decided to get rid of one guitar player at some point in March, 'because he wasn't moving around enough on stage. He wanted a bit more action on stage.' Unfortunately, as a by-product of this change, bassist Dan Kello started taking more control in the rehearsal room, making Strummer feel it was less his band.

However, Dudanski did sense a change in Strummer after the Nashville shows. Perhaps it was, as Strummer suggested in 1979, that it had begun to seem like 'a slog. It seemed after doing eighteen months of [this] we were just invisible. I started to lose my mind.' But the band had gigs booked, and a single due out on the indie Chiswick label. On 12 May, they played the Red Cow in Hammersmith. In attendance were Glen Matlock, Mick Jones, Paul Simonon, and presumably Keith Levene and Bernie Rhodes (it was probably on this occasion that Levene persuaded Strummer to return to the Bush with them). It was certainly the night Strummer returned to his squat on a mission — to persuade Dudanski to jump ship too.

Richard Dudanski: When he wanted to set up The Clash, Joe came back to my room pissed, about two in the morning, said to me, 'C'mon, we're gonna knock this on its head and go with these other guys.' And I said, 'Joe, we'll speak about this tomorrow morning.' The following morning the first person I bump into is Bernie, and he gives me this hour spiel, as was his way, 'You're playing a load of shit! You should be doing this, you should be doing that.' I just couldn't stand the guy. My reaction then, to Joe, was, 'I'm not going with this guy. Why don't you stay here? Let's keep the 101ers, keep with Mickey [Foote] as the manager, and bring Paul and Mick into our fold.' He said, 'No, it's got to be this way.'

The recruitment of both Strummer and Dudanski would have solved a major headache for the still-born Clash. Their need for a solid drummer was as great as for a singer, especially given their determination to persevere with Simonon 'on bass' because he looked good. But Rhodes retained a rare capacity for alienating anyone not snowballed by the Bernie Bullshit; and Dudanski was prepared to run a mile in the opposite direction, even while Strummer had become a full-time apostle of the creed.

As Dudanski observes, 'For the first year he was pretty out on it. It was a big decision to drop the 101ers, [who] were a community-based thing in North Kensington. So [having] knock[ed] that on the head, he went so far into the new movement, he was 100% . . . He *had* to totally believe it.' His faith was such that he began looking for more converts to bring into the circle. A couple of weeks after the Nashville show, Pete Silverton called at the squat to see Strummer and got the spiel, both barrels:

He told me about this fantastic man he'd met – Bernard Rhodes . . . A few weeks later, I got an oblique message that Bernie would like to see me, that I should meet him at Rehearsal Rehearsals . . . He started talking, laying out his strategies, his theories, philosophies. He used a lot of words like that . . . His sound and fury lasted an hour or so. Every now and then, he'd ask what I thought. Quite unable to follow his lava flow of words, I'd agree non-committally. Without seeming to take much notice of what I said, he'd start flowing again. I had no fucking idea what he was talking about.

Though Strummer's course was now firmly set, the 101ers did not formally dissolve till 26 May, over a month after the Nashville, and a

day after Strummer checked out the Pistols again, at the 100 Club. Joe
informed the band that he was, in 101er Clive Timperly's words, 'smitten
by the Maximum Impact – carefully chosen words, *his* words – of the
Pistols. He wanted to go in that direction.' Already he was talking in
parentheses, Bernie-style. Strummer recognized a burning ambition in
Bernie, one that mirrored his own; and one that neither his fellow 101ers
nor his absent girlfriend Paloma seemed to share.

Palm Olive: I remember him telling me about his ambition, saying that he really
wanted to make it, and I was kinda laughing at it. To me, as a true hippy, my
ambition was [to] be happy. Relax. Enjoy life. It was a little foreign to me – that
[kind of] ambition . . . [He] saw the limitations of the [101ers]. By going along
with the status quo of the rock scene, it was never gonna make it big enough
for what he wanted. That [burning] ambition was very real in Joe.

Bernie Rhodes intended to feed on that ambition. But he demanded
100% commitment. His 'he who is not for me is against me' credo
excluded all non-believers, and that included girlfriends. When Paloma
made it clear that she 'didn't like Bernie at all. I thought he was a creep,'
Strummer was obliged to choose. As Mickey Foote told Pat Gilbert,
'Bernie collected together the people he wanted. He was very, very
fearful of people who didn't want to get involved. He wanted people
who wouldn't go against him.'

Terry Chimes, who solved The Clash's drummer problem in the short
term, has suggested that the fact Rhodes 'irritated everyone . . . he met
. . . was a deliberate policy'. Even before the band could start rehearsing
in earnest, Rhodes was enforcer of The View and keeper of the keys.
Journalist Paul Rambali, writing of his first encounter with Rhodes –
when he 'was still the fourth member of the [drummer-less] Clash' – recalls
someone 'wearing the same brothel creepers, strides, leather jackets
covered in purposeless zips, and stencilled shirts, though his clothes
sported a higher incidence of red and black. He asked me more questions
than I could begin to ask his group (and they were obviously *his* group).'
If McLaren was having trouble controlling his charges, Rhodes pulled
the leash a lot tighter; overarching contradictions notwithstanding.

Kris Needs: Bernie was a used-car salesman . . . Bernie didn't see music as
music. He saw it as a vehicle for a message. He liked to tell The Clash he was a
veteran of the Paris riots in 1968. [I guess] he did have some kind of revolutionary

background and a very unconventional upbringing, [which] he wanted to project on the band.

A year on, Bernie would be asked to define his role in the band. His reply reads like the Rhodes résumé: 'My job is to coordinate, understand and clarify exactly what [The Clash] are trying to express, if you like, the melting pot of all their talents . . . I regard my job as being to make sure that we keep to our original intentions and purposes and not be swayed away. I am here to make sure we don't fall into any cheap-trick traps.' He took this job description very seriously. Eventually he felt that he alone understood any underlying programme.

In the six weeks before independence day, when Strummer next shared a stage with the Pistols, Rhodes would push his programme for mass liberation to the band at every opportunity. And as Paul Simonon recently affirmed, 'You can't overestimate Bernie's importance in those early days. He didn't write the songs but he set up the agenda. He set up the whole punk scene, basically. He was always pushing; he always seemed antagonistic.' At this juncture the band welcomed (nay needed) his guiding hand. As Strummer once said, it was Rhodes who 'put the group together. And he . . . put us on the right track.'

Almost immediately, Rhodes went to work on their repertoire. Strummer and Jones had both written the occasional original for previous bands, but almost all were consigned to the scrapheap or recast, as with Jones's 'I'm So Bored With You', which thanks to a new set of Strummer lyrics became 'I'm So Bored With The USA' (though as Brian James caustically recalls, 'The one thing he was *not* bored with was the USA'). Strummer's previous nickname (Woody) and the 101ers repertoire suggested someone as steeped in Americana as any Appalachian backwoodsman. And yet he was soon telling the credulous Coon, 'We sing in English, not mimicking some American rock singer's accent. That's just pretending to be something you ain't.' Strummer was being cajoled by Rhodes into 'writing songs about what was pissing us off'.

Joe Strummer: It was great to meet him. Along comes this guy who says, 'Think about what you're doing, have something worth taking out there. Don't just shamble out there.' [1978]

Less than four months after this statement, Strummer would expel Rhodes from the band he built from scratch. But in June 1976, it was

Bernie's self-belief that was the glue keeping them together; making the Clash Committee – and it was more of a committee than a combo at this stage – a forum for animated discussion. As Strummer would say when edging away from such blinkered commitment, 'We used to sit around and spend a lot of time talking about our songs. Some were . . . like love songs, and we'd keep throwing them away. In the end all we were left with were the heavy songs . . . [but] we were really idealistic in those days, and we really believed in what we were saying.' The love songs weren't the only things thrown away. So was the muse of recent songs.

Palm Olive: [Joe and I] had been together for two years [but] I was getting a bit restless, thinking, 'What am I doing with my life?' . . . I had left the squat and decided to go to Scotland to think about my whole situation. [But] we're in touch on the phone, and he's telling me how he's gonna leave the 101ers, and [what] he's gonna do. So I come back to the squat and he has moved out. I didn't know. So I went to see him [in Camden] and he was very, very different. He told me, 'I don't think our relationship is going to work.' And I was shocked. [Eventually] he changed his mind.

If Strummer was 'the one who actually spouted the communist propaganda . . . on the bus' – as the Heartbreakers' Walter Lure recalled – the others were no less committed at this stage. Alan Drake, Mick Jones's room-mate in the early days of The Clash, describes how, 'Mick was just so intense: he'd stop every two minutes to tell me, "This is very important," and I'd say, "I know, Mick, *I know*. Let's just get on with it and do it."' Looking back, Levene says he realizes, 'We really rubbed everyone's faces in it, [but] we were so fucking young . . . That was a lot of our strength. It gave us a certain tunnel-vision naiveté.'

And yet Rhodes' agenda was just as reactionary as his mentor McLaren. He wanted to recapture a feeling he had had when a young man himself, alluding to such a motivation in a 1980 *Melody Maker* profile, where he talked about how: 'Malcolm and I thought we could do a bit more than what was done before. I was only interested in the political aspect, but . . . I was thinking of what I got from Jackie Wilson's 'Reet Petite', which was the first record I ever bought. I didn't need anyone to describe what it was all about. I knew it.' The echo of such a sentiment can be found in something Strummer said, re London's Capital Radio, in March 1977, 'They could have made [radio] so good that everywhere you went you took your transistor radio – you know, how it used to be when I was at school.'

For now, McLaren and Rhodes shared the same objective. It was one voiced by the usually taciturn Mick Jones in *Melody Maker* that July, when The Clash had one whole gig under their belt: 'We're challenging complacency, standing up for rock & roll. We want to get rid of rock & rollers like Rod Stewart who kiss royalty after gigs.'

If wheels were already in motion, a week-long residency by The Rolling Stones in May 1976 at the 17,000-capacity Earl's Court, part of their last UK arena tour – during which Jagger bounced up and down on a fifty-foot-long, inflatable phallus, singing 'Starfucker' – suggested Camden's Clash still had a long, long way to go. There was 'Rock & Roll Mick', as he was still known to many, seen outside Earl's Court trying to blag tickets for the Stones. He remained in love with *their* rock & roll world, whatever worldview Rhodes reeled off. The revolution remained at least a shot away.

While The Damned were working themselves up to a fevered pitch; and Buzzcocks were looking for a rhythm section they could call their own; the Pistols had finally found a place they could call home – a residency in the heart of the city. They had found the place once before, back in March, but had perhaps seemed a little too combustible that night, what with their lead singer leaving the stage mid-gig to go catch a bus. By 18 May 1976, 100 Club owner Ron Watts was willing to offer them a weekly slot, and the chance to build on the momentum that was already steamrolling most things in its path.

2.2
ARE YOU READY FOR A
BRAND-NEW BEAT?
5/76 - 8/76

We always felt it was important to keep a sense of surprise in the music . . . but it's a give and take, and we also felt that we didn't want to have to play small art clubs the rest of our lives. To me that's not real integrity. The most exciting thing to me is when you take an idea that's completely chance-ridden and get it across to a million people.　　　　　　　—Lenny Kaye, Patti Smith Group

The first collision between punk's transatlantic styles occurred in mid-May 1976, when Patti Smith came to town. Despite it being almost two years since her memorable joint residency at Max's with Television, and her independent 'Piss Factory' 45, she was the first ambassador from the New York scene to make it across that lonesome ocean. Her two shows at London's Roundhouse came at the end of six months' solid gigging, promoting the debut album Charles Shaar Murray compared with those of The Doors and The Who in his much-vaunted *NME* review.

There was already a certain distrust of the woman from diehards; precisely because, as Ingham puts it, 'To her, Keith Richards and Bob Dylan were relevant people, whereas in Britain the reason you were in punk was because you were completely pissed off with those people – especially [after] the '76 [Stones] tour.' She had also gone out of her way to portray herself as a punk Joan of Arc. As she told Ingham – who spent three days trying to keep up with her speeding shadow on that trip – 'This is no avant-garde project . . . Everything I've done has been with one object in mind. Deep in my heart I know rock & roll will be beyond poetry.'

It was a laudable point of view, but Patti was pushing herself to the very brink, disordering her own senses to get where she was going. She spoke to Ingham of 'Self-destruction [as] obviously negative – if you self-destruct . . . [But] the way a snake self-destructs, you know, when he takes that old skin off – he destroys the old skin, but you come out with a new skin, a more developed skin, a more illuminated skin.'

At the Roundhouse the punk fraternity were out in numbers, including members of the Pistols, The Damned and The Clash (and not to see The Stranglers support). Indeed, Rat Scabies and Brian James managed to 'blag' their way backstage, only to find that, 'She didn't seem very interested in any kind of scene happening in England.' Smith also proved surprisingly brusque with those members of the British music press with whom she did not already have a nodding acquaintance. The shows,

though, lived up to the promise of *Horses*, affirming the sense that
something *was* happening in Manhattan. Flitting easily between her own
poetic seas of possibilities and garageband classics like 'Time Is On My
Side', 'Set Me Free' and 'Gloria', she showed that intellect and passion
need not be divorced, and that fifty-foot phalluses were no substitute
for raw energy.

Patti's flaming torch burned out just as the Sex Pistols began their
weekly 100 Club residency, the night after her second London show.
England's appointed heirs had already been obliged to tighten up their
act. The week before, they had found themselves in a real recording
studio, Majestic, with a producer at the console. Chris Spedding had
offered to cut some demos with the band just for the hell of it.

Chris Spedding: I offered to record them because . . . when they started getting
some notoriety . . . I would meet people from the London musical press in clubs
. . . and they [would say], 'Are you also getting involved with that terrible group
. . . the Sex Pistols?' And I was like, 'Well, everybody to their own opinion but
where did you hear them?' 'Oh, we haven't heard them, but we know they're
terrible.'

The three demos they recorded in a single afternoon – 'Problems',
'No Feelings' and 'Pretty Vacant' – proved his point with effort to spare,
though Spedding – who may have been working at RAK impresario
Mickie Most's behest – suspects, 'McLaren wanted people to think that
they couldn't play, that it was just an idea, a way of making all this
anarchy stuff happen.' If so, he need not have worried. The Pistols'
musicianship was already becoming almost a side issue, as they continued
to disturb a whole lot more people than they converted. At the 100
Club, the disturbed had nowhere to hide.

Siouxsie Sioux: I'll never forget seeing the Pistols [at the 100 Club]. As opposed
to people trying to get close to the stage, people were actually backing off,
[almost] like clinging to the walls, saying, 'Let me out of here.' It was great the
way the band, and [in particular] Lydon at the time, fed off of that.

Among the curious at the debut gig of the residency was fellow
musician Tom Robinson, then fronting the antiseptic Café Society,
signed to Ray Davies's Kong label. He remembers that, 'The audience
was still mixed between kids in flared denims and long hair, and a

smattering of do-it-yourself punk types,' but was unprepared for (and appalled by) what he saw, fleeing in much the way Siouxsie suggested.

Tom Robinson: They didn't tune up, and Rotten's first words were, 'Who's gonna buy me a drink then?' The next few minutes completely overturned everything I'd ever understood about entertainment values . . . They shambled on, played diabolical versions of oldies like 'Whatcha Gonna Do About It'. It was totally anti-showbiz and anti-musical, very negative, with these overtones of violence. After about fifteen minutes, I couldn't take it any longer. I had to leave. But it changed my life.

A year later, Robinson was prepared to admit that the Pistols had 'their fingers right on the pulse of a time. And they knew they were right, and they believed in it enough to hold out against everything.' By that time the Tom Robinson Band were grammar school punk favourites, and he had answered the call. The first 100 Club gig also prompted the *NME* to send someone down to see how Spencer's lot were coming along. The final sentence of this interim report – 'It will take a far better band . . . to create a raw music for their generation' – shows just how rapidly the paper went from clued in to clueless.

Three weeks later, Mick Farren was given two pages in Britain's premier music paper to write a valedictory for Rock. 'The Titanic Sails at Dawn' concluded that neither reforming The Beatles, nor 'an endless series of Earls Court-style gigs' is 'going to be the salvation of rock & roll. Four kids playing to their own contemporaries in a dirty cellar might.' But as Ingham says, 'It was like, "You're so far behind the time, Mick. It's already happening. You're six months late."' It would take *NME* until well into 1977 for the penny to drop.

The one critic at the 100 Club that night who was up to speed with punk was not from Blighty. Greg Shaw, freelancer and publisher of *Who Put the Bomp*, had been waiting half a decade for a band like the Pistols to happen. His report in *Phonograph Record* suggested London was fast catching New York up, even making that connection between the original Television and the Pistols:

In music and sheer pop energy, New York is far and away the new Mecca . . . [But] London's big advantage is a circuit of clubs and pubs where bands can work their way up, plus vastly influential weekly papers like *NME* that will support the scene . . . and the Sex Pistols [are] a new band that is causing considerable controversy

. . . Their brand of revolt, though far from spontaneous (most of the heckling in the audience – and there's a lot of it, some of it quite vicious – seems to come from their supporters), has much in common with the 1964 Mods . . . They remind me very much of Television, when Richard Hell was with them and they still did 'Psychotic Reaction' . . . Their sound is a straight blast of tortured punk-rock.

If it had taken over a year for word of the CBGB's bands to reach Britain, America's alternative rock press responded to the Pistols with attitude-driven alacrity. 'Phast Phreddie' Patterson, who had started his own proto-punk zine in LA, *Back Door Man*, remembers Shaw calling him on his return and saying, 'I just came back from England. I saw this group the Sex Pistols. It's real exciting over there. You really should go over there and check it out.' And before *Phonograph* could run Shaw's piece, both *New York Rocker* and *Creem* ran a trimmed version of Spencer's Marquee review. Something about the band's unique DNA (Dynamic Negative Attitude) was still conveyed by this review and accompanying photo. Long Ryder Sid Griffin got the message, even out in Kentucky.

Sid Griffin: Greg Shaw . . . had an article in the summer of '76 on a band called the Sex Pistols playing at the 100 Club, with a black and white photograph of a very chaotic stage. And the article said the Sex Pistols couldn't play, they were very young and enthusiastic, [and] they did a Small Faces cover. I looked at the photograph, and I thought, 'These guys are my age.'

Another American paying attention was already playing drums in a New York punk band. Tommy Ramone remembers seeing 'a picture of a band called the Sex Pistols and I look at it and I read about it and . . . [thought] these guys seem to be doing the same thing we're doing.' McLaren had in mind to go head to head with the New York punksters, when it was announced that the Ramones were coming to London in early July. He tried to convince promoter John Curd to let the Pistols open the show, and got thrown down the Roundhouse stairs for his pains. The not-so-threatening Stranglers got the vote instead.

By the time the Ramones were hearing about the Pistols, the vinyl evidence of a New York punk aesthetic was available to anyone in London who was prepared to pay for an import copy of the Ramones' eponymous platter, issued Stateside at the end of April. *The Ramones* was Sire's first foray into punk, and Seymour Stein had enough street-smarts to make sure an advance test-pressing did wend its way to Nick Kent at the *NME*, who put his reservations aside to give the album a half-page rave in the 15 May 1976 issue (giving the Pistols a cryptic plug into the bargain):

The Ramones are the real inheritors to the Archies' dubious mantle . . . [And] the musical influences are easy 'nough to divine. Classic punk is the meal ticket here – early Stooges retard-bop, plus a healthy surfeit of commercial Anglo-pop . . . [But] after the New York Dolls' pratfall, after the likes of Iggy and Jonathan Richman have been rejected for being the real rock visionaries they are, the coast may be clear for the new wave punks. The Ramones don't say much. They're pretty vacant. But they rock out with a vengeance.

Kent's endorsement alone was enough to send import shops into a tailspin. At least one of London's fledgling punk outfits, The Damned, were one jump ahead of the madding crowd. Because of his friendship with Kent, Brian James now took permanent loan of that fabled test-pressing, 'We took it from his place in Charing Cross Road, where he used to live with Hermione . . . He used to tell us all these stories about the [New York] bands. We used to sit up all night, doing various things to stay awake. So we were well versed in that first album when they came over to play.' Endorsement aside, Kent came to feel that the release of that record at such a pivotal point in punk had a deleterious effect on the maverick movement.

Nick Kent: The Ramones had a big effect. I did see pretty much the first gig The Clash played, which was support for the Pistols at the 100 Club, with Keith Levene, and it was . . . clear that they'd heard the Ramones. It seemed to me that they had a bunch of songs, and they were all ready to go, and *The Ramones* record came along and Mick Jones said, 'Okay, let's play these songs at three times the speed we normally play them.'

This theory is not down to Kent's overactive imagination. The Clash grafted speed to their schtick. Mick Jones's old compadre, Tony James, heard about the change first-hand: 'The early London SS, the early Pistols it was all about The Small Faces, early Who, early Rolling Stones, early Lou Reed. Everything was mid-paced, 130 bpm, 100 bpm regular English garage rock & roll. [But] I can remember Mick calling me, "You've got to fucking hear this record," and he puts on *The Ramones* album. And everybody . . . doubled speed overnight [which] . . . changed the English punk base.'

One might conclude that the same happened to The Damned, especially given such regular exposure to the record at precisely the point when their sound was formulating. Brian James thinks not: 'If it wasn't for that *Ramones* album, we would never have thought of covering The Beatles' "Help" – and speeding it up – but on the stuff we were playing already, the speed I was getting from the MC5.' The recent release of three demos recorded in early June, before they had started gigging, includes foot-to-the-floor takes of 'See Her Tonight' and 'I Fall', which suggest they were in a hurry to hear the starting Pistol.

The demos in question were recorded at the four-track 'studio' in Maida Vale owned by Barry Jones and The Boys' Matt Dangerfield. Damned manager Andy Czekowski is quick to dispel any romantic image the occasion may have acquired: 'It was [done] in the basement of this house which was the coal cellar beneath the street – a squat basically. [We] did the singing in the corridor to get the echoes, and the drums were put in the coal cellar.'

For those who knew what they wanted to do already, *The Ramones* album was a validation. The Vibrators' Eddie Edwards says he felt, 'Yeah, this is exactly the same thing as what we're trying to do.' Tim 'TV' Smith, who heard the album at an old school friend's while in London looking for a flat, says, 'It was fantastic to hear . . . someone being simple and funny, and not pretentious.' Vic Goddard's was perhaps the one dissenting voice. His response to 'every other band in the world suddenly want[ing] to be exactly the same [speed] as the Ramones, including The Clash', was to instigate a one-man go slow.

For other impressionable souls it defined punk at a time when it was still very much up for grabs. Mark Perry, a bank clerk with a yen to publish, says it was Kent's review that drew his attention to the record and that, 'From the minute I digested his description I was hooked and couldn't wait to hear it.' Perry, by his own admission, had been 'reading about the New York scene . . . in *NME* through Nick Kent, hearing about CBGB's . . . It sounded very exciting, talking about things in a new way.' When he decided to start a fanzine – after seeing the Ramones at Dingwall's – he named it *Sniffin' Glue*, in homage to the brat-beaters.

And yet, there in inky, mimeographed grey and white – in his very first editorial – Perry is proclaiming, 'Let's build our own brands up instead of drooling over the NY scene . . . London punk is great, so let's go!' Unfortunately, he hadn't yet seen any actual London punk; rather believing Eddie & the Hot Rods were an exemplar. Implying a precedence to the 'hey ho, let's go' rudimentary Ramones model over what Tony James typified as 'regular English garage rock & roll', he started out already wide of the mark.

The Ramones, at the time, certainly did their best to dissociate themselves from 'the NY scene' about which Perry was salivating. Johnny Ramone told *Sounds*' Susan Shapiro, in a Roundhouse preview-piece, 'We're not art-rock ... We have lots of influences but it all comes down to hard rock and bubblegum. We have nothing to do with the rest of the New York underground or The Velvet Underground or Patti Smith.' In fact, Johnny's first contact with the headliners at their London debut, The Flamin' Groovies, suggested he felt separated from even the grooviest garageband.

Chris Wilson: I think it was at Kensington Close Hotel [where] I first met the Ramones. We'd exchanged room numbers, and later on that evening, I remember us sitting around my room with some room service and I'd just bought a little acoustic guitar in Denmark Street; and John and Joe came in. They had a couple of Coca-Colas, but they looked like they were on something. We just sat and talked for a while. Having been in groups in southern California [that] played in biker bars, seeing guys in ripped jeans and motorcycle jackets didn't mean a thing to me ... Anyway, I passed my guitar to John and said, 'Have a go,' and he went, 'I'm sorry, man. I only know how to play bar-chords.'

Such uncertainty was compounded by the reception the Ramones received at the Roundhouse, which was not all it could have been given Shapiro's belief that 'they're on their way ... to Europe to blow everyone off the continent, [and] to the top of the charts'. In fact, Will Birch recollects that 'the crowd were a bit nonplussed by the Ramones, probably to the extent that there was a bit of hostility. The audience didn't get it all initially.' Nick Kent is quite sure there was some hostility, even 'a lot of violence. It got very territorial.'

MM's Allan Jones, back for some more adrenalin 'n' attitude, chose to see the trouble at the gig as a mere refraction of 'the fiercely retarded music perpetrated by the Ramones, with its moronic emphasis on a violently expressed nihilism'. *NME* also refrained from another rave for the boys. Rather, their correspondent Max Bell predicted a swift dissolution for the boys in the band, and indeed punk itself: 'The Punk syndrome so far has been characterized by its built-in auto-destruction, so according to the schedule the Ramones have one year in which to bank their takings before another sensation replaces them.'

Bell had turned up early enough to see the Ramones soundchecking, and to witness Dee Dee Ramone 'already complaining about the lack of power leaving his stack, and the English sound crew [not] taking the slating too kindly. The grudge will later culminate in a screaming row between band and console at the concert.' It also possibly led to some sabotage. Kent recalls them plugging into the PA and starting to play 'and it just went off. Kaput. It was a damp squib.' Not quite the triumph, then, of legend.

The following night, the Ramones got an even more brazen reception from England's anti-hippies. This time there were some real punk-rockers in the audience to welcome them to Camden Town proper. Joe Strummer may have thought he climbed into the Round-house to see the Ramones – as he seems to suggest in the biopic, *The End of the Century* – but he was in Sheffield, a four-hour drive away, on 4 July. The Clash were opening their live account *way* out of town, supporting the Sex Pistols. But both bands dutifully trundled down to Dingwall's the following night, where the Ramones had a second chance to shine.

As they took to the Dingwall's stage, though, somebody took one look at the New York lads and 'thought, "Let's see how tough you are." And – only because it was a plastic glass – I threw a glass at 'em. And they stormed off stage.' The glass-thrower, Glen Matlock, duly started a tradition of Sex Pistols bassists chucking glasses; and getting banned from venues as a result. Spotted by the promoter, Matlock ensured that the doors of Dingwall's remained closed to the Pistols (Jones lifting a briefcase containing the Groovies' petty cash at the after-gig party probably didn't help their cause either). Matlock stayed to check out the competition, only to conclude, 'We really didn't feel we had that much in common. We considered them more of a comedy band.'

If Matlock was challenging one set of so-called originators, Rotten was at the bar, facing down another. Jonh Ingham was standing there, when Ian Dury came up and said, 'I want to meet this Johnny Rotten guy.' Ingham turned to Rotten, and called him over. 'John comes up, and they both just leaned into each other and it was like one of those "so you think you're tough" [moments]. It really was, "You little punk, everything you got you stole from me." "You wouldn't know originality if you heard it." [Dury]'s razor-blade earrings dangling backwards and forwards. I remember the glints in their eyes – they were just having so much fun.'

What impressed several English musicians at the Camden club that night was not necessarily the Ramones' speed or simplicity, but their staging. Vibrator Eddie describes the set as 'twenty-five minutes of blazing rock & roll . . . I think everybody tightened their whole act up after that, and cut down the gaps between songs.' Brian James concurs, admitting to a debt, just not the one usually assigned, i.e. velocity – 'The way [there were] hardly any breaks between the songs – that kind of thing was an influence: cut out the meaningless chat, keep hitting them.'

Sadly, the most significant event that night, in terms of the course of English punk, occurred at the end, and had nothing to do with the Ramones. Stranglers bassist Jean-Jacques Burnel remembers it this way: 'We were walking Indian file through the crowd, leaving the venue. Steve and Paul from the Pistols were with Paul Simonon . . . In those days Paul had this nervous tick where he used to spit . . . He did it as I walked past and I thought he was spitting at me, so I thumped him. He fell into Steve and Paul, pints flying. Next thing we knew, we were in the courtyard . . . in each other's faces, bit of prodding . . . It just petered out.'

It may have petered out on the night, but it drew a line that separated the Pistols and The Clash from The Stranglers – and anyone associated with them – for good. Always a little too old, and tarnished by pub-rock roots, The Stranglers were now excluded from anything that involved McLaren, Rhodes and/or their charges. Scabies, who caught the tail end of the argument, notes, 'It was a bad move on everyone's part . . . It was the first sign that we all weren't gonna get on.' The Damned would also become tainted as soon as they shared the Stranglers' booking agency. Ditto The Vibrators. When McLaren concocted a punk coming-out ball at the end of August, both bands were noticeable by their absence; replaced by four lads from 'up north'.

– – –

Absent from these London shows, but fully aware of the boys from New York City, were Howard Devoto and Pete Shelley. They had already played the whole of the import album as interval music at Manchester's first punk gig, the Sex Pistols at the Lesser Free Trade Hall. Buzzcocks had also been rehearsing a rendition of 'Judy Is A Punk' that, according to Richard Boon, was 'two seconds faster than the original', with a view to making their debut in the support slot that night. However, sympathetic rhythm-sections remained in short supply, and they finally accepted the inevitable and booked the out-of-place Solstice to open proceedings. The show had already received a surprisingly well-informed, unattributed preview in the *New Manchester Review*:

On June 4 the Sex Pistols board a Manchester stage for the first time at the Lesser Free Trade Hall. If you haven't read any of the articles on them in the music press recently then you've missed some of the juiciest print in months – fans beaten up, abuse, strippers . . . The Sex Pistols are the foremost punk outfit in the country. Every song is so mean, tight, fast and offensive you'll probably be too engrossed to notice the mike-stand John 'Le Demented' Rotten just hurled your way. The element of real danger gives them the edge on any performing band around. If you actually go to hear the music you won't be disappointed either. They're plenty proficient.

The work of *NMR*'s erstwhile pub-rock correspondent Howard Trafford, this plug represented pretty much the entire media blitz. For Devoto and Shelley, promoting gigs was a new adventure. If McLaren had had very little input, he had told Devoto at the outset, 'We don't want to play a pub.' He also sent a set of press packs which – Devoto recalls – had 'all the bad reviews as well'. The week before the gig, Devoto met briefly with McLaren in London, having gone down to see Bowie perform *Station To Station* at Wembley. He sensed that, 'Malcolm looked down his nose at that; Bowie was not to be conjured with in his book.'

Essentially, it was the hardy and the hip who turned up that night to the home of the Hallé Orchestra, drawn by national music-press coverage of the Pistols, or simply part of Manchester's small alternative music network. Peter Hook, later of Joy Division, thinks he went there because of 'getting the *Melody Maker*, and on the front cover there was a picture of a group fighting at a gig . . . and it was the Sex Pistols.' The football-hooligan element had evidently struck a chord. The gang of lads (and lass) that became The Fall were there because, in Martin Bramah's words, they were 'wondering what these "skinheads" were doing covering [The] Stooges . . . I went along thinking I could heckle.'

Yet even with all the media static, the gig was never going to be a sell-out. Indeed, McLaren – who had ventured north for the gig in a surprising gesture of solidarity – was required to become the 'barker' who cajoled passers-by into parting with hard, northern cash. According to Mark E. Smith, already in possession of a ticket, McLaren even ventured into the pub across the road and asked, 'Are you coming over to see the band?' Outside the venue, he continued to accost any likely lad, including one Steve Diggle, who noticed, 'Quite a few people . . . [were] being coaxed in by this strange-looking fella in a Teddy Boy drape jacket, leather trousers and brothel creepers . . . I asked him who was on and he said the Sex Pistols. "Oh, what are they like?" I asked. "They're like The Who . . . Are you coming in?"'

What finally induced Diggle into crossing the line, though, was a serendipitous misunderstanding. He had arranged to meet an unrelated person outside the famous hall regarding an audition as a guitarist. When he volunteered this information to McLaren, the latter assumed he was the bass player Devoto and Shelley had arranged to meet at the gig, with a view to joining *their* band. What he saw that night convinced Diggle to go along with their scheme.

Steve Diggle: Matlock and Cook were so fucking loud but just brilliant together: honestly, forget any of those stories about the Sex Pistols not being able to play. I hadn't heard anything like it in my life.

Future members of The Fall and Joy Division in attendance that night were equally taken with the Pistols. Martin Bramah admits that any scepticism faded fast, 'I was really bowled over. I got my hair cut soon after. I could see something was happening.' Peter Hook remembers that they looked 'like they were having such a fantastic time. It was so . . . alien to everything. You just thought, "God, we could do that."' His mate, Bernard Sumner, looking for an iconoclastic message in the music, felt that 'they destroyed the myth of being a pop star, of a musician being some kind of God'.

Evidently, the lightning conductor could still transmit 'up north'. To those who were along for the ride, this was no great surprise. As Jordan says, 'I really defy anybody in those days to go to a Pistols concert and not be excited by what was going on, because there was a definite static energy in what was going on onstage.' Less than a month later, Marion Elliott caught the band 'on the end of the pier in Hastings. The only people there were little Swedish girls who had come over on the boat for the day! And upstairs there were all these old people doing ballroom dancing . . . It was really funny!' The experience was also enough to convince Marion to reinvent herself as Poly Styrene, and apply her x-ray vision in a similar direction.

Ian Dury was also converted – and slightly cowed – by seeing the band live. Two weeks before his tête-à-tête with Rotten, Dury's re-formed Kilburn & the High Roads were top of the bill at another all-nighter in Walthamstow, north London. Kilburns manager B. P. Fallon remembers, 'After the gig, I took Ian into a classroom and said, "Now do you know what I'm on about?" and that was the end of the Kilburns. It was the turning point . . . The Sex Pistols weren't brilliant musically, but their vibe was fantastic.' The Pistols, it seemed, could both inspire the new, and put the hex on the old wave.

And though still operating below most journalists' radar, Manchester's few fanzines did the Pistols proud. The Stockport-based *Penetration* ran a two-page review enthusing about their capacity to 'blitz the audience with power chords and vocals set in a different key to the music'; while grammar-school pupil Paul Morley used the first issue of his own zine, *Out There*, to describe a band 'as relentless and guiltless as a zipless fuck'. The London critics, though, were not so convinced, preferring to propagate the idea that they couldn't play, until the Pistols' frustration flowered into a song of sorts.

By 29 June, they took to prefacing their weekly set at the 100 Club with three minutes of babbling nonsense over a wail of feedback. 'Flowers Of Romance' was its name, and as Rotten told *Sounds*, it was 'just noise, no music – just to confuse people who said we couldn't play'. That night, at least one member of the band's 'entourage' decided to send a further message to the press, one that only served to reinforce another prejudice – that Pistols gigs were violent affairs. According to the recipient, the attack was carefully orchestrated, nay choreographed.

Nick Kent: That incident where Vicious and Wobble pinned me down and hit me with that bike chain, that's when McLaren turned on me. We were real friends before that – we'd sit down and talk. But for him to [orchestrate] that was just vicious – 'You are now an enemy.' I knew what was going to happen. I was watching this guy like a hawk. Vicious pointed in my direction, and McLaren was nodding his head, like, 'Go on. Do it.' . . . They all had big grins on their faces, then he came back just as the concert began. It was all timed.

In a night of lashings, verbal and otherwise, the Pistols debuted another new song, 'I Wanna Be Me', that continued their spat with the press, specifically those critics 'down in the crypt, where the typewriter sits' who 'wanna be someone/ruin someone'. Though it might seem like Kent had also become a target for Rotten's razor-like pen, the singer never doubted Kent's critical credentials. In fact, Kent recalls Rotten coming 'up to me at the height of the nonsense with Vicious and said, "Listen, you're a good writer."'

If this lyrical vial of bile had a target, it was *Melody Maker*'s Richard Williams, who had written 'this fictional thing projecting the Pistols into the 1980s, with memos from corporate executives. The whole thing was that the Pistols were thinking of doing a reunion tour and Rotten was living in Beverly Hills with a German actress. And apparently he was very upset – so I was told – [saying,] "He's written my bleedin' obituary."'

Rotten considered Williams part of 'the problem – [i.e.] complacent cynics [who]'ve seen it all before, they've been through it, man, they've experienced it. They're just yapping the way bloody parents do.' Williams, an innocuous target at best, may have rubbed Rotten the wrong way by ignoring the band when head of A&R at Island. If so, Williams had abandoned the Island ship long before any signing scrum.

For the Pistols, the grind of gigging was already starting to turn into something of a slog. Out-of-town shows were unpredictable affairs, and like as not resulted in audiences fresh off the boat. The night the Ramones landed, these ideological rivals made a two-hundred-mile trek to Sheffield, playing the Black Swan, a bastion of the pub-rock circuit but the only way to make an impression that side of the Pennines. And at least they had a genuine punk band as support, The Clash having now found a reluctant beatmaster in Terry Chimes.

According to Paul Simonon, Sheffield had 'quite a few hip characters there, who'd picked up on what the Pistols had been doing'. He also claimed he 'used to enjoy those early gigs. Me and Joe Strummer used to leap off the stage to hit people.' It seems highly unlikely that they took on Sheffield's hardiest that night. He had other things to worry about, like someone tuning his bass between songs. Pukka Pistols bassist Matlock remembers turning to Rotten during the set and going, 'What do you think?' Though both were 'keen for something to happen', even Rotten had to admit, 'They're not very good, are they?' This was certainly the view of a paying punter, who wrote to *Sounds* the following week, calling The Clash 'just a cacophonous barrage of noise'; and the Pistols' few fans 'the weirdest bunch of followers' he'd ever seen.

The punk concoction had still barely begun to fizz. All that changed in the three weeks after The Clash broke their mucky duck. In that split-second in Pop Culture terms, The Damned, Buzzcocks and Subway Sect all followed The Clash into the scariest of spotlights, first-night fears. Between them, these four bands would constitute punk's first phalanx, following the Pistols into battle, and providing a real sense of an army on the march.

If The Clash needed more fine-tuning before they could make London sit up and listen, The Damned dove in head-first – indeed head-to-head – taking on the Pistols at their home-from-home the 100 Club, the night after the Dingwall's ding-dong. It was a brave challenge to the original clarion-callers, even if The Damned like to dismiss any debt owed to the Pistols.

Rat Scabies: We always regarded what we did as very different from the Pistols. That was a very essential part of [early] punk, not to sound like another band. It was almost like a Mod inherent cool – if someone else did it, and you copied that idea, you had no imagination of your own.

The Damned certainly weren't interested in anything mid-tempo, flaying away at every song like their lives depended on it. In fact, Vanian felt slightly bewildered by the process, later commenting on how, 'Brian would give you a sheet of lyrics scrawled out, and I'd say, "How does it go?" He'd play the guitar and go (sub-Keef growl), "Yeah, baby, it goes like this! Blah-la-la-la," in your ear – once – and then you had to sing the damn thing.'

James was no less manic once they hit the stage. If the 100 Club show passed without incident, their second show at the Nashville a few days later drew both extremes on the reaction scale. The following month Rat Scabies would bemoan the state of the pub circuit in *Sniffin' Glue*, castigating 'most . . . pub audiences' because they 'like to sit, have a drink and chat about the weather'. No such option was available that night in West Kensington. As Ingham recalls, 'Ted Carroll and Roger Armstrong and me [were] standing at the back, killing ourselves laughing as these hippies scattered to the bar as fast as they could manage . . . It was like four different bands playing together at 78 rpm. It was a spectacle. [But] they [already] had great stage presence.' Ingham's review in the following week's *Sounds* celebrated the sensory overload:

Describing The Damned is pretty hard. You remember the end of a Stooges gig, where they just turned everything up full and walked off, leaving the guitars on the amps to loop out in ultimate white heat feedback? Well, The Damned come on about that strong. They're beyond being good or bad, beyond comparisons, beyond even being ultimately offensive . . . The Damned just are, and if you don't like it, piss off . . . What really made [this gig] unique, though, was their concept of timing. God knows who was making the mistakes, but not once did they make tempo changes in unison. Since all this took place at about Mach 5, the resulting melange sounded positively avant-garde.

The headliners that night, Salt, were less impressed and halfway through the Damned set, bassist Sensible noticed that 'the curtain started drawing in front of us . . . We thought we were just playing songs, but obviously we were doing something quite radical.'

While Ingham remained in no doubt that the Pistols were leaders of the punkpack, The Damned now also became part of his mission statement. But when he saw the Pistols again, at the Lyceum a couple of days later, he recognized how they were outstripping any comers, old guard included. Ingham was not the only one awestruck by the way the Pistols had come on. *MM*'s Allan Jones may have been unconverted by the Ramones a week earlier, but when he caught the Pistols at the Lyceum 'the penny dropped with a very loud clang'. Though The Pretty Things raised the bar with their support set that night, the Pistols responded with vim, velocity and verve.

Jonh Ingham: When it got to the Lyceum gig, and then the Manchester Free Trade Hall, that's when [the Pistols] became a real band. All the stuff before that was like a rehearsal, even though at the time it was great to watch. You would be seeing Jones one week, it would be all feedback, and then a week later it would be clean picking. That night he combined [it all] together. He'd sussed it all.

It had been a hectic fortnight, what with the Clash and Damned debuts, the Ramones leaving for home, and a Lyceum all-nighter alongside a band Rotten openly admired. Yet the Pistols also found time to make a second, more representative set of demos with soundman Dave Goodman at their own rehearsal studio. The repetitive nature of the recording process only made the songs stronger, while giving them the opportunity to hone two new 'uns, 'I Wanna Be Me' and 'Anarchy In The UK', the latter of which would make its feedback-strewn debut when the Pistols agreed to a rematch with the Lesser Free Trade Hall.

This time Devoto and Shelley's own band were opening proceedings. In the six weeks separating the two Manchester gigs, a low-frequency buzz from that first show had made itself audible to anyone attuned, and second time around, the place was three-quarters full. As journalist Paul Morley states, 'The first show you just got the feeling that the Sex Pistols could have disappeared overnight and it would have been one of those things. But with the second show you knew that this was something titanic.'

Again there was something more intangible than simple word-of-mouth at work here. Art student Linder Sterling recalls being 'at some cemetery and [I] saw a van going past, and it had the [gig] poster tacked to the side, the Sex Pistols. Not knowing anything about [any of the bands], I went along that evening with a friend who was a kitchen designer.' Dick Witts, who had played literally hundreds of times in the Free Trade Hall proper, during seven years of playing percussion in the world-famous Hallé Orchestra, just found the choice of venue 'most remarkable . . . I remember thinking, "It's either someone who really doesn't know where to put these musicians on, or they're being deliberately provocative."' He resolved to check it out after reading 'something John Peel said, [suggesting] that [the Pistols] were doing something completely new'.

Aside from those who felt mysteriously compelled to check the Pistols out, there was a sizeable contingent in the audience there to see second-on-the-bill Slaughter & the Dogs, originally given this slot as a safeguard against Buzzcocks faltering again. The Dogs even went to the trouble of printing their own handbills, designed to make some folk think they were co-headliners, before going on local radio to talk about 'punk' as a cross between Bowie and the Stones i.e. their two most obvious influences! If the Dogs were a council-estate lock-up Spiders from Mars, with delusions of relevance, their inclusion on the bill made the difference between originators and imitators crystalline in its clarity.

Ingham, who had travelled up to the gig with the Pistols and *MM*'s Caroline Coon, observed in his review that 'any way you slice it, . . . the Dogs are well outside the boundaries being drawn by the Pistols . . . Pete Shelley reckons they're an offence just to the word itself.' Linder

Sterling concurs, 'Slaughter & the Dogs were not very sure who they were, or what was happening, still [having] one foot very firmly in the past; [while] the Buzzcocks had one foot in the future . . . [They were] playing very badly, very quickly, but it was very, very exciting. [I had] a real sense of never having seen this before.'

Dick Witts: There was an economic reason why [the Dogs] were doing [this], and it showed up in their repertory . . . [whereas] Buzzcocks I found musically very interesting . . . What was interesting was [these] people trying to play instruments they couldn't play and what came out of that – how they negotiated their technical limitations between them to make something that really was exciting and did communicate.

Whatever bad blood there may have been beforehand was already running hot when Buzzcocks launched into 'Breakdown', a highly appropriate opener given how such a possibility remained omnipresent throughout their short set. For Devoto, the show was an attempt to break on through, simply by doing what he later typified as 'that extra-ordinary thing of going out in front of people and opening your mouth'. Richard Boon recognized how, even at this stage, his friend was engaged in 'some kind of existential acting out of being a performer'. The band, on the other hand, remained 'rhythmic to the point of rigidity', as Ingham put it in print.

Devoto says they had in mind to do something that came in 'a direct line with the Sex Pistols doing Small Faces songs – [because] part of the aesthetic was obviously [the] *pre-hippy* sixties'. Hence The Troggs' 'I Can't Control Myself' as a finale. Ingham described it ending with 'a wild feedback solo, Shelley throwing his axe at the amp. When he went on a little too long, Devoto came out of the wings and pulled the guitar from him. He pulled it back. Devoto grabbed all six strings and yanked, ripping them asunder. Shelley propped the now screaming guitar against the speaker and left via the audience.' According to Boon, this climax – captured on silent 8 mm film by a friend of Devoto's – was 'something that had been rehearsed. Peter had this cheap guitar. Howard would rip the strings off.'

Next up were the Dogs, who came on stage with this 'green satin (quasi) Bowie look' that Linder Sterling remembers thinking 'didn't seem right – it didn't seem *new*'. She was not alone in her instinctual antipathy, and the more belligerent Prestwich contingent began heckling them. For Mark E. Smith, it was a matter of principle – 'the glam rock [bands] were seen as the enemy really . . . more so than the hippies, who we personally quite connected with'. Martin Bramah suggests they simply had no idea how many Dog devotees were there: 'We didn't know they had a huge following on the other side of the hall, [and] they came running over. There were a lot more of them, but they were younger than us.'

The resulting scuffle ensured that there would be no third LFTH performance, even though the London headliners were in the dressing room, biding their time. Having survived the Slaughter, Bramah and his buddies watched the Pistols pulsating their way through another 'zipless fuck' of a set; and this time they resolved to begin practising in earnest.

Martin Bramah: For us in Manchester, seeing the Sex Pistols play was totally different than seeing all these American bands or London bands coming in on a tour organized by a major label. It all seemed unattainable – and then suddenly you realized, 'Oh, we can do that ourselves.' . . . It's hard to say which part of the puzzle slotted into place [after seeing the Pistols] but it was the sheer weight of events – the energy that was coming up. [And] music meant everything to us. Just that thought – 'We can do that' – had so much momentum it carried us through to actually . . . gig together.

Dick Witts, ever the trained musician, thought the distinction between the Sex Pistols and Slaughter & the Dogs could be expressed in musical terms, being the 'difference . . . between *repetition* and *insistence*'. Witts had arrived at an epiphany later articulated by *Punk* scribe, Mary Harron; that perhaps, 'Rock is the only form of music which can actually be done *better* by people who can't play their instruments than by people who can.'

Steve Diggle, whose status as a Buzzcock didn't preclude the use of public transport, recalls in his autobiography how he 'stood in the bus queue with all the kids I'd been at the gig with . . . [and] they were all saying, "This is amazing." . . . I could tell that they had got it, they understood what it was all about . . . The message was DO IT YOUR-SELF!' While Diggle was making his way home, Devoto and Shelley were heading for the Conti Club with the Pistols, and a lady they'd met at the gig.

Linder Sterling: By the time the Pistols came on, Howard and Peter came to sit next to myself and the kitchen designer; and the kitchen designer, being very northern, starts talking to them. So afterwards they're all going to the Conti Club, [and] we went along. I started talking to Pete Shelley, 'What do you do?' 'Oh, I do design.' 'Well, we need someone [like that]. Get in touch.' . . . Telephone numbers were exchanged . . . By the time I went back to the Poly in late September in my transformative garb – bondage trousers [and such] – and I met [Peter] Saville and [Malcolm] Garrett, they both [had] mouths on the floor, 'What's happened?' So I took them to the university precinct record shop and made them buy the Modern Lovers' album and the Ramones', and said, 'Listen to these two and you'll understand.'

After the heady high of their Manchester debut (and a positive *Sounds* review), Buzzcocks began the laborious task of developing a scene two hundred miles removed from the King's Road. In the six weeks before their own London debut, Buzzcocks played just one gig, and it lasted no longer than their stuttering start in Bolton back in April.

Howard Devoto: The Ranch was the kids' bar at [Madame] Fufu's, and we'd started hanging out there [with] the Bowie kids. So we approached Frank [aka Fufu] and he seemed to be agreeable to us playing a set at the Ranch. It was a small bar. [But] there was a hatch, and his club was through there. We start up, and [we're] fucking up his act in there. So this heavy started walking in and out, between us, [and] between numbers, he says to me, 'You the boss, then? Fufu says you'll have to stop.' We only played about four numbers.

Meanwhile, the other duo who took something from the Pistols' set at the Marquee, Rob Symmons and Vic Goddard, were struggling to come to terms with some very basic tenets of musicality, or even finding anyone who could bring them to the band. One equally inept friend, Paul Myers, at least seemed on a similar wavelength. He adopted the bass, after Goddard and Symmons 'took him along to see the Sex Pistols. Because he was a soul boy and [had] been to all these clubs, he knew Siouxsie Sioux from when she used to dress up and go to these clubs . . . Paul was into all that sort of thing. [But he] was never really into music.'

Girlfriend of Marquee-convert Steve Severin, Siouxsie Sioux had yet to transform herself into the faux Fräulein-dominatrix that would become English punk's other feminine visual fix (along with Jordan);

and was even some way off seeing the scene as more than a way to pass the time. Paul, though, continued to plunk away, and with a drummer named 'Ray', Subway Sect made a debut of sorts. Symmons believes it was at 'someone's party in a house in Chiswick. And everybody left the room . . . we did copies of the Sex Pistols. Or we tried to. "Did You No Wrong", "No Fun", "I'm Not Your Steppin' Stone", they were the only ones we knew.'

Goddard's contemporary description of this same gig to *Sniffin' Glue* makes it sound even more, er, challenging: 'We did "Steppin' Stone" and a couple of ones I'd written then, which we don't do now. We did a complete "noise" . . . where everyone smashed their guitars around. I just chanted some poetry over it all.' He now admits, 'It was comedy – it wasn't serious. "My Name Is Sue" was one of the songs.'

However, such was the need for bands to fulfill this avowed movement that the act of announcing one had a punk band was enough – at this stage – for McLaren to welcome thee into the fold (especially when he recognized you from assorted Pistols gigs). So when the Sect's original drummer ended up at the 100 Club bar one night, talking to Joe Strummer, and informed the singer he was in a band called Subway Sect, it ended up as a passing reference in *NME*'s Teasers section. When Symmons and Goddard subsequently ran into McLaren at the Screen on the Green, at the end of August, 'Malcolm was at the bar and we mentioned [the band] to him, and he said, "Oh, you're the Subway Sect." ' At this point, McLaren made them an offer they couldn't refuse, but it required them to decide to be something more than a Pistols covers band.

— — —

By this time, McLaren wasn't the only one talking up the tiny scene into a movement of sorts; or referring to something called English punk rock. Matlock certainly assigns the credit elsewhere, 'Punk was invented by Caroline Coon and Jonh Ingham . . . [who] championed our cause and tried to make it look like a movement . . . but there wasn't one really.'

If the idea of a movement was McLaren's, and the name (i.e. punk-rock) was already coined, the codifying of the scene really came with an article by Coon, written on her return from Manchester and published in *Melody Maker* the first week in August. Its title was 'Punk Rock: Rebels against the System', and Coon went to great pains to separate the English strain from its elder New York cousin:

The new British bands emerging have only the most tenuous connections with the New York punk-rock scene . . . The British punk scene, far from glorifying, is disgusted by the past. Nostalgia is a dirty word . . . British punk rock is emerging as a fierce, aggressive, self-destructive onslaught. [*MM*, 7/8/76]

Ingham excepted, Coon until now had been a solitary voice in the music-weekly wilderness when it came to punk. She was also working for the most staid of the weeklies, *Melody Maker*, the very paper that had already dismissed the Pistols as 'doing for music what World War II had done for the cause of peace'. And she had a knack for seeing any rebuff from editor Ray Coleman as evidence of some chauvinist agenda. And so, when Coleman finally agreed to give her a centre-spread on the punk phenomenon, she was incensed to discover that 'they got one of the [other journalists] to do a kind of spoiler piece at the bottom – [saying] it's disgusting, they can't play their instruments, it won't happen.' Where she got her way was calling it punk-rock, and banging that nail into the unyielding ground.

Jonh Ingham: Caroline was really having to fight Ray Coleman, but she took a very feminist, polemical view of all this stuff. My pitch to her – since it was the two of us against the world – was, 'Let's collaborate.' If it's gonna be a movement, it helps to work together to make that point. We just made stuff up on occasion. The bit about 'punks like reggae' was purely because she and I, and John [Lydon] and Paul [Simonon] liked it . . . [But] there was a conversation, 'Malcolm wants to call it new wave.' . . . [It was like,] 'What do you call it?'

Coon never had any doubts about what it should be called, even though – as she says – 'Punk had a very particular connotation in America [that] didn't really translate into English. It's a very graphic term, a four-letter word.' Of course, her own rigid codification obliged her, a mere three months later, to utilize McLaren's preferred term, 'new wave', when describing a related but distinct aesthetic. It also obliged those who'd already wrapped themselves in punk's mantle to start making distinctions based on sound and vision that they had not initially felt any need to do. In this sense, Coon did those who were already causing combustion a disservice.

As early as 1979, Strummer was lamenting this sea-change: 'Punk came out and said, "Bollocks to the lot of you, change is what it's all about, this is new . . ." In '76 it was all, like, individual. There was a common ground, it was punk-rock, but anything was OK, like he was wearing this . . . and he was experimenting with that.' Matlock also insists that the original 'punk scene weren't about [one type of] music; and it weren't about having a carbon-copy look. It was about having ideas, and being forward-looking – being outside the box somehow.' Pete Shelley concurs, 'Punk [at that time] was about taking away all that pretence and actually saying it like it was . . . trying to be direct and open and honest. It was very liberating.' Even the rarely sensible Captain Sensible states that he 'always thought punk was an experiment, about taking risks. We thought the whole idea was, "There are no rules."'

The pressure to conform to certain rules, though, was already gaining momentum. 'TV' Smith, who had now relocated to London, recalls an occasion that summer when he and Gaye 'were at the Nashville, seeing someone else, and Steve Jones said to me, "You should really cut that hair!" I thought, "I'm not going to cut my hair. This is the rebel look. What is the point of a movement that says you gotta cut your hair?" But I still did.'

A cursory glance at the first three or four issues of movement mouth-piece, *Sniffin' Glue*, which began life in late July 1976, suggested no one, least of all editor Mark P, knew where to draw the line. In issue three he was still writing about how 'Eddie & the Hot Rods, the Sex Pistols, The Damned, The Clash, the Count Bishops, the Gorillas, Roogalator, Sister Ray, Stranglers, The Jam, Buzzcocks, Slaughter & the Dogs . . . all need "good" gigs . . . [so] get along and see all the "punk" rock you can.' When he finally saw the Sex Pistols, in *mid*-August, it was brought home how quickly the *diktats* of style and musical taste were ossifying.

Mark Perry: Caroline Coon was the one who told me about the Sex Pistols. She asked if I'd seen them and told me to come to a show. So about a week later, I saw them at the 100 Club in . . . early August . . . I'd never seen anything like that . . . I turned up to this gig with long hair, down to my shoulders, with a brown satin jacket. Caroline said, 'You got to meet some people.' So I met Malcolm, Vivienne and Sid Vicious, who had a shaven head and tissues hanging off him, [going,] 'Who's this fucking hippie?' Caroline said, 'I want to introduce you to Mark – he's done this fanzine about punk.' I remember that Sid picked it up and said, 'Fuck it,' and threw it on the floor. Some hard dude that is! Later on, I realized he was a powder puff, it was just a big show. Then when the band came on, it was just phenomenal. I had my suit ripped off 'cause of the pogo[ing].

It was almost symbolic. 'Right, let's get rid of that.' Within a week, the hair had come off, just cut it all off. [PSF]

The gig that introduced Mark P to the Pistols (and their ministers of propaganda) was almost certainly the one where The Vibrators played support, on 10 August. The Vibrators' own relationship with the 'other' punk bands was already see-sawing. After the Dingwall's incident, Eddie recalls that, 'The people in The Clash – who we'd been quite friendly with – fell out with The Stranglers, so we were tarred with the same brush.' But with the shortage of new bands that played fast and loud, Coon was initially obliged to put The Vibrators in her punk box, as was Ingham.

Knox: We basically were in isolation. We were aware of Eddie & the Hot Rods [and] the other pub-rock bands – [then] towards the summer the press suddenly introduced this term punk-rock and we were there, listed under this term . . . [Then] it became a deliberate policy to play harder and faster because the audience liked that stuff better, but it was quite natural to the way we were playing. I've always played quite hard.

According to Vibrator John Ellis, after 'we had this review . . . [in] *Sounds*, who likened us to the Sex Pistols', they were immediately checked out: 'Suddenly there were all these punk people coming down to see us . . . [Even] the Pistols were in the audience two or three weeks in a row.' Mark P, though, was apparently not impressed by what he saw. In the same issue where the likes of the Hot Rods and the Gorillas gained temporary membership of the punk constituency, he was quoting 'original Damned lead-singer Steve', saying The Vibrators 'won't get anywhere 'cause the drummer's got long hair'.

One band who had now done away with long hair was The Clash, under the tutelage of Comrade Rhodes. Before they were ready to face an(other) audience of paying sceptics, Rhodes arranged for them to do a press gig at the Camden rehearsal space that had replaced their respect-ive squats as base camp. When a laudatory review of the Rehearsal Rehearsal performance appeared in *Sounds*, the accompanying photo drew one's attention, as much as the headline, 'The first band to come along who'll really frighten the Sex Pistols.'

They were now actively courting Caroline Coon, who needed a punk band she could call her own, who would conform to the views outlined in her earlier article. Here was a band who had played exactly one gig, in Sheffield, who were already being shoehorned into second place in the punk pecking order by one or two scenemakers.

Jonh Ingham: I never saw Mick or Paul or Bernie until the Rehearsal Rehearsal's show in August. I had no idea of the existence of these guys at all. So they were really keeping themselves underground.

Others remained highly sceptical about The Clash's actual chops. As Sex employee Helen Wellington-Lloyd states, 'The Clash were great to watch, [but] not listen to.' Even after their public preview, Rhodes held back from thrusting The Clash in front of paying punters for another fortnight. When he did agree to share a bill at the Screen on the Green with Buzzcocks and the Sex Pistols on August Bank Holiday, the reaction (and tape) suggested they were still not match-ready. Charles Shaar Murray's memorable single-sentence critique in his *NME* review – 'They are the kind of garageband who should be speedily returned to their garage, preferably with the motor running' – is certainly borne out by the audience recording.

The Clash at Screen on the Green seemed like little more than Bernie's clothes horses. Richard Boon recollects that they even 'went out into the alleyway to get dressed, so that no one could see that they were wearing slogans and paint-spatter'. Paul Simonon, in particular, preferred to concentrate on looking good, rather than sounding good. (Johnny Green, in his memoir, portrays Simonon as someone who 'thought that the more he moved about the stage, the cooler he looked, [and] the less people would notice that he couldn't play. Not that he cared, really. He was interested in appearances and visuals . . . Give him a new guitar and within minutes he had painted it and carved his name on it.')

At Screen on the Green, the Clash lurched from song to song, with intermittent breaks determined by how long it took Jones to tune Simonon's bass for him. Even at the somewhat sedate pace they were obliged to play, tempo changes were hit-and-miss at best. Terry Chimes and Keith Levene tried their best to hold things together, but on songs like 'I Know What To Do About It', 'What's My Name' and 'London's Burning' their best was never quite good enough.

If The Clash were there to pose away, they were not alone. This was the coming-out ball for the so-called Bromley contingent, which had begun as Steve Severin, Simon Barker and a couple of like-minded friends. As Severin states, 'With the residency at the 100 Club, I just got everybody to come along at some point. Some came back, some didn't, but each week there seemed to be twice as many people there. And at that point, I remember writing to Billy [Broad] in Brighton, telling him he had to come up and see this band.' Broad (aka Billy Idol), who had been a close friend of Severin and Barker since 1972, told *NME* at a time when he needed to assert his punk credentials that the contingent 'was just five people who happened to like the same things'.

Steve Severin: The thing that bonded me and Billy was [our love of] The Velvet Underground. There were a group of us that went to Bromley Technical High School. Billy went to the grammar school. He was friends with another guy . . . who had an elder brother who was in the army in Germany, and he used to come back . . . with these Can and Velvet Underground albums. We just put on *White Light/White Heat* one day.

By the time Severin summoned Broad from Sussex University – where he claims to have fled, because 'otherwise I'd have had to go out and get a job' – the handful of misfits had become if not an army, certainly a contingent. As Severin says, 'It all seemed very organic, the way [the scene] happened . . . There was [even] a coach trip up to Manchester to see [Broad's band] Chelsea play, [with] Suburban Studs and the Worst.' The Bromley contingent's fifteen minutes began at Screen on the Green and ended in the frenzied aftermath of the Bill Grundy interview.

Siouxsie Sioux: For five minutes, a beautiful five minutes, [the scene] really was self-perpetuating, and there weren't any particular reasons why things happened. Days and weeks seemed like very long stretches of time, and a lot happened very quickly.

Siouxsie certainly seemed intent on acquiring a degree of notoriety, turning up at the Screen on the Green looking like a fetishistic mannequin someone forgot to finish dressing. Nor was she the only oddball at this coming-out ball. Phillip Salon turned up in a nightie, a housecoat, turban and slippers, only to later complain 'a lot of them just did not get it' – as if punters had paid to see him impersonating Freddie Mercury undergoing electro-shock treatment. Linder Sterling, who had turned up with Buzzcocks, brought her camera and was snapping away when

Vivienne Westwood came up and asked, 'Who are you a fan of?' Linder replied, 'Me.'

As an honorary Buzzcock, Linder was slightly at odds with the prevailing air of self-congratulation, Manchester's contingent being made to feel slightly self-conscious by the London lot. Steve Diggle said, of the London bands that night, 'You could tell they'd spent a lot of time in front of the mirror getting the look right. All of them had Vivienne Westwood outfits or stuff designed by Jamie Reid or some other art-school toff.'

Despite being made to feel like hick cousins, Buzzcocks were cobbled streets ahead of The Clash. Though they had yet to pen their early anthem, 'Boredom', the songs all had a gritty realism born of a young man's blues, even the one song they never recorded, 'Alcohol' (which like those other lost songs, 'Apollonia's Countdown' and 'Fall Guy', wouldn't even make it to the demo stage). After their set, Devoto wandered back to the sound desk, where he found McLaren, who informed him, 'You know, your songs have got real content.'

This he knew. The following year, he described the figure in Buzzcocks' opening song that night ('Breakdown') as being 'in the position of Camus' Sisyphus – "To will is to stir up paradoxes"'. He also portrayed the song's hero as 'well and truly fucked up, and like all profound but fucked-up heroes [he] wants to cajole others into getting in on the act too,' a sentiment with which the growing legions perhaps found it easier to relate.

In the six weeks since they last shared a stage, Buzzcocks and the Pistols had gone in opposite directions. Though Buzzcocks still had that buzzsaw sound, they had stopped trying to make everything a blur. The Pistols had tightened just about every loose nut. As Giovanni Dadomo wrote in *Sounds*, 'There were no lengthy breakdowns so that [Rotten]'d have to waste time making inane attempts at annoying his audience. Rather than pouring beer over his head and making a general asshole of himself for a third of the set, Rotten is now able to concentrate on his singing.'

They were now opening every show with an 'Anarchy In The UK' that began life as nowt but feedback, à la 'Flowers Of Romance', before devolving into powerhouse chords and a dementoid vocal. As *NME*'s Charles Murray (aka CSM) stated, 'The first thirty seconds of their set blew out all the boring, amateurish artsy-fartsy mock decadence that preceded it purely by virtue of its tautness, directness and utter realism.'

Nor did the band let up for the next fifty-five minutes, as they ran down their entire fifteen-song set, 'Did You No Wrong' included, replete with enough references to remind the many A&R folk in attendance what exactly they were trying to breathe life into. For others, like Robert Lloyd, who had travelled down from the Midlands, the Pistols ended a very long wait.

Robert Lloyd: The kind of stuff I was doing was pretty Kraut-rocky, which was largely to do with the fact that we couldn't play very well. But I was a fan already of The Stooges, the Velvets, the MC5 – the usual suspects – . . . I'd [also] seen Patti Smith when she first came over and just did the Roundhouse . . . [Then] when I went to see the Sex Pistols . . . it was like, 'This is the kind of stuff I want to do!'

Also at the Screen on the Green were the Torquay Two – TV Smith and Gaye Advert – already planning their own punk band, validated by the example of 'someone [like the Pistols] getting up and doing it . . . without having to have the proven requirements that were expected of a band'. Viv Albertine, Mick Jones's on–off girlfriend, also felt a once-familiar frisson, telling Coon the following June, 'It wasn't until I saw the Sex Pistols that I realized what I'd been missing and why I hadn't been to a rock concert for a year.' Though her first attempt at her own punk band would fall apart, she would ultimately slot into The Slits.

Screen on the Green was also the point at which McLaren probably began to wonder if his grand design was coming to naught. Or was, at least, beyond his command. At one of those self-important conferences on 'punk' in the eighties, McLaren would inform the assembled throng that 'the Sex Pistols were part of breaking [rock & roll] down . . . saying that there was no point any longer in playing well . . . I probably sold that [idea] better than anyone, often to the detriment of those working with me, who ultimately really did want to be good . . . [But] it was a philosophical point we couldn't agree on.'

If McLaren had genuinely planned to create a band who couldn't play – but would still succeed despite this – he'd found the wrong fellas. As his assistant at the time, Nils Stevenson, told Jon Savage, 'The Pistols . . . were too good for their purpose . . . The group became the style of the time because they were so good: instead of demystifying [music] and showing that anyone could do it, they proved that anyone couldn't.'

By Screen on the Green, the Pistols were the most exciting, four-cylinder rock band in the country, if not the world. So if the King's Road contingent were going to convince kids that anyone could do it, they were going to have to find another set of willing wannabes to drive the point home. The band that McLaren would later describe as 'a bunch of kids who adopted these attitudes and . . . created a series of discontented shows that provided a barrage of information for kids to use' no longer existed. (Did they ever?)

The Pistols would still help create the right environment for McLaren's cherished movement to emerge. And in the period before National Notoriety undid them, they would still have time to turn a few more heads, and trigger a handful more bands with similar ambitions (and a whole lot more bands without a clue). But it would be The Clash, the geeky garageband, who would reduce their message and style of music to its bare essentials, adding a quasi-political schtick that would resonate with a (largely reactionary) set of souls who were entirely separate from – and subsequent to – those the Pistols prompted into action six months either side of Screen on the Green.

2.3
VINYL QUOTATION
NUMBER ONE
9/76-12/76

SOUNDS/November 6, 1976   15p

ROD ◆ T. DREAM ◆ TROWER

sounds

DAMNED head for the charts.   PISTOLS hit the road

...Punk is on its way! See page 2

DAMNED: their single is selling fast

Colin bought another round ... The tables in which their faces were dimly reflected were dark brown, the darkest brown, the colour of Bournville chocolate. The walls were a lighter brown, the colour of Dairy Milk. The carpet was brown, with little hexagons of a slightly different brown, if you looked closely. The ceiling was meant to be off-white, but was in fact brown, browned by the nicotine smoke of a million unfiltered cigarettes. Most of the cars in the car park were brown, as were most of the clothes worn by the patrons. Nobody in the pub really noticed the predominance of brown, or if they did, thought it worth remarking upon. These were brown times.

— Jonathan Coe, *The Rotters' Club*, Viking, 2001, p. 15

One obvious contender missing from the Screen on the Green punk-fest were The Damned, who were still recovering from a punk festival of their own, held in the south of France by a promoter with only the vaguest notion of who might qualify for the term. The Mont de Marsan punk festival was the brainchild of Marc Zermati at Skydog Records in Paris. Via Bizarre Records in Paddington, he approached The Clash and The Damned. Even after implying that the New York bands would also be represented, The Clash passed. The Damned thought it would be a wheeze.

In the end the festival was — as Brian James suggests — 'basically a pub-rock kinda deal, apart from us'. Jonh Ingham, in his lengthy *Sounds* report of the jaunt, appropriately entitled 'The Lost Weekend', contrasted 'the psychedelic Methuselahs down front [who] retained the [hippy] era's remnants — long hair, Levis, ordinary t-shirts — [with] The Damned, [who] were defiantly 1976. Short hair, winklepicker shoes, and an ever-changing wardrobe, mostly black.'

Not surprisingly, the boys soon went into 'English louts abroad' mode. As Scabies says, the whole trip 'was a bit like the Crusades, with [the] four of us. We just went through, nicking as much as we could.' Along for the ride, in a supervisory role for which he was ill-equipped, was Andy Czekowski, about to be cured of the delusion that band management might be fun.

Andy Czekowski: It was the tail end of the pub-rock scene. You had the Pink Fairies, Dave Edmunds, Nick Lowe. We were the only true punk band [on the bill] ... We were at the back [of the coach] with Caroline Coon. She was very much into the punk scene. The band were well over the top. On nothing but speed from the minute they got on the coach to four, five days afterwards. Everyone else was just having a rest, because they were gigging in two days' time. The Damned couldn't sleep because they were all fucked up on speed [and] couldn't calm down – so they went out drinking – coming back at two a.m. in the morning. Wouldn't get let in, so they tried to climb up outside the building. [Finally] someone let them in, but then they didn't want to go to bed, 'cause two were in one room and two were in another room. And [so] they climbed out the windows, four floors up, to climb into the others' rooms to wind them up – I thought, 'I don't think I can take much more of this.'

Ingham's account of that night suggests Czekowski was the target of the precarious raid – presumably because he was acting the killjoy – and so, '[at] about three a.m., Rat decided to climb out his third-storey, top window, edge along to manager Andy's room and steal all his clothes. Outside, he grabbed a drainpipe, which came away in his hand. He threw it across the alley on to the roof of the next building, where it smashed slates as it crashed towards the ground. Rat cancelled the raid.'

Whatever doubts Czekowski had solidified the following night, when he 'was woken up at two in the morning by the [hotel] manager. He wants me out, them out, everyone out, because they'd started fighting with somebody else in the hotel – I thought, "This is it. This is enough." . . . The next day was the actual gig. They were totally fucked out of their heads and they just wanted to get on and make as much noise as possible. Meanwhile, the promoter was jacking up behind stage. He couldn't take the pressure.' According to Ingham, The Damned's amphetamine-driven set did not sate their desire to play, so there was an attempt to hijack the stage at the end of the day:

It was definitely Dave Vanian's day, fifth time on any stage, the first where he could really move, suddenly discovering the Iggy within him and storming the stage, performing his vampiric rituals with utter conviction . . . [Yet] The Damned had been aching for a second set all night, but after Rat's previous display of drum care, no one would lend their kit . . . They yelled at the audience and the promoters, threw beer, shook fists. Rat tried to deep-six a guitar into the audience. It was the perfect punk ending.

Among the attendant pub rockers who became punk rockers for a day was Nick Lowe, ex-Brinsley Schwarz, now the debut recording

artiste on a new label, Stiff Records. His opinion of The Damned –
'The worst group he'd seen since the Sex Pistols' – expressed to Ingham
on the day, hardly suggested someone envisaging working with them.
But Stiff Records co-owner Jake Rivera – the alter-ego of Feelgood
manager, Andrew Jakeman – was looking for new bands to sign to the
label, and sounded out The Damned at the festival. Rivera had exactly
one producer Stiff could call upon.

Lowe's philosophy of Pop, expressed in the first press story on Stiff,
dovetailed neatly with Rivera's: you take 'a three-minute song, and
every good bit and hook is pushed up on the faders, so that all you hear
are the best parts leaping out at you.' Feelgood frontman Lee Brilleaux
clarified another key aspect of Lowe's philosophy: 'A real one-take
merchant . . . Just bash it down and tart it up later. That really is his
motto . . . Jake used to say, "One Day Basher will do it."' With the
bare-boned budget Jake had to work with, he needed a low-rent producer. Rivera, after all, began Stiff with a simple idea: 'We can do
anything quickly. If someone has an idea, we want to do it in an
afternoon. We're a stepping-stone record company.'

The first Stiff single, 'So It Goes' b/w 'Heart Of The City', released
in August, was Lowe's tongue-in-cheek notion of punk – and a genuine
DIY 45. As he told Caroline Coon, 'All my friends have become punks
overnight and I'm a great bandwagon climber.' Available 'to progressive
music fans who have the complete works of ELP, Yes and Genesis etc.
Just send in all the sleeve artwork (not your precious records) together
with a cheque/PO for only £99.99 to Stiff Records,' the press ad
proclaimed. The single could also be bought through more mundane
retail outlets for a pound.

Though Rivera was pub-rock personified, he already had the punk
attitude down cold. As Paul Riley informed Will Birch, 'Jakeman didn't
mind turning round to people and going, "Fuck you!" That was a phrase
I could understand. I'd had it up to here with hippies by this time, and all
that, "OK man, that's cool, never mind," kind of bollocks. Jakeman
started to get things done.' When Jake approached The Damned on
the bus home from France, he sensed that Czekowski was not long for
this band, and that an association with one of these new-fangled punk
combos would give Stiff a credibility it currently lacked.

Jake's blunt 'charms' impressed The Damned. As Brian James says,
'We didn't want to piss about. With Jake, it was, "Sign this and we'll
get the record out in two weeks." He'd got a lot of attitude. We thought

. . . "What have we got to lose?" ' To seal the deal, the band went round to the apartment Lowe and Rivera shared.

Rat Scabies: They'd bought a five-gallon vat of cider to save money and there it was sitting on the table . . . [Lowe still] reckoned we were the worst group he'd seen since the Sex Pistols, [but] he thought it'd be a good laugh to produce us.

Sure enough, it took One Day Basher a single afternoon – 17 September 1976 – to record 'New Rose' and its B-side, 'Help'. The recording and release of 'New Rose' signalled a significant change in direction for Stiff, which as Wreckless Eric observes, 'was originally set up in part to release a lot of live recordings of pub-rock bands from the Hope 'n' Anchor'. After singles by remnants of that scene, like Tyla Gang, Roogalator, Plummet Airlines and Lew Lewis caused nary a ripple in record shops, a rethink was required. Thankfully for Rivera and his partner, Dave Robinson, 'the music scene was changing and so many new people came along . . . that the pub-rock stuff got buried and forgotten.' Such was the situation when young Eric Goulden, an ex-art student from Hull, turned up at the Stiff office in October★ with a cassette of original songs.

Wreckless Eric: I'd decided I preferred playing music to apologizing for doing crappy sculptures . . . I came down to London because I thought I was a bit out of touch with things in Hull . . . I thought that [Stiff]'d have a big office in an office block, you know. But when I got there, there was only this grotty little shopfront, full of all these people. So I walked in . . . and I just said, 'I'm one of those cunts that brings tapes into record companies.' [1977]

Goulden had one song that Rivera particularly liked, but money was tight, and when another would-be singer-songwriter with acres of attitude sent a demo-tape in, he came up with the idea of a single with two A-sides by different artists (a quite common practice in the fifties). The other artist, Declan MacManus, had already been recorded by Dave Robinson, at his studio above the Hope & Anchor pub. According to Robinson, 'When [I] first played the Declan MacManus tape to Jake, he said, "Next!" '

★ The 'Whole Wide World' session took place the third week in November, so one presumes Goulden turned up with his demo a few weeks before that.

Robinson realized that every act had to be Jake's discovery, and got MacManus to resubmit the tape as if it was unsolicited. Miraculously, Rivera now liked the demos, and put MacManus (aka Elvis Costello) in the studio to record a companion song to the one Lowe recorded of Wreckless in November 1976, 'Whole Wide World'. According to Costello, he scuppered the whole idea by demoing eight songs in a single afternoon, leaving the label little option but to issue the debut statements of Eric and Elvis separately (a version of events Wreckless dismisses in his own autobiography, *A Dysfunctional Success*). In all likelihood, Costello made his feelings known and the idea was dropped. Unfortunately, Wreckless then went temporarily AWOL and it would be some time before Stiff could cajole him into returning to the studio to record a.n. other side. As such, his instant classic appeared first on a Stiff sampler, *A Bunch Of Stiffs*.

If 'Stiff was aimed at people whose arses were hanging out in the industry and couldn't get a look-in' – as Ian Dury portrayed them in 1996 – Rivera's other charges, the Feelgoods, were in fine fettle by September 1976. Signed to United Artists by Andrew Lauder, they had been pushing to make a live album ever since *Down By The Jetty* paved the way. By this time, they were sure enough of themselves to ride roughshod over their A&R man's wishes.

Wilko Johnson: I wanted the album absolutely live, bum notes and all, [because] in those days half the live albums you got there was nothing left from the original recording, but the bass-drum track. Anyway, I wanted to do it without tarting it up, [but] the record company wanted to do it the other way. I wouldn't have it, and it turned into a bit of a confrontation. I got my way. Vic [Mayo] told me later that Andrew Lauder, the A&R man, said [to him], 'Right, we're gonna let Wilko have his way on this, and it's gonna fail, and [then] he's gonna do what he's told.'

On 24 September 1976 *Stupidity* was released. And Wilko was vindicated. By the end of October it was number one, an astonishing outcome for a band without a hit single, and with minimal hype, save the word-of-mouth variety. But, as Will Birch notes, 'By the time that *Stupidity* live album went to number one . . . Hammersmith Odeon was packed with three thousand eighteen-year-old boys, all of whom just had their hair cut short, all of whom had tried to adapt their school blazer into a narrow lapel, all had narrow skinny ties, [but] punk rock hadn't yet really kicked in. All right, the Pistols' "Anarchy" was coming out – and you had The Damned [45], you had the Ramones' album, but . . . it was those young kids at Hammersmith Odeon who were still digging the Feelgoods – they'd bought *Stupidity* [and] they were still loyal. But within three months they were The Clash's audience.'

Wilko Johnson, basking in the afterglow, wasn't sure that he entirely welcomed any direct association between the Feelgoods and these punksters. Though he recognized that 'aggressive excitement [also] underlines our music', he was surprisingly dismissive of 'these new-wave people – [because] it seems that as long as you can put across that aggression and excitement, it doesn't matter what you fuckin' play. Or how badly you play it . . . [And] people . . . are writing about them when they don't even know how to tune up.' The movement's godfather had become a grouch.

Perhaps he'd heard about a recent Clash gig from his fellow Southend pub-rockers, Kursaal Flyers. A week after Screen on the Green, The Clash found themselves playing barely a hundred yards from Rehearsal Rehearsal, at the Roundhouse, supporting a band already flying too close to the ground. Drummer Will Birch was perhaps the only Flyer to sense the future when it came a-knockin'.

Will Birch: We were soundchecking in the Roundhouse – three or four in the afternoon – and they arrived. They came through one of the doors and I saw them and I looked at the guys around me and said, 'Boys, this is over. What we're doing, forget it. Just look at this.' Didn't matter what they sounded like. They just looked fantastic, as Elvis looked fantastic, as the Feelgoods look fantastic. And if you look shit it's very difficult to make it in rock & roll. The Clash just looked great. I thought, 'If those five guys can talk it like they walk it . . .' [But] they didn't go down very well. Nobody understood what they were about. It was obviously [something] different . . . it really came out of Mick Jones's guitar style. I could see it was in a raw state, but I could see it.

Strummer was in a more confrontational mood than at Screen on the Green, perhaps because this audience he now berated, for 'having a good time down the Red Cow', had been his audience. And here he was declaiming, 'Any of you people in the audience who aren't past it yet . . . why don't you get up and *do it*?' which might perhaps explain why 'they didn't go down very well'.

Two gigs clinging to the Pistols' tailgate the previous week had ironed out a number of problems, but the new songs, like the proud-to-be-thick polemic, 'I Can't Understand The Flies'★, were starting to grate on at least one founding member. If one can believe the disillusioned Keith Levene it was at this point that, 'They suddenly came up with this idea for "White Riot". I said, "I'm not fucking singing 'White Riot' – you're joking!" That "No Elvis, Beatles or The Rolling Stones" in "1977" was bad enough for me.'

'White Riot', a knee-jerk reaction to events at the August Bank Holiday Notting Hill Carnival, seems to have been one song written at Rhodes' direct prompting. As he told Vivien Goldman the following year, 'To me, reggae gives the emotional rhythm and punks give the dynamic vocabulary. But the difference is, at last year's Carnival in Notting Hill, I watched the black kids run along the road picking up bricks . . . and while they were running they kept on coming across new sound systems giving out spiritual Jah Rastafari music. So they were getting the spirit, all they needed was . . . the bricks. We've got the means to carry it out, but we lack the spirit.' Joe Strummer gave Rhodes what he wanted – a lyrical equivalent.

The band's problems went deeper than a single song. When Levene re-emerged in a truly experimental combo, PiL, he claimed, 'We had a good thing [in The Clash], but Mick was always Rock & Roll Mick. I didn't realize then just how much I resented rock & roll.' According to Terry Chimes, Mick Jones responded to Levene's bombshell with the retort, 'I'd better learn how to play guitar then.' Strummer's response was to drop some not-so-subtle hints that Levene had a substance problem (not true at the time), and that Levene 'left the group early on saying he had some urgent business to take care of in London'. He who was not for them, was against them.

Jones had two weeks in which to take some guitar lessons, before The Clash re-emerged, still playing second string to the Pistols, at the two-day Punk Festival Ron Watts and Malcolm McLaren were organizing at the 100 Club on September 20–21. The first night would introduce both strands of the nascent new wave, those who wanted to redeem rock & roll, represented by the Pistols and The Clash, and two bands who thought it high time it lay down and died, Siouxsie & the Banshees and Subway Sect.

★ 'The Flies' is a reference to *Lord of the Flies*, William Golding's celebrated novel, a perennial on O-Level syllabuses by the mid-seventies.

McLaren knew the importance of such a gathering of the clan and brought in some superior speakers, hoping to achieve blast off (a curious move if he really wanted people to think the Pistols couldn't play!). Soundman Dave Goodman notes that 'these W-bins' came with a propitious provenance, having once belonged to The Who.

Dave Goodman: They were so big and heavy we just about managed to get them in there. We spent an hour clearing up, and Malcolm and Bernie had to stay behind and help us get them up the stairs.

The Clash and the Pistols both acquitted themselves well on that first night – The Clash debuting their one-guitar sound, and 'White Riot', but thankfully not causing one; while the Pistols ran out of songs to play, so 'Anarchy In The UK' both opened and closed the set, making for one arc of gut-wrenching feedback. But it was the two bands who opened proceedings who took Bangs' punk ideal – 'Can't play, will play' – and ran with it.

Subway Sect may have been the band McLaren had in mind when speaking of 'kids who adopted these attitudes and . . . created a series of discontented shows'. Unfortunately, in order to communicate on *any* level, the Sect required at least a rudimentary 'rock' sound. And when McLaren got to hear them – the week before the festival – he realized they lacked even that. Goddard has no illusions about the Sect's early sound, remarking how many punk 'bands were quite frankly a lot better than they were making out, but we really *were* awful . . . In our eyes, the Sex Pistols were as good as Yes . . . We didn't have a clue.' McLaren told them straight, 'You lot are not good enough to do this thing.' And yet he heard enough there to give them rehearsal space, and a week, to prove him wrong. The Sect decided they would pare their set down to just four songs and spend the whole week 'perfecting' them.

Rob Symmons: He arranged for us to rehearse in this place called Manos in the King's Road, above the old furniture warehouse. I distinctly remember that he went to this guy running the little office and he said, 'You're going to give this [band] rehearsal [time], and they are not going to pay and you're going to come in at eight o'clock and open for them because this group is going to be the biggest group there ever is.' . . . And he talked this bloke into opening the studio . . . And [then] Malcolm said, 'I'll come down and see [if] you [improved].'

The four songs in question were 'No Love Now', 'Contradiction', 'Nobody's Scared', and 'Don't Split It' — of which Goddard says, 'At that point [it] was just a riff that I said whatever I wanted over.' In fact, as he informed a German film crew the following summer, none of 'the words are the words you normally get in rock records — they're like an essay, and from that [I] condense the words for a song, so [that] it doesn't end up being a normal rock song.' McLaren finally gave them the go-ahead. But when they arrived at the 100 Club, Goddard was met by a certain incomprehension from one of his heroes.

Vic Goddard: I was so nervous at the soundcheck. The [other bands] watched us, 'cause they wanted to know what we were like. We only got two bars into the first song and Steve Jones come up on stage and said, 'You can't do that. If that guitar chord goes to there, the bass cannot go to there.' And he started taking our song apart. I said, 'Hang on a minute, our songs are a bit weird. They're not meant to sound like that.' I just ignored what he was saying.

It was one thing to disavow the strictures of rock, it was another to try and completely reinvent a form one had barely begun to master. Goddard's antithetical approach also extended to his stage wear. On a night when everyone else seemed determined to turn up 'in uniform', like a parade of punk peacocks, Goddard took to 'wearing a suit . . . but the top was really a woman's raincoat I bought in Oxfam. We didn't actually have stage clothes.'

Despite staying resolutely sloppy throughout their fifteen minutes in the spotlight, the Sect made at least one convert that night. After the set, Bernie Rhodes came up and made them an offer, 'Every time we play you can be the support band, until you get better.' Ironically, this generous gesture came from the side of punk with which Goddard was already disenchanted. A couple of years later, he would tell Jon Savage, 'Even by the time of that festival all the energy was gone. The Pistols and Clash had already reached their peaks.' His experience that night only served to reinforce the suspicion that would set the Sect on a new course — or put another way, 'off the course of twenty years / Out of rock & roll'. He articulated this direction in *Melody Maker* eighteen months later, when the original Sect had all but run its course.

Vic Goddard: What we wanted to do was become part of what we thought was going to change the face of rock music. Then we found out that wasn't the aim of other groups. When we first saw the Sex Pistols, we thought that was their aim, but then we found all the other groups, such as The Clash, just wanted to put life back into rock . . . and the Sex Pistols seemed to latch on to that and start becoming a real good *rock* band. We wanted to finish rock & roll. All the other groups just wanted to get rock & roll back as it was in the sixties . . . We wanted to change the reasons for playing rock music . . . We wanted it to be a medium for ideas, rather than a release from boredom. [1978]

On the night of the festival, though, the Sect felt they had triumphed over their limitations, at least compared with the act that followed them, who not only finished off rock & roll, but gave performance-art a bad name into the bargain. Suzie & the Banshees, as they were billed (though they bore precious little relation to the subsequent band), had been the brainchild of Billy Idol. It was Idol who had been standing with Severin and Siouxsie at the Screen on the Green, listening to McLaren lament a shortage of bands for the festival he was planning.

Steve Severin: Billy immediately said, 'Oh, we've got a band,' [even though] we'd only talked about it two or three times. Billy could play, he was gonna teach me bass and Siouxsie was gonna sing – they'd [already] done a version of 'What Goes On' together. So Billy Idol was the person who invented Siouxsie and the Banshees. [But] then a week later he pulled out, on Tony James's advice.

What had begun as a serious attempt to put together a post-Pistols band, by the week before the festival had devolved down to an experiment at best, a joke at worst. In fact, so makeshift were these Banshees that they didn't meet their replacement guitarist till forty-eight hours before the gig. Marco Pirroni had gone 'to see Queen in Hyde Park, met Phillip Salon and Siouxsie and all that lot; and they were all going back to Billy Idol's house in Bromley . . . Billy was supposed to be playing guitar for the Banshees, but he wanted to be like a serious musician . . . [so] Sunday night I met them all, Monday we rehearsed, Tuesday we played.'

The Monday rehearsal took place at Rehearsal Rehearsals and, as Severin recalls, 'We had an audience of Bernie and Paul Simonon – with a look of horror on their faces.' It begs the question, how bad must it have been to induce the barely competent Simonon to pull faces? Nonetheless, Steve, Siouxsie, Marco and drummer Sid Vicious convened at The Ship on Wardour Street the following night, wearing their rather risqué stage gear. Pirroni describes how they 'were draped in swastikas. I was wearing an Anarchy t-shirt with a swastika and Luftwaffe insignia on it. Siouxsie had the armband, Steven had a white shirt splattered in paint, with a Union Jack pinned on a breast pocket, and Sid had a yellow Belsen Babies t-shirt.' Not surprisingly, they got slung out of the pub.

Unperturbed, they turned up at the 100 Club attired thus, only for 'Rabbi' Rhodes to get all worked up, and refuse to let them borrow The Clash's gear, spluttering, 'People can do what they want, but we don't think the swastika means anything relevant to us.' Vicious called him 'an old Jew' from the stage. Siouxsie merely asked the Sect if they could use their equipment. They duly obliged, curious to hear how atonal the Banshees could be. TV Smith already knew of Siouxsie's plan to 'just . . . do this Lord's Prayer thing. But then it went on and on. And on,' until, 'It seemed like some horrible sixth-form wind-up arty band. I know they were doing it with the intention of sounding terrible, but they *really* were terrible.' Caroline Coon, there on *MM*'s behalf, made a game effort to describe it:

The [Lord's] prayer begins. It's a wild improvisation, a public jam, a bizarre stage fantasy acted out for real. The sound is what you'd expect from, er, novices. But Sid, with miraculous command, starts his minimal thud and doesn't fluctuate the beat from start to finish of the, er, set. Against this rough corrugation of sound, Siouxsie, with the grace of a redeemed ghoul, rifles the senses with an unnerving, screeching recitative. 'Twist and Shout' and 'Knockin' On Heaven's Door' creep into the act. Sid flickers a smile, Marco, his guitar feeding back, rolls up his sleeves, and Two-Tone Steve two-tones . . . Twenty minutes later, on a nod from Marco, Sid just stops. The enthusiastic cheering is a just recognition of their success . . . 'God, it was awful,' says Howard Thompson, an A&R man from Island. But Siouxsie is not interested in contracts.

If – as Siouxsie claimed – 'the idea was to annoy . . . people so much they'd chuck us off,' they'd have had more success in The Ship. In fact, as she subsequently informed Nick Kent, there was more to it than that: 'All the other bands were talking about not being able to really play, and being unrehearsed and into chaos, man, and we . . . just wanted to take the whole thing to its logical extreme.' They had performed the last rites on that idea – or so it seemed. And the experience had also been exhilarating enough for her to consider doing it for real next time around.

The following night had no such avant-garde distractions. The Damned, Buzzcocks, a hopeless French punk *parodie*, Stinky Toys, and The Vibrators – trading songs with Chris Spedding – were making up the numbers. If The Damned lacked the drawing power to top the bill, they were there because they had another ex-manager, after Czekowski bailed out.

Rat Scabies: We went straight in and played the 100 Club, and talked to Ron Watts, who said, 'I'll get you loads of gigs.' [But] there was an incident where Captain managed to drive the entire audience out of the Nag's Head [in High Wycombe]. We went on stage and there were a lot of hippies [there], and the Captain refused to play if there was anyone with facial hair in the audience. His tirade became so abusive that he drove the entire audience out.

The Nag's Head was Watts' other venue, so Sensible was hardly living up to his name; though the band remained unfazed by the loss of a second manager in a month. Jake Rivera was ready to take up the reins, and on the night of the festival The Damned were animatedly re-reading their one-page record contract.

Buzzcocks were there at McLaren's suggestion, presumably hoping it suggested a national movement. Between their two London showcases, they had played a hotel in Holdsworth and a pub in Stalybridge, but the former was ill-attended, and at the latter, Devoto remembers the regulars 'just lined the doors and looked surly'. Greater Manchester was proving a tough nut to crack. Nor did the Punk Festival lead to a legion of London converts, largely because Devoto and co. closed the show, unaware that 'everyone would leave at eleven o'clock to catch the Tube. [So] it had emptied somewhat by the time we played.'

The Vibrators had already turned down the graveyard slot. Though they were the most professional band spanning the chasm between the Pistols and The Stranglers, especially when Spedding was blazing away on guitar, those into style over content dismissed them. And vice-versa. Knox, with his art-school background, had 'weird friends of ours turning up wearing funny clothes [all the time]. But . . . at the 100 Club, all these guys turned up in rubber with nazi armbands – these heavy, weird gay guys –'cause we'd been on the radio doing this song "Nazi Baby" – and I was like, "What the hell is this?"' Only later did Knox realize that they weren't attired like this because of a Vibrators song!

Sadly, the second night served to mute all the positive clamour from the first gig, ending as it did in a girl blinded, Sid Vicious in custody, and a ban on all punk bands by one of its original sponsors, Mr Watts. Once again, resident headbanger Sid Vicious attempted to live up to what had originally been an ironic nickname. All of Lydon's 'Three Johns' were very different from most Sex habitués, being more likely to be found on football terraces than down the King's Road on a Saturday afternoon. As Helen Wellington-Lloyd observed to Savage, Rotten's 'friends seemed like those National Front types, louts: nudging each other about poofters and yids and blacks . . . [And] John was a bit like that: very suspicious of middle-class people.' If Lydon usually managed to keep Vicious on his leash, tonight he was somewhere else.

Having been adopted as a kind of malevolent mascot by the Bromley contingent, Sid's childlike need for approval led him to act out the violent wishes of altogether more recalcitrant companions. That these Bromleyites shared his sociopathic inclinations was affirmed by Simon Barker, leader of the pack, in an October '76 *Sounds* article, where he portrayed the hippy movement as 'weak and stupid . . . try[ing to] change things with flowers; if you get beaten up you've got to retaliate . . . If you're going to change the world, you've got to use violence.' Steve Severin also proved surprisingly supportive of the decision to chuck a pint glass in a crowded club.

Steve Severin: Sid did throw the glass. Siouxsie and I were standing right next to him. He was aiming at The Damned, so he had my full support . . . [They had] nothing to do with anything.

Vicious proved to be not just a bad critic and a thug, but a lousy shot. The glass shattered against a pillar, its shards taking some innocent girl's eye out. He was immediately identified as the culprit, and when the cops took him away, they dispensed some summary justice in the back of the van. It failed to dissuade the young John Beverley from his appointment with destiny. As Palm Olive astutely observes, 'The whole thing with the hate and anger was it took [Sid] further than he wanted to go. [But] there was a dark force there that was pushing him on. We were all playing with it . . . but you have to be careful you're not taken in by it.'

— — —

Dark but more diffident forces were at work four weeks later, when Steve Severin and his girlfriend caused another stir simply by turning up to see an 'art' show in punk attire. The Institute of Contemporary Art might seem like somewhere the Pistols would have played, but it took until October 1976 for the ICA to let punk in, and just a week for them to change their mind. With the 100 Club's blanket ban, where to play in London had suddenly become a big issue. If The Damned were still prepared to play the Nashville, The Clash – and consequently Subway Sect – were not. In the Pistols' case, previous bans applied by the Marquee, the Nashville, the Roundhouse, Dingwall's and the Lyceum had not left a lot of options.

For new punk bands such difficulties halved their already limited opportunities. That October, Gene October was hunting for somewhere his band, Chelsea, could make a splash. John Crevene, owner of Acme Attractions, seemed to feel that he couldn't carry on selling clothes on the King's Road without his very own punk band; and his plan was to build the band around this gay porn pin-up.

Gene October: I was always under the impression that it cost a lot of money to do a band – you were led to believe that . . . You couldn't even get a gig! The Nashville was tied up, the Marquee was tied up . . . Crevene didn't know how to go about it [either, and so] we put an ad in *Melody Maker*: 'Musicians wanted. Into Television and the Ramones.' . . . This guy called William Broad rang up – in glasses and very straight-looking. [But] he was into Lou Reed and the Velvets, and the Ramones. Everybody had to be into the Ramones. He said, 'I got this mate of mine – he's a bass player – can I bring him along?' And it was Tony James. I didn't like him right away – he was a smart-ass.

James had finished his degree, and was itching to compete with his old chums from London SS, Brian James and Mick Jones. He had met Broad when replying to an ad Billy had placed when there was still a possibility he might form a band with Siouxsie and Steve. According to James, the Broad he met still 'had long hair. He was at university in Brighton. He put an ad: "Wanted a guitarist into The Small Faces, The Who, Beatles, early Stones" . . . I borrowed a guitar, and he was there with Siouxsie Sioux and another guy who played a bit of guitar.'

Chelsea in its original incarnation had two guitarists, both ex-Banshees, Billy Idol and Marco Pirroni. Pirroni had been spotted at Acme by Jeannette Lee and was persuaded to audition, recollecting that

Chelsea 'was supposed to be like the Acme Pistols. It was John Towe, Tony James, me [and] Billy playing guitar and Gene October, doing these silly cover versions.' Pirroni, though, was deemed surplus to requirements as soon as James and Idol began to introduce their own songs to the band. According to Severin, even this early 'it was obvious that Billy was the star . . . Gene just looked an older guy tagged on somewhere'.

For their 18 October debut at the ICA, Chelsea were billed as LSD. They constituted part of an 'art exhibition' called Prostitution, being put on by the ever-eccentric Genesis P. Orridge and his girlfriend Cosey Fanni Tutti, in which mass media 'products' – mostly pages from porn magazines – were exhibited as if they were 'high-art' artifacts, signed and framed. When the *NME*'s reviewer enquired of the 'many kids decked out in punk outfits' why they'd come to the ICA, it yielded a uniform answer, 'We've come to see Chelsea. They're on after the stripper [i.e. Cosey].'

The ostensible headliners were actually Throbbing Gristle, a new noise-experiment from Orridge and Tutti. Severin immediately recognized that their roots lay elsewhere: 'What Throbbing Gristle were doing was an extension of prog-rock, but [then] they got massively influenced by punk. At that show Genesis looked like Peter Gabriel, and he just stood there and made this noise. But somehow you just felt . . . they were now going to adapt to something else. And they did.'

Genesis would subsequently claim it was punk that adapted to TG, but Severin called it right. Indeed, Genesis and Cosey, in a previous incarnation – COUM – had performed at prog-rock shows during its early seventies heyday, but as Genesis later asserted, 'We found that doing rock music for an hour, knowing what we were going to do and just standing there with instruments, was a bit boring . . . So we started throwing in all sorts of other effects, roles and costumes. The music became less and less central, and the actions and images became more and more important.' COUM transferred its energies to the galleries, and its funding to the public purse.

By 1976, Genesis felt that move had been a mistake, and that he should return to the rock/performance arena in a new, challenging guise. In court on an obscenity charge (not for the last time) in April 1976, he claimed, 'I want to be part of popular culture, involved with everyday life and responses; not an intellectual artist, in an ivory tower, thinking I am special, revered and monumental.' The first TG gig – in

July of that year – was advertised with the assertion, 'The music of 1984 has arrived.' The ICA show was meant to signify the end of COUM, and a return to popular media. He would not be alone in thinking he could graft his conceits to the raw energy of punk.

Genesis P. Orridge: At the ICA, the opening night was meant to be the statement: we are now Throbbing Gristle and not Art . . . Now we're going to take the perception of what we did as active performers – and all our ideas – but we want to use sound . . . The punks at ICA thought the songs were really frightening. John Towe said he thought I was going to hang myself at the end. [1978]

Though TG clearly believed they were doing something radical, *NME*'s Tony Parsons, in his review, depicted 'their, uh, music [as] lots of weird psychedelic taped sounds rolling around random keyboards played plink-plonk style, lead guitar that Patti Smith would have been ashamed of, and moronic bass'. And if their intention was – as Cosey asserts – 'breaking down the rock & roll thing', the Subway Sect had already claimed that piece of turf. Perhaps Genesis and Cosey should have caught the 'Lord's Prayer' at the 100 Club by ICA audience members, Steve Severin and Siouxsie Sioux. In fact, it would be Steve and Siouxsie whose picture accompanied a tabloid 'exposé' of the ICA show, which dubbed those there 'wreckers of civilization'. Little did they know.

P. Orridge would later depict TG as 'literally an experiment . . . Let's set up a band. Let's give it a really inappropriate name. Let's not have a drummer, because rock bands have drummers. Let's not learn how to play music. Let's put in a lot of *content* – in terms of the words and the ideas. So . . . we threw away all the usual parameters for a band and said, "Let's have content, authenticity and energy. Let's refuse to look like or play like anything acceptable as a band."' I.e. Suicide crossed with Subway Sect. Cosey's later take on TG has been less self-aggrandizing: 'TG started off as a joke . . . We knew we were giving them a load of rubbish sound-wise, just to get them out of their expectation of music.'

TG would have to rethink their approach if they were to meet this new movement at the crossroads. In the furore surrounding Prostitution – with MPs calling for the ICA's entire funding to be reviewed – TG would be forestalled from further shows until the new year. Chelsea also had very little life left in them, at least as this conflicted combo. Ten days later, they were no more. The entry in Nils Stevenson's diary for 28 October reads, 'Billy Idol, who was to be guitarist in the Banshees, has now left Chelsea and formed Generation X.' Tony James, who went along with Idol, duly informed *Sounds*, 'It quickly became clear that the idea behind the group was nonsense. There was nothing there – just a dopey name.' The pair failed to let October down gently.

Tony James: Billy and I were never totally keen on Gene October. [And] Billy and I were writing the songs – we'd already written 'Ready Steady Go', 'Too Personal', 'This Heat' . . . Chelsea [were] playing at the Nashville. Billy and I had written a song, possibly 'From The Heart', which we hadn't told Gene about, and when we came on for the encore . . . we did that, and Billy sang. And a week [later], we said, 'We're leaving.'

If Prostitution and the issue of public funding caused its own ripple of ructions, the ICA had already agreed to permit another punk show to enter its hallowed halls. Five nights after TG and Chelsea, The Clash and Subway Sect were offering A Night of Pure Energy, and it seems the Sect decided that TG were still a tad too musical for their liking. *ZigZag*'s Kris Needs, who had spent the day with Patti Smith and Lenny Kaye, urged them to come along to check out The Clash. He recalls that the Sect 'came on and did a racket for twenty minutes. Afterwards I went back to the squat in Davis Road with Sid [Vicious] and Mick [Jones] and that's when Sid was going, "They're my favourite band. Because they're so nihilistic." Their first song was called "We Oppose All Rock & Roll". It was total anti-rock & roll stance.'

The Sect now had seven songs, including 'Rock & Roll, Even' (to give it its correct title), which Goddard said 'was about . . . rock & roll as a sort of stance that doesn't need anything to support it . . . It . . . has to do with a way of writing songs that's based on a riff . . . The only things that seem to be getting away from it are things like Television and the Voidoids.' The lyrics took Hell's 'Fuck Rock & Roll' – not that Goddard knew the song – and gave it an agenda: 'Afraid to take a stroll off the course of 20 years / Out of rock & roll / We've just been waiting for it to fall / We oppose all rock & roll.'

If they were keen to undo the precepts of rock performance, the Sect's concept was already streets ahead of TG (as were their musical ideas). As Goddard told *Sniffin' Glue* shortly after the ICA, 'When we play I always take the attitude that we're just practising in front of a load of people. So it seems to me, we do exactly the same when we're practising as when we play live. There's only one difference – when we practise and we do something wrong we stop, but when we play live and we do something wrong, we just carry on.' At the ICA they had little choice.

Vic Goddard: Everyone wrote out different set-lists in different orders. When we went 1–2–3–4, all the members were going at totally different songs and I totally lost it, not knowing which one to sing. In the end, I was singing the lyrics in any old key, 'cause the music was so impossible to sing along to . . . [In fact] the gig was such a big disaster that the drummer left.

Such was the reputation garnered from their previous show no one was sure where artifice ended and incompetence began. As *MM*'s Chris Brazier wrote of the ICA, 'They were so bad, so catatonically unattractive, and yet at the same time so apparently uncaring and in command, that I figured it must all be deliberate.' The Sect made none of the standard rock gestures, so applying its parameters seemed somehow beside the point.

Though the same could not be said of The Clash, they were also unimpressive that night, at least according to John Perry, who had been busy all summer getting a band together with ex-England's Glory frontman Peter Perrett. Having bought a PA with some of Perrett's ill-gotten gains, they 'were hiring it out to The Clash, and it was clear from that point on that there was a different audience and it was growing . . . My problem was that The Clash at those early gigs were so bad – I went along to a few of them with the PA – it wasn't possible to be enthusiastic about them.' However, another guitarist (of sorts) *was* impressed, jumping onstage to share her enthusiasm. Patti Smith, fresh from a sell-out show at Hammersmith Odeon, had found her favourite English space monkeys.

Punk fans Shane MacGowan and Shanne Bradley also found something energizing in the Clash music. MacGowan recalls 'biting each other's arms till they bled – it was a kinda tribal, primeval, love-hate, violence-affection ceremony. It was a hypnotic trance kinda thing . . . Then she broke a bottle and slashed my earhole, causing loads of blood to splatter all over the place; and then cut her own wrists. At this stage the bouncers intervened.' Again, the headlines attendant upon an ICA show were stolen by a couple in the audience; while The Clash remained barely remarked upon. The ICA failed to find any art inherent in either performance, and decided they had dallied long enough with the punk ethos.

The Clash's need for gigs was such that they now turned to an art establishment the Pistols *had* played early on, the Royal College of Art, which provided them with a venue for A Night of Treason on 5 November. Guy Fawkes might have approved of the gesture on the 370th anniversary of his attempt to blow up Parliament, but the fireworks that night were again off stage, as London punk shows became increasingly hairy affairs. It was Strummer who found himself in the firing line this time, someone throwing a bottle that, in Polydor A&R man Chris Parry's words, 'almost took his head off. He was really angry, and . . . he came running down right by where [director of A&R] Jim Crook was, and obviously thought Jim had thrown it . . . Jim said, "If you think I'm signing *that* fucking band, you've got another think coming!" And he walked out.' Strummer, not for the last time, had singled out the wrong target for his pent-up anger.

Parry must have been in despair. Despite being the front-runner in efforts to sign punk's finest to Polydor he had lost out on the Pistols, who had signed to EMI on 8 October, after making a set of demos for Parry that led him to believe the Pistols and Polydor was a done deal. Now The Clash seemed out of bounds, too; while The Damned seemed happy with their independent status at Stiff. He would not find any alternative until the new year, by which time the demands made by many of these musical primitives were out of all proportion to their potential.

The Pistols had already raised the bar, simply by holding out for a real deal, with a 'major'. As the only punk band ready to enter a studio by summer's end, they had been courted by – among others – Atlantic Records. However, Atlantic A&R, Dave Dee, was stunned when McLaren dismissed their offer to sign 'them for a single or an EP and see what happens', bitterly denouncing McLaren for not being 'sensible', instead of 'want[ing] the world'. Dee didn't understand what was happening, and McLaren wasn't about to enlighten him. Instead he pursued EMI with a tenacity to behold, wanting to strike at the very heart of the British musical establishment.

Nick Mobbs at EMI finally persuaded his superiors to take a punt, fully convinced that McLaren was right in portraying the Pistols as a necessary 'backlash against the "nice little band" syndrome and the general stagnation of the music industry. They've got to happen for all our sakes.' Now they needed to make Maximum Impact with 'vinyl quotation number one'. Again McLaren brazenly insisted that the first chance to record the band be given to live soundman Dave Goodman, whose demos had converted many sceptics who'd believed the 'can't play' stories in the press.

On 17 October, less than ten days after McLaren and co. had signed along EMI's dotted line, Goodman and his charges arrived at Wessex Studios to record 'Anarchy In The UK'. Even as EMI artists, neither Goodman nor the band felt disposed to toe the corporate line. As Goodman said, 'I'd never really met anyone from EMI. They'd send people down and we wouldn't let 'em in. The band threw water over one guy. [EMI] were going, "What's going on?" . . . I just thought, "Record everything, this might be the album here."'

The sessions, though, soon stretched into the following week and the members of the band began to get nervous. Lydon, ever the muso, states in his autobiography, 'We could have just fallen by the wayside in the same way The Pretty Things did way back in the sixties with The Rolling Stones, [even though] everybody remembers that The Pretty Things were better [live].'

EMI had its own set of ambitious young engineers anxious to get their hands on the Pistols, and they weren't about to celebrate the work of an outsider like Goodman. Mike Thorne, who would later portray Goodman as 'completely adrift in the studio – balances were hopeless and the music certainly wasn't coming at you as strongly as it should', sought to play on the band's own uncertainties. He convinced Matlock to allow him to do a remix of the 'Anarchy' that Goodman had finally captured.

What Goodman had extracted from these punk proselytizers fully lived up to his espoused intent, to make 'Anarchy In The UK' 'the heaviest piece of music I'd ever heard'. Having been the band's soundman throughout the song's exacting evolution, he knew the elements integral not just to this song, but to their whole aesthetic. The wall of sound he produced was as dense as the Wessex walls, while Rotten's vocals had all the hectoring (yet playful) quality found live. Goodman had also given them a heartstop-ending just as Jones was threatening to blow another set of woofers and tweeters. But Thorne felt he could do better, and Matlock let him loose.

Dave Goodman: Mike Thorne went in with Glen and did a remix and they cut an acetate of that. And that's what they played to the A&R department at EMI, who started throwing doubt on whether it cut the mustard.

Nick Mobbs suggests an alternative scenario. He told Craig Bromberg, 'We were all set to release that, and we would have been happy to do so. It was Malcolm who chickened out and said that he didn't think it was produced enough. He thought it was too raw. Suddenly he seemed to be backtracking to things he had previously denied wanting. Till then, his whole attitude had been unorthodox, to take risks whenever he could.' Whoever nixed this nugget, the decision to re-record the song meant that the single would come out dangerously close to Christmas, when competition for the charts was at its fiercest.

Also recorded in mid-October – as punk's pioneers began to consider their options – were Buzzcocks' first studio demos. Recorded one afternoon on four-track at Revolution Studios, at a cost of 'about £45', the eleven songs served no definite purpose save to document proceedings to date. As Richard Boon says, 'We ran off some cassettes – some [with] ten songs, some six songs with lyrics – and sent them out. It was just a report from "up north" . . . The engineer [at Revolution] . . . didn't get it all. "Is that the take, then?"' Evidently, Goodman was not the only one having to fight received wisdom just to get the punk aesthetic on tape.

Even though these demos – memorably bootlegged as *Time's Up* – were nothing more than a trial run, Boon recalls, 'There was this very strange sense that time was running out. I remember talking to Malcolm at the Screen on the Green and he was desperate to get a record out, [thinking] it was all gonna fade away.' Buzzcocks, though, didn't think a single afternoon at Revolution was the way to announce themselves.

Howard Devoto: When Pete plays the solo in 'Boredom', there's suddenly nobody playing rhythm guitar behind it, and you listen to it [and think], 'That doesn't quite work, does it?' You can get away with it in a gig, but in a recording, you need to double-track it. There were [just] bits that were a bit shambolic, in a way that wasn't quite pleasing.

If the initial efforts of the Pistols and Buzzcocks were destined to fall short of artifact status, the race was assuredly on, especially after Jonh Ingham wrote a rave(ing) review of some Oz band getting the jump on every Pommy punk in the 16 October *Sounds*. The following week, any sense 'that time was running out' multiplied exponentially with another rave from Ingham, for a 'product of four hours intensive care [that] is so hot it's a wonder the vinyl doesn't melt . . . and enough energy to substitute for Battersea power station'. 'New Rose' – The Damned's debut 45 – sent a shudder through every would-be prog-rocker who'd worked away at their craft in the pre-punk years. As Brian James informed *Sounds* the following month, 'Maybe it's not actually new musically but, like with the Pistols, the attitude comes over in the music, and *that* makes it new music.'

The Pistols, meanwhile, returned to the studio, this time with EMI's preferred producer, Chris Thomas. With credits that included The Beatles' *White Album* and Pink Floyd's *Dark Side Of The Moon*, he seemed an odd choice, but Thomas had also worked on the first two Roxy Music albums and Kilburn & The High Roads' final single – factors that ultimately worked in his favour.

Thomas felt that the end-result he got, albeit by following Goodman's notes, was 'really menacing. I know it doesn't go at 150 miles an hour like The Damned, which was another criticism Richard Williams [made], [but] to me it was much closer to The Who than the Ramones.' As it happens, Williams had preferred 'New Rose', blithely unaware that it was him Rotten was railing against on the Pistols' B-side, 'I Wanna Be Me'. *NME* also felt it was 'closer to The Who', though not in a positive way, calling the record 'laughably naive . . . The overall feeling is of a third-rate Who imitation.' Perhaps the Pistols really were destined to be The Pretty Things of punk.

Actually, *NME*'s assessment was more indicative of the way that the paper had lost the plot in the past six months. Kent, after the attack by Vicious, not surprisingly had turned his back on the punk bands. He now insists, 'I could see through so much of what punk was doing. I knew all the lead players, and I knew . . . they were becoming very, very amoral in the way that they behaved.' The paper needed new blood, and editor Nick Logan, to his credit, addressed the problem. In a single stroke he recruited two 'young gunslingers', Tony Parsons and Julie Burchill, to upset the applecart and make hay. If Burchill had no real musical background or critical judgement, she had a tart turn of phrase and a spiky prose-style, while Parsons was working class and wired. His first major feature, on the 100 Club Festival, began by rejecting Coon's previous categorization:

Punk-rock is the term used to describe the descendants of those garage bands in the States, combos like the now-defunct New York Dolls, the Ramones, Tom Verlaine's Television and the Heartbreakers . . . [But] punk-rock just won't do [for the English bands] – the name is too old, too American, too inaccurate . . . Punk-rock is really just a lazy journalist media spiel for a genuine new wave.

Coon responded with a long 'perspective piece' at the end of November, where she defined New Wave as 'an inclusive term used to describe a variety of bands like Eddie & the Hot Rods, The Stranglers, Chris Spedding and The Vibrators, the Suburban Studs, Slaughter & the Dogs who are not definitively hardcore punk but, because they play with speed and energy or because they try hard, are part of the scene.' In two articles, three months apart, Coon had utilized 'punk-rock', 'new wave' and 'hardcore', the three terms that became the battlefield on which punk's authenticity would be fought over the next five years. Though McLaren had hoped, as late as September 1976, that the term 'new wave' would supplant 'punk', or even 'dole-queue rock', punk it was.

Absent from Coon's above list of new wavers was a band that had played a key part in making her rethink her terms, The Jam. Though they had been playing for a year or more, The Jam first came to the music press's attention one Sunday afternoon in late October when – as manager John Weller recalls – 'We played in Soho Market. I got to know this stallholder and asked him if we could use his electricity. We plugged in a three-pin and played off the back of a lorry. Chas de Whalley and Jonh Ingham were there and Caroline Coon took some snaps. From there we went on to the Greyhound, the Hope and the 100 Club.' Ingham remembers Coon deciding that *this* 'was new wave, so suddenly Malcolm didn't like new wave any more'.

Ironically, the fact that The Jam were *not* deemed punk enabled them to now develop a reputation at venues closed to the likes of the Pistols and The Clash. Jam leader Paul Weller certainly did not consider his band to be 'punk', though seeing the Pistols at the Lyceum in July was a revelation reinforced by the Punk Festival in September, and he fully admits that, 'When punk came, at last there were some groups more or less the same age. And . . . they had short hair, straight trousers . . . It made a difference to me, because I was a Mod by this time.' He was also taking more than a few pointers regarding lyrical content from the Pistols and The Clash.

With lines solidifying fast, punk inevitably lost some of its élitist appeal. When the Pistols played a special gig for London Weekend Television cameras at the Notre Dame Hall, off Leicester Square, in mid-November Steve Severin despaired of the audience, 'That was where every suburban kid turned up in a plastic bin liner and jumped about because they thought they were supposed to. And yet it is [now] seen as the archetypal show. For us it was the end. Me and Siouxsie just stood at the back and said, "It's all over. Too many people are into it." '

In the McLaren Master Plan, though, the *London Weekend Show* was a key part of his strategy to take the Pistols into families' front rooms, inspiring a generation of Gaumont geeks. The Pistols had already made an apocalyptic TV debut a couple of months earlier, rampaging through 'Anarchy In The UK', but it was on the regional late-night show, *So It Goes*. The London Weekend footage was at least filmed in front of a live audience – satellite kids or not – and finished with a heartfelt 'No Fun' (then earmarked as a possible B-side for 'Anarchy'). If a rendition of 'Anarchy' subsequently filmed for BBC's *Nationwide* lacked its live intensity, everything seemed to be proceeding according to plan in the days leading up to the all-important Anarchy In The UK Tour, due to begin on 3 December.

— — —

Two days beforehand, though, the Pistols found themselves in front of another set of TV cameras, for Thames' *Today* programme, as their most unsympathetic interviewer to date, Bill Grundy, laboured to get them to admit they were shit; and when that didn't work, to at least get them to say the word. When he made a lame play for Siouxsie Sioux, who was standing behind the band providing local colour, Steve Jones called him a 'dirty fucker' and the world turned upside down; even if no one realized it at the time. In fact, after the live show went off the air, and the phones started ringing from people wishing to express outrage, an unfazed Siouxsie 'picked [them] up . . . and told them to piss off . . . Malcolm was in a right state, though. He was convinced that we'd blown it all for them. I don't think he ever really saw the appeal of just having a laugh.'

If McLaren was a worried man on the evening of Grundy, he quickly pulled himself together. By the time he was summoned in front of EMI executive, Leslie Hill, to 'explain' the actions of his brood, he was telling the bemused penpusher, 'I'm not *going* to control them, I don't *want* to control them, and I *can't* control them. They must do what they must do.' The label had presumably thought 'Anarchy In The UK' was some kinda play on words, not a musical manifesto. As the pressing plants refused to carry on pressing, let alone distributing, the record, Rotten made it clear what he thought of the label and its employees.

Frank Brunger [label manager]: Johnny Rotten made a point of not talking to anybody from EMI. I could be in the same room with him, talking to the other Pistols . . . but Rotten would either completely blank me or, at best, unleash a stream of insults.

McLaren's problems were no longer confined to the Pistols. Having decided to put together a national punk package tour – like those sixties beat-group bills at Gaumont-on-the-Sea – he found it hardly made for happy families. Originally planning to tour with the Ramones (and The Vibrators), McLaren found that the Ramones – and/or their manager/ label – didn't welcome the idea (or the competition). Determined to give the tour a Noo Yawk dimension, he convinced the Heartbreakers to take their place.

The Heartbreakers, though, had lost their main songwriter and frontman Richard Hell the previous summer, and were reduced to quipping with the London boys about how *they* sang songs about heroin ('Chinese Rocks' had actually been written by Dee Dee Ramone, with a little help from Hell). But when the Grundy storm broke, the Heartbreakers hardly lived up to their hellraising reputation. Walter Lure recalls Jerry Nolan buying all the newspapers, 'and the Sex Pistols were on every goddamned front page . . . Jerry threw the papers on the bed screaming, "Look at this shit, man. I knew it was a bad idea. I fucking knew it."'

The Clash were also miffed to find themselves rock-bottom of the four-band bill, almost a footnote to proceedings. Indeed, when Strummer attempted to get his old confidant Pete Silverton, now a *Sounds* journalist, turfed off the tour bus for bringing up his pub-rock past, it took Matlock to remind him that his lot were 'only the first band on the bill'. And for a very good reason. Outside of London, The Clash were largely unknown. Also, every time they seemed ready to roll, someone tired of the party line and quit. This time Chimes rang that bell, citing Rhodes as the reason.

Terry Chimes: I used to argue with [Bernie] because I didn't buy what he was selling. He seemed like this peculiar person with odd ideas and I didn't trust him. I thought he'd be happy when I left, but he was quite upset. He said, 'Look, you're the foil. You say what the man in the street would say. If they can get their ideas past you, they can get them past them.'

Stop-gap replacement Rob Harper found himself thrown in at a truly surreal deep-end, on The Tour That Never Was. Within one date, The Clash did in fact find themselves bumped up the bill, at The Damned's expense. Though the entire Damned had at one time or another entered McLaren's circle of influence, there had been a gradual estrangement, exacerbated by their increasingly cosy relationship with the man McLaren called 'the Bill Brown of rock & roll', Jake Rivera. They had also made it known that they considered the Pistols' signing to EMI a cop-out – telling at least one music paper that they had a new song called 'Anarchy Courtesy Of EMI', and suggesting that the single itself was a disappointment. In Brian James's opinion, 'It sounded nothing like the band I'd seen live – [rather] layers of guitars, big Chris Thomas production'.

Captain Sensible: I remember when they came down to Stiff Records hot off the presses with 'Anarchy In The UK' and we sat round, wondering what our rivals [had] come up with, 'cause they were rough and ready onstage . . . and we all sat there pissing ourselves. It sounded like some redundant Bad Company out-take, with Old Man Steptoe singing over the top.

Once the tour started, it became apparent that the Grundy furore made The Damned a less necessary means of getting bondage-pant bums on ripped seats. As Scabies comments, they 'didn't need us any more. And Malcolm knew it.' After three cancelled shows, the tour arrived at Leeds Polytechnic on 6 December where, as Matlock says, 'Even before The Damned started playing, Malcolm was going, "Oh, I dunno, what do you think? I think they're bringing the whole thing down. They're not very good." It was [all] this politics thing.' But McLaren knew it wouldn't say much for punk solidarity if he gave them the boot arbitrarily. And so, after the Leeds gig, he took Brian James aside, to inform him, 'It's changed now. You're going on first.'

Brian James: I really was at the point of hitting him, [but] he called over two bodyguards. And that's it, we split. We hung around the next day [in Derby], and there was a thing of maybe you can play. We said, 'Well, we're not gonna audition. But we'll play.' Then Malcolm made this big thing [out of it].

McLaren was now able to expel The Damned *and* paint them as the ones who broke ranks. Of course, The Clash were all for their expulsion, knowing they'd be bumped up the bill. But McLaren was no longer letting 'his' boys speak for themselves. Maybe he was starting to enjoy the attention himself, especially after the *NME* devoted two pages to the thoughts of Chairman Malcolm the week before the tour. As Nils Stevenson wrote in his diary the day of the Leeds gig, 'Malcolm has pushed himself into the limelight and is now conducting interviews on behalf of the group. He's in his element, feigning outrage about the way the Sex Pistols are being persecuted.' It was but a small step, in McLaren's mind, to think everything had been his idea all along.

Julian Temple: There was an overall momentum of ideas that hung the thing together . . . It certainly wasn't pre-planned . . . [But] one of the problems was that Malcolm started believing the kind of things that we'd dreamt up to say about him . . . He really did feel that he was some kind of Situationist genius who had planned the whole thing.

McLaren also started to forget not only how good the Pistols were, but how volatile the dynamics of the band had always been. Nick Kent certainly believes that 'the notoriety . . . had a corrupting effect on him, in the sense that he started [trying to] control the group in an obsessive and dictatorial way, which was not gonna work with someone like Johnny.' The frustrations that came with not being able to play compounded any distance now growing between manager and frontman, though the Pistols continued to rise to the occasion when the opportunity came to play their blues away. On a month-long tragical mystery tour this happened just seven times (two of them return gigs at venues they'd already rocked – Manchester's Electric Circus and Plymouth's Wood Centre).

At least, the Pistols retained their capacity to inspire and galvanize. At Leeds Poly, Jon King recalls, 'There was maybe two hundred paying punters, and probably about fifty journalists,' but these included not only King, but most of the future Gang of Four, as well as future Mekon Andy Corrigan, who attracted the attention of a *Yorkshire Post* photographer.

Hugo Burnham: [Leeds] was the first [Anarchy] gig that had not been banned. It was very hushed, 'cause it was like, 'Is there going to be a fight? Are the police gonna come in and gas us all?' There was clearly a lot of off-duty police there. One kid started jumping up and down, pogoing [during The Damned] and these two geezers in plain clothes, the coshes were out, and we were all going, 'Fucking 'ell, I'm not gonna dance too much.' We thought we were gonna get thumped, jumped on, something's gonna go off. It was unbelievably tense, and exciting. Andy Corrigan had a razor blade hanging out of his ear. We wanted to cheer and go mad, but it was just like we gotta be careful. It wasn't packed, 'cause a lot of people were too frightened to go.

Manchester – three days later – was more familiar territory, even if the Electric Circus was not. Located in the council-flat wasteland of Collyhurst, the Circus had been co-opted by Buzzcocks after the Free Trade Hall stopped returning their calls. As Boon says, 'The Electric Circus . . . at weekends was heavy metal, but was quiet in the week. We went along, [and said,] "This is a quiet night. We'll hire it. You'll get the bar. We'll get the door." They weren't that happy to begin with, [but] . . . after the Anarchy tour, the people at the Electric Circus thought, "We're gonna change our booking policy – totally."' For Buzzcocks, the Anarchy tour seemed like an ideal opportunity to give the Manchester scene a kick-start. They even took over The Damned's vacant slot, playing with the same kind of energy, but with a whole lot more to say about life in Mancunia.

The hippy owners of the Circus were astonished to find the venue packed out for both Anarchy shows, held ten days apart. The bands were less happy to discover that provincial punks thought spitting was a gesture of solidarity; 'obviously believing that [it] was the correct behaviour at a Grundy rock-gig', as Silverton reported. At the Circus, Matlock told the crowd halfway through to stop gobbing, or they were leaving. It seemed to work for a while, but as he says, 'Perhaps there'd been some kind of guidelines written in the music papers by then. If you're stuck in the provinces, what do you have to go on? . . . [Previously] the people that were potential scenemakers were all suitably different from each other, and had their own personality.'

Certainly, some punk template had begun to take hold. When Pete Silverton interviewed some likely lads in the Circus audience, he found that 'they were certainly all in the process of forming bands', though Billy 'Massacre' and his friend from Clayton Bridge would have to wait until 'our mums give us the money for the amps'. Bernard Sumner and Peter Hook hadn't made a lot of progress since the second Free Trade Hall gig, though they now had a name for their band, Stiff Kittens. Fortunately for them, that first Circus show attracted its share of suburban punks, among them a public-school pupil called Ian Curtis. To Sumner and Hook, 'Ian just seemed like one of us. He had an Army and Navy flak jacket with Hate written on the back.' Without enquiring too deeply into the 'Macc' lad's background, they asked him to join their gang.

Also at both Circus shows – along with Cleethorpes and Caerphilly – was Black Country punk Robert Lloyd, who had yet to get his own band prefected but had discovered that the promoters of the tour, Endale Associates, were Birmingham-based. They were willing to let him swell the numbers, which outside of Manchester and Plymouth proved disappointing. In Caerphilly, a replacement gig booked at short notice after the Cardiff venue got cold feet, carol singers picketed the show, to very little purpose, save to give great copy to the convoy of journalists and TV crews. Inside, Bristolean Mark Stewart discovered that it was mostly soul boys and the odd provincial punk who made up the low numbers.

Mark Stewart: The underground working-class music tradition, after the skinhead-reggae thing died out, was soul and funk in England. The mohair jumpers, the pink trousers and the pointed shoes is a soul boy [thing]. [But] soul boys had no bands to relate to . . . [Yet from] Manchester [to] Newcastle, there was a synergy . . . Everybody was unaware of each other, [until] suddenly you saw a picture of the Sex Pistols, and you thought, 'This is what we are talking about.' . . . When we went to see the Pistols in Wales, there was only like twenty people there . . . [but] it was [all] mates from the funk scene.

By his own admission, Stewart had already been hanging 'around train stations and [getting] some old bird journalist [to let me] crash on her floor', in order to catch The Clash at the ICA. These two experiences, six weeks apart, convinced him something was happening: 'When I first heard the Pistols and The Clash, you really thought they were questioning the value of everything.' By the following May, he would be ready to help punk get funky with The Pop Group.

During the same four or five months, in Leeds, Jon King and Andy Corrigan, along with their art-student friends, began sharing equipment and rehearsal space, as the Gang of Four and The Mekons respectively prepared to go public. In Manchester, Ian Curtis would provide the necessary catalyst to Sumner and Hook's music-making. Between them, they would build a band called Warsaw, which would within a year of its May '77 debut be dismantled, and reassembled as Joy Division. In Birmingham, Robert Lloyd would finally call the brothers he'd met at a Patti Smith gig in October, and together they would become the Prefects, a necessary antidote to local faves, the Suburban Studs, among the first of a fair few fake-metal-bands in punk clothing.

The Pop Group, Gang of Four, Joy Division and the Prefects would hang around long enough to become post-punk – whatever connotation one may ascribe to that notoriously ambiguous term. The lengthy time lag between genesis and vinyl revelation gave all these bands a chance to shed their punk skins. Yet every one of them assuredly drew inspiration from punk's progenitors at the very outset, taking the Pistols as standard-bearers for a new music that was not a mere replication of the past.

The Anarchy tour may have been the final act in the (original) Pistols' passion play, but at least they had ensured that their legacy outside the capital was not solely copycat combos, for whom three chords and an attitude was not simply a starting-point, but a *raison d'être*. Meanwhile, the camaraderie that had been precariously maintained by the first wave of bands in the three months since McLaren got his movement, was at the point of collapse. The Damned never would make it up with either the Pistols or The Clash. As for Buzzcocks, offered the opportunity to tag along after that first Circus show, Boon admits that the whole situation with the tour 'was too chaotic'.

Even the situation between the Pistols and The Clash was now fraught with difficulties. Rotten had come to dislike The Clash, whom he regarded as second-rate (years later the singer would dismiss them, in his autobiography, as a band who 'looked and sounded like they were yelling at themselves about nothing in particular'). Matlock also found 'the Clash stuff [to be] a bit fifth-form politics, [straight] out of the agitprop pages at the back of *Time Out*'.

However, as tour manager Nils Stevenson noted in his diary, on a personal level, the bassist 'appeared to be happier [spending time] with The Clash. [And] Rotten was not amused.' By the time the not-so-merry band were dropped off in the West End on 22 December, though, nobody was too keen on anybody else. As Stevenson's diary entry reads, 'End of tour. Broke and cold. To make matters worse, Malcolm hits the

roof when he finds out Siouxsie has been using the [rehearsal] studio.'
Stevenson and McLaren were about to go their separate ways. And if
Clash stand-in drummer Rob Harper had no expectation he would
receive another call after being deposited back home, no one (save,
perhaps, Matlock) knew that the Pistols would require their own overhaul before January was through.

PART THREE

3.1
THE ART-SCHOOL DANCE GOES ON
1/77 – 4/77

SOUNDS January 1 1977 15p

GENESIS ◆ FEELGOODS ◆ GLUE

sounds

CLASH
— our pick for '77
More predictions inside

[Punk] was a performance art. It was avant-garde. It was an adventure, some-thing you launched yourself into. It was an alternative lifestyle. After [the Pistols] swore on TV, it then became a way to show rebellion and opt out.

— Pete Shelley, *Mojo*, #70

The English pick up on [punk] and it's made into a whole national movement . . . It's like a coffee thing – it keeps getting filtered into some weird concoction every ten minutes. — Walter Lure, the Heartbreakers, *Sounds*, 1/10/77

When Joe Strummer wrote the line, 'No Elvis, Beatles or The Rolling Stones' ('1977') – during the summer of 1976 – he was envisaging an overthrow by The Clash and like-minded bands. But there was a reason this trinity had resonance – they'd stuck at it. On the other hand, by the end of January 1977, The Clash lacked a drummer, the Sex Pistols a bassist, and Buzzcocks a singer. Just as Television in New York and Rocket from the Tombs in Cleveland had combusted before they could subvert the old order, so the three foremost English punk bands seemingly couldn't make a record, or do a tour, without falling out.

The Pistols manager McLaren had set great store on sticking together, telling a journalist at the time, 'I'm really inspired by The Rolling Stones, because they carried on through thick and thin. I've always felt, right from the beginning, that the group should stay together at all costs.' Yet when the time came, McLaren allowed Rotten to divide and rule, and tunesmith Glen Matlock to just walk away. The feud between Matlock and Rotten – evident as early as the previous March – had never entirely died down, and by the end of the Anarchy tour Matlock was ready to walk the plank.

Glen Matlock: John . . . always thought it was Steve, Paul and me against him, but it weren't like that. Steve and Paul were like Fred Flintstone and Barney Rubble; so it was Steve and Paul, John, and me. But John never saw that. He thought he was always the outsider on it; but only because he painted himself into some corner. John wanted to get his mate Sid in 'cause he thought it would even [things] up . . . [But also] as soon as he got his face in the paper he just became the most conceited, arrogant arsehole going, and when you're in a Transit going up and down the motorway, sitting on top of the equipment, it kinda gets to you. And Steve and Paul wouldn't back me up – John had kinda subsumed [them] and taken over their band; [while] Malcolm always wanted to keep everything in this constant state of flux, playing both ends against the middle . . . [So] we had a meeting when we came back from Holland – John wasn't there – [But] what're they gonna do? Get a new singer or a new bass player?

The Dutch trip, at the beginning of January, was meant as an escape from all the hoo-hah. McLaren sensed that EMI were about to pull the plug (as they were), and wanted to make it as difficult as possible for them to deliver the bad news. Onstage Rotten continued to consider himself leader of the gang. At Amsterdam's famous Paradiso, Rotten tolerated the fans' boorish behaviour, which Matlock and Cook did not. As Phil McNeil reported the show in the *NME*:

There's a long break, with a lot of aural and visual aggro between the punters and the Rotten/Matlock duo, then they resume ['God Save The Queen'], very loud . . . Suddenly a couple of kids at the front . . . start throwing beer. Not glasses, just beer – but for this laidback mob it's the equivalent. While Rotten stands there, Cook erupts from his stool and . . . [begins to] chuck beer back, Matlock kicks his mike stand very nastily off the stage, and the rhythm section storms off. Jones is still riffing, and Rotten sends [someone] to get the others back. They eventually return for the only really furious piece of music they play all night . . . 'Watcha Gonna Do About It', nihilism incarnate. [*NME*, 15/1/77]

Rotten would later recast this incident, claiming Matlock refused to play 'God Save The Queen'. Not true. Though it would take three weeks more for the sword to fall, Matlock now knew he wanted out. And, as McLaren's secretary Sophie Richmond informed Jon Savage, 'Glen could write tunes and they couldn't. They could produce words and chords, but not tunes, and they were finished as a creative unit once he'd gone.' As of January 1977 the canon was essentially set in stone. Nor could they be a live unit of withering fury ever again.

Another career opportunity almost presented itself immediately. Matlock recalls that the day he quit, 'Mick [Jones] and Joe [Strummer] got wind of it, and I met 'em at the Marquee for a drink. But Joe was funny. He said, "Oh, what you gonna do? Good bass player." And Mick was going, "Yeah, yeah." And it was like they weren't [sure] enough to ask me [straight out].' Matlock joining The Clash could have solved a lot of problems, especially if Simonon had swopped bands as well.

As it is, Rotten wanted Sid Vicious in 'his' band; which shows that, for all his street-smart, he never was a great judge of character. Only One John Perry's assessment of Sid is apposite, 'When he wasn't "in character", he was a puppy dog, *desperate* to please. [But] he was a single idea boy at best. He was always somebody else's creation.' When he *was* 'in character', he was a dangerous loon; and joining the Pistols gave him the opportunity to be 'in character' an awful lot of the time.

Steve Jones realized soon enough that, 'Sid really looked the part, but [he] couldn't play. And now we could.' McLaren thought this was a plus point – 'Hey, I thought that's what we were selling'. Even when the inevitable happened, and EMI gave him a severance cheque, he seemed keen to emphasize Sid's inadequacy. When he informed the front runner for the Pistols' signature, Derek Green at A&M, of the change, any downside escaped him.

Derek Green: I asked [McLaren] how [Sid Vicious] played, because I thought Matlock was one of the real players and he said, 'Well, he's never played before and that's why he's perfect for the job.' You would have thought that a regular guy trying to sign a deal would have tried to soften it, but Malcolm made it part of the excitement.

What made this particularly perturbing to Green was that it had been a cassette of the Pistols' latest demos that 'just blew me away . . . I couldn't believe what I was hearing. I was terribly excited . . . [and] I knew *at that very moment* that I wanted the act badly.' These sessions, held on January 17–20 at Gooseberry, Matlock's last contribution, included an incendiary new song, 'EMI', as well as the now-honed 'God Save The Queen'.

McLaren was as interested in A&M as Green was by the Pistols, turning up at their New King's Road offices on 9 January, three days after EMI issued a press release ending their association with the notorious band. Though it would take until the first week in March for both parties to agree terms, Green knew he wanted the band from the date he heard the tapes – even though *that* quartet no longer existed. When Green paid for studio time with Chris Thomas, to record their first A&M single, on 3–4 March, McLaren went to some lengths to persuade Matlock to sit in on the sessions. In fact, Matlock got paid but didn't turn up, leaving Jones to play the bass parts on the two songs recorded that day, 'God Save The Queen' and 'Pretty Vacant'; and at all subsequent sessions.

And still, the A&M deal proceeded, Green duly informing a packed press conference on 10 March that he couldn't imagine the Pistols 'doing anything that outrages people at this stage'. Until, that is, Sid Vicious showed his true colours less than forty-eight hours later by assaulting TV presenter Bob Harris in the Speakeasy. Green awoke with a start. After the Bob Harris incident, he realized, 'I'm not going to be able to defend them to people, because they're . . . serious . . . When these [kind of] incidents occur, [McLaren]'s looking to exploit it. Someone's going to get hurt.' By 16 March, McLaren had another large cheque, and A&M had a lot of copies of a single to dee-stroy. Two days later, The Clash followed in The Damned, Pistols and Buzzcocks' $\frac{4}{4}$ footsteps, issuing their first 45.

Buzzcocks' own first report, *Spiral Scratch*, had appeared in the last week of January (just as Matlock was telling *Melody Maker* he'd had enough). Their first press release, describing the EP as 'almost certainly . . . a limited edition release' was almost immediately followed by a second, penned by lead singer Devoto, announcing that he was leaving the band because, 'I don't like most of this New Wave music. I don't like movements . . . [and] I am not confident of the Buzzcocks' intention to get out of the dry land of New Wave-ness to a place from which these things can be said. What was once healthily fresh is now a clean old hat.'

It seemed like an extraordinarily ill-timed move. Apart from anything else, it jeopardized Devoto's own investment in this self-financed four-track EP, recorded shortly after Christmas 1976, in a single day. Because these Mancunian mavericks had decided not to go the major-label route, it was *their* money on the line.

Richard Boon: On the Anarchy tour in Manchester . . . McLaren was telling me to get my finger out concerning the labels, how the Pistols were getting together with EMI and how Clash's manager was talking to Polydor. After the gig, the band talked it over and we felt that it was not what we wanted to do . . . but we thought it would be worth putting out a record. [1979]

The session at Indigo Studios was produced by self-styled Svengali Martin Hannett, a leading light in the early Manchester collective, Music Force, who was still calling himself Martin Zero, and whose main contribution to proceedings, according to Steve Diggle, consisted of 'every time the engineer got the sound just right, [he would] lean across and fuck it up'. Despite this, Buzzcocks managed to record four songs, overdub a guitar lead on 'Boredom', and put together the £700 needed to make a thousand copies of the EP.

In the process they made the most radical gesture imaginable – a home-made record that overcame all its sonic limitations with an immediacy and desire to communicate not often found. And yet, as Boon said, 'It was out of reluctance, because we didn't want to go to a major label. It felt like it *might* be inspirational, but at the time we were just worried whether we were going to sell the original pressing.'

Howard Devoto: We just didn't have any inroads into the music industry . . . I remember Rough Trade, Bizarre and Virgin's shop in Manchester being our first three clients.

What neither could have predicted was the number of copies these three outlets would shift, though music-press reviews and radio play on John Peel's show represented their sole means of national promotion, and a PO Box address remained their main outlet. After McLaren saw a copy in Rough Trade, he told Devoto, 'It's quite odd seeing this record that has come from nowhere.' It was 'not going straight back there'.

Fellow punksters were bowled over. Wire's Colin Newman did not have even a handful of gigs under his belt when he heard it, but found it to be 'a phenomenal record – it had an intent to it that you weren't hearing anywhere else.' Vic Goddard in Barnes was equally impressed, as was Robert Lloyd in Birmingham. Still not quite the perfect Prefect, Lloyd promptly phoned Richard Boon to offer himself as a replacement singer. The band, though, wasn't making any hasty decision.

Linder Sterling: At the time, [Howard quitting] *was* a shock . . . but I think Howard's got a very low boredom threshold. I think he uses the word boredom in a very specific, philosophical state, so I think when he gets bored by something, that's [almost] a disturbance of the spirit.

On one level, Shelley agreed with Devoto's stance, i.e. that 'what was once healthily fresh is now a clean old hat'. Devoto's decision-process had certainly not been whimsical. As early as the September 100 Club Festival, he had confided in Caroline Coon 'that he is only in a rock band "temporarily" '. And by the time of the two Anarchy shows at the Circus, Devoto had concluded that 'there were just a lot of people writing songs that were to an incredible degree the same as everybody else . . . You know, the whole punk thing happened too quickly for anybody to control it . . . [Yet] it all stayed the same after that initial rush.' When Shelley, intending to continue 'their' experiment, drafted in old Jet of Air bassist, Garth Smith – reverting to lead vocals himself – Devoto felt a certain vindication.

Howard Devoto: There was no way I wanted to go on making that music – it was too limiting, [and] I couldn't see how we could change . . . [When] Garth joined, it was like, 'Yeah, this is one of the reasons why I've left that band . . . Okay, I know he's a good bass player, but what's he got to do with *this*? – that bloke [I] remember in the tuxedo, turning up for the very first Buzzcocks gig?'

Buzzcocks were hardly the only early English punk band with a kamikaze streak. Chelsea, who had played support to Buzzcocks at the Electric Circus's inaugural punk gig in November 1976, had played just one more show before firing singer, Gene October. And another London punk band that defined itself geographically, Sham 69 (short for Hersham 69), had played but a single support slot at the 100 Club before singer Jimmy Pursey asked the other four members, 'Look, do you really believe in the songs we do?' When they questioned the worth of the likes of 'Let's Rob A Bank' and 'George Davis Is Innocent', he proceeded to oust three-quarters of the band.

Another fledgling punk outfit that didn't even make it beyond their squat rehearsal room was Flowers of Romance. Named after the Pistols 'song', they were destined to become another punk prototype à la London SS, with future members of The Slits, the Sex Pistols, Siouxsie & the Banshees and Public Image trading places. The brainchild of squat-mates Sid Vicious and Viv Albertine, they had originally drafted in Joe Strummer's girlfriend, Paloma, now christened Palm Olive, on drums. After banging away with a street theatre group for a few days. Paloma had realized that 'the whole punk thing [was] happening around me', and decided she wanted to be in a band. For Vicious, though, racism and stupidity went hand in hand.

Palm Olive: We were practising at [my squat]. I remember Sid Vicious coming to the house [for] a practice and he was hanging around, and he was telling me that he hated blacks. And I said, 'I hate people who hate blacks.' Next thing I hear, I'm fired from the group. I went right to Vivien's house and she was very surprised to see me – and kinda uncomfortable – and she said, 'It's nothing to do with me. It was Sid who decided.' I confronted him and he just said, 'Well, you're just not right.' So I [told him], 'Well, you need to practise somewhere else.'

By this point, there was a plethora of permutations played out by London's punk ensembles. Ex-Clashman Keith Levene, who flitted in and out of Flowers of Romance, as well as another band called the Quick Spurts (where Chrissie Hynde pops up again!), saw Sid struggle to become the next Simonon.

Keith Levene: If you're talking about some punky bass, just chugging along with the odd change or two then Sid . . . could do it, in time, no problem. He *could* play bass . . . [But] Sid was [Flower of Romance's] main vocalist too, he was our frontman . . . [And] then it all started to fall apart when Malcolm wanted Sid for the Pistols.

By January 1977, Levene had lost another frontman to the lure of the limelight. The Quick Spurts were also losing out to the demands of running a rock club, co-founder Barry Jones embracing his responsibilities as Andy Czekowski's partner in London's first dedicated punk venue, the Roxy. After two word-of-mouth-only gigs in December – the Heartbreakers for pin money, and Generation X, making their official debut – the club announced itself on New Year's Day 1977 with a headlining performance by The Clash, a band who still had a problem with members departing, citing 'musical differences'.

By 1/1/77, Strummer, Simonon and Jones had 'been too long on the dole'. It was time to get serious. Having belatedly agreed to do the Roxy, the band were required to phone Harper, their erstwhile drummer, for an unexpected swansong. But when they needed someone to record some demos for Polydor – who had re-entered the frame for the band's signature – and then CBS, they put their faith in Terry Chimes, aka Tory Crimes, who was sweet-talked into earning some session fees, though no actual credit for holding the whole thing together.

The resultant demos hardly leapt out of the speakers, like Goodman's work with the Pistols, perhaps because the first set were 'produced' by the once-dynamic 'dypso' Guy Stevens (Rhodes: 'We wanted a nutcase to produce the band, because that's what our music is all about.') When that didn't work, they went the Pistols route, letting their soundman, Mickey Foote, twiddle the knobs. Neither set kicked in any jail guitar doors, though this did not faze Polydor's Chris Parry, who knew enough about the band's sound, and probably had an eye on the production chair himself (as he later did with The Jam). CBS didn't seem to know who or what they were getting, but felt they should have their own punk band and correctly considered The Clash main contenders. Throughout January the two industry giants went head-to-head for the signature of London punk's number two band; while steadfastly ignoring the label-less leaders of the entire movement.

Now was the time for Bernie Rhodes to show his understanding of economics to be more Keynesian than Marxist. But the contract he committed The Clash to was the worst of all possible deals. It gave CBS a decade's worth of one-way options while ceding every territory to the multinational for a headline-snatching advance of £100,000, without even ensuring tour support from the label. Strummer admitted this was 'an oversight' though not until 1979, by which time he was obliged to observe, 'I didn't read the fucking thing, I just signed the bastard, like an idiot, because I trusted my manager, and he said, "Sign it."'

The fateful contract was written in such a way that The Clash had almost no prospect of 'earning out' any advance paid; while giving world rights to CBS meant that they could choose not to release records in the USA (something they would do before the year was out), yet stop the band finding their own distributor. Bernie showed himself to be a barrow-boy businessman, rejecting a deal with Polydor that entailed a smaller advance, for far fewer albums, and containing what would have proven to be a quite priceless clause – the cost of any recordings to be borne by the label, not the band. Strummer would insist there was a grand design, but Rhodes does not seem to have known that the devil was in the detail, or maybe he just didn't care.

Joe Strummer: We were being so totally creative . . . business decisions seemed totally irrelevant . . . I was [just] happy that we were going to be able to put our stuff on record. Signing for CBS . . . was a conscious attempt on the part of McLaren and Rhodes to burst out of the confined thing. They'd been to New York and what they hated was that the punk thing was . . . on the Bowery, and that was how it stayed for five years. It never came out of there. [1979]

McLaren was more wary of Maurice Oberstein, rejecting CBS over-tures at the time of the EMI deal. According to Matlock, McLaren even fell out with his old compadre when Rhodes and Oberstein cooked up 'some kind of deal to have a radio station and their own label for a whole host of new bands, and he wanted to go in with Malcolm on it, and Malcolm didn't want to go in.' If so, it was another pie-in-the-sky scheme that came to naught, though Oberstein predictably ended up getting what he wanted.

After all their revolutionary rhetoric, just the association with a label like CBS was not easily explained away. As Acme attraction Jeannette Lee says, 'The Clash were completely humiliated about the fact that they'd signed to a major. They did it – but they were embarrassed about it.' Strummer was obliged to insist, 'Even though we've signed with CBS, we aren't going to float off into the atmosphere like the Pink Floyd.' But Mark P at *Sniffin' Glue* was appalled, and set about calling them to account.

Mark Perry: If you read *Sniffin' Glue*, you see that . . . I was very idealistic. At the time, you had the Pistols, Damned, Clash, Subway Sect, but there was also the indie labels starting: Chiswick, New Hormones, Stiff, doing their own thing. There were a lot of indie records coming out in the States as well . . . I felt that the next stage would have been the bigger bands actually doing that. I started getting really disillusioned when the bands started talking about signing up to this label and that. [When I] spoke to Mick Jones in '76 – he'd say 'the kids that, the kids this, there's got to be a big change'. Then five months [later], it's like, 'Oh, CBS is not going to change us, we're going to record it on our own terms. We made sure we got a good deal.' [PSF]

The one group that supported their decision – the Sex Pistols – had already taken the poisoned chalice, and were still coming back for more. Meanwhile, The Clash set out to rub away the tarnish on their reputation with an album as uncompromising as *Fun House*, as adrenalin-fuelled as *The Ramones* and as righteous as 'Anarchy In The UK'. Beginning 12 February 1977, they were back at Beaconsfield, a demo studio they already knew well.

– – –

Meanwhile, in garages the land over, with bullshit-detectors in vari-able states of repair, were reserve legions taken with the template. For the more attuned souls the Pistols remained the pivotal experience, with bands like Generation X, The Slits, X-Ray Spex, Siouxsie & the Banshees, The Adverts and Wire suggesting a remarkable renewable source of energy. All of these bands made their real live debut at the new punk venue on Neal Street, and between them suggested that English punk could replenish itself as easily as North Sea oil. All were already in motion when the December 1976 issue of *Sideburns*, a Stranglers zine modelled on *Sniffin' Glue*, carried its famous DIY punk-kit: drawings of the A, E and G guitar chords and the edict, NOW FORM A BAND. All they needed was a place to play.

On the first of the first, seventy-seven, punk's favourite accountant unveiled a West End punk palace which he had converted from a gay pick-up joint, only becoming the Roxy when The Clash brought in the year with a loud clang. It was Chelsea singer Gene October who had the connection with this place where bi-businessmen got rough. He thought that the club – called Chagaurama's at the time – would 'be a great place to [play] . . . I need[ed] a base for Chelsea once a week where people [could] come and have a look . . . I went in there one night and there were two people in there. It was dingy, [but] you could get three hundred people in there.' By the time Gene reported back to Andy Czekowski, though, Chelsea had a new singer, Billy Idol, and a new name, Generation X; all of whom were looking to take up October's idea. Tony James voluntered to go with Czekowski to check the place out. In his unpublished memoir, he described the experience:

'It's a seedy club in Neal Street . . . A gay disco drinking club for spade types and what looked like gangsters – night life with gin and tonics – hot chop girls – bow ties on gorilla types – we're gonna be killed . . . Downstairs is a small bar. Coloured lights on the ceiling . . . Mirrors on all the walls – makes it look bigger . . . There's maybe 20–30 people scattered, who eye this new crowd suspiciously – it's small but easily big enough, a stage over there under the stairs, lick of paint, posters. Our own CBGB's.

Since Gene October's expulsion, Tony James and Billy Idol had been busy getting anthemic. By opening night, 16 December, they had songs like 'Ready Steady Go', 'Your Generation', 'Listen' and 'Youth Youth Youth' to hand. They had also punkified John Lennon's 'Instant Karma' and Black Sabbath's 'Paranoid'. With Idol switching to vocals, they required another guitarist. He was found at a youth club in Fulham.

Tony James: Billy went, 'I've seen this kid playing guitar before – he's got long hair but we'll sort that out.' He was like seventeen. It was Derwood . . . Cut his hair the night before the first gig as Gen X. [By then we] had the pop-art t-shirts. I did those with spray paint. And the first one I did was a copy of the [Who] target t-shirt for the drummer. You couldn't buy an Iggy Pop t-shirt – so I copied a photograph of the [*Raw Power*] album cover on to a t-shirt – you couldn't wash them.

If Generation X had the edge on most early Roxy bands it was because they *could* play, had decent equipment and their songs had that classic garage-rock structure. Another garageband, The Clash, were still trying to flay their songs into submission when they gave the Roxy its first real pay day on New Year's Day. They were also plastered across the cover of that week's *Sounds*. Opening the Roxy also gave Rhodes the opportunity to steal a base on McLaren. Czekowski thinks Malcolm 'somehow felt he had the rights to any punk club in London . . . and was reluctant to acknowledge me and what we'd done.' Rhodes agreed to let The Clash make their mark, 'on the condition that we didn't advertise. We didn't tell the papers . . . [But] it didn't need it.'

It wasn't quite true that they didn't advertise the gig. They pasted up flyers all over the West End. In fact, Barry Jones remembers Mick Jones and Paul Simonon helping put those flyers up, 'although Bernie was telling [them] not to, trying to make everything [this great] mystique around the band.' Jones, who had come from Leeds Art School and had already worked for fashion designer Zandra Rhodes, hit upon an original flyer-design that used the new technology of colour xeroxing and juxtaposed discordant images to catch the eye even when no larger than A4. It defined a handbill style that would endure through all the hardcore years.

Barry Jones: The cut-up . . . doing collages was great. I was really into [teen] comics at the time . . . and I'd just discovered colour xerox. At the time there was only one in the West End, a little place off Regent Street; so I'd just discovered how it changed the textures of the colours – how it gave it this look – so I started just pasting things up.

Its flyers were not the only punk visual the Roxy codified. As it quickly became *the* place where London punks came to play, it embraced those who – as Czekowski puts it – 'would come from office or school or whatever, and change into their punk outfits in the toilets, spend an hour and a half in the toilets [and] change from being Miss Prim to Miss Improper.' Mark Perry's then-girlfriend Susie Hulme witnessed many such transformations.

Susie Hulme: I didn't have any money except to get in, [but] when you went to the toilet someone had a bottle of something you could have a sip of. It was really crowded in the toilets. People were changing their clothes from work and ripping things up and fastening safety pins and spraying their hair. You couldn't usually wash your hands because someone had poured sugar into a sink of water and if you had a Mohican this girl would dip your head under and then hold your hair up, pat you with paper towels while it set straight up and then spray you with hairspray. So it smelt of all kinds of things in there.

Helping out on such occasions would be Czekowski's significant other, Sue Carrington, who had previously had her own range of make-up in Woolworth's – until the December day she arranged a photo shoot using members of the Bromley contingent to illustrate a new line, and got fired because 'Berlin had a swastika on his arm' (it didn't help that the contact sheets arrived at work the day after Grundy). So Carrington took her craft into the crevices of Neal Street: 'I used to make up people [like] Billy Idol in the toilet. Gaye Advert used to be always wearing my eyeshadow.' After all, freedom of expression was what this club was meant to be all about.

Andy Czekowski: [In] the early days of punk there was this very liberal attitude to everything . . . a crossover between the gays . . . who'd come down when [the Roxy] was Chagaurama, and the punks. There was just a liberal attitude to style . . . [But] it got round that this [was] a wild club . . . because I used to let everyone get away with hell. [1977]

Czekowski could not have known what he was letting himself in for. What he had, though, was a rare capacity to let things wash over him, and a genuine love of the scene. As Rat Scabies relates, 'You'd go in the bog and there'd be some kid kicking the cistern off the wall and Andy'd be completely cool about it, "You do know that means you won't have anywhere to piss next time, don't you?" His real [agenda] was: Write all over it, do what you want, it's your club. So if you fuck it up, you fuck it up for yourself.'

So-called punk bands now appeared like sewer rats from the squats and garages of every urban wasteland. As Czekowski states, 'We were getting phone calls from all over England, "We want to play the Roxy – we're a punk band."' For these unsigned bands the Roxy was a rare and necessary oasis in the desert of London clubland. Wire's Colin Newman is not overstating the case when he states, 'Before the new wave it was impossible for an unknown band to play gigs.'

Nils Stevenson: The impetus might have fizzled out had it not been for the Roxy keeping it going, and allowing new bands to develop as pure punk bands rather than appearing as supports for naff pub-rock bands.

In fact, some of the first bands to express an interest in playing the Roxy were those 'naff pub-rock bands'. By the third week of January, the club were booking The Stranglers because, as Czekowski says, 'They very much wanted to play the Roxy – Alan [Edwards] wanted them to be there to give them the credibility.' The Boys – who were to The Beatles what The Jam were to The Who – were only ever punk by association, rather than Attitude. But, as Kid Reid commented in 1977, 'Eventually we got called punk and started getting gigs down the Roxy.' There was nothing eventual about it – The Boys played support to The Damned two weeks after it officially opened. The Jam, another 'new wave' band who proved surprisingly keen to get a Roxy stamp on their punk passport, played the weekend before The Boys, above a band named Wire, playing their fourth gig as a five-piece.

Out-of-towners with glam-rock genes also quickly redrafted themselves to fit the Roxy model. As Matlock suggests, à propos Slaughter & the Dogs, who were the first to make the trip south from Mancunia, 'Everything became punk. [But] sometimes you have to jump on the coach, wherever it's going.' That was certainly the view of The Cortinas, a Bristol band that had already supported Patti Smith.

Jeremy Valentine: We used to play R&B, garageband stuff. We like bands like the Shadows of Knight. If you listen to our music, you can hear our R&B roots. We changed when we found out we had a gig at the Roxy the next week, so we wrote about four songs that week. We wanted to write our own stuff and it just came out the way it has. [1977]

Will Birch, who remembered Valentine from Kursaal Flyer gigs in Bristol, turned up at the Roxy one night in January to see these familiar faces on stage, 'Jeremy I remember always had quite short hair, but an art-studenty touch with the Lou Reed shades on, and a lot of that kind of embroidery about him – arty. [Then] when I saw The Cortinas at the Roxy . . . they were [now] doing "Standing At The Bus Stop" [and] "Fascist Dictator".'

Some bands crossing the pub-rock/punk-rock divide found it easier to respond to the demands of this new audience than more 'authentic' punk bands, who were too busy trying to ensure they played in time and tune. There were also the handful of what Stevenson typified as 'pure punk bands' who had been burrowing away before Grundy got pissed. They, too, had the contacts to get through to Czekowski. The Adverts, one of the more incisive second-wave bands, were support at Generation X's second Roxy gig because Gen X's drummer, John Towe, worked at the same music shop as their guitarist, Howard Pickup. The addition of Pickup enabled Tim and Gaye to work up a set that already included the likes of 'One-Chord Wonders', 'New Boys', 'Bored Teenagers', 'We Who Wait' and 'Quickstep'.

TV Smith: I'd [already] written 'One-Chord Wonders' – we were called [that] for a week or two, but the problem was that it was a gimmick[y name]; and then you're [stuck with] the gimmick for however long you last . . . We got a guitarist quite quickly. Howard applied, and not only did he live just around the corner, but he was working in a music store which had rehearsal rooms attached. This solved a lot of problems – we then rehearsed as a threesome in a proper rehearsal room. That helped things get together very quickly.

It was not until the winter nights closed in that they found drummer Laurie Driver, and were able to make that call to Czekowski. Fortunately, TV Smith had found a(nother) suitably punky name, The Adverts, which was the only question Czekowski asked before pencilling them in to make their mid-January debut. As Czekowski says, 'The fact they were linked, in the same group of people, was sufficient for us to give them a try.'

Czekowski was not about to allow *only* the untried, the untuned and the unwanted take over the club. If he was going to repeat the night of The Clash – and he needed to, financially – he had to offer the bands that *NME* namechecked. Hence The Stranglers. Hence, also, The Damned, who played three nights in February as both a little 'thank you' to their ex-manager – and as repayment for their drummer trashing one of his vintage cars after a night out on the tiles. All three nights were damn packed, and for the first time some reviled 'retro' rock stars came down to check out the young tykes. At the end of the first Damned set, Barry Jones remembers, 'This fat old guy get[ting] up onstage, and [he] starts going, "C'mon, this is a fucking great band, let's have 'em up again." I turned to one of the security guys, "Who the fuck's that? Get him out of here." It was John Bonham. He was a big fan.' As were all of Zeppelin.

The Damned's unpaid Roxy residency was a smart marketing move, coinciding with the release of The Damned's debut album, appositely described in Barry Cain's *Record Mirror* review as 'the world's first 78 rpm album'. With songs like 'Neat Neat Neat', 'New Rose', 'Stab Your Back' and 'Feel The Pain', it presented a less po-faced strain of punk than The Clash. As Tony Parsons crowed in his *NME* review, 'They promised, they recorded, they delivered.' *Damned, Damned, Damned* – so good they named it thrice – was the big Stiff pitch that winter. Having finally organized a workable distribution deal with Island, it was time for Rivera to think in terms of twelve-inch units.

For their second and third 'benefit' shows in the Neal Street basement, The Damned were supported by The Adverts, who were threatening to become almost a house band after their Gen X debut, playing the Roxy more times than even the execrable Eater. Their music seemed to share the same *joie de vroom* as The Damned. Of the original Roxy music-makers, The Adverts would be first to get a single on the radio. The Damned connection led inexorably to Jake Rivera and his pub-rock pirates, after an impressed Brian James suggested to Rivera that he 'check these guys out. They were the kind of band, you'd see them a week later and they were that much better. They grew up in public.'

TV Smith: Jake came down [to the Roxy] with Nick Lowe. They had an eye on this punk thing, 'cause they were smart. The big companies move like big beasts, take a long time to find out what's going on; whereas Jake was in there straightaway . . . Jake just said, 'Come down to the Stiff offices and we'll do a deal,' and he gave us a single deal just like that . . . It was strictly a one-off thing.

In keeping with short-standing Stiff practice, Lowe checked out The Adverts one more time, agreed on the A-side, and led them to Pathway Studios to record both sides one not-so-sunny afternoon in March. By the time Czekowski parted company with the Roxy, these one-chord wonders were dreaming of making the charts, and preparing for their legendary 'four-chord' tour with The Damned (The Damned having three chords to The Adverts' one). Though 'One-Chord Wonders' failed to make the big-time, The Adverts were to find themselves in both the album and the single charts before the summer was out.

The 'Roxy' band who struggled most with those chord-charts – but had the *cojones* to carry on – were all-girl outfit The Slits, formed by Palm Olive, after her one-month apprenticeship in Flowers of Romance, and Germanic jailbait Arianna Forster. Paloma was frustrated by her experience in Flowers, and the fact that 'my connection with Joe [was] breaking down, even though we were together from time to time. I decided I wanted to have a girl group. I met Ari at a Patti Smith gig, and I thought [it] was great that she was so obnoxious. I [now] had an understanding of what a front person needed to be in a band . . . This other girl, Kate Korus, I knew from the squat scene . . . Ari was very young – she was fourteen then. I had [already] written, "Number One Enemy", "New Town", "Shoplifting" . . . And Ari had written "Vindictive".'

Such was the post-Grundy tabloid feeding frenzy, and the column-inches these riotous girls provided, that before they even had a stable line-up, The Slits were splashed across the *News of the World*. In the same week they became tabloid fodder, the still-loaded pair bumped into *Sounds* journalist, Vivien Goldman, at an Aswad gig. Goldman felt compelled to write an account of 'Palm Olive and Arianna . . . both wearing elaborate black weals of make-up slashed round their eyes, and the word "SLIT" painted on their necks and cheeks. They'd only just decided on the name, and were justifiably excited about it.'

At this stage, as Paloma admits, The Slits were a *femme fatale* Electric Eels; more concept than band: 'Anything we could do to shock people, we were into. We couldn't play, we didn't pretend that we played.' Ari Up (as she dubbed herself) was not easily knocked off her path, though, and soon dispensed with Kate Korus and original bassist, Suzi Gutz, replacing them with marginally more competent punkettes. As she said at the time, 'People who say they can't get a band together because they haven't found people, or they haven't got the equipment, aren't trying hard enough.' I guess it probably helped that her German heiress mother, Nora, dipped into reserves when so required.

The Slits' new bassist Tessa was from another all-girl punk band, the

Castrators (hence the necklace she wore with a little pair of scissors on it). Viv Albertine, left high and dry by Sid Vicious, had been taking impromptu guitar lessons from fellow squatter Keith Levene, as well as acquiring a few pointers in posing from sometime-boyfriend Mick Jones and friend Chrissie Hynde, whom Albertine described as 'the first girl I'd ever met who played the guitar without looking like Joni Mitchell'. Palm Olive had forgiven her the previous trespass, so she became the missing Slit.

Albertine certainly shared Ari's attitudinal disposition, telling Caroline Coon that she wasn't 'playing in a rock & roll band in a calculated way. It just comes naturally. I don't understand why a great many more women don't do it too.' By March 1977, The Slits were ready to make the transition from concept to combo, joining The Clash, Subway Sect and Buzzcocks at Harlesden's rundown Roxy theatre on the 11th, before a suitably uncritical audience in love with the idea of cacophony as long as it had a beat. Fifteen days later they played the more central Roxy, as support to Siouxsie Sioux and her new Banshees.

The night after Harlesden an equally 'experimental' experience awaited anyone at 14 Woodstock Road, Birmingham, when the Prefects made their debut 'at somebody's house' (little knowing that they would be touring with The Slits and those other paradigms of punk atonality, Subway Sect, barely two months later). Like Ari and Paloma, Robert Lloyd and the Apperley brothers, Paul and Alan, had met originally at a gig on Patti Smith's brief October 1976 UK Tour, after Lloyd had replied to an ad in the local *Evening Mail* for a 'Punk Bassist and singer . . . Into Sex Pistols, Damned, Ramones etc.' Not exactly your usual ad at a time when neither the Pistols nor The Damned had yet released a record!

Robert Lloyd: I was knocking around doing music in my garage in Cannock, and the bass player who was playing with me at the time got to see the ad, and lo and behold we got the gig. The Apperleys, like myself, had seen the Sex Pistols when they'd come to Birmingham . . . and it changed our slant on things . . . I met them when Patti Smith played Birmingham Odeon, but then nothing happened. Then early in '77, [one of us phoned] and said, 'I don't know what happened, but do you still want to do this group?'

March 1977 would prove the high watermark for punk's second wave, as Siouxsie & the Banshees, The Slits, X-Ray Spex and a four-piece Wire all made their debuts at the Neal Street dive; while the Sect and the Prefects continued to plough the more atonal path. If The Slits were 100% womenfolk, the Banshees and Spex made girls the visual and vocal focal point; the early X-Ray Spex providing something genuinely unique, a double dynamic of damsels in lead singer Poly Styrene and schoolgirl saxophonist Lora Logic. From day one, the latter's sax-leads serrated right through the ubiquitous guitar-buzzsaw.

The pairing proved a happy accident. Pop singer Marion Elliott, whose 'Silly Billy' 45 was already a one-flop wonder, had been turned around upon seeing the Pistols in Hastings in early July 1976. Rethinking her musical ideas, she began with a change of brand-name. Poly Styrene was born. ('I thought it would be a laugh to call myself a product. I think all pop stars are products.') In August, Poly checked out the Pistols again, and almost immediately penned 'Oh Bondage Up Yours'.

Poly Styrene: There were these girls that useta chain themselves together with handcuffs and things . . . [But] I didn't write it about them. I just used that kinda bondage theme to express repression. When people see these people wearin' bondage they think they're *for* bondage – but they're not. [1978]

In the sweltering summer of 1976, Marion sat at her typing-pool desk, tapping out songs like 'Identity', 'Plastic Bag' and 'I Am A Cliché', durable statements about ephemeral things. Her love of all things trashy had already prompted her to run a stall off the King's Road at weekends: 'I had little lattice plastic bags and see-through Mary Quant shoes from the sixties: I used to buy up old stock. Anything different . . . It was meant to be an extreme version of tack.' She now wanted to take this 'extreme version of tack' on stage, placing an ad in *Melody Maker* that asked for 'Young punx who want to stick it together'. It brought a response from an O-level student in Wembley who wasn't sure what a punk was, but felt like adding her sax to some kinda musical mix.

Lora Logic: I was brought up in Wembley, near the [Empire Pool]. Bowie was my biggest childhood idol . . . I played piano, then violin, then classical guitar at school, but it was all classical presentation, which I didn't find very inspiring, so I [asked] my dad, who was a big jazz fan, . . . [for] a saxophone, not thinking they'd buy me one in a million years – but they did . . . An advert was put in [*Melody Maker*] by the manager, and it just used the word punk, and I'd never seen that word before . . . Poly didn't really want another girl, but the manager thought it'd be a good idea to have two girls together, especially a fifteen-year-old girl who played the saxophone. Poly had already written a few songs – [well,] she had written the words and had some ideas for melodies – [so] we just, wham bam, put 'em together.

By the time Lora gave Poly's band a new spec, the other elements were already in place. As Lora recalls, 'It was something she'd been working on for quite a while, way before the first rehearsal – the whole concept.' To put their new recruit in the frame, Poly and manager Falcon Stuart took Lora down to a gig 'at the Man in the Moon on the King's Road, just to give me an idea of what punk rock was'. Lora was not the only one Poly felt needed an education in punk.

Lora Logic: At the end of the day, [Poly] was calling the shots. It was her decision as to whether something went, which included cutting off the first [guitarist]'s hair. In fact, he got asked to leave, 'cause he didn't want . . . enough of his hair cut off.

Thankfully for the impressionable Lora, the two girls shared 'the same taste in clothes – we'd go to Oxfam shops and buy granny shirts and stilettos. I felt a lot in common with her . . . [though] Poly had already been involved in designing clothes.' Lora did not yet know that the singer with 'Identity' issues hadn't really wanted another girl in the band. It was Stuart's instincts that proved sound. He knew the look of the band would be all-important, as would their timing. As such, he held back at the turn of the year, believing X-Ray Spex should stand apart. After a couple of pub-rock venue runthroughs, their Roxy debut came on the night most London punks were at the 'other' Roxy, in Harlesden, awaiting The Clash. Their second Roxy date would result in their vinyl debut, affirming their unique identity.

If the progress of Poly initially took place away from any problematic limelight, another punkette with her unique look already defined was expected to whip her own band into bad shape in double-quick time. Siouxsie Sioux, though, also decided to take her time. As boyfriend and Banshee bassist Steve Severin recalls, 'It was six months between the 100 Club [Festival] and our next gig . . . While we were silent, other members of the crowd were saying, "You're gonna miss your chance." By Christmas, everyone's saying, "You've had it." [But] there wasn't any other way of doing it. We [could]n't get any better, quicker; [and]

we hadn't got any equipment or money.' Finding the right sound was bound to be a hit and miss affair.

Steve Severin: [After] we'd done the first gig, almost immediately Nils [Stevenson] was . . . trying to get us to form a [proper] band. Kenny [Morris] came up to us straight after the set and said he wanted to play drums. He was once the Flowers of Romance drummer . . . [but] I don't think they got past one rehearsal. For about two rehearsals [we had] Simone – the black girl with blonde hair on the Grundy interview – [who] was a classically trained violinist. We were gonna do the Velvets. [But] the first songs we started to write didn't sound anything like the Velvets, and the violin seemed a waste of time. I wrote all the early lyrics . . . I think [Peter Fenton] was the boyfriend of one of Simone's friends, and he was the only person we knew who played guitar.

Steve and Siouxsie planned to assimilate elements of each other's record collections into one cohesive whole. As Severin says, 'The only album we had in common when we met was *Fear* by John Cale. She turned me on to Brass Construction, and I would play her my Can and Captain Beefheart albums. We both liked Bowie, [early] Roxy Music and Bolan.' They were also both convinced that punk was already being hijacked by unintellectual forces. As Siouxsie explained the following year, 'What was happening was lacking in certain aspects – it needed a different point of view, a variant on things, but with the same attack, impact.'

Severin admits that 'as far as attitude . . . [and] how to approach the business, how to approach life in general, it all comes from that [Pistols] explosion', but believes the Banshees' music, as constructed, 'evolved from a time before the Pistols'. As Severin told Banshees biographer Mark Paytress, 'There was a huge diversity of sound among all the [initial] bands. No one sounded like Subway Sect, or Buzzcocks, or even The Clash at that point.' The Banshees saw themselves as a necessary continuation of this ideal.

The Banshees emerged from their self-contained cocoon just in time. After warm-up shows in Croydon and High Wycombe, they appeared at the Roxy with a newly trimmed 'Lord's Prayer', covers of Bolan's '20th Century Boy' and TV theme 'Captain Scarlet', and stark songs all their own, with titles like 'Love In A Void', 'Bad Shape', 'Psychic' and 'Scrapheap'. Though Siouxsie still needed to learn the difference between shouting and singing, their first Roxy set, supporting the

Heartbreakers on 2 March, drew praise from a surprised Giovanni Dadomo, who presumed they would be the band from the Punk Festival minus Sid. Instead he found 'an extremely powerful quartet', displaying 'material show[ing] considerable flair and intelligence' and 'a wealth of potential'. Not everyone shared his enthusiasm.

Siouxsie Sioux: I don't remember many early reviews, but I do remember Glen Matlock being quoted [saying], 'I don't know what it is, but it's not rock & roll.' He thought it was an insult, but for us it was the biggest compliment anyone could have paid us.

What the Banshees did have from day one was the most photogenic punkette in London. However, Siouxsie had one rival for the camera-man's click, and it came from another representative of the class of '76. Penetration, named after the Iggy Pop ditty, were the most northern exponents of the new revolution, and were fronted by another girl singer with jet-black, short-cropped hair and manic stare. Pauline Murray and Penetration manager Peter Lloyd had witnessed the Pistols before they even played their fabled first Free Trade Hall gig, in Scarborough and Northallerton at the end of May 1976. They also came down to London on August Bank Holiday weekend, to catch the wave then breaking over Screen on the Green.

With boyfriend Robert Blamire taking up bass, Pauline recruited guitarist Gary Chaplin on their return. With this much-needed tune-smith on board, they began practising in a Ferryhill church hall two nights a week, making their debut at local rock club, Middlesbrough's Rock Garden, in December 1976, working their way south in the new year. After making it as far as Manchester's Electric Circus, to play support at the unveiling of Shelley's Buzzcocks, they found a scheduled show at the Roxy on 14 March cancelled. It would take them till 9 April to make it back, by which time the club already had a death sentence hanging over it. But for Pauline's Penetration – who already had their own message song, 'Don't Dictate' – interested parties were already lying in wait.

Early punk was an equal-opportunity employer. For all the gratuitous, but arresting, images of scantily clad punkettes in *Sounds* or *NME*, young women were empowered by the music like never before. No longer obliged to play the frail or fatale figurine, punkettes like Siouxsie Sioux self-consciously went all out for maximum impact: 'There's so much gone into what I look and why I look, and part of it is to look threatening-looking, part of it is to be confrontational.' Poly Styrene lacked Siouxsie's classic looks, but was nevertheless an arresting presence on stage, accepted by punks even though, by her own admission, she didn't 'play off sex . . . that's not what [this] act's about. It's about excitement, music, songs and havin' a good time.' Outside the clubs, in the music papers and on the King's Road, young women sensed an unprecedented opportunity.

Jeannette Lee: I've never found a situation where I ever felt like I couldn't do something that I wanted to do. There was a big pack of women friends in the whole punk scene that were all really strong women, and I think we felt slightly invincible, that we could do what we wanted. We probably all did find strength from each other. We were too young to think that there was anything that you couldn't do, and by the time that you realized that you could be restricted, you'd already done that stuff.

Women scribes like Caroline Coon, Vivien Goldman and Jane Suck embraced the movement for cultural reasons as much as for the buzz; even if *NME*'s wicked witch, Julie Burchill, was determined to play party-pooper. For Burchill, seeing The Damned at the Roxy, 'made me feel uncomfortable . . . [and] threatened, and that's what rock & roll needs. It's also . . . why the Damned, Clash, Pistols, et al, won't reach the mainstream of kids.' This was one wicked witch lacking a crystal ball. The echo of walls coming down reached as far as New York, where Cherry Vanilla decided to heed the Heartbreakers' advice, and high-tail it to London, where the new wave awaited her. Roxy's first all-American bill, on 1 March, was mayhem magnified.

Cherry Vanilla: The second date we ever did was the Roxy, and it was just unbelievable because there were people between their legs, pulling on their guitar cords, people pulling on the microphone trying to pull us into the audience – it was such chaos. These kids were so wild. That was the first time I'd ever experienced that – kids didn't do that in America. It was crazy how, magically, the music kept going.

— — —

Of the Roxy's music-makers, the likes of X-Ray Spex, The Adverts, Generation X, Penetration, Wire, The Lurkers and The Jam would all make significant seven-inch statements in '77, setting the tone for further revolutions per minute. With 'In The City', 'One-Chord Wonders', 'Bored Teenagers', 'Oh Bondage Up Yours', '1-2-X-U', 'Shadow', 'Your Generation', 'Don't Dictate' and 'Wild Youth', the disenchantment of youth fully spilled over into song. The last of these suggested some commentators were reaching for the minds of a generation *before* they were destroyed.

Tony James: We were walking down Oxford Street and we were waiting for the number thirty bus to Fulham. We just had a song idea and we wrote it at the bus stop. It's called 'Wild Youth', because Billy had bright red hair then and people would turn round and stare. We find it very difficult to write songs like 'Set The Controls For The Heart Of The Sun' because the bus doesn't go there. [1977]

If 'Wild Youth' was an assertion of identity, it was the last such Gen X statement (already preceded by 'Your Generation' and 'Youth Youth Youth'). Others, though, continued to document the scene in all its narcissistic effervescence. Poly Styrene was particularly in love with issues of identity, often addressing them in the first person, as with 'I Am A Cliché' and 'I Am A Poseur'. The latter found her identifying with those who adopt an 'anti-intellectual pose . . . [which is] an intellectual pose in itself . . . Like anti-art, it's just another art form.' Another first-person narrative, 'Let's Submerge', was about the Roxy itself. As clarion calls go, it was conflicted, depicting the place as 'a bottomless pit / [And] the vinyl vultures are after it.'

Poly's vital vignettes were paralleled by the efforts of The Adverts' songsmith. But for TV, writing 'Bored Teenagers', 'New Church', 'No Time To Be 21' and 'Safety In Numbers' – the cornerstones of the positively conceptual *Crossing The Red Sea*, their debut long-player – was already an act of exasperation. As manager Michael Dempsey stated at the time, 'While everyone else was celebrating how "different" they were, how outrageous, Tim was saying, "So what?"; asking them what they were trying to prove.'

Tim Smith: The idea of people hearing about punk rock and saying, 'How do I become a punk?' and then trying to imitate other so-called punks was absurd. The correct question to ask is, 'How do I express myself?' If you do that right, you're a punk, whether you mean to be or not.

For all of the Roxy's catalytic effect on the punk scene – at a crucial nexus in the narrative – there was always a disturbing side to the bacchanalian basement. As Lora Logic notes, 'It was pretty seedy, and a lot of it was directionless, [and] really brainless . . . There was that ridiculous band, Eater, they were dreadful. There was a few bands like that, and you just thought, "Oh, just get off. Go and do something else."' Such a side was evident from very early on. By the second weekend, Dave Fudger was writing about how the 'audience contain[s] a sadly increasing number of sycophants, poseurs, and violent nutters to whom said band is . . . merely a fashion accessory.'

By its March heyday, many of punk's leading lights were already distancing themselves from the club – and the word. Less than a week after The Damned's third and final benefit show, Brian James was telling *Record Mirror*, 'I hate the word punk. It conjures up visions of safety pins and dumb kids. The definition should be someone who plays on stage and really gets off.' In the same month, Joe Strummer told Coon that 'The Roxy is a dormitory' – which was the ultimate put-down from this ex-boarding school pupil – 'the sooner it closes the better.' Before he could get his wish, the *NME* sent down intrepid gunslingers, Parsons and Burchill, to give the club its last rites. For the 'Fear and Loathing at the Roxy' article, Parsons provided the fear, Burchill the loathing:

Around the bar of this decaying temple [the Roxy] cluster professional malchicks redolent of Isherwood's pre-war Berlin, their egos as delicate as painted eggshells, languidly engaged in conversation while their restless eyes cast around relentlessly for someone still higher on the status ladder of PUNKDOM!

Czekowski's hands-off approach to management let loose a Pandora's box of poseurs. Steve Severin certainly does not nostalgically long for these past times: 'You're going down there and you're seeing Eater and Slaughter & the Dogs, and they're all taking some template that we never thought existed, except probably with the Ramones – which [then] culminates in the [next] generation – which is the end of the line – Sham 69, Cockney Rejects, all that absolute bollocks.' King Pin Johnny Rotten proved equally dissatisfied: 'Walking around and seeing thirty thousand imitations. It shows their low mentality level . . . They're people without minds of their own.' Even Czekowski sensed it was not gonna work out fine.

Andy Czekowski: The kids took up the [idea] of anybody can do this, but the answer, of course, is that not everybody can; [even if] you made your appropriate bit of noise and you had a great lot of fun.

The trawl of the talented by every A&R man in town left a fair few unclaimed. It was not just the truly hopeless they rejected, either. Few understood the difference between the avant-garde and the plain inept. Czekowski recollects regularly 'see[ing] the suits coming down and standing at the back, not making head nor tail [of it], but [thinking], "We Must Have One – we'd best get one of these."' If Polydor's Chris Parry was a regular night-time prowler, it was Shane MacGowan – in the process of forming The Nipple Erectors – who put him on to the band he needed to help nurse his wounds.

Chris Parry: In January '77 I was in A&R at Polydor and I'd already been aborted on trying to sign The Clash and the Pistols. I knew a lot of punk people and one day Shane [MacGowan] . . . [told] me . . . [to] come and see this great band called The Jam. I went to the Marquee and liked them and went backstage to arrange with [manager] John Weller to do some demos straightaway. The first session was actually blown out by an IRA bomb near the studio. We did an eight-track tape at Anemone studios and it convinced me. I went into Polydor and told them, 'You've fucked me around on the Pistols and The Clash – don't do it to me again.' . . . We had a contract ready by the next week . . . I said they should record an album at once, and I told them I thought I could produce it. [1980]

The four-album, £6,000 deal made far less of a splash than The Clash, but The Jam proved to be the better long-term bet. Parry had a sense of what the scene was about – while seeing something in The Jam earlier than most. Another label affiliated to Polydor, Chris Stamp's Track Records, needed someone to show them the way. Having courted the Heartbreakers, they put Nils Stevenson on a retainer – as his 25 January 1977 diary entry says – 'to keep them informed about unsigned groups on the punk scene, pay[ing] for the flat I'm sharing with the Heartbreakers and rehearsals for Siouxsie and the Banshees'. Stevenson, though, was not about to sign the Banshees to Track because he considered co-owner Kit Lambert 'completely out of his head', and he had learnt from McLaren never to take the first deal offered.

Others were a lot less judicious. The Vibrators allowed themselves to be sweet-talked by CBS into another cross-collateralized contract after their singles-only RAK deal dissolved in a dispute about potential A-sides. Generation X allowed themselves to be steered by their new managers, Stewart Joseph and Jonh Ingham. The latter had selected them by 'standing at the Roxy, watching all these bands, going, "Who's the best? The Pistols are out. The Clash are out. So who's the next best?" It was Billy and the boys. I was being quite mercenary about it – who's the band that's gonna make hit records?'

If Ingham wanted a return on the revolution he'd kick-started a year earlier, the roster-less Miles Copeland just caught the smell of Opportunity. He also thought he knew whose views were worth hearing, amid the generally banal banter of Roxy's refugees. Czekowski certainly remembers Copeland 'ear-aching me at the back, going, "What do you think of these? What do you think of that?" I'd be telling him like a fool . . . He could see something was going on, he could see what I was doing, [but] he didn't really have a clue.'

Copeland also seemed to set great store by the opinion of Mark Perry, who responded in kind in the February 1977 issue of *Sniffin' Glue*, by bad-mouthing Copeland's only real rival, Track, accusing them of 'telling everybody that "the punk scene must stay independent". Yeah, well I reckon we should stay *independent*, and forget about record companies that had their glory in the swingin' sixties.' Rock managers who'd lost their shirt when the prog-rock bubble burst, though, were just fine and dandy. For all his fervour, Perry remained the man who had lumped Eddie & the Hot Rods in with the Sex Pistols, and Roogalator in with Subway Sect. When Perry and Copeland formed Step Forward Records, their first three signings were Gene October's Chelsea, The Cortinas and Sham 69. Mile wide of the mark, Mark.

Even Czekowski seemed to forget previous nightmarish experiences in personal management, and tried to snap up his own likely set of lads. He chose a band he'd previously told to go away and practise – after their Roxy debut – only for them to return in mid-March a more minimal music machine, after perhaps the most abrupt transition since Pink Floyd dumped Syd Barrett. Dispensing with their guitarist/songwriter four gigs into their short-term 'art project', Wire were unrecognizable by the time their reconstruction made them ready to change the parameters of punk.

The Wire prototype had been a band called Overload, put together in the spring of 1976 by George Gill and a fellow student at Watford Art School, Colin Newman. The pair co-opted an audio-visual technician at the school, Bruce Gilbert, to play rhythm guitar, and the son of actor Jack Good on bass. Playing an end-of-term party, Newman recalls, 'It was all very Chuck Berry meets J. J. Cale . . . but Bruce was very captivated by us playing this music.' By the time Gill, Newman and Gilbert decided to persevere with their 'experiment', everyone save Mr Good had clearly been exposed to the Ramones. A like-minded bassist was now required.

Graham Lewis: I'd met Bruce Gilbert via Angela Conway, [who was] at Hornsey [Art College]. I was living up at New Barnet and he and I had a few conversations – 'What do you like?' And we kept hitting things that we [both] liked. He was up in Watford with the other guys . . . I was at home fucking about with short-wave radio and double-cassette players and making a noise that I liked. Bruce asked me if I would like to go to a rehearsal . . . [I'd] said that I could play bass. They found I couldn't. [But] I owned one, [and] they weren't very good either. It was George, Bruce and Colin playing through one amp and I was playing through another, and we made a racket for a couple of hours and then we went for a drink. George and Colin were [pretty] abusive. They had serious attitude.

Even at this stage, though, Wire had a rare sense of purpose. As Lewis said in 1978, 'Although no one could play or anything, there was a definite idea that we would succeed. What success was, nobody knew – whether it was to get a record out, or what. To play the first gig was a success . . . [But] it wasn't an excuse for everybody to "pull chicks" or get pissed-up.' Lewis also knew how to lay his hands on recording equipment, and even though, in Newman's words, 'It had got to be a bit like The Velvet Underground – messy and heavy and sneering,' they recorded some early rehearsals. Aside from bringing the velocity of the Ramones to J. J. Cale's 'After Midnight' and Jonathan Richman's 'Roadrunner', their early repertoire contained Ramonesque rehashes like 'Prove Myself' and 'Bitch', a technically deficient rock-out called 'Midnight Train', and just three songs that survived their metamorphosis, 'Mary Is A Dyke', 'TV' and 'Feeling Called Love'.

Through their new bassist, Graham Lewis, Hornsey's social sec., Wire were now made aware of the Sex Pistols, trundling down en masse to the 100 Club Punk Festival, where they became part of the throng. As Newman trenchantly tells one, 'I was definitely into the music, and got what it all was, but didn't have the hairdo, didn't have all the right clothes.' The problem, as he saw it, was that, though everyone in the band 'was into the idea of doing something that came out of punk rock . . . it was actually pretty directionless and frankly not very good.'

It was a view shared by headliners The Derelicts on the December night Wire debuted at the Nashville. They came up to the band at the end of the set, to inform them they were the death of cock-rock. Lewis remembers thinking, '"Too fucking right, we've got a bloody right to be here." At least we were trying to do something that nobody else was doing. We didn't want to make a noise like anybody else, and I didn't really have six years to throw away so that I could play bass like Whoever.'

Matters didn't greatly improve at Wire's second gig, at St Martin's School, thirteen months after the Pistols' debut there. Fittingly, Glen Matlock came along to hear them, at least until the sound guy pulled the plug. The following day, Wire again followed in the original spiky-tops' footsteps, playing the Royal College of Art, booked through another of Graham Lewis's art-school contacts. They were enjoying a rare historical happenstance when ideas could yet triumph over technique; and Wire's technical limitations were no more confining than the Sect, who'd played the RCA a month earlier.

Graham Lewis: What we saw in this situation – which was punk – [was] this opportunity. Anybody could get up and do what they wanted to do and that was what was important – whether they had the bottle – and whether they had the 'neck' to do it. You saw fantastic disasters . . . It was fun. It made you laugh. It was great.

Lewis's circle of contacts also provided the band with its first gig of 1977. One of the girls in the house Lewis shared knew Barry Jones, still caught between the Quick Spurts and club management. A tape of those early Wire rehearsals was duly deposited with Jones, who got the idea, and overlooked obvious technical deficiencies. Wire were booked to support The Jam on the second weekend in January, where they made their first media convert, *Sounds*' Dave Fudger:

Klive [Nice, aka Colin Newman] sez that if I say Wire are punk he'll deny it . . . When I told Klive that I thought Wire were good after their set at the Roxy, he didn't believe me. He was figuring that the occasionally lengthy gaps between numbers . . . had detracted excessively from the heartening carnage of their intense, feed-back-strewn and occasionally discordant performance . . . They're [certainly] noisy, messy and raw, [and] they have a healthy indifference to the audience . . . They [also] had the arrogance as support band to refuse to go on until there was a big enough crowd in the hall. [*Sounds*, 22/1/77]

Fudger even offered to raise the money for a single, on the evidence of just this performance. Club owner Andy Czekowski was less impressed, and told them, 'Come back when you can play a bit better.' The rebuff was probably more to do with the way Gill imperiously demanded another booking rather than any actual deficiencies (after all, five days later Eater *headlined* at the club, while the Zips and the Drones both made their Roxy debuts before the month was out). Gill, though, didn't respond well to rejection; and as Lewis recalls, 'George was very much the dominant factor [early on], because his attitude was incredibly strong . . . and he was the lead guitar player . . . He could face anybody down.' Maybe he was still brooding when he indulged in his next confrontation, the one that would take his band away.

Colin Newman: When it starts to get interesting is when George broke his leg. It was very popular at the time to turn up at people's gigs and heckle them. George was heckling this band in Kilburn and decided he hated them so much, he'd steal their amplifier. He was pissed, and he was making his way down the stairs with one of their amplifiers, and fell down and broke his leg. By that time the rest of the band was mad keen to [continue], so we continued rehearsing, [still] with George's songs, but we took out all his guitar solos, and it suddenly sounded a lot more efficient.

Lewis suggests that they also began to write a different kind of song: 'That's when the whole thing gelled because I'd been writing some [lyrics] – like "Lowdown" and part of "1-2-X-U". We rehearsed those and it just went click.' Even Czekowski was convinced that the band had improved dramatically, presumably after he (or Jones) heard another rehearsal tape with the new songs 'Strange', 'Brazil', '1-2-X-U', 'Lowdown' and 'Three-Girl Rhumba'. The four-piece Wire resumed their relationship with the Roxy. Indeed, its owner offered his services as manager. Unfortunately for Czekowski, Wire had minds of their own.

Andy Czekowski: They were arty farty and I was trying to get them into more of the punk scene. They felt they were beyond all this – [being] creative and adventurous and experimental – and I suppose they were. Our level of understanding was different. I'm more straight ahead: get the show on the road, sell some tickets, make some money, and have some fun, whereas everything we discussed with them was all . . . very heavy – big discussions about life and music – and I thought, 'Hang on, it's just a pop band, get on the stage and play.' . . . When I suggested they should wear zip trousers, [our] levels of understanding went in two directions.

Despite their differences, it would be one of Czekowski's money-making schemes – an album memorializing the Roxy, along the same lines as previous volumes from CBGB's and Max's – that would get Wire a record deal with a major label when they had just two gigs to their four-piece name. Other beneficiaries included X-Ray Spex, who were currently recording a nine-track demo with their manager Falcon Stuart, which prompted Julie Burchill to call them 'a garageland Roxy Music'. Czekowski's slightly grandiose idea for the album was also originally intended to include The Damned, The Jam, Generation X, The Slits, and Siouxsie & the Banshees.

Czekowski found that some of these bands weren't interested in deifying the Neal Street dungeon. According to *NME*'s Phil McNeil, Generation X declined to be documented 'partly because they reckoned the Roxy had become "a horror show" by that time, and the album would "perpetuate a legend which wasn't the truth", and partly because they didn't consider themselves ready to record'.

The Banshees had recorded their own set of five demos – four originals and TV theme 'Captain Scarlet' – at Track, a fortnight before they returned to the Roxy at the end of March, to find a mobile truck parked out back, and a mass of wires leading down to the club. Czekowski had struck a handshake deal with Mike Thorne at EMI, through an off-the-shelf company, Sisterdale. EMI would advance all of the recording costs, without any contracts being signed until the recordings were deemed usable, and the bands proved willing.

Siouxsie and her boys agreed to let themselves be captured on 24-track tape, but wisely reserved the right to reject the results. On the night (26 March), sharing a bill with The Slits, the inexperienced Siouxsie shouted herself hoarse by the third song and barely croaked her way to the end of 'Lord's Prayer'. Slits frontperson Ari Up was, if anything, more prone to hollering, but with The Slits it somehow fit. Nevertheless, nothing from the girls' night survived the cut, so it was left to Thorne to get a usable album from two nights in early April.

Neither bill was entirely promising. Eater, Slaughter & the Dogs and The Adverts were booked for Friday, 1 April; with Buzzcocks, Johnny Moped, Wire, X-Ray Spex and the Unwanted due the following night. The best band on night one – The Adverts – failed to rise to the occasion, only 'Bored Teenagers' sounding semi-decent. As TV Smith recalls, 'Everything went wrong. The bass amp stopped working. We didn't [even] have a tuner. We played terribly. But it doesn't matter – all the bands were in a similar position. It's rough and ready. You just can't believe a record like that would ever get released – it showed the interest in it.'

On the other hand, Slaughter were surprisingly spunky, having figured out how they could get away with being dog-rough. Nonetheless Thorne was a worried man, with just another night's truck hire in the budget. Thankfully for him (and EMI) Czekowski had managed to rustle up perhaps the finest triple bill since Screen on the Green, even if he found the whole experience 'crazy – wheel 'em on, wheel 'em off. We had to do that because we thought we'd be kicked out that week.' *Sounds* sent along their latest scribe, Jon Savage, to pay witness:

Poly buzzes round the stage taking hecklers in her stride (Roxy Test 1 is how the bands deal with exploratory barracking) and forestalling most obvious criticism with her songs . . . She needs an audience and projects . . . most are converted, even Ari from The Slits, who came to pull mike wires. Next are Wire: they short-circuit the audience totally, playing about twenty numbers, most around one minute long . . . Image-wise they look convincingly bug-eyed, flash speed automatons caught in a '64 Mod time-warp, but this is buried in the poor sound and the limitations of the format . . . [Buzzcocks'] image/music mesh is good too – the flat Mancunian accent and laconic dryness fitting the lyrics and the cheap-as-a-siren guitar sound. [*Sounds*, 16/4/77]

This was the one and only time Buzzcocks entertained the Roxy crowd. A 25 January show had been cancelled after Devoto dropped his bombshell, and though they had made it to Harlesden in March, much was expected of these headliners this Saturday night. In fact, there were times when new bassist Garth and guitarist Diggle seemed to be playing entirely different songs. Yet the audience seemed delighted with what they got. The sound problems X-Ray Spex suffered were less self-induced, Lora's lacerating fills being buried by the mix; but at least Poly's voice held firm throughout.

The stand-out performance that night, though, undoubtedly came from the largely unfancied Wire, an unknown quantity to producer Mike Thorne, who was finding that conditions in Covent Garden bore little resemblance to his days at De Lane Lea Studios, engineering for Deep Purple and Peter Green's Fleetwood Mac. Graham Lewis first encountered Thorne backstage when 'this character in . . . a Scott Walker cardigan and long hair and pixie boots [came] up and [said], "Oh hi there, I'm the producer and I was wondering if you guys would like to borrow my tuner." We went, "Fuck off, we've got enough problems, mate." ' Any problems essentially stemmed from that decision made at the end of January, to work up an entirely new set of Newman-Lewis songs.

Colin Newman: Myself and Graham went to see The Damned at the Roxy and we were in the White Lion before the gig and [this friend kept] saying, 'You've got to get rid of George. You're so much more interesting without him.' Graham handed me the words to 'Lowdown' and I went away and wrote [the music]. [So] over the next month I sat in my bedroom in Watford and deconstructed rock music . . . The idea was . . . not to do punk . . . [but something] more reduced. [Wire] wasn't done in all innocence, but it seemed to me that doing another punk band was not a good idea. To do something else that was more like what the Ramones were doing, but to not be surf, to do something more serious, and something more rooted in the British . . . '[anti-]rock' tradition. I loved what the Ramones did to that culture [of] 'you got to pay your dues' . . . But [Wire] is a knowing thing. The first conversation I had with Graham . . . we talked about everything from Free to Spirit to The Move. A lot of it was conceptual . . . It was like, 'We don't give a damn,' [so] how do you get to the next stage? You take more elements away.

Their 25-minute set on 2 April comprised seventeen songs (nine of which would constitute the core of *Pink Flag*, an album Newman describes as 'a series of sketches, deconstructing other tunes'). It began with Lewis standing at the mike, saying, 'Pay attention. This is Commercial,' which turned out to be the title of a thirty-second instrumental. The paying pogoers were perplexed by the whole experience, predicating a general incomprehension that would dog Wire throughout. As Lewis later recalled, 'What we were trying to do [that night] seemed to be even more upsetting, because you couldn't even jump up and down to it for any great length of time – the numbers were so short.'

Newman now suggests 'there was no name for what we were doing'. But for Thorne, Wire answered a punk prayer. He had had the Sex Pistols snatched away from him, and though he was talking with Matlock about a new band, nothing like Wire had come his way in the interim. Within a week he would have them in an EMI studio working on a set of demos. By the time the twelve-track Roxy live album appeared in the shops on 10 June, Wire were EMI artists.

Czekowski's suspicion that the Roxy era was already coming to an end was confirmed just three weekends later; Siouxsie & the Banshees headlined a fond farewell to the real Roxy. Though the place carried on in name, Czekowski was no longer involved, nor was Barry Jones, or DJ Don Letts. By the summer of 1977 it had become a haven for what Severin typecasts as 'Sham 69, Cockney Rejects, [and] all that absolute bollocks'.

Fittingly, three of the acts from that 2 April show would go on to greater things, leading punk's next infantry charge. Meanwhile, the live album that was the club's epitaph would make the charts under its own steam. As an *audio vérité* document it did indeed capture a time and a place; and it is somehow appropriate that the last sound one hears on the album is of someone ripping off one of the EMI microphones, strategically placed around the club to capture the Roxy vibe as it existed in that single season.

3.2
NOT LEAVING HOME
1975 – 77

[CBGB's] was . . . people who were enamoured of rock & roll, and had a certain lineage . . . [But] it happened a lot more slowly than one would think in retrospect.
— Lenny Kaye, to author, 2005

Pere Ubu started as an end. Everything in Cleveland was over by 1975. It all existed between '73 and '75, the Electric Eels, Mirrors, us and others. '75 came along and everything was grinding to a halt . . . nothing was going anywhere and we were all breaking up.   — David Thomas, *Record Collector*, #206

When Television and Rocket from the Tombs shared their 25 July 1975 bill at the Piccadilly Penthouse in Cleveland, both bands were on the verge of meltdown, just as plans for vinyl debuts were nudging towards resolution. In Television's case, sessions in manager Terry Ork's loft had resulted in half a dozen songs, including the seven-minute 'Little Johnny Jewel', which was chosen by Verlaine – much to Richard Lloyd's chagrin – as their first single, split over two sides. Lloyd brooded long enough for the single to appear in specialist stockists, before deciding to quit. Unfortunately, like the 'other' Richard before him, Lloyd discovered, 'I couldn't influence Tom, even by quitting. He's a person with a will that's not amenable to anything from anybody.'

In Rocket from the Tombs' case, the Garland Jeffreys garage-classic 'Wild In The Streets', Laughner's choice, was never recorded. Though the disintegration of the Tombs post-Piccadilly killed that idea, plans for a record to 'commemorate' the band continued on at least two levels. Laughner demoed a number of RFTT leftovers, like 'Amphetamine', 'Muckraker' and 'Life Stinks', with RFTT bassist Craig Bell, while David Thomas decided that he'd like to record 'Thirty Seconds Over Tokyo', and set about assembling a band to achieve this single goal. The initial plan was simple.

David Thomas: We wanted to have the record and hold it in our hands and look at it and play it. I was tired of all these bands just disappearing without trace. That was why all those early records were made – because we wanted to leave something behind before we disappeared, 'cause that was expected at any moment. [1978]

Thomas was still not sure he wanted Laughner in this new band, which he named Pere Ubu after Alfred Jarry's caricature king because – as he told *New York Rocker* at the time – 'It would be an added texture of absolute grotesqueness . . . a darkness over everything'. He was already distancing himself from any punk roots, as he began to conceive of them. By January 1978 he would insist, 'Rocket from the Tombs really have no relationship to Pere Ubu other than the fact that I was in them.' But in the fall of 1975 he was fumbling in the grotesque darkness without Laughner as his guide.

Actually Laughner was in New York, as the new guitarist in Television, a dream offer that quickly turned into a nightmare as Laughner found that Verlaine had very fixed ideas about how he might slot into the set-up. When Richard Lloyd indicated that he was prepared to eat humble pie, if not kiss and make up, Laughner found himself surplus to requirements and on the bus back to Ohio. Back at the Plaza, an art community/apartment block that was home to most of Cleveland's underground, he became part of the proto Ubu, which initially comprised him, Thomas and RFTT soundman Tim Wright (whom Thomas figured would 'be an interesting musician 'cause he had interesting ideas'). Along with Scott Krauss, drummer in a number of Laughner's bands, and Plaza resident/guitarist Tom Herman they soon had a working unit, but one still modelled along traditional rock lines. Then Laughner had an idea.

He had already heard a twenty-minute-long experimental piece by the landlord of the Plaza. Allen Ravenstine had used a primitive synthesizer and a four-track TEAC to construct *Terminal Drive*; his only previous contact with the world of music having been as part of 'this community of people . . . working in the art department at Cleveland State . . . [who] were painters and sculptors . . . We went out to a couple of art galleries and we did things with lighting and me making noises with these boxes, playing a processed flute . . . There was no music per se, it was more in the category of a happening, no drums, no guitars, just oscillators, and a flute.' Laughner asked him to combine the two aesthetics.

The resultant single, issued on Thomas's own label Hearthan the first week in December 1975, was a quantum leap from the Tombs. Even the six-minute 'Thirty Seconds Over Tokyo', which ended up as the B-side, had discordant sonic shadows absent from its former self. There was also an entirely new avenue of exploration that had manifested itself at Ubu's very first rehearsal, 'Heart Of Darkness', which these six serendipitous souls worked up from a bass riff of Tim Wright's. Ubu was clearly destined to be something more than a tribute to RFTT, even though Ravenstine turned his synthesizer over to Viet-Vet Dave Taylor when they began gigging on New Year's Eve 1975. Taylor twiddled away on their next single, recorded in February 1976 as RFTT's best riff, 'Final Solution' now became a missing component from the *Apocalypse Now* soundtrack.

Though Ubu remained locked in the Ohio lowlands, these two singles provided an important diaspora for the aesthetic. Unfortunately, this original Ubu line-up proved no more enduring than RFTT, imploding in May 1976 as Laughner and Thomas again came into conflict over its direction. After a well-received New York debut, as part of Max's Easter Festival, sharing the stage with Suicide and coming out ahead on points, Laughner and Wright wanted to commit the band to a programme that took their full-on aural assault over the plains. Thomas was less keen, and unhappier still with Laughner, who was becoming increasingly unstable as the drugs and drink got their maws firmly in his side. A twelve-song set at The Mistake on 5 May 1976 proved the final dissolution.

David Thomas: I broke the band up because . . . I didn't want to play with Peter any more. It was becoming not worth it. That set the pattern in Pere Ubu which is whenever we want to change, the band breaks up.

It was again poor timing from Cleveland's finest. By the summer of 1976 there was the start of an international distribution network for the kind of records Ubu made; and a local club scene that began to tie together the twin towns of Akron and Cleveland and their respective bands. If The Mistake provided a residency of sorts for spin-offs of Cleveland's proto-punk scene, a club in Akron was about to open that would prove equally open-minded. It was here that an art-project of some four years' standing – the De-evolution Band – crossed the great performance-art/art-rock divide. A December 1976 radio-station rap-sheet, compiled by the band, gave their version of the origins of this species:

The present De-evolution band (DEVO) has been together over four years. The group was formed by two KSU art students in the fall of 1972. It began as a multi-media experiment but developed beyond its original purpose into a style of music that can only be described as DEVOLVED. The group has incorporated the musical and theatrical directions of sixties and seventies recording artists with its own simple minimal electronic sound. Sometimes loved and sometimes hated by newly exposed audiences, DEVO always entertains.

Devo were a band designed from the outset to rub people the wrong way. As co-founder Jerry Casale told *Rolling Stone* in 1981, when their mission statement had gone assuredly awry, 'We never did this to be popular . . . To come in the face of a [popular form] that's based on expendable idols and mythological worship with a group of . . . provincial middle-class guys who didn't have big drug habits . . . long manes of hair and codpieces . . . I [couldn't] really expect that we'd be popular.'

Before the revolution, the early Devo felt themselves stranded 'in an area where art is subjected to ridicule, where anybody who doesn't pursue a factory job is suspect.' They took initial refuge in the art department at Kent State, scene of a notorious riot in 1970. It was here they made their live debut, as Sextet Devo, part of an annual Creative Arts Festival in April 1973. Even at this early stage, Mark Mothersbaugh described in his journal how he walked onstage 'in a doctor's robe with a monkey mask on, [before] standing at an organ playing "Here Comes Peter Cottontail".' A set that included 'Wiggle Worm', 'Beehive Flash' and 'Subhuman Woman' apparently provided a 'virtual orgasm for the IQ-conscious Spud'. For most of the audience, though, Devo playing what Casale later called 'this very precise music, like James Brown turned into a robot, . . . really pissed everybody off!'

Amazingly enough, they got another invite the following year. The performance on 23 April 1974 even got plugged by the university newspaper, with an advance set-list and the promise that 'this year's performance will degenerate in the Governance Chambers (as is altogether fitting). Seats will be at a premium, so get there early. Don't miss "Private Secretary", "I Been Refused", "Subhuman Woman", "The Rope Song", "Pigs Waddle", "Be Stiff", "Androgyny", "O No" and "All Of Us".'

As Devo began to emerge from the primordial goo of performance-art, they began to demo the likes of 'Be Stiff' and 'Subhuman Woman' in their basement, alongside equally left-field *leitmotifs*, like the hit-and-run affair 'Auto-Modown', 'Mongoloid', 'Jocko Homo', 'Bamboo Bimbo', 'Baby Talkin' Bitches' and 'Clockout'. At much the same time as New

York's Suicide were wrestling with the same decision, Devo were making a conscious transition which would enable them to be more at home at a rock gig than a gallery. As Casale later observed, 'If [the music] stays [in the galleries], it soon becomes masturbatory and self-indulgent. Rather we decided to take the music and message to the wider public . . . Everything was repackaged to make the songs more accessible.' The laborious process occupied eighteen months or more, during which they amassed enough material for three or four albums while holding down regular jobs.

Jerry Casale: We were all just . . . waiting for an opening . . . Everybody was doing the best they could to keep from entering the wad, the goo, the muckpile . . . the daily existence of hand to mouth. [1978]

By the end of October 1975 they were required to cross Cleveland's city limits, having landed a potentially auspicious support slot (to jazz-meister Sun Ra) at a Halloween show organized by hip radio station WHK. They were now ready to take their anti-star, anti-hippy, anti-progressive message into the rock arena. If, as Casale subsequently told *Rolling Stone*, 'I was always . . . prepared for a negative response,' he got his wish that night. According to brother Jerry, Devo 'managed to clear the entire auditorium' with their twenty-minute set, which as Charlotte Pressler described it in *CLE*, 'would have been a good gig . . . if they had been beer can collectors'. At the end they debuted 'Jocko Homo', a song that Casale claimed 'was conceived as a thirty-minute song [and] was played very slowly with the aim of trying to see who could take it'. The WHK version only lasted twelve minutes, but it did the trick.

The experience only served to galvanize the Casales and Mothersbaughs, who developed their own game of gatecrashing gigs. As Mark Mothersbaugh told Brendan Mullen, 'We'd lie to clubs and say we were a Top Forty band. It was rare if we got to play through the whole night. It incited people to want to get in fights with us. We'd go, "Here's another song by Foghat, it's called 'Mongoloid'."'

One contemporary band press release gave an annotated set-list that included one song – 'I Been Refused' – 'written by Devo for ZZ Top to perform on ABC-TV's documentary on Howlin' Wolf'; another – 'Change' – that comprised 'a short selection from the Library of Congress' edition of *Songs of the African Madmen*'; and concluded with 'Subhuman Woman' – 'the woman every woman wants to be – the woman every man wants. Mechanical on-off pulse.' They were clearly not concerned about making friends. Hence Jerry Casale's definition of perfection at the time: '[A] hundred thousand hippies beating [the] shit out of each other because the beer cans thrown by the Anti-Devos in the middle of the huge crowd are *not reaching the stage.*'

By the end of 1976, things had started to happen both sides of the Cuyahoga; not just for Devo, but also Youngstown's Dead Boys, and Cleveland's reconstituted scene, which now comprised a reconfigured Pere Ubu, Peter Laughner's own band Friction, Tin Huey, the Styrene Money Band and X-Bank-X (where assorted Mirrors and Eels now resided). For Devo, too, Cleveland initially provided opportunities, as they played regularly at the Eagle Street Saloon, the latest bar run by 'Clockwork Eddie'. The Mistake, the club the Agora hid in its basement, through the spring of 1976 was the weekly province of Pere Ubu and Tin Huey.

Tin Huey had been around since 1973, when they rekindled the embers of an acoustic group devoted to 'early Marc Bolan and smoking hash'. By letting the velveteen Harvey Gold hijack their band, local trio Rags mutated into Tin Huey, and their sets began to sound like some Velvets/Stooges hybrid artificially inseminating the child of Sandy Denny and Henry Cow. As their own online history proclaims:

This was not a band for the faint of heart: In addition to the Bowie, Mott the Hoople, Stooges and Velvets covers, the band was investigating the European crazies like Faust, Can, and Amon Duul, as well as the Canterbury gang, Hatfield and the North, Henry Cow, Gong, Caravan, and writing their own ultra aggressive art-rock in the form of original tunes titled 'Kill All Green Dogs', 'Korean Sunset', and 'You Flaked Cod'.

In fact, as Huey's Michael Maylward told *Sounds'* Pete Silverton in 1978, 'We were just obnoxious . . . fucking loud and obnoxious . . . playing Stooges and Velvet Underground shit.' When they added hornplayer Ralph Carney, they moved away from the kind of territory already staked out by Laughner and Klimek, but were still obliged to play the Viking, just like the rest of Cleveland's dementoid detritus. Until they found a regular, three-nights-a-week gig at JB's, near Devo's alma mater, Kent State, and were adopted by Akron.

As of October 1976, Cleveland had a dedicated underground club of its own, the Pirate's Cove. And shortly afterwards, the *Cleveland Scene* reported that Akron outfit King Cobra had 'found the ultimate solution to the problem of having to play what the bar-owner wants – they bought a bar. The Crypt (in Akron) now belongs to the Cobra boys, and they are reserving the stage of their new acquisition for "bands with original music". The Crypt will feature area "underground" bands such as Pere Ubu, Tin Huey, and The Dead Boys.' On December 10–11 1976 Devo made their Crypt debut. By the following spring they were the Rubber City's favourite rebels.

What was needed now was for some more vinyl to come out of Ohio. By November 1976, Allen Ravenstine had returned to the Ubu fold, albeit an Ubu in which Tom Herman tried to replace Peter Laughner; and Tony Maimone, Tim Wright. As the band resumed gigging activities at the Pirate's Cove (with Laughner's Friction), they found that the word was out. The Hearthan singles and, perhaps more importantly, the inclusion of 'Final Solution' on the widely distributed *Max's Kansas City*, had started a ripple effect that would reach all corners of the English-speaking world.

Rob Younger found 'Final Solution' at White Light in Sydney, and immediately loved it. Liverpool art student Julian Cope found the record at Penny Lane Records and felt 'it sounded like it was from deep in the interior of some continent I needed to visit . . . This was the kind of music that I wanted to play. It was rock & roll underneath, but stripped right down and replaced by a kind of ambience of industrial noise.' Miriam Linna, an inveterate collector stuck in Cleveland, and an early subscriber to LA's proto-punk zine, *Back Door Man*, felt these dudes should hear Ubu. As editor Phast Phreddie recalls, 'She sent us the Pere Ubu singles when they were coming out . . . and it blew our minds – [just the fact that there were] other people out there, [who] had their art on the wall.' It seemed like Ubu might yet accomplish their original mission.

David Thomas: All of a sudden we found ourselves in 1976, [having] only played a handful of gigs, . . . [with] people from the mainstream French rock magazine . . . coming over to interview us. So those were heady times, and it all sparked the idea of a new force, a new wave that was going to revitalize music and establish rock & roll as a serious music form.

By this time, Cleveland's own vinyl solution was being run by Johnny Dromette. Dromette had been introduced to Ubu's music by Laughner, who noticed him going through the progressive section of the record store he worked at, and announced, 'If you like that stuff, I think you'd really like the band I'm in.' By the winter of 1977, Dromette had his own store, Drome Records, and had 'loaned the band money from the store to make their third single. I started doing posters for the Pere Ubu shows, that kind of thing . . . [Then] we hooked up with Geoff Travis's Rough Trade Records before it was even a label, it was [just] a store.' Soon Drome was shipping significant quantities of the third Ubu 45, 'Street Waves', to Ladbroke Grove, London – along with sleeveless copies of the earlier Ubu 45s. As Travis notes, importing singles 'was very easy . . . Not many people were doing it and it was a lot of fun to track down the records you liked . . . I bought loads of those [Ubu singles].'

Convinced that there was a market out there for wacky midwest weirdos, Drome began his own label, Clone Records, on which he stuck out Tin Huey's outlandish debut, a four-track EP as radical in its own way as *Spiral Scratch*. Singles by the likes of Styrene Money Band (the priceless 'Drano In My Veins'), the Bizarros and Rubber City Rebels vied with Tin Huey, each purchased unheard by odd little record shops – previously disconnected – in London, Sydney, Manchester, Liverpool, LA, Minneapolis, Seattle etc. Meanwhile, Thomas decided it would be a fitting gesture to put a Mirrors single out on Hearthan.

Not surprisingly, Devo soon felt that this was something in which they could also participate, and began putting out singles on their own Booji Boy label, starting with their mission statement, 'Jocko Homo' b/w 'Mongoloid', in the summer of 1977. Like Ubu's debut, it came in a wraparound sleeve that obliquely placed its protagonists in O-hi-o. Unlike Ubu, they found themselves adopted by an outfit with altogether better UK distribution than Travis's dub-drenched grotto off Ladbroke Grove.

Stiff Records were interested in signing Devo to one of their usual short-term contracts, even arranging to pick up a pallet of 'Jocko Homo' singles from the band when they made their second trip to New York in July 1977. Nor was it Stiff's first attempt to attract the best of the new American underground. Their seventh single, issued in November 1976, had been the long-awaited vinyl debut of Richard Hell, with his anthem for wild youth, '(I Belong To The) Blank Generation'.

– – –

After leaving Television in March 1975, Hell had formed the Heart-breakers with two ex-New York Dolls, Johnny Thunders and Jerry Nolan. Another 'brave experiment to fuse two incompatible forms', the Heartbreakers recorded their entire nine-song repertoire (including 'Chinese Rocks', 'Blank Generation', 'Love Comes In Spurts' and 'Pirate Love') at a studio in Yonkers in January 1976, hoping they might elicit record-label interest.

However, it was not with the Heartbreakers that Hell put his signature song into the world. By April 1976, as McLaren had prophesied, Hell had decided that 'the music was just too brutish for me. It was clear that it wasn't gonna have any kinda musical ambition except to stomp out.' Rather, the EP featured his own band, the Voidoids. Put together essentially to make just such an EP, the off-kilter quartet caused *Sniffin' Glue* to lament that 'there's too much guitar soloing . . . I wished I'd heard him with Television or the Heartbreakers.'

It had all seemed so promising in the summer of 1975, when the Heartbreakers had found a second guitarist (Walter Lure) and a set-list worthy of their pedigree. CBGB's had also become a buzzword beyond the city boundaries, and bands from near and far were appearing on the Bowery, to try their luck in guitar-town. Not every 'old-timer' was entirely wild about the coverage the scene was getting, or its results. After James Wolcott reviewed CBGB's first Festival of Unrecorded Rock Talent for the *Village Voice*, Verlaine remembered 'how different the audience was. It was obviously a group of people who read the review on their lunchbreak and decided they would go to that club this weekend and check it out.'

In fact, Verlaine draws his own line in the sand, talking of 'two periods – there's like Television, Blondie, Ramones. Then two years later [sic] there was the Talking Heads and umpteen other groups.' Of the 'umpteen other groups' at the festival – which ran from 16 July to 2 August – only the Heads impressed Wolcott as much as Television, having both opened (with the Ramones) and closed (beneath Television) the whole shebang. As Wolcott wrote, 'Love at first sight it isn't. But repeated viewings (precise word) reveal Talking Heads to be one of the most intriguingly off-the-wall bands in New York.'

The Heads had certainly displayed an instinct for 'right place – right time'. Evolving from The Artistics, a band formed by David Byrne at the Rhode Island School of Art and Design, Talking Heads came to New York in stages, Byrne in the fall of 1974, Chris Frantz and girlfriend

Tina Weymouth the following year, as winter turned to spring. By May 1975, the trio was ready to make its CBGB's debut, and within a matter of weeks seemed to be darlings of the Lower East Side. Most of the other bands were less than thrilled.

Tina Weymouth: We were always outside the CBGB's scene. They were very snotty to us there . . . The first time we played there was the second time we'd ever performed and we started getting publicity very quickly. The other bands didn't like it and they were very unfriendly . . . Our crowd was very different to the Ramones' and Television's.

Different crowd, but same old club. One band less appalled by these art students in their midst were the seemingly artless Ramones. After opening the festival in tandem, Tommy Ramone tried to ensure that the Heads were on hand at most local shows: 'Right away we saw that it worked . . . Even though the Ramones played hard and raunchy, conceptually there were a lot of similarities: [especially] the minimalism.'

In both cases, the minimalism sprang from technical deficiencies, but whereas the Ramones pretended to be unaware of the effect they sought, Byrne had adopted the self-conscious intellectualism of Television and Patti Smith, and made contrivance a large part of the act. (He recently described most of the CBGB's scene as 'just a sloppier version of the Stones. The same clothes and the same pose. I thought: Let's see if we can just throw all that out, start from square one.') Reversing away from the classic-rock tradition at high speed, Talking Heads were past it by their second album. Other downtown artists, though, found something fundamentally fake contained in their way of talking.

Alan Vega: It was all studied, the songs were all there, all his moves were plotted, he wasn't performing up there, he was just going through the motions . . . He didn't make any twitchy gestures without something in his head saying, 'Make a twitchy gesture now.' It wasn't for real.

Nobody could accuse Vega of not being for real; too damn real for CBGB's owner Hilly Kristal, who continued to deny him access to the Bowery. As Martin Rev observes, 'That [CBGB's scene] was not an electronic scene. It was a traditional scene as far as instrumentation went.' Thankfully, by the end of 1975 there were other options available to Vega and his sidekick. Their friend Peter Crowley had recently begun booking acts at a transvestite bar on 23rd Street, called Mother's; and bwas soon enticing Suicide, Television, the Heartbreakers and the Ramones to venture uptown for some good old-fashioned New York camp.

By the winter of 1976, Crowley had transferred his booking skills to a revamped Max's Kansas City, no longer the private preserve of Mickey Ruskin, who had been bought out by Tommy Dean. According to Heartbreakers manager Lee Childers, Crowley 'walked in and just said, "Oh my God, this place stinks, [but] I can make you a lot of money . . . Get rid of the stained glass . . . let's do rock & roll here."' If Suicide were not rock & roll, they continued to reference it in songs like 'Rocket USA' and 'Sister Ray Says'. A young Thurston Moore, who caught them at Max's at this time, appositely described them in his zine *Gulcher* as 'heavy metal Kraftwerk on drugs'. For Vega, the upstairs room at Max's afforded paying customers few places to hide.

Wayne County: Alan would jump into the audience like Iggy would, and put the microphone in people's mouths and get people to dance and scare people to death. [This was] a place where people ordered their drinks and sat down at tables and watched the band.

By Easter 1976 Max's was preparing to challenge CBGB's hegemony. Taking a leaf from Kristal, Crowley assembled an Easter Rock Festival lasting twelve nights, signalling the New York debuts of Pere Ubu and a new five-piece Blondie (with Jimmy Destri now added on keyboards), and a fond farewell to the Hell-era Heartbreakers. Max's also got the jump on the Bowery bar by releasing an album of bands identified with the club – even if it contained nothing from Max's itself. Tracks by Suicide, Pere Ubu and Wayne County implied something was happening, even if its remaining cuts suggested they were still fighting a prevailing tide of conformity.

Kristal's response was a double-album of genuinely live recordings from his club's second annual festival of unsigned bands, but atrophy had replaced attitude in the year since Talking Heads took the locals by storm. Though Blondie, Talking Heads and Television remained unsigned, none of them saw Kristal's compilation as a good way to introduce themselves to the record-buying public (even though Kristal had Atlantic distribution). Instead, purchasers got the likes of the Miamis, the Shirts and Tuff Darts, bands who were bemusingly bland emissaries for New York's New Wave.

Like Talking Heads the previous year, the only 'new' band to make any impression at the summer '76 festival were out-of-towners, come to CBGB's to make their mark. The Dead Boys, though, were no rock & roll debutants. They had been itching to play this particular rock & roll club since Peter Laughner first told them about it. Formed in Ohio in October 1975 – as Frankenstein, still thinking glam-trash might here its day – Stiv Bators, Cheetah Chrome and Johnny Madansky here emerged from the wreckage of Rocket from the Tombs. They also felt no shame picking through the carrion for some choice morsels. 'What Love Is', 'Never Gonna Kill Myself Again' (risibly rewritten as 'Caught With The Meat In My Mouth'), 'Down In Flames' and 'Sonic Reducer' all became mainstays of Dead Boys live sets. However, they still needed to draw on The Stooges, Mott the Hoople and Syndicate of Sound before they had a set that could impress jaded New Yorkers.

The Dead Boys' 25 July 1976 CBGB's debut came about because Bators had had the brass balls to ask Joey Ramone if he could get them a gig there, after catching a Ramones show in Youngstown. The look of the Ramones did not suggest any great stylistic change going down, so they arrived downtown as long-haired leather-louts with a swastika stencilled to their drum kit. Not cool. Another rethink was required. After all, there was no point in returning to Akron/Cleveland, which was in the midst of an orgy of experimentation.

Roberta Bayley: [The Dead Boys] weren't really punk rock when they came out of Cleveland. [But] they quickly adapted to what the scene needed – which was their own punk-rock band doing Iggy stuff on stage and throw[ing] themselves around and be[ing] outrageous and bleed[ing].

Never again would The Dead Boys share a stage with Pere Ubu or Tin Huey. However, they did end up playing with Devo at CBGB's, when those Akronites came to town in May 1977. As Casale recalled, 'It was the aliens against the spuds. The Dead Boys attacked us on stage during "Jocko Homo" . . . They took [our music] personally – "If the spud fits, wear it" – And the crowd loved it.' But it was not Akron art-rock that did for The Dead Boys. It was the arrival of The Damned, a month earlier. Going head-to-head with The Dead Boys at CBGB's over a four-day weekend, The Damned in one fell swoop rendered our Ohio trend-chasers redundant.

Because the nine months that separate the second CBGB's festival from this second British invasion proved something of an Indian summer for The Dead Boys and their fellow CBGB's rockers, the Hell-less Heartbreakers (who made their CBGB's debut just two days before the Corpse Lads) and the Ramones, they made little attempt to keep abreast of what was going on across the pond. When scenester Lisa Robinson asked the CBGBers for their thoughts on English punk in November 1976, she found, 'Reactions range from "cute" (Johnny Thunders) to indifference by those who feel they have little in common.'

The bands in the New York nexus continued to feel that the world would come to them in time, and save for the Ramones made little attempt to take their music directly to the heartlands, or its homeland. In part, the set-up was already too comfortable. As Lee Childers told *Melody Maker* at the time, 'At the end of a three-day run, [the Heartbreakers] always make about $2,500 at CBGB's. It's not bad money really . . . We're not starving at all, despite what people think.'

There was also an expectation that the 'surefire' success of the Ramones would open the floodgates. The message was already making its way into the world, thanks to two magazines dedicated to New York punk, both founded at the turn of 1976, *New York Rocker* and *Punk*. Even the initial failure of *The Ramones* – despite Paul Nelson's one-man crusade in *Rolling Stone* – did not dishearten The Dead Boys, or dissuade the one industry-type-with-clout who was still in love with black-leather rock & roll, Seymour Stein of Sire Records.

Stein had already put his money where his wife's mouth was, unfazed by the Ramones' rap-sheet. As fellow impresario Bob Last puts it, Seymour 'recognized that the Ramones had some great songs. All the rest of it didn't get in the way for him. Seymour could out-deviant any New York punk, so he wasn't going to be put off by any of the outward signs.' And, as first-album producer Craig Leon notes, those early albums 'were very inexpensive records by industry standards.'

Nor had the Ramones shot their bolt with their numero uno long-player. In January 1977, still ahead of the crowd, came another fifteen slugs designed to dish out more shock treatment. This time, Joey told *MM*, 'We were going after a heavier, more metallic, record. Naturally, we would have liked the first one to sound like that. But we were short on time and the first was a fast record.' *Leave Home* was co-produced by Tommy Ramone, who still thought 'we were making *Sgt Pepper*'s. That was the mentality . . . I didn't think it was gonna sell millions of copies, but I was making like it could.' He was right first time. *Leave Home* was snapped up by the vinyl-starved English punks, though still not in enough numbers to chart. In America it barely blipped across the *Billboard* oscilloscope before it was gone.

Stein was still staking a lot on the success of this sound Stateside. In January 1977, in a fit of faith, he signed The Dead Boys and Richard Hell & the Voidoids, having also recently secured Talking Heads' treasured signature. They had resisted his importuning throughout 1976, making demos for RCA and listening to CBS and Capitol. But with no other rock-solid offer, they had run out of alternatives. For the Steins, it had been almost a year-long courtship. Island A&R Richard Williams recalls seeing Talking Heads at Max's in the winter of 1976 'and Seymour and Linda Stein were sitting in the front row, so keen to sign them that they knew all the lyrics and were mouthing along to them'.

Of course, the act Stein really wanted was Television, but as Craig Leon observes, 'They were looking for massive money, which Sire didn't have.' Television had options New York's other neophytes simply did not have. After Atlantic passed on them earlier in the year, a set of demos with Blue Oyster Cult's Allen Lanier whetted the appetite of Arista, post-*Horses*. But ever unpredictable, Verlaine signed with Elektra in August 1976, because, he says, 'I had a fix on Elektra . . . The sixties acts they had . . . always seemed to be so individual, like Love and The Doors.'

Television's long-awaited debut album, *Marquee Moon*, appeared in February 1977, to some wildly contrasting reviews, especially in the UK. Whereas Nick Kent realized it was 'a 24-carat inspired and totally individualist creation which calls the shots on all the glib media pigeon-holing that's taken place predating its appearance', the increasingly reactionary *Sniffin' Glue* couldn't 'even [be] bothered to review it, 'cause it's got nothing to do with the "new-wave". I can't be blinded by weird guitar runs or off-beat bass runs, no way.'

Mark P's distaste was perhaps understandable on at least one level: this *was* two different bands, the original band that had demoed 'Friction', 'Prove It', 'Venus De Milo' and 'Marquee Moon' two years earlier with Island's Richard Williams; and the altogether noodlier outfit, whose 'Torn Curtain', 'Guiding Light' and 'Elevation' seemed set in deliberate opposition to their original, earthier, aesthetic. Having set the scene with the edgy 'See No Evil', the sensuous 'Venus De Milo' and a frenetic 'Friction', the album veers off into altogether more ethereal territory, promptly earning Television the cruel moniker of The Grateful Dead of Punk.

But for more adventurous anarchists, the prospect of a Television UK tour in spring 1977 was still devoutly to be wished, especially with Blondie holding up the rear. To date, New York had exported only its most reactionary revolutionaries, the Ramones, the Heartbreakers and Wayne County. When Blondie's Chris Stein arrived in Britain, he penned a postcard to *New York Rocker* explaining just how anxious these Limeys were for the revolution to arrive:

In NYC the Ramones explode in the great American vacuum, they run past every-one. In London everyone chases them and when they explode the blast kills half the audience. The Ramones have been a very heavy catalyst here but it is unfair to say the English groups ape them . . . Style is the key perhaps. The difference between how The Clash, Pistols, etc. (revolutionary, idealistic, romantic) and how Elton, Rod, Jagger, etc. . . . come off, is awesome.

If the New York new wavers had been reluctant to take on Blighty before, the spring of 1977 saw the equivalent of an exodus. The Heartbreakers were already settled in, and hard at work on a debut album. They were joined in May by every other important CBGB's band (save the Voidoids), as Television and Blondie criss-crossed the country in one direction, while the Ramones and Talking Heads zig-zagged the opposite way.

Though ostensibly promoting new albums (save for the Heads), it was punk's seven-inch revolution that now hit overdrive. Blondie's 'Rip Her To Shreds' warranted their UK TV debut, while Talking Heads' 'Love Goes To Building On Fire' suggested a basis for the fuss over the original trio (now augmented by ex-Modern Lover Jerry Harrison). NY Punk's first two Top Thirty 45s, however, were Television's 'Marquee Moon' – issued as a 12" single entire – and the Ramones' first UK single, the non-album track 'Sheena Is A Punk Rocker', also issued on 12" (though a 10" 78 rpm might have made more sense).

'Sheena' was the Ramones' big pitch, a song tailored to the punk-rock phenomenon in the only country where it applied. If it seemed to be poking fun at the phenomenon, Joey Ramone did little to dispel such a notion when describing the song to Caroline Coon in May as 'about a surfing girl who leaves that and comes to New York to hang out and be a punk rocker. The song is a fun-spoof on punk rock. There was a TV series in the Fifties called *Sheena – Queen of the Jungle.*'

Despite the Ramones, and their labelmates the Heads, putting in the miles this time, it was Television who took the plaudits. The UK music press ran their own competition in column-inches, the album stayed in the charts thirteen weeks, and a second single, 'Prove It', nudged its nether regions. But already there were mutterings from the English punk fraternity that the whole thing was too cerebral and detached, with Verlaine and Lloyd playing ten-minute virtuoso duels on 'Little Johnny Jewel', 'Marquee Moon' and a stunning rendition of Dylan's 'Knockin' On Heaven's Door', as the audience sat rapt in their theatre seats. A 'Psychotic Reaction' encore failed to convince many that this had ever been a garageband.

No such accusations came the Ramones' way, as they made gabba-gabba-hey while the English sun blinked. The joint tour was a great success, even if the response still failed to match the one The Clash were receiving on the White Riot tour, another distraction and drain on the coffers that month for any attuned English youth. When the Ramones took advantage of a night off to see The Clash, Buzzcocks etc. in Brighton, they perhaps finally realized what they were up against if they were ever going to turn 'Sheena Is A Punk Rocker' into the first of a battery of hit singles.

— — —

The Ramones' and the Heads' tour was scheduled to end back at the Roundhouse, eleven months after that already-mythic London debut. And this time there were antipodean 'special guests': The Saints. In the seven months since Ingham's review turned their world around, helping secure record deals with EMI (UK) and Sire (US) in quick succession, The Saints had kept their eyes firmly on the UK.

EMI certainly seemed to be gearing up to receive them. Having turned their Australian demos into an album, they immediately booked the band into the studio to cut a follow-up single. 'This Perfect Day' was a perfect follow-up to 'I'm Stranded', retaining the same manic edge but with more building blocks of sound. Meanwhile, a copy of the video of their inflammatory Paddington performance, supporting Birdman, was ferried to London to give a flavour of The Saints live to interested parties.

When the *(I'm) Stranded* album appeared in the shops in March 1977, sandwiched between The Clash and The Damned, Ingham was again on the case, insisting that it 'proves that the group's single WAS NO FLUKE'. The curmudgeonly *Sniffin' Glue*, though, called it the 'most disappointing album of '77. It drones on and on and doesn't even make ya fancy turning it over, let alone playing [it] again.' Nonetheless, the title-track continued to sell extremely well on import; and when the opportunity came to support the Ramones at the Roundhouse, someone at EMI jumped at the idea.

The Saints, though, were again ill-prepared. As Bailey duly told *NME*, 'Almost overnight we were thrown from playing small pubs in Brisbane to supporting the Ramones at the Roundhouse.' Their most important press ally, Ingham, turned up at the Roundhouse to find, 'Bailey and one of the other guys . . . standing outside; and Chris was being almost physically ill, he was so nervous. I'd never seen that in a musician before. He was terrified.' Stage fright and jet lag were not an ideal combination, and just as in Sydney, when the threat of Birdman had loomed large, Bailey over-compensated from the outset. Tony Parsons' *NME* account captured Bailey's attempt at career-suicide:

[The Saints] stumble on stage at London's Roundhouse for their UK debut as openers for the Ramones and Talking Heads exuding all the hallmarks of new Bruces in town; an alienated hyper-sensitivity to the hordes of curious eyes, tempered with a violent self-belief founded on snotty cockiness more than genuine self-confidence . . . The amiably belligerent Bailey . . . takes time out to insult the audience when his guitarist breaks a string. 'Right to work?' he slurs incredulously. 'Who wants to fuckin' work anyway, y'trendy Pommie bastards? Why the fuck should I get me 'air cut, mate? I want the right not to work . . .' [*NME*, 2/7/77]

According to Kuepper, the problems had started even before Bailey started bantering: 'We went into our set and two songs in my amp blew up . . . Bailey got abusive, the audience got abusive. I walked off stage . . . It wasn't one of the greatest debuts.' Seymour Stein, who had signed The Saints Stateside, cannot have been impressed. EMI, though, persevered and in a master stroke of timing, managed to get their next single out, and the band on *Top of The Pops*, the same week that the Sex Pistols made their one and only appearance on the nation's Thursday teatime treat.

With the curious and the converts tuning in *en masse*, The Saints mimed along to 'This Perfect Day', making a deep impact on The Fall's Mark E. Smith who later eulogized about their performance, 'They looked just slightly wrong! They all had these pullovers on, and they were really . . . over the top, and the singer stood at this strange angle. I think he had a pint in his hand . . . That was the great thing about them – there was no way the English could televise them.' In fact, Bailey just looked sullen, with the odd glower thrown in for good measure, while making no attempt to convincingly mime the words. The rest of the band were equally dismissive of the exercise, Kuepper barely bothering to make chord shapes on his guitar.

If this was meant as a stand against the antiseptic nature of the show, it was lost on most. The single dropped from the charts, and The Saints were consigned to the punk-rock club circuit, where a lead singer who looked like a pub bouncer was never going to win over any style-conscious Pommie. Even *Sounds* seemed to turn on The Saints. When their Tony Mitchell caught the band in Plymouth, a fortnight after the *ToTP* fiasco, he decided, 'Chris Bailey must be the sloppiest frontman a band's ever had, shirt tails sticking out beneath brown school blazer and ragged curly hair glistening with sweat. There are no introductions to the songs, no attempts to communicate with the audience.'

The lack of communication worked both ways, and though The Saints stuck around – issuing two more fine albums before EMI cried enough at the end of 1978 – a capacity for alienating even their core constituency rarely failed them. When Mitchell asked Bailey what he thought about English punk, he took the opportunity to describe 'most punks' as 'one-dimensional', and to suggest that what had 'seemed so honest' when he was in Queensland, 'having come over here, I see that it isn't true. [That] it's all showbiz – it's a pose.' The rest of the band seemed equally reluctant to join what Kuepper decries as 'this incredibly fashionable movement . . . Only an arsehole would have associated themselves with that!' So much for not being a sap.

Back in Sydney, Radio Birdman were having no such problem riding punk's tailgate, even though, as Tek says, 'We didn't think we were in the same genre.' Younger also felt that his band had 'been lumped in with this punk thing, because we play[ed] upbeat rock & roll stuff, and jump[ed] about the place, get[ting] kicked out of joints. But we'd been doing that since late '74 and we hadn't really changed.' Yet he still got a rush from hearing (about) everything going on in the UK and US.

Rob Younger: By the time punk actually broke, White Light . . . had all the coolest stuff, run by Mark Taylor, who later [formed] the Lipstick Killers. I had 'Final Solution' and 'Street Waves' . . . [and] *Spiral Scratch*, when it turned up in White Light. I was buying *NME* and *Sounds*, and I'd hear about all these things, and White Light was getting them all in. There actually was a woman [journalist] that came out from England, and I was talking to her in White Light, and when she went back to England, she sent me a copy of the first Damned album.

Tek, too, was hearing all this energy whenever he went over to Younger's place, and sensing that the same thing might yet happen in Oz. The gigs were certainly getting more and more jammed, and the audiences were getting more and more into it.

Deniz Tek: I'd been playing the same type of music . . . since 1972 with TV Jones . . . [But] all of a sudden the doors blew open because of punk and . . . it was like, 'Hey, now we know what it is!' . . . In a six-month period in the middle of 1977 we went from getting 30–40 people to as many people as you could get in a room, to 2,000 people at Paddington Town Hall . . . It was the advent of this new vibe – punk – which really sprang up in several parts of the world at the same time.

This sense that the revolution was at hand prompted Tek to write the song which closed their set at Paddington Town Hall the night they whupped The Saints. He says, '"New Race" came out of a suggestion by our producer on *Radios Appear*, Charles Fisher, who [said], "Why don't you write a teen anthem?"' The sentiment of the song – 'There's gonna be a new race / Kids are gonna start it up' – was not seen by everyone as a punk rewrite of Bowie's 'Starman'. More like 'Tomorrow Belongs To Me'.

It took Australian journalist Toby Creswell to point out that 'New Race' 'wasn't a fascist anthem, but a defiant fist at ennui; at the promoters who pulled plugs on the group, at the unwashed hippies hanging on to the faded image of a promise that was reneged years ago'. (When Sham 69 took almost the same chord progression for 'Borstal Breakout', they got no such grief for depicting juvenile lawbreakers running amok.)

While 'New Race' became the band's first single, Birdman put the finishing touches to their long-awaited debut album, *Radios Appear*. It had been a tortuous process, simply because of the endless hiatuses between sessions. As Rob Younger later said, 'We'd never made a record before. [And] I don't think the engineering is all that crash hot. But it's got a lot to do with the band resisting ideas in the studio . . . We really didn't know what was going on . . . We thought . . . you just go in there and play as hard and as furiously as possible, and somehow that's going to translate into a really exciting record. It doesn't [always] work like that in a studio.'

Well, this time it did. *Radios Appear* – the original Oz artifact – is an acetylene torch of a record. From the hollering homage, 'TV Eye', to the band's own call-to-arms, 'New Race', this was a 38-minute freakout straight from the Funhouse. Released domestically in June 1977, it had nothing like the international effect of *(I'm) Stranded*, but in the land of Oz, it heralded the shape of things to come. When Australian rock critics voted for the Top Hundred Australian Rock Albums in a 1990 issue of *The Edge*, *Radios Appear* was fourth, 'placed . . . head and shoulders above punk's blaze . . . a record of mighty connections' (*Stranded* came in at no. 33).

Despite which, the press release for follow-up 45, 'Aloha Steve and Dano', got it spot-on when it described Birdman as 'an obscure international rock & roll unit currently committed to energy transfer through a kind of TOTAL music. Knowledge of this special kind of music is possible only through direct experience, and not from printed description.' Throughout 1977 that direct experience was denied to anyone not antipodean – unless, of course, they found themselves around Sydney, looking to kick out the jams.

As it happens, Mr Sire himself, Seymour Stein, had come to town in the spring of 1977, to finalize a deal with The Saints. Not surprisingly, he heard about Birdman (as Danny Fields had gone to Detroit in 1968 to see the MC5; and ended up signing The Stooges too). According to Younger, Stein 'came and saw us play at the Funhouse, and he was dancing on the bloody table; he really liked the band'.

Stein was soon talking about Birdman doing a UK tour with the Ramones, and putting out *Radios Appear* internationally. Before that could happen, Birdman decided they wanted to tinker with the album as released domestically, and play one last stand at Paddington Town Hall, on 12 December 1977. This time the place was jammed. With no party-poopers from the outback, Birdman tore the place apart with their sonic assault, and the kids tore the place apart, period.* Though the band rarely played better, it seemed that they were leaving just in time,

---

* On the audio tape, Younger can be heard berating some 'chicken shit' in the audience to, 'Come up here – I'll take you, man,' for throwing a beer can at the stage prior to 'Search And Destroy'.

as the new race began to not so much punch the air in solidarity as punch walls in anger.

Deniz Tek: I remember a lot of things being thrown at the stage – I myself got hit on the head with a beer can . . . Rob . . . started fighting with [this] guy [who spat at him] . . . [which had] both a calming effect and an increasing energy effect on you . . . We waited until everybody was gone before we left – we walked into the hall and saw all the damage . . . We walked down the stairs and there was like handprints in blood on the side of the stairs, and all down the stairs was just smeared blood. I remember being thankful that we weren't going to be playing any more of these gigs – for all the highness of it, and the energy of it.

It was time to get out of Dodge. Birdman knew Oz could no longer contain them, or their 'total music'. Though they were given the option of taking on New York's no wave first, they declined. They were as anxious to assault the mother country as those bruisers from Brisbane had been. Tek, though, took time out to convey the tapes of their Sydney swansong to Seymour Stein in LA, to see if he agreed that it captured the 'direct experience' of Birdman live. His reaction suggested a convert in their corner.

Deniz Tek: I played [Stein] . . . a tape of our Paddington Town Hall concert, which was recorded on a sixteen-track mobile truck parked outside . . . and he started going into a frenzy, calling up record distributors all over the country, and holding the phone up to this boom box.

To me, where punk completely lost it – and it happened very, very quickly – was when it became this kinda [thing], 'Anyone can do it.' Well, not anyone can do it . . . It takes a certain amount of ingenuity to turn out a really good three-chord song.
— Nick Kent to author, 2005

If I say I hate so and so, it's cos I know I hate so and so . . . But these cunts think, 'Ah, an obvious case of socio-bollocko fuckism caused by a disillusioned shit.'
— Jimmy Pursey, *Sniffin' Glue*, #12

If the English punk aesthetic was first transmitted by the Pistols traipsing through the land in 1976, culminating in the abortive Anarchy tour, the vacuum their withdrawal from the live scene created in the first half of 1977 was one The Clash were anxious to fill. But they still couldn't find a fourth soul-mate to fill Terry Chimes' shoes. By the end of the album sessions★, he definitely wanted *out*. As he told Marcus Gray, 'I always thought it was a mistake to overemphasize the politics, because implicit in that were things like, "We don't want to become pop stars, we don't want to make a lot of money." And I said, "Well, we *are* attempting to become famous and sell lots of records."' It was a contradiction it was already too late to resolve.

Chimes' replacement, Jon Moss, lasted less than a fortnight, before phoning up a bemused Bernie to give notice and a piece of his mind, 'I don't believe all this political shit and I don't believe you believe it.' Things were getting desperate. Even Strummer's old friend, Richard Dudanski, was considered as a replacement.

Richard Dudanski: Just before the gig up in Harlesden, [Joe] kinda said, 'We haven't got a drummer yet.' But he didn't actually say to me, 'Will you come and be the drummer?' [Anyway,] I didn't like a lot of the things he'd spoken [about] the 101ers.

The Harlesden gig on 11 March was crucial if The Clash were to maintain the momentum accrued despite self-induced setbacks. Dis-

---

★ The sessions for The Clash appear to have taken just three weekends, and the album was delivered to CBS on 3 March; the day the Pistols recorded 'Pretty Vacant' and 'God Save The Queen' at Wessex Studios.

counting the low-key New Year gig, they hadn't played the capital in over four months. With 'White Riot' due to be released the following week, it was time to stake a claim to some kinda seniority. Yet again, Chimes filled the void, but for the last time. Though he'd long suspected the cloth Rhodes had cut the band from was never going to last, even he was slightly surprised how quickly it came apart at the seams. It was as much a surprise for one of the key codifiers, there that night as a spectator.

Howard Devoto: Negative drive was always what I believe the punk ethic was about. Or should have been about; constant change, avoidance of stale conceits, doing the unacceptable. I remember seeing . . . the Buzzcocks and co. at Harlesden in '77 – and being disgusted by the sameness of it all. That sparked . . . 'Shot By Both Sides'. [1979]

Mark Perry was equally despairing. In the early stages of forming his own band – Alternative TV – he already seemed to be reaching for the escape hatch as he lambasted the Clash audience in *Sniffin' Glue* no. 8: 'I'm really fed up with the punters on the "scene" at the moment. At the Clash gig in Harlesden there were lots of stupid kids who kept on acting childish by pogoing in front of the stage. They were going completely over the top by punching and kicking each other. It was like being at a fuckin' football match . . . I may be talking like an old cunt but perhaps I think to[o] much these days.'

The following week, 'White Riot' exploded across the airwaves in all its splenetic fury. The message Strummer was attempting to apply, one of anti-violence ('a riot of my own', y'see) – or so he claimed – was lost in the garbled football chant that passed for his vocal (even Coon's rave review noted that 'the lyrics between verses[!] are largely unintelligible'). It also contradicted statements other band members made, glorifying the threat but shirking the consequences.

Paul Simonon: What we're doing is similar to the hippies in the way that we're . . . protesting against certain things. But the way they done it was different – non-violent: peace and love and all that stuff. Whereas it's not peace and love now; it's . . . hate and war. It's more of an aggressive thing now. We're not saying, 'Flowers, man.' We're . . . pointing out the situation as it really is. [1978]

Even less confrontational members of The Clash adopted this 'tough boys' stance. Linder Sterling remembers Mick Jones, at the Electric

Circus the previous December, 'saying, "You got to be really tough. You got to really watch yourself." And I thought, "I live in Salford. I'm in danger of losing my life every day in my bondage trousers. I don't need to be told [this]." But they were being very macho.'

For now, The Clash certainly had no shortage of apologists in the media. Caroline Coon, who perhaps should have handed in her NUJ card the day she moved in with Simonon, later told journalist Nina Antonia that it was depressing 'to see how the theatre of aggression – which I understood it to be to begin with – got mistaken to be actual aggression. When it's in a group of people who know the rules quite well, it was kind of implicit that the aggression was theatre. That it was pose.' Cultural naiveté, which is the least the Rhodes-era Clash can be accused of, evidently also infected their immediate circle of supporters. Or some of them, anyway.

Rob Symmons: I wasn't a massive Clash fan, to tell you the truth. Before we went on tour with them, I liked them. [But] when we were on tour with Bernie, I saw all sorts of contradictions coming through. The Clash were really out to be big stars . . . They would do interviews with someone like Tony Parsons and then put on a working-class accent – aw roight – it was all fake. [And] I was anti all of that smoking [weed and] drinking . . . and they did all that. I couldn't believe it when they [then] said they were against all drugs and old rock stars.

Tony Parsons readily admits that his famous *NME* piece on The Clash, in the 2 April 1977 issue, 'wasn't objective journalism. It was very much a collaborative piece. They did it with me. I felt very much a part of it all, emotionally.' For he had not so much suspended his critical faculties, as garrotted them. Back then, Parsons was fiercely working class, and both he and 'his' magazine – Neil Spencer excepted – were looking to champion The Clash, having missed out on the Pistols. Like all such marriages of convenience, the divorce would be messy, and the recriminations – notably Nick Kent's scathing review of *Sandinista* – prolonged.

If Parsons simply didn't know, or care to see, the contradictions, others were more worldly wise; but chose to maintain the Clash code of complicity in order to keep those invites coming. Kris Needs was the solitary punk at *ZigZag*, which was still providing monthly manna for hippy musos. Having found The Clash on the Aylesbury–Damascus road, he saw something of himself in Strummer.

Kris Needs: Imagine all the demons raging around in Joe when he was . . . with Mick from his tower block and Paul from Brixton, and Joe comes along as a public schoolboy, age twenty-four. That's why he went so mad and that's why he was so forceful with this Bernie Rhodes indoctrination. That's why he had to wear that shirt with 'Chuck Berry is dead' on it – never mind all the guitar riffs he was stealing [from the man]. Joe was very good at feet first.

Even in these combustible times, there *were* journalists who didn't buy into the Clash spiel, in some cases with information which contradicted a lot of what they heard. Pete Silverton called Strummer to account in his (as-it-happens rhapsodic) review of their debut long-player, pointing out how 'in their interviews, they give the impression that they're poor white trash, straight out of the tower block on to the dole queue. In Joe Strummer's case, at least, nothing could be further from the truth.' But then Silverton was already Persona Non Grata at Rehearsal Rehearsal's. And when Simon Frith, a *Melody Maker* columnist with pretensions of his own, set out to discover what made them tick, he became another entry in Rhodes' black book.

Simon Frith: I felt like a prison visitor, tolerated as a diversion but not much relevant to the boys' real concerns . . . 'Look,' said Bernie, 'what are you doing this for? What do you really know about us? What do you care for?' . . . I asked why punk would be any more effective than any other rock form and they didn't really seem to think it would be . . . [So] why sign up? 'We want our records to get a number one in the charts. We want them on jukeboxes. We want to pave the way for more groups.' . . . In fact, The Clash [proved] as romantic about their audiences as any old hippie, and as confusedly prejudiced about the processes of getting to it. [1978]

Mick Jones was perhaps entitled to tell a journalist (*NME*'s Miles this time) 'of the boredom of living in the council high-rise blocks; of living at home with parents [sic]; of the dole queues and the mind-destroying jobs offered to unemployed school-leavers.' Even though his closest friend, Tony James, found himself on the receiving end of a Clash-induced backlash.

Tony James: [Gen X] got incredibly bad press, because we were well spoken, middle class; and punk was seen as working class – we were always outside of that thing. The first Tony Parsons article in *NME* was [along the lines of] clean punks can't make it. It was a hideous, vitriolic article. I remember reading it at the Westbourne Grove newsagent and thinking everyone was pointing at me going, 'Look! clean punk.'

In fact, Generation X were also flirting with fire. Their own vinyl debut, 'Your Generation', issued in late August, was shameless in suggesting that 'the end must justify the means'. They just didn't look the part of revolutionaries – and The Clash did. In the latter's case, the style had real sonic substance, and the evidence came with their eponymous statement – issued on 8 April 1977 – codifying The Clash in amber perpetuity.

The Clash had been recorded in just six days at what Strummer would later typify as 'the cheapest studio [possible]. I got the feeling they were going to spend the price of an egg sandwich on us.' In fact, it was in CBS's interest to encourage them to run up any and all recoupable costs. It was The Clash who wanted everything to be as lo-tech as possible. Such was their distrust of the process itself that engineer Simon Humphrey found them 'hostile to anything that had been employed as a technique pre-punk. So, if there was like a harmony part, or a double-tracked guitar, or even dropping in . . . they'd think you were trying to polish them up, or break down the whole punk ethic.' Strummer also showed his inexperience (and zealotry), by trying to nail his vocal on each and every take.

Simon Humphrey: [Joe] didn't see a vocal take as being something you worked up to. He just gave it 100% from the word go. Which is why you more or less had to get it first take, 'cause that's the only one you were going to get.

Some years later, Strummer told *Record* magazine he was always 'looking for the ultimate wipe-out, for the ultimate feeling of every song. [But] it isn't something you can just do; you have to work yourself up to some elusive pitch.' If he hit that 'elusive pitch' throughout most of the first-album sessions, it was a strain not just on his vocals, but on his temper. And it was Rhodes who bore the brunt, on those occasions when he turned up to give the troops a rallying address. At the very moment when his disciples were defining everything he'd planted in their minds, Bernie was becoming surplus to requirements.

Simon Humphrey: If [Bernie] was there for more than about half an hour, either Mick or Joe would get fed up with him . . . and they'd just tell him to piss off.

Because he did used to just waffle on. He was doing that big punk manager thing of trying to stoke up an attitude, and he would say all these silly things about anarchy and blah blah blah.

Rhodes' one contribution to the process ensured that the album, and its preview single, stopped just short of crossing into any truly mainstream constituency. He had long ago got it into his head that if one 'important' band refused to appear on *Top of The Pops*, it could snowball into a general boycott, much as America's folksingers success-fully boycotted national TV show *Hootenanny* in the early sixties after ABC blacklisted Pete Seeger. He explained his reasoning some years later to *NME*.

Bernie Rhodes: The idea of [not] doing *Top of The Pops* was that if everyone stopped doing it, we'd have to have a new TV show . . . What I'm saying is – and this is the problem all over with pop – if these fellows [were to] take a united stand to gain the means of production, their statements will be effective, and not peripheral. [1980]

Unfortunately, such a notion presupposed that every other punk band shared Rhodes' ideals. And – surprise, surprise – not one other band bought his hook, let alone the line and sinker. Strummer sarcastically recalled the consequence of The Clash's self-induced boycott in a post-Rhodes press release:

The [first] LP shocked the group by entering the chart at No. 12. But luckily their singles, with a guaranteed lack of airplay, could not get past No. 28. So thus they were saved from Bay City Rollerdom on any scale, and just to make sure, they refused to appear on *Top of The Pops*, which they considered an old pop TV show left over from the sixties, which requires performers to mime along as their record is played at a low volume somewhere in the distance.

Thankfully, album sales were less beholden to the BBC than to IPC (publishers of the *NME*). As such, few at their label saw the album's chart success coming. As Simon Humphrey states, in *Last Gang in Town*, 'It was beyond [CBS]'s understanding that they could release an album and people would simply go out and buy it because they knew about the band.' But know about The Clash the young punk did. And if the didn't know before the band's first completed national tour – due to begin on May Day 1977 – Rhodes was determined they would hear the call shortly thereafter.

Coon's first *MM* 'press release' for the tour suggested that 'one of their avowed intents was to help young bands who, like themselves, had to struggle for rehearsal space and places to play. [They are] now actually putting this idealism into practice.' But Rhodes' idealism was little more than a reheated version of McLaren's. The White Riot tour was the Anarchy tour recast, featuring four or five punk-minded acts. Like McLaren, he needed at least one act with tour-support; and, initially at least, it was the not-so-punk outfit Polydor had signed after losing out on The Clash. The Jam already had their incendiary 'In The City' 45 in the can, and as a live act they could more than hold their own with the headliners. But needs must.

Of the other acts, The Slits and Subway Sect were already part of the Rehearsal Rehearsal's roster, while Buzzcocks were a useful addition, with an acclaimed EP to their name, and a punk pedigree second to one. Of course, as Richard Boon points out, 'We were getting £50 a night, and we were in a tiny little van sitting on the amps in the back, and staying in B&Bs.' The Jam not only had label tour-support, but provided a necessary counterbalance to the three other support bands, who had all had a lean year gig-wise, and were still finding out how to say it loud.

Unfortunately, The Jam had already committed the cardinal sin in Rhodes' book by distancing themselves from the Clash collective, Paul Weller having told *Sounds* back in March, 'We're not into politics and stuff like The Clash and Generation X. We're on the verge of the punk scene but we're also attracting people who are into the sixties.' The same month he had informed a previously hostile *Sniffin' Glue* that 'a lot of the bands about now have got an image of what a punk band should be – going on stage and singing about how bored you are . . . [with] a sort of blank look – it's absolute shit!'

If The Jam lasted slightly longer than The Damned on the Anarchy tour, when Weller gave an interview on the road suggesting he had no faith in socialist solutions, conflict was inevitable (an embittered Weller informed *NME* he was considering voting Conservative in the next general election, a quote that has periodically come back to haunt him). When Rhodes expected The Jam to help subsidize the other bands, they baulked, then walked – amid 'lots of accusations of sound-tampering', according to one Buzzcock. The bad blood endured even after their departure, with The Clash sending the trio a telegram after Tory by-election victories later that month, 'Congratulations on victory on Merseyside and Manchester. Maggie will be proud of you. See you in South Africa for gun practice. The Clash.'

But The Jam were still on board at the Rainbow show, eight days in, which was March's Harlesden gig rewrit large★. It convinced Weller that, without progressive thought, punk was heading ninety miles an hour down a dead-end street. This time Brian James despaired at what he saw: 'The place was full and there's all these people dressed up like people in The Clash. And I remember thinking, "That's it. It's not ours any more. It's gone now. You ain't gonna see nothing more happening. The scene's done now. It's just a regular rock & roll gig."' No less caustic was *NME*'s Neil Spencer, who saw a co-dependency between the destruction evident in the stalls and the anger spewing from the stage:

The prevailing impression is of a deserted, barren landscape patrolled by a bunch of dangerous, half-controlled rock & roll guerillas. That it's a threatening, desperate landscape is an impression enforced by the sheer ferocity, noise and primal aggression of The Clash's music. For the most part it's [also] music without subtlety, or compromise . . . The new wave has helped wash away the accumulated dross left by the ebb of the sixties tide, but in the long run it might just be washing up some more evil pollutant.

The damage to the venue precluded any triumphant London return at the end of the tour, which was probably a good thing given that – even without another London blitz – the tour was not without its casualties. For The Clash, the reaction each night served as a vindication. Indeed, Richard Boon is convinced that 'during the White Riot tour [The Clash] became a great rock & roll band.' If so, it was because they had finally recruited a drummer who knew when to let the pressure drop, and when to top it up. 'Topper' Headon came from a long list of ex-London SS auditionees. Jones had already asked Headon to audition for this lot but it was only when he saw them on the front cover of *NME* that he thought, 'I'll have some of that.' So much for commitment to the cause.

★ The Rainbow show was on May 9, the tour having begun in Guildford, eight days earlier. The Jam left the tour the following week.

Determined to rev the set up to a Ramones-like rpm, The Clash just grew ever more frenetic. As Pete Silverton wrote in a *Trouser Press* retrospective, 'The set started out at 45 minutes. By the end of the tour it was down to 29 minutes and that included all the album plus "1977", "Capital Radio" . . . their truly awful version of . . . "Pressure Drop" and "London's Burning" twice. It gave their roadies something to boast about, but if you wanted to keep up with it, you had to snort at least two grams of amphetamine.' As the sets became a blur of sound and vision, it became more a test of stamina than a set of songs. While Coon describes the tour as 'heart and soul, flesh and blood, total commitment', Jones suggests the toll it took: 'It was really killing me. And [as for] Joe . . . his *fingers* were wore down. We put that much into it.'

The combination of adrenalin and amphetamine kept everyone in the band from imploding before they ignited the flame each and every evening. Every other act, though, especially after Buzzcocks were replaced by the Prefects, seemed to be dancing around rock's charred effigy. Most shows, the Rainbow excepted, began with the one-two combination, Subway Sect and The Slits, which seemed almost designed to disorient. The Sect suspected they weren't quite ready for this.

Rob Symmons: When we first started to play we were absolutely terrible. [We] asked to be taken off the tour. I didn't know you had to tune a guitar. I just turned it till it was tight. The first time we played, it . . . was noise. People would sit in the audience with their fingers in their ears . . . We said [to The Clash], 'We're not a proper group, like you want. We can't do it.' They said, 'No, no, carry on doing it.' . . . Joe and Mick would come onstage, lend me their guitar and tune it up.

The press seemed to share some of the Sect's insecurities. Nick Kent, in his review of Harlesden, struggled to comprehend how any band could have 'such planned obsolescence, so resolute a "blankness" of attitude . . . such crappy instruments . . . and such a determined inability to finger even the most mundane chord shapes imaginable.' Giovanni Dadomo's *Sounds* tour-feature described them as looking 'like displaced schoolboys in third generation hand-me-downs', but with a sound that had 'shades of other, more familiar [New Wave] bands.'

Looking back, it is hard to comprehend what Dadomo thought he heard. Limitations accepted, the Sect were pursuing entirely their own path. As Symmons says, 'We didn't want to be a part of that other thing.

Vic used to get people at the Roxy calling up, saying, "Come and play here." He would always say no. We were fairly insular. We were anti-rock & roll. We really thought the Pistols destroyed rock & roll. That's what I really believed . . . I thought that was the end of rock. I thought playing it wrong was all part of [punk] – playing discordant music.'

For all their deliberate discordancy, the Sect struck a chord with some folk 'who loved all that – just making a noise'. The Pop Group's Mark Stewart was one, having caught them at Harlesden and loved it: 'For some reason the Subway Sect really hit a chord with me. They were wearing grey clothes, [had a] really strong wall of sound and [I loved] their nonchalance. When you are a kid you notice how people stand, and how people carry themselves.' Julian Cope, still waiting for a teardrop, caught the tour at Eric's, punk's answer to the Cavern, and was enthralled, as he wrote in his autobiography:

In plain black shirts and casual black pants, the four members of Subway Sect ambled, sheepishly, onto the stage. The drummer had a tiny kit with one floor tom-tom. The guitarist had a Fender Jaguar and a plain yellow armband. The bass player was totally anonymous and the singer stood with his back to the audience eating a sandwich. Drums and bass started together, a slow-midtempo beat: Boom-bum-bum-bum, Boom-bum-bum-bum, Boom-bum-bum-bum . . . Then a single tiny guitar note: Bow, bow, bow, bow, bow . . . For at least a minute, the riff held steady, then the lead singer carelessly turned half round, the mike in his left hand. With his right hand in the air, he crushed the remains of the sandwich into the ceiling and began to intone into the mike. It was almost puritanical. I had no idea what he was singing about, but it felt as though he'd been into the future and was telling us about it.

Sect's singer was certainly starting to develop a unique style. His stage presence greatly impressed Wire's Colin Newman, who felt he 'was coming from somewhere else, [with] the on-stage conference[s and] the air of general vagueness'. Richard Boon remembers one show on the White Riot tour 'where he had his song lyrics in a notebook, and after every song he'd pull the page off, and tear it up.' Even the band had to admit, they were getting better. So did *Sniffin' Glue*, who asked tongue-in-cheek, 'Whatever happened to the Subway Sect? They used to get up on stage and be themselves. Now they're rehearsing like an established band.'

No one could ever accuse the Sect's partners-in-chaos – The Slits – of not 'get[ting] up onstage and be[ing] themselves'. If, as Symmons suggests, 'they had the same idea of changing music,' The Slits were coming at it from a somewhat less cerebral angle. For co-founder Palm Olive, 'The Slits was more of a statement than a musical [combo]. Yes, we wanted to experiment with music, but it was almost like a little kid drawing. You can see it for what it is. [At the outset,] we were not talented. A lot of it was very, very rough.' That was certainly Nick Kent's memory of these early shows:

The sound would often degenerate into virtual aural torture with guitars wildly out of tune and lead singer Arianna howling and yowling in a style that could be labelled merely puerile were it not so unbearable to behold. [*NME*, 7/10/78]

People really did not know what to make of The Slits, as they travelled from town to town. Certainly, their callowness did not make them any less temperamental, or provocative. Caroline Coon, who was also along for the ride, described the band as deporting 'themselves like lofty viragos storming through life with the lusty abandon of stage hands at the Folies Bergères. Their earthy arrogance and striking mode of attire – an organized mess of dressed-up undress – causes adults to behave with alarming intolerance.' Actually, The Slits 'at their least provocative' were still pretty damn provocative. One of their numerous managers has no doubts what it was that pushed people's buttons.

Don Letts: The Slits were wild, wilder than any girl group I've ever seen in my entire life – wilder than men group[s]. Ari [once] pissed on the stage. We'd walk in the hotel and I'd say, 'Ari, please just be cool,' and I'd be signing in at the desk and Ari would go [gob on the floor]. One day we stayed at a hotel, and in the morning we got a bill for a missing door.

Palm Olive well remembers 'the hassles in the hotels. They wanted to throw us out. We were always the flies in the ointment. We were definitely more provocative than [The Clash] were. And just the fact that we were girls would irk them even more.' There was something rather impressive about the brazen way they carried on, and the fact that Paloma and her girls 'were not intimidated [by] the other bands. We were just there to do our thing – we never wanted to be labelled. There were all these feminist groups who wanted to use us, and we never wanted to go along with that.' So when they did have a fight on stage – as Paloma and Ari did at the Screen on the Green in April – 'People thought we were putting on a show. But it was a real fight.'

Nor did audiences intimidate them. As Jane Suck later wrote, 'The Slits will invite, in their own inimitable way, members of the audience to share the glories of the limelight with them – "Come on, you cunts! Come up 'ere and say that!" – [but] the vicarious experience will last perhaps five seconds before Miss Ari "Von Bring-It" Up directs a forefinger into the solar plexus and shoves the bleeder off *her* stage in mid "I Hate Slits!"'

The Slits and the Sect may have needed a tour like this if they were ever going to be more than just 'a statement'; but what the fans probably didn't need was for the support bill to become entirely 'young bands . . . struggl[ing] for rehearsal space and places to play'. Kicking out The Jam gave The Slits and the Sect more of what was still a four-act bill. But when Buzzcocks also took a sabbatical halfway through the tour – as bassist Garth went off the rails, and through a plate-glass window (courtesy of some bouncers he had verbally abused) – The Clash needed someone to make up a full night's entertainment. After all, they were never onstage for more than forty fiery minutes.

As it happens, Birmingham's answer to the Sect, the Prefects, were there to see Garth's meltdown in Leicester, having turned up simply to see the show. As Robert Lloyd recalls, 'We all liked The Slits and the Subway Sect, though we'd gone off The Clash by then.' The Prefects had already played the most prestigious gig on the tour, at the Rainbow, after The Slits had apparently said, 'We're not playing that seated theatre, it's not punk rock.' The Birmingham-based promoters called up the only punk band they knew who would play at no notice, for no money. This was also doubtless a factor in the snap decision made to ask the Prefects to cover for the band Lloyd had once offered to join. The Prefects, though, were already disenchanted with the 'movement', having had much the same epiphany as Brian James at the Rainbow.

Robert Lloyd: From the Prefects' point of view, we were very fortunate playing with The Clash at the Rainbow Theatre, and it being only our fifth-ever gig [because] we were young and . . . naive, and we thought there was some sort of punk movement that we were part of. But . . . seeing [The Clash] in action from close quarters, and the way we were treated that night, we managed to get really disillusioned, really early on. We could have gone on for another year or so as stupid, naive teenagers but [we had] that disillusionment before we wasted any more time; and once that set in, we were into the humorous, piss-takin' kind of thing.

Their 'humorous, piss-takin' kind of thing' included a seven-second song called 'VD' that impressed John Peel greatly. Whether Rhodes realized it or not, his precious tour had been hijacked by a trio of bands who shared none of The Clash's objectives, all of whom had taken the *Sideburns* strategy to heart – learn three chords, form a band. If the Sect kept their disquiet about The Clash to themselves, and certain Slits still had the headliners by the balls, the Prefects unwisely made that 'piss-takin' kind of thing' part of their general demeanour. The Clash and its crew-cut crew repaid the unpaid Prefects for helping them out of a jam by having a one-sided riot of their own, at tour's end.

Robert Lloyd: The [Sect] would sort of slag off The Clash behind their backs . . . whereas we were just obnoxious. We were just yobs. I really didn't like [Bernie]. I thought he was a complete wanker. And he just didn't like us. But that night, when we were invited to take over, we rang up our drummer and said, 'Can you make it over to Chelmsford tomorrow, and bring the guitars?' And we got put up in the Holiday Inn in Leicester, [so] as you do, you kind of raid the mini-bar and [call up] room service. Not even The Clash were allowed these luxuries, so when the bill arrived the next day, Bernie went absolutely apeshit, [and] we had to sleep on the bus for the rest of the tour as some sort of penance. [But] because we'd picked up the tour in Leicester, we'd got no change of clothes or anything, so they gave us a bunch of Clash t-shirts, with policemen on the front and The Clash stencilled, and because we'd gone off The Clash by this time, we either wore them inside out or someone taped over their name. Bernie [was] like some kind of grandmother, talking about how disrespectful we were . . . [I mean,] we *were* pretty fuckin' disrespectful. But Bernie was like some fascist headmaster. [So] on the very last night of the tour members of The Clash and their road crew attacked a couple of the Prefects and put one of 'em in hospital, which was [pretty] fantastic of them.

So much for solidarity. The Prefects, though, were not swayed from their course. Nor were the Sect. Yet it was only the beginning when it came to The Clash clashing with their early disciples. Next time around, it would be the audiences dispensing summary 'justice' to support acts, having taken the manager's mantra – as spouted on singles, album and interviews through 1977 – at a face value it never had. The Clash, meanwhile, would continue to rail against their more cretinous converts like Cnut at the seaside.

– – –

An altogether more fun experience for fans and bands alike kicked off just as the White Riot tour stuttered home. The Damned, back from the States, were set to headline Stiff's first punk tour, with The Adverts tagging along. Memorably promoted with a shot of Dave Vanian and Gaye Advert sharing a mike on 'Neat Neat Neat', and the classic line – 'The Damned Can Now Play Three Chords, The Adverts Can Play One, Hear All Four . . .' – the tour ran 20 May through 28 June, covering the mainland in spit.

At least the audiences came for a good time. As TV Smith recalls, 'Every place was packed [with] people who wanted it, and were sick to death of the old music.' Gaye Advert also found the fans in the provinces less style-conscious, and more interested in the music: 'It was more DIY. No bondage trousers.' The response confirmed a number of (positive) stereotypes about these out-of-town audiences.

Brian James: You play in London and the audience is super-cool because they don't know if it's hip to applaud, but you go to High Wycombe and you get all these guys who look like fucking hippies from the sticks. They don't know what's happening, they just come along to enjoy it; [and] they just go wild. [1977]

For The Damned, it was a validation they needed, even if they never managed to take it on to the next level. James had already informed west-coast fanzine, *Search & Destroy*, 'We ARE like the Bay City Rollers, we're a pop band . . . We want to get across to a lot of people, sell a lot of records, make a lot of money . . . and do what we're doing in the process.' But this was as close to teen-mania as Brian got. Unfortunately, on punk tours, any adulation manifested itself not in knickers thrown at the stage, but in projectiles of phlegm.

Other bands touring suburbia and seaside resorts in the early summer of 1977 found that – globules of gob aside – there was still a refreshingly open attitude to high-energy bands. But by the time mellow fruitfulness came around, even provincial punks were well and truly rooted in their new-found conformity. The Saint-like Ed Kuepper found that when they ventured outside of London initially, 'It was a totally different kettle of fish . . . Punk hadn't hit them yet and they were [more] responsive. But [when] we came back, like two months later, and we played the same places, suddenly everybody had spiky hair and were calling out to us to get a haircut.'

In the dedicated punk clubs springing up in places like Liverpool (Eric's), Manchester (Rafter's), Middlesbrough (Rock Garden) and Bristol, the response could be particularly combative. The owner of Bristol's BQ Club admitted to one journalist that summer, 'Bands take a lot of stick at the BQ. Have to. The audience is very lively . . . The audience [wi]ll stop at glasses and bottles, but everything else goes.' That such behaviour was a media-induced malady was borne out by The Adverts' January 1978 experience in Belfast, where mainland punks had previously feared to tread. TV Smith describes the experience in Ulster punk history, *It Makes You Want To Spit:*

We hit the stage to the most concerted barrage of gobbing I'd ever seen. The Belfast audience had heard about the spitting craze that had been gathering momentum in the English punk-rock scene over the previous year and were out to show that they were as punk as anyone. For us though, playing under a storm of spittle and having our clothes crusty and reeking for the rest of the tour was something we'd long ago grown to hate. After a few songs Gaye left the stage, and the gig descended into chaos as our manager came on and begged the audience to stop spitting . . . He was met with the inevitable hail of gob . . . That was The Adverts in Belfast. We never went back.

For more perceptive observers, the 'piss-take' now became a necessary antidote to punk's pack-mentality. Some members of the *Sounds* staff even recorded their own punk parody, 'Terminal Stupid' – as the Snivelling Shits – only to have *NME* proclaim it Single Of The Week. And if, by the spring of 1977, *Sniffin' Glue* had settled into its generally negative niche, it had a rival that was less sniffy, more Snuff-Rock. The editorial to the 'first' issue of *Kill It!*, a nigh-on perfect parody of Perry, proclaimed that punk rock's nihilistic impulses just weren't going far enough:

Snuff off pigbrains and welcome to the first issue of 'kill it', the fanzine for snuff rock freaks. We were having to hope an interview with johnny dentle of the 'wakefield dividers', top of the snuff charts with their new record 'off it', but johnnys dead, isn't that great, showing all those old farts where its at. The establishment media honkers of pig street are just scared rabbits. And the news that melody makers jumped of the snuff rock band wagon and changed its name to mortuary maker hasnt half made me sick. Isnt it great that snuff rocks sweeping the country? Three clubs in london got into gear last week by burning their premises down while the people were still inside. This what we need . . . more audience. The news that c.b.s. have signed the crypt for one album is taking it a little bit too far. Everybody knows any snuff band worth its salt should only be round long enough to make a single and we should show them how uptight we are by going along to their gigs and not committing suicide.

Kill It!'s circulation, though, was confined to those attending the latest extravaganza by those proto–punk piss-takers, Alberto Y Lost Trios Paranoias. Formed in 1973 from the remnants of folk-rock bands, these Mancunian madmen were an irreverent, latterday Bonzo Dog Doo-Dah Band that was, as frontman C. P. Lee affirms, 'ripping the piss out of anybody and everything to do with popular music'. For Lee, punk was both an antidote to those bands who travelled 'from stadium to stadium with an articulated lorry each', and the repository of a whole new repertoire.

The snuff-rock concept actually had a punky precedent. Iggy Pop, in the immediate aftermath of The Stooges, had told Danny Sugarman to phone 'every writer in LA and tell them he was going to kill himself onstage that night . . . It was a mess, no staging, no rehearsal. The piece was called *Murder of a Virgin.*' In Lee's version, the singer of Snuff-Rock was convinced it would be a good career move, even as he sang the likes of 'Gobbing On Life', 'Snuffing In Babylon' and 'Kill'. The response to Snuff was such that Stiff Records, who shared offices with Alberto's booking agent, suggested a *Snuff-Rock* EP.

C. P. Lee: We were doing *Snuff** at the Royal Court Theatre. Dave Vanian used to come every night to watch the show. We started about Easter ['77] – for a week. It was a massive success. We caught the zeitgeist, because the set we did as Snuff-Rock was a piss-take of punk-rock. We . . . [even] transferred to the Roundhouse. We were getting coach parties of Japanese tourists. We recorded [the EP] in twelve hours, shot the sleeve in an outside lav in West

---

* Though most people remember the show as *Snuff*, Lee included, the actual title was *Sleak*.

Didsbury, and that was that. It was probably the best thing we ever did, 'cause we didn't piss about.

The EP was such a success that copies made their way across the pond and into the homes of American punks, some of whom, taking it at face value, seemed to be missing some fairly obvious clues in songs like 'Kill' ('I don't give a damn, I don't fucking care / I'm gonna kill my mum and dad, and cut off all my hair', for starters). As Lee wryly recalls, 'I read an interview years later [by] some hardcore punk band, and they were saying, "One of the first records we ever got was *Snuff-Rock* by the Albertos. It was years before we realized it was a joke."'

The line between parody and punk would become ever more blurred, with Manchester managing to produce many of punk's finest piss-takers, including poet John Cooper Clarke, Chris Sievey's Freshies, John the Postman, Jilted John and the Macc Lads; at the same time as it produced some of the dourest, most pretentious, self-important 'post-punk' twaddle this side of Philip Glass. If London punk seemed in an awful hurry to close the door on experimentation, it was still ajar in the spring of 1977, when *Snuff* began doing the rounds at the Roundhouse.

At the beginning of April, *Sounds* attempted to catalogue the bands who constituted a 'new wave' – further blurring any distinction between it and punk – extracting quotes from the would-bes and wannabes, while finding room for the likes of The Police, Iron Maiden and Skrewdriver. Of those included in *Sounds'* shopping list, the first named band, Mark P's Alternative TV, had yet to gig or record, but Perry still claimed they would be 'avant-garde – yeah. Close to Can and reggae-type rhythms . . . Also very fast.'

Already heading in the right direction were Siouxsie & the Banshees ('not just a pretty Rheinmädchen . . . a very fine little band featuring sturdy and provocative original material'); Subway Sect (who 'have been rehearsing for months . . . It was feared that they'd just become ordinary – but we were wrong'); and Wire, already looking to distance themselves from those who 'have assumed social platitudes and attitudes they don't understand'.

If the above bands represented a glimmer of hope on punk's hazy horizon, best of the rest were The Only Ones, who claimed to be 'not punk, but [with] a punk feeling'. Their debut single – 'Lovers Of Today' – already in the can, had all the energy and passion of punk honed to an essential new-wave nubness, a result of the quartet spending six months refining their message-songs at Mano's. Rather than embracing the throng, they had remained cloistered in Chelsea since 13 August 1976, replacing songs from Perrett's previous combos (England's Glory and a prototype Only Ones, which had included Squeeze's Glen Tilbrook) with edgier material, like 'The Beast', 'Another Girl, Another Planet' and 'No Peace For The Wicked'.

Only when the Ones were sure they had something to say, and could say it loud, did they start gigging, debuting at the Fulham Greyhound in January 1977. As guitarist John Perry says, 'At the point we started . . . there wasn't the polarity that became the new wave.' If Perry never entirely embraced the movement, he found that The Only Ones 'were [generally] accepted by the people who *were* of it'. Singer-songwriter and frontman Peter Perrett also shared more than a nodding acquaintance with the Sex set. He shared their anger. As he has said about those early gigs, 'It was like forcing it down their throats. Play it as loud as you possibly can. We tended to play the raucous songs, [like] "The Beast", things that would build to great climaxes and go on for ten minutes. I don't think we started getting tuneful until the album came out.'

Perrett felt enough of a kinship with these three-chord wonders to agree to a show at the Roxy in February 1977, headlining over the Drones, Manchester's musical equivalent to dental repairwork. As he told *MM* six months later, 'At the time the Roxy . . . was accepting new groups, but we weren't a punk group. We fell between the old thing and the new, hardcore punk . . . I just [don't think] you can change anything by singing about the right to work.' The Only Ones would have to continue making allowances, especially when they were obliged to play support to the more established punk outfits.

John Perry: We played a gig at the Red Cow, with The Damned . . . That was the first audience where it was clear that you weren't going to hear the monitors and you need to abandon any attempt to play accurately – there were waves of people crashing into the PA. It was clear that you might just as well play . . . uptempo numbers and just ride it, instead of playing musically.

Though the opportunity to return to the Roxy remained, by March 1977 The Only Ones had bypassed a number of lower rungs, establishing their own residency at a more salubrious Soho watering-hole, the Speakeasy. Having developed a regular pattern of ending 'up at the Speakeasy after rehearsing', Perry believes they 'just said to [owner] Jim [Carterfay], "Can we play here?" and after the first time he booked us back weekly . . . It started to build and it meant that we never had to take tapes to record companies. We were there every week for four or five months and enough people just came by and saw us, and we started getting offers.'

It was here that the band also bonded with members of the Pistols and the Heartbreakers, both of whom had quickly tired of the cliquey-ness found around Covent Garden. At the same time, the experience of alternating between the Speakeasy and more punkified palaces made them a remarkably adaptable outfit, able to slip easily from the utterly mellifluous 'Watch You Drown' into an ever-accelerating 'Another Girl, Another Planet'. It also made them a tighter unit, even if Nick Kent pitied them in print for having to face 'the gruelling extreme of either disorientating the blasé habituees of the Speakeasy or else facing a barrage of gob and heckling from . . . headbangers when it became immediately apparent that their chosen musical perspective was rather more adventurous and varied than the old 1–2–3–4 amphetamine shriek.'

At least The Only Ones had enough band members with capital-A Attitude to face down most crowds. Perry would often tell audiences, prior to 'Another Girl, Another Planet', 'Anyone thinking of singing along – don't!' He also remembers how, 'early on, Peter was looking for confrontation with audiences who weren't remotely confrontational. My suspicion at this point was that it was partly ideology and partly stage nerves, but he certainly got hold of the idea.' One time, when playing Birmingham's Barbarella's, someone spat at Perrett, and he kicked the bloke in the head, only to inform him, 'Look, if you really want to do something, I'd rather you pissed on me because I'm into water sports.' Even more memorable was a show at the Marquee at the end of March, after Johnny Thunders personally asked them to open for his band.

Peter Perrett: The Heartbreakers were at the height of their popularity then, and although I knew it would be a purely punk audience, which wasn't ideal for us, I was into doing any gigs, whether it was a confrontational crowd or not . . . [But] I remember lecturing the audience about replacing one uniform for another uniform, that it wasn't intelligent of them and that everybody should be an individual, [which] was what the punk movement was [supposed to be] about.

Dr Perrett's lecture was lost on most of his students. Indeed, Perry thinks that, 'Thunders [himself] came out and told them to shut up at one point.' By now the Marquee was fast replacing the Roxy as the place where missing links could best blend in with members of the human race. When The Damned attempted to celebrate their first anniversary with three shows there, *Record Mirror*'s female reviewer noted that 'beer cans, glasses and stuff were thrown on stage till it reached ridiculous proportions', prompting her to ask whether 'the fans [had] come to see the band – [indeed,] did they like 'em – or were they trying something along the lines of a darts match?' And when a northern gang calling itself The Fall descended on the famous Wardour Street venue, at least one southern punk wholly misread the situation.

Martin Bramah: We were dressed in our shabby street clothes, and we didn't have the proper hair-dos, we just had this attitude, which served us in good stead. They couldn't get an angle on us easily ... The punks would throw bottles and spit and our attitude was, 'Well, that's asking for a fight.' When we played the Marquee once, there was a super-London punk right in front of me waving a chain and spitting at me, so I just leant down and punched him in the face. That caused a bit of a riot. I think me and [drummer] Karl [Burns] were holding back the audience, while the band played on for a while. But we were quite able to look after ourselves.

This wasn't the first time The Fall had planted a bomb in Wardour Street. In fact, they had been part of a convoy of 'northern scum' who descended on a club called Crackers, at 203 Wardour Street, on Independence Day 1977; requiring Soho punks to decide whether to catch The Damned's Marquee darts match or check out Shelley's Buzzcocks, unknown quantity The Fall and punk-poet John Cooper Clarke at a new punk venue, renamed the Vortex 'for the night'. The Vortex was the brainchild of Andy Czekowski, who continued his painful learning curve.

Andy Czekowski: I saw an advert – two lines in the *Evening Standard* – basement club for hire – Soho – so I go up there to see this place. Two chaps – a little thuggy-looking – took me to somewhere that used to be called [Crackers] at the top end of Wardour Street – very much a disco-ey place. Good size. Had a little stage. Did a deal that I'd rent it off them, me foolishly thinking they had something to do with it. Put together [a bill] to launch what was going to be the Vortex. Turned up in the evening to start the proceedings off and the two chaps I'd been dealing with said, 'Who are you? Never seen you before, never heard of you. Don't come in here or we'll kick the shit out of you.'

The week after Manchester's finest, the Vortex played host to Siouxsie & the Banshees, The Slits and a new band from Bazooka Joe himself. Stuart Goddard had reinvented himself as Adam Ant, with Marco Pirroni returning to the fray as one of his Ants (it was Czekowski, again, who had booked this gig). Such was the need for another dedicated punk venue in the West End that the Vortex endured – despite Czekowski's expulsion; and even though its 'management' displayed an open contempt for their punk payees. Not surprisingly, it was soon hijacked by the sieg-heil fraternity, though through the summer of 1977 it still provided a necessary alternative. The Vortex liked to book triple bills, usually headlined by an ex-Roxy band like The Adverts, Generation X or even The Lurkers, preceded by some out-of-town band desperate to make their London debut at an 'authentic' punk club, and some motor-running garageband opening proceedings.

Hence bands like The Killjoys from Birmingham, Kevin Rowland's first bandwagon jump; The Boomtown Rats from Dublin, a pre-punk covers band now in punk clothing; and The Rezillos, a dazzlingly danceable bunch of headcases from Edinburgh with a bad case of sixtiesitis – all of whom ventured to the Vortex that scary summer. One week the Roxy, the next the Vortex, the bills became ever more surreal, experimental new wave vying with ersatz punk in bewildering battles of the bands. The struggle for the high ground – in music and message – was fought (sometimes literally) on a weekly basis.

Even at this point, the one band which no self-respecting combo liked to share a bill with was Sham 69. Fronted by a man with ambition coursing through his veins, but with all the vision of an autistic gerbil, Sham 69 were on a collision course with punk the moment scribes like Mark Perry, Danny Baker, Kris Needs and Tony Parsons began to take Jimmy Pursey seriously.

Sham could actually lay claim to a certain seniority in dumbcore circles, having made its debut as far back as November 1976 – below the Bishops, one night at the 100 Club – where they had the temerity to heckle the headliners, yelling, 'Stop that fucking row!' after their own, hopelessly incompetent set converted no one. Even teen scribe Julie Burchill's review in *NME* recognized that the only threat posed by this 'pure, incompetent, high-voltage dole-queue rock' was a physical one, coming from people who 'if they weren't on that stage [would] be in a cell or on a railway track'. But Pursey already had a penchant for fantasy, telling Burchill that when he was rich and famous (something evidently already on his mind), he'd give all his money away; and that he hated the Sex Pistols for being 'fucking art students'. Huh?

Pursey at least realized the sheer ineptitude of his erstwhile backing band was holding him back, and broke up the band. It would take another eight months to get this Sham right in his eyes, after another false start – supporting Eater at the Roxy in March – managed to make even these masticators sound good. Meanwhile, Pursey became a perennial fixture on the scene, befriending first Danny Baker, then Mark Perry. With his eyes fixed firmly on the prize, Pursey's 'endearing antics' kept the pair amused, while he regaled them with what he and his gang were going to do to turn punk around.

Baker, in particular, was wide-eyed and willing, having already portrayed himself as 'feel[ing] cheated, because being born on that [south] side of the river, I'm trained to do forty years of manual labour.' For Danny boy, Pursey's working-class rhetoric acquired ever more relevance the more cussedly inarticulate its mouthpiece became. In the final issue of *Sniffin' Glue* (August 1977), Baker and a disillusioned Perry gave Pursey the cover, and four pages, to pour out his invective-riddled doggerel. Baker was already preparing to jump this sinking ship, joining Kris Needs at *ZigZag*, the chip on shoulder intact. Kris Needs had become the new editor of *ZigZag* after a punk coup in May turned the monthly mag a hundred and eighty degrees. He welcomed Baker with open arms, and Pursey by proxy.

Kris Needs: [*ZigZag* editor Pete] Frame said, 'I don't fancy doing this any more.' . . . There was a crunch point when they had to decide what to do with *ZigZag* and the publisher said, 'Make Kris the editor and let's go punk.' So I thought, 'What can I do to piss off your average Jackson Browne fan? Right. The Slits.' So I . . . stuck 'em on the cover, 'Hello we're here.' I got such hate mail from the Jackson Browne fans who thought their lifeline had been cut off, but on the other hand I had a deluge of thumbs-up mail from [lots of interesting] people

... Julie Burchill, Tony Parsons ended up writing for us under other names, so they didn't get [bothered] by IPC ... Danny Baker was doing *Sniffin' Glue* but he became one of my main writers ... I admired his writing – he made me feel like ... I'd been writing a load of flossy bullshit. Baker comes along and all his stuff is *Sniffin' Glue* style, but not like Mark Perry ... Baker would actually make you think with a one-liner. He influenced Tony Parsons a lot, and vice versa ... Me and Baker would go to the Vortex every Monday ... We'd all meet [at Dryden Chambers] and go to this café and [then] go to The Bath House in Dean Street with this guy Jimmy Pursey; [and] Baker was raving about Sham 69 ... Baker was very easily lead. They got by me on the sheer brilliance of Baker's writing, and Jimmy was a really good laugh ... [But] I never thought any of this music was going to be music I was going to take to the grave.

Nonetheless, Needs allowed Baker the forum Pursey needed. Sure enough, in the September issue of *ZigZag*, Pursey bleated about how he had 'taken rich kids' shit all me life. Now while I've got the light, they shall have it back. I'm not in it to sell fuckin' records.' And yet, strangely enough, when major label Polydor expressed interest – after the first Sham 69 single, 'I Don't Wanna', had been put out by Step Forward – Pursey snapped at their heels like a bulldog on heat.

The force was certainly with Pursey that summer. *NME*'s Tony Parsons had also fallen under the man's spell, after noticing the first few cracks in The Clash's class-conscious construct. Desperate to champion a band from the same streets as him, Parsons gave Sham a jet-propelled thrust with his review of their third Roxy gig, in early August, which correctly identified the band as 'ex-skinheads who don't have the cash or the inclination to dazzle you with the mandatory sartorial elegance of corporate-sponsored urban guerillas[!], [but] are content to use their performances to provoke REACTION!' Yet Parsons did not fall entirely under the Sham spell; identifying the real problem – Pursey's monomania – as he 'spits, screams, [and] sings the vitriolic lyrics, with the kind of total self-conviction that is only found in children and the insane'.

Which category Pursey fit into had yet to be revealed, though that first Sham single, 'I Don't Wanna', certainly had all the marks of some brat throwing its dummy out of the pram. Mark Perry, for all his gradual detachment from punk as a brand name, was now the person responsible for signing Sham to Step Forward. He later put a spin on his motivation, telling Jon Savage that he had 'spent a lot of time with people with ideas, and Jimmy was the bit that was missing. He was going to take it down to the gutter again.' At the time, though, he felt that, 'Sham were the band that were going to take Punk to the masses.' If so, it wasn't going to be with Step Forward, but by taking Polydor's pennies – and two steps back.

Having found himself at the crossroads earlier in 1977, Perry was wondering whether he need sell his soul to the devil to gain enough musicality to emulate Can. He had formed Alternative TV with the already adept, but volatile, Alex Ferguson; at the same time going into the A&R business with Miles Copeland's label. Copeland later told *Sounds*, 'Everybody was in A&R. Stewart [Copeland], Gene [October], Mark P, they were always talking about this and that new group they'd seen. I'd been used to artists who were jealous. Screw or be screwed. But these musicians were asking me to help the other guy.' Unfortunately, no one here cited had any instinct for where this amorphous musical movement was going – or whence it came. Having defined punk initially as Eddie & the Hot Rods, Perry now thought its exemplars might be Sham 69 and Chelsea, even if he told *MM* that he was almost taking pity on these bands when he signed them to Step Forward.

Mark Perry: After the first wave of bands had been signed up, it seemed that the ladder had been pulled up on bands like Chelsea and The Cortinas, and they had been left in the lurch a bit. I thought rather than just getting signed up with Polydor . . . they'd like the idea of coming with someone who understood them. [1977]

The initial batch of Step Forward singles gave Chelsea and The Cortinas two bites at the cherry, Sham 69 and The Models one; but even Perry seems to have suspected that no one here represented any real kind of future, releasing his own band's records on the altogether more progressive Deptford Fun City label. Meanwhile, every fanzine or vinyl grotto began to be convinced that they should be putting out vinyl testimonies to a new wave still struggling to wash away the old.

– – –

Of the record-shop labels sprouting up, Beggar's Banquet made perhaps the most impressive start, issuing The Lurkers' unexpectedly compelling 'Shadow' as their first foray in August 1977. The Lurkers, who had been appositely named by drummer Pete 'Manic' Esso, because 'we were always sitting together in one corner in the pub, doing fuck all', had actually made their debut during the long hot summer of '76, supporting Screaming Lord Sutch at Uxbridge Technical College.

Pete Esso: We were suburban pubites who liked Lou Reed and The New York Dolls. I never liked the progressive, hippy music. But I loved The New York Dolls – I liked the campness and the weirdness. But our set [then] was only ten minutes long – four or five songs, one cover, 'Then I Kicked Her'. We finished the set, and I was knackered, and [Sutch] said, 'Is that it? You've got to go on again.' I said, 'I can't. I'm tired.' He said, 'How old are you?' [In the end,] we had to go back on.

For the next six months, they continued to lurk in the shadows; remaining in Esso's view 'suburban weirdos . . . We didn't understand what was going on.' In fact, they represented a strain of English punk – valid, but destined to become all-too-prevalent – that bypassed the Pistols completely, going back to the Dolls, via the Ramones. By Christmas 1976, even these suburban weirdos had noticed that they weren't alone. After asking every band they saw for a support slot, they found themselves in March 1977 at the bottom of the food chain, below Eater, at the Roxy; then supporting Slaughter & the Dogs, the following month.

By June they were headlining gigs at the fast fading punk palace; before transferring their allegiance to the Vortex, where crowds continued to enjoy their no-nonsense na-na-na. If The Lurkers lacked even the basics required to alter time-signatures or tempo, they made no apologies. As original bassist Arturo Bassick (aka Peter Billingsley) told *Sounds*, 'We strip away all the niceties that got into music in the last six years and made it boring.' They still had enough originality to convince an old Mod to invest in their future, via the Ealing-based Beggar's Banquet emporium.

Pete Esso: We started the [Beggar's Banquet] record label. They used to have a little place we used to rehearse. This guy called Mike Stein, a Northerner, was a Who fanatic. He said to the two public schoolboys who owned [the shop], 'You've got to do this. This new thing is happening.' They didn't want to know, 'cause they liked The Eagles. They said, 'It's shit. They can't play.' They were right, but that doesn't matter. [In the end,] they said, 'Okay, we'll do it,' but they [added], 'You've got to record both sides in an afternoon. We've booked . . . a place near Heathrow, and it's got to be done in four hours.' So it was done in four hours. The engineer [actually] said, 'This is shit,' in front of us . . . It sold twenty thousand in two weeks and we didn't have a contract. So we got a contract. But they were our managers, and they were our record company. The contract we signed was unbelievable. When we were done for tax in 1980, this tax bloke looked at it and said, 'Didn't you ever *read* this?'

If 'Shadow' was a three-minute wonder, The Lurkers' follow-up, 'Freak Show', was also surprisingly sprightly. But Beggar's Banquet didn't hit the motherload – dodgy contracts or not – until their fifth single, issued at the turn of the year. 'That's Too Bad', which purported to be by Tubeway Army, was really the product of a single Bowie closet-clone named Gary Numan. It would be Numan's success that would establish the shop as a label. Across town Rough Trade was still deciding whether to follow Beggar's and Bizarre/Skydog into the small-label game. Small Wonder in Walthamstow had no such qualms, though records by Menace, the Zeros and Puncture hardly made a dent in popular perceptions. Nor should they have.

Out in the provinces the DIY aesthetic seemed to be taking an even greater hold, as an encouragingly high number of music-makers claimed the means of production for themselves, though few managed fifteen minutes of inspiration, let alone fame. The first two labels to make more than just a couple of singles for their garage friends were Rabid from Manchester and Raw from Cambridge; both cottage industries made viable by punk-inspired entrepreneurs.

Rabid was the brainchild of record producer and one-man music force Martin Hannett, aka Zero. Having co-run Music Force and 'worked on' *Spiral Scratch*, Hannett should have been in an ideal position to cherrypick from Manchester's nascent scene. At this stage, though, only the now-trimmed Slaughter & the Dogs seemed viable recording artists. Their debut single, 'Cranked Up Really High', showed that they had come on a great deal from the garage-glam of a year previous. An anti-drug song, it eschewed speed for speed's sake, all the while representing garage rock at its most rabid.

Raw Records, on the other hand, was a storefront label, set up by Cambridge record dealer, Lee Wood. An anxious awaiter of any underground scene, Wood was quick off the mark, recording Cambridge combo the Users in March 1977, and issuing the results – 'Sick Of You' b/w 'I'm In Love Today' – on 5 May, two weeks ahead of the Rabid Dogs 45. Though it prompted *Sounds* to enthuse that it 'burns

266 | Babylon's Burning

into your brain without compromise', it was a single shot of inspiration for the Users. Before the end of the year, Wood would find his own saviours, The Soft Boys, who for a short while would put punk and psychedelia in the same blender.

The DIY notion made it a lot further up the A1. Across the border, in Edinburgh Town, The Rezillos had been gigging since August 1976, playing a set largely composed of sixties beat classics, but played at a speed that made The Damned seem pedestrian. By the spring of 1977, guitarist Jo Callis had started to introduce frenetic originals like 'I Can't Stand My Baby' (a song about post-natal depression), 'No' and '(My Baby Does) Good Sculptures' that were utterly original and with all the amphetamine energy of their covers. In August 1977, the band covered both bases with a single on Sensible Records that paired 'I Can't Stand My Baby' with their crazed cover of The Beatles' 'I Wanna Be Your Man'. When it sold 15,000 copies in two months, The Rezillos found themselves propositioned by real record labels, and perhaps over-zealously snapped at Sire, who issued their second single, the classic 'Good Sculptures' – originally also due to appear on Sensible – in December. It was one more before the road, as The Rezillos prepared to join the Ramones on their turn-of-the-year UK tour.

Another band who used their own indie single as a major-label calling-card were The Only Ones. Though they had generated interest from their Speakeasy residency, they felt that they weren't being taken seriously enough, and decided to issue the self-levitating 'Lovers Of Today'. Perrett already had history with the labels, having done demos for EMI as England's Glory back in 1974, hence the choice of label for the single, Vengeance Records. As Perry says, 'He was genuinely pissed off with the record companies. He viewed it as a personal rejection . . . so there was certainly a degree of hatred . . . that aligned him with the punk thing.' When the thoroughly fab 45 became Single Of The Week in *Sounds*, *NME* and *Record Mirror*, the labels finally sat up and took notice, and the signing scrum started; ending in December with The Only Ones being added to a CBS roster that already included The Clash and The Vibrators.

John Perry: Suddenly the companies were looking to sign people, whereas before they had taken eighteen months over any deal and you needed a couple of ex-members of Yes in the band. Anchor were the first to come in, then Island, then CBS as I recall. [But] it was rumoured that Island were having trouble paying their artists . . . [and] CBS seemed like a bigger deal than Island. What we hadn't realized . . . [was that] they weren't allowed to pay their own electricity bill without asking permission from New York.

Some of the larger independent labels were proving surprisingly naive about acts they signed on single-shot deals being whisked away by 'the majors'. Back in March, *NME* had suggested that the contract between RAK and The Vibrators was 'single-by-single type tenuous'; but when Most tried to push The Vibrators into following up their all-original 'We Vibrate' b/w 'Whips And Furs' with a cover of 'Jumpin' Jack Flash', they were off to CBS subsidiary Epic, who issued their classic powerpop single, 'Baby Baby', at the end of May. As Knox says, 'The only real argument we had was about putting tubular bells on the playout to "Baby Baby", as it wasn't *punk*.'

The Adverts were also about to leave Stiff, after the relative failure of 'One-Chord Wonders'. They had recently been taken under publishing magnate Michael Dempsey's wing. He had ventured down to the Roxy, on the grounds that 'anything that the *Daily Express* hated so much must have . . . something going for it'. He liked the band, didn't want any commission, but volunteered – as Smith says – 'to start helping us, just to stop the sharks getting us. [And Michael]'s perception was that "One-Chord Wonders" had not really done it on Stiff; and we were always going to be the second punk band on the label – there was no way The Damned weren't always going to be the leading players. It [became] pretty clear after the [joint] tour; even though we had given them a good run for their money live, and we got on really well.'

By the end of June, Dempsey had signed The Adverts to Anchor; by the end of August they were on the verge of one-hit wonderdom, having always been looking for a mainstream audience. As Smith informed *Sounds* that September, 'It's usual to let the masses hear what you're doing. You either do it in your bedsitting room, or you go out and let them hear it.'

Equally keen to let the masses hear what they were doing were two 'Roxy' bands fronted by arresting amazons, Pauline Murray of Penetration and Poly Styrene of X-Ray Spex. Both had been touting around demo tapes to the labels. Penetration's contained seven songs they'd already circulated to journalists on cassette. X-Ray Spex's was a searing set of nine songs recorded by manager Falcon Stuart. Each demo yielded a single deal with Virgin Records, no longer the tainted label of

Tubular Bells, but of the Sex Pistols. Not surprisingly, Penetration picked the irrepressible 'Don't Dictate' as their introduction to the airwaves, while Poly Styrene decided to declaim 'Oh Bondage Up Yours' across them. Though Virgin gave each 45 a picture sleeve and some basic promotion, they failed to generate enough radio-play, and laudatory reviews were not enough to shake some chart action. Penetration failed to read the writing on the wall, and struck a long-term deal with Branson's boys. But Poly was unimpressed, and jumped across to EMI before turning the charts Day Glo.

In fact, 'Oh Bondage Up Yours' was the last recording by the original Spex, as Lora Logic was unceremoniously given the order of the boot. Styrene had never been entirely happy with Logic, telling one journalist at the time, 'The sax was just something that happened. If I wanted to put a washing machine on I would.' Any sense of competition may have been in her head, but it was no less real to Marion/Poly. According to Lora, Poly even 'stopped talking to me as soon as she knew I'd written a few songs of my own'. When Lora departed for chillier climes after recording her sax crescendos at Virgin's behest, Poly carried out her bloodless coup.

Lora Logic: It was summertime, and things were quiet, and I'd just gone on holiday with my parents to Russia, and I came back and said, 'When's the next rehearsal?' They just said, 'We've found a new sax player.' I rang up the manager and said, 'Is this a nice way to deal with anybody?' He said, 'You must have seen it coming. Look, she's been having some problems. She thinks you're a witch and that you're practising black magic. She can't handle you any more. You shouldn't have said what you said.' That's when her schizophrenia began to come on. She [later] told me that her problems did go back to her childhood, which was very dysfunctional . . . I never knew that she had any mental illness. I just thought she was talented, and we had so much to give the world . . . But Falcon had invested a lot of energy and probably money in getting the band going and he had a hard job seeing that album through. It was a full-time job keeping her head together, so anything that distracted her from doing what he wanted her to do, he didn't have the time to deal with. I was one of those things. [But I sure wish] she hadn't felt threatened by the fact that I got written about as well.

What probably did for Logic was an August review by Ian Birch in *Melody Maker*, which noted that, 'The real points of interest have to be

Poly and Lora, whose sax appeal gives them that distinctive edge.'
Though Poly got her way – and the band acquired a new, *male* saxophonist – the band never regained its 20/20 vision. Even copying Logic's
original parts – using the demo tapes as a guide – the sax lost its rough
rasp, and Poly let the whole thing slip from her grasp.

August proved to be the cruellest month for a number of primary
punk bands. For Siouxsie & the Banshees, firing guitarist Pete Fenton
was to prove a necessary adjustment. Anchor had recently passed on the
band – who had recorded a trio of demos, 'Love In A Void', 'Make Up
To Break Up' and 'Carcass', at Riverside Studios – after deciding they
'weren't rock & roll enough'. In fact, this was as rock & roll as they
were gonna get; Siouxsie having started to tire of 'trying to make
[Fenton] forget what he'd learned. The repetitive, mesmeric drone of
Velvet Underground was the blueprint for what we wanted, but he
wasn't having any of that.' As was Severin.

Steve Severin: [Fenton] was a bit too rock & roll. He would throw in too many
licks, now and then. I think it was because he had an orange cable. No, [really,]
he just wasn't on the same wavelength at all. He was fired mid-set at Dingwall's.
Siouxsie just said, 'This is crap. You're fired.' And that was it.

The Banshees would return a good deal stronger, replacing a guitarist
Pete Silverton described as 'real good at sounding like [a] lorry shifting
gear', with one who had a drone all his own, the mesmeric John McKay.
However, they would continue to struggle to find a label prepared to
take a chance on the ice queen of punk; even though they refused to
pursue the DIY route themselves. Thankfully, manager Nils Stevenson
remained a fearless advocate of the faith.

If the punkettes had few qualms about getting shot of key components
in their soundscapes, the boys were squabbling with the beatmaster
general. By the end of August Rat Scabies and Jerry Nolan, having
huffed and puffed their way uphill for almost two years apiece, quit in
a minute and a huff. In Scabies' case, it had been a long time coming,
the decision postponed every time they returned to the road, his doubts
deferred another day. But when it came time to record their second album,
with Pink Floyd's Nick Mason producing, matters came to a head.

Rat Scabies: Through most of this period I didn't have an address, so I'd come
off the road and I didn't have anywhere to stay. I'd go and doss on people's

floors, so the whole thing of keeping it on the road was something I wanted to do. [But] when it came to the second album, it became obvious that Brian hadn't got enough tunes, and the tunes he was coming out with had a different vibe about them, [they] didn't have the same energy and urgency. Then he started this thing [about how] he wanted us to be more like the MC5, with two guitarists.

Though the album *was* completed with Scabies – as well as second guitarist Lu Edmunds, who had not so much passed, as survived the audition – by the time the band made a return trip to Mont de Marsan, where they were still putting on punk festivals in August, he was rapidly unravelling. And this time there was no one willing to catch him should he fall.

Brian James: Rat had something of a nervous breakdown. It was [the] twenty-four-hour partying. In France, he set up a little campfire in the middle of his hotel room, downed a couple of bottles of brandy and tried to jump out of the window. At that point we'd already recorded the second album . . . To me, The Damned really ended when Rat left . . .'cause me and Rat started the band.

Scabies told the music press that he was 'fed up with the John Wayne syndrome – people poking you in bars, trying to prove how hard they are. But more than anything, it was the pressures of being with four people in a year.' He seems to have been the first member of The Damned to have realized that they had shot their bolt. In fact, the one rough-cut jewel on *Music For Pleasure* was a Scabies original, 'Stretcher Case Baby'; while no amount of psychedelic embellishments could disguise the paucity of material from James's pen.

Having been the first English punk band to issue a single, put out an album, tour the States, and record a second LP, they were now the first to run out of ideas. Though they would stutter into '78, it was all over, bar the gobbing. As Brian James says, 'We kept it going, we had a new album to promote. But it wasn't the same . . . With Dave you never knew what he was thinking; and the clown aspect of Captain had become more and more [to the fore]. I could bear it up to a point, but when I wasn't getting a charge out of being onstage, I couldn't.' That difficult second album would undo many a band following in The Damned's wacky wake.

For the Heartbreakers, too, the act of recording had taken them away from their true strengths, which was to leave any club teeming with converts to gut-wrenching rock & roll. As Only One John Perry eloquently expresses it, 'Seeing the Heartbreakers [in] early ['77] . . . was the first time I'd been to an exciting gig where the audience was really part of the excitement. You're talking about a period where the audience mostly sat cross-legged on the floor at gigs, and suddenly there's waves of people crashing into the PA.' Between delivering some of the most raucous rock this side of the great divide, the Heartbreakers had been labouring to record a long-player affirming their ascendancy. The problem was, as Perry points out, 'They were a one-shot band really. Jerry wouldn't play any slow numbers. It was very quick, bang, bang, bang, between numbers. I [just] think there wasn't enough in the formula.'

To the Heartbreakers, it was sacrilege to fuck with the formula, so it had to be something else. The *LAMF* sessions ran from March to June 1977, an eternity in punk terms, but nothing ever sounded any fresher. Even on the 'Chinese Rocks' single, which had mysteriously acquired Thunders and Nolan on the composition credits, they didn't sound any tighter than in Yonkers, back in January 1976. Meanwhile Jerry Nolan was telling *NME*, 'Ain't nobody gonna hear the "Chinese Rocks" . . . single until we got it *perfect*. We been through too much to screw up now.' In fact, the Hell-less Heartbreakers had recorded the song just fine – along with 'Born To Lose' and 'Let Go' – at a two-day demo session conducted by EMI's Mike Thorne back in February (though it would be six more years before those '77 demos made an official appearance as *Vintage '77*). But then Thorne knew enough to mask their limitations and accentuate the attitude.

And still, the Track single sounded like it had been buried under a large Chinese rock. By the time the madman attached to the purse strings cried Enough, pulling the plug on more recording, the perennial feud between ex-Dolls Nolan and Thunders had gone into overtime, with both insisting on doing their own mixes. By September, it was clear that Nolan was not going to get his way. And so, as he informed biographer Nina Antonia, 'I [told] everybody, you put this record out the way it is, without a proper mix, there's no reason for me to stay in the band.' By the time the album appeared, on 3 October, Nolan was on the boat home. The reviews buried the album even further in the mire, while the likes of *MM*'s Ian Birch exonerated the guilty men:

The fault lies not with the band or the material . . . but producers Speedy Keen and Daniel Secunda. Amazingly they have managed to submit the songs [on *LAMF*] to the most thick-eared, cement-mix treatment since Stone Age man uttered his first holler.' [*MM*, 15/10/77]

Thankfully for Thunders, *Sniffin' Glue* – who had touted Thunders and co. as being 'what rock & roll's all about' back in March – wasn't around by October 1977 to join in the hand-wringing and name-calling. The last issue, dated August, was given over to championing the shameless Sham, and Danny Baker reviling those who pelted him after he announced the death of Elvis Presley at the Vortex on 17 August 1977. For Baker, the reaction was symptomatic of punk's year-zero creed gone mad:

Loads of bands cheered and said things like, 'Fuckin' great.' None of them, I'm sure, knew why. But that's what punks are s[up]posed to do . . . innit? . . . I got up onstage and grabbed a mike, 'cause I was so fuckin' wild about how dopey this whole set-up is getting. But of course who's gonna listen when you can throw glasses at the target?

The reaction that night in Manchester was more measured. The Fall had been called upon to headline at the Electric Circus after The Boomtown Rats consumed the wrong poison; and pulled out a new song, 'Your Heart Out', because – as guitarist Bramah says – 'He [Presley] was a working-class hero to us, so it was a genuine tribute, but it was semi-tongue-in-cheek. We weren't breaking our hearts over it. It was all very distant and removed – he was just an idol who died.' Over at Wessex Studios, applying some more wafer-thin guitar to the basic tracks for the Pistols album, Steve Jones felt much the same, 'I remember it clearly because I wasn't sad. I just thought I'd better get back and do those guitar overdubs.'

Nor was there any tearful bye bye from Johnny. Mr Rotten already knew there was no success like failure, but felt it was high time someone told the truth about the King of Rock & Roll. When *Melody Maker* asked him for his thoughts on the man who started this whole mess o'blues, he didn't sugar-coat it none:

He came to represent everything we're trying to react against. I never wanted to become like Elvis . . . I don't want to become a fat, rich, sick, reclusive rock star

. . . Elvis was dead before he died, and his gut was so big it cast a shadow over rock & roll in the last few years. Our music is what's important now.

There was still a new world order to establish. 'No Elvis, Beatles or The Rolling Stones / In 1977.'

PART FOUR

4.1
AGGRESSION THRU
REPRESSION
6/77-12/77

Sex Pistols' God Save The Queen.
It won't be on the new album and it may not be
out at all for very long.
So get it while you can.
Sex Pistols' God Save The Queen.
Available only as a single from Saturday May 28th
.at shops with the sign.

Virgin Records VS181

[The punk ideal] is all about being honest. This is what happens when you're young – you see what a lie the world is, and in punk there is this recognition of the difficulty of being honest. Punk recognized that it was impossible – unlike previous movements. That's how it built in that it doesn't succeed.

—Richard Hell, to author, 2005

It seems extraordinary that in 1977, the year of punk, the Sex Pistols – the paradigm, the instigators, the Van Der Graaf Generator of a thousand bands – spent the first five months of the year a seemingly spent force, unable to gig, or release records, and with a bassist they couldn't even trust to record his parts in the studio. When *Sounds* profiled every punk and/or new-wave combo the first week in April – after McLaren's hard-won engagement with A&M went pear-shaped – they suggested the unmentionable, that the Pistols might yet become punk's very own Pretty Things.

Time to reclaim the higher ground. The following week, the Pistols returned to the screen of an earlier triumph, the one on the Green, for the first public performance★ of the post-Matlock Pistols. With The Slits as a sonically challenged support, the Pistols were treated like conquering heroes. If they were now playing largely to late converts and professional cynics, it was a necessary reminder that these trailblazers had a purpose above and beyond bumping up tabloid circulation.

Now all they needed was vinyl affirmation as powerful as 'Anarchy In The UK' to set the cities alight. They already knew they had just such a statement. 'God Save The Queen' – the recast 'No Future', already in the can – was one 'potential H-bomb.' Their main problem, acidly articulated by McLaren after the A&M farrago, remained their outsider status:

The Damned are into paper bags and custard pies . . . The Stranglers and The Clash are working well within the industry, but the industry doesn't really want to cope with us. We don't fit into the formula. [*MM*, 10/3/77]

McLaren was going to have to find a new blueprint if he was going to set off any more fireworks. The majors had all turned their backs on

---

★ The Pistols had played a secret gig for American TV at Notre Dame two weeks earlier, but the invite-only audience numbered no more than fifty.

the Pistols, while snapping up their spawn. Only one credible company was still talking to him, and it was one for which he had a deep-seated loathing. Virgin Records had been founded by an ex-Stowe pupil, the bright but untrustworthy Richard Branson, at a time when the British independent sector – led by Chris Blackwell's Island Records and Tony Stratton-Smith's Charisma label – was responsible for the most interesting rock music around.

Virgin had made much of their hippy ethic in the early days, Branson displaying his counterculture credentials by evading VAT on 'export' albums he reimported and selling bootlegs in his stores – both deeply illegal, especially when one got caught. Branson, though, continued to duck and dive, hitting pay dirt with a fifty-minute pseudo-classical suite by ex-folkie Mike Oldfield – the clanging *Tubular Bells* – which rose to the top of the charts, and took Virgin to the edge of solvency.

Back in 1976, Branson had felt he could afford to ignore the punk phenomenon – deeply inimical to the hippy in him – and when EMI's Leslie Hill suggested McLaren contact the bearded one after handing over EMI's golden handshake, McLaren tersely told him he'd approached Virgin 'before we went to EMI, and they didn't wanna know'. By 1977, though, the Oldfield oilfield had all but run dry, and the Virgin ship was again sailing close to the rocks. According to Virgin director John Varnom, Branson cynically decided 'after the EMI and A&M contracts had been terminated . . . that prestige and cash would accrue to the company if they signed the Sex Pistols'. Branson desperately needed both, and McLaren was in urgent need of an outlet for his charges.

Neither entirely trusted the other. Branson told one journalist in 1979, 'We had to watch Malcolm. There was always the danger that he'd try to rip us off, and he'd have been proud of it.' Too right. Thankfully, McLaren was a lot smarter than his erstwhile employee, Bernie Rhodes, and kept rights to important international territories well away from Branson's grubby mitts. Branson knew he had met his match, and saviour; cheerfully going along with every hare-brained scheme McLaren's febrile imagination could conjure – for now.

Where both were of one voice was in the need to get 'God Save The Queen' into the shops in time for the Queen's Jubilee, in June, when the country was expected to revel in its royalty during one nationwide spasm of supplication. Not Johnny and his gang, who caustically spoke of their monarch as 'a piece of cardboard that they drag around on a trolley. Like, go here Queen, go there. And she does it blindly, [be]cause she's in a rut.'

And yet, when the band's art director, Jamie Reid, an old friend of McLaren, came up with an image for the single ad campaign of the Queen with a safety pin through her mouth and her eyes blanked out by swastikas, even his fellow ex-anarchist sent him back to the drawing board. He needn't have bothered. Even the relatively innocuous ad Reid returned with – a portrait of the Queen beside a cup of tea, on a kitchen table – proved too strong a brew for most. *Sounds*, champions of the Pistols for more than a year, found that their printers refused to use the artwork, and so ran the ad minus its image. High-street retailers, en masse, refused to carry the single. Radio stations – both independent and BBC-controlled – banned the record from the airwaves (though only after John Peel gave it a spin or two on his late-night show).

Top of The Pops, BBC TV's weekly allocation of the anodyne and anaemic in the singles charts, simply ignored it – until it became the best-selling single nationwide in its second week on release. Worryingly, the programme's format obliged them to play whatever single topped the charts at the end of that week's show. The industry's corruptible watchdog, the BPI, found a solution. According to Branson biographer, Mick Brown, they 'issued an extraordinary secret directive to the [chart compilers], that all chart-return shops connected with record companies be dropped from the weekly census of best-selling records. Virgin, the store where most Sex Pistols records were being sold, was struck off the list. A week later, the decision was reversed.' In that first week of June, the Sex Pistols' 45 outsold Rod Stewart's overwrought remake of Cat Stevens' 'The First Cut Is The Deepest' by at least 20,000 copies. But it wasn't number one. Officially.

It mattered not. The ban on 'God Save The Queen' merely handed the initiative to the music papers, who stoked the burning brazier with Pistols-packed pages (the most memorable being *NME*'s 28 May 'Sex Pistols Overkill Issue'). The music papers also tripped over themselves to rhapsodize about the record itself. The boy had reclaimed his crown – and every pretender knew it. Meanwhile, across the ocean, Johnny Ramone entered Media Sound studio on day one of sessions for the third Ramones album, carrying a copy of the single. He informed engineer Ed Stasium, 'I want to sound better than this.' I think not.

The only record that summer which sounded better blasting out of bedrooms and bedsits was the next Sex Pistols single, 'Pretty Vacant', issued just six weeks after the Pistols offered a glimpse into the future by declaiming its dissolution. Backed by 'No Fun' in all its Goodmanesque glory, the Pistols again pulled no punches, prompting Charles Shaar Murray in *NME* to announce, 'Another Sex Pistols Record . . . turns out to be the future of rock & roll.' This double shot of Pistols' hate was another McLaren master stroke, a rekindling of a yesteryear when every week seemed to bring a new three-minute stunner from the cream of the sixties' Britcrop. And Murray couldn't help but compare its impact to the likes of 'My Generation' and '(I Can't Get No) Satisfaction'.

The Pandora-like Pistols, though, had unleashed more than they could possibly hope to contain, or McLaren control. As Glitterbest secretary Sophie Richmond told Jon Savage: 'Malcolm always said of the "Destroy" t-shirt that he was making a general point about leaders, [but that] was a bit too subtle for the average NF [skinhead], or even the average Punk. It was a pipe dream.'

Likewise, it was all well and good for Vivienne Westwood to tell *Melody Maker*, 'If someone wishes to wear a swastika they should do it – then people can do what they like in reaction to it . . . I think a young kid's got a right to tear things apart.' But she omitted to mention that their right extended to being torn limb from limb by those who didn't see the ironic subtext in this symbol of mass genocide. Indeed, June saw both Paul Cook and John Lydon targeted by neanderthal nutters. In Lydon's case, it came after a Saturday afternoon session at the studio, followed by one in the pub next door. The attack itself came as no great surprise to a singer schooled on the terraces of Highbury.

Chris Thomas: John started saying, 'Those guys over there are gonna have us,' and I was like, 'C'mon John, don't be so paranoid, people don't go out on a Saturday night to "have" people, they go out to have a drink.' . . . And we went into the car park and there was like . . . eleven blokes.

The rhetoric of violence – a part of punk even before it was stoked by statements from Strummer like 'If you're having an argument which won't resolve itself . . . there's nothing better . . . than smashing someone's face in' – was now generating a backlash that felt more like whiplash. As Murray wrote in *NME*, the week after he proclaimed the Pistols 'the future of rock & roll', 'Punk violence – like most rock & roll violence – is more of a metaphor than an actuality, but the violence with which it is being met is all too real.' Fellow *NME* scribe, Tony Parsons, was one of those on the front line.

Tony Parsons: I'm not saying you took your life in your hands, but you were provoking a lot of people just by wearing a Sex Pistols t-shirt that summer. It didn't make for an easy life, as you wended your way home past north London pubs after another hard day taking amphetamine sulphate in the *NME* offices.

Rotten belatedly insisted – to *Sounds*, at the end of July – that punk 'is not about violence, it's about being yourself and doing what you want to do, and being left alone', but he was whistling in the storm that now surrounded him, and which was blowing the band ever more off course. At the end of June, the Pistols again considered ending it all, the combustible concoction just a hair trigger away from fission. Sophie Richmond described the band in her diary as 'emotionally drained'; and 'at a point where they had to decide whether to patch it up and keep going or split . . . I think that "Then what?" is what pushed them back.'

A week later, McLaren was telling *Melody Maker* that the one thing he admired about The Rolling Stones was the fact that 'they carried on through thick and thin.' But painting over the cracks had now become a full-time job. When the band was interviewed backstage after a secret gig in Middlesbrough, at the end of August, Rotten spoke of his stage persona as 'my act, for all the masses'. The inexperienced interviewer asked him, 'What's underneath the act then?' Rotten replied, 'Skin.' Steve Jones, though, had a quite different answer, 'A poxy little bastard, a poxy little wanker.' It sounded like he meant it.

The band weren't the only ones unhappy with their frontman. Their replacement roadie, 'Roadent', felt he'd seen the man change, 'While he was just "out there" having a laugh, because . . . he didn't think anybody was listening, . . . that was fine. But then he started believing it.' When 'Roadent' decided he preferred The Clash's company, John 'Boogie' Tibieri took his place with instructions to film a gig in Scandinavia at the end of July, 'There was a strong imperative, even then, to get it while we could.' Everyone, it seemed, was living on the same knife-edge.

Meanwhile, those in A&R were wondering when the other punk bands were going to follow the Pistols into the Top Ten, and start paying off all those expense-account dinners. The only punk-like, or punk-lite, band to match the Pistols' chart success in the first six months of '77 were those ostracized oldies, The Stranglers, whose 'Peaches' and 'Something Better Change' both went Top Ten (as did their debut album, *Rattus Norvegicus*). The Jam also came close with 'In The City'. But it was August before the charts rocked to the sound of the Roxy, The Adverts finding the Top Twenty with the ghoulish 'Gary Gilmore's Eyes', a perfect combination of Smith's pithy poesy and pop sensibility.

TV Smith: I was in this habit of picking up papers that had been left on the Tube, and flicking through them, and I saw this little [item] about Gilmore being executed, and donating an eye anonymously – and [started thinking about how] someone's gonna wake up and wonder where his eye came from.

When the call came for The Adverts to appear on *Top of The Pops*, Smith was as keen as his girlfriend to go on, but found it to be 'as ghastly as you can possibly imagine – [with] these ridiculous hardboard painted boxes you had to stand on. You walk in and there's thirty kids. When you watch it as a kid, you imagine the place is packed and glamorous – but it's tacky, tacky, tacky.' Nevertheless, the single seemed to confirm the wisdom of their decision to trade something Stiff for the altogether weightier Anchor.

Stiff, though, were about to mount their own assault on the charts, issuing their three most commercial singles to date – 'Red Shoes', 'Whole Wide World' and 'Sex & Drugs & Rock & Roll' – in the last few weeks of this summer of hate. Elvis Costello had got his way, securing his own shot at success with 'Red Shoes', after 'Stiff had actually considered launching Wreckless [Eric] and myself on the same record.' Despite his *ToTP* debut, though, the single got no closer to the charts than the altogether pricklier 'Less Than Zero'.

Rivera also decided to let Eric have a go with 'Whole Wide World', just as soon as he turned up long enough to record a B-side. Wreckless later claimed he had 'a half-share in a fishing boat in Hull . . . It's in the agreement [with Stiff] that I have to vanish once a year and go fishing in the North Sea . . . That's why it took so long to record the B-side.' In fact, he had spent most of the six months since recording 'Whole Wide World' in November getting pickled himself.

Even when Lowe sobered him up long enough to send 'Semaphore Signals' Stiffward, Mr Goulden seemed reluctant to leave the pub long enough to record any follow-up single. When *MM*'s Allan Jones decided 'Whole Wide World' had the edge on Costello's claim, and set up an interview with the elusive Eric, he found a singer anxious for him 'to hear some of his other songs. Eric, [though,] has had a little too much to drink . . . and keeps falling over and crashing into things.' For Wreckless, such incidents presaged an unequal battle with the demon drink that would ensure he never matched the powerful content of his songs to a strategy for success, like his nemesis, Costello.

What Costello still lacked was a band that could belt out the backing to his bilious barbs with corresponding aplomb. Having already recorded an entire album, with the four-piece Clover, which included his 'most direct and most aggressive songs', hoping 'to hit home – the rhythm of the times [being] like that', he found that no matter how much *he* exuded the attitude of a sawn-off punk, his backing band were hippies to a man, and not about to brave the kind of clubs Costello would have to play to make his play.

With his debut long-player still at the pressing-plant, Costello began the arduous task of putting together a band who could make his verbal arrows pierce the thickest skin. The Attractions were an inspired union of the experienced and the intuitive. With Pete and Bruce Thomas bedding the beat, the sound was capped by Steve Nieve's vamping organ and Costello's staccato guitar. This band stripped the songs bare, and gave every song a jet-thrust up the junction. Starting in July 1977, Costello began to apply lessons acquired from six months of immersion in all this punk plastic to the songcraft already evident on his pre-Attractions album. Though unable to experience these subterranean strummings first-hand, he was anxious to claim its audience for his own.

Elvis Costello: I didn't have the money to go down to the Roxy and see what the bands were doing . . . I just read about them in *Melody Maker* and *NME*, the same as anyone else . . . I was married with a son; I couldn't take the day off. I . . . [was] taking sick time off of my job just to make *My Aim Is True*. [But] I started listening to the records that were coming out . . . When the first few punk records came out, I suddenly started thinking, 'Hang on – this is something a little bit different.' [1982]

Having initially taken time out to work with Steve Nieve that summer, the results proved instantly edgier than anything Clover could manage. According to Costello, 'Watching The Detectives' was something he 'wrote in the first twenty-four hours of constantly listening to the first Clash album, which I'd just bought'. Predating his association with The Attractions, it was originally recorded with two members of Graham Parker's Rumour, only receiving Nieve's evocative noodling after the fact. By the time the song became Costello's fourth single (and first hit) in October 1977, The Attractions had claimed it (and the entire contents of *My Aim Is True*) for themselves, blazing a trail through the land in an amphetamine-fuelled blur of angst, on one of the most (in)famous rock tours of all time – Stiff's Greatest Stiffs.

In the three months preceding this nationwide assault, thanks to some coaching from Jakeman, Costello carefully set about reinventing himself as an angry young man without cause for complaint, save for the weedy frame, the dodgy eyes and the bucked teeth. Bug-eyed and bitter, Declan was a new man. As Graham Parker told Will Birch, 'I'd first seen Elvis in 1975, with Flip City, but he didn't have my aggression or energy. Now he was onstage giving it stick – knees bent and screaming.'

If Parker knew 'Elvis' was the ex-Flip City frontman, he was in the minority. Costello was certainly not about to enlighten the uninformed, telling *Sounds*, 'I didn't appear in a puff of smoke. I've been around a long time. [But] if people weren't interested in what I was doing then, why do they want to know all about it now?' When that didn't work, he insisted, 'I'm not particularly proud of what happened before. It's not worth the trouble of going back to look at it.'

Elvis's reinvention was in real time – as was the anger and energy. Dave Robinson at Stiff witnessed the change, and sensed someone who 'was enjoying being nasty . . . He needed scant encouragement when he found he could be unpleasant to people and get away with it.' Costello also felt he now had the opportunity to settle some scores in song, including some slights that existed only in his powerfully deceptive imagination.

Elvis Costello: I was going in[to record companies] thinking: 'You're a bunch of fucking idiots who don't know what you're doing.' . . . They didn't seem to understand that kind of approach. [But] it didn't make me bitter. I was already bitter. [1977]

The years of being ignored had left a furrow just as deep in Mac-Manus's psyche as the one in Lydon's – prompting songs overwhelmed by negativity. When Costello told Nick Kent that 'the only two things that matter to me, the only motivation points for me writing all these songs, are revenge and guilt – those are the only emotions I know about, that I know I can feel,' he could have been channelling the coruscating invective of Johnny Rotten. He also told Kent that 'Lip Service', a withering rewrite of an earlier Flip City flop, 'was straight from the heart, [be]cause last year I actually went to Island with my demo tape and none of them wanted to know.' Yet 'Lip Service' was a fantasy no more real than Brecht's pirate Jenny.

Richard Williams [Island A&R director]: I kept all my diaries, with all my appointments. I absolutely would have remembered Elvis Costello. The first I knew about it was when Jake Rivera rang me and said, 'We've taken you off the guest list for Dingwall's tonight.' I said, 'I didn't know I was on the guest list for Dingwall's tonight.' 'We've taken you off.'

With Rivera, a man prone to reinvention himself, Costello had found a man after his own wallet. Between them, they determined to create what Costello himself depicted as 'this ugly geek in glasses ramming his songs down their throats . . . That's *exactly* what I'm in it for. I'm in it to disrupt people's lives.' With so much pent-up anger, Costello found a seemingly endless source of renewable energy, which would make the next three years a non-stop succession of albums, shows, songs and speed, burning the brighter because they came from a man who perhaps did not envisage coming out the other side.

Elvis Costello: Gram Parsons had it all sussed. He didn't stick around – he made his best work and then he died. That's the way I want to do it. I'm never going to stick around long enough to churn out a load of mediocre crap, like all those guys from the sixties. [1977]

If Costello was hardly entitled to feel angry at his treatment from the record industry to date, Stiff's other great white hope for the package-tour-to-end-all-package-tours had a lot more to moan about. Ian Dury, though, rechannelled his own frustrations into witty vignettes-in-verse, capturing a world peopled by the ghost of rock & roll heroes ('Sweet Gene Vincent'), diamond geezers ('Billericay Dickie'), the odd smart-ass ('Clever Trevor') and a surfeit of Blockheads. In September, *New Boots And Panties* presented a sharply redefined variant on the Kilburns-era Dury, combining the bawdiness of music hall, some ersatz jazz and a shot (or two) of rhythm & blues.

The Stiff's Greatest Stiffs tour opened on 3 October 1977, featuring a bill that put the fiercely ambitious Costello up against the marginally less embittered Ian Dury. The others along for the ride – ex-Pink Fairy Larry Wallis, Dave Edmunds, Nick Lowe and Wreckless Eric – watched these two contenders slug it out night after night, confining themselves to other kinds of slugs to keep spirits up.

Wreckless Eric: Ian always had to be top dog and for that reason he went head to head with Elvis Costello. Me, Nick and Larry Wallis just stood back in a drunken haze and watched them battle it out . . . I think everyone was glad when it was over. I was never the same again.

Dury was the consummate crowd-pleaser, a vaudevillian out of time, but not out of place; while The Blockheads were as dexterous as Dexedrine, and twice as fast. Costello, on the other hand, made confrontation his crutch, twisting the audience to his way of thinking through sheer animal presence. At Aylesbury, on night number one, he met requests for songs from *My Aim Is True* – which had been out barely two months – with the immortal putdown, 'If you wanna hear the old songs, you can buy the fucking record.'

In the eyes of publicist Glen Coulson, he 'deliberately cut his own throat by doing a set of songs nobody had ever heard before. They were all waiting to hear the tracks from the first album and he did covers and songs from the second album, which completely went over people's heads.' But Elvis was making a point – he was nobody's puppet, and he wasn't gonna be a touring jukebox. His real target was Rivera. As he told a journalist the following week, 'Jake thought we were mad to do all new numbers on the opening night. So it was in a way to get *him* at it. I knew we'd get some stick. I don't care . . . You've got to keep everyone AT IT.'

Nor were audiences any less befuddled by Costello's set as the tour continued on its merry way. Released from chains of propriety by punk, he was howling at the moon every amphetamine-fuelled night. In Leicester, three weeks in, he seemed utterly oblivious to the mobile truck brought in to record the show, opening his set with Richard Hell's 'Love Comes In Spurts' (because Hell was *there*), then taking detours through The Damned's 'Neat Neat Neat', the Kilburns' 'Roadette Song' and Wreckless Eric's 'Whole Wide World'.

Costello's rendition of the Wreckless rhapsody was a substitute of sorts for Eric's absence that night. After the Brighton show, Goulden had been taken to a private doctor suffering from 'exhaustion'. The doctor told publicist Glen Coulson he had never seen a young man in such bad shape. Perhaps Eric's quip to *Sounds* journalist David Brown before the tour, about how he planned to replace his usual two bottles of sherry per day with three bottles of meths, hadn't been said entirely in jest.

That night in Leicester, Costello seemed determined to render as few points of reference as possible to perplexed punters; even debuting one song he'd written on tour – 'Doctor Luther's Assistant' – which would not be released for another three years. Also written on – and indeed about – the tour was a jaunty, if jaundiced ditty on excess. 'Pump It Up' would ultimately depict Costello's own descent into on-the-road mania, but at this time it represented a swipe at fellow Stiffs.

Elvis Costello: I was compelled to write 'Pump It Up' as [a response to the tour]. [After all,] just how much can you fuck, how many drugs can you do, before you get so numb you can't really feel anything? . . . I did go strange towards the end [of the tour]. I'd like blank out and just see red. [1979]

'Pump It Up' was not the only chart-bound chronicle of the motel mayhem that succeeded most evenings' entertainment, as the tour came dangerously close to ending in a real stiff. Nick Lowe woke up one morning to find that Dave Edmunds had been ejected from the tour, and a note lying on his bed from the man himself, 'You missed the sound of breaking glass; make sure you have your boots on when you get out of bed.' It prompted 'I Love The Sound Of Breaking Glass' – Lowe's Top Ten 45 the following year. According to Wreckless, that night's kerfuffle had originated with Lowe's room-mate:

Wreckless Eric: The tour manager was a drug dealer and there was a tour nurse – an American girl who was very popular with . . . The Attractions . . . which almost split up the band in mid-tour. Nick Lowe woke up one morning in a room he was sharing with the drug dealer/tour manager to find the floor covered in blood and broken glass, and the tour manager gone. He'd been whisked off to hospital with the back of his foot hanging off after an offer of a plate of biscuits and a glass of milk from two coke-hungry musicians went horribly wrong.

This was hardly the only hairy incident. Eric recalls that, 'Ian Dury
. . . nearly came to physical blows with Elvis Costello's bass player in
the back of the bus. [And] Davey Payne, an ex-Kilburn who played
saxophone with me . . . was . . . practically psychotic.' By tour's end,
Costello wanted nothing to do with his fellow Stiffs; and when The
Only Ones pulled into the same motorway café, guitarist John Perry
found him sitting on his own, well away from the madding crowd. He
had never felt at one with Stiff's collection of pub-rock refugees, misfits
and madmen; and now he knew he wanted out. As the tour wound
down, 'Watching The Detectives' introduced Costello to the charts, at
precisely the time he and his manager were saying their farewells to Stiff.

Rivera was jumping ship to set up his own label, Radar, with United
Artists' Andrew Lauder; and already knew that he would take Lowe and
Costello with him (along with The Yachts, a Liverpool powerpop
quartet whose 'Suffice To Say' 45 was their first and last word for Stiff).
Dave Robinson was hanging on to Dury, whose *New Boots And Panties*
had just entered the album charts, where it would stay for almost two
years; and Wreckless Eric, who seemed more interested in cirrhosis than
success, but was happy to stay put.

The attitude and irreverence that Rivera and his performing prodigy
had brought to the label would be sorely missed. Stiff Records would
now reinvent itself in a way more akin to Robinson's original vision, in
the days before punk, reflecting his slightly reactionary tastes and innate
conservatism. With Rivera gone, the one genuine punk band still on
Stiff was sunk for good. The Damned needed propping up after a
disastrous second album and Scabies' departure. But, as Scabies says,
'Jake liked the band, Dave didn't. Dave saw us as cash . . . We were
good money, but he didn't like dealing with the delicate egos and the
destruction. We'd get bills for thousands, and we had no idea whether
we'd done it or not.'

Whatever controversies still dogged The Damned, they were as nothing to the Pistols; who, after recharging their batteries and affirming
their live credentials in the hinterlands of Scandinavia, returned to Britain
in mid-August determined to prove they could not be silenced by any
council-imposed live ban. So began the SPOTS sortie (short for Sex
Pistols On Tour Secretly), which began in Wolverhampton and ended
in Penzance a fortnight later, proof that their inability to play a normal
UK tour was not for want of trying. It also gave them the opportunity
to try out the one new song added to their repertoire in the seven

months since Matlock took his leave. 'Holidays In The Sun' was a caustic encapsulation of a trip to Berlin in June, set to a battering-ram riff that bore more than a passing resemblance to The Jam's 'In The City', even after producer Chris Thomas reconstructed the song from the ground up.

Chris Thomas: I remember thinking 'Holidays In The Sun' could have been a single but the construction of the song was wrong and so we . . . redid that. There were verses in the wrong place, the solo was in the wrong place. It started off with a bass drum thing, but I just had the idea of putting goosesteps on it because it was Berlin.

On 15 October, 'Holidays In The Sun' became the Pistols' fourth and last single; backed by the eighteen-month-old (but still utterly fresh) 'Satellite'. Already the doubters were starting to notice something missing, *NME*'s Charles Shaar Murray noting that the A-side 'lacks the structure and immediacy that was, presumably, the contribution of the more pop-orientated Glen Matlock'.

– – –

Matlock himself, who had been silent for some time, began popping up again at the end of August, playing a couple of shows with his new band, The Rich Kids, at the Hope 'n' Anchor and the Vortex – with 'special guest' guitarist, Mick Jones, helping out. Matlock, and cohorts Steve New and Rusty Egan, thought they had found a vocalist back in May, when they convinced ex-Slik vocalist Midge Ure to come down from Glasgow to see if he fit in. Ure – once offered the vocalist slot in a pre-Rotten Pistols – apparently expected more professionalism than he found.

Glen Matlock: I didn't want to have a go at singing myself. I think that's one of the biggest mistakes I ever made. [Anyway,] we ended up rehearsing in this squat in Stoke Newington. By [May], I was exasperated, because EMI were going, 'What's going on?' . . . and I had half of the Rich Kids album written: 'Burning Sounds', 'Ghost Of Princes', 'Rich Kids', 'Hung On You'. We'd demoed them as a three-piece, and they sounded great. EMI wanted to move [ahead], and I wanted to move [ahead, too]. And I went into Leicester Square, into a record shop, and I found a Slik record . . . I remembered [Midge] from back then, and I got EMI to get on to him. He had this PVC-2 [single] going on, which was doing nothing, and I said, 'Would you come down?' The very first time he came down with his manager. We started playing and none of the leads worked, and so we said, 'Let's go down the pub.' And they'd flown down from Glasgow . . . Midge was going, 'It's a bit Mickey Mouse.' But then he came down again. [This time] we learnt a few songs, then went down to the Hope 'n' Anchor and The Police were on. As we were going in, the bloke on the door said, 'The support band haven't turned up.' We said, 'We're a band. We'll play.' [So] we played these six songs we'd learnt, and it was good, except Steve broke all their guitar strings. But it was all a bit ramshackle, [and] Midge decided he wasn't gonna do it.

Ure later exclaimed, 'Jesus Christ they were a shambles! . . . They'd no money . . . they all played out of tune. It was terrible . . . it was great fun, but a helluva racket.' When their singer decided to take the high road, Matlock despaired of ever finding that missing component, and then decided to see if the band could do without a dedicated frontman. The eight-song sets with Jones suggested Matlock might yet make his Beatlesque Pistols a band; while a third gig resulted in a firm offer from EMI, and another call from an auld opportunist north of the border.

Glen Matlock: We did the Brecknock supporting the Tom Robinson Band on the night they signed to EMI. [Afterwards,] one of the EMI [directors], who was really out of it, said, 'Glen, I know you're talking to all the record companies in London. Whatever [offer you get], we'll match it,' and with that he collapsed into his prawn vindaloo. Then it got released in the paper that we'd been offered a hundred thousand pounds. Next morning the phone rang and it was Midge, 'Och, I've reconsidered.'

In October 1977 – a year after Matlock recorded his debut EMI single – the reconstituted Rich Kids resumed recording at EMI, with Ure on vocals. By December, they were ready to hit the road, even though their debut single, 'Rich Kids', wasn't due out till the new year (a Peel session in October certainly suggested cause for optimism). In a surreal twist of fate, The Rich Kids began their pre-Christmas tour at Lafayette's in Wolverhampton – where the Pistols had started the SPOTS tour – two days before the Pistols began another secret sheaf of dates themselves. This time it was dubbed the Never Mind The Bans tour, a play on *Never Mind The Bollocks*, the number one album the Pistols had issued in early November to further controversy, and a court case over the word 'bollocks'; which they won, after proving it was a fine old Anglo-Saxon word no more offensive than 'cobblers'.

The Pistols' nine-date tour seemed to consistently criss-cross that of Matlock's new band. A suspicion of design only grew when Rotten was seen at their final show in Huddersfield sporting a t-shirt that read: Never Mind The Rich Kids, Here's The Sex Pistols – a jibe which undoubtedly stemmed from reviews of *Bollocks* suggesting the two new songs – 'Holidays In The Sun' and 'Bodies' – lacked a certain *je ne sais quoi* in the tune department, perhaps because The Rich Kids had acquired Matlock's powerpop sensibility. The Rich Kids, though, were a band out of time; caught in the glare of a nation waking up to punk, and not ready to move on to cleaner pastures.

Glen Matlock: When I was playing with Iggy, McLaren turned up in Paris, and he did say [to me], 'Where you went wrong with The Rich Kids . . . it was too early.' And he was right. When we went up north, coming on like, 'Here's the new thing after punk,' people who were still only getting into punk thought we were taking something away from them.

The Rich Kids certainly had the tunes – and live, could be a match for most – but Ure had even less in common musically with Matlock than Rotten. It would be left to The Rich Kids' erstwhile second guitarist, Mick Jones – and the band he returned to just in time – to take things onward and upward. Three weeks after Jones had fleetingly felt like a rich kid, Clash fans heard Strummer exclaim, 'You're my guitar hero!' at the end of a Clash single that was two steps forward from 'White Riot' – whereas 'Holidays In The Sun' took a step back from 'Pretty Vacant'. In case anyone was unsure where Strummer was directing his spleen, Rhodes rustled up his own press release, explaining just what 'Complete Control' was meant to mean:

'Complete Control' tells a story of conflict between two opposing camps, both of which are using the tool of change to further their own beliefs. One side sees change as an opportunity to channel the enthusiasm of a raw and dangerous culture in a direction where the energy is made safe, predictable and palatable. The other is dealing with change as a freedom to be experienced so as to understand one's true capabilities.

'Complete Control' came hard on the heels of 'Remote Control', CBS's idea of a single from the debut album. It delivered both a fierce condemnation to their label and an affirmation of an independent voice, even if the band were bemoaning a lack of control that was down to the way their manager had gone about 'negotiating' a record deal with more strings than the man's winter vest.

For now, Rhodes thought he had found a perfect way to reassert the band's stance as punk standard-bearers. He promptly announced their second nationwide stint of the year, prophetically dubbed the Out of Control tour, would begin in Belfast on 20 October. For would-be Ulster punks, this was a hugely symbolic gesture. The Clash were set to become the first English punk band to set foot in the troubled city.

Again Bernie had left a number of loose ends dangling, as he had two months earlier at an open-air gig in Birmingham that ended in chaos. When the band arrived in Belfast, with the media in tow, they discovered that the necessary insurance had been withdrawn for the Ulster Hall, because 'The Clash have a lot of claims in England outstanding against them', and the show would not go ahead. When the day turned into little more than a photo opportunity, local punks left in disgust; and The Clash had a PR disaster on their hands.

Two days later they arrived in Liverpool, to discover that their gig at the so-called Stadium had also 'been cancelled because of insurance problems'. Though Eric's obligingly opened its members-only doors to the band, it was hardly the most auspicious way to proclaim 'Complete Control'. Two days later, in Dunfermline, The Clash were finally joined by special guests, Richard Hell & the Voidoids; and all concerned hoped the mayhem could start in earnest. Richard Hell and his fellow New York renegades, though, were unprepared for the rigours of a Clash tour; Hell having debilitated himself by a disastrous attempt to inject Mandrax directly into his veins before the tour had even begun.

Richard Hell: Not only was I in bad shape [on the Clash tour], but I had this confused attitude towards touring and gigging every night in a new town. I had been playing for three years and it would be playing only every couple of weeks for two or three nights. It's a very different thing to be playing every night.

But it was time to promote the new album in the one territory where it stood a chance (though *not* if one could only get it on import, as was the case for the first two weeks of the tour). *Blank Generation* had been a long time coming. After annual false starts in Television and the Heartbreakers, Hell had taken his time signing with Sire. After recording a long-playing version of his template, he found that the completed album would have to go on the backburner while Sire renegotiated its US distribution. The delay convinced Hell that the album was not all he wanted it to be, and he used the down time to re-record almost the entire artifact. The loss of momentum – combined with a less instinctive approach to the material – made for an album that missed its moment. And though its (US) release was received enthusiastically by critics on both sides of the divide, Hell himself had lost the will to win.

Richard Hell: When [*Blank Generation*] came out I felt like quitting rock & roll. I'd accomplished what I set out to do and I felt like I wanted to disappear, pack my handkerchief and catch a boat to Africa.

The first few shows in Britain did little to convince Hell that he wouldn't be better off on the heels of Rimbaud. As he now admits, 'In retrospect we were kinda naive and very arrogant; but we thought we were really being mistreated by the record company [in England]. We had to travel all around the country – the five of us – in a minibus. But that's what every young band really has to go through starting off . . . [However,] to me it was a little disappointing and humiliating to have to open for a British punk group – period.' The treatment meted out by The Clash audience also hardly suggested he was receiving due deference as an originator and innovator.

Bob Quine: [We were] getting hit in the head with unopened cans of beer . . . I remember one night the drummer had blood in several places streaming down his forehead. The gobbing thing was at its full peak. I can't say I appreciated that . . . It poisoned me permanently against tours. I couldn't have gone on another day.

NME's Tony Parsons wrote of one incident in Newcastle, where Hell 'avoided being blinded in one eye only by a reflex action that caused the firework [thrown] to zip past his head, just scorching the side of his spiked barnet'. Axeman Robert Quine snapped one night in Derby, bringing his guitar down hard on one particularly persistent phlegm-dispenser. Even The Clash were tiring of the tidal wave of gob directed at the stage, Strummer pleading at the beginning of each show for restraint. The results were entirely predictable. Certainly, the oft-shown footage from the final night of the tour, in Manchester, suggested no shelter from the storm, as Strummer ram-raids his way through 'Garageland' and 'What's My Name'.

By this point, Hell had fulfilled his obligations, retiring to London to lick his wounds, and to play two nights at the Music Machine to fans of the Voidoids themselves. Even when his replacement turned out to be punk's favourite china doll, Siouxsie, and her wailing Banshees, the Mancunian malcontents showed that chivalry was as dead as Elvis, cheerfully bathing her in a stream of pure snot.

If Siouxsie decided, then and there, that this was not her audience, Clash roadie Johnny Green seemed bemused to find her quietly seething all the way to the station. The Clash and their attendees still liked to believe they were as one with their fans. Two American journalists caught in the crossfire, Lester Bangs, flown over at *NME*'s expense, and Jack Basher, there for *New York Rocker*, were both given the full indoctrination course, and left as converts to the cause. Basher informed his American readers:

The audience is as important to the gestalt of the Clash show as are the four musicians onstage . . . It isn't until the audience has gone totally berserk and the stage is about to collapse that the band calls it quits . . . I've never encountered a band with a following as ideologically developed and dedicated as The Clash have. Besides going totally bonkers over their music, the fans seem to identify with them, even believe in them . . . The Clash offer, if you want it . . . a direct, almost personal relationship with their audience, based on shared oppression and shared experience.

Bangs was equally bowled over, both by the band's seeming sincerity and evidence of a greatness within their grasp, thanks to two new songs they were trying out live, the new 45 'Complete Control' and a song Bangs described as 'the best thing they've written yet', 'White Man In Hammersmith Palais'. If the tour still didn't take 'Complete Control' into the charts, it whet the appetite of their snotty fans for the likes of 'Jail Guitar Doors', 'Clash City Rockers' and 'White Man . . .', all of which would appear with CBS sticky labels in the next six months.

For now, these English punks would have to content themselves with a copy of 'Complete Control'; or take a punt on some New York punk. Seymour Stein's Sire was attempting to make *Blank Generation* part of a four-pronged pincer movement – issuing it alongside Talking Heads' '77, The Dead Boys' *Young, Loud and Snotty* and the Ramones' third LP, *Rocket To Russia*. It was a belated blitzkrieg, coming at a time when Britain's dam-busters were about to put an end to their own logjam on long-players. Though Talking Heads – and Hell – were still making music a lot quirkier than anything in Albion, The Dead Boys had missed the bus, and the Ramones still seemed to be in second gear, albeit with their engine once again revved to the max.

Tommy Ramone: Everybody was telling us we were good. Phil Spector was telling us we were good. We thought at that point that we were the next big thing. To us it seemed like we should be . . . We were very pleased with [*Rocket To Russia*]. But then we weren't number one, we weren't even number one hundred.

Actually the legendary Spector, who was being courted as a potential producer, had given it to them straight even before work began on *Rocket To Russia*, informing them, 'This is it. For you guys it's downhill from here.' Though he would later attempt a resurrection of sorts, producing their fifth album, *End Of The Century*, Spector read it right that spring. Not that the Ramones' manager, Danny Fields, was helping things. The look was becoming as tired as the sound, yet Fields felt that 'jeans, a black leather jacket and a white t-shirt . . . is an easy and enduring look . . . any kid in the world can create . . . It's male, it's beautiful, it's tough.' More like a gay man's wet dream.

De brudders didn't see it coming, even when some UK reviews for *Rocket To Russia* were less than laudatory. When they arrived to promote their third attempt at album sales that reflected fans' ardour, they were no longer conquering heroes, at least not to the culture vultures hovering overhead. The band, label and management had always been ultra-careful not to allow too much competition on 'their' stage (hence their withdrawal from the Anarchy tour, and their decision at the beginning of 1978 to take The Runaways, and not The Clash, on another American jaunt). But they miscalculated this time, by taking Sire's new siblings, The Rezillos, along for the ride.

The Rezillos may have begun life as reactionary revivalists but by the end of 1977 they were fresh, vital, utterly original and *new*. As Tony Parsons observed at tour's end, 'Even [the Ramones] realized by the last date of their tour that the magic charm of The Rezillos had consistently stolen the Ramonic thunder on this tour.' They did not take too kindly to the usurpation:

Jo Callis: Up to that tour, the Ramones had just walked on water over here. [But] they'd reached that point where the British media wanted to knock them down a bit, and they kinda used us as a tool to do that . . . so they'd give us glowing reviews, and [were] more critical of the Ramones. There ended up being a bit of paranoia in the Ramones camp, and we did find ourselves quite badly treated on that tour, behind the scenes . . . It was almost like Linda [Stein] was their manager. Certainly on that British tour she was there looking after their interest . . . Once at a record signing in one of Bruce's shops in Edinburgh, we were in there lunchtime, and the Ramones came in about an hour or two [later], and Linda insisted we were flung out of the shop because we were stealing her boys' thunder. We were just hanging out in the shop!

Paranoid or not, elements of the press *were* out to get them. The Ramones were being washed away in the tide of new music crashing against the cliffs of Dover – and an attempted rebranding of this music by Seymour Stein along with certain trustworthy American critics was an abject failure. The deeply Anglophile *Trouser Press* were the first naysayers to suggest it was all over – before it had even begun, in vinyl terms. Editor Ira Robbins wrote a long think-piece in the October 1977 issue, suggesting that 'the new wave exists only as long as its enemies believe that it exists. A very shaky foundation . . . From here on in everything that arises will be an imitation. There can only be one set of leaders per movement and this one's have already risen to the surface . . . The style has been set, and now it's the duty of those who pioneered it to give it up.'

Another prior proselytizer was anxious to draw a line under punk and move on to something more akin to his personal preferences. Greg Shaw, publisher of *Who Put the Bomp*, followed Robbins' broadside with an entire issue of *Bomp* devoted to 'Powerpop', scrabbling around to find anything that might resemble the next big thing out of what had been a substratum of punk since day one (with The Boys and The Jam). Peter Case – whose LA-based band the Nerves were one of those co-opted into the concept by Shaw – admits he 'hated it, [but] liked punk 'cause it was a much better word with a much wider scope for interpretation, and [Shaw] was talking up its "built-in obsolescence".'

Much of the impetus for this wholly unsuccessful attempt to rename the music was coming from corporate America, which had decided that 'punk' was unacceptable, and demanded a more palatable alternative. If Powerpop was a non-starter, a newly capitalized New Wave would have to do. In October, Sire unveiled a new slogan, Don't Call It Punk. At the same time, Seymour Stein sent an open letter to FM program-directors in the States, asserting that, 'One of the most significant trends in recent years has been "new wave" rock, all-too-often wrongly referred to as punk rock. The term "punk" is as offensive as "race" and "hillbilly" were when they were used to describe "rhythm and blues" and "country and western" music thirty years ago.' Only now did the term 'new wave' become sullied by association, leaving consumers like Elvis Costello dismissing the New Wave as something 'Polygram Records invented . . . as a slogan to sell a bunch of crap American records like The Runaways.'

This attempt on Sire's part to claim the new wave for its own prompted an immediate retort from the English music journals, who rather than declare the last rites on punk, chose to redefine its terms. On the front line of this fundamental argument about punk's future direction were the new scribes at *Sounds*, natural heirs to Ingham and Dadomo like Jon Savage, Vivien Goldman (now writing about punk *and* reggae, often in the same article) and Sandy Robertson.

In the space of four weeks over November/December, this trio championed the likes of Siouxsie & the Banshees, Wire, The Pop Group, and Throbbing Gristle (plus Ohio's Devo and San Francisco's Residents), all designated part of something called New Musick. As Goldman puts it, 'It was our image to be edgy – that was the whole idea – the feisty little underdogs situation – it behoved us to be extreme.' Though it would be a while before New Musick metamorphosed into post-punk, these cub reporters were already hoping to chart punk's future course.

Jon Savage: I was on a mission at that point. Between November 1977 and summer 1978, I had a very definite programme about the groups that I wanted to feature – the Banshees, The Slits, Subway Sect, Devo, Pere Ubu, The Residents, *et al*.

Sandy Robertson – like Paul Morley, Jane Suck and Danny Baker, before; and Adrian Thrills, Gavin Martin and Dave McCullough, after him – was making the demanding transition from fanzine writer to real journo, buoyed by this exciting wave of music. His quest for something truly atonal did not find its true berth until he came upon Throbbing Gristle's yowl. As he wrote in that first New Musick piece, 'Even punk-rock maestros know a couple of chords, whereas TG have developed their own standards of musicianship to suit their own needs.'

TG had decided to make a vinyl artifact – in the form of *2nd Annual Report*, issued in a limited edition of 985 copies in November (the first annual report being Lou Reed's *Metal Machine Music*?) – and needed to spread the word. However, they still weren't prepared to make compromises to bourgeois notions like learning to play. As Genesis asserted in one 1977 communiqué, 'The enemy is . . . the nice catchy tune, because the nice catchy tune makes the public feel safe.'

Their first gig of 1977, at the Nag's Head in High Wycombe, had inspired one local reviewer to a rarefied kind of sarcasm as he described Genesis inviting 'half a dozen youngsters from the cat-calling and jeering audience on to the stage, and handed them the instruments. They sounded better than Throbbing Gristle, even though they couldn't play a note.' Genesis P. Orridge would certainly assert that this was the *point*. When he wrote a short piece in 2002 on 'TG & Punk', he still retained his love of inspired incompetence:

Punk bands we knew were appalled that we had no drummer; had bastardized the cheapest possible guitar (a Satellite from Woolworth's that we sawed down for Cosey) primarily for IRONIC reasons . . . They were aghast that the two people with guitars could not play and had no intention of bothering to learn . . . Mark P of *Sniffin' Glue* wrote the legend: Learn three chords and form a band. I replied, WHY LEARN ANY CHORDS? That is the essential difference, and vast distance, between TG and Punk. We wanted to explore without ANY connection to inherited rock tradition.

If releasing any kind of document somehow seemed at odds with such a dadaist spirit, Genesis justified the gesture to *NME* in these terms, 'We get letters from kids who wouldn't even know what intellectual kudos meant. Fourteen-year-old kids off council estates in Yorkshire. They don't care about what it means. They just get an instant, instinctive empathy with the noise, and it feels to them anarchic, rebellious, at times potent and strong, angry, but on their side.'

Someone else half in love with this deconstructionist notion was the very man who had appropriated (*not* written) the 'three chords' legend above, Mark P. But Perry's brief sojourn in the sun would only serve to disprove the supposition that ideas need not be tethered to technique. The impressionable lad had quickly fallen in love with TG, which still contained much of the overt sexuality of COUM. Indeed, when Jon Savage asked Perry his biggest influence, at the very time he was forming Alternative TV, he replied:

Throbbing Gristle – they're right maniacs, they're really new wave . . . It's like a society, not really a band. They do sexual depravity exhibitions on stage – [They were] razoring themselves a long time before the punks . . . Every so often their group puts out postcards. One really shocked Ron Watts. This card said, 'Could you please fix us up with a gig?' It showed a guy with a syringe and a bloody arm.

Watts can't have been *that* shocked, as he was the one who gave TG their gig at the Nag's Head. Through *Sniffin' Glue*, Perry was certainly in a position to help Orridge attain his expressed goals – 'to demonstrate possibilities and to communicate information'. And TG were in a position to offer Perry rehearsal space for this band he told *Sounds* would be a Jah Can. At the beginning of April, Perry duly arrived at their Hackney HQ with guitarist Alex Ferguson, who had come down from Glasgow with fellow muso and potential *Sounds* scribe, Sandy Robertson, hoping to surf the new wave themselves.

Perry had already attempted to live up to the *Sniffin' Glue* ideal, at the back end of '76, with predictable results: 'I was disillusioned with the way the old bands were going, the bands that were coming up were a lot of crap basically. I just thought, "Let's have a go myself." . . . [So I] got together with Tyrone [Thomas], who joined me in ATV . . . We just jammed a bit and I shouted. It was rubbish.' At this stage Perry was simply too much of a prog-rock fan (as was Genesis – hence the name) to record a punk symphony with pots and pans, while someone attacked an electric viola with a cheese grater.

That first 'ATV' rehearsal – which, in a TG-like gesture, has now been released on CD – proved surprisingly productive, resulting in two instant anthems, 'Love Lies Limp' and 'Life', giving genuine hope that Perry and Ferguson might help reclaim punk from beckoning conformity. By May, ATV had a higher percentage of pukka musicians than most punk bands, even if they had – for a single gig – the ubiquitous non-musical bassist, Micky Smith. Drummer Towe came fresh from Gen X, in search of some lost beat; while Alex Ferguson, who had had a band in Glasgow, the Nobodies, was an accomplished guitarist with plentiful ideas. Within a few weeks, the four-piece was in a real studio, making their first set of demos.

Mark Perry: We'd been invited by EMI into their studio at Manchester Square, to do a demo. I was dead against it. Miles Copeland wanted me to do it. I thought it would look bad if we went . . . with EMI. He convinced me to just go and use the time and the studio. We went in . . . and recorded four tracks: 'Love Lies Limp', 'Life', 'How Much Longer' and 'You Bastard'. EMI said that they weren't interested, 'cause all the songs had so much swearing, [or] it was too political, or something. But they told us that we could have the tapes . . . So we put out the flexi-disc [of 'Love Lies Limp']. It was a way of saying, 'That's what I did, and this is what I'm doing now.' [PSF]

Genesis, writing at the time, suggested that ATV 'did [these] four demo tapes in the [EMI] studios hoping to get a "proper" record contract'. This seems more likely. Perry's distaste for the 'majors' probably did not extend to rejecting their overtures. As it happens, EMI missed a trick by rejecting ATV for their stance and/or swearing. The recorded cuts were a validation of every claim Perry had made on the band's behalf, being fast, avant-garde and original. Perry's lyrics had real bite and Ferguson showed that simple need not be stupid. This ATV really did seem to stand for Action, Time, Vision.

'Love Lies Limp', in particular, was Perry's autobiographical inversion of Hell's mantra, 'Love Comes In Spurts', set to a kinetic, ska beat by new bassist Tyrone Thomas and stand-in drummer John Towe. In the same issue of *Sniffin' Glue* as the 'Love Lies Limp' flexi-disc, Perry declared, 'Writing is for cunts who are scared to show the[ir] faces . . . your average fanzine writer [being] some frustrated rock star.' The record showed him to be both a better lyricist than critic, and something of a 'frustrated rock star' himself.

Rather than issuing the demo versions of 'How Much Longer' and 'You Bastard' as their first 'official' single, though, ATV re-recorded better sounding, inferior versions, which they released in November – only to second guess the buy-curious by promptly releasing the demos as well. Perry was still hopelessly conflicted about his goals, and the means to achieve them.

Initially, he seemed prepared to allow 'his' band to become an adjunct to the TG agenda. At a show that month, they ended the set by walking off while a set of tapes played, which had been 'provided by Genesis P.

Orridge: little girls scream / Lenny Bruce talks. Genesis' band, Throbbing Gristle, meander through a subterranean instrumental, "Dead Bait" – the tape ends with the Television album played at 45, while Mark stares the audience out.' Genesis, though, already had his doubts about Perry's true goals, asking in a TG communiqué:

So, who DOES own Alternative TV? The whole quality rests on its unselfconscious integrity. This is a joy, a breath of fresh air on the soundwaves. Its weakness is, the one thing this business cannot tolerate is integrity . . . So the choice comes up, do you agree to go under as an honest outsider . . . or do you pretend you believe you can compromise and do a little of what THEY want hoping in the end to slip a disguised version of what YOU want?

It was a question Perry's band resolved for him when the only two true musicians both quit, Towe leaving in September, followed – catastrophically – by Alex Ferguson, four weeks later. If Perry had shown surprising depths as a lyricist, he was an uncharismatic frontman 'with a voice like sand and glue'. Ferguson, as ATV's musical director, provided them with all the minimalist-yet-musical ideas that worked so well on 'Love Lies Limp', 'How Much Longer' and manifesto-song, 'Action Time Vision' (issued as a single after Ferguson quit).

Yet Perry simply couldn't accept that Ferguson was as important to ATV as its ostensible leader, a Cale to his Reed. As he later told Mark Paytress, 'Alex . . . liked to dominate the songwriting, and I wanted to get more involved with that. I knew it was my band.' Ferguson found it impossible to accept Perry's peremptory takeover bid. Matters came to a head one night in Edinburgh, when he pulled the plug on Perry's atonal guitar. Perry seemed happy to see Ferguson go, believing that this would give him the opportunity to change 'musically . . . I wanted to do more interesting, improvised stuff.' He would learn the hard way that vision required technique, and vice-versa.

A shining example of rudimentary technique, realized by a plentiful infusion of ideas, appeared in the shops barely a month after Ferguson bailed on ATV. Surprisingly, this studio debut came in the form of a twenty-one track album, not a double-sided single. For Wire, the refusal to release their initial statement in an easy-to-swallow 7" picture sleeve was as deliberate as the album's stark design, and surfeit of songs (of the 21 songs, six were less than a minute long). *Pink Flag* was as arty as the colleges its makers once attended.

Graham Lewis: After the [*Live At The*] *Roxy* [album] . . . EMI were all for offering us a couple of singles, and we went no way – we've got an album's worth of stuff. We'd [already] had people say to us, 'We'll put out a single' – Dave Fudger, who worked for *Sounds*, had seen us in the early days, and [said he] could get the money together and put out a single.

Issued barely a fortnight after the Pistols' *Never Mind The Bollocks*, *Pink Flag* closed the book on English punk's first wave by being everything the Savage camp at *Sounds* had been hoping for. It was, as *Sounds*' rather partial reviewer Mr Fudger wrote, 'Bleak, morbid but mesmerizing . . . standing apart from this year's other new releases as heartingly as Roxy Music's debut stood out from the pack in 1972.' *Pink Flag* was the lowdown on six months frantically writing and rewriting something that had begun as sub-Ramonesian. It became something else in the six weeks that separate the first set of EMI demos – recorded just three days after producer Mike Thorne caught them at the Roxy – from a second set, which convinced EMI to let them have their way.

Colin Newman: The first three songs, [including] 'Pink Flag' were done to get the [EMI] deal, basically to prove to the record company we could come up with something competent. When we did the Roxy, that twenty-minute set was our [whole] set, and included two covers. So we had to write, rehearse and demo new material. Each set of [demos] . . . were new songs as they were written. Frankly, it was not easy on the ear as far as they were concerned . . . But whereas [other bands] were deliberately dumbing down in order to become popular, Wire were dumbing up. There was a truly moronic side to Wire, but it's contextualized. It's moronic, because it's funny to be moronic.

The lyrics now coming from Graham Lewis's pen were hardly moronic, thanks to a deep-seated hatred for 'all the [rock] clichés, [and] all those bands who were playing songs about cadillacs and chicks and drinking Southern Comfort on their way back to suburbia'. Caustic commentaries on the tabloids ('Field Day For The Sundays'), class-bound conformists ('Mr Suit'), the pop love song ('Feeling Called Love') and even war correspondents ('Reuters') did not suggest any obvious antecedents. Musically, too, they steered clear of most punk parameters, save for brevity and buzzsaw guitars. As Newman told one chronicler, 'It was very obvious what to avoid. We'd seen The Clash, The Damned, and the Sex Pistols countless times, and after the whole media thing had subsided we could see the mistakes they were making.'

Producer Mike Thorne was delighted with the band's spirit of adventure. Though, in his eyes, they 'really . . . didn't know what to do, in the sense of handling their instruments', the fact that they 'decided that they'd like to do something in a new medium – and just did it' made for an album that left any preconceptions acquired at the Roxy where they belonged, down in the crypt. Thorne's only concern was that they were jettisoning material at an alarming rate. He already sensed that when a song was thrown away by these guys, they did not look back.

Wire were moving forward at frightening speed. When they made their radio-session debut on the all-important John Peel show at the turn of the year, just two months after *Pink Flag*, they played just one song from that startling debut ('106 Beats That'). They preferred to preview three songs from the second album they'd not even demoed, including their next-but-one single, the positively deviant 'I Am The Fly', which Colin Newman believes was lyricist Lewis's attempt to 'see us in relation to punk'. If so, Wire were presumably 'the flies in the ointment' who 'spread more disease / than the fleas / which nibble away / at your window display.' They were, for now, England's arch-exponents of New Musick, and the true heralds of what came next.

4.2
DARKEN MY NORTHERN SKY
1/77 – 6/78

When people ask me where I am from . . . I reply that I am from Manchester . . . It doesn't mean I am nostalgic about the place. I was created bitter and resentful by Manchester. I learned absolute emptiness from Manchester. It is not a spiritual environment.
— Genesis P. Orridge

Though one presumes that the band had no hand in scheduling their first UK tour, there is something rather fitting about Pere Ubu, Cleveland's archest art-rockers, making their March 1978 British debut in Manchester; for if there was one English city that closely parallels the development of Cleveland punk, it is Manchester. These two centres of what might be deemed 'industrial punk' both had key bands in place when the starting gun sounded – in Cleveland's case, Rocket from the Tombs; with Manchester, Buzzcocks.

Both bands believed in actively promoting a local scene, bringing the leading lights of their new wave to town, whether it was Television or the Sex Pistols. And, as it happens, each of these bands imploded barely nine months after formation, leaving garageband anthems like 'Sonic Reducer', 'Final Solution', 'Boredom' and 'Orgasm Addict' for their successors to adopt; while producing one radical spin-off band (Pere Ubu/Magazine), along with an altogether more commercial hybrid (Dead Boys/Buzzcocks Mk 2). Both gave an impetus to local scenes tangentially connected to those in New York and London, enabling some important bands to follow in their wake; creating a club scene that became both a reliable stopping-point for every travelling punk combo and a home for local, untutored talent.

If there was an essential difference, it was that it took the Buzzcocks family longer to kick-start Mancunian music; Pere Ubu having found that RFTT, the Electric Eels and the Mirrors had done the hard work. The four (actually, five*) visits by the Pistols to Mancunia in the second half of 1976 had given northern folk the building blocks and blueprint, but local architects took time to realize their plans. Initially, Richard Boon, Pete Shelley and Howard Devoto seemed to have very little to work with; having to resort to 'bussing' in further examples of the form.

* The Pistols did play a show in Manchester between the two Free Trade Hall shows and the two Electric Circus shows, at Didsbury College on 1 October; but because of its student audience, it is generally forgotten.

Richard Boon: There was a missionary zeal [then] about reactivating the potential of Manchester, so we did a gig at the Holdsworth Hall [and] brought Eater up from London, [and] The Drones, [who] had been like a Bay City Rollers covers band. There was an urgency about making something happen . . . I got a phone call from a guy who had a record store in Newcastle, who said, 'I've got this band called Penetration . . .' Interested people came . . . I was doing the door for the [Buzzcocks/]Chelsea [November] gig [and] this guy came up, 'I've just come back from the Mont de Marsan festival.' That was Ian Curtis. He was into Iggy and bits of Kraut-rock.

If the callow Curtis was hoping to make something happen, it was only when returning to the Electric Circus the following month, for the first Anarchy show, that he found fellow sound builders, Peter Hook and Bernard Sumner. At this point, the Electric Circus was Manchester's solitary punk venue and in keeping with the home of English industrial punk, it was 'encircled by broken bricks, shards of glass, and assorted rubble hurled from the derelict forties flat-block opposite', to quote *Sounds'* northern correspondent, Mick Middles. A former bingo hall, it seemed to be the sole survivor from a belated Luftwaffe campaign to flatten parts of north Manchester. To venture into Collyhurst's only Circus was to take one's life in one's hands, even for those born there.

Una Baines: It was a thing with Collyhurst kids, 'We'll show these punks who's hard.' That was the mentality . . . I was beaten up by three girls when I was making a phone call to Mark [E. Smith]. They told me to get out, and I said, 'No,' [so] they dragged me out.

Yet the Circus enjoyed a virtual monopoly of local and visiting punk bands for the first nine months of 1977, save for the fleeting, joyful, month of May when The Oaks, Chorlton, took to persuading remnants of the Roxy to venture north. Siouxsie & the Banshees, The Vibrators, The Adverts and The Slits all gave that side of the city the sights and sound of London punk-rock before there was a vinyl equivalent. But promotion was the key, and printing punk-style gig flyers was no simple matter, especially when they came from Buzzcocks' ex-art-school designer.

Linder Sterling: There was one photocopy place [in Manchester], Rank Xerox in Piccadilly, so trying to photocopy my montages was virtually impossible.

You'd have to take them to the manager, so he would approve them in some way.

Thankfully, when it came to vinyl, Manchester was well served by an array of independent record shops, from Black Sedan in the university precinct, to Paperchase, Virgin and Rare Records in 'town'; all of which served the local scene (Ian Curtis sometimes worked in Rare Records, Paperchase carried most US music mags, while Virgin on Lever Street served as the primary retail outlet in the country for *Spiral Scratch*). Piccadilly also had a late-night bar that resembled Soho's Louise's, where Manchester's more outlandish youth went to, er, express themselves.

Linder Sterling: [We were] going to . . . the Ranch Bar . . . [and] you would see boys as Bryan Ferry one week, in very beautiful white shirts; and those very same shirts next week ripped and torn and painted on. Seditionaries was incredibly expensive, so people had to adapt.

Una Baines: People caught on to it when the main thrust of [punk] was already over. I remember going to the Ranch Bar, and the very first punks turned up. This was when punks started to have an identity, because previous to that, there wasn't anything you could identify it with, as regards a look; and then these kids started turning up with long white shirts, ties and drainpipes. But prior to that it was anti-fashion.

Manchester also had a set of aspiring journalists quite prepared to talk up the scene, even when there wasn't one. Initially, the two most influential were Paul Morley, still trying to get his foot in the door at *NME*, and Ian Wood, *Sounds'* Mancunian reviewer before Mick Middles took his baton. Both had their favourites, revised when ridicule rained down.

By the beginning of 1977, Morley had abandoned editing his fanzine, *Out There*, deciding to go the McLaren route and manage Rockslide, a desperately untalented bunch who thought covering their clothes in slogans and reinventing themselves as The Drones would fool enough punks, enough of the time. Morley informed the national papers, 'We will do almost anything to be successful,' presumably meaning the band. But by inhabiting the same sub-metal domain as Slaughter & the Dogs, they didn't even have that nominal niche to themselves; and Morley soon decided to make a name for himself instead.

If The Drones was an apposite name, it was trumped by another local combo, The Worst, whose spokesman, Allan Deaves, proudly proclaimed, when *Melody Maker* came a-callin', 'We can't play – I don't know one end of a guitar from the other – but what's good about that is that every time I forget how to play or sing things, I have to improvise . . . All we want is to get up there and . . . express ourselves.' Firmly in the anti-competence, if not the anti-rock camp, The Worst were a sub-Sect set of amateurs who preferred to rehearse on stage rather than pay for a room where they might get better. By default, they shared a number of bills with Buzzcocks and The Fall, until the Mancunian punks adopted Birmingham's substitute Subway Sect, the Prefects.

The Prefects may not have been The Clash's favourite sons, but they were quietly championed by both the Sect and Buzzcocks, with whom they shared the majority of their gigs in the two years they stuttered on after White Riot opened their eyes. Vic Goddard was particularly impressed by the fact that these boys from Birmingham 'used to do whatever song was number one in the charts . . . [but] their punkified version of it'. Whenever they ventured north, whether to JB's in Dudley, Eric's in Liverpool or Rafter's in Manchester, the Sect usually called on the Prefects to support, much to the chagrin of their manager. After one show in Manchester, the pompous Rhodes informed Prefects singer, Robert Lloyd, 'I am a patron of the arts and you just abuse them. You are amateur wankers.' Actually, it was Richard Boon who proved the true patron. Rhodes remained a mere rabble-rouser.

Robert Lloyd: Manchester in general was good to us . . . Not only did the Buzzcocks like us . . . but also we played with The Fall and The Worst a lot. Most of the gigs we did, [especially] toward the end, were either in Manchester, or were with Manchester bands. The Buzzcocks and Richard Boon really looked after bands like the Prefects and The Fall, took them on the road, and paid them to be there, when they wouldn't have got gigs under their own steam.

What northern Sect fans particularly seemed to get off on was the Prefects' 'answer' to 'Rock & Roll, Even', 'Going Through The Motions'. According to Paul Morley, an early advocate, this 'vindictive, powerful piece of music . . . [was] born to plug a ten-minute gap in a set'. Actually, it was devised with one simple intention in mind – antagonizing an audience. Before The Fall had refined their own retort to audience expectations, the Prefects had perfected pissing people off.

Robert Lloyd: It was very much our intention to be antagonistic. I don't know if The Fall were trying to do the same thing – they knew more music, and certainly took more drugs . . . but we were so hacked off with this idea of punk that it became our thing. 'Going Through The Motions' was born from touring Yorkshire with bands like Sham 69, and just being confronted with audiences full of Sid Vicious lookalikes and skinheads, and thinking, 'Right, you cunts, we're gonna play a really slow, boring song for ten minutes and really piss you off.' We just got more and more experimental. I think a few audiences, normally in Manchester, loved it. Just about everyone else hated it. We had some terrible reactions, but we used to thrive on it. I wouldn't find it too fantastic now playing to five hundred skinheads throwing bottles at you, but at the time you feel gleeful about it.

The Buzzcocks' patronage of the Prefects displayed a side to the poppiest punk band around that was otherwise kept under wraps. Like his early inspiration, Paul McCartney, Pete Shelley loved experimenting with all aspects of sound, from atonal to ambient. But for now, he needed to reassert the band's pole position after the traumatic departure of wordsmith/singer, Howard Devoto. Though Linder Sterling remembers the split being 'remarkably civilized . . . Peter and Richard were [still] like, [sharp intake of breath]. There were some very late nights talking about, "Can Peter do it?" ' In the end, the alternative – blooding a new frontman – was unthinkable, so they placed an ad representing themselves as a 'leading north-west beat combo, requir[ing a] bass player who is pretty or competent, or pretty competent'.

A change in direction was inevitable. The sardonic quality of Devoto's lyrics Shelley was unable to emulate, though he shared Devoto's desire to express down-to-earth sentiments in a literate lyric. What he definitely wasn't about to do was start 'singing songs about laying all the groupies, [because] then it wouldn't mean anything to women, or the people I work with. I don't like excluding people from ideas simply because of their gender.' With Devoto gone, he was also obliged to consider the songwriting ambitions of guitarist Steve Diggle, who had started penning his own pop songs about 'why a girl might end up working her whole life on a supermarket checkout', or the death of a friend who liked to drive fast cars.

Recruiting bassist Garth from Shelley's pre-Buzzcocks outfit, Jet of Air, was one way of trying to maintain momentum. And yet, Shelley shared much of Devoto's despair at the direction punk seemed to be heading in. Looking for a way to define Buzzcocks in some subtle, new way, he told *New Manchester Review* the month after Devoto dropped out:

[Punk]'s never been a strict rock form. The danger is that people think it is. If punk is just a fashion that includes spitting routines, Nazi salutes and the playing of a token Iggy and The Stooges number, then we're nothing to do with it. Six months ago punk . . . just characterized a form of rock. Suddenly it became a fashion and all these bands pronounced themselves punk. We try through the music to alert people to think for themselves, to analyse and more completely control their lives. The music must be . . . part of a whole lifestyle. We're not content to just end up the way most of the kids do; going to Pips, getting stoned . . . We're making a stand against all this consumption.

One way to shake things up was to define Manchester punk along entirely different lines to the London model. The experience of the band at the Harlesden Roxy, the Neal Street Roxy and the Finsbury Park Rainbow in the spring of 1977 confirmed that the capital's version was assuming a uniform and an orthodoxy for which Shelley and Boon felt hardly any kinship. Something more experimental already seemed to be going on in the provinces. Buzzcocks manager Boon certainly thought so, especially after the release of *Spiral Scratch* resulted in New Hormones 'getting [sent] demo tapes as if we were a real label. Chris Watson from Cabaret Voltaire sent a tape. Dave Allen from the Gang of Four sent a demo.'

For a few months in 1977, Boon, Devoto and Shelley flirted with the idea of making New Hormones into 'a real label'; after Boon had told the *New Manchester Review*, 'It would be good to see lots of local labels flourishing. We would be happy if we could just inspire [bands] to do that.' For now, Buzzcocks confined themselves to giving their favourite northern bands – meaning the Prefects, The Worst, The Fall and the Gang of Four – the occasional support slot, especially when mounting an assault on the brightly lit streets of Soho.

Richard Boon: When we had the opportunity to get gigs in London, part of this [idea of] revitalizing Manchester was to take a local support . . . It was [also] a way of saying that there was contrast in Manchester.

The initial response in southern enclaves proved frustrating for all concerned. As early as October 1977, Shelley was complaining to the *NME* about 'people in London [who] can't appreciate something new and exciting, simply because it hasn't been deemed cool'. Refusing to abandon 'home', he later told one documentary crew, 'Being in Manchester helped us maintain and also build upon our own identity.' The rest of the band were not so in love with Manchester's post-industrial pallor. Diggle, in his autobiography, admits that, 'Manchester was a good place to live back then if you wanted to stay reasonably grounded. Which was probably why I suggested we all move to London . . . but Shelley's Coronation Street boots were stuck firmly in the cobbles.'

The decision to dig in 'up north' did Buzzcocks no favours when it came to getting a record deal. By the time they played the Roxy, they had pretty much decided to sup the poisoned chalice, though not before Boon 'had long conversations [with Shelley] about doing another [independent] EP called *Love Bites*, featuring "Orgasm Addict" and "Sixteen". During all that period we were . . . trying to keep Manchester in the foreground . . . Then [the labels] started sniffing.'

With the reality of running even a small label brought home to them by the success of *Spiral Scratch* – which ended up topping 20,000 sales – the band returned from the White Riot tour prepared to look at what the 'majors' had to offer. It quickly became clear that it would have to be either Andrew Lauder at United Artists or the corporate cash on offer from CBS. As Diggle says, 'The Clash situation put us off CBS, because we knew we'd encounter the same bureaucratic bullshit they were fighting.' United Artists it was – making Buzzcocks the last band on that original Screen on the Green bill to sign to 'a major' – though not before a late intervention by CBS's biggest gun.

Richard Boon: We felt comfortable with Andrew Lauder. The day we were going to sign with UA, Maurice Oberstein had obviously heard and phoned me up – and I had to hold the phone a yard away from my ear – saying, 'What are you doing? What do you want?' and I was saying, 'Your A&R guy passed [on us].' There was a plan of product delivery with UA. The first single would be 'Orgasm Addict', which was like the punk song. The other side would be a bit more poppy. The second single would be 'What Do I Get', which was poppier, with the punky 'Oh Shit' on the back . . . The contract wasn't particularly good. We didn't know what we were doing.

The single-minded strategy of one-two-three 45s, then an album, was a smart one – as were all the singles they now issued, beginning in October 1977 with 'Orgasm Addict' b/w 'Whatever Happened To?'. 'What Do I Get?' b/w 'Oh Shit' and 'I Don't Mind' b/w 'Autonomy' also prefaced the debut album, without ever troubling the charts, despite their obvious pop vérités and a press pack crammed with laudatory reviews. But they could no longer rely on Lauder, who left UA shortly after signing them, to set up Radar with Jake Rivera. It would make for an unhappy relationship between band and label, even after their fifth 45 – 'Ever Fallen In Love' – proved just too damn catchy to be constrained outside the charts.

By the release of 'What Do I Get?', in February 1978, the Manchester scene had begun to take care of itself, even if the first wave failed to take their cue from the Electric Circus, which closed its doors in early October 1977. The final two nights suggested that Manchester was slowly but surely rising above The Worst. Though bands as unremittingly awful as The Drones, The Negatives and V-2 were allowed to say their goodbye to the one venue that had consistently welcomed them, the Collyhurst Circus finale also signalled the emergence of three bands destined to define Manchester's industrial punk: The Fall, Warsaw and Howard Devoto's new band, Magazine.

–   –   –

If The Fall and Warsaw shared a common starting point – the Lesser Free Trade Hall – and a common football team – City – they also each drew encouragement and inspiration from a motley set of musicians known as the Manchester Music Collective, an attempt by two apostates from classical music to help untutored 'musos' express themselves. If it had been a certain show at the Free Trade Hall that had set Hallé percussionist Dick Witts thinking along these lines, it was fellow classicist Trevor Wishart who really set the Collective in motion in the spring of 1977.

Dick Witts: Trevor Wishart, this wonderful composer from the electronic world, like myself had New Left sympathies. We wanted to build connections with this new kind of music [using] public subsidies, which had been corralled on to an elitist contemporary [classical] music scene, because what we were hearing was more exciting than what was being done there – and also [it] had a direct social impact. We thought [what was] needed was a platform for trying out stuff in a public setting . . . and secondly, some sort of developmental fund [for] cheap rehearsal studios . . . Talking to [these young] musicians in the early meetings, what they lacked was the financial capacity to rehearse more than a couple [of times] a week. [And since] no one had worked out a piece of music on score, they actually had to rehearse to work out the music themselves. That was how the music came about. We [managed to get] the basement of North West Arts in King Street, this café, and the man who ran the café was quite sympathetic, so we got Monday evenings for free. That's how the Collective came about . . . [And then] we advertised in the alternative press.

If Witts felt 'overburdened with knowledge about music', he was impressed to find some of the 'musically illiterate' that came along to the Collective were capable of 'playing something from nowhere'. Buzzcocks manager Richard Boon was another early advocate, finding the Collective 'full of all the musicians who had a creative attitude, rather than being slavish copies of punk tabloid stereotyping'.

Among early Collective attendants were members of Prestwich punk combo, The Fall, who had been hoping the Pistols' performances might open Manchester's music venues up to new bands, but discovered that 'every time you rang up a social secretary, trying to get a gig, all they would say is "Send us a tape" and all that crap.' Keyboardist Una Baines avers, 'We were already interested in the idea of the Collective, the idea of having showcases and supporting each other's work was really good.'

It was bassist Tony Friel who first convinced his fellow Fallen to come along, but it was guitarist Martin Bramah who noticed Pete Shelley at the Ranch Bar and told him, 'We're a band. Come and see us.' And he did, bringing Devoto and Boon into the bargain. Before such an exclusive audience, Bramah witnessed singer Mark E. Smith 'just let fly with such venom . . . [At one point,] he just sort of reached into the audience and virtually poked his finger up Howard Devoto's nose.'

The first Fall set-list suggested that the leftist sympathies of the Collective's founders were shared by the band, with songs like 'Hey Fascist' and 'Race Hatred' already written. The energetic ensemble impressed all three New Hormone representatives with their attitude, if not their musicianship. Over the summer the band got used to playing in an encouraging environment before being obliged to perform to those of a less experimental bent, i.e. paying punks.

Mark E. Smith: The Fall kind of got it together through the [Manchester] Collective. It was the sort of thing where you'd have three different bands who wouldn't play together normally. We'd play with an avant-garde tape recorder and a socialist band. [1979]

Through 1977, it was only the Buzzcocks' proactive booking policy and the Collective itself that kept the flame burning either side of the Ship Canal. However, even in the Collective some insiders believed certain members to be more equal than others. As Witts observes, 'There was no hierarchy [initially, but] I think one developed. It depended on who had equipment. If someone came along with some equipment, would they allow other musicians to use [it]? One example of someone who was open, and then turned into a rather embittered character was [Frantic Elevator] Mick Hucknall, [who] . . . started getting embittered about the other people who had more success than him. If Rob Gretton turned up with one [member] of [Joy Division], [there]'d be all this [muttering].'

For the now-radicalized Fall, the move by the Collective to the Band on the Wall in November 1977 signalled the end of its tutelage. Though they shared the opening night at this new location with Trevor Wishart and Pride, all save bassist Tony Friel felt they had transcended the Collective's goals, after recording their first EP just four days earlier.

As a way of signing off, The Fall closed that night with the same song with which they had ended their debut Collective performance, back in May, 'Repetition'. This time the audience was informed, 'This song's gonna last for three hours.' The following month, Friel decided he had more in common with the Manchester Collective than the Smith collective, leaving to form The Passage with Dick Witts, where his love of Jethro Tull and his desire to grow musically wouldn't make Smith go on the defensive, as it had from the very first time they met.

Una Baines: I think [Mark's sister] brought [Tony and Martin] round one night. I think Tony was into Jethro Tull at the time, and there was an immediate argument between Tony and Mark about music . . . We were listening to The New York Dolls, The Stooges, Captain Beefheart, Can, Third Ear Band.

Friel had been one of the original, drummer-less quartet which had decided to get its act together after the Pistols came to town. In defining that initial impetus, Martin Bramah chants a familiar refrain, 'Punk was really an injection of energy into what ideas we already had. It was more the idea we can actually get up and play, rather than just listen to records and jam around the home. We were [already] listening to a lot of the bands coming out of New York . . . but also a lot of German music.' At the time, Friel was the only one who could really play, so was perhaps an odd choice for bassist. The others were obliged to pick up whatever they felt might work.

Una Baines: We talked about how [the band] would be. Mark was originally the guitarist, Martin was the singer, and I was the drummer. But I couldn't afford a drum kit. I had a set of drumsticks and a tray. And Mark [just] couldn't learn to play the guitar. [Whereas] Martin and Tony had [already] been playing, and Tony was already quite good.

Baines relinquished the drums, after remembering how her grand-parents had a piano, and how she 'used to go and play on it when I was a kid'. Instead of a drum kit, she purchased a cheap keyboard – so cheap, she recalls, that the week after she got it, on the 'never-never', 'it got reviewed in *Sounds* or *Melody Maker* as the worst keyboard you could get'. It still arrived too late for The Fall's May debut at the Collective. At this juncture, the band was still, in Baines's mind, 'Four people who just hung out, and did arty-farty things, read each other poems and stuff.' But once the band became a gigging entity, with Smith the singer by default, he quickly began to assert himself lyrically and verbally.

Martin Bramah: The words were where [Mark] made his stamp. He insisted that these [we]re the words we were gonna use. Una wrote some lyrics in the early Fall, [but] their ideas were closely linked. Mark bought a guitar first, and he made noises on it, but he couldn't really play tunes on it. I started off singing because I'd been in other bands, but I gravitated towards the guitar. It gradually took a natural shape. He had a lot of words and a lot of energy.

By the beginning of July 1977, when The Fall played their sixth gig at the Vortex in London, Smith was already the self-appointed group spokesman, informing one fanzine after an unflattering review that 'the original concept of the group was a musical vehicle for the lyrics . . . We would not like to compromise on any terms, be they "old" or "new" wave, and surely the whole idea of what's going down now is to change things both musically and environment/"fashion" wise, etc. . . . The minute we have to speed up/slow down/cut out ANY-THING is the minute we pack it in.'

Smith was not about to 'pack it in'. He had found what he had been looking for, a medium for expression where 'you can use primitive methods to communicate . . . Rock & roll is the only form where you can do that . . . Rock & roll isn't even music really – it's a mistreating of instruments to get feelings over.' It could certainly resemble that when the early Fall played. With a sense of identity that other, more musical bands never found, The Fall were exactly what Manchester's impatient rock critics needed in their quest to make a scene appear out of thin air. By the end of July 1977, Morley was using his most portentous prose to describe them in a two-page profile on Manchester punk in *NME*:

The guitarist's slashing chording is the anger of frustration solidified into burning sound, the simplicity of the lady keyboardist's embellishment a self-mocking intrusion. The singer is an angry concerned narrator, the rhythm clever and neutral . . . Such earnest and undiluted political quests should prove an interesting barrier to overcome.

Sounds' Ian Wood also claimed there was 'an indefinable buzz in Manchester about [the band] . . . You might not enjoy them, but can't ignore The Fall.' As it happens, few were content to just ignore a band whose set included 'Psycho Mafia', 'Dresden Dolls', 'Hey Fascist', 'Frightened', 'Industrial Estate', 'Bingo Master's Breakout', and the in-your-face insolence of 'Repetition', which Wood found could be 'leaden and slow' or 'psychotically rapid'; short, long or excruciating; relentlessly repetitive or surprisingly inventive. If nothing else inspired audiences to voice their feelings, 'Repetition' did it every time. As it was intended to do.

Martin Bramah: ['Repetition'] was very much our 'Sister Ray' – it was our mission statement. It wasn't punk. It had elements of dub reggae and Can. It didn't have a structure – it was just a riff and a beat. Live it was usually a lot longer than it was on the record. [But] it became a war of attrition against the audience. If we were feeling particularly abused, we'd just play 'Repetition' till the audience either walked away or got really violent . . . It was like, 'If you can take this . . .' In the early Fall, confrontation with the audience was sort of the lifeblood. To us, it was taking a gang on to the stage. The Fall wasn't just a violent bunch of thugs, but there was that element to our nature at that age. We had hung out as a gang before we were a band. We were ready for anyone who wanted to challenge us. There was a lot of confrontation, a lot of violence at the gigs, yeah. But we were [also] smarter than that.

Their sonic challenge didn't always go unanswered. Smith, in one early interview, typified The Fall as 'music for the people that don't want it'. Among those who found their 'message' not merely provocative, but inflammatory, were certain right-wing elements who had begun to infiltrate punk shows in the north by the summer of 1977. Statements to the music press like, 'In our political songs we mean what we say,' made The Fall a potential target every time they left the relative safety of Manchester. Things sometimes got out of hand long before they got to 'Repetition'.

Una Baines: We used to get National Front coming to gigs and throwing bottles at us, and I'd hide behind an amp and throw them back. 'Cause we were [still] doing songs like 'Hey Fascist' and 'Race Hatred'.

Sometimes, they didn't even need to start playing before the trouble started. On one occasion, Baines remembers they entered a place to find it full of Hell's Angels. Undeterred, she proceeded to pour 'a pint of beer over this guy's head for grabbing me, and the next minute they're all on Martin on the door, hitting him. We flew upstairs, and locked ourselves in the pub bathroom. We thought we were gonna get stabbed – the landlord was too scared to call the police. Anyway, they got rid of them and we did the gig, with blood pouring down Martin's face.'

Smith, who always liked the way that Lenny Bruce 'used to insult his audience', showed an alarming capacity for starting fights anywhere, anytime, anyhow. As Bramah told Simon Ford, 'If you went out to a club with Mark, he'd pick a fight with someone. But that was just Mark: irrational and erratic.' For the time being, it became a badge of honour.

Smith even told *NME* in 1981 that when he was sixteen, he 'used to take acid and go round clubs wearing swastika armbands – me, Tony, Bramah and Una – and we used to try and cause fights with heavy metal gangs and get bands to play proper music.' None of the others can remember such reckless wilfulness until Smith got old enough to drink, and began his inexorable transformation into a belligerent boozer. The process began when he was required to spend evenings down the pub, hearing about the hellish day his girlfriend had endured, tending to the mentally impaired at the forbidding edifice that was Prestwich Mental Hospital.

Una Baines: [I worked] about eighteen months as a trainee [nurse]. I come from a nursing family. When I left home, I just had loads of crap office jobs. We'd be going to gigs, and listening to music at the weekend, and then have to go to these dreary jobs. It was extremely depressing. I didn't actually want to be a nurse – like my mum and my sisters – but I was always interested in mental illness, 'cause I felt that people with mental illness were far more stigmatized than [other] ill people. I was very naive. I thought I could change the whole of Prestwich Mental Hospital single-handed, but you [quickly] found out that you're up against an entrenched system – it was so regimented, they get up at seven, they have their breakfast at eight, they take their drugs at half-eight. Such human misery in those places! And also the drugs they were on! As far as I was concerned, they were being experimented upon. People who had been on one drug for years, suddenly the whole ward was changed on to another drug . . . I used to go to the pub every night, get pissed and just talk about Prestwich Hospital. I had to witness [electro-shock treatment] . . . This guy Greg, an ex-patient, started the Mental Patients' Union. I got involved with that, and found out all about people's rights. There were informal patients there who didn't realize they could come and go as they please. They'd been given the impression that they had to [stay there]. There were patients in there being given drugs that they thought that they couldn't refuse, and they weren't sectioned . . . [So] we got this van, and we'd get people to the meetings and then bring them back. But patients got threatened by the staff if they went to the meetings again. It didn't last very long . . . I was nineteen, and in The Fall. That's why I left. That was a big tug of conscience for me, but it was making me very, very depressed. You couldn't do anything! I used to bring patients home to my flat and give them tea and coffee, so they started giving me patients in wheelchairs and on crutches. I had to give up in the end . . . [But Mark] used to come to the Mental Patients' Union meetings with me – [he's] quite a sensitive soul really, underneath that exterior.

If these harrowing experiences changed Baines for good, they also seem to have given Smith a subject he could make his own, one worthy enough to allow him to come down from his soapbox. Time spent at the short-lived Mental Patients' Union meetings gave Smith an insight into lives of quiet desperation that now served to inspire his best work.

Dick Witts certainly believes, 'There's something in Mark's past life which relates to . . . Prestwich Mental Hospital. [There's even] that story about Mark going to a local pub and being chucked out because they thought he was from Prestwich Hospital.' A song like 'Frightened', drawing on the experience of people who live their lives 'in a trance', alluded to experiences with which nobody in the band felt entirely comfortable, but which they all seemed to share.

Martin Bramah: Living on the edge of Prestwich Mental Hospital, which was a town in itself and employed a lot of people in Prestwich, we were very aware of it. [Indeed,] a lot of mentally ill people were wandering about Prestwich Village at lunchtime so it was just part of life. There was a woman who insisted on standing in the middle of a zebra crossing on Market Street, just combing her hair and pointing at aeroplanes and stopping the traffic. These people were around Prestwich, and so they found their way into the songs. . . . As children we lived in fear of being dragged in there and never coming out again – as you do – 'cause it's this place where frightening men were living.

Such experiences might have set The Fall apart from their fellow Manchester bands, but even those who wanted to help, and had some common concept of life in the (largely uncobbled) streets of north Manchester, were soon dismissed by Smith. In his first *Sounds* feature, he insisted that 'there's your intellectual bands, like Devo and Magazine, and there's your headbanger bands . . . We want to stand outside of that kind of division.' Smith's paranoia extended to imagining members of Buzzcocks – fans of The Fall one and all – talking to the group behind his back, saying. 'You are great, but you have got to get rid of that singer.' Even Warsaw, who shared the same interest in noise, the Manchester Music Collective and City's soccer team, were treated with ill-disguised disdain.

Martin Bramah: We hated most of the other bands, 'cause we felt that they were just crude punk rockers. We felt we'd left punk behind after just a few months. We didn't really think we were punks, even six months after seeing the Pistols, because it immediately became clear that it had become a fashion movement. It was all about safety pins and bondage trousers. We'd never dress like that. The Sex Pistols didn't dress like that when we first saw them. It was this Oxfam chic. We used to share the same rehearsal rooms on Little Peter Street [with bands] like Warsaw, but we didn't talk to each other even on the stairs. We hated each other. We're doing the same gigs, and just hating each other's guts. I still don't talk to them. It comes from that enmity of young guys thinking they're in a gang, not a band.

They also reserved room in their deep chasms of contempt for most southerners, particularly London's punk fashion victims. When interviewed by *NME* nine months after their first London show, Smith still recalled how, 'Everyone stood there posin' . . . We had no money for drinks or 'owt; and there's all these street kids in bondage suits sippin' vodka and orange.' No way The Fall planned to leave Manchester, in search of the Big Deal. When one came their way, they had no qualms rejecting it.

Dick Witts: I remember this gig we did in Kirkby [with The Fall] – it was in this banquet suite – and there were these two guys who'd come up from London. They came backstage and said, 'We're very interested in managing you, but there are just one or two things we'd like to put in front of you – first of all, your dress – it's a bit of a shambles – and secondly, the girl should be brought forward.' [Surprisingly] Mark didn't hit them, or call them stupid bastards, but all of us creased up, trying desperately not to laugh.

Such integrity left them high and dry when it came to real record-labels, even when the music papers began to take notice, as they had by the end of 1977. If Buzzcocks had hardly been snowed under by the demands of A&R men, The Fall not only made music that was difficult, but were difficult themselves. The one way open in the wake of punk was to make a record themselves, then using it to garner interest.

Though they still 'had no money', they remained in the good graces of New Hormones – whatever Smith imagined – and in October they were invited to tour with Buzzcocks and The Worst. What Boon saw convinced him to make another EP. Still hoping to keep New Hormones going under the United Artists umbrella, he offered to pay for The Fall to record at Buzzcocks' favourite studio, Indigo, where the band liked to demo potential singles for UA. Smith later managed to find a more malign motive for Boon's generosity, suggesting that he 'was pissed off with the Buzzcocks because they were going really poppy . . . so he might have recorded us to piss them off a bit.' In fact, Shelley shared Boon's enthusiasm, willingly writing off the results when a UA-distributed New Hormones became a non-starter; before letting The Fall have the tapes gratis, with their blessing, no strings attached.

The songs The Fall recorded on 9 November were caught just in time. With dissension already in the ranks, they cut four tracks, namely 'Psycho Mafia', 'Frightened', 'Bingo Master's Breakout' and 'Repetition', all of which Paul Eastham – in previewing the resultant EP for the *New Manchester Review* – considered 'consistent with a theme of mental illness'. Perhaps Smith had not expected anyone to notice that the EP was an unrelenting examination of people on the edge of a breakdown, much as he seems to have failed to notice that his old girlfriend, Una Baines, was heading the same way.

Una Baines: By [1978], I was starting to get ill. They kept ringing me up asking me to do another gig, and I'd end up doing it because I didn't want to let people down, but I was getting more and more ill. I had to stop. My brain was totally scrambled. [Then] I had an accidental overdose . . . [so] from being a pretty together, strong person, fighting for all sorts of human rights issues, [I'd] become like a completely fragmented person who couldn't hardly hold a sentence. And . . . I knew that I wasn't going to get better quickly.

Baines was not the first to fly the coop. Barely was the EP, *Bingo Master's Breakout*, in the can than Tony Friel, whose musical ideas were crucial to the early Fall, took umbrage at the imposition by Smith of a new band manager, who also happened to be his new girlfriend, Kay Carroll. As Baines observes, 'He didn't see why this woman could give him orders about our band. It was *our* band. And she doesn't even like the music we play. She [was] into Pink Floyd – which was a Collective no-no.'

He had a point. If Smith had read the situation wrong, Bramah certainly recognized that, 'Tony . . . thought The Fall was as much his vehicle as Mark's. He'd thought of the name and was the primary musician within the band.' Friel also gets co-credit on all four songs recorded at Indigo, so was entitled to feel this way. Smith, in a letter to *Alternative Ulster*, claimed Friel's departure was the result of 'want[ing] to be a musician + study music sheets'. As departures became the norm, he would have to think of ever more inventive ways to deny the obvious – that The Fall was no longer a Collective ideal, but an outlet for Smith's clever lyrics, boorish behaviour and growing egomania.

Martin Bramah: Kay was [already] Mark's girlfriend, so . . . everything Mark said just went. That was the start of the [big] division. Mark was coming forward as the clear leader, with Kay as his enforcer. The rest of us were just the band. Una was the next to leave, because she found it hard to deal with the amount of tension we were subjected to . . . To maintain a kind of creative conflict, you have to be aware that's what it is, but the day-to-day reality is it's just a conflict, and that can get boring.

Meanwhile Smith struggled to find any takers willing to put the EP out, even as an historical document. When he took the tapes to Martin Hannett at Rabid, Hannett was impressed, but was looking to impose himself on any artist he brought into the fold. He suggested re-recording the EP with more guitars, despite Smith telling him that, 'The mis-tuned guitar [on 'Bingo Master's Breakout' was] a deliberate rejection of the first take, which was much more melodic.' When Hannett realized that this guy was not malleable to his will, he carried on searching for some local lads who were.

— — —

Hannett already had his eye on those other misfits from the Collective colony, Warsaw. Unfortunately he was having a problem convincing his Rabid partner, Tosh, to overlook their overt flirtation with Nazi iconography – evident from day one – and sign them to the label. Tosh's response, according to C. P. Lee, was unambiguous, 'I won't have those Nazi fuckers in my shop!' And at this stage Hannett was in no position to override his wishes, nor could he take his talents to somebody more supportive, like New Hormones.

Richard Boon: When we did *Spiral Scratch*, there was no infrastructure to support anything like [it]. You could feel the infrastructure building around you as people said, 'We want to stock this record.' . . . So rather than do *Love Bites* as a three-track EP, we 'betrayed' Manchester by signing to a London-based major . . . [But] we went to a major partly because I had this meeting with John Maher's dad, who [said], 'John's been offered a job in an insurance office. Is there going to be a future for him as a musician?'

After New Hormones' demise, Mancunian 'indie' labels were in short supply, as both The Fall and Joy Division found out, touting around four-track EPs each had recorded at the end of 1977 in local studios.

In the case of Warsaw, the exercise was complicated by the fact that they had decided to change their name, not because of its Nazi association, but because a band called Warsaw Pakt had generated a great deal of publicity by recording and issuing an album in less than forty-eight hours. Warsaw's new name was no less provocative, having been derived from what purported to be an anonymous autobiography of a concentration-camp prostitute, *House of Dolls*. The darkly ironic name given by the Nazis to these conscripted women was the Joy Division.

If Warsaw had already unwittingly lost themselves a record deal because of their (original) name, the new one ended up costing them another, with the hippest new label on the block, Fast Product. Though the block in question was in Edinburgh, Fast had already signed two bands from across the Pennines to single deals, The Mekons and Gang of Four. A meeting with the Manchester band, though, persuaded Fast to pass.

Bob Last: Jo Callis introduced Warsaw to me. We started putting Warsaw on as support to The Rezillos in the Midlands . . . We had a meeting with . . . the guys in Joy Division up in Edinburgh, to try and resolve things, and finally decided we weren't gonna sign them. They were just [flirting] too close to fascist iconography. We had [that] meeting to try and make our own minds up about whether they understood [what] they were playing with, or where they were coming from, and we were [still] a little uneasy. It was tapping into some of Ian Curtis's darker neuroses, and at a certain point we just got uneasy. [When] they became Joy Division, we took the trouble to find out [what it meant and] we saw a process here. We [were] getting a little worried about where it was going.

When the two most productive 'indie' labels in the land – Stiff and Chiswick – decided to stage a series of 'battles of the bands' across the land, early in 1978, Joy Division were just one of seventeen bands who turned up at Rafter's, on 14 April 1978. Down the stairs from Fagin's nightclub, across the road from the ritzy Midland Hotel, the cavern-like club had played host to every important punk band – save the Pistols – in the nine months it had been open, and had just completed a sell-out three-night residency by Costello and The Attractions that ended with bass player Pete Thomas in hospital with a severed tendon.

As Granada TV presenter Tony Wilson recently recalled, 'Every [unsigned] band in Manchester played that night.' Wilson was an enthusiast of the scene, and had been since seeing the Pistols at the Free Trade Hall in June 1976. He was also a local celebrity, because of his late-night TV show dedicated to the new wave, *So It Goes*. Though the show was only screened in the Granada region (which covered little more than Liverpool and Manchester) and London – presumably because these were where this music had a large enough potential TV audience – it was almost the only way for an unsigned punk band to get exposure on the goggle box. And if that wasn't responsibility enough, Wilson also presided over a weekly, teatime TV review called *What's On*, which had already introduced acts like Buzzcocks, Magazine and The Fall to their first TV audiences.

Wilson can't therefore have been greatly surprised that night when one particularly surly-looking singer came up to him and said, 'You bastard! You put Buzzcocks and Sex Pistols and Magazine and all those others on the telly. What about us, then?!' He *was* surprised, though, when the singer in question, Ian Curtis, got onstage at the end of the night and began to perform.

Tony Wilson: Most bands are onstage because they want to be rock stars. Some bands are onstage because they have to be, there's something trying to get out of them: that was blatantly obvious with Joy Division [at Rafter's].

If Wilson was instantly enthralled, so was Rafter's DJ, Rob Gretton, who thought them the best band he'd ever seen; an odd view, given that Warsaw had already played his workplace a couple of times, supporting the Heartbreakers and the Yachts. But that night it was as if he had never seen them before. Unfortunately for the band, by the time they went onstage at two o'clock in the morning, they were playing only to those who didn't need to get up in the morning, a state of affairs that Gretton recalled led them to run 'around threatening everyone. They didn't think they were [even] going to get on.'

Among those they threatened was *NME*'s Paul Morley – and presumably *Sounds'* Mick Wall. The latter certainly went out of his way to badmouth the band in his review: 'For them it's already all over bar the bleating. Mock-heroics all round from Iggy imitators acting out their Sons-of-World-War-Two histrionics.' Morley, who would later suggest he'd been a fan from day one, had already described them in print as being 'doomed . . . to eternal support slots . . . [as] they seem unaware of the audience when performing'. That night they still seemed in their own world, but it was one Gretton found populated by 'blazing madmen'. By the end of the night he was thinking whether to manage them; and Wilson wanted to put them on TV, albeit on *What's On* (*So It Goes* was now off-air).

With their own, self-financed EP due out in a matter of weeks, *What's On* would have been an ideal way to promote the new artifact. Only one problem – the band weren't wild about the results. Indeed, they had all but disowned *An Ideal For Living* by the time it appeared in June, partially because of the lousy sound resulting from cramming fifteen minutes on to a seven-inch single, but largely because it had been recorded too soon. Starting from scratch, it had taken co-founders Peter Hook and Bernard Sumner six months to find a singer, a further six months to get gigworthy (finding a permanent drummer in Steve Morris, after Tony Tabac lasted a single gig), and another half a year for Curtis to discover an independent voice and a commanding presence on stage. So when they were given the opportunity to demo an album's worth of material, a month after the Stiff/Chiswick Challenge, they insisted on re-recording all four EP songs in superior fashion, along with newly penned gems like 'Shadowplay', 'Transmission', 'Interzone', 'Novelty' and 'Ice Age'.

These May 1978 sessions represented both their first studio recordings as Joy Division (the EP having been recorded as Warsaw) and a stark advance on the Warsaw sound. It was almost as if the four band members had retired from punk at the end of 1977, to re-emerge bearing this post-punk prototype at the Stiff/Chiswick Challenge in April 1978. There is much to recommend just such a thesis. Certainly much of the Warsaw set went on the same bonfire as the name, including all the songs they'd demoed back in July 1977: 'Inside The Line', 'Gutz', 'At A Later Date' and 'The Kill' (later rewritten).

Sumner admits that, in the beginning, 'None of us could play a note. So instead we decided to use our brains and intelligence to do something original. We learned to play within our limits.' Those limits were soon tested by a desire – common to Sumner, Hook and Curtis – 'to make extreme music'. In Curtis's case, Lord knows where such desire came from, having grown up in leafy Macclesfield, where he attended the fee-paying King's, a direct-grant school that was closer to a public school than a grammar school. His child bride Deborah certainly never uncovered its source.

Deborah Curtis: From what I can tell it was a fairly idyllic childhood, wandering around fields, building dams in brooks . . . It always puzzled me why he was so obsessed with writing about cityscapes. Maybe he felt guilty that he wasn't trapped in one.

Perhaps the trigger occurred when Curtis came into contact with people like those seared on the consciences of Mark E. Smith and Una Baines. According to Sumner, '[At] the time when Joy Division were forming, [Curtis] worked in a rehabilitation centre for people with physical and mental difficulties, trying to find work. He was very affected by them.' He may also have been affected by The Fall themselves, whose initial ideas seemed like an advance on his own.

Through 1977 Curtis kept tabs on the Collective, though no one seems too sure whether Warsaw ever actually played at their weekly gatherings. Witts thinks not, but Curtis assigned the Collective a key role in the band's evolution in a January 1979 interview, when he had no reason to be economical with the truth, 'The Collective was a really good thing for Joy Division. It gave us somewhere to play, we met other musicians, talked, swapped ideas. Also it gave us a chance to experiment in front of people. We were allowed to take risks.'

Yet even in Swan Street, Curtis and his confederates still felt the same separation from the throng as The Fall, Curtis later suggesting how 'we felt very detached from things. No one was helping us . . . Sometimes we felt like finishing, but it was because everyone ignored us or interfered that we kept thinking, we'll show them.'

Sumner and Hook certainly had mile-wide chips on their shoulders. Even three decades on, Hook likes to portray 'most of the musicians in Manchester then [as] very middle class . . . Barney and I were essentially working-class oiks . . . We had a different attitude. We felt like outsiders.' Conveniently forgetting the two ex-public-school pupils in the band, Hook made feelings of inferiority a class issue, not a musical one. Truth to tell, Warsaw needed more gig opportunities than Manchester could provide if they weren't indeed going to end up 'doomed . . . to eternal support slots'.

It was a recognition of this state of affairs that prompted their reinvention; helped along by the release of a handful of vinyl templates as '77 became '78. Buttressed by Wire's *Pink Flag* and Pere Ubu's *The Modern Dance* were Suicide's debut long-player and The Mekons' single-play. When Ubu came to Rafter's a fortnight after the battle of bands, Joy Division turned out *en masse*, to discover that even the support act, Bristol's The Pop Group, had made some kinda leap into unknown pleasures.

If Joy Division had been unable to play more than three or four songs two weeks earlier at Rafter's, they now had an album's worth of material under their cloth caps, a combination of radically revamped renditions of Warsaw warhorses and startling new soundscapes like 'Shadowplay' and 'Transmission'. Sumner recently described the music of Joy Division as being about 'the death of optimism', but by May 1978 Joy Division were a *cause* for optimism, no matter how cryptic Curtis's lyrics had become. They had grounds for optimism about their own prospects too, as they entered Arrow Studios to begin work on an album for the dance label, Grapevine.

The opportunity had come about through Curtis's careful courting of RCA Promotions Manager Derek Branwood, presumably known to him through Rare Records. Curtis had given Branwood a pre-release copy of the Warsaw EP, which Branwood sent along to London with the suggestion that the label sign the group. RCA, who had been largely silent on the new-wave front, continued to sit on the fence, so Branwood's assistant, Richard Searling, a northern soul DJ, decided to use his own contacts at Grapevine to try and broker a deal. However, when the album was completed – in just four days – both Searling and John Anderson, the head of Grapevine, agreed that they should return to RCA with the results and try to reanimate interest in the band.

The album in question (famously bootlegged as *Warsaw*) should certainly have set somebody's pulse racing at RCA. The eleven tracks were even sequenced in such a way as to represent the quartet's remarkable transition, side one representing Warsaw's best songs, sounding better than ever; while side two depicted their quantum leap into Joy Division. It prompted at least one music journalist, Andrew Harries at *Melody Maker*, to note, 'The band [now] lean heavily towards the austere, experimental German style, influenced by such as Kraftwerk and Eno.' The band, though, were unhappy to discover that Anderson had over-dubbed synthesizer, wanting only guitar and drums in the mix; and began to place obstacles in the way of any deal with RCA.

By September, they were already being courted by TV presenter Tony Wilson, who along with his new sidekick Martin Hannett, had a proposition for the band. Wilson had delivered on his promise to get the band a slot on *What's On*. But despite coinciding with the re-release of *An Ideal For Living* as an altogether more audible 12" EP, the band decided they would rather mime along to the last track on their stillborn

RCA album, 'Shadowplay'. A series of 'atmospheric' cuts to video footage of bridges and cars prompted Hook to tell the director it 'was a load of fucking rubbish'. It was still a startling reinvention for a band who had spent eighteen months as poor relations to The Worst and The Drones. For Julian Cope, who had seen the band in Liverpool a fair few times, it suggested a shift from punk's centre-ground:

One evening . . . Tony Wilson . . . started to introduce this new group. I looked up and recognized them as Warsaw, a bunch who had played Eric's a million times and would never get better. 'Ladies and gentlemen, please welcome Joy Division.' I watched them. Casually, at first, as a name change usually meant sod all. Then I noticed something. They were good. I mean really good. The song . . . was raw as hell, but in a dangerous and suppressed way.

Three weeks later, Joy Division were in Rochdale's Cargo Studios, recording two songs for a double-EP sampler that Tony Wilson was hoping might replicate the spirit of Bob Last's Fast Product. The producer was Martin Hannett, who proceeded to ignore most of the band's suggestions, made them sound like a brittle reflection of their Grapevine self, and ended up mixing the songs without manager Gretton's input, which had been a condition of making the recording in the first place. In short, Hannett was determined to recast Joy Division in his image, and though they voiced their dissatisfaction, the band discovered that the results, issued in December, garnered them the best notices of their career to date. They decided to persevere with Hannett, and indeed with the label this sampler announced to the world – Factory Records.

— — —

Hannett had already been booted out of one session at Cargo, a year earlier, when he had attempted precisely the same high-handed tactics during a demo session with Howard Devoto's second incarnation, Magazine.

Howard Devoto: I can remember . . . kicking Martin out of it, because he wanted to 'faff' around too much. We had so much [we could] spend on these demos [so], 'Sorry, we're not coming back tomorrow. We've got forty quid to spend, and we need to get three songs done, and they need to be done in an hour and a half.'

By this time, Devoto knew he was re-entering the belly of the beast, after a six-month hiatus while he toyed with any number of alternatives to a further bout of public self-examination. For the first few months of freedom, he was content to view Buzzcocks' predicament from the wings, all the while learning 'a lot more about the mechanics of it all, how you went about having a band . . . At that point I don't necessarily think [to myself], "I'm going to be in another band." But then I started to realize, if you're going to do this well . . . there's an awful lot of ground to cover. I don't know if I can be quite motivated enough . . . It's a bloody burden!' Interviewed by Paul Morley for an *NME* feature in July 1977, he started talking about having a band – but 'probably for record only'. Even that concession had only come about because he had found a startlingly good guitarist with whom he wanted to work, come what may.

Howard Devoto: I met John McGeogh through Malcolm Garrett . . . He held a party, and I remember [Malcolm] saying, 'This flatmate of mine is a guitarist. You ought to hear him, because he can play all the guitar parts on *Marquee Moon*.' This is April [1977], and *Marquee Moon* had only been out a few weeks. I registered that. So he came round to Lower Broughton Road a week or two later, and I strummed him the chords of 'Shot By Both Sides'. Obviously I [must have] had half a mind I might want to do another band – enough to check somebody out.

'Shot By Both Sides' began life as a disposition on those punk bands who 'all sound the same when they scream'; something reinforced by his experience of watching The Clash in March – where he 'was shocked to find what was allowed'. But it was Pete Shelley who came up with the riff. When Devoto told him how much he liked it, Shelley said he could have it. Devoto felt impelled to take 'that riff and construct another song around it . . . In many ways Magazine formed to record that song.' As for the band name, it came from the same source as McGeogh's credentials, 'I liked the name Television. So I looked round the room. Carpet. Chair. Magazine.'

So it was that a curious ad appeared in the window of 9 Lever Street, home to Virgin's Manchester outlet, in July 1977: 'Howard Devoto seeks musicians to play slow and fast music. Punk sensibilities not necessary.' The latter sentence said it all. As Devoto later told *NME*, 'Getting Magazine together was a reaction against punk.' And yet, all the interest in the band was as a result of Devoto's punk persona. Asked in September what this new band might sound like, he responded, 'Somewhat frothy – a bit mellow and spiky.' In truth, he wasn't sure himself at this stage. Magazine had begun its real life as a five-piece, with Bob Dickinson on keyboards. But after deciding Dickinson was not quite right, Devoto gave him his marching orders just as a record contract, and session for a single, was looming.

What convinced Devoto that Dickinson did not fit was the set of three demos recorded at Cargo in September, 'Shot By Both Sides', 'Suddenly We Are Eating Sandwiches' (which duly became 'My Mind Ain't So Open'), and 'The Light Pours Out Of Me', the first and last co-penned with Pete Shelley. Despite Dickinson, these were enough to whet the interest of Virgin and United Artists. Devoto, though, found that UA's Andrew Lauder was sending mixed signals, 'He was one of the first people I approached with Magazine, and he kinda [suggested], "You might not want to sign with United Artists." He was gonna leave – that's what he was saying.' That left Virgin in pole position, but Devoto still wasn't sure how long he might stick around, and was interested to see just how flexible Virgin might be. Surprisingly flexible, as it happens.

Howard Devoto: When we were talking to Virgin, and you know, [options to] album one, two, three, four, five, it was all, 'Yeah, right. That's all really hypotheti-cal.' Even that first album . . . 'Album?? Don't push me. Who knows? What the hell am I signing myself up for here?' That's why the contract had all kinds of get-out clauses, [in case] I wanted to 'suspend' my career . . . Virgin came up for the Rafter's gig, but they would have signed us without seeing us live. They were certainly very keen. We were virgins ourselves, so we wouldn't have known a keen A&R person from a hostile one. But our solicitor [knew]. He said, 'They *really* want to sign you.'

Magazine had actually made their unbilled debut at the final Electric Circus show on 2 October, but it had been little more than a run-through of the three songs already demoed. Four weeks later, they made their fully fledged debut at a Rafter's benefit for the beleaguered *New Manchester Review*, with The Fall as special guests after Devoto failed 'to get this guy to go on before us who . . . sticks nails through his tongue, eats light bulbs and things like that'.

The Fall were probably disorienting enough for starters. When

Magazine emerged, it was to perform just eight songs, one of them ('Shot By Both Sides') twice, including an outlandish cover of the theme to *Goldfinger* and the Beefheartian 'I Love You, Big Dummy', Devoto's solitary concession to his punk past. But it was the likes of 'Motorcade', 'The Light Pours Out Of Me' and 'Shot By Both Sides' that suggested Virgin were more forward-thinking than UA. And once they had got Devoto's signature on the contract, just five days later, they could start work on turning him into an obliging little performer.

Howard Devoto: We signed the whole contract with no manager, but I think it was at the meeting where we signed the contract that Simon Draper said, 'I'd just like you to meet Andrew Graham Stewart. He tour-manages Tangerine Dream.' . . . I think in those very early days I kinda thought, 'Maybe we'll play some gigs occasionally. Maybe I'll only do interviews in writing.' But then we get this manager, we've got this record contract, I've got a band – things start to snowball and get their own momentum.

The first matter to hand was recording that all-important debut single. If A-side 'Shot By Both Sides' was a given, the equally seminal 'My Mind Ain't So Open' seemed almost a sop to any punk unpersuaded by the cathartic A-side. Its squalling sax break (à la *Fun House*) and scabrous guitar certainly provided a compelling reason for turning the thing over. For Devoto, the single was not so much a new beginning, as the apex of a less than linear ascent into commerciality and cultural impact combined.

Howard Devoto: I did have this kind of notion that Magazine just came together for me to record 'Shot By Both Sides'. The night I recorded the vocal, I remember thinking, 'In my life there is no more intense moment than this. I've waited two years to pull this together.' It just spoke volumes about how I felt about life, and how I felt up against it all.

Like Richard Hell before him, it almost seemed that with the January 1978 release of this singular statement it was time to take the slow boat to Africa. When *Top of The Pops* asked Devoto to mime along to one of those fake performances of the single, he refused. Perhaps he was too busy packing those books for the long journey into darkness. Eventually, he agreed to do a live vocal the following week, only to then produce an oddly cataleptic performance that all but ended the single's hopes of an upper berth in the charts. As Devoto candidly confirms, 'We didn't play the *Top of The Pops* game very well.'

By early February 1978, Devoto also had an album or more of songs he wanted to record, and some more things he wanted to get off his chest. He was also obliged to admit, in the interviews he conducted when 'Shot By Both Sides' came out, that he was still intrigued by the possibility of a mass audience for something as esoteric as Magazine.

Howard Devoto: I think money can make it interesting – if [one has] to pander to a market then it's maybe a little more interesting than just standing in a corner talking to yourself. It's like deciding what sort of music you're gonna play: [whether] you're gonna play to twenty or so people locally, or if you [want to] see where you can reach the mass market and work out some kind of compromise. [1978]

It was a decision other Manchester bands, bent on impenetrability, seemed determined to avoid. For them there was, by the end of 1978, a label tailored to their needs. Initially, though, Factory would have precious little distribution. In the northern capital of punk, the battle between DIY punks and those who still hoped for fame, fans and fortune was about to begin. Across the Pennines, in Sheffield and Leeds, they awaited the outcome with interest.

4.3
FAST AND SENSIBLE
1/77-12/78

PRODUCT FAST 4   Being Boiled/Circus of Death a 7" single

ELECTRONICALLY YOURS....
THE HUMAN LEAGUE

The new generation in rock has come up with only one brilliant insight. It came
from The Mekons and . . . it is very simple: Rock is the only form of music which
can actually be done better by people who can't play their instruments than by
people who can.   — Mary Harron, *MM*, 26/5/79

Our music is lateral music . . . We're attempting to use our instruments in a
different way . . . looking at it from an entirely fresh position.
                                                        — Mark Stewart, *MM*, 18/2/78

For Pere Ubu, a band who had shared bills with Tin Huey, Devo
and Suicide, the addition of the unsigned Pop Group to their first UK
tour was hardly cause for consternation. For the audiences on that brief
landmark tour, the simple fact that a band like The Pop Group existed,
came from the punk nexus, and held the interest of an Ubu audience
was an inspiration almost as profound as the unearthly brilliance of the
Modern Dance-era Ubu.

Which is not to suggest that The Pop Group in April 1978 were any
good. Just that they hoped to be – sometime soon. Before they got there,
they planned to devise a radical sound that could still strikea nerve with
a mass audience. As band leader Mark Stewart says, 'The whole idea
was to be a pop group – an explosion in the heart of the commodity
. . . In those days if you wanted to get an idea across, you wanted to put
it across in a big way . . . [Yes,] we were interested in slogans . . . [But]
we [also] felt a little let down by the flag wavers, and [so] we took it up
again, and we were younger . . . As soon as punk happened . . . we
made a definite decision that if the whole point of punk is being
rebellious, we can't do it like two months later, four months later – so
we started wearing Val Doonican jumpers.'

This was radical stuff – not the jumpers, seeing punk as evolutionary
– even if it occurred to Stewart before The Pop Group had the chops
necessary to execute much forward motion. It stemmed from the defining experiences of seeing The Clash at the ICA, and the Pistols in
Caerphilly, at the nether end of 1976; which was enough to make him
rethink an earlier inclination to form an R&B band, like fellow
Bristolean 'Jed' Valentine with The Cortinas. By the winter of 1977,
the imposing soul boy was on the lookout for others who could help

him in his quest. But his immediate circle of influence lacked many
like-minded 'musos':

Mark Stewart: '74 [/75], we were getting into The Pretty Things and I was trying
to set up this band called the Wild Boys. We were drawing on the Feelgoods
and Eddie & the Hot Rods and the Count Bishops . . . [But] Jed got in there first
and set up a band, playing dirty, dirty R&B and writing their own covers, unaware
that something was going on [elsewhere]. So they were playing R&B in wine
bars and youth clubs, and a scene was developing . . . [but] I was thinking you
could . . . say something [more] interesting. If you can be dancing and get a
shiver up the back of your spine . . . you can [still] say something interesting [in
song] – [using it] as a vehicle for ideas – that's what I was interested in doing. I
was looking for people from school. Some of them were into Lynyrd Skynyrd –
not naming names. I had to lend them Funkadelic records. One of them was a
machinist on British Aerospace floor, but he looked good. Someone had a
practice room – someone had a car . . . That's how The Pop Group got started.
'Can you play this? Let's go and have a jam.' I was singing – Gareth Sager [and]
Jon Waddington [were] on guitar, Simon Underwood on bass, Bruce Smith on
drums. That was the set-up.

Initially, all The Pop Group were really able to do was indulge in
'experimental jams', and jabber about achieving a 'total disordering of
the senses', proof that they were as busy reading Rimbaud as learning
their instruments. By April 1977, Stewart felt it was time to see what
kind of audience his well-read misfits could attract. He remembered
that he and a friend used to get a funk DJ, and hire local club, Tiffany's,
for the night – so why not hire it for The Pop Group?

Mark Stewart: [So] we got up and played a version of 'Solid Gold Easy Action'
and a couple of [our own] things. We were just playing 'I Wanna Be Your Dog'
and T Rex, and then we tried to play some kind of funk.

If Tiffany's was surprisingly accepting of The Pop Group, other
venues were less so. A gig at the Barton Hill Youth Club apparently
resulted in them tearing the place 'limb from limb with a quite stunning
set', after which a 'large number of . . . malevolent renegades' did the
job for real, thus curtailing any prospect of a repeat booking. Confining
himself to converting Bristoleans, though, was the furthest thing from

Stewart's mind. By September, The Pop Group had 'announced that they were taking some six to eight weeks off to reorganize their set and write some more material, before they assault London . . . [despite having] only performed about half a dozen gigs.' Stewart had always had his eye on London, ninety minutes up the M4, and the place where he'd acquired much of his musical education, but The Pop Group would have to play something resembling tunes if they were going to explode in the heart of the city.

Mark Stewart: Initially, The Pop Group was a little bit of hype – basically manoeuvring to get out of Bristol – but then once we got into [that] position, we were completely open. They were wanking along on their saxophones – and I was just saying whatever I [found] interesting.

Stewart had plenty he wanted to let off steam about. In February 1978, he insisted to *NME*, 'We want to create something that is capable of being good and evil at the same time. We want to be the beatniks of tomorrow.' When the unexpectedly catchy 'She's Beyond Good And Evil' duly entered the set, on its way to single status, it turned out to be more about a 'disordering of senses' than anything overtly political.

Mark Stewart: Just because Nietzsche used the idea of beyond good and evil doesn't mean it can't be used in a different concept . . . For me, ['She's Beyond Good And Evil'] is more coming from a mystical tradition. My grandmother was a clairvoyant, my father is quite an extreme occultist . . . My old man goes on about these different dimensions that parallel this ledge of creativity, where Patti [Smith]'s been, where Lautremont's been . . . Up until the 1920s there were always mystics in society, every court society had its mystics . . . [And] if you try to jam and come to a certain point of free[dom] – like Albert Ayler – it reaches the point where things become interesting. I try and live near that point . . . So it's not particularly about a she. It's [more,] 'Who has the right to judge? Who has the right to say?'

The ambition and ideas – save with a rare exception like 'She's Beyond Good And Evil' – still outweighed the musicality of what Stewart and his band were doing. But Stewart suggested in 1979 that the shortfall between idea and execution was no longer an issue: 'When we started we used to begin by jamming. It was free expression . . . Now we just want to be understood; if it's free, it doesn't have to be esoteric.'

What they were attempting, in Stewart's mind's eye, was to go 'through nihilism . . . emerging the other side with something really positive'. And Stewart talked a good game, using the kind of language journalists love, explaining what he was reaching for, and where he thought punk needed to go.

Mark Stewart: One of the main things we want to do on the tour is smash the barrier between performer and spectator. We wanna try and get audience participation. Maybe we'd like to play without stages and stuff so instead of somebody living out the excitement of somebody and somebody else being a vegetative spectator, we wanna get a whole thing going. Otherwise it's like going to see the film where other people are living out the excitement for you. [1979]

Equally in love with funk and punk were four contemporary art students from Leeds – Andy Gill, Jon King, Hugo Burnham and Andy Corrigan. Though all four attended the Pistols' Anarchy Leeds debut, Burnham believes, 'It wasn't punk rock that really brought us together socially: it was the crowd that had short hair and straight trousers and were always at the weekend disco thing at the bar, dancing to reggae. One of the [social] clubs was called the Grand Funk Society. It was basically a couple of African guys who spent money having huge dances . . . It was like, "OK, we're not like everybody else here."'

Actually Gill, King and Burnham were all southern boys transplanted north by the reputation of Leeds Art School, which by its very location represented a clash of cultures. As Mekon Jon Langford says, 'In Britain, a lot of the universities are shoved out into the suburbs or the outskirts of a town. With Leeds, it's right in the middle and that's . . . where we were all going to school together.' King and Gill came from the same Kent public school, and it was this pair who first began tinkering with a kind of rock music in the immediate aftermath of the Anarchy show.

Jon King: We'd play chess and then write stupid songs [with] faintly funny, off-key lyrics . . . initially [just] to amuse ourselves. It was more like fast R&B. But after a while, we thought, 'If we're doing all this, why don't we get a bass player and a drummer?' Hugo, who used to be part of the Ents department, said, 'Oh I play drums.' He was a brilliant shoplifter, so when he said he had a drum kit, he [actually] went out and progressively stole this drum kit. He'd walk in with this huge artist's portfolio, take down an enormous cymbal, put it in his portfolio and walk out. By the spring of '77 we were all together.

Coming up with the ironic tag, Gang of Four, King and Gill recruited another student, Dave Waterson, known to everyone as the Wolfman, on bass. King recalls how he 'was actually a very accomplished jazz/ funk bass player. He played two shows with us, [but] people [who] are musos [often] think the whole point of music is to play lots, and we went, "No, that's not the point at all." People who can really, really play go into default mode . . . Very many people who I'm amazed by their technical proficiency actually don't have any ideas.' Already Gill and King had definite ideas about what they didn't want. Spartan was the plan from day one. As Gill recently stated, in the notes to the Rhino anthology, *100 Flowers Bloom*, 'The musical form Jon and I loved above all was dub reggae, which is all about space and things disappearing and coming back . . . We were trying to achieve that in a rock context.' All solos because verboten!

Andy Gill: There's a shared interest in avoiding the rock-guitar cliché, for sure. If you think of the first crop of punk stuff, it was all just tedious guitars cranked up through Marshalls. In the wake of The Damned and the Sex Pistols, it was heavy metal. [PSF]

For Jon King, like Pop Group's Mark Stewart, it seemed entirely possible – back then – 'to make people dance and think: a case of using the dominant musical trend to put a message across.' He also shared a sense of frustration at the lack of cultural impact achieved by innovators in more traditional mediums of expression. Even though he was a painter of some promise, according to his tutors, 'After a while I started thinking . . . what point was there in it, [and] about the kind of people who go in the art galleries. It was the same with some of the music I was listening to at the time . . . elitist orchestral pieces.'

Unfortunately, the town King found himself in had a surfeit of teenagers who considered dancing and thinking two entirely distinct activities, the latter to be generally avoided. The Gang of Four would have to show no fear if they were going to take their music into the Leeds clubs and pubs. They'd already had a presentiment of the possible consequences.

Jon King: Leeds was a very violent place. We used to go to these blues dances – where you drink Red Stripe and smoke ganja all night; and [one time] there was an out-of-town gang who came in and just wanted to beat people up. They punched Andy Gill's girlfriend's teeth out; they kicked his face in, broke his nose; and I tried to take on the three guys who were kicking him; and I was hospitalized, bleeding out of my eye and my cheekbone broken. There was always an edge of violence at that time. Leeds was the centre of the British Movement and the National Front. I [even] got truncheoned down by a policeman on an anti-NF demonstration.

Burnham recollects another incident at their local pub, The Fenton, which also 'occasionally attracted the British Movement element. [One time] we walked in [and these guys] kept putting "Glad To Be Gay" on the jukebox over and over again and it was like, "OK, are they BM or are they punk skinheads?" And then, suddenly, there was a hail of glass. Three of us started charging at these people stupidly, but [thankfully] they ran, [all the while] throwing bricks.' Burnham looked like he should have been throwing the bricks, being stocky, with short-cropped hair, a slightly menacing air, and a love for that 'skinhead reggae sound'.

His persona worked in their favour when Gang of Four decided they were ready to face the music, and booked themselves a show at the Corn Exchange in May 1977, where they found that their art-school association attracted one set of troublemakers, and their short hair and punky name another. Burnham believes 'it was quite full – it was all our friends from the college, the art school and the poly, 'cause we had quite a social thing going before then – the art-school crowd. Then there were the people we didn't like, that we drank next to and glared at – the anarchists. Then a bunch of skinheads came in – 'cause it was punk.' And for now, it *was* punk.

Hugo Burnham: It was [soon] obvious that it was easier to do things and be things with this whole movement. It . . . open[ed] up every pub and club; to be able to put something on and get people to come and drink beer, like, 'Can you play? Got short hair? Got any safety pins? OK, you're booked.' Lots of bands took on the mantle. We were not really a punk band . . . but when we first started it was fast and furious. One of our earliest songs was 'Day Tripper', played as fast as fuck. Absurd [stuff] – 'Call Me A Wanker': 'Don't call me a wanker / I'm a bastard'; a song about John Stonehouse: 'John Stonehouse thought he'd jack it in / John Stonehouse went for a swim.'

Sure sounds like punk! As does King's own description of the Gang of Four's early sound – 'very fast and noisy, more like a thrash Stooges version of the Feelgoods.' The skinheads at the Corn Exchange couldn't quite make up their minds. Burnham suspects, 'They were too stupid to work out that we were extremely left wing . . . I looked like a skinhead, and the style of music was verging on marshall music. They couldn't work it out . . . We were all young, and we flirted with that dangerous element, because what we weren't doing was saying, "Fuck Thatcher! Fly The Red Flag! Up On The Ramparts!" It was much subtler than that.' It didn't stop the skinheads taunting Andy Gill, who finally whacked one of them in the face with his guitar.

Despite the air of menace, and the ructions, the general consensus was that the gig had been a great success and plans proceeded for a second show, the following Saturday. This time they would feature the band Andy Corrigan, fellow art-school punk-anarchist and president of the film society, had put together at much the same time. The Mekons, though, were starting from a technical base closer to The Pop Group than their friends, the Gang of Four. Andy Gill, who for a short while stood in on drums for The Mekons, told *NME* in 1979, 'When we were doing our first rehearsals, [The Mekons] would get up when we went for a break and use the gear. When we came back we'd find them making this horrible noise.'

That rehearsal space, according to King, was 'this derelict old warehouse in the slums in Leeds', of which there were no shortage in 1977. Not only did both bands share this vast rehearsal space, and the same watering hole, they also began to assemble a PA both could use. Soon, the two bands would be sharing these venues with the all-girl Delta Five, who were 'girlfriends of friends'. As Burnham suggests, 'It really was a bit of a collective'. If Gang of Four were sure that what they were doing had a value, other than killing time, The Mekons needed the support of friends if they weren't to falter at the first hurdle – playing a gig.

Hugo Burnham: Our second gig, the Saturday after . . . the Corn Exchange, The Mekons opened for us. They had three songs: 'Dan Dare Oh Yeah', 'Fight The Cuts' and [A. N. Other]. They came on in their spaceship, which was a sofa; I was doing lights, Andy was doing sound. It was so fucking art-school, and it was brilliant. Severed Head and the Neckfuckers . . . were the headliners that night.

In those early days, Gang of Four also had another 'support act'. Their drinking buddy Marc Almond had an act at the time which according to King consisted of 'this girl who wore a rubber catsuit used to whip him before we went on'. Whatever gets you through the night. But it was an exciting time to be in Leeds, even if the cellar bar where Gang of Four and Mekons made mayhem that May only lasted as a venue until July, when local teddy boys reclaimed it, after 'object[ing] to the kids taking over what had been, up until then, their rock & roll night'.

Gang of Four had just found a permanent bassist in Dave Allen, a trained musician who knew enough to keep it simple and funky. He had replied to an ad in *Melody Maker* which played dumb, asking for a 'fast ryvum & blues bass player'. They got Allen instead, who as Burnham says, 'was [now] the musician in the band. Andy could play guitar, but if you asked him, "OK, play this song, play that song," [he'd struggle]. I didn't have rudiments . . . I developed my style with Gang of Four. [But we knew] you deconstruct things to rebuild – you're consciously deconstructing what's gone before to fuck with it, to twist it, to some-how create your own concoction.' With Allen on hand, the deconstruction didn't need to end in destruction.

But before their new bassist could bed in, they needed Andy Gill and Jon King to stop gallivanting around New York with the CBGB's crowd, and come home. The end of term had left a three-month hole in the band schedule (and lodgings), during which Gill and King elected to visit their friend, Mary Harron, in New York. Harron, who had been at Oxford, was now a regular contributor to *Punk* magazine, the modelled-on-*Mad* cartoon-zine founded by John Holmstrom and Legs McNeil in the winter of 1976. Harron gave Gill and King honorary entry to the Bowery's inner sanctum.

Jon King: She was round the corner from CBGB's, and she was going out with [Patti Smith Group drummer] Jay Dee Daugherty. We were over there for about six weeks, so rather than study gothic architecture [as we should have], we went more or less every night to CBGB's, and hung out with her mates, Richard Hell, The Dead Boys, Patti Smith and all that lot. I saw the Ramones supporting Iggy Pop . . . In CBGB's they just assumed [we] were in a band because we were two pissed Englishmen, and so we said, 'Yeah, we're in a band called The Mudflaps.'

It seems odd that the pair didn't own up to being in the Gang of Four. Perhaps they still didn't conceive of the band as a long-term project. Certainly few bands suspend activities after two gigs so the singer and guitarist can go on a two-month vacation. But as King says, 'We didn't even think about making a record [initially]. We played for two years without getting any reviews – we were in Leeds.' Harron herself had yet to see her friends' band, and didn't until October of that year. When she did, she was slightly underwhelmed, finding them to be 'just a good R&B band, with clever ideas but no stage discipline or clear direction'. As with so many provincial bands at the time, Gang of Four needed gigs to improve; and that meant venturing beyond Leeds, and/or finding support slots to travelling bands. Steeped in punk lore, they decided to try to gatecrash a Buzzcocks gig.

Hugo Burnham: The Buzzcocks were playing [somewhere] and we [decided], 'Let's do what the Pistols did, turn up and say, hello, we're the support act.' And we just said, 'Hi, we're . . .' 'No, you're not.' '[Well], can we be?' Richard Boon was rather taken by our [nerve], and said, 'All right, then.' And they loved us. So literally two or three weeks later [he called us up and said], 'We're going on tour. Do you want to come with us? You can be an opening act [before] The Slits, who are on tour with us.' . . . We did Leeds University, opening for The Slits and Buzzcocks on the stage where *Live at Leeds* was recorded. We ended up at the Lyceum [in London] – one of those great nights. It was Buzzcocks, The Slits, John Cooper Clarke, The Fall and us. It was unreal . . . We were enveloped by the ruck, 'cause it was very exciting. We were on the road. We were a rock band!

However, the out-of-town band who would make the greatest impression on the Leeds scene were from Edinburgh, not Manchester. The Rezillos would bring with them the man who would make The Mekons and Gang of Four recording artistes, Bob Last. When The Rezillos came to town, in October 1977, they already had a single and a mini-tour of London under their Day-Glo belts; and had garnered interest from Seymour Stein, come to claim Albion's children of the revolution.

Formed by Jo Callis and Eugene Reynolds from the ashes of a previous covers band, the Knutsford Dominators, they had brought in Eugene's girlfriend, Fay Fyfe, to add her pixie presence to the audio-visual mix. When The Rezillos made their debut, a year to the day after the Pistols, it was not as Edinburgh's answer to punk, though it *was* intended as a reaction to the prog-rock torpor into which modern music had sunk.

Jo Callis: We were inspired by the whole new-wave thing, and felt something in common with that initially, because we were bored with endless pub-rock groups doing progressive rock and Genesis on *The Old Grey Whistle Test*. It was all getting a bit staid and boring, and we'd kinda reverted back to our old Beatles records and Johnny Kidd & the Pirates – there not being very much around that grabbed our interest. But we went at it from a slightly different angle – we trawled the past a bit more, initially anyway.

The Rezillos also shared common ground with England's punk brethren thanks to their refusal to allow technical limitations to hold them back. By August 1977, Eugene Reynolds was admitting that 'the actual formation of some kind of punk philosophy [that went,] "Okay, we are no great shakes at playing the guitar or singing, but we are gonna do it, because music is for everybody,"' helped the band greatly. It certainly gave them an impetus beyond their original intent, 'to provoke some kinda response'.

Jo Callis: The first Rezillos gig was Guy Fawkes night 1976, in [Teviot Row] Union at Edinburgh University . . . Our first few gigs were all cover versions . . . a lot of rock & roll things like 'Bony Maronie', 'Something Else', 'C'mon Everybody'; [as well as] 'Sam the Sham', 'Have I The Right?' . . . When we started . . . it was very much 'suck it and see', and it could have been something that we'd have just chucked in after a few weeks; but at least we thought, if we can wind people up and stoke them up a bit, it'll be worthwhile doing it. To our surprise, [at the end of] the first Rezillos gig we got an encore . . . Locally, [it] took off remarkably quickly; and before we knew it, we were getting offered a lot of gigs.

If the early Rezillos essentially took their cue from the back-to-the-roots approach of pub-rock legends, the Feelgoods, their transformation in less than six months into something more original and driven was abrupt *and* unexpected. Part of the process took place at night, when band members tuned into *The John Peel Show*, to hear the latest underground sounds, and find him playing the likes of 'New Rose', 'Anarchy In The UK', 'Blitzkrieg Bop' and 'Boredom'. The last of these, and the EP it came on, had a profound impact on guitarist Callis, and his friend,

Bob Last, who helped the band out by lugging equipment when they began to venture further afield. For Callis, it showed that equally untechnical musicians were penning their own songs, and that any subject matter seemed fair game. For now, he had a band ally in rhythm guitarist, Mark Harris.

Jo Callis: The thing did take off a lot more quickly than expected. With that happening, myself and the other guitar player, 'Hi-Fi' Harris, were quite determined to do original material that fit in with the cover versions that we were doing. I'd written 'Getting Me Down' fairly early in '77, and Mark had written a song, and [both] were done in that R&B/sixties style. [But] we gradually broadened the spectrum a little bit as we went on. Things like 'Good Sculptures' and 'Flying Saucer Attack' would have come quite quickly [after these]. I just [thought] 'Flying Saucer Attack' would be a good title for a song! 'Good Sculptures' was making a bit of a statement about slightly feminist issues – appreciating your girlfriend for more than her physical attributes; and having been to art school, that would have made her a sculptress, I guess. 'Can't Stand My Baby' started out as something I did on cassette to send to my sister, who was at Leeds Art College at the time. I just made this song up in my bedroom, just strumming a guitar and bashing an old World War Two ammunition box with my foot for a drum sound. I'd make up little tapes like that, and send these things to my sister. It just consisted of [the refrain]; and I must have played it to Eugene, and he really liked it, and said, 'We should do that with the group.' It was kinda pushing us in a different direction, so that really was a turning point. It definitely pointed a more original way forward.

That 'original way forward' bore fruit almost immediately – though not every Rezillo seemed in a hurry to leave the sixties behind. For now, Eugene Reynolds shared Callis's delight in the new songs, informing the music papers how Callis had departed from the punk norm, 'Some people write songs that try to tie down all the abnormalities and the crazy things about life to a concise, neat "I've got it sussed" type situation. Our songs completely reverse that and more or less say, "Oh God, this is bizarre."'

Along with live shows in which the dervish duo, Reynolds and Fyfe, danced up a storm on stage, Callis's songs helped propel the band's reputation beyond the city gates, and by the summer of 1977, they had found a manager, Lenny Love, who 'had ambitions of starting his own record label, Sensible Records, and wanted to do a record with us'.

Hence 'I Can't Stand My Baby' b/w 'I Wanna Be Your Man', issued in August.

The insidious idiosyncrasy of 'Can't Stand My Baby' soon attracted the attention of the Leeds lot. Perhaps Callis's sister, Jacqui, in the process of forming Delta 5, shared his original ropey recording with her friends in The Mekons and Gang of Four, before the Sensible 45 arrived. Certainly, the latter band had worked up their own version by the time The Rezillos came to town, though it was so different that when its author later joined them on stage, he 'had to relearn the song to their way of doing it'.

It was The Mekons, though, who first displayed their charms to the Edinburgh band and their 'road manager', Bob Last; supporting the not-so-retro Rezillos at the F Club one October night, having presumably been recommended by the 'other' Callis. According to Jo, his friend 'Bob just signed them there and then. I didn't even know he'd started Fast Product.' If Callis was initially nonplussed by Last's 'leap in' attitude, he shared Last's enthusiasm for off-the-wall acts, and when Last set up a weekend session to record The Mekons' vinyl debut, he came as part of the Fast Product package.

Jo Callis: [Fast] was a side of things that I'd found inspiring, [hence my] helping out when we recorded the first Mekons single. We recorded it at a cottage in the Borders. We just loaded up this three-ton truck with equipment and stuff and all went down to the Borders, and The Mekons came up from Leeds, and we all met in this cottage; and set up this two-track TEAC tape recorder [with] The Rezillos' mixing desk and microphones, and recorded what would be 'Never Been In A Riot'.

For the rest of The Rezillos, Fast may have been an irrelevance, but for Callis it was an alternative path he might take (and later did, with The Human League). As Last suggests, 'Jo had a different set of references [from me] — they came from a totally retro [source] — and that was absolutely not what was driving Fast.' Yet by 'help[ing] out on roadcrew with The Rezillos', Last had 'the vehicle that took me around the country to all of these local scenes'. What he was looking to do was emulate *Spiral Scratch* in some way, which he thought 'had a very modernist vibe, [and] was a self-referential thing about the form'. He also shared Mark Perry's love of Frank Zappa, who was an inspiration, 'not necessarily [because of] what he produces, but the way he works'.

Bob Last: The first record we made . . . [was with] £400 from the Bank of Scotland. I really thought ['Never Been In A Riot'] was a pop record . . . [At the time] we thought, 'If we're smart enough about this we're gonna purposely misunderstand and believe that this is pop. And then we're gonna create the space around it, and the attitude and the circumstances, wherein it will turn into pop.' We didn't think the first records we put out were gonna immediately be hits, but we did think this was a journey. We wanted an interesting platform to barge in.

'Never Been In A Riot', recorded at the end of 1977, lived up to its label as Fast Product 001, being out before the end of January 1978, much to The Mekons' slight embarrassment. As Tom Greenhalgh told *Melody Maker* the following year, 'Our only reason for existing was that we'd made this appalling record, that should never have been a record, but was.' In fact, The Mekons were everything Last wanted from the first Fast band.

Bob Last: It really gets up my nose, all these bands saying we've got to learn to play rock & roll properly before we can do a gig. It means that . . . nothing new ever happens. By the time people learn proper rock & roll, they've forgotten what their original ideas were . . . [but] because ['Never Been In A Riot'] was so obviously crude, somebody who [has] bought the record . . . [might] still want to go out and do it. The Mekons wouldn't be a *substitute* for them going out and doing it. [1979]

Unfortunately for Last, when his partner, Hilary, visited Rough Trade in Ladbroke Grove – a place renowned for taking pretty much any punk single that was not overtly sexist or racist 'on consignment' – Geoff Travis apparently informed the stunned lass, 'This is shit. They can't play. I'm not taking this record.' Coming from a man who willingly sold the likes of Eater and The Drones, this was a dispiriting introduction to the joys of wholesaling. Thankfully, before the venture had time to founder, *NME*'s terrible twins, Parsons and Burchill, decided that the record was awful enough to be great, and made it their Single Of The Week. Fast was up and running.

At the same time, The Mekons began pressuring Last to consider making a Gang of Four record next, embarrassed that they had beaten their friends to the punch, and insisting to the label boss, 'The Gang of Four are the real band – we're just fucking about. You should be signing them.' Unlike The Mekons, Gang of Four had *actually* been looking for a record deal, King informing *Sounds* at the time that 'the only Leeds label, Underground, wouldn't touch us . . . they said we weren't "punky" enough . . . [And] for political reasons we wanted [our first] songs to come out on . . . a small label.' Finally, The Mekons convinced Gang of Four to send Last a tape, which persuaded him he might have made a 'mistake'.

Bob Last: I think it was like locally embarrassing that [The Mekons] might possibly have a record and the Gang of Four not. The first tape had something about John Stonehouse, an excellent piece called 'Don't Call Me A Bastard (I'm A Wanker)', and they also did a cover of [Black Sabbath's] 'Iron Man'. We didn't put those out. [But] I think 'Armalite Rifle' was [also] on there, and that was what I totally got.

Unlike The Mekons, Gang of Four had no intention of letting Fast represent them as if they 'were nobody special', or in the punkish style of those early crude demos. Though they provisionally agreed to make a single before the end of April 1978, it would be some months before they had a sound they wanted to record. Though 'Armalite Rifle' and 'Anthrax' were both 'old' songs, they were now stripped of all unnecessary accoutrements, and lost some of their frenetic quality.

Andy Gill: By the time we came to make our first recordings . . . we'd already assimilated the punk thing and got a take on that element.

As King says, '"Anthrax" itself was a conceptual construct. We had a very clear idea of what we wanted it to be like, which was empty, full of gaps, driving guitar but also not affected.' The reconstruction was radical enough for the band's friend, Mary Harron, to notice. When she caught them at the Electric Ballroom, the month that *Damaged Goods* came out, she found 'the difference [from the previous year] was extraordinary. They still used some of their old songs like . . . "Anthrax", but suddenly everything had become articulated.'

They certainly hadn't approached the session lightly. Burnham is speaking for the whole Gang when he states that the first record should always be 'an absolute statement of intent, of mythology. It's a manifesto – as much about where it's come from as where it's gonna go. You're putting your mark on the table – "Are you with me, or not?"' Such was the sense of destiny with which they approached the exercise that Bob Last found himself immediately at odds with the Leeds lads.

Bob Last: They felt they needed to be more self-serious. For me at the end of the day that was their downfall, because to be serious, they didn't need to be self-serious. They had the clever stuff going on in the lyrics, and the sound was fantastic. It didn't really need to be quite as self-serious. But that was always a source of tension between us – [like] the sleeve thing where they sent us a detailed letter [about the design], so we just put it on the back of the sleeve, and did something totally different. We totally believed in anthemic seriousness, [but] you could be playful around that, and get to more people and make more impact. They just weren't prepared to go that far [with us], and that's why ultimately we didn't go . . . beyond that first single. [I] fought intense battles over the fact that there's some reverb on the guitar solo on 'Damaged Goods' – the only time there is a rock & roll wetness on Andy Gill's guitar; and we nearly came to blows about it at the studio in Rochdale. I don't think they ever forgave me for that.

Gang of Four soon found that they didn't need to forgive Last. Such was the pummelling power of their 'absolute statement of intent' – which refined to an essence some elemental aspect of the rock experience – that real record labels' interest was piqued; and for all of Last's rhetoric about making 'more impact', he simply didn't have comparable distribution. The Gang also suspected that when Last told *NME*, three months after the EP's release, 'Fast Product is essentially me being parasitical on these other people, ripping them off and having them work for nothing,' he wasn't entirely joking.

For now, Last was riding the crest of a whole new wave, using only his instincts to keep himself afloat. Barely had Gang of Four committed to a single, when 'a tape . . . came through the door one morning'. It was postmarked Sheffield, and it contained the songs 'Being Boiled' and 'Circus of Death', songs that – had Last known it – bore all the hallmarks of an English emulator of Suicide:

Bob Last: By lunchtime, I thought, 'We should be putting this out. Let's phone 'em up and see if there's a better quality tape.' Which there wasn't – they'd sent the master. There were some more kind of things that were more overtly Kraftwerky. [But] I didn't have a clue about any of their references [at the time]. To me it was like, if we'd sat down and thought up the next band for Fast

Product, we [probably] would have thought up The Human League. Handily, they'd thought themselves up.

The time Last was obliged to spend on arty, self-conscious types like the Gang of Four and The Human League now allowed The Mekons to start aligning sound and (inner) vision; and despite their best efforts, by the time they returned to record a second single for Fast, The Mekons had no need to skulk in doorways any more. The instantly infectious 'Where Were You?', issued the last week of November 1978, closed out a remarkable year for Fast, as well as Yorkshire's own mini-wave of avant-garage rock. For Gang of Four, though, it was almost too much of a good thing. In January 1979, Jon King, on an impulse, quit the band.

Jon King: After we did *Damaged Goods* we got on the front cover of the *NME*, so I immediately resigned at that point, 'cause I thought, 'This has gone too far.' [Be]cause I [actually] wanted to be a painter. I thought, 'What's going on? I don't want to be on the front cover of the *NME*.' There were [suddenly] all these expectations – 'Oh you gotta tour.' I had a post-graduate place at Chelsea [School of Art]. I was in the Young Contemporaries at the ICA. Everyone was all over us and I was [like], 'Well, I'm not committed to this.' And I didn't want to fuck it up [for the others]. They actually did audition a whole bunch of other [singers]. But of course I wrote the songs with Andy . . . He wrote most of the music and I wrote most of the lyrics . . . Anyway, they asked me if I'd come back again, and I gave in. That meant taking quite a lot of decisions about things. [But] we were suddenly headlining at the Electric Ballroom and the Lyceum.

One of the decisions the Gang of Four were required to confront was the same as every second-generation English punk band at the end of 1978, Where To Now? The emergence of a whole raft of regional 'punk' bands – many of whom rejected the tag, fearing guilt by association – had made '78 a year of almost weekly surprises popping up in the racks of independent record stores. But it hadn't happened entirely by chance. These bands were filling a vacuum created by reactionary racketeers like Crass, UK Subs, Sham 69 and Skrewdriver, then inflicting themselves on London audiences 'in the name of punk'. Perhaps the future direction of rock's new wave could yet be wrestled from these self-righteous oiks.

— — —

Meanwhile, certain first-wave flag-bearers couldn't wait to leave Blighty for the promised land, even if they weren't being received with out-stretched arms, or invited on *The Ed Sullivan Show*. When a request to appear on one of America's 'alternative' TV programmes, *Saturday Night Live, did* come – as it did for the Sex Pistols and, when they bailed, Elvis Costello – it came with strict guidelines concerning what they could play.

Unlike 1964, the US was not quite ready for the reimportation of another American idea, redefined and made accessible by Britain's keener pop sensibility. Perhaps someone needed to shoot another presi-dent. Even New York's Lower East Side seemed a tad unprepared for another British Invasion. When The Damned dipped their toes in the Hudson, in April 1977, they were made to feel like perhaps they should have stopped at Ellis Island.

Rat Scabies: We were incredibly disappointed by [CBGB's] and the audience. We went in there expecting a fight [with The Dead Boys]. [Then there was] the thing with the tables and the chairs in front of the stage. We were used to mayhem, and the thought of arming the audience with tables and chairs [worried us], and they were so lackadaisical about the whole thing, ordering a pizza while The Damned were playing. So we drank way too much and turned it into a comedy event . . . But after a couple of days, we kinda [thought,] 'Now it's time to do it right,' and we kicked it into gear. And then we went to Boston and LA. It was the same thing – we found that the American audiences really had no real idea of English working-class mentality – that driven hunger and boredom. I guess we just weren't used to that American attitude, 'A band is only a band.' To us it was a matter of life and death.

Scabies' first verbal riposte to the New Yorkers, from the low stage at CBGB's, was concise and to the point, 'Awright, we're fed up wiv all you poseurs. We're English and where we come from everyone MOVES. Git up.' It would take another nine months before another set of founders followed in their footsteps, but the seeds had been planted.

Stranglers' manager Dai Davies also found the US was surprisingly soporific, suggesting after a summer trip to Cleveland that, 'The kids there are as bored as they are in Middlesbrough.' Given that Cleveland probably had the most interesting local music scene in the entire US at the time of Davies' visit, this should certainly have been cause for concern. Seymour Stein, after investing heavily in punk, had now begun to have his doubts. As he told *Melody Maker* in November 1977, 'Elvis Costello and the Sex Pistols broke [in the UK] through word of mouth. That hasn't existed in America for years. It's big, big shops with discount prices . . . [and] kids have to go in knowing what they want.' His thesis was about to be tested, as both paradigms were due to tour the States in the next two months.

Costello seemed to provide a suitably acidic test for punk's prospects Stateside. Thought by many in the motherland to be an after-the-fact imposter, he still had the sweaty stench of punk on him when he landed at San Francisco in the second week of November. And, unlike The Clash, he had the backing of CBS-US, who, in order to curtail imports of *My Aim Is True*, had added 'Watching The Detectives' to the running order Stateside. He also had the personal endorsement of the president of CBS Records International, Walter Yetnikoff, who had first caught Elvis 'busking' outside the annual CBS convention at the London Hilton in July, one of Rivera's better publicity stunts.

Costello was prepared to tour this big country till the tyres on his tour bus melted. The month-long tour that began with a KSAN radio broadcast on 15 November culminated in his famous *Saturday Night Live* appearance, where he decided to emulate Jimi Hendrix*, switching from 'Less Than Zero' to an impromptu 'Radio Radio' in mid-song, finding out just how 'live' the NBC show really was. The furore he thus caused kept interest going during the Christmas break he took, before returning in early January for a further two-month stint, covering yet more of the vast terrain that is North America, culminating in a pair of shows at Toronto's El Macambo that were incendiary enough for CBS to issue a promotional album of the final night to radio stations across the land. By the time Costello flew back across the Atlantic in early March, *My Aim Is True* was perched at 32 in the Hot Hundred, and English punk-rock was big news – even if it was the Sex Pistols, not Costello, who'd taken up most of the column inches.

Ironically, Costello's one truly newsworthy moment had been his appearance on *Saturday Night Live* – then at the height of its influence – having been booked as an uncontroversial alternative to the Pistols. Their decision to back out of the show proved to be just the beginning of another McLaren masterclass in creating a stir, while stopping most

---

* Hendrix memorably switched in mid-song from 'Hey Joe' to 'Sunshine Of Your Love' during a live performance on *The Lulu Show* in 1968.

folk catching sight of the band. According to road manager 'Boogie', 'Malcolm's agenda was [always] to avoid the East Coast; he had this thing . . . going back to 1975, about the tastemakers there.'

After warming up with another covert UK mini-tour that began in front of 2,000 students and ended in front of 200 orphans, McLaren devised a US tour that would never leave the backwaters. He told journalist Michael Watts he wanted the band to 'play the "back" towns of Birmingham and Selma, Alabama; Shreveport in Louisiana; Tupelo, the birthplace . . . of Elvis Presley; San Antonio, Tex-Mex country; Savannah, Georgia; and the hard border town of Tijuana in Mexico, where the tour would end'. As he stated after things went awry, 'I wanted them to come in and get lost in the middle of America.'

Unfortunately for McLaren, when the criminal records of Sid Vicious (assault), Steve Jones (burglary), and John Lydon (amphetamine possession) became known to American immigration, he was obliged to think again. Though their US label, Warners, managed to rectify the visa situation with a few well-chosen phone calls, it took time; and the curtailed tour was now just seven shows in ten days. Nor was the finale any longer in Tijuana, but rather at the home of hippydom, Bill Graham's Winterland Ballroom, in downtown San Francisco. And Rotten still hated 'ippies.

Landing in Atlanta on 5 January, the Pistols spent the first week ruffling feathers in cowboy country, playing standing-room-only club shows in the southern towns of Memphis, Baton Rouge, Tulsa and San Antonio. Amazingly, the only actual casualty from this trawl through the Deep South was one particularly persistent loudmouth in San Antonio, who gave Sid a reason for carrying that heavy bass guitar around – to crack a cranium. Though Rotten claims in his autobiography to have 'loved the idea [of the US Tour] . . . one of Malcolm's greatest contributions', Steve Jones retained a greater grasp of the risks involved:

Steve Jones: It was pretty scary. It's more scary now thinking about it than it was at the time. We'd never been anywhere like America . . . Looking back on it . . . we were lucky we didn't get shot.

The shows may have sold out, but it wasn't music lovers or even fashion victims turning up in their droves. US photographer Roberta Bayley, travelling with the band, remembers 'very few people there who cheered for [the Pistols]. It was definitely macho Texans who had come to check out . . . this shit'. As long as the media circus was in town, Sid Vicious continued to play dumb, while the rest of the band just played on. At least Rotten seemed to be enjoying himself, having tired of the unquestioning adulation he now received in Britain. Here his taunts still drew the ire of the idiot fraternity, and with something to play off again, he spat the words with a venom last seen a year earlier.

Before the Bay Area beckoned, McLaren's modified master plan seemed to have worked well enough. Vicious had been kept off hard drugs by the strong-arm tactics of the road crew; the press had talked about everything but the music; and the energy of the shows – in some surreal settings – had papered over the cracks appearing in the band. But McLaren was starting to despair of the direction everything was going in. When Michael Watts came across him in the lobby of the ultra-exclusive Fairmont the night before Winterland, he heard him say, 'It wouldn't matter to me if we gave up.' So much for emulating the Stones.

When the band turned up at Winterland on the 14th, they found those outside to be a distillation of everything encountered in the States to date – just on a larger scale. For the first time, they were due to play in front of five thousand folks; and it was quite clear that the punks dotted around this ballroom were wholly outnumbered by poseurs and voyeurs. And it seemed everyone had been taking lessons in how punks should behave from the *National Enquirer*. Not surprisingly, the local support acts suffered.

Penelope Houston: The stage was already soaked with spit by the time we got up there and the audience was maybe a third punk fans. The rest just wanted to see this phenomenon – the Sex Pistols . . . They were quite hostile actually.

Houston, the singer in The Avengers, later told Gina Arnold that her main memory of the show was 'hordes of strangers [standing] there yelling, "Fuck you! Fuck you!" and spitting, because that's what they thought punks did.' Even the Pistols felt a little out of their depth. Playing the sarcastic spastic, as Rotten liked to do, was a club act. How would it go over in this arena? Who were the Christians, and who were the lions? Lydon later told Savage, 'We were way ahead of ourselves. We didn't know how to get past the first twenty rows.'

Thankfully, the soundman's sound decision to render Vicious's random plunkings inaudible, with a whizz-bang mix especially for Radioland (KSAN being on hand to broadcast the historic event), meant that the Pistols sounded a thousand years ahead of anything the Bay Area's classic rock stations were playing that night. And they continued to make converts right unto the bitter end. Fittingly, Jonh Ingham – who had reported on the band since its beginnings – was there to see the finale, and was still telling it like it was:

By Pistols' standards [Winterland] was ordinary, hardly the stuff of eulogies. Steve's amp fucked up at a few crucial points and John steadily lost interest . . . But in its context it was awesome. In that crowd of 5,000 was a mere handful of punks outdone by Grateful Dead t-shirts ten to one. This was a crowd of the curious, and it was exhilarating to watch practically all of them screaming and waving their arms. [*Sounds*, 28/1/78]

But at least one band member sensed that this might be 'it', and was determined to deliver the band's epitaph. As Rotten began to revert to Lydon, at the end of a world-weary 'No Fun' encore, he uttered the immortal words, 'Ha, ha, ha, ever get the feeling you've been cheated? Good night.' (He later told Savage, 'I meant it at the end of the Winterland show . . . I knew it couldn't go on.')

The broadcast, the bootleg album, the CD and ultimately the DVD of Winterland has frozen this moment and made it the end of Punk to every documentary maker who can hold a camcorder, every sociologist who can tick a box, every smart-ass who sees history as a series of Full Stops. But for those misfits there that night, there was something archetypally punk about Rotten's performance. The Avengers' guitarist certainly thought so.

Danny Furious: I was fascinated [by the Pistols]. They sounded terrible and Sid was trying to be John. John had given up and didn't seem to care any longer. So they finish their set and come out for their one encore . . . and then John's true colours came out. I have *never* witnessed a performance so real, so honest and so full of desperation as that encore . . . I suddenly really got it! What it was that made this punk thing so different and it was John Rotten . . . up there in front of the world, fronting what was at the time the Next Big Thing, and it was all falling apart around and inside of himself, and [still] he put everything he had into that one stupid song.

For the Pistols, it was certainly over. Ray Rumour, writer for local zine, *Search & Destroy*, suggests that even at the time, 'You really had the feeling that [Winterland] was not the beginning, it was the end. After the concert there was a party for them . . . and Sid Vicious drank a quart of vodka or bourbon and then shot up and then passed out . . . It was a shocking thing to see that kind of self-destruction and nihilism.' San Francisco's arty punksters were not impressed.

But for punk rockers and press agents the world over, the fun had only just begun. When it became apparent that Rotten wanted out of the band, and that Vicious wanted out of this world, McLaren issued his last great press release: 'The management is bored with managing a successful rock & roll band. The group is bored with being a successful rock & roll band. Burning venues and destroying record companies is more creative than making it.' When it seemed that there might be a chance it wasn't over, he withdrew this release. So it was left to Virgin publicist, Al Clark, to confer the last rites on the originators:

The fact that [the four Sex Pistols] are now in three different corners of the world . . . could be construed as part of their continuing attempt to subvert authority and achieve world domination. It could also be construed as splitting up.

McLaren, though, hadn't entirely lost his touch. After all, it *had* been he who had ensured that promoter Bill Graham put on a couple of local punk bands – The Nuns and The Avengers – as support to the Pistols; and then expressed the hope that one of them blew the Pistols offstage. He also managed to pick the 'right' two bands (even though Crime had a chronological precedence over both outfits). He had presumably come across the remarkably professional *Search & Destroy* zine, which had been evangelizing San Francisco's punk scene for almost a year; giving him cause to believe that the virus *had* successfully crossed the Atlantic, and that the original plague-carriers had not laid down their punk lives in vain.

PART FIVE

5.1
THE WEST RIDES
THE CREST
1977-79

America will fully test the credibility of every new-wave band that decides to have a go there, because they are going to either have to stick to their guns, risking rejection, or go undercover.
— Harry Doherty, 'Will America swallow the new wave?', *MM*, 12/11/77

I think America is really ready for the other new UK bands. There's such an interest . . . I was very surprised. Especially in places like LA . . . they're just waiting for something to copy. — Dave Vanian, *MM*, 30/4/77

When the Sex Pistols came to San Francisco, there was a contingent of LA punks and punkettes who made the eleven-hour trek up Highway One, determined to catch this key inspiration. Nine months earlier, the traffic had been the other way; as the Bay Area's new beatniks headed down to see The Damned make their West Coast debut at the Starwood. These 'suburban weirdos' needed to stick together; and generally did, crashing on each other's floors in a mutual city swop whenever English (or each other's) punk combos came to town. In the sun, sea and sand culture of California, punks in their undertaker make-up stood out like an untanned surfer-dude on Venice Beach. Mick Farren said as much in his *NME* report from LA in November 1977, which suggested the local punk scene was still at the copycat stage:

The new wave in Los Angeles is hardly more than a ripple. The smart joke is that there are just seventy punks in the whole city, but they move fast so they look like more. This may be snide but it's also, unfortunately, close to the truth . . . They seem to spend an awful lot of time poring over the pages of London and New York rock papers to cop the turn of the trends. [*NME*, 19/11/77]

Aside from sharing each other's bands, and cramped living conditions, the San Francisco and Los Angeles scenes had their own scene-making, even scene-creating, fanzines; professionally printed by, and for, punk artists only. *Slash* and *Search & Destroy* enjoyed a healthy rivalry, and a mutual respect. Both were remarkably quick off the mark; starting up before they had (m)any bands worth an endorsement. As *Slash* editor Claude Bessy told Richard Meltzer, 'For the first two or three issues we pretended there was an LA scene, when there was really nothing. But before we knew it . . . some bands started forming because of the paper, and before we knew it we had a scene to report on.'

The first issue of *Slash* appeared in July 1977, two months before the opening of the Masque – which would provide LA punk with a home. However, the story of LA punk starts with an earlier rockzine, *Back Door Man*, which propounded a punk aesthetic as far back as 1975, before there were *any* bands prepared to live up to such an ideal. As editor 'Phast Phreddie' Patterson points out, 'We had Ted Nugent and Blue Oyster Cult on the cover – [At least] it wasn't The Eagles or Elton John! The image was very important to [*Slash*]. [But] to us, it was [about] rock & roll.'

Back Door Man was obliged to admit very little was happening out west in the mid-seventies – especially after Patterson started receiving early singles by Television, Pere Ubu, The Damned and the Sex Pistols – so the magazine attempted to start its own indie record label, much like Greg Shaw's Bomp. Unfortunately, they took the garageband aesthetic a little too far with their first single, issuing an actual garage rehearsal of the Imperial Dogs, an LA Dolls, with all the slop, but none of the chops. After that disaster, they decided to recoup some money before any further 'new' releases, issuing a bootleg EP of Velvet Underground demos. The coffers refilled, they proceeded to issue a Zippers single, but it got caught in Glam's tail-light, even though it came out almost a year after Phast Phreddie sensed the new vibe emanating from the east, reaching all the way to la-la land, via Seattle.

Phast Phreddie: Everybody was reading the English [music] papers. They were really influential because of the photos, [which said,] 'This is what the punks look like.' . . . So I'm standing in the Whisky one day, and in walk Tomato du Plenty and Tommy Gear from the Screamers and they look just like these creeps on [that week's] *Melody Maker* cover, the spiked hair [etc.] – they could have walked in off the photo shoot – and everyone's looking at them. So I go over there, and they [tell me], 'Oh, we just came down from Seattle, we have this band called the Screamers.' They were getting their message out before they had a [gig].

The Seattle-based Screamers had begun life as the Tupperwares, before coming to LA to introduce their art-school ideas where they might yet make a splash. According to Black Randy, though, the article that charted a new course for the Screamers was not in *Melody Maker*, it came from the Sunday *LA Times*, which ran a feature on English punk a week after the Grundy brouhaha. Randy took 'a copy of that article to my friends in the Screamers . . . [and] I said, "This is going to be what happens next." . . . As soon as they read that article, the first thing they did was to shred their clothes and chop their hair.' Again, the image was reaching interested folk ahead of the music; and a lot of imagination was expended on how these English punk bands might sound. Mike Watt, not yet ready to become a Reactionary, let alone a Minuteman, was at Long Beach State College in the fall of '76.

Mike Watt: I found that the library [had] *NME*, *Sounds* and *Melody Maker*, among the reference material, and I would find a cubicle downstairs in the corner and I read this stuff. [But] I didn't really hear the [UK] bands [till later] . . . We saw the pictures [long] before we heard them, and we imagined what they were like. We thought it would be like synthesizer or space music, they looked so freaky. The pictures made it more alien than it was in reality. I remember hearing 'New Rose' and . . . it was guitar music – it freaked us out.

Meanwhile, Robert Lopez in San Diego was having the same problem with New York punk bands. After reading 'about bands like the Ramones and Richard Hell and Television and Patti Smith . . . I'd have to imagine what they sounded like.' On 8 December 1976, Lopez had the opportunity to remedy this deficit, when the Ramones played LA's Roxy Theatre, a club modelled along the lines of New York's Bottom Line, a place familiar enough to the four brudders.

Black Flag founder Greg Ginn believes that the Ramones concert may have been the turning point. Long Ryder Greg Sowders also subscribes to the view that early live shows by 'the Ramones and Blondie . . . turned on the people out here'. But both Ginn and Sowders were mere bystanders to the initial wave of LA punk bands. Germ Chris Ashford is speaking for the Screamers and the Reactionaries when he says, 'The Ramones or the CBGB scene in New York weren't factors in the formation of the Germs. It was all about The Stooges, Bowie, and Joan Jett . . . and then it was all about the Sex Pistols and The Damned.'

If it would take Watt a while to find the sound of The Minutemen, or for Lopez to construct a set of Zeros, others in LA were in more of a hurry to 'go punk'. Cliff Roman, who formed the Weirdos in the winter of 1977, told Gina Arnold he'd heard 'about' the Sex Pistols in *Interview* magazine. Having still not heard them, but determined to play 'weird, loud, fast' rock, he wrote seven songs in his bedroom and taught them to friends.

Cliff Roman: I used to be into jazz . . . like John Coltrane, in high school. Then I got bored with it . . . When I went to Cal Arts College there were guys hanging out all day just playing free-form jazz. It got real boring. Then I got into Bowie, Lou Reed, Iggy and the Dolls . . . I think punk really means the extinction of hippiedom. [1978]

By spring 1977, there were already a handful of LA bands attempting to play weird, loud and fast; but without anywhere to play. Enter the Nerves, a band from San Francisco who had driven to LA at the tail-end of 1976, despairing of anything happening in northern California before hell froze over. Though they were no more than a powered pop band, Nerves singer Peter Case told the others, 'We're gonna rent out some hall and we'll put on any bands we can find. Punk rock's happening, [so] we'll call it the Hollywood Punk Palace.'

The first band Case approached were the Screamers, who coincidentally lived next door, looked outlandish and were telling everyone they *were* a band. But Case found them to be 'too over-controlled about everything', and still not ready for live performance. Determined to make it happen, Case began to ask around, and was told about Cliff Roman and his Weirdos: 'They didn't have a drummer, so at first they were saying, "We can't do it." [So] we said . . . "You don't need a fucking drummer. Just show up, you guys are like the greatest group in the world."'

Further enquiries yielded a young quintet still revving up in the garage. The Dils were the construct of two brothers, Tony and Chip Kinman, who had recently sacked their singer and drummer, changed from the Duds to the Dils and moved to downtown LA. While there Tony 'met a guy named Peter Urban who . . . would end up becoming [our] manager. It happened [he] was a hardcore communist. We'd sit around and talk about it, and we started writing songs with more aggressive themes.' Their early songs – notably both sides of their first single, 'I Hate The Rich' and 'You're Not Blank' – suggested that Mr Urban had a touch of the Bernie Rhodes about him.

The Dils duly found themselves part of the Hollywood Punk Palace. On 2 April 1977, the Nerves held LA's first punk gig, with an action-packed bill. The slightly incongruous presence of the Zippers, still caught in a Glam time warp, meant that Phast Phreddie was there at the birth of a local scene at last adopting aspects of *Back Door Man*.

Phast Phreddie: The first Punk Palace was at S.I.R. Studio [in] early '77 – they just rented out the studio. Maybe seventy-five people showed up for this. The bands were the Nerves, the Weirdos, the Zippers, the Dils and another band. It was before the Weirdos had a drummer . . . They only knew about seven or eight songs, they came out and did the set and people loved them. So they came back and did their whole set over again, 'cause that's all they knew. They'd all dressed up in weird shit that they'd stapled on to themselves. Then the Dils played – at the time they were a five-piece – and they all had Soviet Union flags draped from their amplifiers. But they were horrible – they didn't have songs, and the singer was not good. The week after that, they did another Punk Palace at this place called the Orpheum, a 99-seat theatre . . . The Zeros came up from San Diego. Their big thing was Johnny Thunders.

According to Tony Kinman, the 'other' band that first night were these New York 'rockers who were trying to be punk. They called themselves the Dirty Diapers, and they were like these long-haired rock dudes, playing what they thought was . . . punk rock.' Needless to say, they were not invited back. By the second show, the Nerves were down to the last of their cash, and were already starting to feel out-of-step with what was going on. When another show was booked at the Orpheum, this time by the Weirdos, the Nerves were left behind, replaced by another downtown band with a lot of nerve, and precious little else – the Germs.

Like the Screamers – and, lest we forget, the Electric Eels – the Germs were a concept before they were a band. According to guitarist Pat Smear, they even 'made t-shirts with iron-on letters that said THE GERMS in the front, and AFTER YOU on the back . . . long before Lorna even had a bass. We'd make posters and put them around town, not for gigs, just to advertise the band.' The method by which Pat Smear and Bobby Pyn (later Darby Crash) recruited a rhythm section suggested that the early Germs were as attention-seeking as a baby's wail, if not quite as musical.

Pleasant Gehman: Auditions were held at the swap meet in the Capitol Records parking lot, where anyone who looked halfway interesting was accosted and offered the position of bass player or drummer. [1981]

When the Germs were added to the bill for the third Punk Palace gig, the Weirdos hardly planned to set the musical bar high for the other acts. However, at this stage, the Germs didn't know a bar-chord from a rip-cord. As Weirdos frontman John Denney told LA punk chronicler Brendan Mullen, 'They were just snickering, massively intoxicated kids who were literally just playing random feedback and banging around . . . The gag wore out fast.' While bemused, paying customers looked on, the Weirdos took steps to remedy the situation.

Phast Phreddie: Up till then, the Germs had just been a bunch of kids hanging out at Bomp records, spitting on each other. They'd never even rehearsed, they couldn't play their instruments, and when they did [appear], Bobby Pyn's idea of a show was dressing up in a jockstrap and spreading peanut butter on other members of the band . . . They were up onstage for maybe five, ten minutes before the Weirdos' roadies pulled them off. They didn't do a song – 'cause they didn't know any songs.

If the Weirdos had made a miscalculation – allowing the Germs to do their audio representation of an action painting – they had had the wit to invite along the Screamers' temporary house-guests, The Damned, who had come to LA to play the Whisky with Television. However, at the last minute, Verlaine apparently refused to share a bill with the Brits, and The Damned found themselves gigless, broke and an awful long way from home.

Fortunately, Screamer Tomato du Plenty saw an opportunity to acquire some first-hand pointers, and offered the London band a floor to sleep on. It was at his place that Weirdo John Denney tracked the Brits down and invited them to the Punk Palace, where Captain Sensible was impressed enough with them to jump onstage during the Weirdos encore. LA's seventy punks were given a chance to see how English punk should sound a couple of nights later, when The Damned managed to pack out the Starwood, after Stan Lee of the Dickies pulled some strings to get them a gig and (hopefully) enough money to fly back home. The great plan nearly backfired when one-man guest list, local DJ Rodney Bingenheimer, decided to honour the lads with an appearance.

Rat Scabies: When it came to our gig at the Starwood, Rodney Bingenheimer turned up with this guest list with two hundred names on it, like a who's who of [LA] rock. We just gave it to Jake, and Jake just tore it up and said, 'We got no fuckin' money. Listen, they're all rock stars, they can fuckin' pay to get in.' He [then] pinned this note up over the celebrity entrance: 'The Damned do not have any money. If you do not pay to get in tonight, they will not be going home, and you will have them here for good. You will not like this.'

That night The Damned proved that punk was not merely an excuse for fashion statements and loose living. Exuding more energy in their twenty-five minutes on stage than Led Zeppelin would manage in the three and a half hours they hung around at the Forum two months later, the quartet lit another fuse, this one six thousand miles from home. As Zero Robert Lopez has said, 'After . . . The Damned at the Starwood, it seemed like everybody in the audience started their own band.'

Those duly inspired included The Damned's short-term landlords, the Screamers. Though Brian James compares the stage Tomato and Tommy had reached by April 1977 to the period he spent 'sitting in Crawley listening to a Stooges album, and not being able to find anybody else that wanted to listen to that kind of music', the Screamers considered themselves ready to roll by the end of June. Unveiled at a private party for LA's new punk magazine, the Screamers also found themselves on the cover of its first issue.

Phast Phreddie: When they finally played, they didn't even have guitars – it was basically two keyboards, a drummer and a singer, but noisy – like Suicide, but more so . . . [And then] they're on the cover of [the first] *Slash* magazine – before they've even done a gig – [because] they were [also] totally into the look, more than anything . . . *Slash* have a full interview, but nobody knows what they sound like. After the first magazine came out, the magazine had their [launch] party. Then everybody heard them.

If the Weirdos, the Zeros, and the Dils all had a greater claim to appear on the cover of LA's first dedicated punk zine, it was the look of the Screamers, a cross between Plastic Bertrand and The Clash – rather than their 'anxious sound' – that appealed to publisher Samiof (and editor Bessy). Indeed, the early issues of *Slash* seemed more concerned with providing pointers on fashion than championing punk's underlying 'do it yourself' message. In one early editorial, Bessy showed just how superficial was his sense of how one became a punk:

Stand and face yourself in the mirror . . . look vicious, mean, uncaring . . . remember, it's your STANCE that's all important . . . dig up some pegged pants and some cruel-looking shoes (kats, pointy toes – kittens, spike heels) then rape the shit out of the ugliest shirt you've got (tape it, tear it, adorn it with anything that's offensive). Don't forget your hair (see Screamers interview for tips). Myself, I prefer a nice white cotton shirt with a narrow tie . . . If you've got a little money to spend, move quickly to Granny's on Sunset – they've got all the stuff from Malcolm's shop Seditionaries in London . . . insane clothing. [*Slash*, #2]

Though Bessy would like credit for inspiring the first wave of LA punk bands to form, it was really a happy confluence. For Bessy, the events at the movable Punk Palace had been almost an irrelevance, hence the reference to 'this madness [as] mostly an English phenomenon' in his editorial to issue one. Much like Mark P before him, though, Bessy hoped that local 'punks set this rat-infested industry on fire. It sure could use a little brightness.' By the time he made his call to alms, LA already had punk bands that beggared belief.

Altogether more significant was a real-estate deal then being conducted on North Cherokee Avenue, off Hollywood Boulevard, between a self-styled mad Scot and a hard-up landlord. According to the former, one Brendan Mullen, he had been looking to rent a single room 'where we could be left alone, but this real-estate agent . . . said, "Listen, I'll make you a good deal; for a couple of hundred bucks extra, why don't you take a sixty-day first option on it, and lease the whole goddamned basement!"' In a moment of clarity, Mullen decided to take the option, much like Andy Czekowski had with a certain Covent Garden basement six months earlier. Like the Roxy, no serious attempt was initially made to turn the Masque – as the cavernous complex became – into a legitimate exercise.

Brendan Mullen: [The Masque] was just this huge basement where people could bring their own booze and just whoop it up. It had no licences, it was completely underground, it was completely illegal, so therefore we could do anything we wanted.

By the end of the summer, the Masque was up and running, minus all necessary permits, passing rapidly from a rehearsal facility for bands like glam rockers the Berlin Brats and power poppers the Motels, to a place where 'no-cover, open-door BYO parties' became the order of the day. When the Weirdos demanded some recompense for getting up, a standing charge was imposed. But, as Mullen ruefully observes in his oral history, *We Got The Neutron Bomb*, 'Everybody was on somebody's list somehow.' The pitiful pay may have irked the Weirdos, but there was no shortage of LA emulators happy to take their place in line.

Deadbeat Geza X's claim that the Masque was 'the catalyst for LA punk rock to make a break from the past' may be overstating the case, but the 'club' *was* a breeding ground for a lot of things, notably a genuinely underground scene. An ad for the Masque, from December 1977, appositely described its activities as 'a cabaret of the macabre . . . a spectacle of simulated London street desperation in the promised land, filtered through a rock & roll sensibility of carbonated freeway fury and terminal swimming-pool despair'.

One might have expected LA to be full of souls wanting to share their 'carbonated freeway fury and terminal . . . despair', but the early punk scene was not only tight-knit, it was – as Mick Farren discovered – minuscule. New entrant to the scene and potential knitter in the sun, Exene Cervenka – who was soon fronting LA's most promising punksters, X – says she still can't believe 'we all found each other and knew we were supposed to be together – outside society'. Mike Watt asserts that the way the scene coalesced was an inevitable by-product of a definite lifestyle choice.

Mike Watt: Punk was more than just music, it was a way of doing things. So people gravitated to [the scene] . . . It seemed to us that if you met [a punk musician] before or after the gig and talked to him, [what he did] on stage was like an extension of what he was thinking about. [So] if he was worried about how things are being run, it was gonna come out in his music . . . I found out about [the Masque because] one of the Weirdos was a Pedro guy. We were jamming with some guy at the old army base [at McArthur], and this guy's walking around with [coat-checks] around his neck, and he told us about this scene where people were writing their own songs, playing their own music. At that time, any band you'd see copied records. But this was guys going out expressing themselves, and not caring about how much they knew how to play. This [had a] profound [effect] on us.

Ex-rock journalist Richard Meltzer, now based in LA, believed it was meant to be this way. In a 1980 article he would suggest the LA scene 'respects its own privacy, and thus at least contains the seeds of its own potential survival: it's UNDERGROUND AND PROUD OF IT . . . Fuck 'em is exactly the line this time around, LA's punk-derground wantsa *stay that way*.' Unfortunately, Meltzer's assertion came barely months away from meltdown.

Meltzer's willingness to participate in punk stemmed from a sense that he'd helped start the ball rolling, back in 1968, when he penned his monstrously indulgent undergraduate thesis, renamed 'Aesthetics of Rock' and published by *Crawdaddy* editor, Paul Williams. As an equally cantankerous contemporary of Lester Bangs and Ben Edmonds, Meltzer had been suggesting that rock was a car crash waiting to happen for almost a decade. Punk gave him a name for the way he'd always felt.

Indeed, he would later claim that 'what appealed to me about punk rock, *real* punk . . . was that it wasn't rock & roll at all, it was something else . . . [When] I realized punk took in all these vast disparate turfs from primitive chunka-chunka to the most bizarre and experimental, it was like being in love again . . . For [these] blazing, incandescent moments it oozed and spurted something *antithetical* to rock: it was honest.' Meltzer even joined in the fun himself, forming his own punk-rock band, Vom (short for Vomit). In a *New York Rocker* feature he explained why:

A lot of people want to define the New Wave . . . Essentially it's a sense of it all as thoroughly stupid, and unselfconsciously inane. All of these groups, even the serious ones, have at least one foot in the stupidness bin, and if they didn't, they'd just be folk rock or heavy metal . . . So Vom's trying to focus exclusively on the stupidity.

Unlike Lester Bangs, who seemed to have some semi-serious intent underlying his musical endeavours with the Derelicts and Birdland, Meltzer was playing it strictly for laughs, as one look at your average Vom set-list should make abundantly clear: 'Electrocute Your Cock', 'Getting High With Steven Stills', '(I Am) The Son Of Sam', 'Broads Are Equal', 'Vom All Over', 'Invasion Of The Surf Commies', 'My Old Man's A Fatso', 'I Hate The Dils', 'Beaver Patrol', 'I'm In Love With Your Mom' and 'I Live With The Roaches'. Distilled, degenerate punk rock.

Vom were not the only band on the LA scene playing strictly for kicks in those blessedly naive times. As journalist Kristine McKenna has written in *Make The Music Go Bang!*, Mullen was a 'promoter' had 'the instincts of a hardcore Dadaist . . . The work of several acts he consistently showcased – Nervous Gender, Black Randy and the Metro Squad, the Screamers – was virtually indistinguishable from performance art in its use of irony, overkill, aggression and humour.' One band Mullen featured, Arthur J. and the Gold Cups, was actually formed as a way 'to get back at *Slash* for bitching editorially about irrelevant, uncool joke bands misrepresenting what the scene truly stood for, by taking stage time away from "real bands" with important messages and directives'.

If *Slash* always preferred a more po-faced punk, there was at least one LA band who maintained a distance from the afterhours high jinks of partying punks. They even informed *Search & Destroy* – *after* they moved upstate – that 'the whole [LA] new-wave scene is treated like a party – but you're not going to produce anything that will cause *change* if you treat yourself like a joke.' The reason the Dils refrained from any alcohol-fuelled hedonism was because, Tony Kinman explained, 'You're no threat if you're lying in the gutter. It's just a nuisance. Eventually you just become part of what you said you were hating all along.' One way they kept themselves apart from any Masque madness was by insisting they play the last set of the evening, much to the owner's repeated annoyance.

Brendan Mullen: On every occasion I booked the Dils during the heyday of the auld pit and other venues I was involved with, they insisted on playing last on every four-band bill I promoted during '77–'79, rather than second or third – the most advantageous spot, unless it's overwhelmingly your own crowd! Everyone would go home or to the after-party . . . with my staff chomping to close out and get the hell away from the venue so they, too, can go to the same party. No one wanted to hang out to endure the Dils working a twenty-minute version of 'What Goes On'. What little audience was left from the other bands would dwindle to nothing during their sets.

Despite the Dils' disdain for LA Punk's extra-curricular activities, they were one of the first local punk bands to get vinyl out, and on two different labels, first 'I Hate The Rich' on What? Records in September 1977, and then *198 Seconds Of The Dils* ('Mr Big' b/w 'Class War') on Dangerhouse three months later. This was quite a coup. Although LA remained the home of both record industries, legit *and* bootleg, it was proving unresponsive to anything as alternative as punk. Thankfully, there was always the Rhino Records store. As Jeff Gold says, 'At Rhino we would literally take *any* record on consignment . . . and KROQ would play a lot of them'.

Once again it was the Nerves who had shown LA's purer punks the way, issuing their own eponymous EP in March 1977. It sold well locally, and the lead track, 'Hanging On The Telephone', sold spectacularly when covered by Blondie the following year. However, it took the ousting of synth player David Brown from the Screamers in the summer of '77 for someone to start the record label that would document LA's most fleet-footed scenesters.

David Brown: Dangerhouse, created by the triumvirate of yours truly, Pat 'Rand' Garrett and Black Randy, was a highly naive attempt to create a politically and artistically correct playground for the unique, nihilistic talents of the LA punk 'scene'. It was clear something needed to be done. In the beginning, there was a lot of musical talent which was going to unrecorded waste . . . The very lack of commercialism implicit in LA punk seemed to drive away potential resources.

The first two Dangerhouse singles were by co-founders Pat Garrett, as The Randoms, and Black Randy (and the Metro Squad). Neither suggested any great 'unrecorded waste'. Both did, however, display a certain playful quality, in keeping with the Masque's manifesto. The Randoms' 'Let's Get Rid Of New York' came with the immortal legend across the top of its sleeve, 'Recorded at home in their spare time'; while Black Randy hid the deliciously silly 'Loner With A Boner' on his first B-side.

It would be December 1977 before Dangerhouse started releasing anything important, but a quartet of singles in the next four months suggested West Coast punk might yet do more than 'cop the turn of the trends'. Starting with the Dils' double-header and The Avengers' 'The American In Me', Dangerhouse hit the motherload with the Weirdos' 'Neutron Bomb' and X's 'Adult Books' b/w 'We're Desperate'. All were fiercely inflammatory tracts on the American nightmare. In the case of The Avengers and the Weirdos, they were also defining statements, never surpassed.

Like the Screamers, the Weirdos 'were from art school, [and] they all had spray-painted pants and plastic wrappers wrapped around their legs, [with] shirts made of trash bags' (Robert Lopez). But, for all their art-school pretensions, they remained fashionably dumb in execution –

even if singer John Denney had the wit to cut up hi-fi magazines, to make a montage for a flyer, describing the Weirdos' early sound euphemistically:

Superior noise . . . incredible range . . . flawless attack and sustain . . . a hint of harmonic distortion. The cardoid pickup pattern feedback with rich sustaining sound power together in lightning fast runs . . . thereby enabling the playing of amazingly the full spectrum of sound in any proportion combined.

Such humorous invention, evident in the lyrics to 'Neutron Bomb' and 'Destroy All Music', was generally offset by a live sound that had all the nuance of a jet engine in reverse thrust. If the Dangerhouse 'Neutron Bomb' showed that a little pop sensibility never did any harm, it was something the Weirdos had acquired in the studio. Onstage, 'Neutron Bomb' was usually an excuse to give their instruments a final, potentially fatal pounding. When Denney talked about the Weirdos as 'like some fantasy group [formed just] for fun, with a bit of art damage thrown in', this was the damage part of the formula.

If the Weirdos blew their wad with 'Neutron Bomb', X were a different proposition. Though they began by playing songs as dripping with dark humour as Vom – of which 'We're Desperate' and 'Adult Books' are all-too-rare remnants – ditties like 'Cyrano De Berger's Back', 'Sedation TV' and 'At The Cross' were dumped before long, replaced by more widescreen songs from the pens of the couple who started X, John Doe and Exene Cervenka.

At the time they were approached by David Brown of Dangerhouse, X really *were* desperate to be recorded and recognized. Unlike the other Masque bands, X were primitive by choice, not by default. Both John Doe and Billy Zoom could play already – indeed, both had solid pedigrees. The Billy Zoom Band, a ramshackle rockabilly band, broke up on Halloween 1976. On the same day Doe arrived in town from Baltimore, where he had played in a bar band: 'We tried to play originals . . . The name of the band was Howdy Duty . . . [But] the only good band I remember in Baltimore was a dyke band that played Hank Williams songs.' It was that kinda town, and Doe couldn't wait to get outta there. The crucial shove came from *Horses*: 'When I discovered Patti Smith's first record I realized something big was going on. I could've moved to New York but the East Coast felt stagnant to me, so I came to LA.'

While Doe pursued a poetess he'd met at a reading, the florid Exene Cervenka, Zoom set about checking out the Ramones. He had seen a review of the Roxy gig in December 1976, which 'just trashed them, said they were awful – the songs were all too fast, they didn't have enough chords, there weren't any guitar solos, and everything was real loud.' More intrigued than appalled, Zoom told himself, 'I'll have to check them out.' By February 1977, Zoom alone, and Doe with his new girlfriend Exene, were running ads in the LA *Recycler* looking for like-minded souls 'to play music that isn't bullshit'. Killing three birds with two stones, they replied to each other's ad. The name was Exene's idea.

John Doe: I was driving by the Starwood with Exene and she said, 'If I had a band, up on that marquee would just be a big black X.' I said, 'You'd name your group, Big Black X?' [1980]

For the first nine months, progress was constrained by the lack of a regular drummer, despite papering the walls of the Masque with flyers, pleading, 'We want a drummer and we want 1 now! Fast: yes; Typical: no; New Wave: ?' Throughout this period they were obliged to 'borrow' other bands' beatkeepers, until they permanently borrowed DJ Bonebrake from The Bags in January 1978. Bonebrake, like Zoom, was a trained musician who had learnt the virtues of simplicity from listening to NY punk. He later claimed that when he first heard Tommy Ramone, he realized 'that simpler was better. Just play what fits into the song. A lot of drummers try to throw in every lick they ever dreamed of.'

If the early X had suffered similar drummer problems to The Clash, they shared little of their Masque contemporaries' adulatory regard for the UK scene (though they were still clearly taking note of the more noteworthy). When the Camden band's name came up in an interview with SF zine *Search & Destroy*, Exene let rip, 'I don't think anybody in our band *owns* a Clash record. We'd never think of imitating a band that *imitates* – that's all English bands do to be in rock & roll – is imitate American culture . . . There IS a rivalry, or should be, because everybody thinks in terms of England.'

Though her outlandish claims for 'American culture' were positively porous, Exene's declaration of independence showed X to be the one LA band that recognized the need to stake a claim for a punk sound not referential either to New York or London. 'Adult Books', with its faux reggae intro and sped-up groove, gave the game away – these boys could play. From January 1978, when DJ demobbed from The Bags, X accelerated past the competition, until they were ready to stake their claim to fame, with a whole album of shorthand snapshots of life in *L.A.*

If the first X record suggested hidden reserves of talent, the first Germs record set a standard for ineptitude that would have challenged Eater. 'Forming' (another release on What? Records), recorded when the Germs were still forming, and featuring stand-in drummer Donna Rhia, was a formless forum for Darby Crash to live out his punkified Ziggy fixation by asking his virtual audience to let him be 'your gun / pull my trigger'. Not everyone, though, bought his messiah schtick. When he got into a stand-up argument with Alice Bag in which, according to eyewitness Mullen, he suggested 'that a performer is supposed to cultivate a deity-like untouchability, Alice rightly took this to be the antithesis of the punk position, settling the argument by punching his lights out'.

Crash would ultimately get to stage his own rock & roll suicide. For now, though, he contented himself with performances that were a discordant disordering of the senses. If Long Ryder Sid Griffin describes Darby's 'painful howl' as 'the white man's suburbanite version of the blues', Mark Stern of Youth Brigade opines, 'Most of the time it was fucking awful. He couldn't sing worth a shit, and half the time he was so fucked up, he'd be rolling around incoherently.'

Even when the Germs got to play the relatively prestigious Elk Lodge, which had considerably better sound than the concrete bunker that was the Masque – as they did at a 'Save the Masque' benefit in February 1978 – the songs were a blurry backdrop to 'Ziggy' Crash. Indeed, when he *became* Ziggy for a buzzy 'Hang On To Yourself', it barely sounded any different from the surrounding sonic sludge.

This made it all the more surprising when, in May 1978, the Germs issued a second single (SCAM101), on the newly formed Slash Records – a spin-off from the zine – and 'Lexicon Devil' actually suggested some kind of focus forming. Evidently guitarist Pat Smear had decided that, whatever trip to nowhere Darby may be on, it would be useful to set it to some vaguely tonal noise. Though the Germs still made the Ramones sound like ELP, the aural action paintings were no longer so awful they made one sick.

Phast Phreddie: The Germs knew they wanted to be in a band, but they had no concept of how it was really done . . . [Yet] they wanted to be rock stars so bad that they actually went back to the drawing board, learnt to play their instruments, they got a real drummer and became a real band. They wanted it so bad!

By May 1978, when 'Lexicon Devil' appeared, Dangerhouse Records had shot its bolt. The appearance of a second LA punk label, Slash, should have been a cause for celebration, but instead resulted in bitter backbiting. Black Randy complained that 'as soon as we finally got this damn Dangerhouse thing set up . . . the Weirdos and X called up and bailed'. Exene Cervenka retorted that they had never seen a penny from Dangerhouse 'because we wouldn't sign their contract that said they owned our names, our faces, our music'.

For now, Slash would paint itself as the scene's saviour, though many of the same accusations would also come *its* way, further down the line. Whisking the likes of X and the Germs their way, Slash took over the mantle from Dangerhouse at much the same time as the Whisky superseded the Masque as the punk venue of choice for any 'semi-serious' band. After all, there was underground and there was plain subterranean.

— — —

The Avengers would also grow increasingly unhappy about Dangerhouse's lack of accounts, let alone royalties. But when Dangerhouse released their memorable 'The American In Me' in December 1977, they were not just the only outlet available, but a blessed opportunity no other San Francisco punk band really had.

The Avengers had maintained close contact with the LA punk scene right from their summer '77 formation, thanks to singer Penelope Houston's friendship with the Screamers, dating back to a common starting-point, an art college on the outskirts of Seattle. They even made their Southern Cal debut at a landmark gig, The Punk Rock Fashion Show, held at the Hollywood Palladium on 23 September 1977. The Avengers were SF's representative on a bill that drew from all the key American punk enclaves: New York (Blondie), Cleveland/Akron (Devo), and LA (the Weirdos).

By the end of January 1978, they not only had their first single out but had supported the Sex Pistols at *the* infamous Winterland finale.

They certainly seemed to have the punk gods on their side. And yet, when it comes to San Francisco punk, The Avengers almost qualify as the last gang in town. Both the Nuns and Crime predate them; as does the Bay Area's one punk palace, Mabuhay Gardens, and its magazine mouthpiece, *Search & Destroy*. Yet The Avengers seemed to sidle in and steal the crown.

What The Avengers had was a phosphorescent frontperson, peroxide punkette Penelope Houston, who immediately engaged the eye; and short, snappy songs with terse titles, like 'My Boyfriend's A Pinhead', 'Car Crash', 'I Want Into Your Heart' and the assertive 'We Are The One'. Unlike Crime and the Nuns, The Avengers' antecedents were kept well hid beneath their buzzsaw, having been quietly buried after their first gig. According to Houston this 'was at a warehouse party, and there was about two hundred people there. We just played covers.' The set that night essentially comprised early Stooges and Stones standards.

In keeping with the art-school/punk symbiosis, Houston had first come to San Francisco in January 1977 to attend the prestigious SF Art Institute. Even at college in Washington, she had found that 'people used to call me Penelope Punk, because I'd put my hair in pigtails that stood straight up on end and I wore a black vinyl jacket. Then a friend of mine told me there were these punks in England who ripped up their clothes and pinned them back together.' It was at SFAI that she encountered Danny Furious, who immediately recognized someone who stood out from the collegiate crowd.

Danny Furious: I was totally floored with this 'Marilyn-type redhead' who also attended the SFAI and [who] would dress in these vintage fifties clothes, in stark contrast to the other painters at school . . . She was the most fascinating girl I'd ever seen! So I . . . popped the big question, 'Do you want to sing in our band?' She said, 'No, I wanna be an actor. I know nothing about rock & roll.'

Actually, Houston knew plenty about rock & roll, even if she was not as immersed in The Stooges as her fellow Avengers, Danny Furious and Jimmy Wilsey. As she told *Search & Destroy*, 'My main turning point . . . was when I heard Patti Smith's *Horses* . . . I loved her visuals, the way she sounded . . . [She showed] you don't have to compromise your intelligence to be attractive, punky or sexual onstage.' Though Houston says she 'had no intention of being a punk-rock legend . . . I was going to be a painter', the experience of performing at the loft party convinced her otherwise. But she had a condition – original material.

Danny Furious: Our first real show [at the Mabuhay, 11/6/77] was th[is] show-case gig for the [Nuns] and we played only original material. This was partly due to Penelope taking a trip down to Hollywood and kickin' it with the Screamers for a few days . . . Upon her return from Hollywood . . . she announced that, 'We must have our own songs!' . . . [So we] wrote the first five or six songs . . . [which] included 'I Want In', 'Fuck You', 'Vernon Is A Fag', 'My Boyfriend's A Pinhead', 'Teenage Rebel' and 'Car Crash'.

If everything here was familiar punk fare – of the 'fuck your mother, shoot your father' variety – Houston soon advanced to writing altogether more biting, non-PC material, including 'We Are The One' ('I am the one who brings you the future / I am the one who buries the past'), 'The American In Me' and 'White Nigger'. And though they remained in San Francisco, The Avengers started taking regular rides down to LA, alternating between the Masque and the Whisky. With their Screamers connection, they soon became part of the Dangerhouse roster. Recorded in ten hours straight, the Avengers EP would prove to be the label's most popular release and a clarion call to California's disenfranchised and dispossessed to start believing in themselves.

For The Avengers, though, the *American In Me* EP preceded eighteen months of frustration, as production deal after production deal failed to become record deals; while the Mabuhay scene stayed resolutely inside its Bay Area bubble. Even a projected single recorded at the end of 1978, 'White Nigger', on which Sex Pistol Steve Jones produced his famous guitar-soup, failed to smooth the transition into recording artists. By the following June the will to thrill had gone. After sharing the Old Waldorf stage with another short-cropped punk diva, Penetration's Pauline Murray, Houston called time on The Avengers, just as the results of the Jones session were about to see the light of day.

On the other hand, San Francisco's *original* proto-punks, Crime, seemed quietly determined to stick around. After all, they had been around since 1975, which was when Frankie Fix and Johnny Strike finally found a rhythm section of their own. As the latter says, 'Before that it had been me and Frankie sitting in our apartments with our guitars and tiny amps, calling ourselves something different each week: the Bloody Children, the Noisemeisters, the Space Invaders.' Crime lasted long enough to tangle with punk's Anglophile strain, but they drew primarily on what Johnny Strike calls 'the US bands who initially imitated the Brits, but who were as wild on their own turf'.

Being around SF when it was all tarnished Glam, did not dissuade Strike and co. from a life of Crime, and in 1976 they issued their first independent 45, 'Hot Wire My Heart' b/w 'Baby You're So Repulsive', following it a few months later with 'Frustration' b/w 'Murder By Guitar'. Despite the most brutal guitar-sound this side of The Stooges, no national record labels responded to these ultra-obscure garage-rock bulletins.

The advent of SF punk allowed Crime to carry on doing what they had always done, believing that a record contract was just around the corner. In the opinion of Raymond Rumour, they were 'really on the make from day one . . . Lynn Hirshman, a freelance curator from the SF scene . . . was helping them, packaging [them]. [The first time I saw them,] they were doing a show on the street – in the now so-called Jack Kerouac Alley behind City Lights. They were out there in their uniforms, and they had searchlights and spotlights – it was a piece of street theatre – they were very good, but there was definitely a reaction from a lot of punks, "These guys are too professional, they aren't really one of us."'

The leather and shades failed to mask a seventies garageband, trying on the punk attitude to see how it fit. Songs like 'Hot Wire My Heart', 'Terminal Boredom' and 'Baby You're So Repulsive' suggested a band who were San Fran's answer to the Suburban Studs or Slaughter & the Dogs, not The Clash or The Damned. Nor were they ever entirely accepted by the LA punk scene, for whom they were an all-too-uncomfortable reminder of proto-punk/glam hybrids like the Berlin Brats. Crime proved as *Doomed* as their one album, which stayed unreleased until 1990.

By 1976, the town on the bay already had proto-punk's greatest secret, the experimental-equals-weird wackiness that was The Residents. Five years of record releases hadn't resulted in any actual sightings, as The Residents confined themselves to sporadic bulletins on their own Ralph Records. But recognition of an art-punk association came in issue three of *Search & Destroy*, which contained the Complete Residents Handbook, a nine-point programme for musical freedom that any punk could relate to:

The Residents think the music rules book is funny. They sometimes read it when they go to the toilet . . . They try to make the most interesting series of recorded noises that have ever been heard. These noises sometimes sound vaguely like music . . . The Residents isolate themselves from their audience to assure that the works are a product of their own desires.

S&D – which followed hard on the stiletto heels of LA's *Slash* in the summer of '77 – was having the same problem as *Slash* finding enough of a scene to champion. So The Residents were a perfect reference-point for editor Vale to pull out of his hat. But it took an altogether more venerable advocate of free speech to keep the fanzine afloat in those early days. Vale's day gig was working at City Lights, the book-store that doubled as west coast HQ to the Beats. Here he convinced Allen Ginsberg, once charged with obscenity for his poem 'Howl' by the elders of San Francisco, to do a benefit reading for *S&D*, which raised a thousand dollars, enough to do a second and third issue. By then, the likes of The Avengers and the Nuns, and LA bands like the Dils and the Weirdos, were providing a reason to believe nightly at the 'Mab'.

In fact, the Dils had quickly tired of what Chip Kinman called 'outrage for the sake of outrage' – LA-style – and what brother Tony typified as these 'kids [who] don't translate the boredom into political thoughts'. After well-received sets at the 'Mab', San Francisco began to seem a better option. Avenger Danny Furious suspects that, 'The Dils [in LA] . . . were perceived as "piss-stained commies", or some such nonsense . . . so they decided to move up north where politics was not a dirty word (yet).'

Though yet to jettison the 'hammer and sickle' backdrop, or Marxist manager, the Dils started allowing a little Americana into their San Francisco set. *S&D* scribe Ray Rumour recalls, 'Chip and Tony Kinman [being] . . . like mountain people. They were hillbillies and they had a kind of Everly Brothers thing going with their voices. In fact every now and then, for an encore, they would do an Everly Brothers' song like "Cathy's Clown".'

What the Kinmans also found during their time in San Francisco was another guitarist-songwriter, Alejandro Escovedo, then playing in the Nuns, who was starting to tire of the city's new wave at the time the Dils came north. Between the Kinmans and Escovedo, SF punk would start to acquire a country twang but it would be 1982 before Rank & File made LA sit up and hoe down.

The Nuns would suffer a personality crisis throughout most of their brief life, caught in cracks opened up by The Stooges and the Dolls, yet never clambering to the ledge that marked out new territory. According to Escovedo, the Nuns were originally the product of a film project he and Brooklyn buddy Jeff Olener were putting together back in 1976, which seemed like a cross between the Germs and Alberto Y Lost Trios' *Snuff-Rock*:

The last scene was where [the kid] goes and auditions for this band – and he's a real Iggy character – only we didn't know any San Francisco bands that were into the kind of thing we wanted – kind of a trashy rock & roll band. We didn't play any instruments ourselves but we said, 'Fuck it, we'll be the band.' I picked up a twelve-string guitar with six strings on it and banged out the only three chords I knew . . . It turned out to be 'Decadent Jew'.

Gradually the Nuns expanded to a six-piece, adopting another of SF's female artists, Jennifer Miro, and another New Yorker rocker, Ritchie Detrick, whose one claim to fame was membership of a pre-Ramones combo with Dee Dee. But for all their nudge-nudge song titles – like 'Fat Girls', 'Getting Vicious', 'Suicide Child', 'Decadent Jew' and 'Child Molester' – Howie Klein called it right in a *New York Rocker* feature in which he wrote, 'Even a dopey A&R man can tell that a band like this is gonna mean nothing but trouble and ulcers.' The art-school experiment ended with school's out at the end of '78.

All these bands were firm favourites at SF's one-stop club for punks on parade. At the 'Mab', there was also ample opportunity throughout punk for anyone wanting to play. As Raymond Rumour recalls, 'In terms of a scene – every night of the week – the Mabuhay was the place. There was this guy called Howie Klein who was definitely a big early promoter of shows, and was always at the door. If you wanted to play, you just spoke to him and there were always three groups a night, nine, ten and eleven o'clock, and you just signed up and you got on the bill. If you were any good you suddenly had a following – then you were on for other shows.' If no one broke out on a national level – at least until the Dead Kennedys came along in 1979 – there was no shortage of wannabe punk bands in the Bay Area, some containing the forward-thinkers of American post-punk.

Steve Wynn: My 'bad' new-wave band, Suspects . . . was with Kendra Smith and Russ Tolman, [later] of True West . . . We used to play the Mabuhay, support[ing] Crime and the Dead Kennedys. [But] when we played there, it was usually pretty empty. We were just a little band from Davis, with no real following. [Yet] Dirk Dirksen, the booker for the Mabuhay, would book us whenever we wanted to play. He'd always be a little rude to us, but would then book us a month later. We thought to be fourth-billed on a Tuesday night at the Mab and play to ten people was the greatest thing in the world.

In the main, though, SF punks came to the 'Mab' to see the same three or four 'local' bands, and the usual interchange of LA acts, almost all of whom considered the place a second home, even if Germ Chris Ashford bemoans the fact that, 'It seemed like it was . . . much more of an art-school crowd.' Some LA combos found more favour up north. As Penelope Houston says, 'We brought X up and we brought the Alley Cats up. Oddly enough people really liked the Alley Cats and they didn't like X.' Evidently, they had their favourites, thinking they were simply waiting for the rest of America to catch up.

Unfortunately, as Dead Kennedy Jello Biafra informed Gina Arnold, 'It became obvious by mid-'78 that none of these [SF punk] bands were ever going to be let in the door. I remember once I was in Aquarius Records and Penelope was in there and some woman came up to her and said, "Hey, when are you guys going to make an album?" and Penelope burst into tears!' Indeed, one of the factors that ultimately did for the first-wave 'Mab' bands was Jello Biafra's own band, whose summer 1978 debut came at the opposite end of the bill to the then-ascendant Avengers.

Ray Rumour: The name [the Dead Kennedys] was definitely the most shocking name at the time . . . [even if] there was an element of homage to it. I produced the first gig they did, at the SF Institute, and for three weekends in a row – maybe there was a week off – I had the Dils, The Avengers, the Dead Kennedys, the Mutants, and a reggae band from Oakland, because we wanted to make it a somewhat interracial scene. The first week the Dead Kennedys opened, the second week they were second, and the third week they were headliners. Thereafter, they were just the hottest thing on the scene.

The Dead Kennedys had as charismatic a frontperson as The Avengers, but if Houston had a small stock of anthems she had been recycling for more than a year now, the Dead Kennedys had a set of songs that actually pushed punk's thematic boundaries, aligned to a genuinely inflammatory stance. 'Kill The Poor', 'California Über Alles', 'Holiday In Cambodia', 'Forward To Death' and 'I Kill Children' could have come from Throbbing Gristle's locker of lost songs. But the Kennedys' music didn't hide behind the kind of atonal ambiguity TG liked. It was punk – fast, powerful and raw. But these boys could also play well enough to take their razor-backed riffs to ostensibly incongruous covers like 'Rawhide', 'Viva Las Vegas' and 'Back In The USSR'.

By the end of 1978, *Search & Destroy* were obliged to share in the excitement, depicting these Dead boys as 'the fastest-rising new band in the Bay Area . . . They've only played seven times but [at] all events [there] have been Disruptions – after their third, [Mabuhay owner] Dirk Dirksen [even] gave them his stern lecture on "violating the theater of illusion".' Unfortunately, for all the smart subtexts in their driller-killer ditties, the Kennedys quickly began to attract an audience more interested in the spectacle of Biafra bouncing off walls. As a self-confessed Suicide fan, with a dose of Iggy there too, Biafra soon decided he should have what Lester Bangs once typified as 'the most fucked-up band in history so as to externalize his own inner turmoil'.

Biafra also realized that the 'Mab' punk scene was never going to be self-perpetuating. Even the local audience for punk was looking to the UK and/or New York for most of its inspiration (as one look at the ads in *Search & Destroy* confirms). For all the fun and frolics a weekend at the 'Mab' offered, the first-wave SF bands were caught between UK punk-rock and a hard place. As Mab regular Steve Wynn recalls, 'Anything on import, I wanted to know about – so Eddie & the Hot Rods would be as interesting as XTC as the Buzzcocks as The Boys. We didn't make any distinction. Maybe because California was [my home], *there* I made the distinction. [When] I saw the first two Dead Kennedys shows, I said, "This guy's a big poseur." The Dils would [also] be the kind of band where I'd say, "I don't know if I'm buying this." I'd get these records on Dangerhouse [and] they were okay, [but] then I'm getting the first Clash album and [thinking], "This is what I'm talking about!"' At the same time, most interested parties were reading pieces like Greg Shaw's 'New Wave Goodbye?' (in the September 1978 *NYR*), which suggested that America remained a closed shop when it came to these new sounds:

The major labels that have dabbled in New Wave are now backing out: Mercury and Ariola have closed down their Blank and Zombie subsidiaries. Warner Brothers has indicated that they'd like to see Sire stop signing new bands (in fact Sire is about to drop many of last year's signings) and while most of the token New Wave artists signed to majors will probably be kept, it's been a long time since any signings of American bands to American labels have been reported.

When The Only Ones – who, for all their drug use, were hardly as deranged as The Damned – arrived for their first US tour in the winter of 1979, they found their US label, CBS, had already lost interest. Guitarist John Perry recalls how 'it quickly became apparent that this was a tiny phenomenon that hardly registered on their radar at all. [In fact,] you got the impression that the distaste [for this music] was such that even if the things had been selling, they would have preferred to cut their own nose off rather than be associated with something so . . . unpalatable. And we weren't going in and kicking over the tables at the record company . . . We actually wanted to work and sell records. The attitude was all on their side.'

While the likes of Sire and Blank (who had signed Pere Ubu and Minneapolis's Suicide Commandos) were curtailing their activities, the US label which had the likes of The Clash, The Vibrators and The Only Ones under contract couldn't even be bothered to give their albums a domestic release. So what chance The Avengers and X, let alone the Nuns and the Germs? The West Coast vanguard would have to reinvent itself if it was going to lay claim to a national audience of outsiders and misfits. Which bands like the Dead Kennedys would, though not in a way that would send the major record companies running their way. As their brethren in LA found out on St Patrick's Day 1979, those bearing down on punk nightspots were now carrying nightsticks, not record contracts.

5.2
LAST PUNKS IN TOWN
12/77–1/79

Joe Strummer [said that] his ambition was to be bigger than the Sex Pistols. Talk about missing the point – we didn't give a damn whether we were big, small or anything, we just did what we wanted to do. Success was not something we sought out.
— Johnny Rotten, *Arena*, 1995

There has not been a hint of hypocrisy [from The Clash] for all the obvious strains of being an honest punk in a dishonest commercial world . . . [But] there's still a big gap between the group's critical and [their] commercial success. The singles don't make the Top Twenty, the album sold steadily but nothing like the Pistols' or the Stranglers' . . . A year ago, punk was a gesture – spontaneous, explosive, necessary, but with built-in self-destruct: exit the Sex Pistols. The Clash survived and now it really is down to them to tell us what happens next.
— Simon Frith, *Creem*, 7/78

By February 1978, it was apparent that the Pistols' split was for real. And that the only possible heirs who could build on their legacy were The Clash, who had finally issued a single – 'Complete Control' – which could stand alongside the Pistols' first three 45s. The pressure, though, was starting to tell on the Camden clan. In a series of press interviews that month, Strummer admitted, 'We have worked ourselves into a corner'; and that 'this political stuff . . . [is] a trap – a hole to get shut up in. We wanna *move* – in any direction we want, including a political direction.' The real problem was, whither now?

Joe Strummer: I remember what a fuck-up it was after the first record. We wrote all those songs, believed in them, dead sincerely, maybe naively. But after we'd done that, we kind of turned round and said, 'Now what are we going to do?' We just couldn't think of anything to follow it with. [1979]

A lack of direction was evident as soon as the band issued its follow-up to 'Complete Control' on the 17th, a tame retread of the sentiments of 'The Kids Are Alright' set to the riff of 'Can't Explain'. To compound the disappointment, 'Clash City Rockers' was backed by an old 101ers song, 'Jail Guitar Doors', that hadn't even featured in early Clash sets.

Equally disturbing to anyone who bought into the band's early rhetoric was the news that the band was looking to bring in an American producer for that difficult second album. Surprisingly, such an idiotic idea had *not* come from their UK label. Maurice Oberstein, the man who countersigned their contract, had been delighted with the first album, explaining to a TV crew the previous summer how he had made 'the decision of letting [The Clash] go in and record themselves, with a studio engineer as someone to work the controls, [because] as long as we're careful to understand that what we see live is what we want to put on records, then . . . we will not then destroy what excitement there is in the music. But if we apply the same techniques to recording The Clash as we record a heavy-metal band, we will not end up with a very good recording of The Clash.' And still they were talking about using the man who coined the term 'heavy metal' as their producer.

As far back as 1964, US labels had been pressuring the British pop bands dominating their charts to record there. Even though The Beatles, The Kinks, The Who, The Small Faces and The Move all managed to resist their importuning and still record a succession of classic 45s, the Stones – Mick Jones's true rubric of inspiration – had been recording Stateside since June 1964. Now CBS, a label who were recording major rock acts with in-house producers long after rival labels allowed more sympathetic input, were pressuring the premier punk band to bow and give in. Among their all-knowing sages was A&R man Bruce Harris, who informed *NYR* of the many flaws he found on *The Clash*:

There's an overall sloppiness in production, and overall this is an album with an inferior impact. Radio is just not interested in this record . . . The Clash record is also impossible to decipher lyrically. Listeners would have to pay attention much too much.

Unfortunately, the US-based label had the band over a barrel. Not only were CBS refusing to issue *The Clash* – an album with more honest-to-goodness energy than any American artifact since *Fun House* – but they were telling the band they wouldn't issue the next one either, unless it was done their way. And the man they had in mind to achieve the magical transmutation was already telling the *NME* that The Clash 'are being accepted [in the UK] on the basis of stage presence, their material and their performance, not on the basis of what they sound like. Their sound is not good enough to succeed in the States.'

Sandy Pearlman's credentials, as ex-*Crawdaddy* scribe and Blue Oyster Cult's studio overseer, might have impressed Radio Birdman, but the idea of using CBS's appointed producer now drove a deep wedge through the Clash organization. This manifested itself the minute Pearlman ventured backstage to say hi after a show at Lanchester Poly in January 1978, and roadie Robin Banks took it on himself to dissuade the white man from taking his interest any further.

Robin Banks: I knew exactly who [Pearlman] was, and I'm glad I hit him! I took the first opportunity I got, because he was a fucking MOR producer brought in for the American market. In The Clash there was one faction who wanted him. And one who didn't – which was me, Johnny Green, Paul . . . and Joe.

This division over direction was wide, and getting wider. Jones, in particular, seemed in danger of becoming permanently *persona non grata*, as he slowly reverted to 'Rock & Roll Mick'. When he turned up at a studio session wearing a Bruce Springsteen t-shirt, the rest of the band ragged him mercilessly (all the while considering Strummer's H-Block t-shirt, which resulted in a death threat from an Ulster militant group, entirely street-cred!). When Pearlman 'turned up to see them rehearse at a place near the 100 Club on Oxford Street . . . all of a sudden [Mick]'s out of the band for a few days . . . [and] Steve Jones . . . was playing guitar.' Rhodes had meanwhile informed the band that Mick was letting the punk side down.

Yet it was only Mick Jones's presence in the studio that was keeping The Clash from scooting off the rails, having assumed a new role at their most recent session with revolutionary results. According to engineer Simon Humphrey, 'Mick had [taken on] more of a producer's role – he seemed the one with the vision – [whereas] Joe . . . had no interest in what was happening in the studio.' The session at Marquee Studios in Richmond had resulted in a single at least the equal of 'Complete Control', a clash of reggae and rock, 'White Man In Hammersmith Palais'; along with three possible B-sides, of which the Maytals' 'Pressure Drop' would have been the most apposite, though they plumped for Strummer's homage to cult TV series, 'The Prisoner'.

Debuted back in October 1977, 'White Man' had convinced Lester Bangs that these guys could go all the way. Writing in *NME*, Bangs found The Clash 'actually play better, and certainly more interestingly, when they slow down and get, well, funky. You can hear it in . . . "[White Man] In Hammersmith Palais", probably the best thing they've written yet.'

Another man who recognized 'White Man' as a real breakthrough was Tom Robinson, whose own band were starting to draw favourable comparisons by the time he was writing for *Melody Maker*, asserting that 'White Man' showed 'a new side to The Clash, [one] that can afford to admit the contradictions we all face, that there are no easy answers, whether we indulge in an ironic laugh, or the romantic self-image of the drug-prowling wolf in the sun'. The single showed – to anyone save CBS execs – that Sandy Pearlman was *not* necessary. Here was a record that demanded attention, with layers of sound that Pearlman, for all his endeavours, couldn't replicate (his own, inferior attempt at 'White Man' the band stuck away on a various-artists charity album).

And still, the reconstituted Clash dutifully turned up at Basing Street Studios in May, expecting to record their second album with Pearlman at the helm. The studio had been home to most of Island's best work in the past decade, but as Clash roadie Johnny Green has written, 'Those sessions at Basing Street were interminable.' *Sounds*' Pete Silverton was one of the few outsiders to witness first-hand what Pearlman was doing to make the process as close to heavy-metal perfection as he could:

In a break from blowing bubbles with his gum, [engineer] Corky noticed a small mistake on Paul's bass track. Paul couldn't hear it [at] all. Joe could, but still wondered, 'Why can't we leave it as it is?' Pearlman: 'Because people will notice.' Joe: 'Only ten million Hitlers will notice . . . Anyway, you won't even be able to hear it once I shout over it a bit.' Mick: 'And I'll be twanging over it.' The bass part is redone. [*Sounds*, 17/6/78]

Meanwhile, Strummer unwisely started a campaign to talk up the potential of a second album, while lashing out at everyone from Elvis Costello to Tom Robinson. He was also implicitly laying into Mick Jones, a friend of the latter, who had played guitar on a recent session with the former. Writing to *Melody Maker* at the end of May, he began by taking Jones's ex-London SS buddy, Brian James, to task:

I'd like to reply to the *MM* Brian James interview where he was advising The Clash to give up. We have just recorded, sung and mixed 54 minutes of brand-new Clash music as a dry run for our album, and though the operation only took nineteen hours, if Brian James heard what we got up our sleeves he'd shit his pants and choke on his love beads. Yes, it's back to Bohemian Bournemouth for you, Brian . . . [because] we've taken punk and put it where it belongs – way out in front of everything else, and that includes the tedious four-eyed school of Van Morrison imitators. [And] now I told what it ain't like, I better try to tell what it is like. Best way I can describe it is sort of Shakespeare Meets Chuck Berry On The Shepherd's Bush Roundabout or even Penthouse Incredibility Meets Commercial Suicide At The Dyed Roots of Punk. [*MM*, 20/5/78]

Strummer here gave himself more than enough rope for his own hanging. The nineteen-hour 'dry run' he was referring to – at Utopia Studios in April – predated the Basing Street marathon, which became a prolonged 'dry run', too. Pearlman found the band constantly distracted, and let down, by Rhodes and his roadies. Strummer actually admitted to Silverton that the endemic disorganization 'starts with Bernie and it comes down to us. Bernie lives in another universe to most people.'

Whatever the cause of the torpor, The Clash entered Basing Street having recorded their first album in two weekends, and having apparently demoed a second in nineteen hours; and left three weeks later with barely a single, usable cut. Evidently, this 'American' method of recording was a fine way of keeping studios in business, though not a particularly good way of making records. On the other hand, the four-song sessions for John Peel's all-important BBC show – which in the years 1977 to 1980 produced more great music than any record label, large or small – were done in an afternoon, at an eight-track studio in Maida Vale. However, when The Clash agreed to do their first (and last) Peel session in June 1978, the (lack of) results became a source of embarrassment to the band, and annoyance to Peel himself.

Johnny Green: We were asked to go to the BBC's Maida Vale Studios to record a session for the John Peel show . . . [but] after Basing Street, we weren't used to recording entire tracks in half an hour. Spliffs abounded, to the growing frustration of the BBC engineers. The session was never finished, and Peely vented his anger . . . with some sarcastic comments on air.

Rhodes was also starting to lose patience with his punk prima donnas. When the band decided, at extremely short notice, to do a show in Paris at the end of May, they arrived at the rehearsal studio to find that, 'Bernie had just done a runner on the band, taking with him not only the car but all their passports. Paul had irked him by painting his naked portrait on a blank white wall, and then drenching him with a hose. When he returned, he explained he'd only gone to get some petrol . . .

[but] the journey out to Heathrow in the Clash-mobile was rather tense, enlivened only by Paul's incessant practical jokes at Bernie's unwitting expense.' (Pete Silverton)

The source of Simonon's animosity was an incident at the end of March, when he had been firing his air rifle using pigeons as target practice, only to find himself and Topper arrested and imprisoned for killing some rather valuable racing pigeons. Rhodes seemed reluctant to spring his charges from incarceration, deciding – in Caroline Coon's view – that 'it will do them good to be in prison for a couple of days . . . You don't do that to people.' Bernie did. Hence the mural on the rehearsal studio wall, which actually depicted a large pigeon defecating on a naked Rhodes.

If Rhodes was fast losing allies in the Clash camp, he was hardly going out of his way to build bridges. When Pearlman – hoping to remove Rhodes from the process – convinced the band that they should resume the water-torture sessions in San Francisco, after the completion of their first UK tour of the year, Bernie gave his protégés both barrels in one of his press releases:

If the group wants to go to Boston tea parties and do the rich things, then they should let me know, and I will accept *Top of The Pops* and all the other expected things for them, and I will go and look around for another band that has the capacity to express the ideas The Clash started with, when I formed the band . . . I'm tolerating their 'bad boy' attitude at the moment, but they've taken eighteen months or whatever for the second album, while the first took ten days. I hope it's good, and good for the right people[!].

Which begs the question: Who exactly was looking to wash their hands of whom? Rhodes seemed intent on instigating a campaign to claim 'the ideas The Clash started with' as a result of the band betraying those ideas by going 'to Boston tea parties'. In fact, he had already started his search 'for another band that has the capacity to express the ideas The Clash started with'.

Six months earlier, he had predicted a five-year hiatus before 'punk will emerge again, redeveloped and with a stronger appeal, mixing the current audience with the new audience of young kids that will make it stronger. At the moment it is in cold storage, or suspended animation, just lying back in its coffin.' He had also suggested that, 'The scene is getting predictable – there's not enough spice getting into things.' This was all part of the announcement of Subway Sect's eagerly awaited vinyl debut, which he presumably hoped would find punk's 'current audience'.

'Nobody's Scared' b/w 'Don't Split It' seemed like an audacious 'preview' of the album the Sect had been recording for the past six months with Clash soundman, Mickey Foote. Save that it wasn't. In fact, Rhodes had lifted (uncredited) two songs from a 1977 John Peel session, and issued them as the Sect's debut single without even relaying his decision to the band. As guitarist Rob Symmons says, 'Me and Bernie used to have arguments about all the little things he'd come out with . . . [and because] Bernie didn't let us know what was going on.' At least with Goddard, Rhodes seemed to have met his match.

Vic Goddard: [With The Clash,] Bernie wasn't like a normal manager. He was one of the band really, 'cause all the ideas that went into the songs, a lot of them came from him . . . [But] if he told us to do something, we just did the exact opposite, deliberately. He insisted that he didn't mind what the [next] drummer was [like], as long as he had short hair, so we got the first bloke who had hair down to his arse. Most of 'em, we didn't even let 'em set their drum kit up, 'cause they had short hair.

Rhodes found he was being constantly second-guessed by the Sect frontman, who was determined to prove he had a mind of his own. The goading of Rhodes extended to preferring the Prefects to any other support act. As Robert Lloyd says, 'Bernie was still their manager, [but] things never calmed down between us. He just looked ridiculous, in those crepe shoes, and skinny trousers with zips on, and his leather jacket.' Rhodes may even have been 'the idiot of all . . . just dressing up / Ready for the great downfall / He may be an exception to the rule / But he's a very special kind of fool,' memorialized in 'Enclave', one of the songs the Sect had recorded for that great lost album.

If so, Rhodes had the last laugh, by not allowing the Sect to fulfil their awesome potential. In the summer of 1978, with an eleven-track album he'd paid for in the can, Rhodes convinced Goddard to disband an outfit that had been good enough to give the Patti Smith Group a run for its money on their spring 1978 UK tour. And whenever Goddard's boyhood friend Symmons 'tried to ring, he'd just say, "Oh nothing's happening," and put the phone down'. So much for sectarian solidarity.

Rhodes discarded the album – and mislaid the master tapes* – save for two songs he salvaged for a single; 'Ambition' acquiring a synthesizer loop before becoming Sect's second single in October 1978, to accompany another 'special guests' UK tour, this time with Buzzcocks. This Sect, though, was a different story, consisting, in Goddard's words, of 'a jazz funk bassist, a rock & roll guitarist, a cabaret pianist and a Bethnal Green docker on drums'. As he candidly admits, 'I knew the band wasn't going to go on. The keyboardist was only engaged for the tour.' 'Ambition' b/w 'A Different Story' (aka 'Rock & Roll, Even') was a helluva mantle for this ersatz Sect to adopt on tour.

Not surprisingly, audiences were perplexed by a band with all these newly acquired chops, but none of the old edge. The musical papers found no such conflict, all three main players proclaiming 'Ambition' their Single Of The Week, while still wondering where that long-awaited LP might be. Rhodes had other plans, and after Goddard took his backing band – as the Sect now were – into BBC's Maida Vale Studio for another Peel session, he set about convincing Goddard to front a different set of misfits he was looking to mould, the Black Arabs.

Rhodes had already attempted to graft another frontman to the Black Arabs, but the Specials singer Terry Hall took this as his cue to tell his erstwhile manager to get lost. Another band member, Roddy Radiation, later spoke about Rhodes' proclivity for 'put[ting] musicians together like that. Rhodes wanted to split us up. But you can't do that with people.' Bernie thought it was something he could do, having already done it with London SS, The Clash and Subway Sect. Why not a bunch of hopped-up Coventry skins in love with punk and ska?

After Rhodes saw the Coventry Automatics – as The Specials were originally called, when adopted for the Out On Parole tour – he immediately wanted to turn them into something else. It was Strummer, though, who first fell in love with the manic Midlanders. As he later said, 'A lot of bands were doing the punk-reggae thing at the time, us included, but they were taking it very seriously, very rootsy.' Rhodes, though, kept

---

* The great lost Subway Sect album has never subsequently surfaced, though six songs from an early bootleg version have recently been utilized on the 2-CD Vic Goddard overview, *A Different Story*. Track-listings for the original album abound but perhaps the most reliable appeared in a contemporary article by Jon Savage in the 1 July 1978 *Sounds*: 'Chain Smoking'; 'Birth And Death'; 'De-railed Sense'; 'The Ambition'; 'Staying (Out Of Touch)'; 'Imbalance'; 'Eastern Europe'; 'The Exit Of No Return'; 'Forgotten Weakness'; 'Enclave'; 'Rock & Roll, Even'.

telling the Automatics that their sound 'was much too jumbled up'. Rather than let them develop at their own pace, he sent them to Paris to play a set of shows at the Gibus. Sir Horace Gentleman later described it as 'like a Peter Sellers disaster movie. We started [out] playing punk rock and heavy reggae . . . but it [just] didn't work.'

On their return, Rhodes put the renamed Specials in cold storage, presumably awaiting the next wave. Instead, in the words of manager Rick Rogers, 'They started cracking up. They really needed to be seen.' When Rhodes produced a contract that verged on the feudal, the band as one refused to sign. Instead, Jerry Dammers wrote a song, 'Gangsters', that 'was as much a reaction against Bernie Rhodes as anything else. He didn't think it was good enough. He had no confidence in the band. I was determined to prove him wrong.' 'Gangsters' became The Specials' debut single – on their own 2-Tone label – and the first of seven consecutive Top Ten singles, six more than The Clash ever managed. Could it be Bernie didn't really have his finger on the pulse?

The positive reception the Coventry Automatics received on the Out On Parole tour was seen as a vindication by The Clash, given their oft-voiced intention to inspire by example. As early as October 1976, the usually taciturn Mick Jones was telling *Sounds*, 'A lot of things we do [are designed] to encourage kids to do it themselves and be creative themselves.' And by the beginning of 1978, Paul Simonon was claiming to an American journalist, 'What we've done, it's made loads of kids that would normally go around wrecking streets and fucking up cars form groups.' It's hard to think whom Simonon had in mind.

Singer Strummer certainly didn't seem convinced, dividing those taking up the 'White Riot' banner into two camps in his May 1978 rant to *Melody Maker*: either 'dry, humourless, po-faced, gloomy, boring rip-off stuff like Sir Tom Robinson', or 'moronic, unintelligent, badly played guitar-thrashing with only one tune for both sides'.

In the case of Crass – a new band from North London, who believed that the world owed everyone a living – they managed to combine 'dry, humourless, po-faced' lyrics with 'moronic . . . guitar-thrashing'; but then, by their own admission, 'The music is just the icing on the cake . . . We try to live without institutions and the conditioning that's been applied to us – without normal structures like family, church, finance.' With such distractions, was it any wonder that they couldn't find the time to learn how to write tunes or spout anything more artistic than anarchist rhetoric recast as rhyming doggerel?

More obviously drawing on the Clash template, at least as diffused through Rhodes' rose-tinted lens, were Newcastle band, the Angelic Upstarts. As singer Mensi duly admitted, 'Seeing The Clash was the first inspiration. They weren't really a brilliant band, but I really got a hit off them and I thought, "Fuckin' 'ell, I can do that."' The Upstarts' compelling 'The Murder Of Liddle Towers', a damning indictment of police brutality, centring on the death of a homosexual in police custody, set to the old 'Cock Robin' template, was issued in May 1978 (three months before producer Dave Goodman – and 'Friends' – issued their own, protest-punk classic about the case, 'Justifiable Homicide').

Though they never improved on that first single, the Upstarts were the first mainland evidence that The Clash might spawn their own legion of energized musical revolutionaries. Coming only a matter of weeks after the appearance of the Tom Robinson Band's *Rising Free* EP – which included the ever popular '(Sing If You're) Glad To Be Gay' – and an incendiary debut single by Belfast's Stiff Little Fingers, 'Suspect Device', it suggested perhaps this new Clash-consciousness was seeping into the punk worldview.

But when The Clash took to the road again at the end of June, determined to blow away all those bad habits acquired at Basing Street, they found that punk's thick-skinned, thin-haired reactionaries still felt threatened by anything remotely challenging musically; even if it represented the starting-point for so much of what they pogoed along to. Failing to heed any lesson from the treatment doled out to their last NY guest, The Clash chose Suicide to preface their brand of righteous rock.

Suicide had already given fair notice of their anti-rock stance on their self-titled import-only debut album. During a handful of pre-tour interviews, Martin Rev even told one journalist, 'If a group . . . cause people to get suicidal, then just the impact of the performance alone is successful, even though the effect may not be what you want.' He presumably didn't expect such an antithetical aesthetic would end up being more life-threatening to the performer than the audience. This time it would be Rev's partner-in-sound, Alan Vega, who would take a beating night after night for refusing to condense his message down to neat little platitudes wrapped in bar-chords.

Alan Vega: The skins got me a bunch of times, the Nazis, the National Front, the swastika armbands. I got my nose busted onstage at Crawley. The Sham 69 guy got a thousand skins with him to come to the gig . . . [and] they didn't like me. They jumped me from both sides, [even though] they had these huge barricades. They crawled over the barricades. They got me and busted me up . . . In Plymouth, the Nazis got me in the dressing room [while] Marty was still onstage with his keyboard thing. I got into the dressing room, and there's all these guys with armbands.

If The Clash were awed by Alan Vega's bravado, they were infuriated by the response of *their* audience, who treated these New York originators even worse than they had the Voidoids. At the Music Machine in Camden Town, Strummer saw 'a bottle miss [Vega's] head and he bent down to pick it up and threw it at his own head . . . The skinheads weren't gonna stand for it . . . [Yet] he'd [always] face them off.' Unbeknownst to those skinheads Johnny Green saw 'climbing up the PA stack like cockroaches ascending a dinner table', the tour proved a parting of the ways for many who had followed punk from the outset, but now despaired of its fixed direction. Cabaret Voltaire's Paul Smith, who caught the Sheffield show on 30 June, was one of those who drew a line behind him:

This gig was for me the turning point in witnessing punk in the UK as no longer being a small, self-consciously elitist, arts-led community, frank in its opinion and expression, but fundamentally open to new ideas, rhythms and sounds. The Clash, while eclectic in their own musical tastes, were naive well-meaning messengers of small political activism . . . [playing to] an audience . . . who took onboard the fad rather than the real culture, and which almost instantly crossbred with the UK's inherent, class divisional culture of soccer violence and the love of a good alcohol-fuelled punch-up.

The Clash's failure to maintain Complete Control was just one of the dichotomies their position as No. 1 Punk Band now threw up. Another was the continuing shortfall between their concert attendances and their records' chart placings. Despite two singles of paint-stripping power, and persistent pushes from the press, nothing by The Clash rockers was piercing the Top Thirty. Meanwhile, bands from punk's junior league were passing through the veil with ease.

The Jam had continued on from 'In The City', charting with 'All Around The World' and 'This Is The Modern World'. Mick Jones's pal, Tom Robinson, could also do no wrong, storming the charts with his irrepressible debut 45, '2–4–6–8 Motorway' and following it up with a live EP, *Rising Free*, which hid its more controversial side away, while the gesture-politics of 'Don't Take No For An Answer' got that all-important airplay.

Robinson himself seemed a most unlikely candidate for punk spokes-man, with his wavy, shoulder-length hair, and BBC-radio voice. He even had a dodgy past, fronting the bland Café Society, a Konk Records katastrophe that sunk without trace sometime in the summer of '76. In his favour was his friendship with the likes of Glen Matlock and Mick Jones, an openly gay stance and unapologetic attitude to his essen-tially middle-class appeal. As he openly admitted to *NME*, 'I'd like to say our audiences are comprised of people whose rights are being eroded, but I think most of the kids who come to our gigs are middle-class rock fans.'

Robinson was, however, a true convert from the exclusive 100 Club school. Caught in the glare of a May '76 Pistols onslaught, he took his time reconsidering his initial reaction (storming out). But by October 1976, he had revisited the 100 Club and witnessed both 'top dogs', before having an actual epiphany, at exactly three a.m. on 12 October 1976.

Tom Robinson: I looked around and saw the Sex Pistols exploding all over the country, The Clash tearing the place apart, and here was I sitting in my bedsit, kidding myself. [1977]

Almost immediately, Robinson started penning fiercely political material, including a rewrite of an earlier, innocuous paean to homo-sexuality, '(Sing If You're) Glad To Be Gay', which became the Tom Robinson Band's defining anthem, having been debuted at a well-received solo club residency during Gay Pride Week at the end of 1976. As he would observe, 'In two years of Café Society we'd had two reviews. I did four nights by myself and got reviewed in *Sounds* twice and in *Street Life*. So I thought I must be doing something right.'

By December 1976, Robinson had his own band. By the spring of 1977, when the Tom Robinson Band began gigging in earnest, he had a set of rabble-rousing anthems offset by some distinctly British pop songs, betraying the influence of early mentor, Ray Davies. Initially, Robinson seemed to think that his more apocalyptic songs – like 'The Winter of '79', 'Up Against The Wall' and 'Ain't Gonna Take It' – might even make a difference, telling *Melody Maker* that October, 'We're sticking our necks out. With The Clash and the Pistols, they equivocate . . . [But] you've got to face up to '77, live for today, [and] say things today that need saying.'

But when it came to making a statement on record, the most pressing thing on Robinson's mind seemed to be how a long-distance lorry driver managed to keep awake (it's 'the little white line' – nudge, nudge). That, after all, was the theme of TRB's first single, on the establishment label Rotten had once called to account, EMI. It hardly smacked of leading the charge, or mounting those ramparts in a single leap.

By the following spring, one of the best sellers at Better Badges mimicked the TRB clenched-fist logo, but bore the legend 'Gay Whales Against The Nazis'. 'Earnest' Robinson was already catching a backlash, before he had issued any actual call to arms. Nor did side one of the *Rising Free* EP suggest he was about to torch Westminster, though it did at least draw on one of the band's strengths – their power live.

With their third single, 'Up Against The Wall' b/w 'I'm Alright Jack', TRB finally gave the fist-clenchers something to pump the air to, at the expense of its contemporary long-player, *Power In The Darkness*, much of which sounded like half-baked leftovers from Robinson's Society past, passed off as agit-prop anthems. The monumental 'Winter of '79', one of the band's most reliable rabble-rousers, *was* there, and remained a piston-powered preview of a dystopian future that was all the more terrifying for being five years ahead of 1984. But no matter how many power chords guitarist Danny Kustow hit, or how sincere Robinson sounded, *Power In The Darkness* contained song after song culled from the Phil Ochs school of journalist-songwriters.

Spent of songs, and boxed into a corner by critics latching on to contradictory stances on any perceived injustice – whether it be 'the working class, women being raped, blacks getting beaten up, [or] gays getting their pubs bombed' – Robinson lost his nerve, and with it, his actual audience, reaching for one he was never gonna claim. During the long, hot summer of 1978, he blinked and his moment in the sun was gone. Robinson proved, once and for all, that sincerity was not enough; and that chart success does not, *per se*, change a damn thing.

Altogether more credible claimants to The Clash's crown – as and when they abdicated – were a set of lads from Southall. Like Robinson, The Ruts had become disillusioned by the hippy movement, despite finding aspects of the rock-star lifestyle thoroughly appealing. Left at the starting-post by punk, its two founders, Paul Fox and Malcolm Owen, had retired in the early seventies to a hippy commune on a rock off Wales, where Druids supposedly used to sacrifice the odd virgin. Here they tinkered with a band called Aslan.

So when punk turned up, engine revving, Paul Fox and Malcolm Owen were pulling at daisies in Anglesey, watching the world sail by on a cannabis cloud – or as Fox portrays it, 'playing patience, drinking tea and growing weed'. Owen, though, must have been paying some attention, because in the winter of 1977 he took Fox aside, played him 'Anarchy In The UK' and informed him, 'We can do that.' London was calling, and burning, again. For Owen, it came as something of a relief.

Malcolm Owen: I was really delighted when punk happened because as far as I was concerned all the English rock bands were just a load of old shit. Led Zeppelin had just gone too far over the top . . . I was a regular at the Vortex. I used to be tied up in all sorts of . . . [bondage gear] . . . It turned me on so much, 'cause it was so energetic. [1979]

By August 1977, Owen was turned on enough to want to do it himself, and again called up his friend Fox, already a resplendent purveyor of riffs. The last to leave Wales, Fox had been playing in a good-time dance band, Hit and Run, for the last few months, having been buying records from Hit and Run bassist, Dave Ruffy, a City record dealer who specialized in US imports. Ruffy had been among the first London dealers to bring in the first Ramones album, which he proceeded to play to anyone who would listen – including Fox (and one 'Seggs' Jennings). When Ruffy finally met Owen, he was not what he expected.

Dave Ruffy: By the time I met Paul . . . I think Malcolm had [come] back to London with his girlfriend. He became a trendy DJ in London. Hung out with the stars. He knew Phil Lynott. He used to knock out a bit of 'charlie' to all the stars, and he used to get really good stuff. He was a great DJ. He used to play Kraftwerk – no one at the time played Kraftwerk – all manner of [strange] things, and [then] he'd drop in an ELO song, because he liked it.

On 18 August 1977, the trio congregated for their first rehearsal, with Paul Mattocks from Aslan on drums. It was time to see if Owen was more than a druggie wannabe. He was. Ideas for songs came with astonishing ease, and though early lyrics like 'Lobotomy' and 'Rich

Bitch' could have sat on a second *Snuff-Rock* EP, there was already a distinct sound, founded on the same tenets as the early Pistols, a bedrock beat, melodic bass parts and a guitar-sound set to eleven on attack and sustain.

Less than a month later, The Ruts were ready to make their debut at local watering-hole, the Target, during a break by headliner, Mr Softy. Owen's 'wife', Rocky, was stunned at the transformation, exclaiming, 'That's not my Malcolm, is it?' Also there that night were other members of Hit and Run, unamused by a perceived conflict of interest. They told Fox and Ruffy to choose between funk and punk. When they chose the latter, Hit and Run also lost its roadie, 'Seggs' Jennings, who now joined The Ruts on bass, as Ruffy reverted to drums.

Seggs: Ruffy said, 'Do you wanna be the bass player? You have to get your hair cut.' I went to the audition – which consisted of going round to Fox's house. Malcolm sat there, and we all had a pipe [of weed], and then he laid out a line of coke; and I just remember my head hitting the ceiling; and Paul [is] teaching me the next song, which was 'H-Eyes', ironically. And that was it, 'You got the job because you can get to the toilet and come back, and still pick up the bass.'

The Ruts were entering an already troubled landscape when they began aiming beyond the Target, in the winter of 1978. With songs like 'SUS', 'Society', 'Give Youth A Chance' and the combustible 'Babylon's Burning', Owen was clearly not afraid to write message-songs. But there was no ghost of Ochs in Owen's stuff. On the last of these – an anthem for anxious souls – the original idea came from guitarist Fox, who suggested to Malcolm that he convey something of the tenor of the times. Owen fused his love of reggae and The Clash in a two-word, four-chord encapsulation.

Malcolm Owen: 'Babylon's Burning' . . . that's the whole world. The shit's going down. People are so anxious; they're burning everywhere. You must have had that feeling where you're frightened sometime and you can't think why . . . So I thought why not go, 'Babylon's burning / You'll burn in the streets / You'll burn in your houses' – it's a short, simple statement. [1979]

The Ruts weren't the only new band to come from multicultural Southall; even sharing with dub-drenched contemporaries, Misty, a love of reggae, Rasta culture and ganja, and a hatred of all forms of racism.

Not surprisingly, both bands found themselves being roped in by Rock Against Racism, an ostensibly non-partisan lobby group but with close links to the Socialist Workers Party. RAR, to the SWP, was one way to further the revolution, but to The Ruts it was simply a cause worth fighting for, and fight for it they did.

Paul Fox: We did three nights at the Nashville, and the first night we got all these NF geezers kicking the fuck out of one harmless bloke. Next night, a mate of ours, Rod McAlpine, a complete psychopath, who [had been] learning karate, brought all his mates down from the karate class. So when [the skins] started, they chased them out the door.

Seggs: It was pretty scary. We started getting loads of grief at the Nashville, [with] all these famous skinhead clashes that we had because we were playing with Misty . . . We [also] did one pro-communist thing with [actress] Vanessa Redgrave. I just remember [someone shouting,] 'The skinheads are coming over the hill.' And they were.

Drummer Ruffy admits he doesn't 'know how to get across to people how violent it was. [But] it was a great learning curve.' Despite their best endeavours, though, the band never entirely quenched the thirst for a punch-up among their more fanatical fans, and by 1979, it had become a serious problem. *Sounds'* Phil Sutcliffe, witnessing a show that summer, felt obliged to report on how often 'songs started, stopped, [and] resumed again. There were quite a lot of fights in the crowd, which also distracted the band, who take the responsibility for helping to keep the peace very seriously. A drunken friend . . . got up onstage . . . and disgraced himself by giving "Sieg Heil" salutes to the beat.' It was all becoming too much for the band who, like The Clash, were obliged to back away from any overt political association.

Seggs: In the end, we stopped using the Rock Against Racism banner 'cause everyone was coming up and putting [banners up] for 'Punks Against Battered Wives' [and the like]. So both us and Misty said, 'Look, it's obvious it's Rock Against Racism. It's a black band, it's a white band, and then we're coming on and jamming together.'

The association with Misty continued. Indeed, such was the bands' kinship that Misty offered to finance The Ruts' first single, 'In A Rut', a three-minute contagion for its time. Though the band credit the memorable phrase – 'You're in a rut / You've got to get out of it' – to a fireman named Ken Felloon, who shared the band's squat, it surely originated with something Joe Strummer said to Caroline Coon back in November 1976, 'I'll jeer at hippies because . . . [perhaps] they'll realize they're stuck in a rut and maybe they'll get out of it.' In ex-hippy Malcolm Owen's hands, 'In A Rut' became a ripsnorter of a rock & roll 45, set alight by a superb band in Fair Deal Studio one afternoon in the summer of 1978. However, it had to await Misty's own debut single before it could be released, which was not until the new year.

Dave Ruffy: 'Cause I'd been in retailing, I went off with it to Rough Trade – [and] Geoff Travis bought five hundred, cash . . . On the way home I dropped one in John Peel's box. And he played it that night, and every night for weeks and it was like, 'Whoa.'

Seggs: It was £100 to press up a thousand 'In A Rut's . . . and we had a thousand records under Ruffy's bed all of a sudden. We said, 'God! We're never gonna sell these.' And went on to sell 32,000. Which was largely down to John Peel.

Before The Ruts had time to get in a rut, John Peel's producer, John Walters, was on the phone, asking them to come in and record a session for the show. The 23 January 1979 Peel session, oft-repeated in the coming year, did as much to spread the word as their indie single. It also introduced bedsit punks to the two songs the band planned to record for their next single, 'Babylon's Burning' and 'Give Youth A Chance'. Already a debate was raging within the group as to which way to go.

Seggs: Me and Ruffy didn't want to sign to a major – Malcolm did, because he was hanging about with Phil Lynott, and he wanted to live the pop-star lifestyle. And Foxy was very similar . . . They'd get off and go partying, and me and Ruffy would come back with all the gear and unload it.

After a year or more of flame-grilling audiences with the sound of Babylon, The Ruts needed to decide which side they were on. Initially, it looked like the rhythm section might prevail, the band entering Underhill Studios in February, to record 'Babylon's Burning' for the third time. But the results failed to put fire in Owen's veins. He perhaps suspected the song needed the kind of production a proper record label would facilitate, if it was going to have the impact it could and should.

Enter Virgin, who by now knew that most working-class lads could be dazzled by an advance with lots of zeros. When they offered the band twenty-five grand, their car-dealer manager signed the band's life away. Afterwards, he turned up at the Queen's Head with a grand each for the band members. As Fox says, 'I'd never seen a thousand pounds. I did £150 in the pub that night – a gram of charlie, bought everyone a drink.' At the time, he doubtless thought there was more where that came from. There was not.

Seggs: We signed with Virgin because they were wearing jumpers [not suits], not realizing their jumpers were worth a grand; and not realizing the [whole] cross-collateralization deal. We were so green. We had legal representation, but we said we don't want to have anything to do with the music business, so we don't want a music-business lawyer. [Instead we got] this guy on Regent Street who did Arab divorces . . . It started a twenty-eight-year period of being ripped off.

Yet The Ruts already knew that there was an alternative, and it came from Ulster. Talking about the punk movement, in the wake of 'In A Rut', Owen complained to *NME* about 'all these people saying . . . that punk is dead. [So] what happens? The first real punk album that comes out in a long time . . . goes straight into the chart at number 14.' The album he was referring to was *Inflammable Material*, by Belfast band Stiff Little Fingers, and it came out on a record label, Rough Trade Records, founded by the same man who bought the first five hundred copies of 'In A Rut', Geoff Travis. This label was being run out of the back of the man's record shop.

– – –

Even more ironic was the fact that Rough Trade had been founded on the back of the success of a single that had been paid for – and then rejected by – Island Records, the label that Travis most admired, and which he admits was still 'what we aspired to'. By 1978, Travis had more than enough examples of independent record shops transforming themselves into labels, all of whom still came to him for capital distribution. For the provincial labels, in particular, Rough Trade was the most reliable, reputable outlet west of the west end.

The most recent entrant to the 'indie' arena was a Belfast retailer Travis knew well. Terri Hooley's Good Vibrations shop had been taking a steady supply of punk singles from Travis for two years now. But in April 1978, Good Vibrations also became the latest label bearing a shop's name, issuing their debut single – 'Big Time' – by Belfast's premier punk band, Rudi.

Actually, Rudi should perhaps be deemed the last proto-punk band, bearing a core of musical influences – UK Glam, The New York Dolls, the Feelgoods and, ultimately, the Ramones – which would have seemed less recherché anywhere else in the UK. In Ulster the showband tradition died hard, and even punk bands were expected to prove their worth by covering mainland sounds. The early Rudi duly attempted their own renditions of '96 Tears', 'Roxette' and 'Gloria' (à la Eddie & the Hot Rods, *not* those original Belfast punks, Them). Unfortunately, Brian Young and his Rudi boys lacked the chops necessary to emulate other heroes, even ones as dissolute as the Dolls.

Brian Young: I had bought *Melody Maker* for a [T Rex review], and there was an article on The New York Dolls. Those were the days when you just knew from the picture of the band if you liked them or not. I raved about The New York Dolls without hearing a note of them . . . Then they were on *The Old Grey Whistle Test*, and that was it. Once you saw Johnny Thunders, you knew that that was right and everything else was wrong . . . We actually thought we sounded like . . . The New York Dolls, [but] we sounded absolutely nothing like [them] . . . The reason we started writing songs was [because] we couldn't play covers properly – the only New York Dolls song we could play was 'Pills', and that was Bo Diddley.

Rarely able to play out – save at local discos and youth clubs – Rudi remained largely an excuse for ramshackle rehearsals through 1975 and 1976. By now, though, Young had found the Ramones debut on import at Caroline Music in Anne Street. At last here was a band who, in Young's terms, 'were almost as musically inept as ourselves . . . writing such killer stuff [that] we started knocking out our own songs'. Though Rudi added 'Blitzkrieg Bop' and 'Let's Dance' to their repertoire, their own songs didn't sound much like their chordically challenged cousins from Queens, betraying a greater influence that the Ramones unquestionably shared, Marc Bolan.

By 1977, Rudi were obliged to institute their own aggressive booking policy, at places like the Strathearn Hotel in Holywood, The Trident in Bangor or the Glenmachen Hotel, ostensibly offering a disco 'with band', in order to have a place to play. As of October, when The Clash were due in town, Rudi were one of a handful of bands playing regularly at the Glenmachen, as was a band named after a Vibrators B-side, Stiff Little Fingers.

Jake Burns: A lot of people, ourselves included, hired the stable block of the Glenmachen Hotel on the outskirts of town. Ostensibly this was booked for a party, but the reality was that the band were in the car park selling 'invites'! Having said that, the majority of the audience was made up of the folk from the two or three other like-minded bands in Belfast at the time, such as Rudi and The Outcasts.

On 20 October 1977, mainland punk finally came to Belfast. The Clash had been booked to play Ulster Hall, and though they failed to perform on this fabled occasion, the day-long deliberations brought Ulster's punk clan together like never more. As Protex drummer Owen McFadden states, 'All the bands who had been doing this quietly in their bedroom met up. We didn't know anybody else existed, and suddenly there was this crowd of people who'd all been denied access to this gig. That's when the scene first gelled.' By the time The Clash returned at Christmas, Rudi were the hottest band in town, and their biggest song was about the Ulster Hall fiasco.

Brian Young: 'Cops' . . . was about the Ulster Hall thing – and everyone thought . . . this'll be their first record. But even as naive sixteen-year-olds, we realized after a while [that] people [were] read[ing] all their own things into it, and you can't do that in Northern Ireland. It's fine for Joe Strummer to wear his H-Block t-shirt [in London] – but you can't do that in Belfast!

As it happens, the night Rudi debuted their other 'big' song, 'Big Time', at The Pound on 12 January 1978, proved to be the night Terri Hooley came down to see them. And he recalls, 'The cops turned up with the UDR, and all hell broke loose.' Perhaps this helped persuade Rudi not to make 'Cops' their first single. Instead, with Hooley's encouragement, Rudi entered a recording studio on 15 February to cut 'Big Time' and 'Number One'.

Released in April 1978, Good Vibes 001 created quite a stir locally.

As Owen McFadden says, 'That [single] was absolutely revolutionary. Local groups didn't make records. [So] to have the band you'd just seen down the local pub have a record was incredible.' Unfortunately, Hooley had not as yet thought about second base. Young remembers 'the records arriving in the shop – [but] we had no idea what to do with them. Nobody had thought the next step. It was like, we sell it in the shop. "How do you get into other shops?" Duh.'

By now there was no shortage of local punk bands anxious to record for Good Vibrations, and Hooley's A&R policy was simplicity itself, 'If I fancied your girlfriend, you were on the label, or if you had bought me a drink in Lavery's one night before you were in a band, then once you got a band together, you were on the label.' No matter how unorthodox his *modus operandi*, it seemed to work. The second Good Vibes single introduced a band that had yet to even play out.

'Strangers By Night' by Victim proved that some diamonds are best left in the rough. Victim were seemingly determined to make the ultimate punk statement: issuing one inspired single, playing the most important gig in Belfast punk lore, and then promptly breaking up – only to ruin the legend by re-forming in Manchester, sticking around for another two years, then letting their drummer join The Smiths. But back in 1977, Victim were a three-piece formed by cousins Wes Graham and Colin Campbell, after catching the likes of Rudi and The Outcasts at The Trident in Bangor. Modelling themselves on The Jam, they even made 'In The City' part of their repertoire. Yet the single they recorded for Hooley in March 1978 sounded more like the up-tempo marriage-march of Little Johnny Jewel and Sheena the punk rocker.

In the winter of 1978, with this cult classic in the can, Campbell and Graham stumbled upon a Belfast city-centre pub that had its own stage, and proceeded to convince the owner he should let them play there. Supported by the equally short-lived Androids, Victim were the first punk band to play the Harp Bar, on 21 April. It quickly became the one place local punk bands could call their own, even if an afternoon soundcheck was sometimes the backdrop to the local stripper performing for the Harp's other regulars, Belfast dockers.

Owen McFadden: The Harp was an amazing place. On the surface it was a really traditional Belfast city-centre nightspot, where it could get heavy. Yet they welcomed this whole bunch of very strange young people with open arms. Suddenly there was this place where everybody could go.

In terms of Northern Ireland, every punk band was obliged to pay its dues at the Harp – even Stiff Little Fingers, who already seemed to have bigger fish to fry. Sadly, as Gavin Martin wrote after himself quitting Belfast for a mainland music weekly, 'The trouble with the Harp Bar is it never progressed beyond its adoration for primal thrashings . . . [But] Bondage gear, Vaseline'd, peroxided and geometrically shaped hairstyles and groups blueprinting the first Clash album all sound[ed] retrogressive and smel[t] rotten [by 1980].'

By then, Stiff Little Fingers were long gone. Though they didn't officially form until the spring of 1977, they had their first single out by February 1978, and a major-label deal – apparently – just four months later. In fact they sailed past the other Belfast bands, and out of the harbour, less than a year after their first gig, which a mighty miffed Brian Young chanced to see.

Brian Young: I was at The Outcasts' first gig, and I was at the Stiffs' first gig and there was a week between them. They both played a pub in Ballyhacamore called Paddy [Lam's]. We'd seen it in *NME*. It said Stiff Little Fingers, and we thought, 'That's the title of a Vibrators' song.' Henry had [the] *Teenage Depression* [EP] broken up, on a string, round his neck. But they all had hair [down] to here. We were sitting there all smug, thinking, 'We're top dogs here, look at these long-haired hippies.' Jake had a cheesecloth shirt with 'Repression' stencilled on, and was still wearing flares. But Jesus Christ, they could play every bloody song. They played all the first Stranglers LP, all the first Clash LP, half the first Vibrators LP. I thought, I'll be a smart-ass, and shouted, 'New York Dolls', and Jake played the 'Jet Boy' riff. That just shut me up! They could really play. And The Outcasts absolutely couldn't play.

There was a reason SLF were this good from the get-go. They had been here before, their previous *nom de plume* being another song-title from a live album every self-respecting rock fan owned back then, Deep Purple's *Made In Japan*. As the name Highway Star suggested, the proto-Fingers were firmly in the tradition of Ulster covers bands, playing a diet of Purple, Led Zep and Taste. But already, by 1976, the two band leaders, singer Jake Burns and guitarist Henry Cluney, were tiring of the bombast.

Jake Burns: Henry, our rhythm guitarist, got heavily into the punk thing right off . . . By then even I'd gotten fed up with heavy metal . . . I was buying records by . . . people like Graham Parker and Dr Feelgood . . . Henry bought the Damned [album] and Sex Pistols records, and kept bringing them over to my place, and we'd be saying, 'This is what we should be doing.' The other guys in the band weren't so convinced. But the big watershed was the first Clash album. That was 'go out, cut your hair, stop mucking about' time . . . [because] they were singing about their own lives growing up in west London.

Hey, what an idea – write about one's actual environment, no matter how bleak it may seem! Initially, though, Burns' band 'just did what bands in Northern Ireland [always] did, and became a human [punk] jukebox'. Even this reinvention came at a price. As Burns says, 'No one would book us. We came up against the old, "Oh you're not proper musicians." I'd be [saying], "Well, you fuckin' booked us a month ago, when we were Highway Star."' If promoters couldn't look them in the eye, Belfast's proto-punks continued to look down on these long-haired punk pretenders. News of their transformation even reached as far as Derry, where The Undertones' guitarist heard all about their miscreant past.

John O'Neill: We were such purists about everything. We knew all the *Nuggets* stuff, the New York Dolls, the Velvet Underground, we knew all that stuff back in '75–'76; and Stiff Little Fingers were [still] doing covers of Thin Lizzy and Doobie Brothers songs, which was anathema to us. Then they started getting into far more exciting stuff, but they'd already committed the ultimate sin [in our eyes].

The Fingers' 'exclusion' from the local punk scene actually worked in their favour, making them look for other ways to generate attention. In particular, Jake Burns had his eye on a column in the Belfast evening paper, written by Colin McClellan, who had 'gone to Canada and seen some rock group in a club and they were [apparently] far better than anything in Northern Ireland. I wrote more or less *the* cocky punk band letter.' It seems unlikely that Burns was unaware of the fact that McClellan had also posted the *NME* report on The Clash's abortive trip to Belfast in October 1977. McClellan agreed to meet the band, and brought along a fellow journalist, Gordon Ogilvie, who seemed at least as interested in the band as McClellan.

Jake Burns: Gordon . . . mentioned straightaway, 'Have you got a manager?' . . . We met up the following week and Gordon asked [whether] I had written anything pertinent to where I'd grown up. This was just on the back of my hearing the first Clash album, and I'd written the song 'State Of Emergency'. And he reached in his inside pocket and said, 'What do you make of this?' and handed me the finished lyrics to 'Suspect Device'. I thought, 'I can't believe this. Here's someone who is actually thinking along exactly the same lines.' The following week [I] played them [the finished] 'Suspect Device', and they put up the £500 to make [a single].

When tabloid journo Ogilvie suggested the Fingers use the Troubles as subject matter, in December 1977, the band had serious reservations. Finally Ogilvie told them, 'Fuck it, you're not exploiting anybody. You've been through it as well. Write about it, if you believe in it.' If he succeeded in persuading the boys, the subject remained a no-no to other Ulster bands. Rudi's Brian Young refrained from public put-downs of the Fingers, but makes it plain that he considered punk to be 'our escape from all the day-to-day shit ya had to put up with living here'.

And The Undertones, in Derry, may not have been SLF's fiercest critics either, but they inevitably became the most quoted. Songwriter John O'Neill suggested in 1979 that SLF 'seem to be exaggerating something everybody [here] is used to'; and that 'if they're trying to tell people in England about the troubles, they haven't a hope' (he now feels faintly embarrassed that The Undertones didn't show a greater sense of solidarity, back when). It was singer Sharkey, though, who really laid into the Belfast boys, describing 'Suspect Device' as 'just cheap shit', and asserting, 'No way we're ever gonna use our background as a sort of gimmick.' The contradictions in Sharkey's stance seem clearer with hindsight.

Owen McFadden: It's a big irony about punk in Northern Ireland – this was the one place where it would have been legitimate to claim we're from a wasteland and there is no future. 'Cause that's what it was like. It's hard to convey how desolate it really was, no bands ever came here, there was absolutely no night life . . . And yet, only really Stiff Little Fingers approached the subject of the Troubles, and . . . there was real suspicion from [the] other groups. People here really didn't want to go and see a band singing about the Troubles.

At the time, SLF were obliged to defend themselves from the sniping of their equally troubled peers. Actually, one of Burns' contemporary retorts – 'I don't think our records would sell in Belfast if there weren't a lot of kids who are aware or fed up of the prejudice' – is a hard one to refute. Nor can the parochial sniping by figures like *Alternative Ulster* editor Gavin Martin contend with the most compelling riposte, the song itself. If the searing vocal on 'Suspect Device' isn't from the heart, Burns should have been on the first plane to Hollywood.

John Peel certainly recognized the record for what it was, a *cri de cœur* the like of which had not been heard since 'Garageland'. And he immediately tried to get the band to come over to London to record a session for the BBC. Finances, though, were not *that* flush, and Peel was obliged to make do with a six-song demo tape Ogilvie sent along in early April 1978, containing a cover of Bob Marley's 'Johnny Was' and five new originals, including one called 'Alternative Ulster'.

The latter song was originally supposed to be donated to the fanzine of the same name, but Ogilvie realized it deserved a far wider audience than as a flexi-disc freebie in a xeroxed zine (perhaps this induced the enmity Martin bore the band henceforth). The song had a wider remit than 'Suspect Device', being a proclamation from Burns to the youth of the province to 'get off your arses and do something for yourselves . . . [instead of] sitting there complaining you're bored, and that there's nothing to do.' It also had a riff for the ages.

Peel was delighted by the tape, and played four songs, including 'Alternative Ulster' and 'Johnny Was', on his 13 April show. Accompanying the tape was a note from Ogilvie/Burns which suggested 'no real response as yet from record companies, but we are plugging away at what we believe in'. If so, the 'session' broadcast did the trick. By the end of June, it was reported that SLF were about to sign to Island Records for thirty grand, and 'are off to London shortly to start recording and gigging'. The band had already decided on their second single, '78 rpm', with 'Alternative Ulster' relegated to a B-side. But things did not prove as cut and dried as they'd been led to believe.

Jake Burns: Island brought us over and stuck us in the Cunard Hotel in Hammersmith. 'We will make you stars, kids.' You know the kind of thing. We thought: 'Fuck! This is great. Is this what it's like to be a pop star? Let me have it.' They put us in the studio and let Ed Hollis produce us, just for demos. We'd been playing Hot Rods covers for the past year, and we thought, '[Wow!] *Their* producer producing *our* demos.' We were totally overawed by the whole thing. Then they just ditched us. They'd hammered out a contract, made us an offer, and told us all to quit our jobs. [Then] Chris Blackwell . . . decided he didn't want us . . . The basic objection was [that] they didn't know how on earth they were gonna market this stuff in America. By that stage, we had quit our jobs . . . [Thankfully,] Gordon happened to be in the Rough Trade shop, and happened to mention this [saga, and they said,] 'Oh, we put out the odd record. We might be interested in helping you out with a second single.' . . . [So] Gordon went round to Island studios and said, 'I'm from Stiff Little Fingers. I've come round to pick up the 24-track masters. We did some stuff here the other week.' And they basically gave him the boxes of tapes [no questions asked], and he fucked off with them. We remixed them and put them out on Rough Trade. [1979]

By October 1978, when the two songs appeared on Rough Trade, SLF had inverted the sides. The newly recorded 'Alternative Ulster' had such an irrepressible riff, it picked itself; even if it set the Belfast backbiters off again. But they no longer mattered. Indeed, the fact that the Fingers had chosen to pass over an opportunity to join the bill for the Battle of the Bands at Belfast's Queen's University, back in June, suggested they no longer felt they had anything to prove. Their decision left the field clear for another band whose relationship with Belfast punk was destined to be conducted largely at arm's length to steal the show – Derry's very own, The Undertones.

Brian Young: We were the headline band and [The Undertones] blew everybody off . . . It was one of Terri's usual, the PA didn't turn up. [Then] they turned up, the whole backline's set up. Everyone's raking about soundchecking. We were more interested in how many bottles of cider we could get into us before we went on; and they set up, and started to play. Then this fella who'd set the PA up – who we thought was their roadie, wearing plastic trousers and these horrible plastic seaside specs – started singing. That was Feargal. But once they started playing, the twin guitar parts were [wholly] worked out. We were mostly interested in Johnny Thunders poses.

Like the Feelgoods in their Canvey Island hideaway, The Undertones had given themselves a long gestation period seventy miles removed from the Big City, having formed in 1975 with a familiar, reactionary remit – to return music to its perceived heyday. As the band's songwriter and chief architect, John O'Neill, says, 'I'd started getting into music at a time when The Beatles had just broken up, and it read romantically about how great it would have been in the sixties . . . [And] they just weren't making the same kinds of records . . . I mean, I liked T Rex,

[but] I'd talk to a guy who was trying to get you into Led Zeppelin or Yes, and I'd say, "I like T Rex," and they'd go, "Pop shit!!" ' If the band had an unspoken agenda, it was 'that music should be exciting and spontaneous' – though O'Neill admits, 'We never really talked about it as such.'

Formed by John O'Neill, his brother, Vincent★, Billy Doherty and Mickey Bradley, the unnamed combo lacked a singer for the time it took to decide on the kind of combo they were. Only when they were 'getting semi-serious' did O'Neill and co. realize that if 'we wanted to take it out of the bedroom and into playing somewhere . . . we needed a singer. [So] there's this guy in the same class as Billy, actually his second cousin, called Feargal Sharkey, that was known in Derry as a singer of Irish traditional-type songs. He looked a bit odd. But Billy just asked him, "Would you like to come to a rehearsal?" . . . He wasn't really into the music. I remember being round at his house one time and looking through his record collection, and . . . there wasn't really anything rock. He never really got excited about records.'

Despite his lack of education Sharkey was a compelling singer with a voice that for all its raspy quality had a surprising command of melody. The band was ready to gig. On 17 March 1976 they made their debut at the local school, introduced as the Hot Rods after Sharkey decided that was a good name; oblivious to the fact that the name was taken, and that the band played Hot Rods-style covers. In fact, by O'Neill's own admission, The Undertones' early version of 'Gloria', the true starting-point for all Anglo-punk, was based on Eddie's version, not Them's – even though at least two other Them garage-punk anthems featured in their early sets, 'One-Two Brown Eyes' and 'Don't Start Crying Now'. The influence of the Hot Rods on their early sound cannot be underestimated.

John O'Neill: It was all very R&B . . . [When] Eddie & the Hot Rods came along, they were the youngest of all those pub-rock bands, and they were a huge influence on us. We started [out] playing early [R&B] stuff, more or less the same as the record. Then the Hot Rods EP came out, and they did 'Gloria' twice as fast as Them. [So] we started [playing] all our songs twice as fast.

Already the band's repertoire was in a state of flux, having been exposed to records they had previously only read about in *NME*, thanks

★ Vincent O'Neill was replaced by his brother, Damian, early on.

to local 'muso', Donal McDermott. That rare combination, a fan of the Velvets *and* The Doors, McDermott had access to import shops in Dublin, so the still-unnamed band asked him if he could possibly get hold of anything by The Stooges or New York Dolls. Thanks to his friendship with Derry's one known rock band, Radiators from Space, McDermott 'was able to get imports of The Stooges, the MC5 and The New York Dolls – and he reluctantly lent them to us. I remember listening to The New York Dolls' records and it was like a veil had suddenly been lifted . . . hearing a band sound like how The Rolling Stones *should* sound in 1975.' (John O'Neill)

As Undertones' bassist Mickey Bradley has written, Donal's 'records . . . provided The Undertones with a whole new repertoire. Out went The Rolling Stones, Dr Feelgood and Eric Clapton. In came Iggy and The Stooges, the Ramones and the Shadows of Knight.' Another of McDermott's records, Lenny Kaye's *Nuggets*, inspired them to come up with a proper band name. To the likes of O'Neill, The Undertones 'sounded like a *Nuggets* band. In Derry, there were two camps: people who weren't really interested in music . . . [and] people who were so-called serious rock heads. We hated *both* camps with a passion. [And] The Undertones sounded like a name that [would make] people who were into "Rock" [go], "What sort of a name is that?"' At this formative moment, McDermott produced another import album, *The Ramones*, and the picture was almost complete.

John O'Neill: Hearing the Ramones the first time, you knew that as well as the New York Dolls and the Stooges influence, you'd also hear the Ronettes, and the Shangri-Las, and that's why it was such a huge influence on The Undertones. We virtually made a career of ripping off the Ramones, but a lot of it was to do with [the fact that] we knew their influences – [the ones] that weren't necessarily obvious – like the uptown R&B sorta thing.

For O'Neill, there was another by-product of all this immersion in R&B and garage rock. Like Them's R&B-infused frontman, George Ivan Morrison, O'Neill transmuted the excitement from these influences into something uniquely his own. Rather than 'ripping off the Ramones', he took the template, twin-guitared it, injected all that indigenous love of Britpop, and found his own subject matter, far removed from the world of letter bombs and sectarian violence.

John O'Neill: The things I was most interested in were my wife, arguments, seeing other people and things that had happened to them, day-to-day normal things that go on, even in a place that has abnormal politics . . . The first song I wrote was called 'I Told You So' – which was a straight rip-off of a Doctor Feelgood song. After that, [it] was 'I Don't Want To See You Again', which lasted about forty-five seconds . . . Billy was a better guitar player than me, as [was my brother]. That was [also] one of the things that made me try and start writing songs, because I knew at some point the chances were I'd get kicked out of the band, 'cause out of the three of us I was the least proficient.

This, though, was Northern Ireland and, like Them and their fellow Maritimers, The Undertones were expected to stick largely to covers if they expected to play anywhere public. When they finally obtained a gig at a local pub, the Casbah, Bradley remembers, 'Feargal and Billy really get[ting] worked up at the end of our version of "Gloria" . . . Maybe they really needed to go out in a blaze of glory. Whatever, the manager of the bar thought we should come back – and that was the start of eighteen months of regular bookings in the Casbah.' The Casbah became their very own Canvey Island, even if Damian O'Neill depicts the usual Casbah audience as 'long-haired hippies, drunks, stoners and mavericks, or what my dad would call "ne'er-do-wells", with a few prostitutes thrown in for good measure'. Increasingly confident of a good reception, The Undertones' set-list ventured into ever more audacious realms.

John O'Neill: We were playing the Casbah every two weeks in 1977. To make it fresh for ourselves, we always had a target of doing one or two new songs, even if it wasn't our own song, so we went through an amazing list of songs – two-thirds of *Nuggets*, two-thirds of New York Dolls, [the] Ramones, Sex Pistols, Clash, The Damned. People who were coming along to see us might've been hearing about The Clash or the Sex Pistols, but they mightn't be aware of The Stooges, so it was almost like an evangelical thing, that we had [to] play The New York Dolls. [But] when we started writing songs, people didn't know. They might've thought 'Babylon' was our own song and 'Teenage Kicks' was a Ramones song . . . We just basically built up a following.

Playing their steady diet of proto-punk widened the already-evident divide in The Undertones between musos and non-muso, fostering a source 'of tension between us and Feargal. The four of us were a bit of a gang . . . But he'd go for a month, and not turn up for practices. The band meant so much to us, but didn't mean as much to him. A famous time, at the end of one show, Mickey had to pull Billy and Feargal apart [because] they were hitting each other. Feargal might have said, "This is a song by The Stooges," and we played [the Dolls'] "Personality Crisis". Billy would take such umbrage.' (John O'Neill)

Sharkey's real problem was Derry itself. He couldn't wait to leave. As he sarcastically stated in the band's first national write-up, in November 1977, 'We conquered Derry and now Derry is conquering us.' Though finding gigs in Belfast, or Dublin, seemed like the only way the band could survive and grow, they were reluctant to play either, for entirely different reasons. At the second of two Dublin shows in June 1977, playing support to Radiators from Space, someone in the audience had been stabbed to death and then, to compound the sense of disorientation, Billy Doherty was initially arrested as a suspect. Belfast made the band equally nervous. As O'Neill says, 'Even though Derry and Belfast are only seventy miles away', anyone from Derry back then 'thought they were gonna get their head kicked in, the minute they heard your accent'. Little did they know how much Belfast's derivative punk scene needed a band like The Undertones.

Such was The Undertones' feeling of disconnection from Belfast that when the band made its first trip to the city, it was not to gig, but to record a demo tape, with which they hoped to engender mainland interest. Make no mistake, The Undertones were as keen to make it to London as SLF. But recording a demo did not prove so straightforward. As Brian Young notes, 'There was no recording industry here for local bands – no studios interested in local bands . . . Greg from The Outcasts told me they went in to do a demo in some home studio, and they literally played every song they knew in half an hour, and the fella [then] handed them a tape.'

The first Undertones demo wasn't much more professional, being recorded in a room at the university, using a single mike. Though that five-song tape contained the likes of 'Teenage Kicks' and 'Get Over You', its positively primeval production values ensured that the likes of Stiff, Chiswick and Radar were more flummoxed than poleaxed by the tape when it hit their doormats. Again, though, someone up there was looking after these good Catholic boys.

Mickey Bradley: We got over the fighting long enough to make some demo tapes . . . One of the tapes got in the hands of a man called Bernie McAnaney.

We knew Bernie through his brother Sammy, who worked in Radio Rentals with Feargal . . . Bernie was at college in Belfast, and knew Terri Hooley, who owned a record shop. Terri had at this stage also been making records with some Belfast bands and so Bernie gave him [our] tape.

Though Hooley had yet to meet the band, or their girlfriends, he managed to peer through the murk and the mire and see potential there. He invited the band to return to Belfast, and make a record for the semi-established Good Vibrations label. But they were also expected to play for the locals first. On 14 June, the day before the session for their first EP, The Undertones turned up at Queen's, nervous as hell: 'We felt like a lot of people were looking down on us country bumpkins, but Brian Young come along and said, "Fuck, these guys are brilliant!"' What really surprised, and impressed, the other bands on the bill, was not the MC5, New York Dolls and T Rex covers they played at the soundcheck, but the original songs now rolling free from O'Neill's pen.

John O'Neill: By the time it came to Belfast, it was [almost] all our own songs; whereas some of the other bands, like Protex, were doing mostly obvious cover versions.* We were doing the same thing six months earlier, but [back] then six months seemed a long time.

Four of O'Neill's best were earmarked for their debut EP, which O'Neill hoped might emulate *Spiral Scratch*, which was 'the benchmark for us – the idea of doing four songs seemed [so] cool. And again back to that sixties thing, the Them EP . . . [But] I remember when Terri sent us the test pressing, we were appalled, "It sounds tinny." But at least, we'd made a record . . . I can now look at it and go, "It's a great record," but ["Teenage Kicks"] is pretty clichéd . . . To us, "True Confessions" was our best song.' Others thought otherwise, airplay deciding the shape of things in favour of that most perfectly compressed pop song, 'Teenage Kicks'.

If Hooley sent The Undertones a test pressing, it appears he must also have sent one to his buddy, John Peel, because before the EP had even appeared, Peel wanted an Undertones session for his radio show. The

---

* Headliner Rudi's set that night featured covers of 'Suffragette City', 'Wild Thing', '96 Tears', 'Shakedown', 'Teenage Depression', 'The Kids Are Alright', 'Blitzkrieg Bop', 'Pills', 'Let's Dance' and 'Gloria'.

band were bemused by Peel's evident enthusiasm, especially as he had been a recipient of the earlier demo of 'Teenage Kicks', which had failed to register at all. At the time O'Neill wasn't sure what to make of it: 'We thought there must be something wrong. "Why is he saying that? Is it because we come from Northern Ireland and he's sympathizing with us 'cause we're war babies?"' But Peel's enthusiasm was genuine.

Unfortunately, BBC budgets still didn't stretch to five Belfast–London airfares. Unperturbed, and with the example of SLF to hand, Peel managed to book the band into a local BBC Belfast studio, where they recorded four more songs, including the one that pleased O'Neill most as a songwriter, 'Get Over You'. The results were equally pleasing – 'the best demo we'd ever done'. As a follow-up to 'Teenage Kicks', Peel decided he would play the tape through on air, all seven and a half minutes, uninterrupted.

Yet by the time the session could be aired, The Undertones had been spirited away to London, not at the licence-payer's expense, but at Sire's. According to Hooley, 'Seymour Stein heard ["Teenage Kicks" on] the [John Peel] show and . . . the next morning, Sire phoned and wanted to license The Undertones . . . Any other person would have rushed to Derry and got the group to sign a contract. We . . . told them to come over and sign up the band. They came over a few days later and made the band an offer. Ian Birch from *Melody Maker* and myself advised against it . . . but they went for it.' In fact, Sire were just one of the labels now interested in the band – Peel having again done their A&R – though Sire had certain advantages, one of which was the fact that they were prepared to come to Ulster and see The Undertones play.

Mickey Bradley: Sire were American, they were the Ramones' record company, and we were flattered that they were even interested. Their London manager was a man called Paul McNally, immediately christened 'Noisy' McNally by us, for no reason whatsoever. On a Thursday night he saw us play, liked what he saw and wanted to talk to us the next day about the contract. So . . . we all met in Feargal's mother's front room – the band, a few of our friends, Terri Hooley from Good Vibrations, and Paul McNally from Sire Records.

Once again, a record label seemed to be offering money up front that was intended to be endlessly recoupable. But to Bradley and the boys, the advance figure of £40,000 sounded 'a lot, and in 1978 it was a lot. Money that we couldn't even imagine having . . . We didn't know then that the royalty rate was the important figure, and in our contract it was pathetically small.' Sire certainly seemed in a hurry to start recouping. Barely a month after Good Vibrations had put out their version of the EP, Sire were reissuing it with their snappy yellow label, and pulling enough strings to get the band on *Top of The Pops*, even though at this stage, the single was only 'bubbling under' (it continued to simmer outside the Top Thirty for a couple more weeks, and then went off the boil completely). In case the band was thinking of getting too big for its Derry roots, they were flown back home the day after their *ToTP* recording, to fulfil an earlier obligation in their hometown.

Mickey Bradley: Two days after our first *Top of The Pops* appearance, we played on the back of a lorry in a playground for a local youth club, it was Halloween night, and we'd agreed to do the show a few weeks before. We were only on for one song, when out of the sky came a shower of eggs.

The eggs were probably directed at singer Sharkey, who had made no secret of his desire to leave Northern Ireland, telling *MM* the previous November, 'We want to leave Derry . . . to go anywhere. Dublin first, but the goal is obviously London. We have no choice but to move out. We can't move in this place.' Something deeply embedded in the Ulster psyche meant that locals turned on anyone who threatened to make it on the mainland, as if it was the ultimate betrayal to want to leave such a hopeless situation behind. The Undertones' songwriter suggests that the aggravation was not confined to the odd soft-shelled missile.

John O'Neill: We put up with a lot of stick . . . [just] walking down the street . . . A lot of stick. Some of it really quite violent. Especially [with] Feargal. On numerous occasions he was stoned and spat at. People took punk as a media thing – safety pins and dyed hair. We got enough stick looking like *we* did, just [because] it was something different. It became like a sport, slagging The Undertones.

Bassist Bradley relates one truly scary incident: 'A few months after our first *Top of The Pops* appearance, while we were in the first flush of stardom . . . we did a benefit show for Women's Aid, playing in a community centre in Shantallow, a housing estate in Derry. While the support band was onstage, some fellas came up to me and asked, "Where's Sharkey?" . . . Now these boys didn't seem to be looking for

Feargal's autograph. His blood, yes, his autograph no. They must have seen the look of fear on my face, because one of them told me not to worry – it was just Sharkey they were after . . . For some reason he brought out a particularly vicious streak in the youth of Derry.'

It was a replay of the situation Them experienced after their initial chart success, back in 1965. The Undertones took to the mainland, where records were sold and careers made, joining the other contemporary Ulster band to realize that there was an alternative, Stiff Little Fingers. Those left behind would mutter long and loud enough for fanzine editors to hear – and, when they also left to join *NME* and *Sounds*, reiterate – the myth that Belfast's best punk bands stayed behind. Meanwhile, The Undertones would find the chart success their songs deserved, albeit after their best two shots missed the target; and Stiff Little Fingers would place a whole album's worth of *Inflammable Material* in British record shops – and in the charts – proving that it was possible to engage a wider audience with content as political and inflammatory as the troubled times.

5.3
THE YEAR OF LIVING DANGEROUSLY
1978

Punk is there for those who want it. If it's dead, show me the alternative . . . It's a feeling. It's basically a lot of hooligans doing it the way they want and getting what they want. And it definitely carried a loaded bomb behind it . . . Punk is against hypocrisy, monotony, consistency. It's against the unacceptable face of capitalism, against religion . . . I don't want to be categorized in any other term but punk. That's where I come from and that's where I'm staying.

— John Lydon to Caroline Coon, *Sounds*, 22/7/78

At the end of 1977, *Sounds* produced an extraordinary document in the guise of an end-of-year list. Singles Of The Year, which in previous years had been eked out to twenty-five halfway decent pop productions, was a hundred strong this year, and still missing the odd indie nugget (the *Burn My Eye* and *Nerves* EPs, and the Users' 45, for starters). As further evidence of a revolution in artifactual statements, nearly a third were on independent labels, and three-quarters came in picture sleeves, a vital visual counterpoint to so many of these audio assaults.

In the album department, though, the English drought had not entirely abated. Yes, the Pistols, The Clash and The Damned had all issued twelve-inches of rapier-like thrusts at rock's cadaver; but of the other UK bands playing the long game, just Wire's *Pink Flag*, Costello's *My Aim Is True* and that clever bastard Ian Dury's *New Boots And Panties* warranted comparison with the body of work coming out of New York in its homecoming year. *Marquee Moon*, *Leave Home*, *'77*, *Blank Generation* and even *Blondie* suggested that previous hype hid a hard truth – New York punk was ready to rock and roll. By March 1978, the gap in ambition seemed to have grown more acute, the new year bringing Suicide and Pere Ubu albums that required others to travel at warp factor ten just to keep up.

But if the tide washing across the Atlantic was high, the UK new wave was ready to proclaim, Surf's Up. The month of *The Modern Dance* also saw *This Year's Model* and *Another Music In A Different Kitchen*, first forty-minute forays for The Attractions and Buzzcocks. These added Attractions made all the difference to one angry young man. No matter how good the songs on *My Aim Is True*, or acerbic the voice, Costello had been hamstrung by those dudes diddling away in the background on every track.

By the time work began on *This Year's Model*, Costello had stockpiled yet more twisted dispositions on life as a gnarled nerd, and The Attractions were lighter fuel to the man's flame. With a blade now tempered by touring, the results suggested a man awaiting his own public execution, lashing out at every enemy who put him there. When Costello sang, 'If I'm gonna go down / You're gonna come with me / Hand in hand', few dared disbelieve. With the full resources of Radar at his disposal, he knew his time had come.

If Costello had been accumulating songs till he was almost blue, Pete Shelley was not far behind. Like Costello, he and his manager had planned a strategy of singles to announce the brand, but had been perplexed at their lack of chart success. 'Orgasm Addict' and 'What Do I Get' were as good as it got. When it seemed Buzzcocks' best was not quite good enough for mainstream success, they approached the album differently.

Steve Diggle: It took so long for us to get a deal, we'd progressed quite a bit . . . By the time we got to record *Another Music*, we wanted to experiment a bit more. We wanted to have a different approach, rather than the straight punk thing. I had been experimenting with sounds on an old Akai 'sound-on-sound' tape machine . . . [but] didn't realize till later that both [Pete and I] had been doing stuff like that.

In an ambitious attempt to document the many stages the band had already passed through, Buzzcocks constructed almost a song-by-song chronicle of their passage out of 'punk', excerpting part of 'Boredom' at the LP's outset to reinforce the point. All the Devoto-era material that had served them well – including 'Fast Cars', 'You Tear Me Up' and 'Love Battery' – was to be found on side one; with the other side reserved for more 'experimental' material, concluding with their own 'Going Through The Motions', the five-minute 'Moving Away From The Pulsebeat'.

It was an audacious effort, well received but just oddball enough to dissuade the leather jackets, and as such it never quite captured the crest of its own wave. It also suffered by comparison with a rival album that appeared shortly after its release, in a garish red sleeve, recorded in a single afternoon in October 1976 on the cheapest possible equipment. *Time's Up*, that fabled bootleg of the band's first set of demos, served as a nerve-tingling reminder of the journey's start for those who liked their meat raw.

If *Time's Up* confirmed that this wasn't the same band, neither was Howard Devoto the same man. Now able to control himself, but no longer prepared to remain a drop in the ocean, Devoto's Magazine hit the bullseye with 'Shot By Both Sides' in early January. Their first London show at the end of the month – the night after their disastrous *Top of The Pops* appearance – debuted six more new songs. Evidently, there was an album there, but a punk album it was not.

Howard Devoto: With Magazine I felt I was doing something that I knew would be referenced against 'punk' for very obvious reasons, and that was a thing to be played with. [But I didn't think] I was going to take the whole thing somewhere else. I don't think I thought in those ways. I was [recently] asked to pithily place Magazine in the whole thing, and I said, 'Chronologically and aesthetically, somewhere between Ultravox and Joy Division.'

Perhaps Devoto was on to something, making music that was *not* punk, but was 'referenced against "punk"'. Even before the album was recorded, *NME*'s Charles Shaar Murray thought he had a word for it. In a February 1978 feature, he described Magazine as 'the most convincing post-punk band so far'. Devoto insisted that 'the new songs are about the same sort of things that the songs were about [in] the Buzzcocks'. It wasn't immediately clear how the rumbling 'Motorcade' – a song about 'a man with all the power, all the assets anybody could ever desire . . . [who] sit[s] in . . . his big car and feel[s] nothing' – had its roots in 'Boredom'. Or how 'The Light Pours Out Of Me' was an update of 'Friends Of Mine'. And yet they were. *Real Life* was the statement *Another Music* had hoped to be, and a leap Shelley was not quite prepared to make.

Devoto's rival in the Whither Now quest was not *Another Music*, but a somewhat more decadent debutant. The Only Ones' eponymous entrée had been issued a month earlier, in the slipstream of another mystifying chart failure. 'Another Girl, Another Planet', a triple Single Of The Week in the weeklies, had fared even more disappointingly than 'Shot By Both Sides', its only equal from the winter Pandora's box of pop singles. Constructed to the exacting specifications of perfect pop, right down to the rifling riff Perry paraded as its intro, 'Another Girl' was issued a second time by CBS, in disbelief at its failure. Same outcome.

Perhaps The Only Ones were destined to be an album act. They certainly had the songs, shot through with Perrett's unique worldview. Beguiled by Aleister Crowley's 'whole of the law' – 'Nothing is forbidden. Everything is permissible' – and De Quincey's bared soul, Perrett's languid lyrics were an effective counterpoint to the band's surges of speed. If Perrett had any actual peer, it was over the pond, where Television's Tom Verlaine claimed to 'understand all destructive urges'.

So when The Only Ones were added to the May 1978 Television UK tour, it seemed like a perfect romance. For Television, though, everything had gone disturbingly quiet since that glorious validation, *Marquee Moon*. Verlaine seemed to be planning to follow his Rimbaud into darkest Africa, telling a journalist in May 1977, 'Once you have a recording contract, it's a struggle not to go out and play every night. The company wants you to do it. Your manager wants you to do it . . . [But] it's really destructive to do that. You defeat the whole purpose.'

Thankfully, guitarist Richard Lloyd's own destructive urges had got the better of him, and shortly after Television returned home from their spring '77 tour, he was laid up in hospital with hepatitis, freeing Verlaine of both any obligation to tour or to include Lloyd in the decision-making for Television's second album. The result, *Adventure*, was an album which aside from a pair of gratuitous 'oldies' – 'I Don't Care' (renamed 'Careful') and 'Foxhole', both over two years old – was a dry run for Verlaine's imminent solo career.

Carelessly failing to issue 'I Don't Care' as an introduction to the album, Elektra saw *Adventure* enter the UK Top Ten for a single week – on the back of its illustrious predecessor – but drop away entirely by the time of the UK tour. The 'Foxhole' 45 also flopped, despite its promo video (featuring a superior version of the song). The tour, booked in expectation of another season of press hype, was played out in half-empty theatres, save for the single London date, which though critically acclaimed suggested a pyrrhic victory at best.

Television had already made their defining statement, but hadn't done a Pistols – bowing out when their guitarist got 'sick', and the world cared. When they did finally call it a day, in August 1978, there was a surprising lack of interest from even the UK music media that had lauded their coming just eighteen months earlier. By then any transatlantic attention seemed to have shifted to the flatlands of O-hi-o, from whence came Pere Ubu and Devo, bearing disturbing tidings of the end of punk.

David Thomas: Punk . . . wasn't what we were doing. We weren't doing loud, thrashing, antisocial, adolescent music . . . We were embarrassed to be associated with the punk movement. We had done that three years earlier . . . in

Rocket from the Tombs, but we had passed that stage . . . [In fact,] the English [punk] scene was characterized by a sort of vacuous, culturally alienated fashion fixation that was eventually responsible for the destruction of what we had been working on.

Nonetheless, it was to England that Thomas's band came in April 1978, to see if the message underlying *The Modern Dance* might yet get through. As Thomas had previously informed *Search & Destroy*, 'We are presently searching for what lies Beyond the New Wave . . . We're not concerned with pop music of the past.' In this sense, *The Modern Dance* served as a clearing of the decks – an abnegation of the 'Life Stinks' point of view championed by the late Peter Laughner, who had died in his sleep the previous April. Its penultimate cut, 'Sentimental Journey', suggested the need to move on.

David Thomas: The last thing you hear [on 'Sentimental Journey'] is all the glass being swept up. It seemed to us to be the finest, subtlest touch. It seemed so apt, after this extravagant thrashing around and chest-beating and adolescent sorta psychodrama, [that] in the end . . . you gotta sweep it up.

To their initial despair – if ultimate resignation – Ubu's attempt to delineate the future route of punk was forestalled by the appearance of Devo in the UK on a tidal wave of hyperbole that washed away much of the impact of Ubu's altogether more avant-garage street waves. Indeed, when Thomas was asked about the Akronites, in May 1978, he insisted, 'I like all of Devo . . . but I don't want to discuss their work. The two bands are diametrically opposed. Our whole outlooks and attitudes are totally different. Devo has some kind of fixed plan, whereas Ubu must remain flexible, changeable and contradictory.'

Since the start of 1978, the word on Devo had become a sentence, a paragraph, a feature and finally a whole press-pack. Barely had the effusive praise heaped on the March release of *The Modern Dance* died down, when the prospect of a Devo album that would knock it sideways began to be talked up. Also the main Devo spokesman, Jerry Casale, was loudly proclaiming a radical agenda that didn't just go beyond the new wave, but beyond rock itself.

Jerry Casale: With music, a group comes out, they start the same boogie beat, and somebody says, 'Do you dig rock & roll?' They think that by saying the word they're gonna make it happen . . . They beat the same dead horse over and over, but they're not getting any response because there's nothing there any more. Devo breaks up the picture, reconstructs things . . . so that the picture is changed . . . [Now that] the breaking down musically has occurred – punk . . . Devo are here to mutate. Devo's just the clean-up squad of the eighties. [1978]

The three Devo singles on Stiff – 'Jocko Homo', 'Satisfaction' and 'Be Stiff' – issued between January and July 1978, seduced the punk-aware into believing that these mutants might hold the key. Each single suggested a rare intelligence at work, and a sound as isolated from punk as the mainstream. And there was a whole new set of post-punk journalists – the likes of Ian Birch at *MM*, Jon Savage and Sandy Robertson at *Sounds*, and Paul Morley at *NME* – anxious to ignite their own revolution. Having proven unable to aggrandize the aggressive elements of punk from their grandstand seat, they were determined to make anything that came after the fact theirs, and theirs alone.

While Ubu talked in codex, Devo talked in riddles. Unable to decide if the spiel was real, these neophyte scribes deferred judgement until they had a whole album to assess. Meanwhile, a trio of UK shows in March – where Devo's slick programming was offset by altogether more anarchic sets from Alberto Y Lost Trios Paranoias – seemed to suggest the seed of something new. Unlike Ubu, though, when the full artifact arrived, it was deeply disappointing, the sessions for *Q: Are We Not Men? A: We Are Devo!* having stretched the patience of producer Eno to the limit.

Eno: 'Anal' is the word. They were a terrifying group of people to work with because they were so unable to experiment . . . Their picture of recording, for me, was very old-fashioned, like a Platonic Ideal of recording, that somewhere there existed the ideal state of this song. [1995]

When Thomas accused Devo of 'some kind of fixed plan', he presumably didn't know quite how fixed. Arriving at the March 1978 sessions in Germany, the band not only had the album sequence worked out in advance, but also had one for the *next* album. Save for the omission of 'Be Stiff' and 'Social Fools', which were given to Stiff to fulfil their three-single deal, *Are We Not Men?* barely wavered in detail, Devo passing into the mainstream with nary a pang. In hindsight, Casale admits, it is about this time that they 'finally bend over and bed down with Bugs Bunny (i.e. Warners) . . . [and] even though we fight the good fight and win for a while, Devo's heretical question, "Are We Not Men?" is forever transmuted by the sublime irony of becoming part of the corporate feudal state.'

If Ubu lived to fight another day, Devo did not. Subsumed into orthodoxy by the surprise success of their first Warners LP and single ('Come Back Jonee'), they were struck off the list of potential prophets by England's post-punk penmen. If Devo's commercial success coincided with critical rejection, The Adverts, The Rezillos and Radio Birdman found their commercial chances already compromised by their labels of choice. Each of these bands issued their debut album (in Birdman's case, reissued *and* revamped) in the space that separates *The Modern Dance* from *Are We Not Men?*, but despite delivering everything expected of them, were undone by the record companies they had been led to believe would nurture them.

When The Adverts had entered the studio in October 1977, they could only have been optimistic about their prospects. 'Gary Gilmore's Eyes' had been one of the best punk singles of the year, and the deal their manager, Michael Dempsey, had made with Anchor seemed like a very good idea at the time. Unfortunately, before they were ready to repeat the success of the single, Anchor ceased to be such a smart move.

TV Smith: We went to Anchor because they were a subsidiary of ABC . . . But then . . . ABC pulled their support from Anchor, so the whole American connection was gone. The in-house publisher of Anchor took over our deal, and formed this label [Bright], and put out the record on that. At one point, *Crossing The Red Sea* . . . [which] was [already] recorded, suddenly didn't have a label to release it. [It finally came out] six or seven months after ['Gary Gilmore's Eyes'] . . . but one week in the lower reaches of the chart, for what was a classic punk album, is obviously not right.

Like that other arch commentator Poly Styrene, TV Smith had had the set of songs he wanted to record for some time, though in keeping with punk's value-for-money aesthetic, decided to omit 'Gary Gilmore's Eyes' (despite re-recording the song for inclusion on the American version of the album – which never happened). Opening with new versions of the two other songs for which they remained best known – 'One-Chord Wonders' and 'Bored Teenagers' – Smith documented the collapse of the ideals with which punk had started. 'New Church', 'No Time To Be 21' and 'Safety In Numbers' became the last few downbeat chapters to this heady hiatus; and 'Great British Mistake' and 'Drowning Men' its bitter epilogue. As Smith says, '*Red Sea* just seemed to close the door on that version of the band – we'd said what we wanted to say ... Job done ... Now, what's next?' Unfortunately, letting Bright release the results proved to be a not-so-bright idea, and the band would have to regroup before they could record again.

Radio Birdman, who arrived on this sceptred isle as *Red Sea* departed from the charts, were sure of just one thing – they didn't want an international release for the Australian version of *Radios Appear*, a sheer cardiac attack. As Younger says, 'We decided to fix up a couple of songs that we weren't satisfied with: there were a couple of remixes, a couple of new versions entirely and a couple of actual extra tracks.' Tek believes they were attempting to 'fix the problems' on it.

In fact, they gutted the beast. Instead of an artifact worthy of Prada's punk collection, they had a convincing, seemingly authentic imitation; but an imitation *Radios Appear* nonetheless. The album that appeared in March 1978, in a resplendent white sleeve, scrapped four of the ten tracks on the original *Radios Appear*, and re-recorded versions of at least two other songs. It still had some residue of the perspiration of inspiration, but the rough edges had been sandpapered, a key reference point forsaken (a cover of The Stooges' 'TV Eye' being replaced by 13th Floor Elevators' 'You're Gonna Miss Me'), and its utter urgency honed away. It still blew hard, but no longer was it a full-force gale. Nonetheless, it should have been more than powerful enough to blow any damn Limey's woofer – if, and only if, the album hadn't become *Radios Disappear* at the whim of Monsignor Stein.

Deniz Tek: As soon as we got over there, Sire lost their distribution deal with Phonogram. And Polygram was supposed to provide our tour support. So, one, our tour support vaporized; and two, they weren't interested in distributing our album. We would show up [in a town], play a set and people would say, 'Do you have an album out? Are you going to record?' It was very frustrating.

In fact, Tek had only just spent a week in LA with the Steins – and Seymour, at least, couldn't have been more enthusiastic. But Stein had long proved adept at keeping his cards close to his chest; and though he started to suspect he had lost his bet on punk, he had probably not yet decided whether Birdman should make the cut in the coming cull. Only when he turned up one night at Friar's in Aylesbury did Tek suspect that they might be in trouble.

Deniz Tek: In fact, they dropped [almost] everybody. They kept the Ramones and the Talking Heads . . . My understanding was that when they had to switch distributors, they [found themselves] in a cash crisis and they had to drop some bands. When Seymour came to see us in Aylesbury, he was disappointed: 'Where's the uniforms?' Then the next thing we knew, we're not on the label.

Stein may have been partly persuaded by ill–informed elements in the UK music press. *NME*, reviewing the single 'What Gives', depicted it as 'the Aussies catch[ing] up to Brit rock a year late (as usual)'; while Mick Wall's review of a Rock Garden gig in *Sounds* concluded that, 'Radio Birdman repulse rather than attract positive response. They draw insult more than they could possibly threaten. They play loud (*too* damn loud), but they say nothing.' Perhaps Birdman threatened some values this *Sounds'* scribe held dear (on the very same page, Wall managed to dismiss Joy Division at Rafter's, so that's pretty much both punk pillars pulled apart). And yet many of the English fans who did catch Birdman live departed converted to the cause.

Deniz Tek: We didn't have any problems with [most] audiences. We played at the Marquee twice, and the second time we played people were showing up with our symbol spraypainted on their jackets. So it didn't take very long for people to get their heads round it. The only [exception] was at the Vortex. It was the last night that the Vortex existed – we closed it out – and there were some pretty hardcore fashion punks and sociopaths that were just throwing stuff; and some of the guys who were with us [took exception]. It ended up in a big brawl and we had to stop playing. The bouncers and the police came.

Thanks to Sire's right hand not knowing who its left hand was jerking around, Birdman's cord wasn't cleanly cut when the cull came. Instead, they found themselves at a studio in Wales recording a second album for a label that had seemingly dropped them. As Tek has said, 'We knew that the structure was collapsing around us, but we were getting everything we could out of it now.' As such, 'Nobody told us not to go to Rockfield. I think Sire probably forgot, because they probably had a million things to cancel . . . We showed up and they were expecting us, so we went into the studio for three weeks and recorded. We got out of there with a pretty rough mix of the album and a safety copy . . . I just took it home and stuck it in my closet.'

It would take until 1981 for that fabled album, *Living Eyes*, to appear. By then, the rights had reverted, and Radio Birdman's cult status – at least in their homeland – was assured. However, by the time they returned from Blighty in the summer of 1978, Birdman was in tatters. Ron Keeley and Warwick Gilbert had quit the band after Rockfield. And when Younger and Tek returned from a holiday in America, Tek found that, 'Chris had already formed The Hitmen and said he didn't want to do Radio Birdman any more. And Pip was doing his internship in Newcastle. So it was . . . not enough critical mass to call it Radio Birdman any more.' Stein still had the option of releasing the Rockfield album, but despite having a large studio bill to pay, he opted out of that too.

Deniz Tek: [Stein] has no problem with cutting people off, cutting your funds, leaving you stranded in a foreign country . . . having your great album in the can, [but] not releasing it out of spite. So he's really got two sides. And his wife Linda really doesn't help at all. She's a fairly malignant personality . . . and just used to having her own way.

Tek wouldn't have found many on Sire's roster to contest this assessment. Certainly on his side were members of The Rezillos, who found themselves on the wrong side of Linda S, after being hung out to dry by the Phonogram farrago. Having issued their consummate classic, '(My Baby Does) Good Sculptures', as a taster for the album, they saw the single sold short because of Sire's strained relations with Phonogram. They also found themselves twiddling thumbs, in a limbo of Stein's making.

Jo Callis: The album was about to come out when the Sire deal with Phonogram fell through, which initially to us was a bit of a disaster. It held up the release of our album for five or six weeks, which seemed like an eternity. We were all set to go off on tour and promote the album, but everything ground to a halt while Sire renegotiated their distribution with Warners.

At least *Can't Stand The Rezillos* did not suffer the fate of *Radios Appear*, sitting in Phonogram warehouses, wearing out its welcome. When it appeared in late July, alongside Talking Heads' *More Songs*

About Buildings And Food, the album gave Sire an opportunity to start all over again. At least the delay did not hinder The Rezillos' frenetic forward-thrust. The album's single, 'Top of The Pops', was adopted by BBC Radio and TV, and sent chartward, much to Fay Fyfe's amusement: 'It was great to get "Top of The Pops" on *Top of The Pops*, but you also have to remember, as well as singing about daft groups that go on *Top of The Pops*, we were on it ourselves; and that we hated and loved everything in the music business and ourselves simultaneously.'

Seemingly unaware that 'Top of The Pops' betrayed the same underlying contempt for the show as Elvis Costello's 'Radio Radio' – which would also find its way into the charts – the arbiters of the airwaves beamed their benificence on the canny Caledonians. Unfortunately, The Rezillos lost the plot at a party to celebrate the Warners/Sire deal, where Linda Stein showed her sense of humour was as good as her ears.

Jo Callis: There was a Sire party . . . an after-the-event party for the changing over to Warners. And we got a bit out of hand. Coming down from Scotland, we just didn't think it was rock & roll enough – so we thought we'd liven it up by starting a bit of a pie fight. They had these meringues as part of the buffet. The whole thing culminated in Faye shoving one of these meringues into Linda Stein's [face]. Stein had just had a sixty-pound haircut – and she went mental. Something as petty as that might have gone against us . . . Bob [Last] was managing us, and he had to get . . . Faye to apologize to her the next day, and buy her a big bunch of flowers. It really wasn't in our nature to do that, but we bowed to the pressure.

Whatever mean spirit was now abroad at Sire, The Rezillos were unfazed, delivering an equally compulsive non-album single with which to further their reputation. 'Destination Venus' was an attempt to develop a sound more akin to what Callis wanted. And so, as Fyfe said, 'We had a one-minute reprise of electric buzzing guitar which sounded like a distorted radio . . . [But Sire] reckoned it wouldn't get airplay so they chopped it down to a twelve- or fifteen-second reprise, which means nothing.' The single flopped. Suddenly, despite previous chart success, the band's future hung in the balance. Their friend, Bob Last, now Mr Fast, was asked to salvage the situation.

Bob Last: There were pressures from Seymour, but they just didn't know how to respond. Generally, for British bands, understanding any kind of corporateness was really problematic. But it was a rollercoaster, and at some point it was gonna break down. There were tensions. Jo was very interested in a lot of things that we were doing at Fast, whereas for Fay and Eugene it was just about that retro thing; and the punk thing happened to provide a level of energy. Success always exacerbates tensions, 'cause suddenly you've got all these possibilities to worry about . . . Some of them would [probably] tell you that they broke up the band to get out of the Sire contract. [But] both things were gonna happen: Sire was gonna implode, and The Rezillos were gonna split up.

By the end of 1978, it seemed everyone wanted out. After farewell shows at London's Lyceum and the Glasgow Apollo, The Rezillos went their separate ways. Sire no longer had any way of making The Rezillos pay for Mrs Stein's next perm; while Fay Fyfe laid the blame squarely at Sire's door: 'They have all the bad things about being a big record company, and haven't got any of the good things about being an independent. I was prepared for certain bad things to happen, but I'd no idea just how bad it was going to be. You just have to compromise *everything* you're doing.'

Callis suggests that everyone was pulling in opposite directions: 'I think one school in the group thought things should go back to more like they were originally; I wanted to move on, and for the material to mature, have a bit more depth to it . . . Other people in the group wanted to write [their own] songs, and they weren't really very good.' It is Eugene Reynolds, though, who probably has the most cogent take on the whole absurd affair: 'I was in favour of it all falling apart. We were surfing on the crest of a wave, but we fell into it and drowned quite spectacularly.'

– – –

For Eugene, his relationship with Fay took precedence. And he probably knew that he was never going to dictate the band's direction when neither wrote the songs. A band from the other side of the Tweed had similar powerplay problems, save that in Penetration the ambitious Pauline and her paramour, Robert Blamire, believed that the loss of songwriter Gary Chaplin at the end of 1977 need not be the end of the band, but rather an opportunity to change direction. As such, the slow-to-appear *Moving Targets* LP reflected a band in transition, with its best songs – 'Don't Dictate', 'Duty Free Technology', 'Silent Community' and 'Firing Squad' – all demoed back in June 1977, when Chaplin had written the tunes.

Another band unable to overcome the loss of its songmaker at the end of 1977 – *or* transcend its early demos – was Mark P's Alternative TV. Though *The Image Has Cracked*, issued in June 1978, contained a handful of punk standards, the soapbox element in Perry's make-up was fast becoming a substitute for the songs of Alex Ferguson. Indeed, on the opening song, 'Alternatives To NATO', a soapbox was literally featured, Perry having decided to place one on the Marquee stage, and record the rants from that night's residents. Perry admits he 'had a bit of a row with Miles Copeland to get that in . . . He just thought we didn't programme [the album] right. His idea would have been to start with "Action Time Vision" and maybe have "Alternatives" at the end. But I said, "We want to make our statement, and say we're different, right from the first note."'

Different, yes. Interesting, no. 'Action Time Vision', the anthem that was Ferguson's last contribution to the set-up, and already a 7" successor to 'How Much Longer' and 'Life After Life', was that all-important rallying cry. 'Alternatives', on the other hand, was Perry the lapsed hippy getting into spontaneous happenings, and forgetting that such 'spontaneity' rarely endures. Never the most convincing frontman, Perry soon found his time was pretty much up.

As punk bands became consumed by the same raging egos that had debilitated the previous generation of rockers, one frontperson who'd expelled her saxy sister was finding it awfully hard to come up with an album affirming the wisdom of her decision. Even when chart success seemed to provide that affirmation – as 'The Day The World Turned Day-Glo' touched a populist nerve – Tony Parsons, once Poly Styrene's knight of the purple prose, was suggesting that 'the [single's] production has a faint whiff of HM about it that was absent on their first demos'.

The production was not actually the real problem – the lack of Logic had changed the sound. All her replacements found Lora to be the mother of invention, copying their parts from the demo tape manager Falcon Stuart had made during the Logic-era. Indeed, when she heard the album, Logic just thought, 'That saxophone player is playing all of the riffs that I used to play, [but] in a stylized studio version.' The departure of Logic also seems to have operated as a break on Styrene's songwriting. Perhaps without such an expressive sounding-board, she found it hard to maintain interest.

Styrene certainly seemed to sense that any strategy for success would be strictly short-term. As she told an American journalist in June 1978,

'We didn't want a long contract because they wanted to tie us up too much . . . So our next single, "The Day The World Turned Day-Glo" . . . will be on our own label . . . distributed by EMI International . . . You don't make any money until you sell a few records, but . . . you've only got to sign up for three years.' Even three years was a stretch as the new Spex songs reiterated T. Rex riffs, suggesting Styrene was failing to live up to Parsons' and Burchill's risible depiction of her as 'the finest imagination of her generation'.

By the summer of 1978, even the paler shade of song had dried up, just as Styrene complained to *NME* that 'some bands . . . shove out stuff like a factory. I couldn't enjoy that . . . Besides, it takes me quite a while to write songs.' In truth, her mind was no longer like a plastic bag, it was more like a blank page. And though she had told *Sounds* in April that 'as soon as I can't write songs any more, I'll pack it up', she was still driving herself to complete that one album of validation.

Unfortunately, the walls had started to close in on Poly again. Worryingly, she also stated in the *Sounds* interview, 'I don't know who my friends are any more.' The following month, she was complaining, 'You feel all the time that people are draining you, draining off all your energy all the time until you think, "Blimey, I haven't got anything to give. Leave me alone."' She hoped that moving back in with her family might make her 'feel *normal* again.' But one night in Doncaster, everything came to a head.

Poly Styrene: It was . . . after a gig, and I'd been smoking and reading lots of funny things, and I hadn't ate or slept for days. Suddenly I started seeing all these terrible things . . . I must have been hallucinating . . . [But] it was much stronger than an LSD trip or anything! [1978]

She later told Jon Savage, 'I had a kind of breakdown. I wanted to take a break and rethink what I was doing, everything that I was involved in, because I saw . . . that I shouldn't continue.' But continue she did, touring on the back of an album which Styrene and Stuart seemed determined to also issue in single form, releasing no fewer than four singles from the static Styrene canon. None replicated the success of 'The Day The World Turned Day-Glo', and by 1979 Styrene had become an unstable person to be around.

One night at the home of John Lydon/Rotten, she apparently had another breakdown of sorts, hacking off her own hair, convinced that there was some occult ritual occurring at Gunter Grove (which was just about the only activity *not* happening there). By August 1979, her ever-tolerant band felt they could no longer identify with a singer who might at any minute 'look in the mirror . . . smash it quick . . . take the glass / and slash [her] wrists'. Though Poly would not be Marion's last reinvention, neither the singer nor her songs would ever be the same again.

Styrene's state of mind, and the suspicion that *Germ Free Adolescents* is all we would get, certainly coloured the *NME* review, which reads like a 'get well' card, even referring to the album being 'delayed while Poly Styrene recovered from the effects of letting her particular worldview get the better of her'. Also reviewed in the same issue was the debut long-player of Siouxsie & the Banshees, but no such concern for Siouxsie's mental well-being was displayed here. Instead Julie Burchill spent almost the entire page-long review decrying the anti-semitic sentiment underlying one line from a song that didn't even appear on the album ('Love In A Void'). It was not so much pop journalism as the polemic of a petulant schoolgirl, but it was one more obstacle for the Banshees to overcome.

As far back as December 1977, naysayers with media access had driven Siouxsie to put pen to paper, sarcastically apologizing in *Sounds*' letters page for not 'subscrib[ing] to the standard "Punk ethic". "Mimicry is the sincerest form of flattery" seems to be [your] maxim to judge "interesting unknown bands". Maybe they should remain unknown if they sound "like" the Pistols, Ramones or Clash.' For all the Banshees, the longer they stayed out in the cold – and it would take until the summer of 1978 to sign a deal – the more they despaired of punk's direction.

Steve Severin: There's no one reflecting real life except us. Everything else is totally escapist . . . With us it's complete confrontation from the word go. Tom Robinson gets to a lot of people that he wouldn't get to if he was playing truly radical music. [1978]

The Banshees remained a refreshing change to anyone weary of the bam-bam-bam of bar-chords. They had found the right equation by systematically removing elements that didn't fit (i.e. Fenton), and honing those that did. Severin claims that, in performance, 'Siouxsie [even] used to take [Morris]'s high-hat away from him – move it two feet away –

so he had to go on to the tom-tom . . . We wanted [the drums] somewhere between Mo Tucker and the Glitter Band.'

The recruitment of guitarist John McKay in September 1977 was another master stroke, though Severin suggests he needed some coaching in the Banshee aesthetic: 'When he joined the band he was playing like a semi-acoustic Gretsch copy, and Nils made him change over to a Les Paul, [saying] "You gotta use the same guitar as Steve Jones and Johnny Thunders."' By November 1977, when the (still-unsigned) band appeared on the front cover of *Sounds*, and recorded their seminal first session for John Peel, it seemed certain that any dissenting voices would become but straws in the wind.

Steve Severin: [Peel's producer] John Walters had been to see the band and he was a fan. Peel was a bit harder to convince. He came to see us and The Slits at Croydon Greyhound . . . but he left saying yes to a session . . . [That] got us straight on to the cover of *Sounds* . . . We thought, 'OK, we got the front cover of *Sounds*, we just done a Peel session, we're gonna be signed any minute.' . . . [But by winter 1978,] Nils was ready to throw in the towel. [He] would get lots of people to see us live – we were playing lots of live shows – and they never came back again. We nearly signed to Radar. Andrew Lauder was quite interested at one point. Mike Thorne was [also] interested, until he actually heard us . . . [But] Nils [kept] thinking, 'Let's just keep holding out, until we get it exactly how we want.'

That first Peel session suggested they were almost there. 'Metal Postcard', 'Mirage', 'Love In A Void' (the one remnant of the Fenton era) and 'Suburban Relapse' were stark postcards from the edge, and refreshingly non-conformist in tone and tempo. Their content also showed Rotten's lapsarian lyrics had not eluded everyone from Bromley. But something was holding the labels back. Perhaps it was the tone the press adopted whenever their name came up. As Severin says, 'Our first big feature in *Sounds* was headlined "The Most Elitist Band In The World" . . . I took that as a compliment.' However, in a movement that prided itself on its egalitarian ordinariness (though only after most of its original elite had fallen on their swords), a band so brazenly convinced of its own importance was a slap in the face to the misguided many.

Needless to say, almost the only way that occurred to those whose feelings were so affronted was physical challenge. But as Nils Stevenson stated, 'Siouxsie became a formidable presence on stage, showing no fear in facing up to fucking ferocious audiences.' Without the usual macho recourse, Siouxsie was obliged to devise a way to 'put them off with the way I behave'. High on adrenaline, she sometimes used whatever weapon came to hand: 'Anyone who spat at me or behaved like a "punk" just incensed me, so I'd kick them or hit them with a mike stand.'

It didn't always work. Severin recalls one time Siouxsie was performing 'at the Nashville, [and] she's wearing her eyepatch, which most people thought was a fashion statement, but was actually because she got conjunctivitis from somebody spitting.' Yet the Banshees never deviated from challenging those peacock punks who had replaced one conformist straitjacket with another. Siouxsie would later describe one particular show with Sham 69, at the Croydon Greyhound, where 'the skinheads were intimidating certain parts of the audience and saying, "You better not come down looking like that again!" . . . I *hate* that: it's like going back ten years.'

Thankfully, as 1977 turned into 1978, the Banshees began to find an audience of their own, who were delighted by the band's austere direction and stark visuals. With McKay now making himself a vital component in the songs' construction, the band began to emerge from the subterranean clubs, taking more prescient punks with them.

Siouxsie Sioux: Everyone else that's attempted to get across to [punk fans] has tried it in the most moronic way; and that's brainwashed people into blanking off to anything that's not acceptable on their terms . . . [In our case,] it's not a political message, 'Do this, do that.' It's just to think, really. To go overground and subvert everything. [1978]

'Overground', the Banshees' answer to Bowie's 'All The Madmen', was one of the new songs aired on their second John Peel session, in February 1978. Severin considers this song the point when 'we suddenly realized we're very different from everybody else'. It also spoke for a band that didn't see the point in subversion which didn't strike at the heart of the machine. Everyone in the band was holding out for a major-label deal, Siouxsie claiming, 'It would be pointless to have that [musical] freedom and not be heard. The most important thing is to get into a big record company and do the damage there.' By the spring of 1978, they were starting to doubt it was ever going to happen.

Steve Severin: At that point, we'd turned down a deal with Rough Trade, and we were considering [the Peel Sessions] being released by BBC Records. [We did] a little series of gigs – like Reading, Bristol and Newport – and Nils didn't come with us. Basically, those were going to be the last gigs. He was saying, 'If we don't get a record deal in the next month, that's it.' We'd done a show at Alexandra Palace, and sold it out. We just couldn't understand it, but Chris Parry at Polydor saw that [gig] and, just as [it seemed] all was lost, he signed us.

What had persuaded Parry, first and foremost, was another song aired on that second Peel session, 'Hong Kong Garden', which he heard while lying in the bath, contemplating his navel. Manager Stevenson subsequently claimed that the band knew this 'perverse love song to a Chinese take-away . . . was a delightful piece of nonsense, designed specifically for chart success.' In fact, there was some discussion about the band's first Polydor single before everyone agreed it would be 'Hong Kong Garden'. By the time the band played the Roundhouse in July, to celebrate signing with Polydor, the single was already recorded and their course set. For all the Banshees' brinkmanship, their period in limbo had only made them stronger. As Nick Kent wrote, in his Roundhouse review:

What hit home most forcefully on Sunday . . . [was] not that the Banshees' maverick attitude has reaped an army of support, but that the support is totally warranted. Here is a group in the intriguing position of having started with all manner of musical shortcomings but with a coherent vision, who've worked consistently to overcome their liabilities and who've succeeded moreover in forging a style that is at once riveting and absolutely their own.

Pop confectionery, though, like 'Hong Kong Garden', was ancillary to the main plan, and was omitted from debut album, *The Scream*, in favour of longer, more ambitious songs like 'Jigsaw Puzzle' and 'Switch', the latter an audaciously ambient coda after the storm. Again the band remained sure-footed, and whenever producer Steve Lillywhite failed to follow, Severin or Siouxsie would bring in records, saying, 'This is how we want the tom-toms to sound, this is how we want the guitars to sound.' Issued in October 1978, it took NME a month to decide to let Burchill vent, by which time the charts had already confirmed the viability of the Banshees' blueprint, and the increasingly poor aim of *NME*'s young gunslinger.

Where the Banshees now perhaps got ahead of themselves was in their ambitious plans for their first headlining tour of UK theatres, due to begin in late October, a couple of weeks after the album hit the racks. Hoping to 'introduce' their audience to ex-Velvet Underground chanteuse, Nico, they were surprised to find their own fans no more discerning, or restrained, than those who followed The Clash.

Steve Severin: It was a mixture of the old punk crowd and the new audience that had come because we'd had a hit and they had never seen us before – so a lot of those shows were hit or miss because people were just [like:] Where's the band that did 'Hong Kong Garden'? You know, here's this band playing 'Metal Postcard' and stuff like [that]. So it wasn't the triumphant tour that it should have been . . . I don't think they knew what to expect every night – [and] if it wasn't Nico, it was Human League [and] Spizz Oil.

Nico fled from Siouxsie's stage after only a handful of gigs, her strident delivery of 'Deutschland Über Alles' being met nightly with a battery of abuse and the odd missile. The Human League fared only slightly better, but could hide behind a slide show and synthesizers, and endured for the sake of their CV. The problem, as one *Sounds* scribe suggested, was that the Banshees were, by the end of 1978, 'in the position of being the only band currently touring who emerged from the 100 Club/ Roxy/Vortex gobbing route to fame. And that means they attract, whether they like it or not, every knucklehead who thinks the true spirit of punk is the North Bank on Saturday with a few chords thrown in, so you can jump on the guy next to you in time with the beat.'

In fact, the band with whom the Banshees had shared their one and only Roxy bill, The Slits, were also 'currently touring', and were if anything finding it even tougher to tie a label down. In Kent's view, the problem remained The Slits' 'lack of direction, paired with only the barest hints of musical progression, [which] can be viewed as being directly at odds with the Banshees' career thus far, of constant gigging and self-improvement.'

Actually, The Slits' 'lack of direction' was probably more the result of musicians pulling in opposite directions than any obstacles their technical limitations were throwing up. By September 1977, when they recorded their first Peel session, The Slits had their sound down cold.

But the battle for the band's soul was being fought out onstage every night, and there was no doubting which way Fräulein Ari Up wanted to go. As Palm Olive says, 'The whole reggae thing was Ari. We all started getting into it, but . . . that was the direction the band [really] went in after I left the band.'

As the least musical member of the band, Ari was obliged to achieve her goal by sheer will, and by imagining herself to be anything but spoilt, white and wilful. Don Letts, who had his own spell managing the band, was amazed to find this daughter of a German 'heiress' become 'so engrossed in [reggae] that she had longer dreadlocks than me, [and] spoke Jamaican heavier than me. It became quite disconcerting.' And yet, as Vivien Goldman archly observed, 'The Slits are (for me, blissfully) the antithesis of the Rasta ideal of a . . . good little woman.' The Slits' sheer lack of manageability meant they spent large tracts of time not only managerless, but rudderless. Stubborn determination kept them going after even Malcolm McLaren was rejected as a suitable Svengali.

Palm Olive: People thought that we hadn't had a deal because we couldn't get one. But that's not true. We didn't want a record company to rip us off. We [also] went through eight managers whilst we were together. So we were very self-sufficient. If we didn't think they were going to give us a good deal, we'd rather wait till we had more of a following. So that was a conscious decision . . . McLaren wanted to manage us at one point. At our first meeting, he said he hated women and he hated music. But he liked hate. He thrived on it. [I thought,] 'I don't like this guy. I don't like to work with someone like that.' But the [other] Slits were very taken with him. [Before this,] all our fights were little fights, like sisters' fights, but that was a real disagreement, and I managed to persuade them.

If Palm Olive managed to see off McLaren, the next potential powerbroker was Magenta De Vine, who had seemingly convinced Real Records – where Johnny Thunders had fled after having his heart broken – to sign the band for a one-off single, 'So Tough' b/w 'New Town'. Both had been aired on Peel between September 1977 and April 1978, reassuring Real that this was no longer the band who beat every song into bloody submission, while Ari danced on its grave. Peel versions of 'Love Und Romance', 'Shoplifting', 'So Tough' and 'New Town' also suggested their anarchic quality *could* be contained and codified.

However, on the verge of a record deal, the band started to doubt their own strengths, and in particular the commitment (and competency) of co-founder Palm Olive. Apparently overlooking the number of songs in their set which originated with Paloma, the others began to speculate whether they might not be better off with another, more malleable drummer. A statement issued by the rest of the band in October baldly claimed 'that the musical direction and accomplishment of the band was being restricted by' Paloma; and she was gone. According to Paloma, the real cause of their final disagreement was that 'they started talking about the [nude album] cover, and I did not want to do that cover. To me, it was like an affront. To use [an image like that] was like selling out . . . that was not what we were about.' It went a little deeper than that.

Palm Olive: I wasn't a Christian [yet] . . . [but] I just had this very strong sense that I was surrounded by people who didn't have a clue . . . It was just the whole [scene] was not standing on solid ground.

The band now began to lurch ever closer to the Jah Punk Ari considered an ideal state. But before The Slits could unleash their grand design, they still needed a label that would let them loose in a studio (other than the BBC's). It would take till the winter of 1979 before The Slits found a label prepared to suck it and see. For Chris Blackwell's Island – which had such a resounding say in the direction of rock and reggae before punk – The Slits were almost the last punks standing. Paloma, meanwhile, had landed safely in another barely formed all-girl band, The Raincoats – who still managed to release their post-pop classic, 'Fairytale In A Supermarket', five months ahead of The Slits' vinyl debut. She left behind two years of cathartic live performances, two John Peel sessions, no shortage of press, and a whole set of personality crises.

— — —

By the time The Slits began recording their debut album, in spring 1979, Viv and Paloma's ex-boyfriends, Strummer and Jones, were working on their third, itself a reaction to the rocky reception The Clash's second instalment received. *Give 'Em Enough Rope*, released in November 1978, was a self-referential title, presumably designed to deflect criticism. It failed in its task. Jon Savage's review, in *Melody Maker*, hit the nail on the head, then hammered it home:

[The Clash] sound as though they're writing about what they think is expected of them, rather than what they want to write about, or need to. It's as though they see their function in terms of 'the modern outlaw' . . . and conservationists of the punk ethos they so singularly helped to create . . . [Admittedly] it's hard when you define a period so accurately. The Pistols broke up and neatly avoided the issue. [But] here, The Clash seem locked in time, stranded on their conception of what the problems are, where solutions are to be found, and what problems face their audience. [*MM*, 11/11/78]

Listening to it now, the second Clash album sounds like the work of people with their minds on other things. Indeed, it was just such a suspicion that prompted Pearlman to move the sessions across the Pacific. As he told *Trouser Press* way back then, 'At a certain point . . . I told them that if they didn't get out of England, they would really have trouble finishing the record, because of their constant fights with Bernard . . . [who] would come in, and they'd argue for five hours, and then no one would be able to play.'

Jones, in particular, proved a willing co-conspirator. As Johnny Green records, 'Mick the muso was keen to play about in a "proper" recording studio, and also for The Clash to break America. The others went along with him.' Pearlman claimed motives more high-minded, though no less misguided: 'To get this amazing revolutionary consciousness . . . on to vinyl and make it sound good enough that American radio wouldn't throw it in the toilet bowl.' In reality, removing a band like The Clash from its wellspring was tantamount to a name-change. As Al Clark, Virgin publicist, observed back in 1977, when it was the Pistols being offered the corporate chalice, 'What happens to a [punk] group . . . when it starts making records in America with quite polished producers, under the guidance of the record company, it just loses its purpose.' Amen.

To Rhodes' credit, he understood this, and was determined to keep the pressure up from his side of the pond. A man who never shied away from the brink, he doubted the whole process, until the band was obliged to snap back. Topper Headon proved a surprisingly articulate spokesman, telling *MM* in September, 'It always seems to happen this way between Bernie and the band – a battle of wits between him and us. Something has got to be done . . . if this sort of thing [continues to] happen . . . [because] it seems to be a question of him trying to manipulate us into doing the album a lot faster than we want.' Simonon then threw in his thrupenny's worth: 'Bernie Rhodes makes us look daft, and it gets our fuckin' backs up – the way he assumes he can speak away for the four of us. He can't, right.'

Rhodes, though, continued to call them to account – knowing that the end of his cosy cabal was in sight. One night he asked right-hand roadie, Johnny Green, 'Which way are you going to jump? . . . Are you into the politics? Are you into change? Or are you in this just for the money?' When the band gave Bernie his marching orders at the end of October, he promptly claimed his due, informing *NME*, 'McLaren and I built the audience up . . . The Clash became popular because of a direction and because we worked as a team.' He also froze the band's assets, a reminder that he still held the purse strings.

Strummer, to his credit, didn't dispute a lot of what Rhodes now said. But he did point out two home truths: 'That Bernie . . . can't, you know, do sums . . . [and] Bernie thought punk rock meant low over-heads . . . He didn't want us to become what we'd started out against. All credit to him. But his method of preventing this was . . . to come in with scorn.'

Caroline Coon, who had already formed an anti-Rhodes bulwark with Simonon, suggests that Rhodes 'couldn't cope, [and] rather than say I can't do this, [he] decided to kinda set the band against each other.' This seems a rather pat analysis of something made inextricably complex by being built on contradictions. In the end, the band just realized they could do without Rhodes. Their time in America proved that, and provided them with a different directive – to convince America they were the future of rock & roll.

Joe Strummer: After two and a half years . . . you kind of lose your amateur status . . . We realized that we had to face . . . those three thousand people . . . every night, just the four of us. Our manager wasn't going to be out there facing them. [1979]

The CBS strategy for making FM-friendly punk rock, though, proved to be an unmitigated failure; while *Give 'Em Enough Rope* lost The Clash their share of once doting devotees in Britain. Marco Pirroni speaks for many when he says, 'I listened to the first track of The Clash's *Give 'Em Enough Rope* and that was it. I didn't buy any more of their records, or go to any more of their gigs.' At the same time, the album convinced few Americans that they were anything more than another

English hard-rock band. *Give 'Em Enough Rope* on domestic release would sell only nominally more copies than *The Clash* had sold on import. If anything, the months of studio bills merely rendered Strummer's lyrics even more unintelligible; while the vying textures of sound evident on 'White Man In Hammersmith Palais' and 'Complete Control' were subsumed by a concept as redundant as AOR (Adult Oriented Rock) radio, for a network of radio stations who thought Blondie were too radical to be pop.

If The Clash had stretched out recording their not-so-fabulous sequel to counter-productive proportions, fellow first-wavers Buzzcocks seemed in an undue hurry to follow up *Another Music In A Different Kitchen*. Appearing at the end of September, alongside their fifth 45, *Love Bites* suggested no clearer direction than The Clash. Continuing to slip in the odd audio experiment, but ever reliant on Shelley's pop credentials, the album was a minor hit on the back of 'Ever Fallen In Love', but a critical miss ('Buzzcocks made this album in a rush, and it's not very good,' was *NME*'s judgement). Shelley was finding it just as hard retaining their core audience when courting the fleeting success of a 45.

Pete Shelley: You get people now who see punk in the same way the real ardent teddy boys see rock & roll – that '76 was the only time that it worked, and if you develop you're selling out. [1978]

The clash of cultures reached its head on the last night of their autumn tour, at Brighton's Top Rank, when Buzzcocks decided to make a stand about punk attitudes to its stars and stages. As Diggle says, 'We'd had beer glasses thrown at the stage, so we finished the set and decided to fuck the encore. Bad mistake! The whole place erupted. A tidal wave of bottles and glasses pelted the stage.' Actually, it was a full-scale riot, some fans walking out with amps under their arms, others pelting anyone trying to protect the equipment. For Buzzcocks, the appeal of such nights was wearing thin.

If some old heroes seemed to be outstaying their welcome, one 'latecomer' seemed to be stealing by on the inside track. A week after Nick Kent pummelled everything save the opening track (the perfectly magnificent 'Safe European Home') on The Clash LP, his compadre Charles Shaar Murray reviewed a record he described as 'one of the handful of truly essential rock albums of the last few years . . . [and] the album that'll make Bob Harris' ears bleed the next time he asks what has Britain produced lately. More important, it'll be the album that makes The Jam real contenders for the crown.' *The Jam!!*

All Mod Cons was not The Jam's difficult second album, it was their transcendent third. *The Modern World*, released back in November 1977, was their disastrous sequel to *In The City*. Its one worthy proclamation, the title-track, had taken a sideswipe at carping critics – 'Don't have to explain myself to you / Don't care two shits about your review' – before they got those barbs in, but get them in, they did.

Many years later, Paul Weller admitted in a *Mojo* interview that 'some of those early Jam songs were awful, my attempts at being socially aware. But that was me just aping The Clash, after reading interviews with Joe Strummer and Mick Jones, saying people should be writing about what's happening today. I'd never thought of it before.' At the time, though, he still seemed to think he could ride out the storm, and immediately began work on a third album, a move producer Chris Parry considered premature.

Chris Parry: When they were preparing for the third album, in [early] '78, Paul's writing came to a grinding halt. Eventually they came to me with a tape of several Foxton songs, a couple of good Weller ideas and a few half-thoughts. I told them it was crap, and they shouldn't do the album on that basis. That whacked them hard. Buckler and Foxton never forgave me, but a week later Paul told me he agreed, and they cut the Ray Davies song 'David Watts' as a single to give themselves a breathing space. [1980]

Given cause to pause, Weller began to re-examine his own songwriting. Just one song from the scrapped third album seemed to suggest a better road. 'A-Bomb On Wardour Street', first issued on the double A-side 'David Watts' b/w 'A-Bomb' single, was presumably prompted by the IRA bomb-threat that almost cost them the Polydor deal back in March 1977. This time he envisaged a real bomb, as Weller found the apocalyptic tone he had been searching for in The Clash's cast-offs. The choice of 'David Watts' as its alter-ego was equally inspired, a reclamation of the quintessentially English strain of pop-rock first alchemized on The Kinks' *Something Else*.

The 'nod to the past, look to the future' approach was retained for The Jam's next singular preview of *All Mod Cons*, 'Down In The Tube Station At Midnight'. This time it was The Who circa '66 to whom

Weller paid homage, revamping 'So Sad About Us'. But it was 'Down In The Tube Station' that suggested England had finally found a commentator able to address head-on the paranoia and aura of violence that so defined the late seventies. As CSM wrote in that vital NME review, 'Weller [has begun] depict[ing] himself as the victim who doesn't know why he's getting trashed, at the hands of people who don't know why they feel they have to hand out the aggro.'

Weller admitted he'd been inspired by another Roxy refugee: 'I feel that I'm really doing the same as Poly Styrene, taking a situation like a tube station [at midnight] . . . an everyday experience, and turning it into art.' *All Mod Cons* placed The Jam in punk's premier league, where Weller fully intended to stay by continuing to develop: 'I wanna keep it simple all the time, but . . . you can't suppress progression.'

Weller had learnt the hard way that it was either stagnation or progression. Wire took to the notion like proverbial ducks to H_2O, having steeped themselves in other strains of English quintessence – like Syd Barrett-era Pink Floyd. Or The Move, who – as Colin Newman points out – 'could be Mods on Thursday, and hippies on the following Wednesday, and no one batted an eyelid'. If *Pink Flag* was the most radical English punk album of 1977, *Chairs Missing* – its sequel – was even more avant-garde, in an altogether more radical year.

Like The Jam, they signposted the change with a series of singles that bridged the chasm separating *Pink Flag* from *Chairs Missing*. If 'Dot Dash' had all the freneticism of *Pink Flag*, it had a greater dose of the same strange brew found in so many sixties Britpop singles. It also had a hook to die for – 'dot dash, dot dash / dip flash, dip flash / don't crash, don't crash' – which Lewis recalls coming 'from a specific experience on tour, . . . being terrified crossing the Fens between Nottingham and Norwich on an extremely winding road, with visibility down to four, five yards.' What could be more quintessentially English than a song about lousy weather!?

'I Am The Fly' was both *Chairs Missing*'s first 'preview' single and its first 'insect' song. Premiered on their January Peel session, Newman recalls using 'a blues change, a simple E to A – which is really un-me – but it was acceptable because the sound was weird.' If the sound was a little too weird for daytime playlists, the lyrics were off the dial altogether: 'I am the fly in the ointment / I can spread more disease / Than the fleas / Which nibble away / at your window display.' Yet they were topped by those on Wire's next single, 'Outdoor Miner', which Lewis explained to *NME* was about 'an insect called a Serpentine Miner that lives in the leaves and eats chlorophyll. I just couldn't quite comprehend what the reality of being a Serpentine Miner must be if there is a roof fall in a leaf.' Here was the most vivid imagination of a generation, finding subject matter within the most incongruous places in the whole wide world.

Graham Lewis: [It's not so important] what metaphors you come up with in describing Love, Security, Insecurity – that's what the song [Outdoor Miner]'s about – it just so happens that it uses the example of a very specific small creature . . . I didn't feel there were any boundaries to what you could not write about; and [when you] couple that with the power of [the] melodic and discordant [elements] that we could put together, you can present unusual things – [which is] what we thought you should be doing. That's the power of working in a popular medium.

'Outdoor Miner' was the flagship single for *Chairs Missing* (an added middle-section was required to get it to single length, the album version having all the girth of a *Pink Flag* track). Left behind were a whole stockpile of songs that could have bridged the gap, making for a releasable missing link. Newman is quite clear why it didn't happen, 'Doing the same thing again seemed irrelevant really. So we just junked a whole load of what could have been another album – we just threw it away . . . When *Pink Flag* came out, we were already probably playing sixty per cent of the material from *Chairs Missing*, which is where we were going. That was the only way we could stay ahead of what was going on . . . and we felt *that* was [the] confrontational part of what we did live.'

Three songs on *Chairs Missing* not only originated in the *Pink Flag* era – 'Practice Makes Perfect', 'Sand In My Joints' and 'I Feel Mysterious Today' – but all three were demoed for *Pink Flag*. Newman remembers the session he played the last of these to the rest of Wire, and everybody saying, 'That's for the next album.' For Newman, though, the key track that brought on *Chairs Missing* was 'Practice Makes Perfect'. It was the first song recorded for John Peel at the turn of the year, and the lead-off track for the fourteen-song LP on its September 1978 release. Waving goodbye to *Pink Flag*, the wired ones leapt every which way but the one of least resistance, unashamed to align ideas to technique; even if their producer, Mike Thorne, suspected that, '*Chairs Missing* was almost an attempt to make a really special album. [Like] we felt, "God, we've got to do something different." ' Again, Wire proved to be one punk band whose self-conscious approach was hardly a hindrance. By the autumn of 1978, they even felt they had some peers to invite along.

Graham Lewis: There are obviously people that we are in some way associated with . . . People like Pere Ubu, Siouxsie & the Banshees, Buzzcocks and Magazine . . . we're all working in completely different fields – but there's a common aim, in that they don't want to do what every other fucker is doing, because . . . it's already been done. [1978]

Following hard on the heels of Wire were the Cleveland contingent, Pere Ubu following *The Modern Dance* with an album as breathlessly executed as *Chairs Missing*, and just as ambitious. Obliged to jump labels by the lily-livered label-makers at Phonogram, Ubu made their second album, *Dub Housing*, for Chrysalis, and prefaced it by reissuing all the non-album Hearthan tracks on two Radar 45s, both named *Datapanik In The Year Zero*. Rarely can such a body of work have been placed before such a polarized public in such a short time – barely eight months for the sweep of four years' work to appear on four platters.

If *The Modern Dance* was a sweeping-up exercise, *Dub Housing* was a concerted attempt to put yet more clear blue water between these navvies and the next wave. Thomas even obligingly explained to the papers what Ubu continued to stand for: 'The only things I can ever break Ubu down into is (a) we want to try and keep pushing further, reach further than you know you can grab on to, and (b) to never repeat.' Yet Thomas was still reluctant to draw more than a thin red line between Ubu music and more commercial noisemakers. He semi-seriously claimed to have 'always thought we were a real pop band. [Even though] I'm obviously wrong and I'm living an illusion.'

For all its dissonance and fascination with dub-like space, *Dub Housing* was as close as Ubu came to the main punk currents. As they toured Britain throughout November and December 1978, the shows they gave proved simply too powerful to ignore. And with a figure like Crocus Behemoth stage-centre – pounding out time on an anvil – no one was about to gob on these guys.

The same, though, could not be said of John Lydon, who was preparing for the live debut of his post-Pistol self. The Public Image Ltd LP, *First Issue*, had been issued on the day Ubu concluded their second UK visitation – 8 December 1978. PiL's album, a slightly hurried affair, was eagerly awaited by the legions, not just because it was by the late Johnny Rotten, but because the preview single, 'Public Image', had seemingly taken up where 'Pretty Vacant' had left off. Lydon himself had also started to make some extravagant claims for his new band:

Y'know it'd be very easy for us to . . . churn out the same old lalala hard rock & roll that's as dead as a doornail anyway, and then we could earn lots of money and be good little pop star rebels . . . [Instead] I'm just a member of a group who has the freedom to record just what we feel like . . . I feel we're closer to disco than anything right now. Certainly not rock music! . . . I thought the idea was to start up a million different groups, not a million groups all playing the same decaying, feeble rock.

The starting point for Public Image Ltd seemed to have been the moment when the Pistols stopped playing Rotten's (preferred) 'Rubbish Rock', and began to believe they could redeem 'the same decaying, feeble rock'. However, after his experience with Sid Vicious – now on bail for the justifiable homicide of poisoned dwarf, Nancy Spungen – Lydon wanted musicians willing to play rock music all wrong, rather than being too inept to play it right. Initially, he rehearsed with two old friends, Jah Wobble, a novice bassist but a quick learner, and Keith Levene, who could play all of Steve Howe's Yes solos – backwards. Straightaway, there was a connection.

John Lydon: The three of us were wanting to do something, but didn't know what. The anger in us, different kinds of anger, kinda formed something . . . The little bit Wobble knew he knew well, and Keith's jangling over the top – the two formed such a lovely hook for me. It was like a gift from the gods.

The non-rock side of Rotten had always been there. When London's Capital Radio had famously given him two hours of air-time to spin some of his favourite tracks, in June 1977, he turned up with the likes of Peter Hammill's 'Institute of Mental Health Is Burning', Captain Beefheart's 'The Blimp', Kevin Coyne's 'Eastbourne Ladies', Nico's 'Janitor Of Lunacy', and Can's eighteen-minute 'Halleluhwah' from the irreducible *Tago Mago*.

Lydon later claimed, in his autobiography, that 'if the [*Bollocks*] sessions had gone the way I wanted, it would have been unlistenable for most people, because they wouldn't have had a point of reference.' But the Pistols' musical direction was one area where he had never had the upper hand. So PiL started with a single premise, that 'the Pistols finished rock & roll. That [it] was the last rock & roll band.' If Lydon had once done his best to revive its ailing self, he'd decided it had been a forlorn exercise.

John Lydon: My whole attitude with [the Pistols] was to better ourselves and not to wallow in working-class peasantry and love the idea of being downtrodden and broke . . . The Pistols was to make things better! The end of rock & roll. Get rid of that music, there is life beyond. [1981]

If Lydon decided on PiL's *leitmotif*, it was Levene who was the true leader of the band, the others being required to follow this often-pie-eyed Piper. Levene planned to rely on happenstance, improvising around Wobble's bedrock bass (and drummer Jim Walker's whomping beat). Meanwhile, Rotten dropped in and out of the performance with acidic asides about how he wished he could die, or that the public image belonged to him. Lydon made light of the process to *Sounds* just two months after PiL began rehearsing: 'The way we write songs is so easy. Someone will just bash out something and everybody will fall in and I'll babble over it.' Levene's own description, in 2002, to Perfect Sound Forever's Jason Gross, embellished on the process somewhat.

Keith Levene: We thought we were doing something quite radical, by making the songs up literally as they went along. It was quite daring . . . If we did something and made a mistake, I'd say, 'I'm not going to go in and fix that, because it's only a mistake if you underline it – otherwise, it's just something else . . . There was a sort of cohesive disintegration within the band . . . [Wobble] couldn't play [so] he made up his own bass lines pretty much from scratch. [But] he wouldn't mind me editing them, like me saying, 'Don't play those two notes.' . . . We were getting away with being very audacious and saying, 'We can do whatever the fuck we want. We're PiL, fuck you.' People never knew if we were serious or playing a joke on them. But we were serious. [PSF]

The first public display of their approach was the 'Public Image' single, issued in September, and judiciously edited to suggest a whole lot more structure than it originally had. As Levene says, 'Even when we recorded it, we didn't have it exactly the way we wanted, until we edited about two inches out of a 24-track. It was a bold edit and it worked.' The song shared an insidious riff – something Levene had been fooling with before he ever gave Chrissie Hynde guitar lessons – and some caustic lyrics with those classic Pistols' 45s. These particular words reclaimed Lydon's identity from McLaren. But it was recorded – as was the remainder of *First Issue* – with what Levene later called, 'as much bass and treble as possible, and with as little rock & roll as we could get away with'.

Though the single was righteously received by press and public alike, charting at the same position as 'Pretty Vacant', *First Issue* was another tale altogether. Containing at least one song, 'Theme', which seemed to be the bastard son of 'Halleluhwah' and 'Sister Ray' – and with a lot less in the way of judicious edits – the album was greeted with howls of indignation by those music papers who felt slightly duped. Only *ZigZag* championed the album, and the band's daring in making it. But Public Image Ltd seemed unfazed by the reception, and when Keith Levene was asked by *Rolling Stone* about those initial reviews – in the spring of 1980 – he pointedly contrasted the PiL approach with the output of one of his previous bands:

They all slagged [*First Issue*] because it was self-indulgent, non-simplistic and non-rock & roll. Those are all good points . . . That's the kind of music we intend to make. We don't want to be another Clash.

By December 1978, few expected 'another Clash'. But, despite the caveats critics now directed at PiL, there were plenty of folk who turned up at the Rainbow, in Finsbury Park, on Christmas Day, to see the rebirth of Johnny Rotten. Boy, were they set to be disappointed; not to say, disabused.

PART SIX

6.1
OUT OF PUNK –
INTO THE LIGHT
1979

The rise of the New Wave has coincidentally paved the way for groups of musicians who do not fit into the conventions of 'punk' or 'New Wave' . . . but are also far too experimental to be accepted into the mainstream of rock. In America, groups such as Pere Ubu, Devo or Suicide play in 'underground' clubs and make their appeal to the New Wave audience . . . These bands are conceptual art commandos in New Wave guise.

— Richard Grabel, *NYR*, 1979

1979 is the year of Afterpunk and there's a battle of ideas going on that is much more interesting than the original punk argument about commerce and cop-out . . . Now the ideas that kept punks uneasily together are whirling apart . . . The debate is about the meaning of music not as a commodity but as art.

— Simon Frith, *MM*, 31/3/79

By the beginning of 1979, everyone save perhaps the odd modern Mohican was looking for the Next Big Thing. In the somewhat unseemly haste with which the British music press sought to bury punk, journalists lined up with their chosen term for what might come after it. Jon Savage's New Musick had sunk like Brian Jones. New Wave had been sullied by Sire's shameless rebranding exercise. Powerpop had barely held enough power to stutter out of the garage. Perhaps surprisingly, Charles Shaar Murray's use of 'post-punk', back in February 1978, had also failed to catch on.

So when *NME*'s new boy, Paul Morley, wrote an effusive celebration of New Pop UK that January, rather than brand the bands, he posited a distinction between 'indie' rock and the 'major' label variety. Implicit for some time, this was now increasingly an issue simply because the likes of Rough Trade, Step Forward and Factory were serious about providing a credible, financially viable alternative. Morley predicted an increasing profile for these 'indie' labels and their bands:

Here's a whole mass of diverse and distinct new rock musicians whose activity is implicitly concerned with preventing [a] suffocation of choice . . . This genuine underground music reaches a small, enthusiastic audience, and despite the reserved and/or reactionary decisions of many fans who . . . continue to demand the vague ideals of '75/'76, dourly dismissing the eclectic . . . with depressing abruptness, this audience is going to flourish as it becomes obvious that the major labels have manufactured a new pop muzak. [*NME*, 13/1/79]

Morley's own adoption of the term 'post-punk' was still a step or two away. In March 1979, Simon Frith suggested using Afterpunk in his weekly *Melody Maker* column, and though the term was a non-starter, he did recognize that punk was changing, nay evolving; and, like Morley, he predicted that the battle would be between the chart-conscious and the art-conscious, or as he designated them, the populists and the progressives:

In the tattered corner, bouncing aggressively . . . are the populists . . . their criterion of musical excellence is accessibility . . . [But] populism [often] slides, with a plop, into philistinism. Its disdain for difference and difficulty is a familiar form of pre-judice . . . In the smooth corner . . . are the progressives . . . They have a complex notion of popularity that I'm not altogether sure I understand . . . draw[ing] on the populist ideal – performer/audience fused in one emotion – to legitimize an account of performance in which intellect is as important as feeling . . . The populist/progressive debate has no conclusion. Its terms were held together in the punk moment, but only because punk was originally incoherent. [*MM*, 31/3/79]

It took an American to point out what most progressive punk bands had in common – an art-school background. As Mary Harron, fresh from *Punk* herself, wrote in a May *Melody Maker*, '[Over here] an art-school band . . . is *not* a correct thing to be. The music that is emerging in Britain has carried on some of punk's attitudes, [but] the words "art" and "avant-garde" continue to be deadly insults – meaning effete, dilettantish, irrelevant to rock. The only problem with this is that the new music is firmly grounded in art and the avant-garde.' What Harron didn't explicate was that this art-school connection went deep into the marrow of English punk, dug in from day one. As such, the progressive impulse was part of punk's original DNA, prior to infection by that most virulent virus, Ramonesitis.

The search for a convenient moniker for 'the new music' wasn't confined to the pop scribes and sociologists. Those engaged in selling this music were as keen to apply a brand name as any manufacturer of pop muzak. Tony Wilson, Factory Records impresario, told *New York Rocker* the following March that he had a term for the likes of The Pop

Group, Gang of Four, and Factory artists like Joy Division and A Certain Ratio: 'Post-Modern Funk – as I call it – has the superb dance rhythms of the early seventies . . . combined with the aggression and explosiveness of '76.'

It was a nudge in the right direction for anyone determined to label the music of those punk bands who had dared to develop, and were now deemed something *separate* from their point of origin. When post-punk as a term cropped up again in the early eighties, it was with the clear implication that it was really shorthand for post-(modern) punk.

What does not seem to have unduly concerned the moniker-makers – or their heirs – was the fact that those designated post-punk probably had been, at some point, pre-punk, proto-punk, or simply punk. As such the progressive side of punk was unwittingly merged with combos who formed after punk; or had no overt relationship with punk, being in many cases prog-rock gatecrashers afraid to apply that tarnished moniker. Here post-punk – at least before Simon Reynolds decided it was All The Music I Liked When I Was Young, a somewhat broad, not to say solipsistic, view of pop – was made to represent two separate strains of punk colliding with an entirely separate strain of rock, that might more appositely be termed anti-punk.

These two strains of punk included those bands who – starting from scratch – took so long to learn their instruments that by the time they'd mastered the basics, weren't sure if they actually wanted to play punk any more. Simply by failing to put out any major artifactal statement in the interim, thus freezing their punk status, these bands were free to reinvent themselves. Members of this fraternity included The Fall, Warsaw, The Pop Group, Gang of Four, the Prefects and The Slits, all of whom were entities by the winter of 1977, and already following the edict of the enormously influential Subway Sect in advocating the anti-rock aesthetic that was always an integral part of punk.

A second strain constituted bands formed by those punk originators convinced that their artistic goals couldn't be achieved in their original guise. From this vantage point, if there is a 'true' starting-point for English post-punk, it may be Siouxsie & the Banshees' recruitment of guitarist John McKay, *or* the formation of Magazine and PiL, which places it somewhere between August 1977 and May 1978. Or perhaps Wire's decision to turn from a quintet into a quartet and slow down the songs in January 1977; or the reformulation of the Banshees after the 100 Club Punk Festival the previous September? Even this early the evolutionary process was already underway in America, where Pere Ubu were Rocket from the Tombs' final solution, and the Voidoids resulted from Richard Hell realizing the rest of the Heartbreakers were dead-end kids looking to evade responsibility.

Evidently, this honed-down thing called post-punk was never *post* punk. It just seemed like a convenient way of killing off punk (at least in name), while many bands continued to live out its 'original' directive. It also meant that someone needed to take credit for inventing something that by its very name *succeeded* the still-sprightly punk phenomenon. Tony Wilson again stepped up to the bar, in a recent *Mojo*, on behalf of the charges he let down so badly back in 1980.

Tony Wilson: Sooner or later, someone was going to take the energy and inspiration from punk and make it express more complex emotions. And that's what Joy Division did. Instead of saying: 'Fuck off,' they said: 'I'm fucked.' In doing so, they invented post-punk and regenerated . . . rock & roll.

If Joy Division's message can be codified as 'I'm fucked' – and I'm not convinced it can – they neither invented post-punk, nor regenerated rock & roll. The former was a message proclaimed loud and hard by both Peter Laughner and Richard Hell some five years before Joy Division started playing in its house of dolls. As for the regeneration claim, rock in 1979 had rarely been so rambunctious. Anyway, it is hard to see how a band whose one hit single came in the summer of 1980 – as a direct result of its singer 'topping' himself, thus ending the band – can claim to have regenerated something sailing past its wild youth. Even the suicide-as-route-to-recognition ruse had already been thoroughly tested by the late Laughner, who signposted his road of excess with songs like 'Ain't It Fun' ('to know you're gonna die young'), 'Life Stinks', 'Never Gonna Kill Myself Again' and 'Dear Richard' (his 'answer to an unwritten suicide note').

In truth, post-punk, just like punk itself, was a construct of scribes, not songwriters. And like punk, it was an attempt to draw a line in the sand; to say this is Now, and to sideline much of what came before. And that process predated the wholesale adoption of the term. Perhaps the starting gun for post-punk's clean-up brigade can be found in an attempt by *NME* to disown its own pre-punk view of rock. Over eight weeks, at the end of 1978, it published in instalments *The NME Book of Modern Music*, an elitist exercise that unilaterally decided which pre-punk music it was cool to listen to (which now included Can and Captain Beefheart, but not Pink Floyd or Frank Zappa), and which punk bands qualified as Modernists. 'Punk', as here defined, 'didn't last long. Not even with the great records that were released.' Apparently, it was all over – even with all that shouting.

In fact, *NME*'s adoption of such a contemporaneous creed – like *Melody Maker*'s equally belated conversion – was largely a riposte to its rival in the 'credit where due' war, which had been raging since *Sounds* surprisingly pre-empted its two more illustrious sister-papers at the birth of punk. *NME*, or more accurately its new scribes, with a little help from Nick Kent and Charles Shaar Murray, had decided to champion the progressive strain of punk. Effectively this was a rejection, by new editor Neil Spencer, of the Burchill-Parsons 'let us now praise gutter-snipes' school of criticism, in favour of a newer, hipper generation of wannabe *wünderkinds*, including Paul Morley, Ian Penman and Adrian Thrills.

Though their recruitment was probably partially a response to *Sounds*' earlier staff-revamp, which had seen the likes of Jane Suck, Sandy Robertson and Jon Savage take the baton from Ingham and Dadomo, the *NME* need not have worried. By the summer of 1978, *Sounds* editor Alan Lewis was no longer convinced that his weekly was on the right tack with all this New Musick, and decided to recruit someone who could engage the disenfranchised ex-*Sniffin' Glue/Oi* constituency. His choice was Gary Bushell, a fan with his own fanzine, who 'landed the *Sounds* job in July 1978 . . . [after] I showed [Alan Lewis] a Sham interview I'd done . . . He asked me to show him what I could do, so I went out every night, saw bands like UK Subs and stuck the reviews through the *Sounds* office door the next day.'

The fact that Bushell still hadn't seen through Pursey's Sham should have been cause enough for Lewis to return his CV. But Lewis liked Bushell and, as features editor Vivien Goldman states, he 'liked *Oi*. I think he thought it was going to sell more papers than this multicultural rubbish, [even though] I knew Alan Lewis from *Black Music* magazine . . . [Though] I was terrified to go freelance, [I thought] there's [got to be] more to life than going into an office where this *Oi* aesthetic is being perpetrated.' After Goldman quit *Sounds*, Savage wasn't far behind. The New Musick programme, though, wasn't entirely done for. News reached the disillusioned pair that an old friend had taken over as editor at *Melody Maker*, after finding out A&R wasn't for him.

Richard Williams: I came back in '78, by which time it was rather difficult to know what to do. I brought in Vivien Goldman and Jon Savage. I just wanted to make it broader. The *Melody Maker* I loved – the *MM* of the late sixties – covered a huge spectrum of stuff, and rather idealistically and unrealistically, I wanted to recreate that – to make it a cross between that and the *Village Voice*.

As *Sounds* returned to its strange netherworld – the uncool alternative to the hipper music weeklies – punk figures like TV Smith despaired of both the paper and punk's direction: 'I really hated to see it descend into [all] that fake working-class agenda, which had nothing to do with [punk]. It was like Gary Bushell introduces the Right To Be Thick.' And yet, Bushell's *Sounds* was the one weekly still championing the last punk bands in town, outfits like The Ruts and Stiff Little Fingers, without indulging in that classic 'build 'em up to knock 'em down' game that was an *NME* trademark.

For readers of the post-punk *NME* and *MM*, it sometimes seemed like rock itself had become a tiresome distraction from the altogether more important sociological implications of a fracturing audience. Delighted by the anti-rock strain of (post-)punk, these weeklies documented its increasingly doomed efforts to engage with the leather jackets. In March 1979, *MM*'s new editor even attended a Pop Group gig in Portsmouth. The band, which had finally released their defining artifact, 'She's Beyond Good And Evil', might have found another of Nietzsche's aphorisms more apposite – 'Communication is only possible between equals'.

In Portsmouth, response [to The Pop Group] was swift. As the [set] dragged on, a youth in what looked like a Seditionaries t-shirt took to the stage and helped himself to the microphone. Joined by several of his friends, including a couple of punkettes, he proceeded to bellow through the PA: 'What a load of crap! . . . What a load of crap! What a load of crap!' And then: 'Anarchy! Anarchy! Anarchy!' The punks and punkettes danced, strummed the guitars, and took over the drums. The musicians' attitudes were markedly different. Mark Stewart appeared to welcome the intruders, giving up his mike and encouraging them to bash along on the instruments; bassist Simon Underwood and guitarist Jon Waddington played along as best they could; Gareth Sager picked up his saxophone, clarinet and guitar and made as if to carry them to safety. It [quickly] became obvious that the intruders had not arrived in a spirit of community. They had not been moved to participation by the nature of the music. They simply wanted to interrupt, to take over, to impose themselves on the occasion. What they wanted was a two-chord 4/4 thrash. [*MM*, 24/3/79]

Stewart wasn't the only one who found a Portsmouth punk audience unreceptive that night. Support act Alternative TV had been met by the same wall of blank incomprehension, prompting Perry to yell back, 'You thick bastards! That's not what the punk spirit is about, just giving you what you want!' Presumably Perry hadn't bothered to check out 'The Return of Johnny Rotten' at the Rainbow, just nine weeks earlier. If he had, he might have had an inkling of how deep the division had become.

Public Image Ltd hadn't quite been presumptuous enough to make two London dates at the end of December their debut performances, warming up for the occasion with shows in Brussels and Paris. They couldn't have yet heard the June 1978 Suicide set in Belgium's capital city, *23 Minutes In Brussels* (curtailed after that by a full-scale riot), issued as a limited edition flexi-disc with the UK edition of the Suicide album, which suggested Brussels was a bad idea. According to Wobble, PiL's reception was not dissimilar: 'It was a fucking riot. I ended up kicking a geezer in the face [who] was the head of security . . . It really was a riot – we ended up barricaded in the dressing room.'

Paris, where even Subway Sect had found a small fan-base, was considerably more receptive; and was rewarded with three encores. The Rainbow on Christmas Day, though, was decidedly short on festive fun. Though the sound of the band was akin to a set of sledgehammers with pick-ups, the audience quickly polarized and by the third song, fights were breaking out like waves on a desert shore. By two-thirds of the way through PiL's 45-minute set, the *Oi* fraternity had forced its way to the front, and was mercilessly heckling Lydon. When he attempted to calm proceedings, by handing out cans of beer to thirsty fans up front, he got one back, unopened, full-square on his forehead.

Still Lydon continued to define the public image until, after a single, dismissive encore, he courageously stood at the side of the stage, castigating a particularly persistent throng of Mohican-heads for imagining that 'pink vinyl 12" singles' was what punk had ever been about. This was indeed the same man who had been 'so real, so honest and so full of desperation' at Winterland eleven months earlier; but the audience – in London at least – had changed. It would be three years before London caught sight of Lydon again. By then, the circle was complete.

Even in the winter of 1979, the strain of 'leadership' was already taking its toll. As Jah Wobble has said, Lydon was 'under great pressure. I see now, in some respects, classic signs of depression. He would spend an inordinate amount of time quietly watching videos, for hours on end. I remember feeling at the time, "For fuck's sake, John, come on!"' The depression might have had a more immediate source – the death of his mother from cancer – which in the spring of 1979 prompted PiL's true masterpiece, 'Death Disco', the product of Lydon's cathartic grief and Levene's rich instrumental imagination, both plugged directly into the moment.

Keith Levene: [John's mum] was going through the glorious process of dying from cancer, and it was all a bit heavy I suppose, for everyone. That's what John was singing about – very passionately, I might add . . . I would play the E chord and it would be like breaking glass in slow motion . . . The whole thing was in E. That opened it up, cos it was all literally in one note. I realized that this tune that I was bastardizing by mistake was 'Swan Lake'. So I started playing it on purpose, but I was doing it from memory . . . When he'd stop [singing], I'd play 'Swan Lake'. When he'd sing again, I'd go back to the harmonic thing and build it up. [PSF]

Issued as both a punk-size seven-incher and in six-and-a-half-minute sensurround on a twelve-inch 45, 'Death Disco' appeared after a six-month hiatus, interrupted by a single show in Manchester. In that time, some folk *had* caught up, and the single received an unexpectedly glowing series of reviews. Roy Carr in *NME* asked, on our behalf, 'What is one to make of "Death Disco"? Is it just another con-game? . . . Are, as some people insist, PiL incapable of writing songs? . . . [Well,] whether it is a hoax or a signpost for the future is open to interpretation. [But] it exists, it irritates, it intrigues. You just have to keep on playing it. Mission accomplished.'

And yet this radical fusion of Tapper Zukie, Tchaikovsky and *Tago Mago* was compelling enough, and Virgin's marketing sufficiently shrewd, to send the single into the charts and the band into the *Top of The Pops* studio (where they refused to mime along to the song). There they met old friends Siouxsie Sioux and Steve Severin, who were there to perform their third Polydor single, 'Playground Twist'. Though it had a lot more structure than 'Death Disco', the Banshees' 45 also seemed too twisted for the charts – but there it was. In fact, Severin remembers going into Polydor 'and the head of A&R . . . said, "I would have bet money that a song like that would have never got in the charts." I don't know what we were thinking of, but such was the momentum of the group.'

It was the Banshees' third hit single in less than a year, and probably the best. But they still couldn't bring themselves to play the game. When The Police also performed on that week's show, the Banshees cold-shouldered them, prompting Stewart Copeland to complain about their snottiness in the following week's *NME*, much to Severin's evident amusement – 'He said it was obviously a punk elite thing. I remember [thinking], "Fucking right it was. You're just rubbish, mate."'

Unlike PiL, though, the Banshees felt a certain pressure to keep 'the momentum of the group' going; and responded by releasing a hasty second album, *Join Hands*, at the end of August. As Severin readily admits, 'We were really struggling to get the material. There was only six months in between making the two records. And, of course, it had to be totally new . . . If we had had three more months we would have come up with two or three other songs, and it would have been a great follow-up album. But we were already booked into Air Studio, the clock was running.'

In fact, two of the most popular Banshee-screeds had been omitted from *The Scream*, and would have been ripe for revision. 'Make Up To Break Up', though, was firmly in the band's punk past; and Burchill's barbs made Siouxsie reluctant to put 'Love In A Void' on *Join Hands* (though it appeared in the interim on a German single). The desire to produce something 'totally new' still led the Banshees to revisit their starting-point, filling out the second album with their fabled arrangement of 'The Lord's Prayer'. The transition from live encore to studio jam session was not a smooth one. The Banshees simply weren't used to improving in the studio – unlike their post-punk stablemates, PiL.

In fact, so in-the-moment were PiL sessions now that when ex-101er drummer Richard Dudanski was summoned to the studio to sit in that spring, he found himself recording a side's worth of songs while flying by the seat of his pants.

Richard Dudanski: Keith did know me from the 101ers and just rang up and said, 'We're recording in the Townhouse. Can you get over here?' And in fact [over] the next ten days, we recorded like five songs. The tape was just left running. Basically, me and Wobble would just start playing, and maybe Keith'd say something like double-time. But it was a bass-drum thing which Keith would stick guitar on, and John would there and then write some words and whack 'em on . . . once we'd got the [basic tracks]. I think the first day we did 'No Birds Do Sing' and 'Socialist'. Then we did 'Chant', 'Memories'.

Brought in after Jim Walker quit, and Karl Burns changed his mind, Dudanski says, 'I was really thrilled when first joining PiL. I shared the whole [idea] of wanting to do something different and not controlled by the industry. And Virgin would have done anything [for them]!' For PiL were in a unique position, treated like rock stars, feted by the press, but quietly determined to upset the cart at every turn. At the reins was the charismatic Lydon, someone who Dudanski promptly realized 'really loved music. I'd bring tapes and records over, and we'd swop stuff. We'd listen to a little madrigal, or Renaissance music, a lot of Irish folk music, [smoked] a lot of weed. I had Bulgarian voices, Indian stuff, a lot of Islamic percussion stuff.'

Another, non-musical member of the Gunter Grove group was Vivien Goldman, now successfully transplanted to a *Melody Maker* under Richard Williams' tutelage. She had first met Lydon in the pub opposite the Rainbow, before a Burning Spear gig: 'He knew who I was – he said, "You're that bird who reviews the reggae records. You're always out of date. You're always late." He was so funny. He made me laugh even then. If he hadn't come up with an insult, one could almost be offended.'

But when she 'really got friends with him [was] at the time when he was leaving the Pistols, moving away from that laddish scene to be a bit more experimental.' She even became a 'mystery woman' in the tabloids for a day, snapped in Lydon's company on a Virgin-sponsored trip to Jamaica in March 1978. One of several substitute mother-figures at Gunter Grove in those years, she had a vast knowledge of reggae and the resources to surprise the sponge-like singer.

Vivien Goldman: I went to Gunter Grove all the time. I used to bring a lot of reggae artists over there . . . When you are mates you tend to hang around at the biggest place and his was the biggest place, and he had the sound system – the fetishism of the pre-release and the 12 inches and the dub platters – very exciting period – much easier to be on top of everything than it is now, because there's so much audio information. At that time you could totally know what was going on – it was such a small scene.

Having block-booked time at Virgin-owned studios to record further extemporizations for their ever-obliging label, Lydon roped Goldman into recording her own single, 'Launderette' – 'in their down time . . . We were out at The Manor and nobody knew what to do. Everybody was just stuck – because they were trying to find something really, really, really new. Well, in the end they did find something fairly newish . . . [since] those were the sessions that resulted in *Metal Box*. [But] I remember [Keith] saying he didn't want to play guitar in any way that anybody had ever played in the past, otherwise it wasn't even worth it . . . Talk about hubris! But, of course, nothing exists that's really different, [and] that idealism can lead to people's own destruction.'

Goldman's delightful single wasn't just a way to use up down time. Lydon and Levene were imbued with the notion that PiL should be more than just a band (their refusal to call Public Image 'a band' on US TV in 1980 would lead to their most memorable media appearance, on Tom Snyder's *Tomorrow Show*). This was a limited company, and limited companies don't do side projects, just projects *per se*. And initially there was a nominal attempt to live up to this ideal, Wobble issuing his own satirical dub 12", 'Dreadlock Don't Deal In Wedlock', and Wobble and Levene joining forces with Don Letts for the *Steel Leg Versus The Electric Dread* EP. But Goldman's 'Launderette', a female 'Jilted John', would be the last such project the band officially endorsed. When Wobble continued to pursue his own projects, it became a source of tension, rather than part of the master plan, even with others growing increasingly frustrated by the general lack of activity.

Richard Dudanski: The whole thing ground to a halt. Apart from those first recordings at the Townhouse, [and a session at] a studio in Bermondsey, [where we] recorded 'Graveyard'/'Another' . . . we never, ever played. Jah was into it. He wanted to do something. We'd try and set something up. But it would just not happen. Keith would not turn up. It could have worked – there was this band with [all] this potential – but we seemed incapable of actually *doing* it.

None of this was apparent that summer/autumn, as the band drip-fed their audience the songs they'd recorded with Dudanski, following 'Death Disco' in late September with the memorable 'Memories'. But the momentum of the band, inspiringly maintained for most of 1979, ground to a halt the first week in September, when PiL played its third gig of the year, headlining the first annual Futurama Festival at Leed's Queen's Hall.

Leeds was a bad idea from the get-go. It had been a particularly notorious battleground ever since the Pistols' first Anarchy gig; and as a long-time Arsenal fan, Lydon should have known something of the reputation of Leeds FC's lunatic fringe. But ever the Londoner, Lydon equated Leeds with Manchester, where PiL had played its only two gigs of the year to date, one to 4,000 fans, the other (a secret gig at the Factory) to maybe 250. Both shows were well received by fans used to the likes of Magazine, The Fall, Joy Division and the Prefects. Leeds, though, was both a wake-up call *and* a nightmare.

Richard Dudanski: [Futurama] brought everything to a head. Again, no rehearsals, shitty sound, John was in an awful mood, Keith was out of it, and [we were] hanging around all day. And I had a big row with Keith after it . . . It was [hard] not only for the audience, but for the musicians as well, 'cause we hadn't played for about four months.

One major problem that night was the disorientating material PiL elected to play, in a place with ping-pong acoustics and a two-stage set-up that resulted in fans being herded from one side of the arena to the other. Opening with 'Chant', they proceeded to preview both sides of the 'Memories' single. In this acoustical graveyard, when the befuddled reached for the bottle it was generally to lob it stageward. Lydon's response was to turn his back on the audience, performing the remainder of the set that way. The show undid a lot of the good press previously directed at 'Death Disco'. Afterwards Dudanski tendered his resignation. An explanatory letter he sent to *NME* was the first public indication that all was not well in the PiL camp:

What could potentially be a great band will probably do just enough to retain its guaranteed success. Perhaps exactly because of this guarantee, the really good ideas behind the band will never be more than just that. [*NME*, 10/79]

Given that the following week 'Memories' appeared, succeeded in October by the magisterial *Metal Box*, it initially sounded like sour grapes. In fact, just as Dudanski's arrival spurred PiL into action, so did his departure. As if determined to disprove Dudanski's doomy view, they promptly returned to Townhouse with Martin Atkins – a northern fan of the band who wanted in – and recorded 'Bad Baby' as both Atkins' audition and the track needed to complete *Metal Box*. Once again, the song was largely improvised, Lydon writing the lyrics when the backing track was done. If they were continuing to rely on happenstance, it wasn't all accidental. As Atkins says, 'There was attitude galore – and gleeful excitement at messing with people. There was . . . [also] disregard for the rules.' And a great deal of thought still being put into PiL's sound.

Jah Wobble: As we went into *Metal Box*, what we were doing really became something else. It was a partly industrial sound, which was quite appropriate . . . The way the music felt was often so near perfect, there wasn't that much to do mix-wise. There was a minimum amount of movement on the faders, a touch here, a touch there. Masterfully done. If there's loads of pyrotechnics going on at the mixing desk, it tells you you've probably done something wrong when you were recording.

In early November 1979, Lydon invited the one reliable media supporter of the 'band', *ZigZag*'s Kris Needs, to hear the finished artifact, which Lydon insisted was 'not an album. You don't have to listen to the songs in any order . . . Albums have a very strict format, the eight tracks, difficult to find.' Needs remembers he 'sat there – John got lots of beer, watched TV till the little dot went off – "Right, come and hear my album." Obviously speeding. Three in the morning. I was blown away . . . John said, "We're not giving any of this out." [But] he wrote all the words out by hand, which I've still got, and he gave me a cassette, and I did this very last minute thing for *ZigZag*.'

If Needs gave the album two thumbs up, Lydon was still ambivalent about any kind of critical acceptance, hence his single-sentence, self-deprecating radio ad for the 'album': '*The Metal Box* . . . twelve tracks of utter rubbish from Public Image Ltd.' This time, though, Lydon need not have feared the media behemoth. There were plaudits galore for PiL's post-punk classic:

[This] is light years away from the Sex Pistols . . . Everything is refracted and bent through PiL's need for sparseness . . . *Metal Box* is a vital ending to seventies pop culture and a sizeable nod in the direction of a real r 'n' r future. The last laugh is with John Lydon and no mistake. [Dave McCullough, *Sounds*, 24/11/79]

Don't matter a tawny owl's hoot whether any of this album is accidental or intentional . . . in terms of impact and effect *Metal Box* is pulverizing . . . All this forward flow in twelve months – it's almost frightening. PiL are miles out and miles ahead. [Angus MacKinnon, *NME*, 20/11/79]

Lydon was as put off by the acclaim as by the panning its predecessor received, informing *Trouser Press* the following spring, 'I don't like that "masterpiece" shit; that's a real put-off. The normal person just reading that thinks, "Fuck you."' Ever the anti-intellectual, he continued to distrust the critical consensus, believing he could buck their expectations – with disastrous results next time around. Meanwhile, *Metal Box* came at the end of a year of retrenchment for Lydon's immediate contemporaries. Disappointing releases by Siouxsie Sioux and Howard Devoto may have been more about lack of material than any lack of direction, but for Wire and Pere Ubu it was a case of a middle-eight too far.

Magazine's *Secondhand Daylight* had been produced – at Devoto's insistence – by Colin Thurston, engineer on Iggy's *Lust For Life* and Bowie's *Heroes*; but perhaps it needed Berlin's brutal backdrop to acquire the full *Heroes/Lust* ambience. Perhaps Devoto had also lost some of the sureness evident on *Real Life* after 'Touch And Go' and 'Give Me Everything', two highly worthy shots across the singles chart's bows, missed their target.

Wire's third album in two years, *154*, appeared in September 1979, after another year of bemused audiences expecting to see the band promote its latest long-player. At least the label still seemed to be willing to take the long-term view. As Newman told Simon Reynolds, 'EMI saw us as the progressive element coming out of punk, with longevity and a more artistic approach – slower pieces, more depth and space in the sound, different noises that weren't just thrash, thrash, thrash.' But single success continued to elude them, despite another terrific non-album single, 'A Question Of Degree', released as *154*'s loss-leader.

Touring as 'special guests' to other EMI artists didn't help much either; perhaps because, as one sarcastic scribe noted that summer, 'As a promotional tour for their fourth album, Wire's latest series of gigs are a useful affair. There's just one minor snag; they don't actually release their third album till September.' In fairness, Wire had given plenty of notice as to their live *modus operandi* during interviews at the time of *Chairs Missing*.

Colin Newman: We don't present a rock & roll show so if people want to see or get off on a rock & roll show, they'd better not come and see us. Plenty of other bands can do that . . . When we see a[nother] band, we always think, 'Oh God, I hope we don't end up like that'; and we'll try to avoid falling into that trap – it all comes down to the fact that we're not really happy being a rock & roll group. [1978]

An appearance on a *Rockpalast* 'in concert' during February had previewed half of *154*, but fans of *Pink Flag* had to wait until the final song of the hour-long set to hear any of its twenty-one songs. As Graham Lewis says, 'We got bored very quickly and we had a very strong critical "board" if you like. If two people went, "I think I've had enough of this one," we'd go right – it was dropped.' Their boredom threshold was so low that by the time the sessions for *154* began, there were few vestiges left from the psychedelic punkiness of *Chairs Missing*. *154* was intended as a more 'industrial' record, an attempt to keep one thread ahead of Gang of Four, The Pop Group, and PiL, as well as the one US band they deferred to in the innovation stakes, Pere Ubu.

But Ubu were already wandering from their remit as a (post-)modern pop band. Their own tertiary artifact, *New Picnic Time* – issued the same week as *154* – had the working title of *Goodbye*, almost as if they *knew* it qualified as career suicide. A tongue-in-cheek Thomas likes to blame the record company for not keeping their excesses in check, complaining that they 'would just let us do anything we wanted, which was really a mistake . . . because it encouraged us to try and go further and further. Every time we'd get away with something, we'd think, "Wow, I wonder what else we can do."' *New Picnic Time* – no fabulous sequel to *Dub Housing* – ended up sending the band into the altogether more receptive arms of Rough Trade, for whom no Ubu album could be too weird.

– – –

The sentimental Geoff Travis had been following Ubu since journey's start, buying their singles direct from Hearthan prior to the Phonogram deal. In fact, Rough Trade had acted as a one-stop shop since year zero for everyone from John Peel to the provincial punk paying his annual visit to Portobello Road. As of autumn 1978, they finally began putting out the odd (and the very odd) single. Within six months, they had ten singles to the Rough Trade name, at least half of which were five-star 45s: Subway Sect's 'Ambition', Electric Eels' 'Cyclotron', Swell Maps'

'Read About Seymour' and the first two SLF records. But only when they also issued the Fingers' debut LP, in February 1979, could their finances start to match their ambition.

Geoff Travis: Stiff Little Fingers charted and sold a lot of records, and that gave us confidence to be a label. There was a few years' hard work of distribution before the label started, so by the time the SLF album came out and sold a hundred thousand we knew we were totally capable of doing that – [even if] we had no idea back then [about how] you have got to get someone under a contract, in case they disappear or someone bigger comes along and entices them away.

Rough Trade had timed its intervention astutely, if a little fortuitously. Travis thinks, 'If we'd have been a year earlier, then you'd like to think we would be making records by The Clash – rather than the next generation.' But this new generation was cut from a different cloth. For them, 'indie' was good, majors were bad. And it was deals like the one The Clash signed that made many feel this way. As Travis told *Melody Maker*, the month *Inflammable Material* made its mark:

Rough Trade has that chance to provide an important middle ground. What you have [now] is people who are doing interesting things, making music, and there's not many places for them to go. Traditionally, they just go in that very small funnel towards stardom. What's important . . . is to get rid of the idea that it's important to be a star, and to make the funnel wider, so as to include as many people and ideas as possible. [*MM*, 2/79]

In such a fertile climate, it wasn't hard to sign bands. As Travis observes, 'Our third record was Cabaret Voltaire – and that was because Jon Savage wrote an amazing review of the demo tape that stirred our interest, so we went to see them . . . We were in a great position – the distribution was very much the gathering point – musicians were coming down to see us and giving us their tapes.' With the notable exception of SLF, Travis's label 'wasn't punk but post-punk – Cabaret Voltaire, Metal Urbain – and women's music: Kleenex, The Raincoats,' though some label-less punk stragglers were also welcomed into the fold. Lora Logic's first post-Spex single, 'Aerosol Burns', was one such early Rough Trade coup that turned into a long-term arrangement.

Lora Logic: [After Spex] I thought, 'I'll take a break. I don't like this business any more.' I was very, very hurt. [Then] I got a place at St Martin's School, studying photography there, but I was [quickly] disillusioned by the art-school crowd. It was just cocaine down the pub at lunchtime. Geoff Mann, [who] ran some seedy club in Soho and [wanted to] set up a record label, found out I was there, and he kept approaching me, saying, 'Why don't you just do something by yourself?' . . . Eventually he talked me into doing something. It was easy. He just said, 'Write two songs, and I'll pay for you[r studio time]. You got nothing to lose.' And that was 'Aerosol Burns'. It took a couple of hours – it was all very punk style . . . Geoff Mann [then] took 'Aerosol Burns' to Geoff Travis.

'Aerosol Burns' was a classic Rough Trade single – flagrantly uncommercial, yet overtly musical, it came at everything from an oblique angle, informed by the punk spirit, but assuredly art-rock. Another band so inclined was Subway Sect, who effectively ceased to exist after 'Ambition'. Travis, though, was not dissuaded. When Goddard decided to market himself as Vic Goddard and the Subway Sect – à la David Essex in *Stardust* – Travis was waiting. Also approached slightly too late were the Prefects, who by the end of 1979 were on their last legs, and whose sole releasable recordings had been made for Peel's radio show. Travis ended up releasing the BBC 'Going Through The Motions' as a memento of this northern Sect.

Robert Lloyd: We always had [this] thing – we never wanted to make a record – [but] Peel had seen us at the Rainbow with The Clash, and he kept going on about [us] in his column in *Sounds* . . . Eventually, John Walters did get in touch with us and said, 'Would you come in and do a session?' That was the first time we'd ever been in the studio. We'd never recorded a single thing [previously]. Thankfully, Peely thought it was great, and so he asked us back to do another one, a few months later. Shortly after that, the band kinda fell apart . . . [Then] within a month of splitting up, I actually got a telegram from Mayo Thompson at Rough Trade, saying Rough Trade wants to record the Prefects immediately . . . So I called up Geoff [Travis] and said, 'Well, the Prefects have split up.' And so he said, 'Can't we release some of your recordings anyway?' And I said, 'There aren't any. We did two Peel sessions.' He said, 'Can't we take two songs from that, and release it as a single?'

Travis and his label were providing a genuine alternative largely because they refused to perceive themselves as just a smaller version of a major. Of all the figures there from the beginning, Travis seems to have been the one paying attention when the shit came down; and his point of view was simple, 'I would always argue very vehemently against the idea . . . that the thing to do is to get inside the system and become very big, and then manipulate. I haven't seen anybody who has ever [actually] done that.'

The evidence was increasingly with him. As he also later observed, 'It doesn't matter how much "creative control" a band is given [by a "major"]. You're still indentured. Long-term contracts will put a band in debt from recording and touring costs. Then you have to produce when you're not ready. You have to write songs when you have nothing to say.' Unfortunately for Rough Trade, post-punk seemed as prone to rapid deceleration in the quality of ideas as its former self. By September 1979, Travis was already complaining to *NME* about the standard of what he was being sent:

Every morning there's about five demo tapes sent in the post . . . There are a lot of people that seem to be influenced by Cabaret Voltaire and Throbbing Gristle. Then there are a lot influenced by The Fall . . . [But] we haven't actually found anything on any of the tapes that we would consider putting out as it is.

The influence of Throbbing Gristle was proving particularly deleterious. Like those fellow libertarians, Crass, TG were an ideas band whose musicality advanced in infinitesimal increments, while their ideas came in fast-flying flurries. Their notion of a punk blitzkrieg was to take the idea 'of all these women queueing up nude to go in the [gas] chambers, and . . . [create] a factual description of a traumatic image . . . We used to introduce [the song] by saying, "This is called 'Zyklon B Zombie' – it's a bit like Coca-Cola except worse for your teeth." . . . It was meant to be a pastiche of heavy punk.'

'Zyklon B Zombie' – the central track on *2nd Annual Report* – sounded a lot like a pastiche of early Black Sabbath. But for the anti-rock fraternity in the music press, TG took up where Subway Sect and the Prefects had stopped short – selling the idea that anyone can make a racket like TG, so everyone should. Even by 1979 it was still music for anyone who wanted to test a set of earplugs. Or as Richard Meltzer memorably put it, in a 1979 *Village Voice* review:

Monotonous but only half-assed synthesizer whitenoise; spastic 'sci-fi' upchuck; workaday factory cacophony; barely audible production-camouflaged vocalizings on thematic grotesqueries like germ warfare and fistfuck rapes in the local men's rm. It's reliable obnox-noise alright, clinically colored and all that but basically just your standard unpalatable racket, big deal.

TG, in the years after *2nd Annual Report*, when a semblance of a live set began to emerge, were obliged to live out a number of punk-like contradictions, the most worrying of which was the steady stream of product they released. This seemed like a marked departure from an aesthetic originally performance-based and confrontational, questioning why the audience was even there. But because their records were distributed through Miles Copeland's International Record Syndicate (IRS) – as were Rough Trade, Step Forward and Faulty – TG had an international profile by 1979 (hence Meltzer's review), at a time when a sizeable audience thought it a mark of good taste to test the boundaries of what their ears could stand.

Where Copeland showed himself to be a smooth operator, for all his punk-like rhetoric, was the deal IRS made with A&M in America, whereby these 'indie' labels acquired US distribution, but A&M were not obliged to pay them any advances. Copeland was on a similar wavelength to Travis, pushing for 'total freedom. [And] the minute you take an advance, they're going to have the right to say, "This isn't commercial enough. We won't get our money back on this one."' One of the immediate beneficiaries of the IRS set-up were The Fall, whose nominal leader had been making a great deal of the fact that major labels spelt death to musical freedom.

Mark E. Smith: When you leave work to concentrate on rock & roll you're really swapping one trap for another . . . The music industry is the most medieval system there is . . . [But these bands] really do believe that by having eight hit singles and getting the status of Elvis Presley or something, they can then say, y'know, 'Stop! We're gonna change everything.' [1978]

The underlying irony in Smith's stance was that no major label had shown the slightest interest in The Fall in the six months they had been touting the highly worthy *Bingo Master's Breakout* EP around. When they finally let Step Forward issue it, in June 1978, it was more from a lack of options than any high ideal. Even that offer came about because, as Martin Bramah says, 'Mark Perry was aware of us, and was championing our cause in London.' In Step Forward's microcosmic world of five-figure sales the EP qualified as a roaring success, and encouraged them to offer The Fall the opportunity to finally make a full-length album. Yet The Fall remained a conflicted band, and one of the issues came down to what kind of album they should make.

Martin Bramah: *Witch Trials* isn't that representative of what The Fall were doing [by then], 'cause Mark wanted to get some of the older songs on record for 'posterity'. In fact, there was a lot more free-form stuff going on by the end of that period, in the vein of what Public Image did on their first album. My feeling was, 'Let's do the later stuff. It's more interesting. It's more experimental.'

Smith may well have realized it was now or never, when it came to documenting the likes of 'Frightened', *Witch Trials'* electro-shock opener. And perhaps Smith thought he should represent the tortuous route away from 'Repetition'; a long-playing document of that journey, as it were – even if he was no longer interested in playing the band's defining song. As he told *NME* at the end of 1979, 'You get kids asking for "Repetition", and I say, "Do you go to the same school as you did two years ago? Do you go to the same pub as you did two years ago? I know I don't."' Actually he did.

By the time *Bingo Master* appeared, The Fall barely resembled the band it had been two years earlier. Both Tony Friel and Una Baines had left. In the latter's case, as she says, 'I just couldn't do it [any more]. My head was in bits . . . The last [gig] I did was particularly horrendous . . . I just stood there looking at my keyboards. I think people thought it was just part of The Fall.' Smith's feelings about her departure were expressed in shorthand to *Alternative Ulster*, 'Easter '78 – [Baines] quit – freak-out'.

The *Live At The Witch Trials* sessions were perched on a similar precipice. Ever since ex-nurse Kay Carroll had moved into the Smith/ Baines household, because 'she needed somewhere to stay', Baines found there was 'a clash of ideas. Maybe that's what started Mark off . . . just doing things because they're completely strange.' Certainly Baines believes it marked the beginning of the end for the original collective ideal – 'We['d all] agreed that we'd never have a manager . . . it was about being equal. I wouldn't have been a part of something that wasn't.'

Carroll was soon installed in Una's place. The dynamic became doubly difficult at this time because Bramah had moved in with the slowly recovering Baines. In December 1978, Smith discovered that drummer Karl Burns 'wants to be a musician and get crowd reaction. [So] he quit – dog shit.' By then *Live At The Witch Trials* was complete, and though it veered off at a tangent from the blistering *Bingo Master*, was still a recognizable relative (Friel's contributions were confined to 'Frightened' and 'Industrial Estate', but Bramah got co-credit on seven of the eleven cuts).

The reviewers just seemed relieved that The Fall had finally delivered a full forty-minute bulletin, *Sounds*' Dave McCullough calling *Witch Trials*, 'a confident, deadly exciting step forward'. But The Fall immediately took two steps back, Smith (via Carroll) again upsetting that delicate equilibrium on which most bands – even Pink Floyd – continually teeter. Barely had *Witch Trials* been shipped to the shops than Carroll was on Bramah's case, regarding time spent looking after Smith's ex-girlfriend and The Fall's former keyboardist.

Martin Bramah: I felt that I was giving everything that was required to The Fall, and I was getting little back . . . I missed a rehearsal because Una – who I was living with – had to go to hospital, and I went with her. So the next day Kay came round and started tearing a strip off Una for making me miss a rehearsal. That was the last straw.

Bramah believes to this day that 'Kay hated the fact that Una hooked up with me, because Una was a big threat to her . . . Mark really loved Una, and if she wanted to, Una could have got him back.' She didn't. The Mark E. Smith she once knew so well – the one who believed The Fall was a unit forged in friendship, and he was but a cog in the Collective – no longer existed.

Una Baines: I think Mark always had his own ideas of what the band was, and ultimately it was his idea that dominated it. He definitely was trying to wrestle the thing away from anybody else, and making it his own thing . . . Maybe Mark only pretended [to share our ideals] at the time; or maybe he thought, well it's not worked that way, so I'll do it this way instead.

Once, when asked why so many band members left The Fall, Smith came up with the understatement of the decade, 'Because I'm hard to work with.' He still had a fiercely Puritan work ethic, and was soon hard at work on the first post-collective, 'post-punk' Fall album, *Dragnet*. Issued just seven months after *Witch Trials*, it didn't really venture in any 'free-form' direction. Rather, it attempted to make a virtue of the absent melody makers, Friel and Bramah; substituting the clang of industrial noise. Its press release reflected both Smith's irreverent humour and his obsession with change for change's sake:

Dragnet is white crap let loose in a studio but still in control. Sung in natural accents in front of unAFFECTed music. *Dragnet* isn't a mass of confusion covered by reverb and a control board. This sound could catch on . . . The follow-up to 1st LP *Live At The Witch Trials* (Much OK'd and acclaimed), that's as much as *Dragnet* has in common with that record. This is band and fate's policy. Change equals growth.

Another band who equated change with growth were The Slits, who now held the record for time elapsed between debut gig and debut album. *Cut* appeared in September 1979, thirty months after their live debut at the Roxy. Ari Up explained why the process had taken so long: 'We know what we wanted in our own heads, and we couldn't express it. That's why we got really frustrated after a few recording sessions.' Six of the ten songs had in fact been previewed – and some would say, never bettered – on John Peel in September 1977 and April 1978.

Replacing Palm Olive with the ultra-reliable Budgie for the Island sessions, The Slits came out with a minor dance-hit, 'Typical Girls', along with a surprisingly proficient set of songs perhaps best left sloppy. But with their one-album Island deal done, The Slits preferred to join Palm Olive's Raincoats at the Rough Trade haven, where Ari Up knew she could deal in dreadlock-rock ad infinitum.

The Pop Group were another band who revelled in their role as harbingers of punk's warped mutation, having also taken an eternity to get some of their mutable ideas on black vinyl. The delay was partially because of unrealistic goals. As they told *Sounds*, back in December 1977: 'When we go into the studios . . . we're going to spend the time trying to capture the atmosphere – and it's difficult because it's only one sense that's being hit.'

Mark Stewart recalls The Pop Group's attempts to 'capture the atmosphere' of the band involved 'a session with Andy McKay which was very interesting, 'cause we were all Roxy boys . . . [Then] we started doing recordings with Charles from This Heat, who we really got on with. [We] also had a meeting with John Cale, who came down to Bristol.' But nothing came of the interest expressed by these parties, and it was 1979 by the time they'd settled on Radar, or Radar had settled on them. Even then, the label wasn't entirely au fait with the status of their Lamarckian evolution.

Gareth Sager: The record company expected something quite different from what we gave them, something closer to what Echo and the Bunnymen and Joy Division went on to do. But we'd already been through that.

Coming out the other side, The Pop Group's *Y* appeared in April 1979, a daring but doomed attempt to reconcile their original intent – to be 'an explosion in the heart of the commodity' – with some fairly outlandish musical ideas. Guitarist Gareth Sager now suggests they 'were fighting against the conservatism that had immediately crept into the punk movement . . . We took the punk ethic and ran into space with it.' Back in March 1979, he was more circumspect, admitting to *Sounds*, 'We don't really know what we're trying to do. We're just questioning everything.'

They were certainly starting to question the kind of audiences they were attracting. In June 1979, drummer Bruce Smith complained about their last London show on the grounds that 'we were preaching to the converted. It was sick. Everyone was so into us that it was easy.' Not quite everyone. *MM*'s Simon Frith described the experience as 'like outguessing a psychologist . . . The church is a vision of hell: other people grooving on a noise I can't quite hear.'

In the same month, the band managed to alienate Andrew Lauder, their chief advocate at Radar, to such an extent that he showed them the door; then washed his hands. Not surprisingly, The Pop Group promptly joined the babble emanating from the ever-expanding Rough Trade throng. Indeed, Stewart immediately gave them the inflammatory 'We Are Prostitutes', which he says 'came from a German Action Painting, [or maybe] something written on an advertising board, [suggesting] the lunatics have taken over the asylum'. Rough Trade was a perfect place for such a group of intense individuals, who were always destined to be off the commercial radar.

Thankfully, while also being the year the majors regained the initiative, 1979 was proving to be a year rich in regional diversity. If a John

Peel session was no longer the route to a record deal, and the London punk clubs were too scary for your average A&R person, the provinces were now producing most of the interesting progressive punk bands. Rather than continuing the flood of one-off singles which sank without trace, many bands began to contribute to regional anthologies, of which Brighton's *Vaultage '78*, Liverpool's *Street To Street* (originally called *World Shut Your Mouth – Don't Be A Twat Sunday!*) and *A Manchester Collection* proved the pick of the bunch.

Even here, among the Grand Cru of regional vintages, there was a sense that many of these bands had been caught just in time. Though *Vaultage '78* went into a second and third pressing, and produced pop possibilities for the Piranhas, the most original cuts came from all-girl outfit, Devil's Dykes (the hypnotic 'Plastic Flowers', that band name, and credits that include 'costumes from Resource Centre jumble sales', say it all) and The Vitamins ('New town, honey, so alone / New town, so fuck off home'), neither of whom lasted long enough to feature on *Vaultage '79*, an abject affair.

A Manchester Collection (subtitled 'Bands of the Manchester Musicians Collective') could have been the first hard evidence that the Collective was providing a sounding-board for more than The Fall and Warsaw, save that The Passage had already prefaced it with their own sonorous EP. If the likes of Grow-Up, I.Q. Zero and Fast Cars had been built along Buzzcocks-like lines, Mediaters managed to match the spirit of The Fall's 'Repetition' with their absurd 'Monotony', while FT Index produced the best white man's reggae-protest song this side of the Irwell Delta, 'Working On The Line'. As to the method of recording, it was much the same as other Object Music releases.

Dick Witts: Each band had fifteen minutes in a recording studio. You had to get in there and do it, and you had to get out for the next band. Just enough time to go bang-bang-bang, get some sort of sound level, and then do a couple of numbers.

Meanwhile, *Street To Street*, caught the last vestiges of Liverpool's first wave of bands, including the legendary Big In Japan in instrumental guise; The Id, who by the time the LP appeared had mutated into Orchestral Manoeuvres in the Dark (OMD); a band called Tontrix, who broke up after recording their one and only song, 'Clear On Radar'; and – presciently positioned as last of Eric's own crop – Echo

& the Bunnymen, whose demo of 'Monkeys' had been recorded some months before their 'Pictures On My Wall' single, but still appeared on LP three months after that record became *NME*'s Single Of The Week.

Further evidence that the previously latent Liverpudlian punk scene had spent two years steeling itself for post-punk and/or stealing some synthesizers, came with another single issued in May 1979. Somewhat impertinently, 'Electricity' was on the Manchester indie label, Factory. OMD's entry into post-punk annals was a perfect record for Factory to release, were it not from a bunch of Scousers. Their pop sensibility ensured that by the time they found the charts with 'Messages', the following May, OMD would be on their own properly distributed DinDisc label.

With the departure of OMD, Factory could at last concentrate on the Mancunian music scene. Tony Wilson, Factory's founder, still pictured himself in the Bob Last mould; and his approach to setting up Factory mirrored much that Last had done with Fast Product. Wilson fully admitted as much when talking to Ian Wood in March 1980, shortly before Ian Curtis's death changed his worldview.

Tony Wilson: I realized that . . . Bob Last . . . had proved you could do it, it wasn't all that difficult [to set up a label] . . . So we started off there, thinking we'd put out a sampler and see what happened . . . Manchester, I knew, was the most important musical city in the world, more vibrant than London. And . . . it needed a new label! . . . My mother left me some money and some unit trusts. The sampler cost £3,600 altogether, and I then left the proceeds in the kitty and sold the unit trusts to pay for the recording of Joy Division's album . . . The [idea] was to put out an album . . . which would be in its own way as successful and important as Stiff Little Fingers, which in many ways it is. [1980]

A fierce regionalist, Wilson was highly dismissive of 'those idiots in London' (his term for the major labels in August 1979). He saw Factory as 'an attack on the music business – to show them that *we* do what *you're* supposed to do a lot better [than you do] . . . and that's why we want to get in the charts . . . I'm playing with pop culture.' The first one now will later be Last. Even if it had taken all of his powers of persuasion to convince Joy Division to remain in the chill Mancunian air. By January 1979, when Curtis spoke to *NME*'s Paul Morley, it was clear that the band was anxious to clock in.

Ian Curtis: We'd like to stay on the outside. [And] we'd love it if Tony Wilson said he'd pay us to do an album on Factory . . . We can't afford to do it ourselves . . . but you either stay outside the system or go in totally, and try and change it. [1979]

Financing an entire album from Wilson's income as a TV presenter, and the odd bequest, obliged Joy Division to hang fire until the returns on *A Factory Sampler* were in. The *Sampler*, released the previous November, was bolstered by two of their tracks – 'Glass' and 'Digital' – which according to Factory's press release were 'typical Div with bass heavy stomping rhythms and menacingly dark sounds . . . threaten[ing] to burn through the speakers if you so much [as] breathed whilst it played'.

In fact, these October 1978 Martin Hannett recordings were hardly typical of that period Joy Division. A comparison with takes of the same songs recorded five months later by Martin Rushent, for a possible record deal with one of Factory's rivals, Genetic, shows that Rushent caught a lot more of the band's live sound – splintered guitars on a bed of rock.

However, just as the band bought into Wilson's spiel, so Wilson bought into Hannett's, and it was Hannett who was assigned the task of capturing Joy Division on their (second) debut album, to be recorded at state-of-the-art Strawberry Studios in Stockport, built on the proceeds of local boys 10cc's lucrative chart career. Given the precarious financial nature of the Factory operation, the choice of both studio and producer was curious indeed. The former was probably the most expensive studio in the northwest, and Hannett's working methods – as Howard Devoto could have told Wilson – were hardly conducive to cost-cutting.

Howard Devoto: Martin tried to adopt a kind of mystical role, where he didn't communicate with you much . . . I'm not sure that when he was working with engineers, they'd got much confidence in him . . . Martin did his mysterious stuff, hunched up with the engineer, and you'd vaguely hear, 'You just can't do that.' . . . [But] once you've got a recorded sound, and you've got Hannett squeezing the sound like he did, then you've got something very characteristic – which you're [then] referring to when you see [the band] live. As someone who saw Warsaw and then the early stages of Joy Division, I [still] wonder if there [really] was a quantum leap.

If Hannett had engineers reaching for their revolvers, the band were no nearer to understanding the methods of the man Wilson had put in charge. Peter Hook told Pat Gilbert about how he 'talked to you like a mad professor. He'd say, "Make it softer but harder. Wider but not too wide." "Jesus, it's only a fucking bass line, Martin!"' Perhaps, like another Martin, he fancied himself as the 'fifth' member of (what he hoped would be) the most important band of the era.

Certainly, this was the view of journalist Paul Rambali, who in a *Trouser Press* retrospective suggested that 'Martin Hannett . . . defined Joy Division's sound to a large extent. He's obsessed with electronics; he'd buy all the latest equipment he could get his hands on. He'd arrive at the studio with these big boxes, hook them up and start recording.' The problem – as C. P. Lee suggests – was that what Hannett really cared about was how to 'manufacture sound as he heard it in his head – and he was obsessive about that'. He wasn't very good at hearing how others wanted *their* music to sound.

At times, Hannett clearly supposed Joy Division's music to be his own creation. He told Martin Aston in 1989, shortly before his death, that 'Joy Division were from the north side of Manchester. It's a science-fiction city. Not like the south side, at all. It's all industrial archaeology, chemical plants, warehouses, canals, railways, roads that don't take any notice of the areas they traverse.' What he meant was that *he* was from this science-fiction city (which was part north Manchester, part back cover of *The Modern Dance*). Curtis and Morris were from the verdant valleys of Cheshire. With Hannett at the helm, Joy Division's Bernard Sumner realized he had 'inflicted this dark, doomy mood over [every-thing] . . . We resented it, but . . . the press loved it, and the public loved it . . . We swallowed our pride and went with it.'

For some, this was New Musick eighteen months late. Now on the inside track, having relocated to Manchester, Jon Savage proclaimed *Unknown Pleasures* 'a brave bulletin, a danceable dream; brilliantly, a record of place. Of one particular place: Manchester . . . [But] Joy Division are vulnerable to any success the album may bring – once the delicate relationship with environment is altered or tampered with, they may never produce anything as good again.' Max Bell at *NME* compared the album favourably with the 'German experimentalists' (i.e. Can and Neu) and *Strange Days*-era Doors.

Only *Sounds*' Dave McCullough found Hannett's ice-age sound a tad chilly: 'The black, over-seriousness denies any real, life-like communication and [what we] are left with is by its very nature a contrived, engineered set of songs.' It would be hard to argue that *Unknown Pleasures* is anything but 'a contrived, engineered set of songs'. The question is whether the sound Hannett gave these lads was an asset or a curse. Anyone who had the good fortune to see the band in the first nine months of 1979, when the instruments were still doing the talking, would probably aver that it was a curse.

Another 'northern' band with a surfeit of ex-public-school pupils, also making their own 'contrived, engineered set of songs' at much the same time, had relocated to London to do the deed. But the Gang of Four needed little help from EMI in-house producer Rob Warr to get the ultra-austere sound they had in mind. Two years on, their capacity to translate ideas into sound was still founded on the virtues of exclusion. By stripping the sound bare, they hoped to make an overtly modernistic projection of a particular path down which punk could yet travel.

Andy Gill: Although I used feedback, I was using Solid State amplifiers, and the distortion was reined in. We'd had years of listening to reggae. We didn't want to do reggae – we wanted to do loud guitars. But as a rhythm, like building blocks of riffs. I wanted a harsh, angular, clipped approach to take it away from clichéd rock posturings . . . The drumming was basically funky, but not through copying various icons of black music, more through simply deconstructing the nature of drumming, and where you place the beats. It was like starting from ground zero with the drumming. Hugo and I would argue endlessly about what the drum parts would be like. Anything that sounded like rock drumming, I would change . . . You could tell by listening to Gang of Four music that punk had happened, but it definitely wasn't punk music.

Their experience with Fast had convinced the Four by the end of 1978 that they should look at what the major labels had to offer. Jon King says he doesn't 'know whether we should have gone for the money or not . . . [but] we just wanted to be artistically in control'. In a November 1978 article referring to the Four's search for a label, Hugo Burnham cited 'the Sandy Pearlman affair with The Clash' as 'an example to us of what can happen' when one does not have 'control of things'. In the end they went with EMI, on the understanding that they had the final say on most 'things'.

The studio which got their vote, the Workhouse in London's Old Kent Road, was chosen because of *New Boots And Panties* (not your most obvious reference point), and was given a try-out when Gang of Four recorded its first EMI single, 'At Home He's A Tourist' b/w 'It's Her Factory', in March 1979. When the band reconvened for the sessions-proper in the summer, they decided to re-record 'Damaged Goods' and 'Anthrax' from the Fast EP, and this time *no* reverb. King believes they recorded the album 'in three weeks . . . Andy finished his degree, we went to Wales for a week and knocked a few ideas around, and then went in to do *Entertainment!'*

The album that resulted shared much of *Unknown Pleasures'* austerity, but the guitars had not been sacrificed at the altar of the producer's own ego. The Four also did not draw any ker-plunk noises from the Industrial Sound Effects For Post-Punk Producers library. Naked and unadorned, *Entertainment!* showed it didn't need to be just a game. If *Unknown Pleasures* would have a greater effect on the course of English post-punk, Gang of Four's EMI distribution meant that their reach was greater. And, like it or not, Wilson had picked on the wrong band to represent post-modern funk. These primary proponents of English post-punk, both cauterized in the cauldron of punk, were heading off in opposite directions.

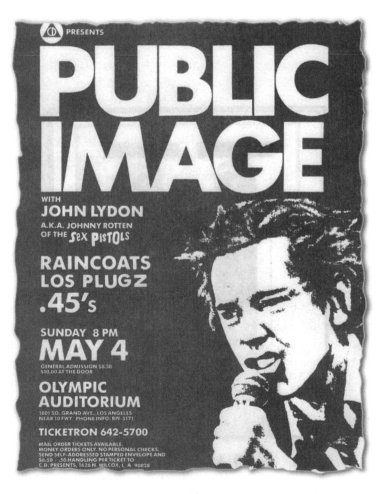

[The new bands] seem to be trying to reflect life as it really is . . . They're pressing against the globe, but they're never going to break out of it. When punk dies out, which it will in about two years, people like us will still be going.
— Genesis P. Orridge, *MM*, 20/11/76

I thought Teenage Jesus and the Jerks . . . were trying to sound so weird they were ordinary . . . Whereas I could watch the Prefects, who, in their own bumbling way, were doing something more weird . . . than anyone in New York.
— Colin Newman, to author, 2005

When Richard Meltzer dismissed Throbbing Gristle as 'your standard unpalatable racket' in New York's trendy weekly, *Village Voice*, he was preaching to the converted. By 1979, it had been over a year since the five boroughs had felt the charge of the 'no-wave' brigade – defined by the Eno-produced *No New York* album, and the artists thereon, Teenage Jesus & the Jerks, DNA, Mars and James Chance and The Contortions – as well as the SoHo bands like Theoretical Girls overlooked by Eno. Like Throbbing Gristle, all of these bands had a theoretical basis with which to bolster their own unpalatable rackets, an arty background and in certain important cases, a solid background of musical training they preferred to reject.

Lee Ranaldo: In that early period, everybody that moved to New York, like Arto [Lindsay] and Mark Cunningham from Mars, and Glenn [Branca], were theatre people, painters [and] writers. There was this homogeneous community – it was intellectuals exchanging ideas. A lot of these artists fell into music because a) it was something you grew up loving, b) it was easy to fall into. [So] you were taking your art school and applying it to this new discipline . . . All the no-wave groups were completely different, and the things that they have in common are very formalist things, stripping music that we all grew up on down to these very primal elements. The drummer in Lydia's group had one drum. That's exactly what was happening in the art world.

Tom Verlaine has talked about the 'two periods' to the New York new wave, commencing with 'bands that were in New York, that played there'; followed a year or two later by 'bands that came to New York, decided to live there and played there'. He wasn't just thinking of Talking Heads. There was an entire school of art-rockers coming to town. Many of these folk arrived after the fact – turning up at CBGB's and Max's just as the likes of Blondie, Television and the Ramones stopped frequenting the Bowery. As Trudie Arguelles told Brendan Mullen, 'When I travelled to New York during the summer of '77, Patti Smith and Television and the Ramones had already been the big thing for a while. It just didn't seem as much of an exciting, new, growing thing – it had already happened.'

If Arguelles elected to try her luck in LA, one would-be punk who arrived in New York during the winter of 1976 from the mundane municipality of Milwaukee – calling himself James Chance (né Siegfried) – caught some glowing embers of that first blaze. Despite his jazz background, Chance was particularly taken by the Heartbreakers: 'I liked their whole style. They were just such an ultimate rock & roll band with Hell. After Hell left they kind of devolved into a caricature of what they were before.'

Even when back in Milwaukee, Chance had been reading the *Voice* and noticed 'these little ads for CBGB . . . it [always] looked interesting.' So he headed straight for the place when he arrived in town. At a Ramones/Heartbreakers gig he found his first New York girlfriend, Nancy Arlin, also his first connection to the nascent 'no wave' – she played drums in a band called China, who later moved to Mars. Chance was no musical novice, having studied music at a conservatory in Wisconsin while – in his spare time – playing in a band which sounded like a cross between the Electric Eels and Tin Huey.

James Chance: I had . . . the first free-jazz group in Milwaukee – and I was also in this band called Death, which was a Stooges/Velvet Underground-type band. I would come out at the end of the show . . . like a Steve McKay-type thing. The lead singer killed himself. That was another reason I wanted to get out of Milwaukee . . . This was '73, '74 and there was just nowhere for us to play. It started out as a club band doing Velvets and Stooges covers – that was before I played the sax . . . We also had a contingent of dancers who would take over the dance floor . . . and the singer . . . dyed his hair silver and he put this silver glitter all over his face . . . He called himself Sterling Silver . . . We had some gigs opening for Dr John, but then after that . . . the only gigs we had were two high-school graduation parties. One of them was for his girlfriend's high school – the audience . . . were too stunned to be mad.

Arriving on the eastern seaboard, Chance wasn't sure whether to pursue his 'free-jazz' muse or to continue hanging out 'down at the rock & roll club'. For a while, he even tried to juggle these two quite different disciplines: 'When I first got to New York I had a jazz group that did a few of these loft gigs, and I was even doing some of that shit [like] jumping in the audience . . . Jazz people were so uptight at that time – they liked this adventurous music, but their whole attitude in . . . other ways was so square – so first I wandered around and sat in weird places on the stage, and then I did this leap with the saxophone . . . [The band] was [called] Flaming Youth after an old Duke Ellington song . . . [but] it sounded like a heavy-metal band.'

His distaste for the jazz *scene* – rather than the music, which he continued to dig – eventually got the better of Chance, 'I just was bored with the idea of people standing up there and not having any theatrical element . . . I was hanging around more and more at Max's and CBGB's, and I could see that the jazz thing wasn't going to go anywhere – there were just too many jazz musicians all trying to make it, all good musicians . . . it wasn't going to happen. But then at CBGB's, at the beginning, I didn't know anybody . . . and I got a real chip on my shoulder . . . [Frankly] I thought Death was better than most of them.' Nothing came together until he met lunatic princess Lydia Lunch (née Koch), a sixteen-year-old cocktail waitress and another out-of-towner, who turned up at CBGB's later in 1976, as NY punk made its last death rattle, The Dead Boys now often being the best the Bowery could offer.

James Chance: The way I met Lydia was she was dancing by herself in the aisle at CBGB's to The Dead Boys . . . and I just went up to her and started talking to her. She'd just come here from Rochester . . . She showed me this thing she had written – this long prose poem – and it was really good . . . By this time I had my own apartment on Second between A and B and [it] cost like $115 – it had black walls and a red ceiling and the windows were all boarded up . . . on the top floor of this fifth-floor walk-up. One night my doorbell rang and it was Lydia. She needed a place to stay. So we lived together [for] a year . . . [But] she wasn't my girlfriend . . . She had a whole list of people in bands that she wanted to fuck, and she went down the list . . . I think she got all of them. She was very aggressive . . . Anyway, she started playing me these songs . . . She couldn't play any chords, she would just bang out this atonal accompaniment to the vocals. I think most people would have said, 'Forget it.' But I actually encouraged her.

Lunch already had her own agenda, partially related to that list of people 'she wanted to fuck'. She wanted to make a splash. To be someone, she felt, would be a wonderful thing. When a documentary crew turned up at CBGB's in early 1977 to film The Dead Boys, she could barely contain herself, proudly proclaiming that The Dead Boys had named a song after her, 'I Need Lunch' (the opposite seems more likely).

Over time Lydia's love for the CBGB's bands – which had, after all, compelled her to go there – has diminished in her eyes. By 2004 she could claim to Simon Reynolds that 'everything [which] had influenced me up to that point I found too traditional – whether it was Patti Smith, The Stooges, [or] Lou Reed's *Berlin* . . . I felt there had to be something more radical. It's got to be *disembowelled*.' In truth, she came from classic punk stock; i.e. lacking in even the most basic technique, versed in a particular strain of US underground rock, utterly determined to have her say, but without the means to communicate anything save angst. To this day, Lunch isn't sure whether she views punk as an attitude or an art-form.

Lydia Lunch: Punk can be an attitude or a fashion statement or a lousy, three-chord music. Take your pick. I always thought I was anti-punk. I got lumped in with punk because I wore black and I dyed my hair. I thought punk was lousy Chuck Berry music amped up to play triple fast. I didn't like the chord structure, or that they used chords. I thought it was really too much orientated towards fashion. A lot of the groups that were in New York were diversifying more and trying to find a new genre – groups like Mars or DNA or the Contortions . . . I think *that* [scene] was very anti-punk. When I think of punk, I think of the Sex Pistols and The Clash. But . . . those are *rock* bands. [PSF]

With the encouragement of Chance, Lunch persevered with her atonal yowling. But she was still not sure a place existed for her – until she saw Mars, who sounded like that's where they came from, and were busy compiling a soundtrack to *The War of the Worlds*. Lunch was now 'very encouraged. They were so dissonant, so obviously insane. There were no compromises or concessions to anything that had existed previously.' But Chance didn't think the world was quite ready for the full three-course Lunch, so began performing some of the songs Lydia had played him with another downtown band, the Screws – renamed The Scabs specifically for this purpose. It was here that Chance first crossed paths with the versatile Jody Harris, who would help him with later musical contortions.

James Chance: The Screws mostly played in SoHo and Tribeca. It was Jody Harris, Donny Christianson [and] bass player David Hostra. And a singer. I used to sit in with them. They played once a week in this bar in Tribeca . . . I used Donny's studio to rehearse my jazz band, [which] I still had all through '77 . . . [This was also the] period where I tried to have a band with me and Lydia, doing my material. I had her singing some of the early songs that I had, like 'Dish It Out' and 'Roving Eye'. It was Jody on guitar and Wreck on bass.

The Scabs, though, became surplus to requirements when Lydia decided her landlord had got things the wrong way round – they should be doing *her* songs, with the spotlight firmly on *her*. If recent statements can be believed, Lunch had awfully high ambitions for the band she now formed with Chance, the cathartic but cacophonous Teenage Jesus & the Jerks: 'It was almost as if my job was to dispute the "alternative" that had already been established. Although . . . the groups that had originally made me want to go to New York – and which originally had made me run away at fourteen to go and investigate – . . . attracted me there, I wanted to create something that would completely divorce myself from that, break away and shoot forward.' A familiar refrain; made possible thanks to Chance. And New York, circa '77.

Lydia Lunch: [New York] was glorious. It was a mass insane asylum . . . It was easy to get by in 1977 . . . Obviously, I went there for a creative outlet and for the stuff that was coming out of there. I didn't go there to embrace what existed. My whole theory was to stick a thorn in every side that had come before me. I still found that a lot of things I was drawn to didn't go far enough, or were still too based in a tradition. [PSF]

New wave or no wave, Teenage Jesus came together in a familiar way. As Chance states, 'If you saw someone, or met someone, who looked like they should be in your band, it didn't matter if they could play or not . . . We saw this Japanese couple . . . And then Bradley Field came here from Cleveland . . . Lydia had this idea of having him play a cymbal and a snare drum . . . It was totally Lydia's concept. All I did was come up with a saxophone part, and go along with what was going on . . . I used to sing one song with Teenage – "Jaded" – that was my big moment. But Lydia had this thing of wanting the music to be really severe and stripped down.'

The original Teenage Jesus were severe enough for Lester Bangs to compare it to the noise made when 'guys in my sixth-grade neighbour-hood used to entertain themselves by tying the head of a cat to one hot-rod fender and its tail to another, and driving the cars apart slowly.' Lydia had her own explanation – given in 1979 – of what Teenage Jesus had been intended to represent: 'You punched people on the head with the sound. The audience is either going to say, "Ugh," and leave quickly, or they're going to be masochistic and want to be punched again.'

By the summer of 1977, Teenage Jesus were playing the downtown clubs, either in tandem with Mars, or with the residue of bands they intended to leave in the dust. The one band who remained spiritual godfathers to no wave, Suicide, were still part of the Max's scene; and it was here that Teenage Jesus found their true home. Peter Crowley continued to book the bands and, as Chance recalls, 'Crowley really liked the whole no wave. If it wasn't for him we wouldn't have had hardly any work. But . . . Hilly [Kristal] did not get [it].'

Disturbed Furniture's Phil Shoenfelt suggests that 'the no-wave bands were far more monochromatic [than Suicide] . . . This out-of-towner element, combined with their more ascetic instincts, tends to make me see them more in the family tree of bands like Pere Ubu and Rocket from the Tombs.' In fact, the no-wave scene had more than just a stylistic connection to the Cleveland scene. Parts of Ohio seemed to be emptying by 1977, in the wake of The Dead Boys' relocation; while an April 1976 Ubu show and July 1977 Devo residency at Max's reinforced the idea that Ohio art-rock was always welcome there.

When psychobilly's Ohio offshoot, The Cramps, realized they were fish out of the Cuyahoga and would be better off in New York, they helped bring Cleveland's art-rock into contact with its cacophonous cousins. Sharing rehearsal space with Mars and the early Teenage Jesus, they ended up introducing their friend, Bradley Field, to Lydia and James. Field had the necessary interest in horrible noise, and was willing to bang his drum.

Mars also brought another band into the clique. DNA were formed by Arto Lindsay and Robin Crutchfield, the latter of whom had some unique ideas about the relationship between maths and music: 'I was an artist before this, so I relate to the piano sculpturally, pretty much in patterns of black and white, in groups of two and three keys, and I see these symmetrical patterns on the piano . . . Sometimes it doesn't sound good to the ear, but it's a real nice geometrical pattern I'm using.'

Lindsay, a friend of Mars, had been watching them make their mark, and helping them with their equipment, when he was approached by Terry Ork.

Arto Lindsay: He asked me if I had a band. 'Oh sure,' I said, even though I didn't have a band. He asked me if I wanted to play the next week and I said, 'How about next month?' . . . I just went out and got a band, cobbled one together. Ikue Mori was living here . . . She never played an instrument, but I liked her and I invited her to play drums. [And] there was a guy called Robin Crutchfield, who was a performance artist – very . . . striking looking. I thought it would make a great outfit. I wanted to do something really extreme. I thought that was the route to success, which didn't turn out to be true . . . I very consciously wanted to do something that was very different from Mars, because we were all very close . . . They were more of a Velvets/Roxy [Music] sounding band so I wanted to do something that was very angular, involving a lot of starting and stopping . . . the opposite of what they did. [PSF]

If punk proved anything, it was that two bands might be a coincidence, but three bands is a scene. Suddenly, local critics began to talk about this as the sound to supersede punk-rock. And the bands were happy to provide obligatory anti-rock rants. Chance, in particular, provided good copy, telling *New York Rocker* in 1978, 'I don't identify with any kind of group, or anything like rock & roll. That's just another example of maudlin sentimentality – people having this big love affair with rock & roll. I have nothing to do with rock & roll.'

By then, Lydia and James had parted company. Chance claims it was Lunch who wanted a change, 'She decided that she didn't want me in the band any more. She [said she] wanted the sound to be more minimal. I don't know if it was strictly a musical thing, or if she was threatened because I was getting some of the attention. [But] after Lydia kicked me out of Teenage Jesus, I decided to start my own band. I still had the idea of having a girl singer, [and] for a while I had Alan Vega's girl-friend. She had a little homemade synthesizer . . . Then I had another girl . . . Finally I said, "To hell with these girls, I'll just sing." I decided if Richard Hell can do it, I can do it.' The band Chance now formed, the fabled Contortions, were not as abrasive as Teenage Jesus; but included one more Cleveland conspirator, Adele Bertei, who co-founded Laughner's last band, Peter and the Wolves, before coming to Manhattan.

James Chance: I wanted something danceable that would communicate to more of an audience than just these arty types. It wouldn't be such a high concept as Teenage Jesus . . . I wanted it to be completely uncompromising, but I didn't want to make it so 'out there' that it had no chance at all . . . After Lydia left the storefront, she and Bradley got a place on Delancey . . . I met Adele there . . . She'd been in bands in Cleveland . . . I told her she was going to play organ.

The first Contortions gig was 4 December 1977 at Max's. Initially, though, the line-up was extremely fluid, with Chance and Bertei holding their musical work-outs together. At various stages it also featured a Japanese drummer, a British lead guitarist and the drummer from Chance's jazz band, Steve Moses. Little Moses played just a single gig, but it was where The Contortions found an important new convert.

James Chance: This benefit for *X* magazine [was] at some kind of hall in the East Village . . . The whole thing was so pretentious. At this gig they were actually sat on the floor, which was the one thing calculated to get me really mad – so I just waded into the audience and started pulling them up on to their feet, but that wasn't enough so I started smacking a couple of them . . . I worked my way to the back of the audience and I saw Anya Phillips back there . . . I thought should I attack her and I thought no, better not. I talked to her after the show. She said she really liked the band.

Whether Phillips felt more kinship with the band's music, or Chance's compulsive acts of confrontation, she knew everyone on the downtown scene; and, as Chance states, 'Because of Anya . . . we start[ed] to headline. She was really respected and she'd been there from the very beginning.' Chance, meanwhile, was (over?) compensating for a previous self-consciousness onstage by becoming increasingly physical, determined to make people love or hate the band. Bertei thinks Chance was displaying 'a strong masochistic streak . . . He'd jump into the crowd and start kissing some girl. The boyfriend would push him off and a fist-fight would ensue . . . James, being [always] the worst for wear . . . would get the brunt of it.' Bertei and bassist George Scott would often have to jump in. Indeed, she increasingly felt that the band should be James Chance and The Distractions, as the music became increasingly sidelined.

James Chance: I did a gig with a horrible band from England called Crass in a big gym-type place that you could rent out. That was another one where I attacked people ... I remember Adele saying to me after that gig, 'You're pimping the band.' I hated Crass. They were some quasi-fascist thing that was supposed to [contain] some kind of irony ... [But] the New York bands were not imitating English punk, [well not] until much later ... It wasn't shocking to us. Swastikas and safety pins and chains – big deal – [even if] I liked the pure energy of it.

Chance's antic disposition was not overly selective. He would challenge *anyone* in the audience. When *Punk* writer Legs McNeil started heckling one time, he jumped on him. Likewise, he decided that the self-styled dean of New York rock critics, Robert Christgau, was due an introduction – and took the opportunity at a festival of 'no-wave' bands in May 1978. Roy Trakin's review in *New York Rocker* suggested Chance – or maybe the audience – got the worst of it:

Mr Chance immediately established his personal space at the top of his performance by kicking out all those artist-types sitting cross-legged within about a six-foot radius of his band, as he snarled and smirked with unmerciful obnoxiousness ... [until] 'Dean' Robert Christgau ... found himself on the floor in a fierce imbroglio with James Chance ... The aroused rock crit admirably acquitted himself by pummelling the lead Contortion into bloody submission ... [However,] the music featured ... was [so] aggressively ugly, often gratingly so ... [that] it is difficult to imagine an American audience ... being attracted to this kind of melodic chaos. It is a sound akin to the mutilated narrative in literature.

The festival, held at SoHo's Artist Space over five nights in early May, yielded a promise from Brian Eno – ever attentive to challenging new sounds – to make a sampler album documenting this atonal adjunct to New York's new wave. In fact, the 'no-wave' scene seemed to have dramatically expanded in the past six months, and the original quartet of bands – bound by mutual relations – found themselves beset by other art-rockers experimenting with noise.

If Terminal, Tone Death and The Gynecologists were formed with obscurity in mind, Glenn Branca's Theoretical Girls could easily have joined the 'no-wave' camp, having been formed by an arty out-of-towner with a musical background, who created a band interested in 'just trying every possible idea that came to our minds. We really didn't care what the audience thought. And all of a sudden we had this . . . audience that was coming from the art world.'

But the original no-wave bands were the ones that piqued Eno's interest, and they were not wild about the idea of sharing their chance with anyone from the wrong side of Houston Street. As Arto Lindsay suggests, 'We very deliberately kept the *No New York* record to just those bands. We thought it would make sense and it was a little bit of a turf thing – we convinced Eno that Glenn Branca's band shouldn't be on the record.' The result, as Sonic Youth's Lee Ranaldo recalls, was that *No New York* 'created a heavy schism in the New York scene, because of who he chose and who he didn't.'

There was probably a certain inverted snobbery underlying the decision to exclude Branca, whom the others considered very much part of the 'art' scene, not the 'rock' scene. A theatre major from Harrisburg, and founder of Boston's Bastard Theater, Branca thinks, 'They thought we were . . . "art fags".' If Theoretical Girls liked to play places like the Kitchen and Rhys Chatham's place, Arto Lindsay's DNA refused to play somewhere like the Kitchen, because it was an art-crowd and 'we avoided situations where we would have an audience more easily . . . We wanted to play to *people* at places like CBGB's and Max's.' And the original no-wave bands had Eno's ear because of Anya Phillips, ever on the inside.

James Chance: Anya was having this kind of affair with [Eno] . . . I met him through Anya a couple of times even before he heard the band . . . One morning, Adele and Pat knocked on my door . . . and said, 'This is it. We're doing it today.' And we went over and recorded it . . . all in one session . . . It was a nice pretty good studio in SoHo. [But] we set it up in such a way like we were doing a live gig. He didn't even put me in a booth . . . everything [was] leaking on to the other tracks, and [we] just played the songs like we were doing a gig. Except for 'Can't Stand Myself'. That was kind of improvised in the studio . . . At the end I wanted to redo a part of the vocals, but it was impossible . . . I guess he did that on purpose. It was more like an anti-production method.

Eno subsequently implied to Lester Bangs that 'he deliberately mixed them muddy, hoping to reproduce the lazy kineticism of The Velvet Underground.' But he also managed to capture the 'raw, feral intensity' of these bands at the point of critical mass. By the release of *No New York* in November 1978 the bands were already evolving into something less noisesome; or deciding that those with the shortest fuses burn brightest. Before the following spring, Mars and Theoretical Girls considered their job done. Teenage Jesus were also ready to call it a day, though not before enjoying a brief, introductory tour of Europe.

Lydia Lunch: All the 'no-wave' bands just self-destructed. They were all so concise in the music, the delivery, the point and they just ended. It wasn't a premature death, it was an immediate and accurate one.

For DNA and The Contortions, the end was not so immediate. Lindsay and Chance were less in love with the idea of 'premature death'. In both cases, they replaced those mainstays of their sound disinclined to pursue new directions, as Robin Lee Crutchfield quit DNA and Adele Bertei left The Contortions at the end of 1978. Lindsay recruited the man who had told the *Cleveland Plain Dealer*, back in December 1975, that he was 'going beyond commercialism . . . going beyond music'. Tim Wright had been co-founder of Pere Ubu with Laughner and Thomas. Quitting Ubu shortly after Laughner, Wright had disappeared into the dark regions of South America, but returned in time to help Lindsay record the final word on the no-wave sound, the *A Taste Of DNA* EP. By then, Lindsay had formed The Lounge Lizards, an equal and opposite reaction to no wave that eventually took over from his failing trio.

Chance, meanwhile, debuted a more soulful alter-ego, James White, at Club 57 on 2 February 1979. At the time, he intended to keep The Contortions going – much as he had kept practising those jazz scales while the original Teenage Jesus were scratching blackboards. But his attempt to record both a disco album, as James White and the Blacks, and a Contortions album, *Buy*, resulted The Contortions' demise in any meaningful sense, and a new solo career for Chance. In the end the *Buy* album was completed with a little help from session men, who resembled ex-Contortionists.

James Chance: Michael Zilker, a rich kid [whose] family owns the Mothercare stores in England, came to town . . . He wanted to start ZE Records and he wanted to sign The Contortions . . . but he also . . . wanted me to do a disco album . . . Anya came up with the name James White and the Blacks . . . We spent most of the money doing the first side of the album . . . so I just did instrumentals for the other side. That was totally uncompromising . . . The idea was to put out The Contortions' album at the same time . . . but by this time there was tension in the band . . . We were all making pretty good money at Max's for the time . . . As soon as people started making money, then they all started fighting over money, and resenting that Anya got anything because she was my girlfriend . . . There was [also] tensions between Jody and Don, who were trained musicians, and [the] other [non-musicians] . . . We had recorded a whole album's worth of songs. [But] George's attitude was so bad. He would stand there with these bad vibes just wafting off him like a cloud . . . so the next session . . . without even playing it for them to see if they would agree, I just said the tracks are no good, we're going to do it over and they all just walked out. Jody and Donny came back, but George didn't.

By the time *Buy The Contortions* appeared, in 1980, the no-wave scene had lost any forward impetus; and the locals seemed more interested in travelling bands, usually ones from over the pond, where those trying to redeem rock had not entirely sunk into apostasy. When *NME* sent Max Bell to New York in the summer of 1980, to report on the local music scene, he concluded that New Yorkers 'now appear . . . indifferent to . . . local talent. The British Invasion 1977 style has had much to do with this uncertainty. The clubs resound to imported sounds . . . The least convincing groups are apt to ape their British counterparts with an attention to lifestyle that is hilariously misguided, while the genuinely inspiring and aspiring New York bands struggle to make headway.'

— — —

Since February 1979, New York had received a steady stream of UK bands providing first-hand evidence that the hoopla was justified. In that month, both The Clash and The Only Ones gave New York their all, and were received rapturously – even if New York was just the gateway to the west, and the rest of America proved a tougher nut to crack.

John Perry: We were surprised how well known we were [on the East Coast]. We got there, and people knew the songs. If the whole of America had gone the way Boston, New York and Philadelphia had gone, we'd have broken it . . . but once you got outside that area . . . people really didn't have a clue.

Strummer believed that hard work was the key. As he wrote in his *NME* account of their dozen-date Pearl Harbor tour, 'To break, crack, storm or blitz America, you have to work as hard as Elvis Costello, shake hands and smile like The Boomtown Rats, and sound like Dire Straights [sic]. Of the three, we could make the first, but not the rest.' Their February shows, though, were little more than a fly-past. Yet in the few punk havens that existed, writers like LA-based Mikal Gilmore questioned their goals, getting Strummer's stop-gap retort, 'We've got loads of contradictions for you. We're trying to do something new; we're trying to be the greatest group in the world, and that also means the biggest. At the same time . . . we aim to keep punk alive.'

The contradictions were now tearing at the seams of their carefully stencilled jackets. Having made all sorts of compromises in order to get a domestic US release of album # 2, they now allowed CBS to issue another LP that was little more than product to peddle while The Clash passed through. This US edition of the first Clash album was almost a throwback to those travesties US labels perpetrated on The Beatles and the Stones pre-*Sgt Pepper*, comprising little more than half of the correct album, book-ended by random singles and B-sides from the post-*Clash* canon.

Evidence, were it required, that The Clash were now prepared to play the game could be found in their choice of Caroline Coon as their new manager. Coon was of the opinion that 'it was getting very big. One had no idea it was going to get so big . . . [but] my feeling is [Rhodes] would rather have seen The Clash break up than [him] not be able to handle it.' Rhodes probably just realized that the contradictions were bound to come out in the wash, once the Coon-led Clash decided to capitalize on America's love for rhetoric-wrapped rock. CBS were happy enough with their new recruits, who had come through their punk training with flying colours. The Clash proved to be a surprisingly malleable band to market. Even when they refused to meet CBS employees backstage in LA, it proved little more than a newsworthy nod to punk values.

During these 1979 shows cartoonist Ray Lowry, who was there at the band's behest, felt that 'something was . . . being lost in the sheer grind of getting up onstage night after night . . . [even if] Joe and the boys still had remnants of that ferocious intensity . . . they'd embodied a couple of years earlier.' John Perry, who was in New York with The Only Ones and caught the fabled February Palladium gig, offers a less circumspect assessment: 'By that time they were a good rock & roll band – [though] not as good as the Pistols in '76 – but at the expense of everything they claimed to stand for.'

Like The Clash, The Only Ones were only sparring with the Yankees that winter, returning in September to make a proper fist of it. This time they had tour-support on the 26-date trek, though they were also obliged to accept another idiotic, CBS-induced idea. Exercising their contractual clout, the US label decided to issue a single-album 'sampler' (*Special View*) drawn from the first two UK albums – rather than releasing the second UK album, *Even Serpents Shine*, which would have been a flaming torch next to the post-*Rumours* cold cuts being marketed domestically by the snow-blind majors. Unfortunately, the experience of that US tour proved particularly dispiriting to Only One Peter Perrett, who seemed in danger of giving up before the final curtain.

John Perry: It seemed to me there came a point with The Only Ones where he became disillusioned. I think he had rather a simplistic view of how it would go – bang, bang, bang, bang, we'd be huge. And it seemed to me that, after that, he didn't really write any great songs.

Drummer Mike Kellie has a simpler explanation: 'Peter . . . just got too stoned and nobody slapped him.' By the time The Only Ones returned to the States again the following year, promoting their disappointing third album, *Baby's Got A Gun*, Perrett was in danger of losing the plot completely. Though not in charge of a gun, he was deemed to have been guilty of assault with a deadly weapon when he reversed at speed into an overly officious parking attendant in a multistorey car park in San Francisco. Thankfully, by the time the writ could be issued, he was already on the plane home. But for The Only Ones, it was the end. As fellow user, Nick Kent, told Perrett's biographer, '[Perrett] was a good-looking guy and he had everything too easy, and in the process, it had made him weak.' Kent knew what he was talking about.

If The Only Ones found breaking America an uphill task (with Perrett in the role of Sisyphus), others found the Americans energized by their post-punk sound. The problem for Perrett and his posse was that CBS 'knew' best. Other UK labels seemed more reluctant to thrust these bands on their American partners, perhaps because the bands themselves were distinctly antagonistic to American corporate values. When The Specials came west in 1980, Roddy Radiation discovered that 'America was still hippy land . . . The Chrysalis USA guys came in wearing suits and ties, smoking cigars . . . and Jerry just told them to fuck off. Most of the band joined in. They stopped pushing the record after that. But I must say it felt good.'

If Chrysalis caught a cold, their distributors, EMI, had already tested the temperature by sending Wire for a week of shows at CBGB's in July 1978. The locals were surprised to find that a UK punk band could play this hard, without doodling or delay. Indeed Lewis recalls audience-members coming up to him and saying, 'What's cool about you guys is you fucking rock – you ain't jocks, you know.' The following summer, Gang of Four followed in Wire's footsteps, venturing far enough inland to make an indelible impression.

Hugo Burnham: [The Americans] were taken aback [when we toured] because we fucking *rocked*, rather than standing around in long macs looking miserable, like your typical post-punk band. That's why we did so well in the US. The propensity to *rock out* is more ingrained in the young American psyche than in Europe. It's the same reason The Clash were so successful in America.

The Gang of Four were determined to break America, perhaps because Funk was so integral to their austerity. Either that, or Gill and King couldn't wait to show those New Yorkers who remembered them from the summer of '77 that they really were in a band. Initially, the Gang of Four had not signed a US deal, having seen the way that had worked out for others. Instead, they made their own way there, building an audience from the ground up.

Andy Gill: We recorded *Entertainment!* around May or June, 1979, and soon as we finished that, we went straight off to the States. We didn't have a deal for the States at that point. We signed to EMI, but it was for the rest of the world. We wanted to do another deal and get a bunch of money for that. It worked, but the downside was that it took quite a while longer . . . We went on tour in America in a little van, playing little clubs with a couple of hundred people. It grew from there.

The Gang of Four were unwittingly adopting someone else's template, Miles Copeland's. With Squeeze and The Police – two pop bands smart enough to wear skinny ties, while issuing catchy singles – Copeland had been flying to the States beforehand, hiring a truck big enough for the band, a roadie and a small backline, and then he went into the smaller towns and stopped any kid wearing a new-wave badge, or with a punk haircut, and asked about venues to play. Backtracking to the independent record shop, or the local college radio station, he would eventually find someone willing to promote an unknown English band with a new-wave feel. Genius.

It was also much the same criteria that allowed The Only Ones to sell out two shows in Minneapolis on their first tour, thanks to Peter Jesperson's independent record store, which for the past eighteen months had a policy of 'stop[ping] people from walking out the store without the [latest] Only Ones'. But whereas Jesperson's enthusiasm drove a tiny, local scene in a particularly cryogenic part of the midwest, Copeland extended the policy nationwide.

The problem was that in most places there were enough punks in town to fill a little club, but a theatre show was out of the question. Exceptions, even for England's finest, were still rare. As Sylvie Simmons wrote, in her February 1979 *Sounds* review of The Clash's Santa Monica show, 'In LA anything that doesn't make a big profit is considered neither art nor desirable. Little bands are pretty much banging heads against the brick wall. The so-called "new wave" scene is barely holding its own. That The Clash sold out the 3,000 capacity Santa Monica Civic Auditorium is a good sign, [but] the numbers were padded out by press and posers and probably members of every quasi-punk band in town.'

The only other 'punk' band capable of filling the smaller theatres in the larger cities were Public Image Ltd, who had Johnny Rotten, the backing of Warners and a lot of positive press preceding their first US tour in the spring of 1980. Arriving in New York for a 20 April show – having made their US debut just two days earlier – PiL found an audience not quite ready to give up on rock, and nonplussed by Lydon's repeated attempts to break down the divide between audience and artist, which extended as far as pulling a young kid onstage to sing 'Bad Baby', and handing the mike around the crowd during songs. When Lydon and Levene quit the stage after an hour, the rhythm section – Wobble and Atkins – played on, suggesting that the PiL corporate view was not necessarily shared by all employees.

Two weeks later, Public Image reached the West Coast, after zig-zagging across the midwest. In LA Lydon and Levene turned up at a hastily arranged press conference, where Lydon continued to preach the gospel of life after rock & roll, 'I think rock & roll is media manipulation and exploitation and corruptness and bullshit. I'm anti-anything to do with it. It's a vile culture that has to slide into the sea.'

At this point, neither Lydon nor Levene knew quite what to expect, though they presumably knew LA professed to have its own punk scene. They could have asked Clash roadie Johnny Green, who would have informed them that, 'LA's idea of punk was the Addams family. Its idea of dancing was to cram in as much angel dust as possible and do the Worm across the stage.' Or they could have read Greg Shaw's assessment of the place in an August 1979 *NME* feature: 'Punk was a totally English phenomenon and the kids here [in LA] are just kidding themselves that they're a part of it . . . A year ago they were a year behind England, now they're two years behind.' Finally, there was another feature, in a September '79 *Melody Maker*, in which Mark Williams depicted LA punk as 'a crude, white-knuckled swansong for apocalypse now . . . Not the gratuitously adolescent sound of the suburbs, [rather] it's a furious blast of accelerating decay.'

The following month Slash Records managed what no US indie label had achieved to date – issuing and distributing the debut album by the Germs (*GI*), even if label boss Bob Biggs considered, 'The marketing campaign for our artists [to be] put an ad in our paper and give it a great review. That was it. The ethics didn't bother me.' Biggs had committed himself to a Germs album with no illusions: 'It wasn't about musicality. It was about sheer aggression – a feeling that what you were hearing was not complicated by any poetic relationships.' When *GI* appeared in October, few outside the scene knew what to make of it, even if the man from Vom, Richard Meltzer, gave the Germs the benefit of the doubt in his splenetic *Village Voice* review:

Darby loses you by keeping everything basically at one overwhelming speed (super-overdrive) and when he slows things down in a song like 'Manimal' it's like he's got peanut-butter in his mouth anyway . . . Backed against as nasty a wall as ever there's been, you're left with SELF-DESTRUCTING CLUMSY UNMUZZLED HEAD-BANG DOGGEREL as the only language that's truly hokum-free.

Here was a band who had achieved a no-wave-like aesthetic by alternate means, down to that decelerated buzzsaw which resembled a school of gnats having a spat. With Darby as their Teenage Jesus, the Germs were LA's own Jerks. But they were three thousand miles away from any other point of reference; and *GI* was an impenetrable whirlpool of noise to most folk who heard it that fall.

It also seems to have sent a signal to the LAPD that it was time they put these headbangers out of commission. As Tony Montesion told Mullen, 'When the *GI* album came out, [and] the *LA Times* said they were the next Doors, . . . it seemed like, at every show after that, they couldn't get through three songs without cops showing up with dogs on short leashes . . . They'd unplug the equipment in the middle of a song. Darby would be on his knees onstage, going, "Don't let 'em do this." . . . He tried to inspire us to . . . trash the place.' But having already peered over the parapet, LA's punks knew what happened if they fought back. It had been back in March when they first tangled with the cops, at an Elks Lodge, St Patrick's Day punk all-nighter:

In addition to the [punk] concert, which featured some of the best LA new wave acts, including 'X', The Zeros, the Alley Cats, and the Go-Gos, the Elks Hall had also booked a wedding reception and a party of Vietnamese emigres in adjoining rooms. It was to prove a recipe for trouble. Kids from the concert, which attracted about 800 people, over-spilled into the lobby and the stair-well, dropping beer cans and Quaaludes and occasionally bad-mouthing wedding guests, the majority of whom were middle-aged and middle class. The confrontation between Punks and Straight America proved too much for the sensibilities of the off-duty cops moonlighting as security, and the riot squad was called in. [John Trux, 'Punks Riot in L.A.', *NME*, 31/3/79]

The Baton and Shield Squad called by 'the off-duty cops' went about teaching these punks some manners with relish, cracking skulls indiscriminately. By the end of 1979, the remnants of the punk scene realized that funtime was over. As Masque's master of ceremonies Brendan Mullen puts it, 'By early 1980 female attendance fell off at Germs (and other hardcore) shows, which had degenerated into bizarre post-pubescent all-male warrior bonding rituals with frequent inter-ventions by SWAT teams and helicopters . . . Most of the original Hollywood punkers either OD'd, went back to school or got jobs with their family businesses. Many turned to rockabilly.'

Mullen dates 'the end of Hollywood punk, and the final nail of the Naive Picnic Period' to a Christmas 1979 Germs show at the Whisky, where a 'horde of rabid ignoroids on the floor' took an altercation between Germs guitarist Pat Smear and the Whisky security staff 'as their cue to invade the stage . . . The show came to a shuddering halt with a dozen people brawling onstage before the Whisky management killed the stage lights.' It was the last time the Whisky gave punk-rock the time of day, and signalled a marked change in the demographics of any LA punk gig.

Lydon and his fellow directors of PiL were entirely unaware of this when they arrived at the Olympic Auditorium for a sell-out show on 4 May 1980, to be supported by the Plugz and Los Lobos. If the Plugz were deemed just about degenerate enough, Los Lobos were strictly *non grata*. Louis Perez says they 'hung on for about ten minutes until serious projectiles began hitting the stage; [but] finally we were run off'.

When Lydon took to the stage, he faced an audience the like of which even he had never encountered. As Mikal Gilmore has written of that defining moment, 'Lydon was plain transfixing, but the audience that assembled to celebrate the band's appearance, a crowd of thuggish-looking jar-head punks who eventually became dubbed the area's "hard-core" subculture, very nearly upstaged the show. It was the first time this audience had made its identity felt in such a large, collective and forcible way.'

New York Rocker's LA correspondent, in the year's round-up, explained that this was 'the new tidal wave of beach punks. Like killer bees, they had been breeding in the coastal suburbs for a couple of years until last spring, when they began invading the Hollywood hierarchy of new music . . . At the Public Image gig, the beach kids turned a lazy show into something akin to Judgement Day. Only I still haven't figured out who was being judged. Was it . . . the rotten old idol, face to face with the "real thing" that he created?'

Rotten, to his credit, managed to maintain a degree of order by sheer force of personality, and the power of PiL ultimately carried the day; but the Lydon that looked out on his 'own creation' that night wanted nothing to do with the crazies careering away at the Olympic Auditorium. It was time to put a halt to the rock & roll spectacle. Returning to Britain, Levene informed the *NME*, 'What [touring] America amount[ed] to is that we don't ever want to do gigs again – and we definitely don't want to be a rock & roll band . . . All they want is rock & roll stuff.' Well, 'rock & roll stuff' with a little ritualized violence thrown in for good measure.

6.3
THE DARK STUFF
1979–80

FINAL SOLUTION PRESENTS

THURS. AUGUST 2ND. 7.00PM
ESSENTIAL LOGIC
JOY DIVISION
THE TEARDROP EXPLODES
ECHO & THE BUNNYMEN

FRIDAY, AUGUST 3RD 8.00PM
THROBBING GRISTLE
CABARET VOLTAIRE
REMA REMA

SATURDAY, AUGUST 4TH 7.00 PM
THE TILLER BOYS
PRAG VEC
LUDUS
CLOCK DVA

SUNDAY AUGUST 5TH 7.00PM
RED CRAYOLA
SCRITTI POLITTI
GOOD MISSIONARIES
THE TRANSMITTERS

AT THE PRINCE OF WALES CONFERENCE CENTRE, BELOW THE YMCA
CORNER OF GT. RUSSELL ST. AND TOTTENHAM CT. RD, LONDON, W.C.1.

ADMISSION EACH NIGHT £2.00 OR £1.75 IN ADVANCE. FOUR DAY TICKETS £6.00 IN ADVANCE FROM
SMALL WONDER, ROUGH TRADE AND HONKY TONK RECORD SHOPS

What I liked about punk was that 'This is who I am – like it or not – in your face'. It was a perfect way to channel [that] out . . . [but] that initial feeling of liberation is not real. It's like a kid running in the middle of the highway. He may have an initial sense of liberation, but it's a false sense.   — Palm Olive, to author, 2005

It was nice that the punk thing collapsed. It was tiresome to have Sham 69 and 999. If you really want to go for the scorched-earth policy, well, if these people pop up, you want to scorch them as well.   — Richard Boon, to author, 2005

February 1979 was perhaps not the ideal time for The Clash to make their first Stateside sortie. The UK reception to *Give 'Em Enough Rope* had been lukewarm at best. Even the more worthy singles from the album, 'Tommy Gun' and 'English Civil War', had garnered disappointing sales (and B-sides). The competition for punk pennies was hotting up, with the release of compelling cuts like SLF's 'Alternative Ulster', The Ruts' 'In A Rut' and The Undertones' 'Get Over You' in those all-important picture sleeves.

One of these bands, inspired to say it loud and proud by *The Clash*, were now issuing their own debut LP to almost universal acclamation. SLF's *Inflammable Material* even reproduced the unexpected chart success of *The Clash*, the Fingers' protestations of oppression and depression acquiring a special resonance now that these avatars had seemingly reneged on their revolutionary remit. Even when *NME*'s Paul Morley raised the thorny issue of the authorship of the band's lyrics, their sheer commitment to the material garnered them the benefit of the doubt:

Three of [*Inflammable Material*] side one's outbursts, and four of side two's have words written by *Daily Express* man Gordon Ogilvie . . . [leaving] the suggestion of a presence of cynically motivated Svengalis using the group for mischievous or disturbing ends . . . [But] if McClellan and Ogilvie . . . are 'up to something', then the snarls and sourness in Fingers' execution wreck it all. There is just no sign of lack of commitment or identification with the words. [*NME*, 10/2/79]

Inflammable Material was a punch to the gut, its impossible-to-ignore message unrelenting, right from the opening line of a re-recorded 'Suspect Device': 'Inflammable material planted in my head / It's a suspect device that's left two thousand dead.' And yet, no one back in Ulster seemed too happy to have the profile of Ulster punk, and its travails, highlighted in song. The sound of knives sharpening was audible even across the Irish Sea. When *Alternative Ulster* overseer Gavin Martin managed to abandon the fanzine trail for a staff-job at *NME*, he couldn't wait to deliver a hatchet to his old friend Jake's head:

It's impossible to ascertain the personal influence Ogilvie has over Jake, with whom he shares a flat, or how easily led the group are; maybe they don't really know the truth themselves. Let's just say that since the day I sat in a bollock-freezing church hall and watched as Gordon instructed Jake how to phrase his vocals on 'Johnny Was', I'll always have my doubts. The process used to bring today's SLF into being was slow, deceptive and cunning. Gradually their set became infiltrated by their own compositions, but right up until their last gig in Belfast, before leaving to join Island Records . . . these were buried in a morass of Clash, Pistols and Damned. This disorientating slapstick made it hard to put the new 'politicized' Stiffs in serious perspective. [*NME*, 29/3/80]

Martin later justified his attack by claiming 'they'd had a critical joyride up to that point in the music press; I put the other side of the story.' Actually Martin showed the very side of Ulster that had convinced the Fingers to leave in the first place, a proclivity for backstabbing anyone who blew the whistle on Belfast's closed circle of hate and war. But Martin's piece was the least of the band's problems. As Morley wrote, at the end of his album review, 'Now that they're isolated from the tragic ingredients of the inspiration . . . they'll probably never again communicate similar grievances and discontent with such raw exasperation.'

In that sense, their problems were little different from The Clash, and their chosen path depressingly similar. Burns admitted as much at the time of the album's release, 'It's quite possible that we could blow it, dissolve at the end of this tour. I mean, what *can* we do next?' But rather than dissolve, they chose the path of least resistance. Having charted with the first Rough Trade LP, they promptly went with the first major to sell them a line about international distribution – perhaps because they stuck out like a reactionary thumb amid all the post-punkers signed to Travis's label, and were unhappy sharing some of the oddest bills of the era (SLF, Essential Logic and Robert Rental, anyone?).

Signing to Chrysalis, the Fingers still asked Geoff Travis and Mayo

Thompson if they would consider producing their next record. Travis says he 'thought, "This is a bit cheeky," but we went to rehearsal, and we listened to the tune, and we said, "We're not sure about that, Jake." He was really annoyed and that was the end of it.' Travis's instincts were intact. The single they heard – 'Straw Dogs' – had none of the fulsome fury or clashing chords of 'Suspect Device' or 'Alternative Ulster'; and though SLF tried on major-label marketing for size, Morley's suspicions proved prophetic. Stiff Little Fingers' first raised digit to the world had managed to both break through and break the mould. What does one do next?

Meanwhile, their fellow Ulstermen, The Undertones, must have wondered where they'd gone wrong, having issued in quick succession, the *Teenage Kicks* EP, which had *two* A-sides to demise for, and the equally compulsive 'Get Over You', without registering more than a murmur on rock's Richter scale. Part of the problem was that they simply had not planned on a long career. Nor had they planned on leaving home. When the opportunity arose to support The Clash on their September US tour, they just weren't prepared to sign up for the duration.

John O'Neill: From thinking we were gonna make one single and break up, to suddenly get[ting] signed, and making one LP and break[ing] up; and then it does quite well, [so] we think, 'Oh, let's do another one.' But by that stage the rot had set in. The split had come between me and Billy – [who were] always reluctant to go away – and Damian and Feargal – who couldn't wait to get away. The Clash tour we had a choice of going for three weeks or for five weeks. Looking back, I think what an idiot [for picking three].

For The Clash, the September/October tour was make or break, after a difficult year without Rhodes. Determined to press home any advantage derived from February's fly-past, they premiered half a dozen of the better *London Calling* songs, including the foot-stomping title-track, though the album itself was just barely completed and was still a good two to three months away from release.

London Calling saw The Clash raise their game; and the stakes thereof. An album that embraced a plethora of styles, it had more in common with the 101ers than anything Rhodes might condone. But their new mentor was twice the maniac Rhodes had ever been. Guy Stevens, Mott the Hoople producer and unreconstructed alcoholic, was someone who went straight to Mick Jones's rock & roll heart. When engineer Bill Price, who had worked on *Bollocks*, delicately adjusted the fader on his own studio desk during one Wessex session, Stevens leaned over and told him, 'Stop fiddling around like a girl's blouse. Into the red! Into the red!' The results were still top-heavy, and the disparity between those styles the band could carry off, and those they couldn't, marked. But The Clash certainly displayed a great deal of nerve, in daring to make their own *Exile On Main Street*.

In fact, the critical reaction back home was surprisingly positive (though nowhere near as fulsome anywhere else as in NME, where Shaar Murray applied to join their press corps), even if many lapsed fans remained outside the fold. As Kris Needs, the first journalist to hear the finished album (albeit while trussed up on a pool table in the studio), suggested, 'If you hold them to their past you're strapping on a strait-jacket.' This was The Clash attempting to belatedly take up a definition of the music Pete Silverton had incorporated into his review of their first album, back in '77, 'Rock & roll ain't about being only anything, it's about trying to be everything and wanting to be more.'

With *London Calling* The Clash didn't resolve the contradictions, but they finally learnt to live with them. Perhaps they always knew this is the way it had to go. Strummer had told Coon back in March 1977, 'In three years what do you think I'm going to be doing? I'll still be walking around muttering to myself. [Our fans] are still going to be shovelling shit down some old chute, and maybe with their wages they'll buy The Clash's fourth album. Rock doesn't change anything.' At least with this double-album, they finally got CBS-US to sit up and take notice, even if the now-mainstream message alienated some of their natural constituency Stateside.

Kurt Cobain: The Clash were always a bad imitation of The Rolling Stones . . . I blame [them] for not letting me get into punk. [1992]

By the time The Clash played their penultimate show that fall, in Seattle on 15 October, their preferred support act, The Undertones, were already back in their unsafe European home. For The Undertones, the opportunity to tour the States had come just as the word was seeping out about their Derry ditties, and Sire began acting like a US major. In April 1979, their third single, 'Jimmy Jimmy', had finally done chart-bustin' business; and their eponymous May debut album went

Top Twenty. The decision was then made to reissue the album with the A-sides to their first two singles, 'Teenage Kicks' and 'Get Over You', added to its already generous fourteen cuts. It was in this form that the Americans (and some tardy Brits) were introduced to the band that fall.

Thankfully, The Undertones had found a wily chaperone, Andy Ferguson, who according to John O'Neill, had 'started out selling bootlegs, and ended up with Sire. [But] the record deal we signed with Sire was one of those classic record deals. The advance . . . wasn't bad, but we just thought this was money we were given. Andy could see we didn't have a manager, and that we could make some really bad decisions here. So he took great pains – showed us the ins and outs of publishing, PRS, and all these things – and renegotiated the contract.'

Ferguson also found festering tensions – a result of Feargal Sharkey's separation from everything the rest of the band was trying to do. As such, despite further chart successes – including a Top Ten album, *Hypnotised* – the Undertones were destined to become another Rezillos, never quite making the transition from pop band to cultural force.

John O'Neill: [Feargal] was never really into the pop culture. Later on, I started getting more into things like Al Green and Tamla, naively thinking I could write songs that would phrase things off the beat, but it used to be a constant source of arguments with Feargal. 'It's got to be on the beat! It's got to be on the beat!' I used to play [him] The Pop Group and the Gang of Four, but it *had* to have some pop element. So it was always a bit too much of a compromise.

The Adverts were another punk band for whom the unequal struggle between commercial success and cultural impact ultimately did for them. They were on their last legs by the summer of 1979, when they began recording one last statement of intent. *Cast Of Thousands*, issued in October, was an audacious last throw of the dice, imbued with the clarity of cynicism. However, there was no tour support from their new label, RCA, and no way to go out with a bang. One song on *Cast Of Thousands* said it all – 'I Surrender' – which Smith admits, 'was [me] trying to say . . . that I didn't want to be part of something that couldn't move forward. It felt like we were being blocked by . . . the expectations of the punk audience.' Meanwhile, their third record label in as many years couldn't wait to say goodbye.

TV Smith: By '78, it was clear that the punk scene was already going, and [equally] clear that we were already going, as well . . . Our audiences were diminishing alarmingly, we had no [label] support, we were struggling to find enough money to make the record. Michael [had] scooped us a deal with RCA, but they didn't really want us. He did it through the marketing manager, not through the A&R department at all. [The manager] had only been at the company a few weeks, and a couple of weeks after he signed us, he was out. And [of course] the A&R men were pissed off with us, 'cause they didn't sign us. They put the record out theoretically, but they dropped us at the very first opportunity. Our morale was [already] very low. We were getting through members like nobody's business . . . Gaye had had a totally punishing experience for the last year of the band . . . It was just a question of how to finish it.

The Adverts were not alone in deciding to do the decent thing after issuing that difficult second album. Pauline Murray's Penetration felt the same way. *Coming Up For Air*, which came out the month before *Cast Of Thousands*, was one of those second albums made doubly difficult by the loss of the band's tunesmith, Gary Chaplin, and the dispiriting failure of their April 1979 single, 'Danger Signs', the best new song in the post-Chaplin set. Like The Rezillos, Penetration returned home to record their final show at year's end; but the Newcastle City Hall show, released posthumously, simply showed how the piston-driven band of '77 had suffered an irreversible pressure drop.

The punk spirit seemed to be dying on the dance floor. If it was ever going to find a way to renew itself (again), it was going to have to find a way to bring together the various warring factions that represented fractured youth in the seventies – skinheads, punks, Rastas, soul rebels. For a heady six months at the end of the decade, it seemed like one band could. The Specials (aka the Coventry Automatics), the ska revivalists who survived a baptism of fire with Bernie Rhodes, were a unique hybrid of punk, ska and reggae and they had taken two years to get it just right.

Jerry Dammers: When we started off, we were trying to mix modern heavy reggae with punk rock, but the two styles were so different that they didn't mix . . . So we have gone back to ska because it's much closer to R&B . . . What we're trying to do is form a new British beat music from the influences of British rock and Jamaican music . . . In a way, it's all still part of punk. We're not trying to get away from punk. We're just trying to show some other direction. [Sometimes] you've got to go back to go forward. [1979]

The early Specials were an intoxicating mix of dangling rhythms and dynamic presentation – masterminded by highly driven Dammers. They knew they had something unique. As Simon Frith wrote, as early as May 1978, 'The mood of the music was punk, the sound was reggae.' Actually, The Specials were already turning to ska, that 'other' aspect of sixties Mod culture, leaving the Britpop to The Jam. Ska had nothing like the reactionary connotations of Britpop, perhaps because it had never really broken out of that sub-culture, and therefore was ripe for reprocessing in an increasingly multicultural Britain.

If Dammers took a great deal of inspiration from the cross-cultural Midlands dance scene, he had been paying attention throughout the whole arc of punk. And he sang a familiar song to *MM* in 1979: 'It wasn't until the Sex Pistols came along that you realized that you could get away with doing your own songs . . . They were the first group a lot of us could relate to . . . We could identify with them . . . They were a real inspiration for me.' Dammers loved the idea of creating a scene, akin to Pistolean punk, but dance-oriented and Midlands-based.

Initially, he hoped to co-opt Dexys Midnight Runners, another band who had sailed close to Bernie Rhodes' wind, having been formed from the tattered remnants of those party-poopers, the Killjoys, Birmingham's answer to the UK Subs. The other band that interested The Specials were not even honorary Midlanders. Madness were London's ska-infused answer to Kilburn & the High Roads. By May 1979, The Specials were already speaking of new ska as a punk-derived movement.

Sir Horace Gentleman: We want to start recording other bands who complement us . . . That way it'll come over as more of a movement, which it is. I think people are more interested in a movement than a particular group. [1979]

The Specials still weren't sure they had enough of a reservoir of talent on their home patch to localize the label they had set up, 2-Tone. By the summer, though, it became apparent there were at least two other ska specialists ploughing their frenetic furrow in the clubs and pubs of the Black Country. Of Selecter and The Beat, the latter had the greater pedigree, having been formed by Andy Cox and Dave Wakeling after a punk-disco epiphany, still blithely unaware of the then-Automatics.

Dave Wakeling: If [a DJ] played too many Punk songs in a row everyone would get burnt out and if you played too many Dubs all in a row then everybody was just leaning against a wall nodding their heads. [But] the combination was glorious. And it happened in an instant, me and Andy [Cox] sitting on the floor, watching the crowd from the corner, saying, 'What if you could get both of these elements going in the same three-minute song?' . . . We started The Beat on that basic premise . . . [Then] David Steele walked in with the *Melody Maker* or *NME* and said, 'Look!' . . . and we said, 'The Specials!!! Oh God, they beat us to the punch.'

Selecter were more directly inspired by Dammers' directive, Noel Davis reinventing reggae band Hard Top 22 along 2-Tone lines. As their bassist Charlie Anderson admitted, 'What we're aiming for is a family of music in Coventry, the Coventry Stax if you like. That is what 2-Tone is about . . . The idea has been in Jerry Dammers' mind for some time.'

By October 1979, 2-Tone had a roster of sorts, having announced itself six months earlier with debut 45s by The Specials ('Gangsters') and Selecter ('The Selecter'). Dammers had negotiated a deal with Chrysalis which allowed him the studio time to record up to ten singles a year, by bands of his own choosing, all contracted on a by-single basis. Chrysalis were obliged to release at least six of the results. When both The Specials and Selecter charted, followed by Madness ('The Prince' b/w 'Madness') in August, they began to believe Dammers knew what he was doing, and 2-Tone was fêted as the next big thing – post-punk for populists. On 21 July they solidified the brand name, reopening Camden's Electric Ballroom with a night of 2-Tone, featuring The Specials, Selecter, and Madness (Dexys Midnight Runners, still ostensibly a 2-Tone act, bailed at the last minute).

For 2-Tone it was probably a case of too much, too soon. Though Madness had agreed to play a 2-Tone package tour that autumn, alongside The Specials, Selecter, and The Beat, they had decided they had more in common with the likes of Ian Dury and Wreckless Eric, joining the Stiff roster for subsequent examples of their 'heavy, heavy monster sound'. Meanwhile, in November, The Beat became the fourth 2-Tone band to chart with their debut single, a hopped-up remake of 'Tears Of A Clown'.

As for Dexys, the July no-show seemed indicative of a general unwillingness on frontman Kevin Rowland's part to subvert *his* identity to any collective ideal (though they did intermittently change places with Madness on the 2-Tone Tour). This was a man for whom the new wave was a career opportunity. When Killjoys didn't work, it was time to ditch the dirges, drop some dexies and *dance*! Though Rowland would be responsible for the best dance album of 1980, *Searching For The Young Soul Rebels*, he wasn't even prepared to share success with his band, let alone someone else's label.

And The Specials had their own momentum carrying them along. Quite simply, by October they were on a runaway train of rhythm, consolidating everything with their own forty-minute moonstomp, *The Specials*, a tonic for the 2-Tone troops, from which they pulled 'Rudi, A Message To You', another compulsive hit single for the label. On 7 November 1979, the ska revival reached into even the most detached front rooms in Britain, when a single edition of *Top of The Pops* featured The Specials, Selecter and Madness.

But by the summer of 1980, the revival had run its course. Madness and Dexys, disinclined to make their 2-Tone status anything more than honorary, were already tiring of the format, the former preferring a more obviously English sensibility, the latter (re)discovering Celtic soul. Selecter then announced they were quitting the label in July, singer Pauline Black placing the blame at Dammers' door:

Every 2-Tone single has reached the charts . . . [which has created] a situation which the Selecter feel is ultimately stifling new talent, leading new bands to feel they need to stereotype themselves to what they believe to be the 2-Tone sound. 2-Tone was intended to be an alternative to the music industry, a label that took risks and . . . injected some energy into what had become a stale music scene. The time has come . . . to take risks again.'

Black need not have worried about all that tiresome chart success – Selecter never troubled the Top Thirty again. The Specials, though, remained a force to contend with, especially after pro-contraception polemic, 'Too Much Too Young', topped the charts in February 1980. Yet the band had their own issues to resolve. As Roddy Radiation says, 'Due to internal conflict, and the sudden success of the 2-Tone movement, we found it hard to address all the world's problems! Our own problems were challenging enough.'

Jerry Dammers suggests success wasn't the problem, merely a symptom: 'It became difficult when there was nothing left to rebel against.' It was a conundrum that punk – for all its right-on rhetoric – had never really resolved. Another punk-derived activity now rebounding on The

Specials came about because some of their audience decided they were entitled to share the stage with those more Special. As Dammers recently told *Mojo*, 'At first, [a stage invasion] was a great laugh, "We're all in this together, there's no stars here." Then people were getting onstage two numbers into the set.' Footage of The Specials onstage in German TV documentary *Punk in England* shows how ludicrous the situation quickly became.

By the end of 1980 Dammers had had enough, yet was determined to go out with a bang. 'Ghost Town', issued in June 1981, was the most muted of explosions, but it was everything Dammers had been working towards. Tom Robinson may have been a year out with his 'Winter of '79' but there was some tough medicine being dished out by decision-makers in the winter of 1980, and this punk survivor was determined to have his say. Written after he found something he *did* want to shout about — urban decay — it was a number-one single at a time when Babylon really was burning. That summer shots rang out and fires raged in Moss Side, Toxteth and Brixton.

No Pistols, Clash or Damned, in 1979. The soundtrack of the times was now being written by The Specials, The Jam and The Ruts, all of whom released defining singles in the first year of Thatcher's Tory government, powerful seven-inch warnings that the shit was about to hit *their* fans. The Jam had slightly lost their way in 1979, with two disappointing 45s 'Strange Town' and 'When You're Young', a case (or two) of All Trad Cons. But they came good again in late November, delivering a necessary shot in the arm, 'Eton Rifles', their first Top Three single, followed by the punchy (if patchy) *Setting Sons* LP, their first Top Five album. The following month they topped the all-important *NME* Readers Poll. And in March 1980, they achieved something only Slade and The Beatles had managed before — a single that *entered* the charts at number one.

'Going Underground' more than warranted the company, bearing comparison with the very best The Jam's more 'authentic' peers could offer. If Weller was one Woking lad who had made good by getting good, The Jam never quite passed that crucial acid-test, cutting it live. Though they had energy aplenty, the musical limitations of a set-up without a lead instrument, and Weller's one-dimensional vocals made for some so-so shows, for all the strong songs and their fanatical fans.

The Ruts, on the other hand, had risen on a groundswell of concert-converts from eighteen months of solid gigging. Turn-screw tight, The

Ruts were the best musicians to play hard and fast since the proto-typical Pistols imploded. When they signed to Virgin, in the spring of 1979, they confirmed their credentials with a secret gig at the Marquee (billed as The Human Punks) recorded for a possible live album. Though the album didn't happen, 'Human Punk' became the final track on their October long-player, *The Crack*.

Before that, they planned to set Britain alight with their second attempt at a follow-up to 'In A Rut', and their fourth recording of 'Babylon's Burning'. Recorded with Mick Glossop at Air Studios, it was the beginning of a chart career even shorter than the Pistols', giving notice that the end of that moment when English punk mattered was nigh. In capturing that moment and containing it for four whole minutes, 'Babylon's Burning' emulated 'Pretty Vacant', charting at seven and holding its own through a third summer of hate and war. While The Ruts finished up the album, Virgin hurriedly released as a follow-up the belligerent 'Something That I Said', but the moment was already gone.

Initially, Owen had threatened that 'the punkier tracks, the faster raw tracks, we're gonna do in an eight-track studio', but in the end they returned to Air. As Ruffy recalls, Glossop 'took a day and a half to get drum sound, [but] once we had it – it was there. And we worked really well together – we weren't about to be produced.'

Owen promised that *The Crack* would 'be most of our established set, all the original numbers from the early Rock Against Racism gigs till now. We have got a lot of other stuff held back . . . but the album will be all the familiar stuff.' He was true to his word, though the album also delineated a pronounced forward motion with the side-one closer, 'Jah Wars', a six-and-a-half-minute fusion of reggae and rock that was Owen's account of the treatment dished out to black friend Clarence Baker by over-zealous police when the right-minded of Southall went on the offensive during a National Front march.

'Jah Wars' was everything The Clash had been striving for in their ersatz reggae excursions – some of the best protest lyrics this side of Donovan, the G-force of a seminal rock band and a dub sound dripping with dreadlocks. From Misty, The Ruts had evidently acquired what Vivien Goldman called 'the semi-mystical totally musical way Misty create their music . . . free-form from spontaneous jams, [which] they assured me springs from the ideology whereby if you're not poverty-stricken you can't be *roots*, and if you're not *roots* then you can't make decent music because you're "too much gimmick".' As Seggs suggests, 'If you're jamming, and you don't want to play "Johnny B Goode" then you play reggae – if you love it [as we did] . . . so we used to jam a lot on reggae.' Such practice served them well on 'Jah Wars', an invariable highlight of any later Ruts gig.

They now felt they had made their punk statement, Owen telling *Sounds* in October, 'A lot of [the early material] we play because people still want to hear it. But it is slap-bang-crash.' He hoped that 'Jah Wars' could point the band in a more original direction. Yet, inexplicably, at a time when dance and punk seemed like partners again, the single release of 'Jah Wars' at year's end made almost no impression on the audience who had snapped up *The Crack* (which, like *Inflammable Material*, had found a deserved berth in the Top Twenty), or turned up on their forty-date tour. Perhaps it was because it was already on the album, and punk principles still demanded non-album singles, but more probably it was because radio stations weren't wild about the sentiments, or the portrait it painted of the police, and didn't give it the time of day.

Unfortunately, for all the ideas Owen had for new songs, he was slowly turning into another Peter Perrett, debilitated by the very thing he had warned about on the B-side to their first single, 'H-Eyes'. In July he had even admitted, 'I've taken [heroin] . . . [But] let's face it, it's no good for you. It's nice when you take it, but it's going to fucking kill you.' And still he 'dabbled'. And like The Only Ones, the rest of the band weren't immune to a little Cocaine Charlie either – or his friend, Morphine Sue.

Paul Fox: [Malcolm] was ill at the end. He was doing gear, and he couldn't get onstage unless he had his fix. We got to Plymouth and he couldn't get any gear, and he couldn't get out of bed – he was a skeleton, grey. [But] we were a druggy band – we did love a bit of 'charlie'. Malcolm's drug-dealing paid for all our rehearsals, all our drugs, for cabs to get to rehearsal.

The fate of Sid Vicious barely a fortnight after 'H-Eyes' hit the shops, given a fatal overdose by his own mom, had posted clear warning that this generation was no more invincible than the turned-on they had turned on. But Owen dismissed Vicious as an idiot, having already meted out some summary justice on behalf of Kent, Harris and the 100 Club girl (In Fox's words, 'Malcolm gave [Sid] a right hiding one night in the foyer of the Speakeasy. He'd tried to give [Malcolm]'s wife a slap, and Malcolm steamed in and beat the crap out of him'). Worryingly, Seggs suggests it was 'through coke and alcohol that . . . Malcolm discovered . . . he had this front.' He was also hanging out with Sweet-singer Brian Connolly and Lizzy's Lynott, rockers well on their way to the undertakers.

By the new year, the band needed to decide what to do. A January John Peel session had previewed the next single, 'Staring At The Rude Boys', a righteous update to 'In A Rut', that pondered whether violence was the only way to gain elbow-room on the dance floor of life. Though it had nothing like the impact of The Jam's fully fuelled 'Going Underground', its March release signalled a welcome return to the charts. At the same time, though, Owen was sinking fast.

Seggs: No one wanted to believe [drugs were a problem] . . . First of all, I said, 'What are you doing?' and he said, 'I know what I'm doing.' Before you know where it is, it's nine months down the line and it's too late . . . It was between 'Jah Wars' and 'Rude Boys', when we went to Europe . . . [Before a French TV show] he cut out a secret compartment in his brothel creepers and he . . . took a gram of Chinese rocks that he'd bought off [a prog-rock bass player], and he then started to disappear into the toilets. Twenty minutes later, he'd come out, 'Sorry, couldn't get my laces done.'

For a minute there, the rest of The Ruts did the honourable thing, turfing Owen out of his own band, hoping that it would serve as a much-needed shock to his rapidly depleting system. In fact, he was due to go into hospital for an operation on his throat, but when he got there, he was told he would have to detox first. When he finally came out, it seemed like the old Owen was back. He even had a new song, 'West One', he wanted to record.

Seggs: He came up with this thing, 'Shine on me, shine on me.' It's all about being in the West End. And [we're] driving home [from the hospital] in the car, and Barbara Dickson was on with this song, 'Shine on me, shine on me.' He's been listening to hospital radio.

If the refrain did sound surprisingly MOR, when The Ruts re-formed and recorded 'West One', it proved that 'Jah Wars' and 'Staring At The Rude Boys' were no flukes. Just as The Clash had superseded their early, amphetamine-fuelled material with slightly statelier, but equally incendiary singles, like 'Complete Control' and 'White Man', the Ruts seemed to have achieved a comparable breakthrough.

Also recorded at that final session was yet another fab flirtation with all things dub. 'Love In Vein' had its own unbearable refrain, 'Don't want you in my arms no more.' The second anti-heroin song from Owen's pen, this message to the rude boy – which had convinced the band to give him another chance – went as unheeded as the first. Having successfully detoxed, Owen now made the classic junkie error. He decided on a celebratory fix at its previous potency. On 14 July 1980, Owen was found dead in the bath of his parents' home, and that difficult second album, already half-written, would stay that way.★

'West One' b/w 'Love In Vein' appeared at the end of August, to the laudatory reviews it deserved, as another departure from the riff-driven Ruts repertoire that had grabbed an audience there for the taking. Like 'Jah Wars', 'West One' didn't rely on Fox's fretful guitar, but was a rare blend of dub and northern soul. But its chart failure suggested that The Ruts would have had no greater success taking their audience dancing than the band who inspired them to aspire. For those who thought punk need not go post-modern to remain in the modern world, Malcolm Owen had been something of a great white hope. Those left were, at least to Misty eyes, 'too much gimmick'.

— — —

Strangely enough, in the melting pot of all things post-punk, some so-called progressives had been doing almost as well as the populists during 1978–9. The likes of Magazine, PiL and Siouxsie & the Banshees had suggested that a chart-sized audience existed for some pretty unearthly music. But in the Banshees' case there was already a battle going on within the band as to their future direction, even as 'Playground Twist' went swirling on high. Commercial success was now placed at the top of their agenda by the band's founders.

Steve Severin: [Kenny and John] had a distorted view of the thing. They thought it was an art event . . . But Siouxsie and I were very clear – this was a pop group

---

★ Virgin did issue a second Ruts album, *The Crack*, which mopped up the various non-album B-sides and A-sides, two unreleased songs from the final Peel session, and three songs from a gig in Paris. Aside from this material, the only known song from the final sessions appears to be a backing track called 'Last Exit', to which no vocal was ever added.

... I wanted to get Siouxsie and the Banshees on *Magpie*. That would be an achievement ... But John and Kenny would have just preferred to have support[ed] Throbbing Gristle. All the way along the line Siouxsie, myself and Nils were much more vociferous [about] what we wanted and why we wanted it – 'We want to do this kind of music on a major label. That's the only way anything's going to change' ... They'd go and see Cabaret Voltaire and say, 'Why can't we have films being projected on us?' and I'd say, 'Why do you want a film projected on you? You've got Siouxsie. What's the point in covering up this [charismatic] front singer ... There's a reason why [Cabaret Voltaire are] hiding behind a film – they don't actually perform.'

In early September 1979, matters came to a head in dramatic fashion when drummer Kenny Morris and guitarist John McKay disappeared on opening night of the *Join Hands* tour in Aberdeen. At the time, the gesture threatened to undo everything the Banshees had achieved to date. As Severin says, 'There was a harsh reality to this, because the whole tour was partially self-financed. We had no tour support.' Without label support, the entire financial future of the band had been compromised, and Siouxsie was understandably incandescent with rage. When she came onstage to explain the situation, her version of events was, 'Two original members of the band are here tonight. Two art–college students fucked off out of it.'

In fact, there had already been an inkling of trouble in store, as Siouxsie admitted to an attendant journalist: 'When we went into rehearsals for this tour I asked [McKay and Morris] outright whether they wanted to be a part of Siouxsie and the Banshees, or if they were going to be total voyeurs and dilettantes all their lives.' If she actually phrased her concerns this way, one can hardly wonder that they 'fucked off out of it'. When McKay and Morris finally came up for air, the rationale they gave in a letter to the papers suggested they no longer felt part of the decision-making process:

Over the period of time which elapsed between *The Scream* and *Join Hands*, the emphasis shifted from what we as a unit wanted, to what we as a unit ought to do to retain our tenuous grip on commercial success . . . [and] now we had a unity of three against two.

This was a reference to the power-block that Siouxsie, Severin and Stevenson had formed. When Siouxsie and Severin had ended their personal relationship, the previous September, Stevenson had made his move on the lady. Yet this only made the triad stronger, and more intractable. Siouxsie admitted to her biographer that, in hindsight, she could 'see how difficult it must have been for [the other two]. We always said that the band was about four individuals, which it was – so long as John and Kenny agreed with me and Severin!'

What was not initially clear was how sound the instincts of McKay and Morris proved to be – the band *had* stopped doing what it wanted, and was now doing what it thought it should 'to retain [its] tenuous grip on commercial success'. With their departure, that process would only grow more pronounced. Perhaps the remaining Banshees would have liked to stay among the madmen, but they decided instead to 'perish with the sad men roaming free'.

One band who remained resolute in their career path – to destruction, via innovation – were Wire. The commercial failure of *154* hadn't affected their determination to continue upsetting the commercial cart. When they were asked to record another session for John Peel – who had never convinced the band he was a fan – they again decided to make no attempt to promote their latest album. Instead, they recorded a fifteen-minute experimental piece called 'Crazy About Love'. Coming from the band who once released a 21-song album, it was a statement unto itself.

Colin Newman: John Peel didn't really like us that much . . . We never fitted into his category [of] weird and out of it. He was suspicious of it. Like a lot of people, [he felt], 'That's not proper rock & roll, really.' So [though] Peel was quite supportive early on, [later on] I think it was just a matter of the producer saying, 'These people are important. You must give them a session.' So instead of promoting *154*, [we thought why don't] we do [something that means] he has to give over fifteen minutes of his show to us.

This gesture can't have endeared the lads to EMI, who were still struggling to understand the band's terminal dissatisfaction with everything they did, the minute they did it. The problem, in Graham Lewis's opinion, is that by 'having three writers in the group, we were producing a large amount of material – [but] there was a small funnel for that to go through . . . [And] by the end of *154* the coziness had very much gone out of the situation . . . It had been a very accelerated period of creativity . . . [But] EMI at that point were a little bit rudderless . . . the people you'd made your marriage with had moved on.' Those left behind weren't enamoured with the group's idea of promotion, or their refusal to do the standing still. When erstwhile producer Mike Thorne mentioned the possibility of another Wire album to the head of the company, his reply was to the point, 'A record company is not an Arts Council.'

EMI decided to cut their losses – though they did throw Wire one last lifeline. Newman recalls there being 'an option for another album. In the contract they had to give us an advance. At that point we owed them £70,000. They said, "We'll pay for the record, we'll support you touring, but we won't give you an advance." That was what we lived off, so that was not practical.' Wire's rejection of EMI released them from any last commercial restraint, and in February 1980 they reincarnated themselves again, at London's Electric Ballroom.

For some time, Wire had been reluctant to meet their audience even halfway when it came to playing the 'old' songs. As Newman had informed *Sounds*, at the time of *Chairs Missing*, 'I've never understood this idea of "You've heard the album, now see it on ice" . . . If the music is good it should stand up on its own; it shouldn't *need* to be familiar.' The Electric Ballroom show included exactly one old song, '1-2-X-U', which as Newman says, 'was [meant as] a parody. It was [deliberately] absurdist.'

The rest of the performance, which was recorded for a live album (later issued by Rough Trade), was a totality unto itself. Newman calls it 'a piece which had humour, lots of elements, not just something to wind up a bunch of pissed skinheads'. The reaction on the night, and indeed the following week in the papers, suggested Wire had stretched themselves to breaking point. With everyone pulling in opposite directions, they finally accepted that one outlet was not enough. It was time to lower the flag on punk's most daring practitioners.

In fact, commercial hara-kiri was something of a fad that winter. The following month, The Slits and The Pop Group announced that they were forming their own label, Y Records, for all future bulletins, and that Rough Trade would provide distribution. In both cases, the frontperson seemed to believe they could dictate the direction henceforth, as each band duly began to tear itself apart, again. The Slits became ever more the projection of Ari Up's vision, save that the new songs were few and far between, and no longer qualified for top ranking. After a US tour in the spring of 1981, they called it quits.

In The Pop Group's case, guitarist Bruce Smith was not alone in suspecting that, 'Mark saw the music as just a vehicle, a platform for messages.' He was reluctant to go the Crass route. But bassist Simon Underwood was the first to quit, at the point 'when the band started becoming overtly political, as opposed to esoterically political'. The musical quality of The Pop Group's best musicians – Smith and Sager – would survive the transition into Rip, Rig & Panic, leaving Stewart to continue exploring esoterica in both ideology and musicology.

One man, though, who was greatly disappointed by the path The Pop Group ultimately took was an Aussie émigré by the name of Nick Cave, who suggested in 1981 that they 'sacrificed the music for that soapbox, toilet-roll politics'. Cave had come to England in the winter of 1980, with his Melbourne group, The Birthday Party, expecting to find 'a real upsurge of new young groups and incredible records like "She Is Beyond Good And Evil"'. Almost immediately, he caught Stewart's band at a London show and it 'blew my mind. I saw [this] gig where they just marched on stage, picked up their instruments and it was [just] so random, extreme, strange, angry.'

Cave, and his friend Rowland Howard, had been stuck in Melbourne throughout the whole of punk's pomp, 'obsessed with the English music scene. The *NME* was shipped to Australia three months late [but] [Rowland]'d have it, and he would get anything that sounded good, and he would play these records to us round at his place: Echo and the Bunnymen, Pere Ubu [etc].' The band that *really* inspired Cave and Howard to get serious, Radio Birdman, first came to town back in 1976. At the time, Cave and Howard already had the makings of The Boys Next Door. But, as Barney Hoskyns rightly wrote, back in '81:

The Birthday Party, whatever they may say to the contrary, bear the memory of seeing Birdman for the first time as powerfully as anyone. As a rather average five-piece combo called The Boys Next Door, all of whom, except Rowland Howard, had been playing together since third form in high school, their conception of music was radically changed by the experience.

But something made the nascent Birthday Party turn their backs on Birdman, possibly a distorted account of the Saints/Birdman showdown in Sydney that they had been given first-hand, when the boys from Brisbane came to town. According to Deniz Tek, 'The first time we went [to Melbourne] The Boys Next Door invited us to a house party, and they were very friendly and interested . . . and had been pumping us for information about what music we listened to, all night long. Then the next time we came down they didn't want to know us, or know *about* us.'

The Boys Next Door would take their time preparing the ground for their emergence into the post–punk light with their particular brand of the dark stuff. By 1978, when they started regular gigging locally – with Birdman and The Saints already little but an antipodean race-memory – The Boys Next Door were deemed too straight for most other Melbourne art-rockers.

Nick Cave: The university crowd, some really interesting bands, [ultimately] saw us as a rock & roll band who sold out to Mushroom Records. They probably were a lot more interesting and radical, and their music came out of a fundamental knowledge that they would never, ever be given a record deal. There were very weird, extreme bands in Australia. There was Filth, who were just chainsaws, and punching the shit out of each other onstage . . . There was an electronic thing going on across the river, closer to early, live Suicide. [Even] we were a very different band than what was recorded.

Perhaps it was precisely because The Boys Next Door – for all of Cave's baroque imagery and their love of random background noises – had some relationship to rock, that they drew the attention of at least one intrigued businessman, Barry Earl. Cave, at the time, liked to typify what they were doing as 'the biggest musical cliché in the world . . . When the history of rock music is written – which, since it's practically dead, will be soon – it'll just be remembered as a sordid interruption of normality.' But they were still mad keen to record something more than demos. When the opportunity came, they were practically foaming at the mouth.

Nick Cave: Earl was head of a subsidiary of Mushroom Records, called Suicide Records, that Mushroom set up when they heard that this punk-rock thing was happening in England. We were playing a gig at the Tiger Lounge and Barry came up . . . the archetypal fat [cat], cigar-smoking, silver jewellery on every finger, and he said, 'Hey, do you guys wanna make a record?' 'Fuck yeah.' . . . [Then, after we signed] we were called into Barry's office, [who] says, 'I've just been on the phone to England. Punk's out. Powerpop's in.' They got a guy from Skyhooks to produce the record, and his brief was obviously to make us sound poppy. And we had no idea how to operate in a studio. It seems absurd that we couldn't stop the process, but we were just kids, and we made this record we're totally ashamed of, [because of] how clean and neat the whole thing was.

Neither 'Mr Clarinet', the first single, nor *Hee-Haw*, the first EP, sound 'clean and neat' to *these* ears – more like the work of musicians who love the sound of breaking glass. They were enough to get the Boys' wheels rolling, and for the band to be given the opportunity to come to England. By the time they landed in the winter of 1980 they had decided to call themselves The Birthday Party (just to confuse anyone who imported their EP); and to immediately check out the post-punk scene they had read so much about in those air-freighted *NMEs*. But those three-month-old weeklies had been writing about a scene that no longer existed, having seemingly vanished into the London fog.

Nick Cave: I remember looking at the back pages [of *NME*] and seeing the gigs that were on. So we came over to England thinking it was just the swingiest place we could come to, and it was the most dismal hell-hole. It was too late, and our circumstances were diabolical. We'd actually signed a thing saying that [our manager] would collect all the money and distribute it to us. He lasted a week, [before] he went back to Australia, and left us in a one-bedroom bedsit with all our girlfriends in Earl's Court. We thought, 'At least we've got the music to go to,' and then we went to a gig that had Echo and the Bunnymen, Teardrop Explodes and the Psychedelic Furs, and it was fucking abysmal. It was a crushing night. The way The Birthday Party became onstage came out of seeing that gig, with everyone staring at their shoes and playing this boring music. It was like, 'Fuck this, we didn't come here to do this!' And we just went nuts . . . The confrontation was genuine, born of a real frustration with our situation, [and] with the English.

By the time The Birthday Party had any records out in England ('Mr Clarinet' was reissued, followed by 'The Friend Catcher' and a hastily compiled LP of Australian recordings, before the end of 1980), they already had a 'rep' that made The Saints seem almost saintly. If Vic Goddard had set out to destroy all rock & roll, Cave felt that something more extreme was required to finish the job. For the next three years The Birthday Party were an abscess on rock's wounded self, which continued to turn ever more gangrenous.

Nick Cave: Something would [always] happen onstage with [our] kind of music – it required a certain kind of confrontation. And we were enormously drunk at the time. We would drink the rider as quickly as possible, and stumble out on stage. [So] we were attracting a certain element who came along to fight us. We did [one] tour of Europe where we were billed as 'The Most Violent Band In The World', and we were doing concerts where people were coming along to beat the shit out of us. I was enjoying that aspect, for some reason. If people were just standing there, I thought it was my personal responsibility to bait, antagonize and intimidate, and if that didn't work, [get] physical. [Guitarist] Mick Harvey got quite irritated with this type of shit. He was trying to do great music, and a lot of the time I was just fucking up the whole thing, [being] more interested in the people in the front row than singing the song properly. [But] I lost interest as soon as I found it's what people [actually] wanted.

The Party even generated enough interest to carry them across the pond, to New York, though as Cave recalls, they didn't get very far: '[Of the] five dates, three of them were cancelled from what happened at the first one. We were booked to play [like] a singles bar in New York. We played one song and the owner was like, "That's it. Off." We said, "Let us play one more song," and we played a really long version of "King Ink", [in which] we were strangling beautiful women with mike leads. We just got thrown out.' So much for no wave preparing the way!

There was another post-punk band at the time still smarting from their failure to get through to the Americans that rock & roll was if not dead, certainly a dead-end. Having returned to Gunter Grove in June 1980 to lick their wounds, Public Image found itself reduced to a three-piece comprising Lydon, Levene and Levene's girlfriend, Jeannette Lee, previously of Acme Attractions, who had been a fixture at the place since PiL formed, having switched from Don Letts to Levene in mid-stream.

Lee's presence had prompted Wobble on several occasions to ask out loud, 'Excuse me, love, but what do you actually *do*?' Wobble, though, was no longer a part of the commune, having grown weary of spending 'a lot of [time] watching *Performance*.' Meanwhile, Lee *almost* defined her role to *NME* the following March, suggesting that being 'there means I'm contributing to the clash of personalities. There is no band, there are no rules and there are no managers.' She remained ensconced with Levene, who maintained little more than a nodding acquaintance with the outside world. It was a strange set-up all round, as John Perry discovered when he occasionally called round with a mutual drug-dealer friend.

John Perry: The PiL house as I recall it was: Keith lived in a sort of rabbit hutch at the back, which Lydon occasionally came through to cast his eye over. His comment, first time we were there, was, 'Nice to see someone here who's awake.' Keith's usual friends would be face-first-in-the-soup. On the ground floor was Dave [Crowe], who was the bodyguard. All four walls were decorated with cutlasses and knives. Lydon was *very* paranoid about being attacked. [And] Keith . . . couldn't sign cheques on his own, but he had some deal going with Dave.

Such was the oddly detached existence enjoyed by Lydon and Levene in their little commune that drummer Atkins, (temporarily) ousted after America, 'thought that Keith (and Jeannette) lived MILES away . . . Then one day, after a call, Keith came upstairs and I realized he lived downstairs.' In the nine months after their return from LA – and a notorious appearance on *The Tomorrow Show*, where Lydon memorably described rock as 'a disease, it's the plague, it's not achieving anything' – the trio embraced its insularity. Lydon confessed in a piece he wrote for *Smash Hits*, 'I'm a TV addict. It all started when I used to lock myself up trying to avoid people.' Into this unreal world came the occasional intervention by the arm of the law, but otherwise it was all one blur.

Martin Atkins: [Gunter Grove was all] speed, cases of Red Stripe, spliff, reggae on John's huge speakers, *Apocalypse Now* on [the] TV, mad people knocking on the door all the time, the police . . . kicking the door in.

Finally, the realization dawned that Virgin expected another album. Levene and Lydon were unfazed, having already convinced themselves that they could reproduce the inspirational, improvisational approach used on *Metal Box* without the input of Wobble, Walker, Dudanski *or* Atkins. Levene recalls how they had 'three weeks of blocked-out studio time, which was a fucking fortune . . . We'd turn up there and go through the process of setting up the instruments. And nothing was happening. Nobody was doing anything.' Finally, a call was made to Martin Atkins, who arrived 'excited to hear what they had done in the preceding two weeks [!] up there – NOTHING!'

The results, when they did actually get down to business, might have made for a terrific EP – headed by the title-track to the ensuing album,

Flowers Of Romance – but Levene's belief that they had delivered 'a truly commercial album that had a string of production values all the way through . . . because of the drum sound we had' was even more off-beam than the music. The title-track warranted another slot on ToTP, and a berth in the lower reaches of the Top Thirty, but PiL was in danger of disappearing up its own backside.

Levene, meanwhile, felt he had some unfinished business in America and in May 1981 – on a busman's holiday in New York – he was approached about doing a PiL gig (or two) at the Ritz Ballroom. Levene sounded out Lydon, and the pair agreed it might be time to realize some of the ideas expressed on *The Tomorrow Show* a year earlier. Presenter Tom Snyder had asked Lydon if their gigs still involved musical instruments. He had replied, 'So far'; going on to claim PiL had 'worked very hard to break down those barriers' that separate a band from its audience – 'but it's not working, so it's time to think again'. What they came up with for their Ritz appearance was the ultimate confrontation between a band and its ostensible audience.

Keith Levene: I told [the venue] . . . 'We'll do the gig if we can use all the equipment and do a video gig.' They said, 'What's a video gig?' – I was making this up as I was going along – and I said . . . 'You should advertise it as Public Image Ltd Video Appearance Live.' They said it didn't make sense – 'You can't appear on video live.' I told them, 'You watch us do it.' . . . It turned out that the Ritz was a 'Bridge and Tunnel' club. I had no idea – I was expecting a New York audience. So I had an audience that had more or less come to see the Sex Pistols . . . [Lydon, though,] sussed out the demographic of the audience, [and] he started playing whatever would piss them off, just to get a response. [PSF]

Lydon, Levene and their co-opted drummer, Sam, had no intention of performing any kind of ordinary set. Having set up *behind* a video screen, they began banging the odd drum and hitting an occasional guitar string, while Lydon persistently goaded the crowd. After a perfunctory attempt at 'Banging The Door', Lydon – still behind the screen – asked, 'Did you like that? Is that what you want? Are you getting your money's worth? Isn't this what rock & roll's all about, maaan?' The audience finally did what it was being provoked to do, and PiL's 'performance' broke Suicide's previous record, instigating a full-scale riot barely fifteen minutes after Lydon sauntered behind the screen.

As journalist Tim Sommers wrote at the time, 'Beyond a certain point, the [resultant] riot became a certainty, and PiL did nothing to forestall or divert this . . . The fact that no one was killed or seriously injured, or the fact that the riot really didn't *blow*, was pure luck. It just as easily could've gone the other way.' But then Lydon had informed Sommers before the show, 'If anything gets busted up, if everything gets broken, we can just catch the first plane out tomorrow.'

On one level, the ensuing riot was the culmination of everything Lydon had been saying since PiL began – that rock is dead, that it was time the audience moved on, and that this was a band who was not interested in playing 'the game'. On the other hand, it was largely born of those endemic PiL traits, indiscipline and inertia. There was a reason why the first song Lydon ever wrote was called 'I'm A Lazy Sod'. But the Ritz was not the end of PiL. The events that night *might* have retained an aura of integrity akin to Winterland *if* Lydon, Levene and Atkins had not returned eighteen months later, playing the PiL hits at US concert venues. So much for killing off rock & roll!

The one thing the Ritz gig succeeded in doing was getting Lydon out of England, and the doom and gloom that now bathed this once 'green and pleasant land' – which, sadly, was not the case for another post-punk singer-songwriter who felt the walls closing in, Ian Curtis. On 29 December 1978, just four days after PiL's UK debut, Joy Division's singer had had his first full-blown epileptic fit. It was a sign of things to come, but the rest of the band seemed strangely unperturbed by, or just plain ignorant of, the seriousness of Curtis's condition. According to Dick Witts, when The Passage played a show with the band in Bristol, and Curtis collapsed beforehand, 'Barney and Hookey were incensed that the manager closed the gig down. [But] we all knew there was something not being spoken about Ian's health.'

Like other equally tragic figures before, Curtis spent the next year caught up in the momentum of a band suddenly going somewhere at speed. The release of *Unknown Pleasures* and singles like 'Transmission' and 'Atmosphere' (on an impossibly rare French-only EP) had gained them a great deal of critical kudos, but it was really their magnetic live performances that continued calling to so many lost souls, performances at odds with the slightly stilted sound of the records Factory made with them. As Ian Wood wrote in March 1980:

Joy Division makes the stage an emotional trapeze wire; what holds me is the feeling, like a kid at the circus, that Curtis is going to break down and fall off. But outside of a live gig, without this intensity, Joy Division's apparent unwillingness to make definite statements – either in their material or in interview – worries me. [*NYR*, 3/80]

Wood wasn't the only one worried. Genesis P. Orridge had been talking to Curtis about the ideas underlying TG, as well as 'about militaria, transgressive acts, sociopathic tendencies, and a good deal about depression and isolation'. After catching a Joy Division show in November 1979, the reasons 'underlying [the] desperation of our late-night phone marathons became much clearer . . . as I saw this dynamic within Joy Division; and the trap, the predicament that so unnerved Ian Curtis and that remained so shockingly consuming of him. I feared for his life from that evening [on].'

And yet everyone around Curtis continued to walk in silence. Even when Curtis told Sumner, 'I feel like there's a big whirlpool, and I'm being sucked down into it and there's nothing I can do,' no one in the band felt compelled to examine the subtexts of the lyrics Curtis was now churning out with a bewildering regularity, as if in a hurry to get it all out. Sumner subsequently admitted to Savage, 'We never talked about Ian's lyrics . . . I felt that if I thought about what we did, then it would stop. I thought, if something great is happening, don't look at the sun.'

One man who was certainly imbued with the idea of making Joy Division sound as doom-laden as possible was their producer, Martin Hannett, who started work on their second album in March 1980, fresh from working on a third Magazine album, *The Correct Use Of Soap*. Though Devoto had expelled Hannett from a demo session back in 1977, he continued to rate his work as a producer – as long as he was kept on a tight rein. As this smart singer says, 'I got my hands on the mixing desk when we did [*The Correct Use Of Soap*], and it was a negotiation.'

The result was a real return to form, with Devoto showing a surprising flair for the absurd in his remarkably affecting cover of '(Falettinme Be Mice Elf Agin)', while delivering his most effective shot in the dark since Magazine's debut 45 – even if 'A Song From Under The Floorboards' enjoyed minimal chart action. An energized Virgin encouraged Devoto to embark on a promotional tour of America, but when he found out that 'my father [had] died while we were on tour in America . . . I no longer had the semi-megalomaniacal drive to front a rock band.' There would be one more Magazine album – *Magic, Murder And The Weather* – but the defection of McGeogh to the Banshees, after the completion of *The Correct Use Of Soap*, effectively consigned the band to rock's back pages.

Meanwhile, Hannett had the opportunity to regain control of the mixing board at Strawberry. Factory funds were relatively flush and it was time to record Curtis and co. again. But Hannett was dissatisfied with the results (or maybe the sarcastic comments of Strawberry's engineer finally got to him), despite producing a dance version of 'She's Lost Control' for the US market, presumably to prove that Joy Division were post-modern funk, as well as the anthemic 'Love Will Tear Us Apart' 45.

And so Hannett took the Manchester band to Britannia Row in London, where *Closer* was completed, closing the book on the band who had allowed him the greatest latitude. This time Hannett really went to town, using the full palette of industrial sounds he heard in his monochromatic imagination. The sound of a drowning man was submerged beneath Hannett's concrete mix. Curtis, already starting to shut down, continued to go along with Hannett and Wilson. But, if what he told Genesis P. Orridge can be relied upon, he already felt the ideals that originally inspired the whole band had been fatally compromised.

Genesis P. Orridge: He knew if he went [on the US tour] he'd be trapped into carrying on and on and on with Joy Division. That there would always be new 'convincing' reasons and persuasions as to why he should do just one more record, just one more tour, just one more interview, ad nauseam. Until there was nothing left of him, or the integrity of his original idea.

He wanted out – of his tangled relationships with his Belgian girl-friend, his wife and his daughter, out of the whole treadmill on which he felt bound, out of the whole spiral down into nothingness. One evening in May 1980, he put himself in a suicidal frame of mind by watching Werner Herzog's blindingly bleak *Stroszek*, before putting Iggy Pop's *The Idiot* on the turntable, tying a noose above his head and making the fateful decision 'not to be'. If Malcolm Owen had been a little too in love with the rock & roll world, Curtis found a little too much self-hate in his dead soul.

Inevitably, the act alone ensured Curtis joined a sainthood of rock

Suicides — along with the kind of success he feared, but never found. 'Love Will Tear Us Apart' seemed such a summation of these sentiments that it couldn't help but climb the charts — with *Closer* close behind. Meanwhile, in London, Virgin missed a trick by not issuing 'Love In Vein' as Malcolm Owen's last will and testament. But then, they probably spared Owen and The Ruts the cast of inevitability that has shrouded the music of Joy Division for the past twenty-five years. What the eulogies both singers received uniformly missed was that the premature deaths of Owen and Curtis deprived punk, in both its populist and progressive guises, of the two most powerful, dynamic and compulsively visual performers of the post-punk era, and with them, lost any real sense of a way ahead. Fade to black.

PART SEVEN

7.1
TALES OF WARF RATS AND
SUBURBAN WEIRDOS
1980-82

No political consciousness has filtered through to these kids. Their hatred is immediate and directed at the most available targets: parents, hippies, the polyester and soap opera people of Beverly Hills and Hollywood . . . They even hate the commercial new wave – 'powerpop queers in narrow ties' . . . but the majority of these Reaganland kids have no way out. They have short-circuited, they are locked into a going-nowhere spiral of hostility. They hate so hard that they have no space to grow. — Mick Farren, LA Punk, *NME*, 11/4/81

Years ago Iggy Stooge used to damage himself in performance, throwing himself on broken glass or into the audience. Now the audience completes the cycle. — Richard Harrington, *Washington Post*

However much self-hatred resided in Curtis's soul, it was matched by at least one LA punk progenitor, Darby Crash, who proved to be equally in love with the rock & roll suicide; Crash finally sparing the world any more of his Germs by taking a fatal overdose in December 1980. As ever, his timing was awry – Lennon's death the following day obliterated any nominal media interest. But for many, it 'was really the signal here in LA for people to say, "Okay, we've pushed it far enough – we're at the edge of the cliff right now."'

Such was the view of Penelope Spheeris, who had spent the previous year documenting the LA scene in its transition from punk to hardcore. When her film, *The Decline of Western Civilization*, finally appeared in 1981, she was criticized for concentrating on hardcore bands (though X and the Germs were totemic representatives of the 'original' scene). But as the title of her film made clear, this was a morality tale, and Crash was a court jester who came to play the fool full-time. Mick Farren found his performance in Spheeris's film deeply disturbing:

[It takes] rock & roll incompetence to new peaks. Too out of it to form words, he howls and grunts and falls gracelessly from PA stacks hard onto the stage. As he tries to stagger to his feet, hands reach out from the crowd and draw on his back and face with felt-tip pens. He's oblivious. It's a matter of screw art as long as he can't feel the pain.

Everything Crash had taken from punk was a *by-product* of the music – its Iggyesque performance-art, the 'fuck you' attitude, the love of confrontation, its 'anyone can do it' aesthetic. However, its main message – be honest in a dishonest world – eluded him. Yet Crash *was* speaking to an audience that believed in his brand of nihilism. When Kurt Cobain first drafted a list of albums that most influenced him, *GI* was there. A punk, but no punk rocker, Crash was the harbinger of hardcore, which embraced many of punk's 'cultural values': adopting the DIY mantra wholesale; having an almost fundamentalist belief in breaking down barriers between artist and audience; but disavowing its musical message of constant revolution.

Hardcore proved yet again that those who do not learn from history are destined to repeat its mistakes, infecting itself with the violence that had plagued the movement from day one. At the same time, it proved strangely detached from the musical heritage it ostensibly drew upon – caring little for the distinction between the Yardbirds and Led Zeppelin; nor seeing the great chasm between Sham 69 and the Sex Pistols. Figures like DOA's Joey Shithead liked to feel that 'when the hardcore thing happened in 1980, it defined a different form of punk. We played with The Clash and thought they were. *wimps.*'

In one sense, hardcore does represent a clean break from English punk, which was as self-referential as it could get. American hardcore not only fanatically applied the 'he who is not for me is against me' credo but set it to a very basic backdrop – how loud, fast and furious can one get. If most hardcore bands made a virtue of their limitations, it got very silly, very fast – especially in California where The Stains proved a blight on the post-Hollywood scene.

Tim Kerr: The Stains played this 'Hardcore versus New Wave' rift to the hilt, which up until Black Flag came to town wasn't even in the picture – Punk was all-encompassing: Sex Pistols and Joy Division were the same thing. The Stains put up posters around town: 'Are you Hardcore or are you New Wave?' They listed bands that were Hardcore and that were New Wave.

The term 'hardcore' – adopted Stateside with its exclusionist, transgressive connotations intact – had actually been around since the birth of punk rock, being used by Caroline Coon in her seminal November 1976 *Melody Maker* piece on punk and the new wave. The following month The Stranglers' Hugh Cornwell bemoaned an element in punk he called 'the hardcore, manipulated people', a reference to those who refused to consider The Stranglers part of *their* thing. Nine months later,

The Rezillos' Eugene Reynolds used the term in a similar way, when suggesting his band 'obviously don't fit in with what . . . so-called hardcore punks in Scotland think is punk'.

Evidently this sub-genre's exclusionist connotation did not originate with The Stains (cough) – or even in America, where it was seemingly first used in its destined sense in the ghettos of Washington DC. Here hardcore made a distinction between 'true' punk (DC hardcore) and 'fake' punk (everything which came before), reflecting a determination to move year zero forward by five full years. Mike Watt, in San Pedro, certainly thinks he 'heard of hardcore first from ads by [DC label] Dischord Records. Ian [MacKaye] called it hardcore: 'At the time, it was the young people coming to punk, 'cause the seventies [punk] was not teenagers, but people from the glam scene and artist types.'

MacKaye's Minor Threat, and fellow DC bar-chord barnstormers like SOA and Bad Brains, were by their very proximity to New York – which had its own *reductio ad absurdum* variant, no wave – fighting a little aesthetic turf war of East Coast regressives. In fact, such was the rapidity with which the term was adopted that MacKaye himself was obliged to disown it by 1981: 'The whole "hardcore" thing . . . [has] become a selling point now. You see albums saying "hardcore" on them and I'm not into that. I consider myself a punk.'

In LA, the turf war became, de facto, a territorial one – a punk *West Side Story* – with the original Hollywood brats appalled to find satellite kids from Orange County moving in. For the hardly objective Brendan Mullen, 'the suburban OC thing [just] destroyed the initial impulse . . . There was a certain psychopathic type who invited themselves to the ball. It was largely a lot of upper-middle-class kids trying to get back at their parents for having too much money . . . It was not about music.' Others were more willing to see LA hardcore as a necessary step away from imitation of the UK.

Steve Wynn: In '80–'81 the most exciting thing was [hardcore:] Black Flag, Circle Jerks, Social Distortion, TSOL, Agent Orange. These bands were actually real punk bands . . . Hearing Black Flag [didn't feel] like somebody trying to be like The Clash or the Ramones. It was a whole different thing! It sounded like skateboarders who didn't like their parents and didn't like their life – it sounded like LA . . . [because] LA's all about nothing fitting – there's no centre emotionally and no centre musically, and it's just about alienation.

Wynn had come back from SF in 1980, expecting to find LA still in the grip of the weirdos, but found a heavier, more abrasive strain had invaded the body-punk. It came from 'the Valley', that geographically defined suburban bleed north of LA, via a band with the punk moniker to end all monikers, Fear. As Mullen says, in *Neutron Bomb*, these guys were 'not influenced by Bowie or the Pistols, [but] fused an aggressive, revved-up take on punk with unapologetic out-and-out heavy-metal riffs pulled from the Unholy Book of Sabbath and Motorhead.'

In this sense, Fear were innovators, and the true progenitors of grunge. They were also largely despised by their peers. As Minuteman Mike Watt recalls, 'I remember some of the Hollywood [punks] being angry, thinking that Fear was heavy metal. To me, it seemed like weird Beethoven.' Heavy metal remained a no-no, despite its status as an essentially American hybrid of another authentic English strain from the great mid-sixties rock explosion, prog-rock.

And heavy metal wasn't about to go away. It was already embedded deep in the American psyche (the term having been coined by the man who had put the second Clash album through the mangler, Sandy Pearlman). In fact, hardcore was to punk what heavy metal was to prog-rock, an attempt to strip the music down to an essence based on immediacy of impact – hence its proclivity to sink to lowest common denominator. This process, evident in a century of American popular song, placed 'authenticity' above any other aesthetic criteria – even when it meant minus any nuance, musical or lyrical.

The heavy-metal/punk symbiosis had been largely held at bay in the UK, even though the godfathers of HM were exclusively English – Led Zeppelin, Deep Purple, Black Sabbath etc. Even in LA, sounding like HM was a guaranteed way to wind up punk audiences. But then, as Fear frontman Lee Ving says, 'Rankling people . . . was definitely a part of what Fear wanted to do as a band. And . . . we were looking directly at the punk audience as a prime target.' Their emergence at almost the same time as the Dead Kennedys in San Francisco suggested that West Coast punk was looking to ratchet up the shock content. Fear's own set included songs like the anti-semitic 'Waiting For The Gas', the homophobic 'Homo-cide', the anti-social 'We Destroy The Family', and the gung-ho 'Let's Have A War', while Ving seemed to have very much the same approach to PR as Jello Biafra.

Lee Ving: If they hate [the songs], chances are they're the person we want to hate it. And I'd just as soon beat the fuck out of 'em anyway, as look at 'em. [1978]

Fear, though, were not the Kennedys. There was little beyond shock value in their lyrics, the heavy-metal element was not cleverly disguised, it was in-your-face, and as Greg Sowders says, though 'they could really set an audience off — Lee was just an instigator and a provocateur.' Ultimately their role as precursors to hardcore would go largely unrecognized because another suburban band, Panic, adopted the Black Flag moniker (a suggestion of band leader Greg Ginn's brother, visual artist Raymond Pettibon), and began to lay aural waste to the punk netherlands of LA in the early months of 1979. As Steve Blush asserts in *American Hardcore*, Black Flag ventured where even the Germs feared to tread:

If the Ramones and Sex Pistols defined Punk, then Black Flag defined Hardcore. Inspired by the Germs, but unashamed to display gnarly Rock influences like Black Sabbath, ZZ Top and the Grateful Dead, they were the most important band of American Hardcore . . . The punk vibe was urbane, elitist and exclusive. Everyone preached DIY, but few practised it. Black Flag, on the other hand, merged the basic constructs of aggression, anti-stardom and alienation with a blue-collar mindset.

Formed by Greg Ginn in late 1977, Panic were already demoing tracks at a local studio in Hermosa Beach that December. Aside from that mock exam, they seemed content to let Hollywood punk run amok for a while longer. When he attempted to document Black Flag's early years in 1981, Ginn dared to call the album *The First Four Years*, suggesting that — much like the antipodean Saints — every shambolic jam with friends was a band rehearsal. Ginn was asserting a primacy over the Hollywood bands, even though his band did next to nothing during the period of its brief dominion.

Brendan Mullen: [Ginn] will insist that Black Flag began as Panic in '76 and was unable to book a single show in the Hollywood area for a full three years (until summer of '79) because they were suburban (from the South Bay), and not part of some imaginary 'in-crowd' they invented. [In fact] their first gig as Black Flag was the Moose Lodge in January '79 . . . and they only began to get noticed when their seven-inch EP came out, summer of '79 . . . Meanwhile, tons of other suburban bands with long hair and intense fast downstroke beats seemed to have played around the Hollywood area with no problem. Fear was already doing the 'proto-hardcore' thing a full year before Black Flag . . . [Whereas] it was the dumbed-down, fucked-up crowds from Hermosa Beach (not originally even their turf) that Black Flag began openly pandering to (though he'll vehemently deny it); [and] which gave the scene a bad name.

Perhaps there was an element of panic at the prospect of playing live. Original Flag singer Keith Morris says that, at the time, all of the band looked 'like we were roadies for Peter Frampton. We were wearing flannel shirts and deck shoes.' That alone might have ensured any punk audience was too busy hurling missiles to accept their take on punk. By 1979, though, they had a record to promote and a suburban audience to energize.

In fact, they had spent most of 1978 waiting for Greg Shaw at Bomp to issue their single, 'Nervous Breakdown'. According to SST discographer Michael Bonner, Shaw decided 'to sit on the record for nine months, before deciding that punk was over and returning the tapes to the band'. Singer Keith Morris suggests the fact that Shaw expected the band to 'pay for everything, and he was gonna put it out and own the masters and the publishing' drove Ginn to finally put the EP out himself, forming SST Records for the very purpose. Whether Ginn knew it or not, he had created the label the west had needed since What? issued forth in 1977.

But releasing records required some promotion, and in LA that meant playing gigs, airplay being about as likely as Fleetwood Mac recording their next album drug-free. The first gig was in the incongruous setting of a Moose Lodge on Redondo Beach, where singer Morris recalls being chased around the auditorium by forty senior citizens when he decided to start swinging from the American flag. Altogether more successful was the Flag's second gig, which took place in Pedro shortly after The Clash's Santa Monica show. The support band was a local outfit, the Reactionaries, with whom Black Flag were set to form an almost symbiotic relationship.

Mike Watt: We got our first gig because when Black Flag was handing out flyers the first time The Clash came [to LA], they couldn't believe there was a band in Pedro, [so when] one of their first gigs . . . was in Pedro, they asked us to open. It was . . . one of these centres for young people. They rented it out.

The Reactionaries were Black Flag's brothers-in-arms, sometimes quite literally. Formed by Mike Watt and D. Boon, the Reactionaries were a powerhouse quartet fronted by singer Martin Tamburovich, who were opposed to rock & roll. As a laughing Watt observes, 'We thought that jazz was closer to punk than rock & roll. That's why we called the band the Reactionaries. We were kinda anti-rock & roll . . . I mean, Albert Ayler, John Coltrane . . . they were just punk rockers that came before . . . Part of it was reacting against rock & roll. Part of it was being in a scene where experimentation and little stories counted a lot more than technique and notes.'

Watt and Boon had fully immersed themselves in the LA punk scene, in a way that Ginn never really did. As Watt memorably wrote in his 'History Lesson Part II': 'We learned punk rock in Hollywood / Drove up from Pedro / We were fucking corn-dogs / We'd go drink and pogo.' Initially, though, neither was sure they could live up to the LA punk ideal. As Watt has written, in his *Spiels of a Minuteman*, 'We felt tainted by knowing rock & roll off of records, and unoriginal compared to these cats who were writing tunes just after picking up their instruments.' Watt didn't feel compelled to emulate the punk directive until he examined the lyrics, which 'were more like personal statements, and reflected what was going on in the person's head who was singing them'.

It would be 1980 before the Reactionaries dumped Tamburovich, dropped down to a trio, and reinvented themselves as The Minutemen. But from the outset they constituted part of the SST family, sharing with Flag a common ideal, looking beyond the narrow confines of the local LA scene, realizing the need to connect up the dots Stateside, to replicate the situation in Britain. The logistics in the US, though, were entirely different – the country was big, the scene was not.

Mike Watt: Punk rock was really big in England when we started, but in America it was really small. With it being small, you had to get this kind of fabric. It wasn't just the bands, it was the artists, the fanzine people. We created our own parallel universe . . . We had to or it would have died. There wasn't really a market for it, so we set up our own little world . . . A lot of Hollywood bands never toured – I think only the Dils had a van. Maybe it was from Greg [Ginn]'s experience with ham radios, but he believed that if you try, you can get things beyond your little group. He said, 'Let's not hide this as a secret. Let's get out and play.'

There may have been another reason Black Flag seemed so keen to expand their frontiers – they didn't feel entirely welcome in LA. Their options, few enough already, got fewer after a free gig at Manhattan Beach's Polliwog Park in the summer of 1979. According to Morris, they secured it because, 'Greg had persuaded the guy from Manhattan Beach Parks & Recreation that we had some Fleetwood Mac songs in our set.' When asked to furnish some evidence, Ginn kept stalling the promoter: 'I kept promising to give him [some] of our music, but I knew I couldn't because he would never have let us play.'

When Black Flag unleashed themselves on a picture-postcard after-noon in the park, they were pelted with assorted foodstuffs by the unamused, picnicking old-timers. The experience garnered them their first publicity, as well as an apologetic press release from a shame-faced Special Events Supervisor. Returning to their Huntingdon hideout, they were made to feel no more welcome there. As Morris says, the locals 'considered us anarchists and terrorists – like we were building a nuclear device in our rehearsal space', but such hostility only fuelled the band's determination to show 'em.

Keith Morris: Our dedication to our cause was ceaseless. We were going to make as large a racket, piss as many people off, go apeshit as we could, and we had no choice but to play to please ourselves and a handful of friends. This noisemaking unit was too obnoxious to fit in with most of the other musical outfits.

Morris, though, wasn't just singing 'Nervous Breakdown', he was heading for one. By his own admission he was 'soaked in alcohol, [and] freaking out on alcohol and speed', and singing with the Flag was becoming too demanding. After a studio session in October 1979, he quit. If he would form the equally hard-nosed Circle Jerks in the fullness of time; for now he left it to Ron Reyes (then Dez Cadena, and finally Henry Rollins) to do Ginn's Black Flag bidding.

Having overtaken Fear, Black Flag began to develop the 'complete fearlessness' that SST's Joe Carducci considers their trademark. When the hardcore audience began to demand they conform to its hard, fast and loud mantra, they challenged even this constituency. In March 1980, they sparked a riot at the Fleetwood when they apparently played a 55-minute version of 'Louie Louie' that made even Mancunian John the Postman's legendary 20-minute version seem concise. But the Flag's face-offs with their fans were less of a problem than their constituency's constant confrontations with outsiders. Even a natural supporter like Richard Meltzer – who had championed punk as a necessary breath of fresh air from day one – was appalled by the element Black Flag attracted:

The last [punk] show I willingly went to was in some black neighbourhood around Inglewood: Black Flag (playing under an assumed name) and three Orange County bands whose identity you'd have to hypnotize me to recall with any certitude . . . Midway through Black Flag, who had the good sense to go on first, bottles started flying – full bottles . . . tables got smashed, chairs, windows. (Rock as usual.) After the cops closed the joint, the kids . . . went out and trashed the ghetto, pissing and puking in doorways, hurling bottles through the windowglass of fried chicken stands, ripping wipers and antennas off old Buicks . . . I never went back.

It was inevitable that such ritualized violence was going to be noticed and, when that happened, amplified for the sake of 'a good story'. Sure enough, at the end of June 1980, the *LA Times* ran a story focusing on Black Flag's hardcore fan-base, called 'Violence Sneaks Into Punk Scene'. This kind of publicity, as Danny Weizmann wrote in *Hardcore California*, 'was a disaster for such bands as Black Flag, the Circle Jerks, Fear, China White, etc. It banned them from clubs, jeopardized any party they played, flyer they put out, and even fans that wore their stickers. The Huntingdon Beach PD [even] began to refer to the bands as "gangs".'

Ginn, as ever rewriting history, is being disingenuous when he claims that 'before [that article], it was more intellectuals and other thinking people involved; after [it], every interview[er] was [asking], "What about the violence?"' The rituals of hardcore were already well established, notably 'slamming in the pit', that charming pastime which Mick Farren described in his 1981 *NME* feature as a 'set piece of mindless mayhem . . . I suppose it is a dance. If not, it's something altogether new; spontaneous and pure, random, motiveless violence to a background of super fast rock & roll.'

It was Mikal Gilmore, the most open-minded rock critic in town, who pointed out that 'the music for these melees – a rabid, samely version of early, monorhythmic, nonmelodic punk, usually dispensed by Fear, Black Flag, or the Circle Jerks – is both prompting and incidental: merely a relentless agitating soundtrack or backdrop for the real performers, the audience.' And that, really, was the rub. The music, even at the volume Black Flag played, was becoming a sideshow. The inmates had taken over the asylum.

For which Ginn must share the blame. As LA rock scribe Michael Schneider pointed out in the January 1981 issue of *Bay Area Music* magazine (*BAM*): 'Although Black Flag don't encourage the violence, they don't discourage it, much less acknowledge it onstage.' Had Ginn simply not noticed the fate of Sham 69, who by the end of 1978 literally could not play a major city in the UK without trouble in the stalls bringing the show to a series of abrupt halts, while Pursey whined about how he hadn't meant to spark class war by writing inflammatory, class-conscious diatribes directed at 'the kids'? The contradictions wrenched *them* apart in triple-time. What made Ginn think he could buck the trend?

If anything, the propensity for violence was greater in LA than in London; as not only did the police carry guns, but the LAPD seemed to act with a rare impunity from repercussions which went unabated until the Rodney King riots in 1992. As DC degenerate Henry Rollins discovered, when he became Black Flag's singer in 1981, 'The police experience in DC was getting told to get your skateboard off the street. The experience in California was to be intimidated, threatened and made to feel powerless.' Black Flag gave the LAPD an excuse it didn't necessarily need to crack craniums.

Sid Griffin: I loved Black Flag because of their power and passion, though I didn't believe a lot of what they said . . . [But] there was a lot of trouble at those gigs. I can remember leaving the Whisky after seeing Black Flag, and the LAPD were [there], wearing their navy-blue uniforms, riot batons out, motorcycle crash-helmets [on]. They were clearly spoiling for a fight. Okay, someone threw a bottle, [but] all hell broke loose. They were hitting women – and the smallest little farts. Black Flag . . . were a lit match to the LAPD – way more than the Circle Jerks or the Adolescents.

Back in the Washington home of HarDCore, where some of the same kinda shit was going down at punk gigs, it was generally left to the hardcore punks (and local hardnuts) to get on with it. And get it on they did. Henry Rollins' own version of events is that 'by late summer of 1980, [the] violence started as new people came in [to DC] from the suburbs. We'd get marines, bikers, rednecks, tough guys, thick-necked young wise-asses. We'd fight outsiders. We didn't care if it was fair, this guy was fucking with our little piece of the world, so we'd stomp the shit out of him. That was our attitude.'

For HarDCore's godfather Ian MacKaye, the source of the problem wasn't hard to see. He encapsulated it on Minor Threat's 'Said Gun', 'You're looking for a reason to hate, so you can fuck somebody up / You'd hate yourself if you got the chance – I guess you already do / You fuck yourself up every night . . . If you have to fight / Then fight the violence that rules your life.' One implicit target herein was his old friend Rollins.

Ian MacKaye: I was in a lot of fights. I'd just try to teach the guy a lesson, no permanent damage . . . [But] I'd look over my shoulder and Henry [Rollins] would be dragging his guy down the stairs and kicking him! I'd have to go and try to stop him.

Rollins paid little heed to MacKaye's cautionary wail. When he was offered the opportunity to join Black Flag after Dez Cadena, its third singer in two years, reverted to guitar, he seemed hell-bent on taking on all comers. According to Black Flag's roadie, 'Mugger', MacKaye had been in the frame for the Flag singer slot 'but he was too like, "This is *my* personality," and [Ginn] couldn't really mould him. Ian knew what he was. They were looking for somebody young, who they could kinda work on.'

Initially, Ginn seemed content to let Rollins get on with fighting the whole audience while the band played on, convinced that the contradictions would come out in the wash, like the kinks in those blue collars. As SST's Joe Carducci says, 'Greg wasn't very kind to Henry. Henry would be getting beat up, and Greg would consider that he brought it on himself. And yet, Greg knew that the whole band brought it on themselves.'

The problems facing Ginn and his SST co-workers were affecting every part of the Flag family. Mike Watt – who by the summer of 1980 had his own investment in SST, after they released The Minutemen's vinyl debut, 'Paranoid Time' – recalls that 'the LAPD had this whole idea that [SST] were not a record label, but some kind of front for something else. There was this whole trumped-up, weirded-out [drug charge] the judge threw out in chambers. There was an organization in

Orange County called Parents of Punks! A lot of 'em couldn't figure on it being [self-]expression. It had to be some socially deviant thing.'

SST, which had made its first appearance back in the summer of 1979, two years on still only had three Black Flag singles and two Minutemen 45s to its name. But Ginn had big plans. For all the SST rhetoric, he was enough of a businessman to know that the majors had the US distribution network sewn up, and agreed to talk to these companies, even when the likes of Keith Morris thought it a cop-out: 'While Greg was talking to some record company guy, I unzipped my pants and urinated on the backs of this guy's legs.' When Black Flag recorded its first LP, *Damaged*, in summer 1981 – with new recruit Rollins learning the songs from tapes of the material made with Cadena – Ginn decided to approach Unicorn Records, who had major-label distribution through MCA, hoping to get the album available all the way from the Grand Coulee Dam to DC.

Ginn knew this distribution deal was Black Flag's big chance. And *Damaged* delivered its 'deviant' goods with spades of attitude, from its declamatory opening, 'Rise Above' ('We're tired of your abuse / Try to stop us – it's no use'), to the scary closer, 'Life Of Pain', a paean on self-harm that ends with 'Self-destruct . . . There's got to be a way to get out.' The album proved that Black Flag could be a whole lot more than 'a relentless, agitating soundtrack' to ritualized violence, given even half a chance to grow. Sadly, that possibility was curtailed – probably for good – on 27 September 1981. That morning the *LA Times* quoted MCA chief Al Bergamo's reaction on hearing the album: 'I found it an anti-parent record . . . it certainly wasn't like Bob Dylan or Simon & Garfunkel'. (Er, 'Your sons and your daughters are beyond your command' is a *pro*-parent sentiment, then, Al?)

When the story got picked up, the moral majority started hyperventilating and MCA promptly refused to distribute *Damaged*. This left Unicorn in a precarious position, which became only more precarious when it filed Chapter 11, a 'voluntary' way of staving off bankruptcy that convinced Ginn they were intending to default on any monies owed to SST. In that fine American tradition, Unicorn's response to being caught with their hand in the till was to countersue – issuing an injunction precluding Black Flag from releasing their records through any other avenue of distribution. When Ginn tried to sneak out a Black Flag double-album retrospective, *Everything Went Black*, as an official bootleg, without the band's name anywhere on the record, the judge almost threw him in jail for contempt of court. Meanwhile, Unicorn continued to mysteriously fund their network, until SST discovered the source of its sprightly situation.

Joe Carducci: We found out they were taking checks that were supposed to go into the Chapter 11 account, and putting them into one of their non-bankrupt corporations. When they did that, the judge threw them into Chapter 7 and foreclosed on 'em, and that freed us – much to the judge's consternation, 'cause he fucking hated us. He looked at those Raymond Pettibon drawings on *Everything Went Black*, and wanted to lock us [all] up.

It had taken Ginn eighteen months to extract his band from this self-inflicted catastrophe – at any time he could have disbanded Black Flag, and re-formed under another name – during which time the impetus of the band had been fatally forestalled. As Carducci says, 'It was one frustration after another. They couldn't release anything, they couldn't tour because they'd over-toured *Damaged*, and he didn't want to play the new stuff because other people would copy it.' Ginn was attempting the trickiest of balancing acts – retaining their live audience, almost their only source of revenue, while essentially disowning the hardcore template Black Flag had espoused for so long. And which its audience still craved.

The Minutemen had already made such a transition themselves, even before *Damaged*, providing Black Flag with fair warning of the rocky road ahead. As Mike Watt suggests, hardcore very quickly 'solidified into a kind of orthodoxy of that fast guitar style. Opening for Black Flag, [we raised] a huge question in their mind – is this really punk? I thought the idea was anarchy, not orthodoxy ... There were [real] contradictions there. [After] the espousal of going for it, and try anything you want, [we were] being expected to deliver a certain thing.'

With the Unicorn lawsuit at last resolved, Ginn knew he needed to get the message out that Black Flag had evolved, if they were ever going to pick up the pieces. The toll this legal matter had taken was evident when he told *BAM* in August 1983, 'We're years behind in recording and showing the public what we want to do with the basic ... groove of the music ... We play seven- and eight-minute songs now, which forces audiences who think of us as exclusively two-minute songs to realize Black Flag has changed. And they can get violent about that ... We do analyze our impact from time to time. We don't have a frivolous attitude. It's important to us that we be a positive influence . . . We're not just looking for a random reaction . . . We're not [just] trying to shock.'

And yet for all the fear-mongering Black Flag engendered in the media, Ginn had succeeded in giving both the hardcore scene and the local post-punk scene a kick-start it assuredly needed. In the eighteen months they were embroiled in ancillary matters, the SST roster had gone from strength to strength. By the end of 1983, when Black Flag resumed releasing records, SST was the communal command HQ for the likes of Saccharine Trust, Hüsker Dü and The Meat Puppets, as well as the increasingly quirky Minutemen. None of these bands were content to confine themselves to that tunnel-vision hardcore sound.

But then, the SST bands had some catching up to do. In the past year and a half LA had witnessed a calypso of contemporary sounds, from punkabilly to the Paisley Underground. Everyone from The Blasters to The Gun Club, The Cramps to Blood on the Saddle, Lone Justice to Green on Red, Rain Parade to Dream Syndicate, seemed to have a different idea about the message to take from punk, and/or the best way to reclaim Modern Music. Evidently, 'going for it, and try[ing] anything you want' was a credo that did not need be confined to the suburban weirdos of SST.

— — —

If 1980 was the year of hardcore, 1981 saw punkabilly steal much of its thunder. The following year, the cowpunkers moved their herds in, before the Paisley Underground began to clear them out. Los Angeles was setting itself on fire again (and again), each mini-scene renewing itself in punk's phoenix-like flames – even as its post-punkers began acting like a lot of reactionaries. As Greg Sowders says, 'It [was] a logical progression [sic] – from seventies punk, if you start to back it up, what else is raw and vital – oh, here's sixties punk.'

Just as the British punk strain drew self-consciously on its garagebands of yore – taking the sixties model, and stripping it down till it was barely street-legal – this generation of LA bands were tipping their hat to the last set of LA bands to shake some action. Love, The Byrds, The Doors and Buffalo Springfield (along with Oakland's Creedence Clearwater Revival) were designated the acceptable face of mainstream mid-sixties 'mericana, their sounds and songs dusted off by initially derivative combos from the same concrete jungle.

Some generation-jumping connections proved particularly surprising. When the first X album, *Los Angeles*, appeared on Slash in April 1980, it was produced by The Doors' Ray Manzarek, and included their own cover of Doors classic, 'Soul Kitchen'. As Doe told Mullen, 'We didn't have any illusions about wanting to do it lo-fi or anti-establishment . . . We wanted to go in there and make the best record we could.' The exercise was repeated the following spring, when the more cocksure *Wild Gift* appeared (also produced by Manzarek). By this time, though, it was clear that X hadn't merely improved musically. They were starting to show all those wares kept under wraps through the Masque years.

John Doe: I knew about blues and country in 1977, and I said, 'Fine, I want to do what I'm doing now.' You just put it away, and it bubbles around in your musical knowledge . . . 'Adult Books' is as much a Ben E. King song as it is an X song. If you listen to only the drum track of 'In This House That I Call Home', you hear 'Iko Iko'. [But] it was important to put all that stuff away for a while.

Those reference points hadn't been lost on everyone during the days of Whisky and whine. The first time Dave Alvin, guitarist in The Blasters, saw X he was knocked out by Billy Zoom's guitarwork, which he realized had 'a lot of references in there . . . rockabilly stuff flying around with surf stuff thrown in, and [then] Ramones power-chord riffing.' John Doe was determined to keep adding textures to the canvas, telling *BAM* in 1980, 'We require a lot from an audience. We challenge them with the music . . . We're not like the Ramones or The Undertones, who are easily grasped.' (A not particularly well-targeted sideswipe.) The point was driven home when X decided to include on *Wild Gift* re-recorded versions of the 1978 Dangerhouse single cuts, now humming along at garageband speed. No more bushel-hiding for these boys (and gal) – time to let it shine.

X, though, were finding it difficult to gain an audience outside LA, and began to suspect that this would be the case as long as they remained on Slash. As Exene told *Sounds* shortly after *Wild Gift* appeared, 'No one's going to make it easy for Slash. There's all this stuff that exists, that's been built up over the years, radio and all that, and it's very hard to infiltrate.' *Wild Gift* would be X's last album for the label. For all of Bob Biggs' protestations, by the time X jumped across to Warners in the summer of 1982, they had outgrown the label; and Biggs had already found two more homegrown punkabilly bands to take X's place.

The Blasters and The Gun Club both made their Slash debuts in the second half of 1981, though The Blasters had already recorded a homemade album of revved-up rockabilly for a tiny San Fernando record label, Rollin' Rock Records, in the fall of 1979. The Alvin brothers, Dave and Phil, had also been keeping tabs on the Hollywood bands, believing that they needed to integrate some of punk's more progressive elements into The Blasters if they were gonna levitate.

Dave Alvin: With our background in blues and R&B, we knew we couldn't honestly be a true punk-rock band. But we could take what we learned from [R&B musicians] . . . and mix it with what we learned from the English punk 45s.

Phil Alvin: No other bands were really doing it our way . . . We were like real raw . . . and the fact that we were also doing blues, and didn't know any contacts in Hollywood *and* we weren't cute – it was just like, 'Well, who the fuck wants *you*?!' [1984]

Thankfully, The Blasters *were* adopted by a handful of journalists as part of a (somewhat arbitrary) hybrid of rockabilly and punk in the months after X's debut album. After a rave review from Chris Morris in the *LA Reader* of their *American Music*, they were soon sharing bills with the likes of X and Peter Case's Plimsouls.

In other words, The Blasters were X in reverse – two bands attacking the problem from opposite sides, but still coming at it from ninety degrees. But another Masque regular, who gave Slash the first Gun Club album, arrived at his rockabilly/punk fusion from a more unexpected trajectory. Jeffrey Lee Pierce was another Laughner-like character, who was a little too death-ridden for his own good. Initially just a pen-wielding enthusiast who effused on behalf of X and the Germs for *Slash* or its New York doppelgänger, *New York Rocker*, he continued to take notes on the LA underground throughout the Hollywood years, until a September 1980 *NYR* piece on his favourite band suggested someone about to make a play himself:

LA's small punk scene . . . has nothing to do with record companies, nothing to do with The Knack or the Motels. It has no Clash or Ramones to look up to as heroes – it's too new for that, because it sprung up late and from completely nothing . . . [but bands like X, who] were originally crude and bashing . . . instead of self-destructing they grew and grew.

Kid Congo, who co-founded the band (as Creeping Ritual) in 1980, but had left before the first album, says he and Pierce both agreed that they would 'do something other than basic punk-rock'. Congo also claims they 'were very influenced by The Slits and no wave and blues and reggae and dub . . . That was the genesis of us wanting to play.'

Meanwhile, Pierce was being introduced to a lot of blues and jazz by Back Door man, Phreddie Patterson. Yet he still wasn't sure which elements fit together, until he bolted them on and saw if they rattled or shook. As Steve Wynn asserts, no matter how much The Gun Club showed 'all the[ir] delta blues and country influence . . . it was still punk-rock.'

Fire Of Love, issued in August 1981, was just the kind of 'vision of things' which the west had been struggling to muster. Simply put, *Fire Of Love* had an ambition found repeatedly in punk's island home in the past five years, but not previously sighted in this western land of plenty. The first LA (post-)punk album that could stand alongside the likes of *Marquee Moon*, *Modern Dance*, *Pink Flag* or *Even Serpents Shine*, it proved that no rock genre was safe from the punk aesthetic.

An isotonic rush of swampy R&B, the album was an utterly original way of plugging in to the blues. Pierce even had the bravado required to write an R&B song called 'She's Like Heroin To Me'; while the one 'cover' they tackled, Robert Johnson's 'Preaching The Blues' – one of Johnson's 'demonic trilogy' (along with 'Hellhound On My Trail' and 'Me And The Devil Blues') – was perhaps the first electric rendition to have the same hellbound sound Johnson got out of his beat-up acoustic forty-five years earlier.

However, there no longer existed that old Hollywood scene, just its offshoots, none of which seemed too keen to conscript The Gun Club. According to Congo, 'The Gun Club didn't fit into any sub-genre. We were too arty to be in the rockabilly scene, but too rock to be in the arty scene.' Caught between camps, Congo quit and joined The Cramps.

It seemed like the same problem which had led the Dils to flee the city back in 1978/9. As Chip Kinman says, 'When punk started changing into hardcore, we realized we didn't want to be part of that scene . . . It was time to move on.' Barely had Pierce settled on his swampy variant of the punk muse, though, than the Kinmans returned, renewed. And they weren't calling themselves the Dils any more. Now it was Rank & File. Once again, their initial instincts were good, as they found that LA punk had acquired some American roots while they had been away.

Brendan Mullen: By the time Chip and Tony [Kinman] returned here circa '82 . . . interest was already ragin' locally for mutant rockabilly, blues, country, folk and other US roots rock inspired by X, The Blasters, The [now transplanted-to-LA] Cramps, Ray Campi's Rockabilly Rebels, Levi and the Rockats, Jimmy and the Mustangs (from OC), Top Jimmy, Los Lobos – the Flesheaters, Tupelo Chainsex, Screamin' Sirens, Blood on the Saddle . . . even The Gun Club was already locked 'n' loaded. The roots scene [was] sustained [by] those disinclined or too-long-in-the-tooth already to go the 'hardcore' way . . . [and] nurtured by Slash Records, where Anna Statman and Chris Desjardins were key A&R reps.

The Kinmans' new band had another West Coast punk in tow. After Tony had quit music altogether at the end of 1980, Chip had formed an alliance with ex-Nun Alejandro Escovedo. The combination seemed to have so much potential, Tony couldn't help but want to be involved again. Their designated direction, 'country-hardcore' – as they called it – was a genre Tony felt had 'the same sincerity as punk, same delivery, it's just a different bass pattern'.

After several months of testing out new songs in a small club in Austin, the Shorthorn Bar, they wound their way back to LA, playing to 'West Coast Dils fans . . . who had no idea who Lefty Frizell was'. Thankfully, they snagged a support slot with The Blasters, immediately making an ally of Dave Alvin. According to the Kinmans, it was Alvin who persuaded Bob Biggs to sign Rank & File to Slash in May 1982. Emerging from the Dils counted for little, whatever the label's now-masked origins.

If Rank & File were not quite sure how they might fit in alongside LA's punkabilly bands, the next mutation was already underway. And they were assigned the John the Baptist role in this as-yet-unnamed creed, cowpunk, lighting the way and preaching on behalf of a young lady who had taken to joining the Kinmans for Rank & File encores of revved-up country standards. Maria McKee had the most direct connection of any post-punker to the mid-sixties LA garage-rock scene – her (half-) brother Bryan Maclean had been a guitarist in the classic Love line-up responsible for the timeless *Forever Changes*, back in 1967.

Though McKee was still young enough to marry Jerry Lee Lewis, she had already sung with her brother's band, while comprising the blonde half of a country duo with local lad, Ryan Hedgecock. By 1982, inspired by her punk idols, she was immersing herself deep in country music. As she later admitted, it was when she saw X's John Doe wearing a George Jones t-shirt that she went to Tower Records and 'bought every George Jones album I could get my hands on'.

She would soon be performing Hank Williams and Merle Haggard songs (with Dave Alvin) on local TV programme *Cutting Edge*. Meanwhile, during an acoustic residency at the Cathay de Grande, McKee and Hedgecock met Marvin Etzioni, 'who came in and started helping with the writing'. Soon, they found a drummer, the already accomplished Don Heffington, and began playing country classics hell-for-leather under the legend, Lone Justice.

Ryan Hedgecock: As a band, when we started, we were doing hardcore honky-tonk music . . . [because] there was [initially] an inability to play more complicated music. Then I got into Gram Parsons, and from that into the Stones . . . Gradually we started incorporating those elements. It has never been a conscious thing. [1985]

Through 1983, Lone Justice were just about the most exciting band in LA, as they went through all their changes in a whirlwind moment, writing a battery of country-punk songs like 'Cactus Rose', 'Soap, Soup And Salvation' and 'Workin' Man Blues', while also countrifying 'Sweet Jane' and punkifying 'Going To Jackson'. Fronted by a real firecracker, they were too good, too soon.

Certainly other LA post-punk music-makers feared for the band's future. As Long Ryder Sid Griffin states, 'Early on Lone Justice were terrific, [but] the moment they polished up – and got signed – it was over for me . . . We used to call them the New Stone Ponys, 'cause it was the Stone Ponys, then they were the Stone Ponys featuring Linda Ronstadt . . . then it was Linda Ronstadt. There was [just] so much focus on Maria.' At the end of 1983, another hot property with their own country/punk fusion, Jason and the Nashville Scorchers, came to town and caught Lone Justice at the end of this particular trail.

Jason Ringenberg: I was a big Lone Justice fan. When we got our record deal with EMI in late '83, we opened for Lone Justice [in LA], and they were already a well-developed band. I thought there was only so far Rank & File was gonna go with what they were doing, but I felt with Lone Justice, the sky was the limit . . . She was so young and so good. But she got told that *way* too much.

By then, 1983 was shaping up to be the season of the big hype. At the end of 1982 all the punkabillies and cowpunkers – still landlocked at the 'indie', Slash – had been joined by LA's last wave of post-punk bands, the Paisley Underground. A&R hardly knew where to turn. Thankfully, these bands at least seemed to have a point of reference – invariably sixties-based – to which they could relate. With Lone Justice, it was Creedence Clearwater Revival. In the case of The Dream Syndicate, the Paisley's premier band, it was The Velvet Underground. After all, how could that particular name not be a direct reference to the Velvets (Dream Syndicate being the 'nickname' for The Theatre of Eternal Music, from whence John Cale came).

Steve Wynn: We got the name one step removed – from a Tony Conrad record called *Outside The Dream Syndicate*. Dennis, our drummer, was into Kraut rock and he was a big Faust fan, and from that he got the Tony Conrad solo record and said, 'Look at this record! It's a cool name.' To us, it was just an album title . . . [Eventually I would have to say,] 'We're ripping off lots of bands, not just the Velvets. We steal from The Fall, Creedence, Black Flag, The Stooges – big time.'

The Dream Syndicate was one of at least two bands with which Steve Wynn had been playing in the fall of 1981. The other was a spin-off from one of the last punk bands in town, the Unclaimed – a punk band in the *Nuggets* sense. Formed in April 1979 by Sid Griffin and Shelley Gans – after Griffin was thrown out of another Hollywood punk band, Death Wish, because 'my guitar-tone was too country' – the pair decided, 'We could do a sixties punk band, à la the Shadows of Knight or The Seeds. It was us and the Chesterfield Kings. We played punk venues and people didn't know what to make of us. We dressed in black, but it was black Beatles boots, black Levis, never torn, and black turtlenecks. We [even] put out an EP.' However, when Gans proved opposed to anything remotely original, Griffin was obliged to point out, 'We can't keep playing obscure *Nuggets* songs.'

Griffin was a Masque regular who had been following the progress of LA punk as it was blown every which way by the latest wind of change, so when 'the cowpunk thing [came along] – and things shifted [again] . . . I clocked it, and I knew that it would be good for a guy like me, who wasn't inherently angry and self-hating, but I didn't really know *where* it could possibly go.' Realizing Gans wasn't about to sway his way, he put in a claim; forming another outfit with Unclaimed bassist

Barry Shank and Steve Wynn, this young, knowledgeable guy who worked at Rhino Records and DJ'd at the Cathay de Grande, a favourite haunt of the Unclaimed.

Sid Griffin: We quit to form the Long Ryders. Barry, Steve Wynn and I had a band that was gonna be the Long Ryders. We had rehearsed for like four months, and [Steve] always wanted me to feedback à la The Dream Syndicate. I had a Super-Beatle amp . . . and when I fed back, I'd blow the horns. I said, 'Look, I can't keep just feeding back all the time, it's knocking the top end off of my amp.' So Steve Wynn quit, to go with this other band he was rehearsing with.

Though it would take Griffin a little while to overcome this setback, Wynn was almost immediately up and running with his 'other' band, who had been in the background all along (Wynn admits that while he 'was playing with [Sid] and having a good time . . . [I was] also playing with . . . the band that became The Dream Syndicate'). The problem for Wynn had been that the Unclaimed Ryders [sic] were doing mainly Griffin's songs, and his choice of covers; and Wynn felt it was time to wend his own way.

Drummer Greg Sowders joined Griffin's group just as Wynn left, and recollects, 'Early on rehearsals [were] very sixties, Yardbirds, *Nuggets*, very psychedelic, and a few Velvets songs Steve left behind for us – [like] "Run Run Run". Sometimes Steve would sit in with us, so we'd play "White Light/White Heat".' This was Wynn's preferred reference-point. And for some time he had been wanting to put together a band with his long-term girlfriend, Kendra Smith. When Wynn found the versatile Karl Precoda, things started to happen apace.

Steve Wynn: I met Karl Precoda, and he and Kendra and I started jamming on 'Susie Q', and anything else, in the basement . . . and liked what we were doing. [It was] a very quick transition from jamming for fun to, 'Let's go in the studio for one day and make a demo, so we can play local shows,' to, 'Hey, this is good. We should put this demo out as an EP,' to lots and lots of press, to signing with Slash. [It was] all within a matter of months.

Wynn had songs he could draw on from earlier bands like The Suspects and 15 Minutes (the latter's version of 'That's What You Always Say' had already appeared as a single). But The Dream Syndicate were an altogether more ambitious agglomeration of influences. Wynn typifies their early sound thus: 'We were doing long songs, very few chord changes, with noise, with feedback, with dynamics – almost a hippy kind of thing. There was a radio show that we did a month before recording *The Days Of Wine And Roses* . . . that [best illustrates] what we were doing. Very extreme noise, cacophony to a beautiful ballad, back and forth . . . We were [trying to] mix the artier, janglier stuff with punk-rock, and that wasn't happening around us.'

That hour-long September 1982 KPFK radio show (subsequently issued on CD) showed how a band that 'came out of punk rock' might tackle the likes of Buffalo Springfield, Bob Dylan and Donovan ('Mr Soul', 'Outlaw Blues' and 'Season Of The Witch' respectively). The *Nuggets* element of the Unclaimed, which had appealed to Wynn, was here fused with a kind of atonal repetition befitting any band that (even unwittingly) took its name from La Monte Young's Theatre of Eternal Music. What took the quartet by surprise was how eagerly their art-punk was embraced.

Steve Wynn: We really thought we'd be hated. We expected no one wanted to see a band play 'Susie Q' for twenty minutes – we wanted to see how far we could go with it. We liked that [idea]. When we were on good behaviour, we'd play the songs like they were on the [first] album. But other times we'd play a Creedence song for half the night, or what became 'John Coltrane Stereo Blues' for the whole show.

In fact, The Dream Syndicate were adopted by the local press with such rapidity – after making that first, souped-up demo into their own indie EP, on Down There Records – that they were signed to Slash (where else?), and cutting an album, barely nine months after they had rehearsed in earnest for the first time in late December 1981. They had certainly sailed past the one local psychedelic band who could claim a chronological precedence over them. The Rain Parade, though, were not a garageband with psychedelic undertones, they were a psychedelic band with a garage.

Sid Griffin: Rain Parade really started the [Paisley] thing . . . [And] the Rain Parade were probably going to be the best studio band of all of us . . . If Rain Parade with [David] Roback had stayed together, I think they'd have been [big]. [But] I can remember [Matthew] Piucci explaining to me their material. It wasn't based on like Am-G three times, it was just based on a riff that is repeated, there's no chord structure to it. So they were completely different to all of us. [With the other Paisley bands] you could write the song down with a chord chart. You couldn't do that with Rain Parade.

Actually, the Rain Parade had little in common sonically with the likes of The Dream Syndicate, the Long Ryders and the Bangs (later The Bangles), all of whom shared a love for the rawer representatives of sixties rock, and a baptism through punk. Membership of the Paisleys, though, was largely a matter of personal connections. As Wynn points out, 'Because I was at Rhino, people'd bring [their records] in, and I would meet them. I went out for coffee with [the Bangs'] Vicki and Sue and said, "Here's how you get your single pressed. We should do a show together." And we'd talk about the Velvets . . . for an hour . . . It totally came from a record collectors' perspective.' Only when the term Paisley Underground got coined did everyone start feeling a whole lot better about this art-rock adjunct to LA's post-punk scene.

Sid Griffin: The Paisley Underground started out as The Dream Syndicate, Green on Red, The Bang(le)s and Salvation Army. [Then] the Long Ryders latched on. Steve Wynn knew [some of] The Bangles. I was sharing a home with Debbi Petersen, and I was going out with Vicki . . . who wasn't the bass player yet (Annette from Blood on the Saddle was the bass player [originally]). Steve introduced me to Dan Stuart (of Green on Red), who I was appalled by. He was so drunk he could hardly talk, and he kept talking about Pink Floyd . . . Everybody was fixated on sixties music, although different genres: the Velvets were the great influence for Steve's mob, The Byrds for my mob, Green on Red had a Doors/droney organy thing going on . . . Michael [Corseo] of the Salvation Army came up with the phrase Paisley Underground, in an interview. Within weeks, everyone was talking about it. A lot of people pooh-poohed it, but . . . I realized, 'No, we want to be part of a scene,' like UK Punk or Merseybeat. I really wanted to [be] the acceptable face of this LA [post-punk] scene. There was no way X and The Gun Club were gonna be commercially successful in Fresno, California – but they might go for us.

By this juncture, Griffin had gotten over Wynn's defection; and after several months of rehearsing as a three-piece with bassist Tom Stevens and drummer Greg Sowders – the latter recruited from punk/ska band, the Box Boys – guitarist Stephen McCarthy answered an ad Griffin had placed in the *LA Recycler*. It read, 'Singer/guitarist wanted for sixties-influenced group . . . [who] want The Byrds, Standells and Seeds to ride again.' Quite why McCarthy responded to the ad, nobody knows; for as Griffin says, 'When Stephen walked in the door that changed the equation; he's extremely country and you can't get it out of him.' This whacky combination somehow worked.

Greg Sowders: [When] we get Stephen McCarthy it's a bit more countryish – he doesn't really know those [*Nuggets*] songs, [he's] just playing a lap-steel guitar, tuned to some psychedelic tuning . . . playing all these country licks where they're really not meant to go.

Though the Long Ryders musically had a lot more in common with the cowpunk bands – as Sowders readily admits – the bills they found themselves on were 'with The Dream Syndicate and . . . with the Rain Parade – [who] were doing a really psychedelic, acidy kinda thing. Then there was the Three O-Clock, [who] were really into Mod, [Brit]pop stuff. It was a little *scene*. I mean, one day you wake up and you go to a club and there's a bunch of kids that look like you do. And they're forming bands.' Actually, they were doing a lot more than forming bands, they were making records – sometimes with a little help from the Syndicate.

Green on Red had arrived from Tucson, Arizona, the previous year, hoping to make their noisy garage-rock audible over the city's own relentless racket. Originally one of Arizona's more popular punk bands, The Serfers had even opened for the likes of Black Flag, DOA and Fear when they played Tucson's one punk palace, Tumbleweed's. The name change, from a song singer Dan Stuart had just written, coincided with the move west, and the realization that The Serfers might suggest an unwanted association with hardcore.

Green on Red's own garage-sound was held together by vocalist Dan Stuart's drawling delivery and Chris Cacavas's Farfisa-keyboard sound. But they weren't yet ready to rock the west's punk capital. This became apparent when a $1,200 loan from a friend resulted in an EP, the so-called *Two Bibles*, at the end of 1981. The six tracks therein revealed a band with no clear identity. But the band kept on playing the plentiful local clubs until one night they shared a bill with The Dream Syndicate at the Cathay de Grande. After the show, Green on Red invited the Syndicate to the LA equivalent of a Sunday roast.

Dan Stuart: [Wynn] showed up at one of these barbecues we used to have. I played him a tape we'd recorded for less than $200 at this rehearsal space we used, that had an eight-track upstairs, and he said, 'I got a label, let me put it out!' So that whole tape became the [*Green on Red*] record. We owe a lot to Steve! He [also] helped us get the Slash deal. The Dream Syndicate . . . was leaving [Slash] for A&M, so he confirmed that they sign Green on Red.

The Green on Red mini-album, issued in September 1982, almost a year after *Two Bibles*, confirmed that the lights downtown had at least changed to amber. With Wynn's endorsement, they became the latest recruits to the proto-Paisleys. A couple of months after its release, Wynn produced three demos for the band, including the strident 'Gravity Talks', and by the new year they were on Slash.

Indeed, by the end of 1982 it seemed like only the Long Ryders were still unrepresented on vinyl. As Griffin admits, 'The Long Ryders were always slightly last. There's that album *Warf Rat Tales*, which was an anthology of LA bands, and I was heartbroken that we weren't on it; and Rain Parade were on it, and wanted to get off.' In fact, the album in question, issued in September 1982, had very little going for it, save for the two Rain Parade cuts ('This Can't Be Today' and 'I Look Around'), but at least it showed a refreshingly non-conformist approach to permissible post-punk sounds, from garage to powerpop, to the Rain Parade's slightly redolent psychedelia.

At the same time The Gun Club, already locked and loaded, were issuing their second Slash album, *Miami*, before their moment slipped away. If *Miami* was a strong follow-up to *Fire Of Love*, it didn't provide the same visceral shock. The Gun Club's swamp-rock was no longer such an unexpected place to find the punk aesthetic at work. Also that fall, Slash released both Rank & File's *Sundown* mini-LP and Dream Syndicate's *The Days Of Wine And Roses*, each a slightly more unexpected way of updating the sound of those quintessential punks, Hank Williams and Lou Reed, to make them relevant in a post-punk world.

The Gun Club may have defined their own, uniquely backwoods strain, but Rank & File had found a different stroke – stumbling upon that authentic voice the Kinmans had been searching for since the Dils first drilled for black gold back in 1977. On *Sundown*, Rank & File did for country what *The Ramones* album had inflicted on sixties pop. And Slash, with its Hollywood punk association and a roster that already included The Blasters and The Gun Club, seemed like the place Rank

& File needed to be. Meanwhile, in Pedro, Blood on the Saddle were getting ready to ride, and in LA, the Club Lingerie beckoned for Lone Justice.

The Dream Syndicate were another band for whom *Fire Of Love* was 'a huge influence' (though not necessarily an obvious one), even if they were not so sold on Slash. A matter of days before they started recording *The Days Of Wine And Roses* on the label's tab, Wynn had semi-seriously asked if anyone in the audience at KPFK wanted to sign the band for five dollars, and spare them from Slash. With no takers, they entered Quad Teck Studios with Gun Club producer, Chris D, proceeding to record this stunning debut album in just three all–night sessions.

Despite all the limitations – notably Wynn's unexceptional vocal range – the Syndicate's songs fizzle and flow from the first. 'Tell Me When It's Over', the album opener, is a collect call to California to wake up. In the words of Syndicate advocate Byron Coley, it 'cascades forth with a fully matured RIFF, and its whole revolves around this riff's expansion and contraction. Now holding back for a trice, next stuttering wetly like a drunk's feigned apology, then surging forward once more.' The rest of the album follows suit, riding its repetitive waves.

With critics like Richard Meltzer and Coley converts from the off, *The Days Of Wine And Roses* did not merely register with the same Slash constituency as *Fire Of Love* and *Sundown*. Major labels now wanted to sign the Syndicate. Rather than play the 'indie/good, major/bad' card, Slash thought they could hold on to Wynn's outfit by taking a leaf from the Morris Levy school of band management.

Steve Wynn: By the time Slash came around we were already getting a lot of press, and playing headlining shows and having a following. They'd [already] done X, The Blasters, and Gun Club. [By then,] the X records were popular, so they were happening. About three months after *Wine And Roses* came out, X signed with Warner Brothers . . . We did the record for Slash in three days, for a few thousand; and then we had a signing frenzy: we had Geffen, A&M and EMI [saying], 'What do you want?' . . . [But] the [real] reason we left Slash was we had a two-record deal, and when all that press happened with *Wine And Roses*, their business manager said, 'I want you to sign a seven-record deal. If you don't, I'll put out the next record and let it bomb!' We were just stunned . . . [So] they were bought out.

When X – who'd signed the same two-album deal with Slash – had looked to leap labels, Slash boss Bob Biggs said he 'felt betrayed . . . [Warners] have no ideas conceptually how to sell the music, how to get people to identify with it, how to get a cultural object, not just something that's out there in Musicland for three months, and then it's gone.' It was a perfectly fair point, somewhat undermined six months later, when Slash signed a distribution deal with Warners, on their way to being swallowed whole by the Warners' whale, early evidence that the US indie labels were as keen to bed with the majors as the bands.

The subsequent feeding frenzy over the Syndicate indicated that by 1983 LA's better post-punk bands were prepared to consider swimming with a bigger school; and Slash was no longer the biggest fish in the pond. The indie ethic was not dead in the water – LA still had the surprisingly strong SST – but even they were having to look this larger beast square in the eye.

7.2
JOINING THE MAJORS
1983-87

Usually the people who are saying, 'You're not punk,' are the ones who have set up the genre so defined that they have no room to move. Even if you set yourself up as anti-everything, pretty soon you become the anti-everything.

—Lenny Kaye, to author, 2005

Punk is something you have to do to know it . . . Punk was about more than just starting a band, it was about starting a label, it was about touring, it was about taking control.   —Mike Watt, to Gina Arnold, 1992

By 1983, the word was out. Just as 1976 marked a watershed for New York's downtown scene, with out-of-towners taking up where the locals left off, so seven years later the idea proved ripe for a Hollywood remake. The two independent labels, Slash and SST, both now acted as magnets for mavericks; and when the former struck up a distribution deal with Warners in the spring of 1983 – coinciding with the release of The Blasters' second Slash LP, *Non Fiction* – it seemed that word might yet wander far and wide.

Already arrived from Arizona were Green on Red, whose mini-album had attracted favourable notices the previous fall. The qualitative leap from their so-called *Two Bibles* EP, wisely issued in a limited edition of five hundred copies, was pronounced. After recording a three-song demo in November 1982, produced by Steve Wynn, labels like IRS and Slash sat up and took notice. Ever prepared to press self-destruct, singer Stuart was unimpressed by Miles Copeland and, according to keyboardist Chris Cacavas, 'Just told him to fuck off!' He evidently felt Biggs was the better bet, despite Wynn's flight to A&M.

With Slash paying the bill, Green on Red recut 'Gravity Talks' – as the title-track to their first full album – and a dozen more sixties-inflected nuggets. The results suggested a line of attack absent from earlier efforts, straight to the heart of Stuart's darkness. It was a blistering blast from the present, suggesting Green on Red might yet give Slash another lease of life. Yet *Gravity Talks*, issued in the fall, was another terrific post-punk statement that remained below the radar of popular consciousness; and frontman Dan Stuart's frustrations with Slash began to runneth over. Like X and The Dream Syndicate, Green on Red were soon looking for an offer they couldn't refuse. Phonogram duly obliged.

Altogether more happy with the way Slash plied their wares were a trio of midwest refugees that went by the name of the Violent Femmes. From Milwaukee, the Femmes' frontman, Gordon Gano, had been stockpiling songs for at least three years when Slash issued the Femmes' first album, in January 1983. A&R Anna Statman had managed to convince Bob Biggs to issue what the Femmes forwarded her 'as is' – meaning Slash did not have to pay for the Femmes' album, because the drummer's dad had; the album having been recorded the previous July at a 24-track studio in Lake Geneva, Wisconsin. The band, though, had had only enough money to record ten songs (to save on tape, they even recorded a number of them on 'twelve-track', getting twice the mileage out of expensive two-inch reels). The question was, which ten songs from their brimming drawers?

Brian Ritchie: We just thought these songs kind of belong together; they show a unified viewpoint, which was: what's it like to be a fucked-up teenager?

According to Gano, the idea was 'not to break [the flow] with . . . the more country type of material we had – that would take it musically into another direction.' Gano had a definite idea of how he wanted to introduce the band to the world-at-large. *Violent Femmes* was a stripped-bare affair, the semi-acoustic trio playing their hybrid punka-billy as if it were pure skiffle, but with a lyrical content that crossed Jonathan Richman's gauche honesty with a Pentecostal brand of brattish-ness. Catchy enough for college radio, the likes of 'Blisters In The Sun', 'Prove My Love' and 'Add It Up' were soon perennials of the subsidized airwaves, even if *Billboard* studiously refused to acknowledge the impact the Femmes made on a demographic looking for the energy and honesty of punk, minus a degree of amplification whose one enduring result was damaged eardrums.

The following year, the Femmes issued a follow-up, *Hallowed Ground*, that exposed their true roots. There was nothing un(self)conscious about this band's sound, or the blend of influences evident therein. For all of the best efforts of SST and Minneapolis's Twin/Tone, *Hallowed Ground* was the most radical American rock album of 1984, the Femmes drafting in a four-piece horn section, the Horns of Dilemma, to make their punkabilly swing. Its blend of Beefheart, *Fun House*-era Stooges, Modern Lovers and Carter Family may not have been *precisely* what The Meat Puppets had been reaching for on *their* second album, but it was a fusion of punk and Americana that, the Femmes excepted, only the Puppets dared to execute – albeit at tinnitus-inducing volume. Its key pairing – 'The Country Death Song' (a cross between Dylan's 'Ballad Of Hollis Brown' and Suicide's 'Frankie Teardrop') with 'Never Tell' (a truly psychotic take on traditional murder ballads like 'Pretty Polly' and 'Omie Wise') – both dated from the Femmes' first demo tape in the fall of 1981. No matter; the Femmes always intended to make records that 'would sound out of time'.

Unexpectedly, for all their Appalachian weirdness, the Femmes found their music more enthusiastically received in safe European homes than in the backwoods and boondocks of America. Nor were they alone. Green on Red, despite their best efforts, couldn't get arrested in LA. On tour in Europe in 1985, though – where they were promoting their first Phonogram product, *No Free Lunch*, letting new guitarist Chuck Prophet cross Crazy Horse with The Clash – they were something of a sensation.

By the decade's mid-point, new American music was generating a great deal of interest overseas, but not a lot outside ivy-leafed college campuses back home. And the two most exciting exports were both bands who had sealed their compact with the majors in the cauldron of LA: Lone Justice, for whom almost two years of incubation at Geffen had failed to fully put out their fire; and Jason and the Scorchers, who had come to town at the end of 1983, on the heels of an EP and a mini-album on their own Nashville label, Praxis. Given that their brand of cowpunk had been fermented in the country capital itself, Jason and the Nashville Scorchers represented a one-band battleground in the punk/country conflict. Even its singer was conflicted.

Jason Ringenberg: Most of the stuff I listened to [growing up] was what you'd probably expect – Hank [Williams] Senior and Gram Parsons. But I had a younger brother, who was heavily into first-wave punk-rock, and so just by osmosis I got into the Pistols and the Ramones. I played in one real punk-rock band called Shakespeare's Riot in Carbondale, Illinois in 1978. We were essentially doing covers of the Sex Pistols and people like that, but we were also starting to do revved-up versions of Johnny Cash, even at that time. We [also] did a version of [my song], 'Help, There's A Fire'.

In 1981, Ringenberg had elected to move to Nashville, which 'was only four hours from where I was living', even though he didn't know anybody and wasn't necessarily thinking of playing country music: 'I wanted to make a real high-energy roots band. I knew I wanted to do that.' But, as Ringenberg discovered, there was '*no* rock & roll [in Nashville]. There was one little club, called Phrankenstein's. Then Cantrell's started – and all kinds of bands came through Cantrell's. The first [rock] band I saw in Nashville was REM, playing in this little club. They were just starting out. Black Flag [also] came through that summer. And the Circle Jerks. [But] if you were a Mohawk walking round Nashville, you could get beat up. It happened quite often.' In this time-warp town, Ringenberg had a simple choice – cowpunk or cowpoke. At least he had found his 'high-energy roots band', which made its debut on New Year's Eve 1981 with a name that suggested their game away, the Nashville Scorchers.

Jason Ringenberg: I was a hillbilly punk rocker in those days. I had a shaved head, I'd wear a priest's robe onstage and a cowboy hat. Everyone in the band was a punk rocker. Warner had this hair stuck [across] his face, Jeff wore a Mohawk and his pants backwards. Perry had cigarette burns all over his arms. It was a punk-rock band . . . I think Jason and the Nashville Scorchers became much more punk rock than I ever expected, because the [rest of the] band were all-out punk-rockers, especially Jeff. I envisioned sounding like a hopped-up Jerry Lee Lewis or *Highway 61 Revisited* with a modern sort of edge. That was what was in my head, but they took it into a punk-rock world . . . It was so revolutionary at the time that people really respected us, even if they didn't like our music. The punk rockers [certainly] loved it. We opened for the Circle Jerks at the 688 [Club], at the height of their popularity in late '82. It was anarchy-skinheads, and we walked on with our cowboy hats, playing all this hopped-up Hank Williams stuff, and they ate it up . . . Because we were so explosive, it had such an energy and we attacked the stage so fiercely, that they allowed the twang.

Just ten days after their first gig, the Nashville Scorchers were in the studio, cutting their first EP. The impetus to get things going was coming primarily from their manager, Jack Emerson, who was from the school of punk impresarios. As Ringenberg recalls, 'Emerson was adamant that we get out a record as quickly as we could . . . even if it wasn't quite developed. We'd only been together for a few weeks when we made that [first] record, and had only done one show. But Jack wanted to show that we were the first of this roots-punk movement that he felt was going to just explode . . . Two weeks later it was out on the street.

Jack worshipped Jake Rivera – he was very into Stiff Records and that whole "can do" spirit.'

The *Reckless Country Soul* EP was a declaration of independence from the genre-defined strictures of American radio. Yet Ringenberg was soon despairing of the state of the union's music, 'It was a battle all the time. I remember *Billboard* came out with an article [about] a convention of radio programmers, listing all the bands radio shouldn't play because they were too radical, and they listed us, X, The Blasters, Gun Club – all our friends, all our people. That was the kind of attitude that all of us were fighting . . . We were all in the same boat.'

On their first EP, the Scorchers even dared to take one of country's most wistful standards, 'I'm So Lonesome I Could Cry', and pummel it like a punk. Egged on by Emerson, they continued to espouse the right ideas, compiling a musical manifesto when external influences had yet to make themselves felt, and the band were four strong winds, whipping through every song like their lives depended on it. And the independent single was by now a defined way to create interest locally, perhaps also sending the first formative flickers out into the ether.

For the Scorchers, the EP succeeded in introducing their music to a buoyant campus-based music scene in Athens, Georgia, just across the state line from Tennessee, where bands like Pylon and REM were setting their own ripples in motion. Both these bands had already adopted a similar blueprint, knowing that issuing *any* indie single at this point was tantamount to throwing a stone in the product-pond. In Pylon's case, 'Cool b/w Dub', issued in January 1980, was cool enough to get them a gig supporting the Gang of Four in New York. Wasn't that the way it was supposed to work?

Curtis Crowe: 45s were really the unit of currency for that whole movement. It was one of the few accessible things where four kids with day jobs could go out and raise enough money to make a 45. You distributed them by throwing them into your car and driving to the towns that you played in. You could go to a record store in any town and they'd go, 'New 45? We'll take 5 of 'em.' They'd throw them into the store and it didn't cost them anything. They thought that somebody'd buy them, even if they were terrible, because there were people out there every day buying every new 45 that was on the shelves. [PSF]

REM's approach was a little more measured. The band had come together when bands like the B-52's and Pylon had already opened the town up. Initially chasing their tails, playing sets of garage covers and red-raw originals, they seemed to grow surer of themselves with every passing gig. The release of their own single, in December 1980, blew more than a few local fuses. 'Radio Free Europe', despite being about as intelligible as a Clash '77 encore, showed a mineshaft-deep knowledge of the rocky road from *Nuggets* to new wave. It also showed a sense of ambition altogether rare in garageland USA.

By the time the Scorchers were giving themselves an Extended Play, REM were already looking to tie the Nashville/Athens scene together. As Ringenberg says, 'We were essentially a part of the Athens scene as much as the Nashville scene for a while. We knew REM, Pylon. All those bands we were friends with, played with. I had a girlfriend in Athens.' The first time REM brought the Scorchers to town, they ensured the word got out. As their soundman Woody Nuss told Denise Sullivan, 'In order to build a hype for the [first] Scorchers show, REM played the night before, unannounced, and then told everyone to come down the next day for the Scorchers show.'

It was to become a gesture typical of the Athens band, though after the first Scorchers show, they needed little further hype. Word of gaping-mouth sufficed. Through 1982 and into 1983, the Nashville band pursued its scorched-earth policy, even as copies of the *Reckless* EP became harder and harder to find. That seven-inch bulletin had served its purpose. Its successor, *Fervor*, a six-track mini-album issued a year later, achieved fission. If Rank & File were cowpunk's Ramones, the Scorchers were its Matlock-era Pistols; content to leave their roots showing. Unfortunately, like the Pistols the Scorchers were always a combustible concoction. On *Fervor*, thankfully, the singer still held the upper hand.

Jason Ringenberg: *Fervor*, to me, was the least punk-rock record we made in the eighties. Some of that stuff really took our fans back – it definitely had as much to do with Gram Parsons as the Sex Pistols . . . *Fervor* put us on the map, and it did change the way people saw southern musicians. It had a big influence on other bands. *Fervor* and [REM's] *Murmur* changed music in the south. We knew something special was happening . . . [But] me and Warner fought all the time. Maybe not verbally fighting, but there was always a tension. *Fervor* was kind of a big accident. That was me and Jack . . . planning the whole thing. Warner would show up kinda drunk, and we'd change his amp setting to make it real clean and country sounding; and he'd do it, but he wasn't really into it . . .

He had some country influences, because his dad and mom were country singers, and he played with them in their little band ... – his parents were stone-cold country – [but] his favourite band is AC/DC. He always said that country music was shoved down his throat, and he hated it.

Where Hodge had the upper hand was in front of the band's audiences. Already the Scorchers were having to spin their fans' wheels, and there were precious few coming to the shows who had arrived at the Pistols via Parsons. It was time to make a play for the majors, knowing that if 'you play with matches, you're gonna get *burned!*' – as Ringenberg memorably sang on 'Help, There's A Fire'.

Jason Ringenberg: Jack had big ambitions for us, and we did too – though there was some dissension in the band about that. Jeff the punk rocker was not so into the idea of chasing a record contract with a major label. But we went to California, and we played the game perfectly. *Rolling Stone* came out with a great review of our independent record, which was almost unheard of, and we were starting to get airplay. Every label in town wanted the band – A&M, EMI and Chrysalis all made pitches for the band. We signed a huge deal with EMI finally, [who] were then like, 'We need to keep some momentum going here. Let's [release] "[Absolutely] Sweet Marie",' [which] was on the demo tape that got us the deal.

The first concession EMI-America extracted was to get the band to drop Nashville from the name. It was just the opening volley in a five-year campaign to turn something unique into America's answer to AC/DC. Already, by the time the Scorchers started to singe LA, the country had started to give way to the reckless. When Long Ryder Sid Griffin caught them at the Palomino, he felt they 'weren't doing the hybrid as we saw it'. With a major-label deal on the table, Warner Hodge began to take first, an interest, and finally, a firm hold of the reins; even if Ringenberg managed to get a scorching take of Dylan's seminal '66 cut, 'Absolutely Sweet Marie', by the simple ruse of not telling Hodge it was a cover. EMI-America promptly added it to a revamped *Fervor*★, which was reissued in the winter of 1984.

★ The original six-track version of *Fervor*, on Praxis, featured different mixes, vocal and guitar parts to the EMI-America version, as well as an entirely alternate version of 'Pray For Me Mama', which can now be found on the *Reckless Country Soul* CD, a collection of early Scorchers studio recordings issued by Mammoth in 1996.

Still cracking the whip, EMI-America ushered them into the studio before the year was out. On their first EMI-America album (*Lost And Found*), Ringenberg thinks Hodge still 'walked a fine line between Johnny Thunders and Albert Lee, [but] he never quite got to [it] again ... [If] my sort of vision predominated on the first two records, then [Warner] pretty much took over. By and large, after the summer of 1985, it was his show.'

Lost And Found, for all its signs of pending schizophrenia, still sat easily between a magnificent remake of *Reckless Country Soul*'s 'Broken Whisky Glass' and a kick-ass cover of Hank's 'Lost Highway'. But by the time the band came to Europe, later in the year, Hodge was revolting against that goddamn hillbilly music! Once the Scorchers started rolling down that lost highway, there was no going back. By 1989, there was no one still standing.

At least the Nashville Scorchers had documented their faltering from grace with some trailblazing indie bulletins, thanks to Jack Emerson. For Lone Justice, who signed to Geffen Records on 21 October 1983, less than nine months after their live debut, there was barely a lonesome whippoorwill left of their original sound by the time their debut album appeared in June 1985. In the interim, the label had drafted in producer Jimmy Iovine, that nemesis to all things authentic, who had already sucked the life from the likes of Patti Smith, Bruce Springsteen and Bob Dylan – who, after a single session, knew enough never to work with the man again.

Maria McKee: We were fairly radical. We had all these punk-rock influences. We signed to a major label and ... it began with, 'Can't you keep your guitars in tune?' and ended up, 'Maybe you need a new band.' ... Jimmy Iovine was warning me that I would make enemies if I was too punk or too arty. And I believed it ... My style of music [which] has always been very raw and urgent ... got sublimated by people who thought it would impede commercial progress ... The minute the record business was involved, I was fodder to these satin-jacketed men. [1996]

Drummer Don Heffington, the one band member with previous recording credits, soon realized that Iovine held ideas above his station: 'I was under the impression we were going in to make a quick album, but we cut a bunch of things and it was extended and extended, and there wasn't enough communication among the members of the group

. . . to stop what was happening.' When Lone Justice insisted on cutting one of their early stage favourites, the spiky 'Cactus Rose', it was relegated to a B-side.

The result was one of the most disappointing debuts in a long summer's day. Live, though, McKee remained a powerhouse, and their 1985 shows – often opening with John Fogerty's bitterly ironic 'Fortunate Son' – were still fanned by the fire that burned in McKee. But the 'satin-jacketed men' weren't about to admit that the commercial failure of Lone Justice was down to them. Disbanded in all but name before they made 'their' second album (*Shelter*), the story of Lone Justice was a cracked-mirror reflection of the *Give 'Em Enough Rope* saga. Unlike The Clash, though, McKee's band never recovered, and twenty years of intermittently superlative solo work has still failed to heal the scars on her soul.

At least McKee survived Geffen's a-star-is-born circus – unlike its early-nineties nominee – but she was not alone in feeling the pressure to mainstream what had originally been a refreshing alternative. The Scorchers were slowly being melted down by EMI-America; and Dream Syndicate were finding their berth at A&M an unreliable place to be docked. In a worrying flash of déjà vu, they had been assigned Sandy Pearlman to produce their second album, determined to see if he could spend more of A&M's readies than CBS's (as Steve Wynn ruefully recalls, Pearlman's favourite movie was Coppola's *Apocalypse Now*, something which 'showed . . . in his regard to schedules and budgets'). The process exacerbated tensions within the band. Karl Precoda began to baulk at the changes in direction that the perfectionist Pearlman imposed on another band who'd made a classic debut platter in three days, without his 'input'.

Steve Wynn: It was a real ugly time. Karl and I fought a lot. Eventually we weren't talking. The band broke up making that record. Nobody from the record company checked up on us . . . They just kept paying the bills. We were in our own little world.

Before *The Medicine Show* – another Pearlman patchwork quilt – appeared in May 1984, Precoda had quit. By the time of the attendant tour, so had bassist Dave Provost (who had replaced Kendra Smith after the Syndicate's first tour of 1983). The band was collapsing around Wynn, and though a sort of Syndicate would record two more albums, the dream was already over.

Life in the indie lane was proving no less problematic for Wynn's fellow Paisleyites. By the end of 1983, Green on Red were already whining long and hard about Slash, despite their new-found Warners' distribution. The Long Ryders, meanwhile, elected to go the indie route, using the best independent distribution network around, with a view to getting major-label interest somewhere down the pike.

Sid Griffin: I took the first ever Long Ryders demos to Chris Hillman, and he said, 'It's not there. Do a bunch of gigs.' I took him the second batch of demos we did with Ethan James, months later, and he said, 'Much better,' and I took him the *10.5.60* EP, a year later, and he said, 'You got it.' [Though] I shopped it around, I was working for the people who [ended up] put[ting] it out, JEM Records. I took it to Marty Scott . . . and he said, 'We'll put it out . . . on a packaging and delivering [deal].' Which means you never see any money. Every time we were due some money, they'd say, 'We've printed up some more.' But it got us nationally distributed – [and] people wrote about it in New York City and London.

By 1985, the *10.5.60* mini-album had spawned a full-blown follow-up, *Native Sons*. Issued through Frontier Records, it garnered further plaudits and helped secure a deal with UK's Island Records. Even then, as Sowders says, 'We didn't take tour support. We wanted to control our own art. It was just a very do-it-yourself attitude that we learned from the punks . . . [But] we *wanted* to be on the radio. Even though we had this DIY attitude, we were not anti-success.' Yet success proved hard to come by in the States, even after *Native Sons* gave rootsy rock a good name in post-punk circles.

Sid Griffin: In America, the Long Ryders had a Number One indie album, and a Number Four indie album. The only indie band that was bigger than us in the mid-eighties was The Replacements. The difference was, we'd go to cities where we'd have a huge following – like Chicago, where we'd sell two thousand tickets at the Metro – and then the next night we'd have a four-hour drive to Milwaukee and sell seventy-five tickets. That's the States.

A classic fable of the eighties 'Biz', the Ryders seemed fated to fail. Barely had they signed with Island than their A&R man Nick Stewart left the label, leaving their *State Of Our Union* in the can, and a potential chart single, 'Looking For Lewis And Clark', there for the hyping. It was not to be. As Griffin candidly recalls, the new A&R man 'called me in his office. The next single was [gonna be] "Lights Of Downtown". Within ninety seconds he looked at me and said, "I'm not gonna release 'Lights Of Downtown' as [the next] single 'cause I only release hits, and this ain't a hit. [In fact,] I don't like this band, I don't like this single, I don't like this music, I don't like this band's name, and I don't like *you*." He really said that to me.'

By the end of 1985, the Paisleyites were back underground, while the cowpunks were being boxed into AOR corners by an uncomprehending machine. All the warnings from advocates of the indie sector seemed to be coming home to roost. Whatever salutary lessons may have been learnt along the way, most unregenerate punks took it as vindication-by-proxy of their DIY ethic, and an affirmation of the essential worthlessness of the promises major labels made before turning more commercial contemporaries into model citizens of Stepford.

— — —

While those post-punk combos interested in commerce were learning the hard way that it was called the music *business* for a reason, the eighteen months after a district judge made Unicorn extinct represented something of a heyday for SST and their punk partners. Though none of the three albums Black Flag issued in 1984 (save the retrospective double, *Everything Went Black*) greatly furthered their damaged reputation, this Orwellian year represents the zenith of SST's arc.

Three bands already established at the label, The Minutemen from San Pedro, The Meat Puppets from Tempe, Arizona, and Hüsker Dü from Minneapolis – all of whom issued debut records in 1980–81, at the height of hardcore – took leave of the Luddites at the first turn-off, to make a trio of landmark albums in 1984 (*Double Nickels On The Dime*, *Meat Puppets II* and *Zen Arcade* respectively). Meanwhile, Twin/Tone's favourite sons, The Replacements, finally delivered the goods with *Let It Be*; and Homestead continued the tortuous task of turning New York's Sonic Youth into a name to drop, with their über-electrical exegesis, *Bad Moon Rising*. REM, on the ostensibly independent IRS, also continued to consolidate their grip on collegiate types with *Reckoning*; while the Long Ryders evoked the frontier music of *Native Sons*.

Of all these 'success stories', SST's seemed like the most hard-won. Having triumphed over the legal system, the confining creed which spawned them and a precarious financial situation, they were due some good times. Actually the start of SST's arrested ascendance dated back to the end of 1981, when Greg Ginn cajoled Joe Carducci to come down from San Francisco, where he had overseen Rough Trade's transition from distributor to domestic label. Almost immediately, two bands were brought into the family of Huntingdon hardcore labels, one on SST, the other on The Minutemen's New Alliance.

Joe Carducci: The first band we talked about adding [after I joined] was The Meat Puppets, because I'd been distributing their seven-inch, up at Systematic. I was [also] in touch with Hüsker Dü at Systematic, 'cause I was distributing their first single ['Statues']. Then they sent me *Land Speed Record* on cassette. They were looking for a label to release it. We were [only] doing seven-inch records. I knew that SST couldn't do it, but I didn't know what New Alliance could do. Mike Watt agreed to do it over the phone – unheard.

Both bands were out-of-towners who originated with a hardcore point of view. If The Meat Puppets started life so inclined, after the release of their first LP, in June 1982, they felt they had got out of their system the need to flay songs to the edge of extinction. They had come with a pre-punk proclivity for Classic Rock they shared with bands like X and The Minutemen, but temporarily suppressed. Their audience, though, was still one step behind. As Carducci suggests, the Puppets 'would react in a number of ways – making some shows really good, and others just noise. Eventually they didn't let the audience determine what they were doing.' Drummer Derrick Bostrom suggests it helped them make the decision to leave the Luddites behind.

Derrick Bostrom: It seemed that everywhere we went, punkers would take one look at our long hair and begin to shower us with spit and beer cans. Our covers of songs by Neil Young or Creedence Clearwater Revival did little to alleviate the situation. Clearly, a break from the hardcore movement was in order.

By the time northwest punk musician Mark Arm saw the Puppets play second string to Black Flag at a Seattle show in the winter of 1983, they had figured out the necessary combination, even if 'people were throwing ashtrays at them'. What particularly set the 'big dunderheaded audience' off were the songs from their second album, which was already in the can. After the show, Arm and a friend went backstage to interview the band for a local fanzine, 'and they're going, "Well, you know our next record is going to be very different? It's really going to be *a lot* different." '

The Puppets seemed in quite a hurry to leave the 'loud fast rules' of hardcore behind, demoing a number of the songs for their second album in August 1982. One of these ('Teenager(s)'), which they gave to Michael Koenig to include with his zine *Take It!*, showed the then-and-now feel of the new material, switching from a hardcore flaying to a slow jam (originally called 'Tribute To 45 Grave') in mid-song. The album took a while longer to pull together, but when it did appear, the cautionary 'Lost' ('I know there'll come a day when you say you don't know me'), the gorgeous 'Plateau' and the rabid 'Lake Of Fire' suggested they were learning to fly even as their audience remained grounded.

If once diehard devotees were nonplussed by the Puppets' hardcore hillbilly, their label didn't consider it a problem. But then, Ginn was a closet Deadhead. The Puppets were one band unfazed when they found the flagship hardcore label being run by a bunch of stoners. (As one employee has said, '[All] these [other] bands would come into town with their leather jackets . . . and they'd come down to SST and find these people who looked like a bunch of derelicts from Appalachia sitting around their trailer'). As for the music the SST staff personally *liked*, Henry Rollins affirms that 'all the ZZ Top records were in the Flag lexicon, as well as . . . early Nugent, Sabbath, AC/DC with Bon Scott, Captain Beyond – stoner rock. Not much punk rock. The only punk you'd see around would be SST stuff.'

Nor were The Minutemen unduly different in outlook, having 'gone to arena gigs all through high school, [so] at odd times they'd start talking about the time they saw Gentle Giant open for ZZ Top at the Long Beach Sports Arena, or Uriah Heep headline over Mavinushu at the LA Forum, or some other such crazy bill.' (Joe Carducci) However, the music that The Minutemen were now referencing was an entirely different kettle of cod. What was really inspiring Watt and Boon by 1979 were the records coming out of England's progressive punk pulpits, where technical limitations in no way hindered exploration.

Mike Watt: We really liked [bands like] Throbbing Gristle, but a lot of it we couldn't relate to as far as working [an] instrument. Wire was very profound for us – but they wouldn't come over. The same thing happened with The Pop Group. Those bands existed for us only as sounds. But they were incredible –

this idea of putting Beefheart with Parliament. It sounds very simple – why not? – but it was profound.

For Watt, in particular, *Pink Flag* provided a paradigm of how to disguise the fact 'that we knew how to play . . . We tried all these real extreme devices to hide it, [most of] which we picked up from . . . Wire – [who said] you don't need verse/chorus, you don't need solos, you don't need shit.' But then, as Colin Newman points out, that first album 'had national distribution, [so it] was very influential on *all* the American hardcore scenes'. Along with the Pistols, The Clash, the Ramones and The Saints, Wire's first provided an all-important template of brevity and wit. Twin-Tone's Peter Jesperson acknowledges the impact that defining debut had in the midwest by admitting that, 'When we made the first Replacements record [it was with the] goal to try to make an album with twenty-two songs on it, because *Pink Flag* had twenty-one.'

By the time of *Double Nickels*, Watt and Boon were prepared to go one better, issuing a 43-track double-album, with yet shorter songs, more diverse styles, and rhythm tracks that bordered on dance music. The latter notion they acquired from The Pop Group, who by mixing Captain Beefheart with George Clinton 'blew away what we thought were "the rules of rock & roll"'.

There was another, more direct imperative driving The Minutemen to think in such grandiose terms; an urge to match and raise contemporaries who had upped the stakes. The band in question was Hüsker Dü, whose first album (*Land Speed Record*) had appeared on Watt's own label, New Alliance. The Minneapolis band had now recorded a double-album, *Zen Arcade*, partially to see how SST responded to the challenge (its release was delayed while the label raised the necessary funds!), and in part to see how many former punks could stomach an entire final side devoted to a fifteen-minute jam. *London Calling*, *Zen Arcade* ain't.

Over the remaining three sides, Hüsker Dü charted both the band's bruising side and its bruised soul, reflecting the band's ongoing internecine strife. As Grant Hart told local journalist Mark Weingarten, 'I was challenging the punk stuff with more pop things, and Bob was more into hardcore.' In fact, the conflict between pop and punk had defined Hüsker Dü from the beginning. Formed in 1979 as a backing band for some optimistic frontman who had some dates at a new-wave club, Hüsker Dü soon jettisoned their own George Gill.

Grant Hart: Greg and I really didn't have to talk Bob [Mould] into it. It was only [meant to be] two nights. We weren't looking for anybody long-term. Personalities were too different . . . We played covers, everything from Elvis Costello to the Buzzcocks . . . We had a few practices. [But] when this [other] guy couldn't come, we enjoyed it more than when he could.

If the decision was made to jettison the singer *and* all that powerpop, a little of the latter stuck to the underside and – despite systematic efforts – resolutely refused to be dislodged. In time-honoured punk fashion, one way to deny poppier roots was to play at the kind of speed where even Beatlesque melodies decomposed within the blast furnace. And it had the added bonus of pissing off any pop fans in the audience, like Twin-Tone's Peter Jesperson, who immediately sensed that they seemed to be 'trying to play faster than anybody else'. Mould was determined to carry on with the experiment: 'We just sort of came out of nowhere, playing this real, real fast punk stuff and people hated it. We just kept playing faster and faster to get people to hate us more.'

Actually, the general reaction in their midwestern home was mystification. As Grant Hart recalls, it was mostly people muttering, 'Who are these uncultured people who play too fast? Don't they know the first Ramones album came out two years ago?' But for every new waver alienated by the Dü, there were a similar number of converts – just not quite from the same demographic as fans of Wire and The Only Ones.

Peter Jesperson: Hüsker Dü were never my cup of tea, musically . . . But when they started playing the Longhorn, they definitely made a splash. You could feel a whole new crowd of people coming in to see them, some [of whom] I was a bit scared of. There was some real sinister-looking skinheads and leather-jacketed guys.

At the time, Jesperson's tiny Twin-Tone label was the only game in town. However, when Hüsker Dü approached the owner of Minnesota's solitary punk outlet, he passed on them. The band's response was suitably punk-like. They did it themselves, issuing 'Statues' b/w 'Amusement' on their own Reflex label, so-called because the label was a reflex to being rejected by Twin-Tone. But midwest hardcore 45s tended to be about as well marketed as Victorian hardcore pornography, and as soon as The Replacements entered the frame, Hüsker Dü began feeling the squeeze on all sides. Their response was to look west, buoyed by sales of their single achieved by Joe Carducci at Systematic. With New Alliance/SST, Hüsker Dü found a hardcore home willing to build extensions to house their kind.

Meanwhile, The Replacements proved to be just that for many Minnesotans at the turn of the decade, being a necessary antidote to the detritus on America's atrophying airwaves. It seemed a long time since Minnesota's Suicide Commandos had shared a label with Pere Ubu (Blank Records), or shared a stage with each other. Though they had been playing garage rock since 1975, the Commandos had steadfastly stayed a secret society anywhere east of Lake Superior. In fact, when Peter Jesperson heard an advance of the first Ramones record, his first reaction was, 'Wow, this is a band from New York, and they're doing the same thing Suicide Commandos are doing.' But, unlike the Ramones, the Commandos failed to deliver any knock-out punches on vinyl and when they got blanked by Blank, they stopped playing Russian roulette.

Part of the problem for the Commandos was the lack of any kind of midwest scene at the time. As Jesperson says, 'They used to [just] play a place called the Blitz, which was a really crummy basement club in downtown Minneapolis.' The one young journalist on the *Minnesota Daily* with a punk sensibility, Andy Schwartz, moved to New York at the first opportunity to work at *NY Rocker* (much as the best Minnesotan writer on folk music, Paul Nelson, had left for *Sing Out* twelve years earlier). So much for press coverage. What the twin city needed most, though, was a record label, and finally importer/retailer Jesperson decided to do the decent thing.

Peter Jesperson: What I wanted to emulate when we started Twin-Tone was Beserkley. *Beserkley Chartbusters* was a Bible at our place . . . There's three of us started the label . . . We felt that we were forced into existence by the sheer number of incredible [local] bands. June of '78, we did three EPs. We made two thousand of each and sold them all . . . one was called Spooks, [which was] really Kurtis A., [one was] Fingerprints, and [finally] a group called The Suburbs.

Shortly after Jesperson's necessary deed, the twin cities got a dedicated punk club, the Longhorn, where bands like The Only Ones, the Sonic Rendezvous Band, Destroy All Monsters, Pere Ubu and the B-52's would find themselves booked, as and when they made it to the frozen north. The better local bands would invariably find themselves requisitioned to entertain the early birds, while the headliners imbibed Grain Belt.

One of the bands who'd already sampled said gut-rot were Dogbreath, a punk quartet caught between their love of the Pistols and The Clash, and a furtive allegiance to the Diplodocus that was Classic Rock. When the young Paul Westerberg began to eavesdrop, and then sit in, on rehearsals, Dogbreath became The Replacements, and Westerberg (along with Jesperson) set about educating the band members about those points of reference they needed to subsume.

Peter Jesperson: [Paul] didn't even really like The Clash that much. He loved the Pistols. He was pretty fussy, and pretty old-school. In the early days, riding in the van, whenever I'd put in a tape and it would inevitably have The Only Ones on it, Westerberg [would] holler at me from the back of the van, 'Take this fuckin' junkie music off.' . . . What The Replacements wanted to be when I [first] ran into them was Johnny Thunders' Heartbreakers. I think they did three Heartbreakers songs the first time I saw them. That was Westerberg's main thing. Thunders and The Raspberries were the first couple of bands we shared a fanatical love for.

For now, though, those references remained one mushy mess, as the band put some of their stinkier songs into the hardcore blender. The *Sorry Ma, Forgot To Take Out The Trash* LP and *Stink* EP, both put out on Twin-Tone, may have been 'Westerberg's attempt[s] to do something a little contemporary, a little more hardcore'. (Jesperson) But the band, and Westerberg in particular, were already developing a contrary reputation. As soon as someone put them in one pigeonhole, they flitted on to the next branch. Road manager Bill Sullivan told journalist Michael Azerrad about one occasion they 'were in Nashville and the whole place was packed with country music executives. They played all their punk rock – just as loud and fast as they could, until they virtually cleared the room; until there was nothing left but punks. And then they played country music the rest of the night.'

The Replacements inverted every expectation, pulled every chain, upset every cart, and refused to conform to any musical stereotype. When their reputation as the hardest-sounding band around reached New York, they underwent that rite of passage for all punk bands, a CBGB's weekend residency. But when they turned up 'in flannel and long hair', and announced they were The Replacements, cranky club-owner Kristal exclaimed, 'The fuck you are.' Yet when they were given just enough slack, and didn't bridle at some (probably imaginary) sleight, they could fire up the very furies.

Peter Jesperson: When they were on, there were times when I would be sitting, watching, and I'd go, 'It is not humanly possible that there is a better rock & roll band on the planet right now.' . . . [But] it was unpredictable for a million reasons, depending on how much they'd had to drink. Sometimes if they were playing in a club where they didn't feel like they were being treated with respect, that could send Paul spinning off into some tantrum, where he'd pull out a cover and trash it . . . I'd try to manipulate them, without them knowing it. They'd say, 'Hey, can we get some beer in the dressing room,' and I'd [think], 'Shit, it's six o'clock, they're gonna be falling down drunk by eleven,' and then I'd go to the club guy and I'd say, 'Whatever you do, don't put the beer in the dressing room yet.' I'd hold them off as long as I could ... It was not a pleasant job. I remember being in Houston one time and the promoter came up to me and said, 'Everyone's asking for their money back,' and I said, 'Well, I guess you should give some refunds.' He said, 'No, no, I mean *everyone* who's paid wants their money back.' The band was still attempting to play, [but kept] falling down on the stage.

By 1984, with two Twin-Tone albums and one EP under their belt, people were beginning to wonder, when are these guys gonna stop pissing about and get serious? Evidence that they could be the most infuriating band on earth came with a cassette-only release from Twin-Tone, *The Shit Hits The Fans*, a November 1984 set that showed The Replacements in slaughter-Classic-Rock mode, a way to jerk the chain of every yahoo who shouts requests at rock gigs.

Taking requests from the thirty-strong crowd in Oklahoma city, the 'Mats (as fans called them) perform thirty-second versions of dinosaur ditties like Sabbath's 'Iron Man', Zeppelin's 'Misty Mountain Hop' and 'Heartbreaker', Bad Company's 'Can't Get Enough' and Lizzy's 'Jailbreak'. They even pull out REM's 'Radio Free Europe', X's 'New World' (though they miss a trick by not doing thirty seconds of 'Thirty Seconds Over Tokyo', as a reformed Ubu liked to do in the late eighties). Then they wrap things up with 'Let It Be', not the title-track of their latest fab waxing but the McCartney melody murdered.

Despite such teenage perversity, labels higher up the food chain were expressing interest in the band – on the back of the eclectic *Hootenanny*

– but, as Jesperson says, 'They were notorious for biting the hand that fed them, from pretty early on. They had [this] sense that they were selling more records than they really were, and that they had more money coming to them than they really did. They started to get belligerent about Twin-Tone at some point. They wanted to make a bunch of money, and they believed they deserved it. But when we'd meet with Bob Biggs from Slash . . . they'd act like The Three Stooges.'

The album they recorded in spring 1984 was probably the last chance saloon for the 'Mats. And Westerberg knew it. Finally, he began to pull out of his bottom drawer songs he seemed almost embarrassed to have written. As Jesperson says, 'While The Replacements were doing their thing, [Paul] was [always] recording a lot of solo piano, solo guitar, very sensitive demos in the basement of his parents' house, and he would give those to me, and swear me to secrecy.' *Let It Be* was hardly the musings of a Laurel Canyon loser, but it showed a band prepared to let melody be the mother to an intervention. And 'I Will Dare,' issued as an advance single, was the perfect riposte to any doubters.

Paul Westerberg: It's kinda hard to put attitude down on tape. But we tried for, like, three records. We kinda gave up the ghost on *Let It Be*, and let a little bit of music happen, too. [1989]

Jesperson was certainly impressed: 'When we heard "Within Your Reach" and "Colour Me Impressed" and those songs, it was like, "Oh my God."' Nor did he need to feel alone any more. The majors had picked up on the stink, and were starting to sniff around. Thankfully, Twin-Tone felt none of the conflict that an SST might have when those calls came. As Jesperson says, 'Twin-Tone wasn't interested in trying to hold The Replacements back. We were approached by EMI, we talked to Columbia . . . [and] everybody said, "Well, these guys are ready now."' The band also felt that it was 'time for a major label to take over'. All they needed now was to deliver live, at a show that actually mattered.

Peter Jesperson: They were always throwing a wrench in the works . . . they sort of pissed on the very thing they wanted – which was to be able to make a living at it. It was like, 'Jeez, if we let everybody know we're serious, and we fail, we're gonna look really stupid; but if we look like we're kidding around and we fail, then it's not as big a deal.' . . . There'd be ten people turn up to see the band in Wichita and they'd put on the best show I'd seen all month, and then we'd go to New York [and fail to deliver] . . . There's a famous show they did at CBGB's in December of '84, when Alex Chilton opened up, and every A&R guy in the city was in the room, and they were falling down drunk and they didn't finish a single song . . . Then, a couple of nights later, they played Irving Plaza and they just kicked ass from the first song. That's the show Seymour Stein saw. But that's why I never would tell them [if] it was an important gig.

The ever-impulsive Stein, whose Sire label was now fully integrated into the Warners network, was just as convinced as the night he caught Birdman burning up Paddington. By 1985, Twin-Tone had handed the flagon with the dragon to a label Jesperson hoped might do something with a brew so true. Westerberg, as ever, was determined to strike a cautionary note, informing *Rolling Stone* that if the label 'leave us alone and give us a little push, they're going to have much better results than trying to steer us in directions . . . If anyone tells us what to do, we're real immature about it, and we'll go in the exact opposite direction.' He wasn't joking.

Yet the 'Mats needed (and received) minimal interference in order to deliver their most disappointing album to date, *Tim*, which started the bandwagon rolling – backwards. When Hüsker Dü repeated the same trick the following year, with their Warners debut *Candy Apple Grey*, Warners must have begun to wonder what happened to these underground bands when they signed a contract worth the paper it was written on.

Others were already starting to wonder why, with the indie scene having so many firelighters to hand, its alternative rockers were failing to set American would-be fans on fire. Even REM's Peter Buck, whose band had the greatest momentum and seemed closest to that tipping-point, was perplexed; voicing his mystification – and celebrating his counterculture contemporaries – in an article in the October 1984 *Record*:

I guarantee that I have more records from 1983 in my collection than any other year . . . All over the country we go, and every town has at least one really top-notch group . . . Los Angeles . . . has a million good bands now – Dream Syndicate, Rain Parade, Black Flag, Channel Three, Minutemen – [but also] The Replacements and Hüsker Dü from Minneapolis . . . [and] Jason and the Scorchers from Nashville. There are good bands all over America doing exciting things, and no one really hears them . . . I don't know if any or all of these bands will eventually be famous, rich [or] even remembered but as a movement they're inspiring kids to pick up instruments and work in ways that aren't prescribed. I talk to kids all the time who are excited by bands like [ours] because, first of all, they like our music; but mostly because we show that you don't have to knuckle under to the dictates of the music business to be successful.

Sadly, without a major label, many of the above bands were never going to bend the European market to their will; and, as of the end of 1984, that market remained a lot more receptive to America's new underground than its homestead. The second half of the year and the first half of 1985 would see the Long Ryders, Jason and the Scorchers, Green on Red, Lone Justice, The Dream Syndicate and REM find adulatory audiences at every Euro-turn – but these were all bands with some kind of label support. For others, even venturing overseas involved a huge financial gamble, even if it was one they needed to take simply to survive.

One such band was Sonic Youth, the one solid-state legacy of the 'no wave' aesthetic prevalent in New York at the time its members gathered downtown. Frontman Thurston Moore recently described the effect of arriving as a gangly geek, and discovering that 'downtown NYC had a developing post-punk community of artists and musicians exhibiting a new radical style of nihilism and producing sex/danger noise/vision. This was "no wave" and it was committed to destroying any strain of rock & roll still alive in punk . . . Seeing, hearing and playing atonal guitar monotony in a Broome Street gallery was formidable and it was a formulative experience for my eighteen-year-old psyche.' Guitarist Lee Ranaldo had a similar galvanizing experience in the same neck of the grid.

Lee Ranaldo: The [new wave] records that really got me were the first Talking Heads record, the first Devo record, the first Costello record and the first Television record. Overnight, I cut all my long hair off, got rid of the hippy clothes . . . I was in college in Binghampton, New York, and we would drive down on Fridays and crash on people's floors . . . That was my first experience of CB's, and Max's and loft parties. [I'd] see bands like Teenage Jesus, The Contortions and Mars. I moved to New York in the thrall of bands like Television and Talking Heads, but once I was in New York, that was the first movement that I was here to experience – that fleetingly short eighteen-month period when those no-wave bands existed.

For Europeans, the fact that 'no wave' had travelled about as far as New York Transit made the racket Sonic Youth extracted from these influences sound both exotic *and* esoteric. As guitarist Lee Ranaldo has said, 'We'd go to Europe and . . . after shows people would be just like, "We've never seen anything like this." They'd never experienced any of that New York stuff that we were coming out of, so we were like this apparition that came out of nowhere. They didn't know the Contortions or DNA, or any of the stuff that inspired us.' The accumulation of coincidences that spawned these new Sonics had begun with the one key 'no-wave' figure excluded from the *No New York* scene, Glenn Branca.

Lee Ranaldo: Glenn was working both with the Static and starting to do this multiple-guitar thing. [Rock] was the music he grew up with . . . but he didn't want to be in a lowly rock band, he wanted to do something different with it. He had this grandiose vision. I answered an ad in the *Village Voice* for Glenn – looking for adventurous guitarist, or something like that. Glenn was the guy at that point, and [his idea] was to take this thing he loved in his youth, which was rock music, and combine it with all his art-school and theatrical training. And he did it . . . [but] he got a certain degree of success, and I think he didn't know where to go with it, and he got sidetracked into learning how to write for classical instruments.

While Ranaldo was paying his dues with Branca, Thurston Moore – who had also played with Branca – had formed The Arcadians with his girlfriend Kim Gordon, drummer Richard Edson and blonde keyboardist Ann DeMarinis. On occasions Ranaldo's own little side-project, Plus Instruments, would jam with Thurston Moore's Edenic alternative. But DeMarinis – never entirely with the programme – quit in summer 1981 and, as drummer Edson recently wrote, 'One day I showed up for practice, and there was this other guy there. His name was Lee . . . It was different. Louder. More streamlined and focused. There were two guitars searching for a way to make a beautiful racket.'

Though drummers came and went, the unholy trio of Gordon, Moore and Ranaldo would remain the fulcrum of the Sonic sound. And Branca would continue to take an active interest in the one concrete legacy of his brand of no wave, even founding Neutral Records in 1982 simply in order to put out Sonic Youth's first mini-album, an audio action-painting of random ideas that collided more often than they coalesced.

Initially, Sonic Youth lacked a clear idea of how to fuse their diverse *non*-no-wave influences with the industrial noise which was an integral element of all they did from day one. In fact, when Moore penned their first press release in 1981, describing the band's sound as 'crashing mashing intensified dense rhythms juxtaposed with filmic mood pieces – evoking an atmosphere that could only be described as expressive fucked-up modernism', he seemed resistant to any of the rock vérités, pre-punk *or* post-punk.

Not surprisingly, the atmosphere (and aesthetic) sometimes became as strnen (sic) as the quality of mercy. As their first drummer, Richard Edson, once stated, 'What they loved to do was just crank up the amps and just play with sound. And for a drummer, it was like, "Um, I don't have an amp." So I'd have to play myself raw. I would always insist, "We've got to have a form, we've got to have a form. Otherwise I'm going to die here." So I kept forcing them, "This isn't a song. I just played twenty minutes without a break."'

Perhaps the others still thought they were playing one of Branca's pieces. His overarching influence in those years cannot be overestimated. Aside from providing an outlet and a *modus operandi*, he also represented a way of introducing their own noisefest to the Europeans. Because Moore and Ranaldo continued to offer their services when Branca took his multi-guitar suites overseas, they had the perfect opportunity to get a little word of mouth going here.

Lee Ranaldo: Thurston and I were playing a tour with Glenn in Europe, and every city we went to, Thurston and I would say to the promoter, 'We have this little band Sonic Youth, and we'd like to come [back] next month.' So we managed to get a European tour two or three years before anyone else in New York did. We had this foot in the door.

That 'foot in the door' proved to be all-important because four years on New York had done very little for the Youth's prospects, even when they made contact with a concept. By the time Neutral put out their first full album, *Confusion Is Sex*, at the end of 1983, the band knew enough to accept chaos. By 1984, they were no longer tied and bound to no wave. With their second album, *Bad Moon Rising*, they were looking to lead. Unfortunately, as Ranaldo says, 'There was a period when we were kinda despairing, where we literally did not have anyone interested in releasing the records we were doing . . . [but] Paul Smith said, "I'll put it out in England."'

Paul Smith: I just put this cassette [of *Bad Moon Rising*] in . . . and thought, 'My God, somebody makes music like this.' It was just . . . a really interesting blend of what at that point was . . . industrial, but then with guitars . . . [that] were all really weird and fucked-up, and there were sort of pop and rock bits in there, but it wasn't a pop or rock thing.

Youth had come upon Smith, overseer at Mute, via Lydia Lunch. Initially Smith thought Cabaret Voltaire might be happy to put it out on their label. Even when they demurred, Smith was not dissuaded and originated Blast First 'in order to put *Bad Moon Rising* out'. The reaction in the UK to this sonic smorgasbord was extremely positive, and very soon word was making its way back across the pond, to the 'big city / where a man cannot be free'.

Lee Ranaldo: *Bad Moon Rising* was really the first record that brought us to anyone's attention anywhere, and it happened stronger in England just because of the way the music press is over there. We came over, we made a good impression, the music press wrote these huge articles on us, and that started it rolling in a lot of ways. Immediately, it seemed like we were bigger in England than we were here. Then it all reflected back on America. Paul knew how to work that stuff; but here none of that stuff was in place for underground music, so it took a lot longer to get the word out . . . [The UK press] were writing about us long before anyone over here gave a shit.

Unfortunately, the UK music press chose to lump Sonic Youth in with all the 'Green Ryders' (which was how these East Coasters typified the Paisley bands). As Ranaldo says, 'We were like, "Wait a minute, we're so much more weighty than those bands." [But] it was [all] American guitar-music [apparently] . . . We just couldn't figure out why they were listening to them and us in the same breath. We felt that we were *not* a nostalgic band.' Though Dream Syndicate were the only West Coast band Sonic Youth considered a kindred spirit, they decided it was better to go with the prevailing current.

Thurston Moore: People tend to think of our music as . . . industrial. But there's this big American uprising of Byrds-like jangly guitar bands . . . We feel akin to all that, in the same manner of bands like Green on Red. Only we don't sound the same. [1985]

Outside the system Sonic Youth may have been, but they needed to belong to *something* with its (ostensible) origins in punk. But whereas the 'Green Ryders' were all looking to be bailed out by the big boys, the New York band was still patently in love with their outlaw status, adopting producer Steve Albini's astute aphorism, '[If] to make a record [a band] have to use outside money . . . there's a presumption that those other people are gonna have a say in how the record comes out.' Though the relationship with Blast First was going swimmingly, they needed a similar situation in the States. When they finished *EVOL*, in March 1986, they were looking no further than SST − not that they could see any other riders on the horizon.

Lee Ranaldo: SST was the place we wanted to go − that was the pinnacle at that point as far as US labels . . . Every good record you had in your collection was on SST − The Minutemen, The Meat Puppets, Saccharine Trust. All those bands were our heroes, and they were all on that label . . . [But] Blast First masterminded everything for a while there. Paul Smith was our de facto manager, he was the one we were sitting down with and making plans, and everything else would fall into place around that. I'm pretty sure we shopped *EVOL* to SST when it was done. SST were the only ones really interested in us at that point. There was no major-label interest in any part of that scene.

The whole of Youth had been following the hardcore conflagration since its early days. Indeed, for a while, Moore had published his own fanzine, *Killer*, containing interviews with and features on Minor Threat, Black Flag, The Minutemen and Flipper. But, as Ranaldo says, the band also 'knew we weren't *of* it. We were apart from it in a lot of ways − [ours was] more art-schooly kind of music.' For another label this might have been a problem. For SST it represented an endorsement.

Unfortunately, SST was not the label it had been. Signing Sonic Youth gave it a much-needed shot in the arm, but the prognosis was still not great. Barely had the NY band signed than they learnt of the defection of Hüsker Dü to Warners. The Minnesotans had been unhappy with SST since *Zen Arcade*. As Mould has said, that album 'was sort of the beginning of us knowing that things were a little askew. When we're out promoting the record and doing in-stores, and the best we could do was make special flyers to give to people, because we had sold all thirty-five hundred copies that got pressed.' If Mould had doubts after *Zen Arcade*, he gave SST the benefit. After *Flip Your Wig*, their October 1985 follow-up, though, he had just one single thought, 'We've got to get out of the punk-rock ghetto.'

When it came to the SST set-up, Mould didn't know the half of it. West Coast promotion-man Ray Farrell had joined SST just at the time that *Meat Puppets II*, *Zen Arcade*, and *Double Nickels On The Dime* were all coming out, and found that 'these were the first records that were beginning to sell for those bands'. He immediately discovered that their most, er, important distributor, 'Important Records, were frustrated at the fact that we ran out of *Zen Arcade*. They would [even] offer to pay for private pressings of this stuff so they would have something to sell.' But where Farrell was most alarmed was with the label's attitude to college radio, which suggested that SST was not so much anti-success as plain un-businesslike.

Ray Farrell: SST didn't send college radio records out, except maybe [to] three or four stations. So I'm going through [letters] from college stations saying, 'Dear SST, we'd love to be on your mailing list. We love The Minutemen. Can you send us the record?' Another twenty playlists go by, you'd come across the same station again, 'We wrote to you about two months ago asking to get the Hüsker Dü and Minutemen records. Individual DJs are bringing in their own copies and taking them home again. We would play this to death if we had it.' Then [another] twenty playlists go by, you'd see the station again, 'What the fuck is wrong with you guys?'

Ginn seemed unprepared for success even on this nominal scale, afraid that things were going to slip from his control. And control was very important to Greg Ginn. Joe Carducci, who had had enough by 1986, feels that there was an element of deliberate sabotage to what happened next – a flood of product which even a major might have struggled to promote.

Joe Carducci: Greg was of two minds on the label. One was that he only wanted to do stuff no one else would do, and not have expectations about the label. But I had the feeling before I left that he'd regretted [how] the label had become a home to this clutch of bands, and that it was known in some kind of aesthetic way. So in a way that barrage of releases in the late eighties was his way of exploding that reputation.

Having issued some fifty-eight records between 1979 and 1985, Ginn issued forty-six artifacts in 1986 alone, and more still in '87. The SST quality control could not possibly be maintained. In fact, Carducci's doubts became manifest almost immediately after his departure, when Ginn came up to Ray Farrell and said, 'I want to sign a bunch of instrumental bands.' He had already been playing without the increasingly detached Rollins, as Black Flag Instrumental, and was now convinced it was the way ahead. Actually it was as regressive as it got – but those stoner roots were starting to show through.

Ray Farrell: Black Flag Instrumental could play the Anti-Club, and there wouldn't be an enormous amount of people. It was the backyard stuff, to be able to play out without any pressure. [And SST] was about Greg Ginn's vision . . . There were some bands on SST that were purely backyard signings, sub-metal bands. Bands like Worm were just guys that hung with Chuck [Dukowski] in high school . . . [But] in a way, it was the beginning of the end for SST, because a lot of stuff was coming out – three Zoogz Rift albums in one month, just crazy stoner stuff . . . He really wanted all the bands to stay in line, behind Black Flag. But at the same time he knew that if those bands were representative of an SST ethic, more and more people would say, 'What's this Zoogz Rift about?' That didn't happen.

As SST's original ideals went down the pan, Sonic Youth were going from strength to strength, issuing *EVOL* in 1986 and *Sister* in 1987, two albums that solidified their reputation as a band which harnessed all that was best about guitar-noise, and still made it adhere to the rock from which most of their essential sources had been hewed. In Europe, their sales continued to parallel their ascending reputation. But in the States, something was up, and it was at base camp that the problem lay. If the band's profile had begun to paddle the mainstream, their status at SST seemed to be lagging behind.

Lee Ranaldo: Somewhere in the period after *Sister* was done, we saw that our records were selling, they were making money somewhere along the line, but SST never seemed to have money to pay, and that brought things to a head.

Basically, we left the label for Enigma over frustrations with the finances, and with distribution – [just] so we didn't go some place and people were saying, 'We heard about this record, but we can't find it anywhere.' . . . We had to go through a legal process, [where] we threatened to sue them for non-payment of back royalties, and constructed a deal whereby we bought the rights to all those records back from them . . . We had to have discussions, and in some cases arguments with [Ginn] over the whole thing. They were not happy at all that we wanted to go. And in a lot of ways, it was the start of their troubles. A lot of bands that were deserving of financial remuneration from them were not getting it. Up until then they had coasted along on their notoriety, and all of a sudden there were bands like The Meat Puppets [saying], 'We're not getting paid for the work that we're doing, and other people are interested.'

Ranaldo suspected that 'whatever records were making money was being used to fund a bunch of lame-ass records', and he was almost certainly right. The SST label was in free-fall, and with it the American indie dream. Black Flag existed only in name. The Minutemen had disbanded, after a devastating car crash in December 1985 had claimed D. Boon. Hüsker Dü went Warners-ward in 1986. The Meat Puppets were running out of reasons to press record. Sonic Youth defected to Enigma (and then Geffen) at the end of 1987. Reasons for not going major were fast fading from the frame, and in their place came a realization that maybe independent labels were stepping stones, not final resting places.

In 1988, SST signed their first Seattle band, Soundgarden, a sub-metal outfit with a punk attitude but few of its key musical reference points. By then, as Farrell observes, 'Soundgarden were playing SST in a way, because they were going to do a Sub-Pop record, an SST record and then go to A&M. And musically, Greg was really into it, but by that time he knew that some people were using SST as a possible stepping stone.'

Whether Ginn then knew that Soundgarden were chancers is not clear. He certainly preferred them to another Seattle band who'd sent him their demo tape in January 1988. Perhaps the choice of name offended him. After all, wasn't Nirvana the name of that hippy Island duo who had recorded the classic curio, 'Rainbow Chaser', back in 1968? It sure didn't sound like the name of an SST band. As for the tape this northwest power trio sent, his opinion 'was that they were not that original . . . they were by-the-numbers alternative. It wasn't bad, but it wasn't great either.' Perhaps Ginn no longer knew what to look for. Or perhaps he was content to let the next wave crash on another shore.

7.3
THE BLACK
MUDDY RIVER
1984-91

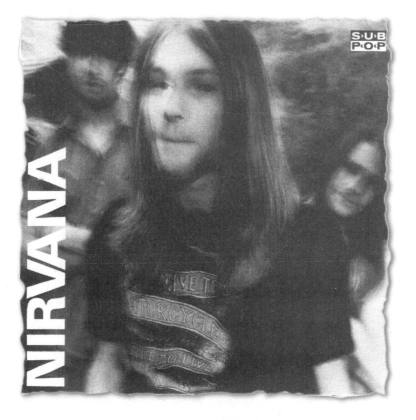

Anything after, oh, 1983 [ain't punk]. Doesn't matter if it's ostensibly punk – up the yingyang – 'cause by then the moment had passed, the world which gave it rise had expired, the market was no longer resisted, and whatever it then was, was no longer anything remotely else.

— Richard Meltzer, *A Whore Just Like The Rest*

We never considered anybody to be grunge . . . I always thought we were a punk band – [that is,] punk with a little 'p'. I always considered myself a punk rocker, I always will . . . In 1995, we came out of the closet and said, 'Fine, we're grunge. If anybody fuckin' is, we are.'   — Steve Turner, to author, 2005

The Clash, in their apocalyptic countdown at the end of '1977', had given young punks seven more years. So maybe Meltzer was a year out in his estimation, but by 1984 all those underground streams were flowing into the same old sea of tunes. If grunge – and specifically Seattle grunge – wasn't so much punk's final solution, it *was* its final mutation, i.e. the last recognizable mutant strain. And, fittingly, it came with its own set of reactionary roots.

When the world sat up to the sounds of Seattle, in the early nineties, there was an attempt to reconstruct a history of punk rock in the northwest that gave it a precedence over even the *Nuggets* bands. For this purpose, it became necessary to define its genesis as the Kingsmen's 'Louie Louie', a 1963 cover of a 1957 Richard Berry rock & roll original. Or even the Wailers' version, cut in Portland a couple of years earlier, from which the Kingsmen nabbed the nub. The Sonics – later, but wilder – also found a berth in the birth of northwest punk.

One soul who definitely wasn't buying into such prehistoric sounds, though, was Nirvana singer Kurt Cobain. In a draft band-bio written in the summer of 1988, he described his band as 'a trio who play heavy rock with punk overtones . . . Nirvana has never jammed on "Gloria" or "Louie Louie".' Cobain, to his credit, considered 'Seattle grunge rock' to have begun in Portland, sixteen years *after* the Wailers first wailed. He gave the credit to The Wipers, a three-piece fronted by the enigmatic Greg Sage, who issued their ferocious first album, *Is This Real?*, on their own label Trap in 1979, only to realize that to get anywhere they needed to start from somewhere other than here.

Greg Sage: The Wipers came out of nothing. We wore flannel shirts because that's what we'd be wearing anyway. If you wanna know how much we thought about Portland and its underground music scene, look how quickly we split for New York.

Other Portland punk bands of the period, notably The Neo Boys, all girls and much lamented locally, stuck around and ran aground. The distance from anywhere else was debilitating. Joe Carducci, who moved down to San Francisco in 1979, defines Portland punk in a nutshell: 'There really were [only] about twenty or thirty kids [in Portland], and they'd mix 'n' match in three or four different bands . . . The Neo Boys just died on the vine, 'cause [it was] Portland. There'd be some traffic between San Francisco and Portland . . . but everybody was against broadening the scene. It was a cool little club, and there were four college stations . . . [but] ultimately each of those [West Coast] towns was too far apart. It wasn't like Boston, Philadelphia, New York and DC.'

For anyone in Portland, only Seattle was a practical drive away. But Seattle's own take on punk left town, before the fact. Tomato du Plenty's band, the Whizz Kids, whizzed down to LA and became the Screamers. Left behind were bands like the Telepaths (who became the Blackouts), the Snots (who did at least issue one cult classic 45, 'So Long To The Sixties') and the Refuzors, who showed that the punk spirit could infuse even the most diehard redneck.

Steve Turner: The Refusers . . . never put out a record, but they were serious thugs. They had long hair; scary, scary men. Are *you* gonna go up to the Refusers and tell them to cut their hair? They weren't teenagers – [more] like the evil Ramones. More mid-tempo [though]. Big logger boots on. They looked like biker trash.

The one band who might have held their own with the Refusers, musically and physically, were Flipper, a Bay Area band formed shortly after the Kennedys, who made the effort to trek up to Seattle on a regular basis. Their cataleptic version of punk rock seemed to find surprising favour in the northwest. Elsewhere, it was not so welcome. As Dead Kennedy Jello Biafra commented in 1981, 'In a day when punk is sometimes safe family entertainment, Flipper draws strong opinion be it for or against, and when you see them you'll know why.'

Ray Farrell, then working at the SF label Subterranean, where he was sometimes required to chaperone the cavorting combo, remembers them as 'always slow and meandering, and looking like they're gonna fall apart. You couldn't figure out how it could sound as bad and as good at the same time. The guy couldn't really play bass; and the guitar player masked what he did by having all these effects over it.'

Farrell also recollects how 'occasionally one of them would come in [to the Subterranean office] and open up a can of catfood or dogfood and eat it in front of us' as a way 'to say that they didn't have any money'. If ever there was a band with the punk attitude – and 'loud fast rules' go hang – it was Flipper. According to Farrell, when 'they were opening for a band they didn't want, Ted Falconi would just go and cut the wires off their amps, so they couldn't play. That way Flipper would be the last band on the bill.' When they opened for PiL in San Francisco in 1980 they thankfully didn't go that far, but their sludgy sound and singer Will Shatter's brazen histrionics were a deliberate digit to these supposed parents of post-punk.

It would take until 1982 for Flipper to make the album that ensured their legacy would not go unacknowledged. *Generic Flipper* was the first true punk album to be played at the coagulated tempo of Black Sabbath, but with the atonality of the Velvets and the lyrics of a literate lout ('We're living like cockroaches in this place / Sprayed with insecticide that leaves no trace / And if we could crawl on you at night / You could be sure we'd love to bite . . . This song rhymes and we play it in time' – 'Living For The Depression'). At the time, the fact that *Generic* was issued by a label called Subterranean was rather fitting. Yet up north, *Generic* was a treasured artifact in the tiny punk enclaves of Oregon and Washington.

Kris Novoselic: I liked prog-rock, and then I discovered punk-rock. In 1983 . . . I listened to *Generic Flipper* and it was a revelation. It was Art . . . Then I tried to turn people on to it, and they'd be, like . . . 'Ah, that punk-rock stuff . . . all it is, is I want to fuck my mom!'

It would take Novoselic a further four years to find soulmate Kurt Cobain, and attain Nirvana. In the meantime, Flipper's Will Shatter would follow in Malcolm Owen's footsteps, ODing after cleaning up, unable to stop himself from dipping his toe into the jet-black pool one last time. Those four years perhaps represented the true heyday of the

Seattle post-punk scene. When Cobain talked eulogistically, in 1994, about how 'we did have our own thing for a while – for a few years in Seattle, it was the Summer of Love and it was so great', he was surely referring to these years, when Seattle was on no one's radar, and the scene had time to gestate and grow, much like the original CBGB's scene in 1974–5.

Mark Arm: There was no sense among the people playing in these bands [like], 'We got something special here.' It was like, 'This is what we do to pass the time, [and] how we get together with our friends.'

Like those on the CBGB's scene, a number of musicians forming bands in Seattle in the early eighties were novices unfazed by a lack of musical training. As guitarist Steve Turner says, 'I didn't touch an instrument until I was supposed to be in a band.' His attitude impressed fellow 'muso' Mark Arm, who remembers 'growing up in the seventies, [when] you had to be a good player to even be in a band. It didn't seem like unless you started playing when you were thirteen it was even possible.' Turner and Arm became fast friends, and started a series of proto-grunge punk bands, some of whom existed simultaneously with legends in their own lunchtime, the Thrown-Ups, Seattle's answer to the Prefects.

Steve Turner: We never practised once. It was improvised, but actual songs. We'd write down ridiculous song titles and then Mark would click off a song and we'd start it off. Leighton [Beezer] had a theory about music . . . Improvising music is real easy 'cause you can't really ever be more than one fret off from each other. If it sounds real bad, you move one fret. So we basically distilled the essence into 'harmony is one fret away'. Some of the [Thrown-Ups] songs are surprisingly poppy.

Arm had originally wheedled his way into the Thrown-Ups (on drums!) because 'Scott, the previous drummer, [liked to] change beats in the middle of whatever, for no apparent reason, and throw everything off.' In fact, during the early to mid-eighties Seattle was a surprisingly diverse place to be – both post-punk and after hardcore. Arm and Turner's first 'proper' band, Mr Epp, was if anything even more 'experimental' than the Thrown-Ups, being *designed* to wind up the hardcore headcases they satirized with their variant on the TV Personalities' 'Part-Time Punks', 'Mohawk Man'.

Steve Turner: [Hardcore] became this rigid style of music and dress code and dance-fight. There was a whole art-thing that got lost with hardcore – which was really unfortunate 'cause that was like the kinda cool-weirdo creative side of stuff. [With] Mr Epp, which Mark played in with me and these kids from high school, these [hardcore] guys called us Art-Spaz, and [would] throw shit at us, and all we were doing was making feedback. We weren't arty, but we weren't wearing leather jackets [either].

If Mr Epp had a primary contemporary influence it was The Dream Syndicate, who were important enough for Arm to brave a U2 concert, in order to see their support set. Not surprisingly, he found himself surrounded by the congenitally clueless: 'They're playing, and Karl Precoda got out in front of the PA stack, there's a little ledge, and just getting feedback thru the PA. And this kid in front of us is going, "There's something wrong with his guitar – it's feeding back."'

Mr Epp were hardly the only art-rockers in town. In fact, as Turner observes, 'There was this whole English-sounding scene in Seattle . . . the Three Swimmers opened for Gang of Four, and were very much a Gang of Four-sounding band. Even the early Soundgarden stuff was very English-sounding: post-punk arty, flange guitar, bass heavy, very Bauhausy.' At this time, the two coolest bands in town were The U-Men, a band so art-rock they took their name from a (actually, *the*) Pere Ubu bootleg album, and The Melvins.

The U-Men were raucous rabblerousers who started something in 1981, but finished before the rest caught up. The Melvins were actually from Aberdeen, a place that another resident, Kurt Cobain, described a few years later as consisting 'of highly bigoted redneck moose-chewing deer-shooting faggot-killing logger types who "ain't too partial to weirdo new wavers"'. When they formed, in 1983, Turner considered The Melvins 'the fastest, tightest hardcore band in Seattle.' To a sixteen-year-old Cobain, stuck inside of Aberdeen with the Seattle blues again and again, they were manna from heaven. In his journals, he described the epiphany experienced seeing The Melvins live in 1983:

They played faster than I ever imagined music could be played and with more energy than my Iron Maiden records could provide. This was what I was looking for. Ah, punk rock. The other stoners were bored and kept shouting, 'Play some Def Leppard.'

Melvins' frontman Buzz Osbourne *could* have played some Def Leppard, if he'd felt like it. As he subsequently confessed, 'I liked all the really heavy stuff at the time: Nugent, Aerosmith, Kiss, Black Sabbath, AC/DC . . . Then I met this guy who had moved to Seattle and joined the Lewd, moved to San Francisco, and now was moving back to Aberdeen . . . He had an immense collection of punk-rock records and it was a really good education. I never would have found those records.'

Like every American teenager who touched that radio dial from the mid-seventies on, Osbourne's indoctrination by the metal-merchants made him a musical Manchurian Candidate. The cancer of 'Classic Rock' had seeped deep into the marrow of America. By the time The Melvins had slowed down, in the mid-eighties, what they were playing sounded like a contradiction in terms, prog-punk.

For if it was hard to really hate the early Led Zep albums, it was necessary for the sake of one's punk soul. As Peter Prescott of Boston-based Mission of Burma told one sympathetic writer, 'I heard in [grunge] the kind of stuff that I had always wanted to get away from. Not that I hate Kiss and AC/DC and Led Zeppelin, because I think they were sort of hovering in the background of a lot of that stuff, but that's what I played in my basement in high school.' For Kris Novoselic – and Kurt Cobain – the desire to be a punkified Led Zeppelin never went away.

Even after *his* punk-rock epiphany, when bassist Kris Novoselic 'totally disavowed all this stupid metal – Ozzy Osbourne, Judas Priest, Def Leppard, it was just shit, I just could not listen to it any more . . . I was still into Zeppelin and Aerosmith and [that] stuff.' It was a distinction that would have sent Johnny Rotten rabid. In fact, Nirvana's very first gig, at a friend's party in March 1987, featured two Zeppelin covers ('Heartbreaker' and 'How Many More Times') in an eight-song set. The clearest indication of how Novoselic and Cobain saw themselves probably resides in their first ad for a drummer in local listings magazine, *The Rocket*:

SERIOUS DRUMMER WANTED. Underground attitude, Black Flag, Melvins, Zeppelin, Scratch Acid, Ethel Merman. Versatile as heck.

But perhaps the most ubiquitous pre-punk influence on the northwest scene was another set of Black Country bashers, Black Sabbath, whose leaden brand of heavy rock almost never made it on to Classic Rock FM, perhaps because they sounded at times like the house-band of

Bedlam. Mark Arm admits, 'I didn't get into Black Sabbath until '83, but it was definitely a point of reference for us . . . It wasn't played on the radio . . . Maybe "Paranoid" [was played] on Top Forty radio. [But] by the time I was listening to FM rock . . . Black Sabbath was hardly ever played. [Whereas] Zeppelin was played all the time.'

As the prog-rock precursor to Flipper, early Sabbath had an unearthly quality not found in the more FM-friendly Zeppelin and Purple. By adding this to the punk gene pool, and fusing it with accelerated bursts of hardcore riffing, The Melvins and their northwest brethren produced an altogether more glutinous variant of punk-rock. And they called it grunge (though not right away). Before that could happen, Soundgarden would have to start dredging from the same sludge, and the two bands that ultimately spawned Mudhoney and Pearl Jam – Green River and Mother Love Bone – would have to live and die in relative obscurity.

Aside from The Melvins, Green River were the 'other' early Seattle band that seemed to warrant the epithet grunge – the result of a sharp deceleration from hardcore's high tempo, but retaining the same volume and hard edge. As Turner says, everyone in the band – himself included – 'came from the hardcore thing, [but] didn't want to play hardcore. We wanted to broaden what we were playing, I guess. The things I was really into at the time were like the first couple of Replacements albums . . . [Then there was] the first Dream Syndicate [album] – I really, really love that record.' When Green River supported Sonic Youth at a landmark show in Seattle in August 1985, the New Yorkers were taken aback by the weird blend of acceptable and unacceptable influences.

Thurston Moore: [In the early eighties] discovering anything that was pre-Sex Pistols was kind of *dangerous*. But all of a sudden, it became the healthy thing to do . . . I remember playing with Green River in Seattle. They seemed genuinely influenced by hard rock from '75 on, but they were punker kids.

Green River brought together art-punks Arm and Turner and careerist Jeff Ament. Ament had been in his own hardcore band, back in Montana, called Deranged Diction. Their mantra was 'No Art, No Cowboys, No Rules' (apparently unaware that the first two *are* rules). Turner and Arm knew that Ament could give them something their previous art-rock experiments lacked, and so Turner 'took a job at a coffee shop that Jeff worked at, to slowly convince him to be in a band with me and Mark. He hated our band, 'cause we were a shitty art band.

He liked proper musicianship, and we didn't have that . . . [In fact,] I can't think of someone I disagreed with about music *more* than Jeff.'

Turner and Arm were obliged to put up with Ament's Classic Rock tastes, while drawing on a number of pre-punk American rockers themselves. Though the band they came up with, Green River, was ostensibly named after a notorious serial killer, the Creedence song was another, welcome association. When Ament introduced Stone Gossard to Arm and Turner, Green River was ready to flow. By the end of 1984 they'd issued their first album, *Come On Down*, though this heavy hybrid failed to rattle many cages.

The 'grungey' Green River was destined to remain another brave attempt to fuse two incompatible aesthetics. Much like the Hell-era Heartbreakers, it had barely begun to 'make the grade' before its diametrically opposed elements began to pull the band apart. For Turner, the most disturbing turn of events came when Ament and Gossard said 'that they planned to make a career in music. They started calling going to practise going to work. I just thought, "What are you sniffing? You're insane. There is no career in music for anything like this."' By 1985, Turner had quit the band, replaced by Bruce Fairweather. Ament and Gossard now began to push the band down the pike toward prog-rock.

Until the summer of 1987 – and the release of an EP of Green River studio recordings, *Dry As A Bone*, on a new Seattle label, Sub-Pop – they remained just another band with a reputation based on live shows and two songs on the seminal *Deep Six* compilation LP, recorded with Turner back in 1985. *Dry As A Bone* broke the dam, and Green River began recording an entire Sub-Pop album, *Rehab Doll*, with Jack Endino in the Nick Lowe role. Seemingly destined for greater things – maybe even a career – tensions became accentuated by the album sessions, its members arguing about whether to look for a major-label deal, or whether to stay within Seattle's indie cocoon. Matters came to a head when the band played a showcase in LA, and Ament and Gossard invited along a lot of no-show A&R folk. As far as Arm was concerned, the whole thing was starting to resemble a twelve-step programme to sonic sobriety.

Mark Arm: I had brought tapes of the Scientists and Feedtime [on the road]; and Jeff had brought tapes of the latest Aerosmith record and a Whitesnake record, and he was just going, 'Listen to the production.' I [just] couldn't wrap my head around that idea: 'Whaddya mean, listen to the production?! Who cares about the drum sound. The whole fucking thing *sucks*!' But I was totally outnumbered, taste-wise.

Ament and Gossard were not about to be dissuaded from carving a career out of replicating FM radio riffs, and soon hooked up with Andrew Wood from Lords of the Wasteland, and Greg Gilmore of Ten Minute Warning. Together they formed Mother Love Bone – a band so in love with rock & roll mythology that singer Wood elected to OD before the release of their major-label debut album, *Apple*, in 1990. It seemed that West Coast hard rock and Chinese rocks went hand in hand.

Whatever grunge elements remained – and according to Wood, four days away from that OD, there was 'still a little grunge in the guitars from the Green River days . . . but we may be right in throwing some of the ugly grunge away. It's called stale grunge' – these were eradicated along with Wood. When Ament and Gossard found singer Eddie Vedder, Pearl Jam emerged fully formed for FM-sound.

If the pair of Polygram recordings Mother Love Bone made didn't suggest a worthy hybrid of prog and punk, the release in October 1988 of another Sub-Pop mini-album, *Superfuzz Bigmuff*, by Mark Arm and Steve Turner's new band, Mudhoney – so named after one of Russ Meyer's monster-mammaries movies – confirmed that theirs had been the part of Green River where the mud ran deep. *Superfuzz* was both a distillation of earlier Seattle sounds and the template for all future 'grunge'. At last, Arm and Turner had found a double-D sound.

Steve Turner: I was trying to do a proper band with Ed from the Thrown-Ups and Dan Peters playing drums, [but] Ed really didn't want to deal with a real band. So as soon as Green River broke up, Mark joined up and the three of us started practising. We practised through December '87, just the three of us, and then [we] got Matt, who had just been fired from The Melvins . . . January 1, 1988 was our first practice. The band wasn't started to be anything more than a[nother] project. We knew Bruce Pavitt, and also Tom Hazelmeyer of Reptile Records, who'd put out the Thrown-Up records and said he'd [like to] put out 'something'. So we had two different labels saying, 'We'll put out a single.' We're like, 'This is gonna be great. We'll put out a single or two, then I'll go back to school.'

Mark Arm: I was working with Bruce Pavitt at Muzak and I remember bringing in boom-box cassettes of what we'd been doing, and he's like, 'I can't tell what's going on. Why don't you just go in the studio?' He gave us a couple of hundred bucks to record with Jack Endino.

Another powerhouse trio that was a tad slow coming off the Seattle starting-block had also been making their own set of tapes with Jack Endino. On 23 January 1988, Nirvana – comprising Kurt Cobain, Kris Novoselic and temporary drummer Dale Crover (from The Melvins) – recorded and mixed ten songs at Seattle's Reciprocal Recording Studio in five hours, before driving thirty miles to Tacoma to play a gig at the Community World Theater. Frontman Cobain had apparently asked Endino to produce the session because he liked the sound of Soundgarden's Sub-Pop 45, 'Screaming Life'.

Nor were Soundgarden alone in considering moving to SST for their next artifact. Cobain evidently shared similar ambitions. But when Ginn expressed no interest in the tape, Cobain began dubbing copies to give out to any able-bodied punk he came across between Aberdeen and Seattle. Endino also did his bit, passing out cassette dubs of his remix to local journalist Dawn Anderson, DJ/writer Shirley Carlson and, most importantly, to Jonathan Poneman, co-owner of the Sub-Pop label (along with Bruce Pavitt).

Whereas Nirvana could easily have fallen through the capacious cracks now forming at SST, with Sub Pop they were assured of the astute attentions of Poneman and Pavitt. It was the latter of the pair who had come up with the Sub-Pop imprimatur, back in 1983, as the title of a column in *The Rocket*, long before he was thinking in terms of a record label. Like Bob Last at Fast Product, Pavitt dreamed of taking underground sounds overground, but initially was a proselytizer without product, trying to celebrate everything that was alternative to AOR.

Nils Bernstein: Bruce wanted to showcase bands that operated outside of established media centers . . . He was going to write about Ohio bands, Atlanta bands and whatever, [hence] subterranean pop . . . [Initially] it couldn't be about things happening in Olympia or Seattle because there was nothing happening . . . So Bruce put out cassettes with the zine, and then decided to put out an album version of the cassettes that he had been putting out [*Sub-Pop 100*] . . . It had some Seattle bands on it because [by] that time some of our bands were really good – Green River's on it, The Wipers are on it . . . [But] Bruce was into the variety and the artiness, so he wanted to do spoken word, he wanted to do stuff that was cabaret noise . . . [Then] with the promo copies of the *Sub-Pop*

100 that he sent around, [he] put in a copy of the Green River single . . . [But] I don't think Bruce set out thinking I'm going to be to the late eighties what Fast was in the late seventies.

— — —

By 1988, everything was in place for the last flare to be fired from punk's pistol – and again it would be in a place that had a couple of good clubs, an independent label, a dedicated fanzine and a handful of bands to get excited about, some of whom had been on the scene since before The Melvins, having taken their time getting a handle on a post-hardcore world.

Steve Turner: It seemed like all the Seattle bands were starting to meet at some place. Soundgarden started out as one thing and were going this way; we started out as [another] thing; Melvins started out as something else [again]. I guess, everyone was starting to influence each other.

The only real problem was that not one of these bands sounded like the Pistols, the Ramones, The Clash – or even Black Flag. Perhaps it was time to rebrand again. And where better a place to start than Green River's *Dry As A Bone* EP, which the Sub-Pop catalogue described as 'ultra-loose GRUNGE that destroyed the morals of a generation'.

Turner, for one, is unsure where the term originated. He believes he first came across it in the liner-notes to a late-seventies Johnny Burnette and the Rock & Roll Trio reissue, which described Paul Burlison's guitar tone on 'Train Kept A-Rollin' as 'grungey'. Given the overwhelming influence of Burlson on Zeppelin's Jimmy Page, it's a fitting place to first find the term. Though Turner's partner-in-punk, Mark Arm, co-opted the term in a 1981 fanzine article, it remained a descriptive term, not a genre. When it did mutate, the suggestion that grunge was a heavy-metal hybrid rather than any part of punk would send some folks crazy.

Kris Novoselic: It's the attitude that sets it apart. When you think of heavy metal, you think of sexist innuendoes and pseudo-Satanism . . . We're heavy, but we're not heavy metal. [1992]

One thing was for sure, Sub-Pop had stumbled on their very own attitudinal clique of bands that they could brand and market. And as Turner says, 'It's rare when it all combines at once, where there's a label actively willing to promote [the local scene], and a guy with so many connections from doing his fanzine . . . The *Sub-Pop 100* compilation was like the across-America compilation, but after that record, [Bruce] only focused on the Seattle stuff for the next couple of years.' Pavitt would later claim a clear sense of where he was going, with happenstance just a willing partner.

Bruce Pavitt: From the very beginning, I had a really focused agenda: I was trying to promote America's regional scenes . . . We were caught up with all the quality music here [in the northwest] – and with the whole romantic notion of a regional scene . . . I had a very strong image of the small regional scene erupting into an international phenomenon. But, remember, we were shut out of the US media. And England has such a relentless . . . schedule for writing music, we knew that the only way we could maybe break through was to use the British press . . . [So we] released *Sub-Pop 200*, which documented a lot of local bands. And Peel was playing it – then he wrote a review in the London *Times* [sic] stating that the music was the most distinctive regional sound since Detroit's Motown. [1994]

Actually, it appears to have been Pavitt's partner at Sub-Pop, Jonathan Poneman, who first suggested that if they were really going to make Seattle's 'small regional scene erupt into an international phenomenon', they needed to sell the scene to the English music press. Having found the air fare to fly over *Melody Maker*'s Everett True to do a piece on the Seattle scene in the winter of 1989, Poneman gave True a single-sentence quote that would come to define this slow-moving juggernaut:

There isn't so much a Sub-Pop sound as a readily recognizable movement happening in the American northwest right now, which is heavy, confrontational guitar-based rock. [*MM*, 18/3/89]

By this time, Sub-Pop had begun to produce the kind of anti-muzak that warranted more than this slightly half-baked hype. Between August 1988 and June 1989, the label issued the last Soundgarden statement with grunge in its grooves (*Fopp*); Mudhoney's first two singles, 'Touch Me I'm Sick' and 'You Got It', and their blunderbuss of a mini-LP, *Superfuzz Bigmuff*; Nirvana's 'Love Buzz' single plus the coruscating *Bleach*; and the first recorded works of the Crocus Behemoth of the Seattle scene, Tad ('Ritual Device' and *God Balls*).

In the middle of all this, the label also issued the all-important twenty-track sampler, *Sub-Pop 200*, devoted solely to Seattle and its surrounds, which served as both a crash course in the origins of northwest 'heavy, confrontational guitar-based rock' – with Green River, The Thrown-Ups, Nirvana and Soundgarden (doing 'Sub Pop Rock City') – as well as introducing the less 'grungey' strains emanating from Olympia's oft-overlooked Beat Happening and the country-grunge of The Walkabouts.

The release of the 'Love Buzz' 45 and 'Spank Thru' on *Sub-Pop 200* may have started a Nirvana buzz before they even applied *Bleach*, but in the spring of 1989 Sub-Pop were staking their reputation (and depleted funds) on Mudhoney. With this in mind, they somehow slotted them on to a European tour by Sonic Youth, hoping to align Seattle's finest exponents of 'confrontational guitar-based rock' with the East Coast's most respected representative of that club. In an inspired move, they also issued a double-sided single that made the connection explicit, Sonic Youth covering Mudhoney's 'Touch Me I'm Sick', and Mudhoney reciprocating with 'Halloween'.

Sonic Youth by 1989 were perhaps at the height of their cultural importance, and were happy to join Sub-Pop's band of supporters. They had finally found the sound *they'd* been searching for, issuing the seismic *Daydream Nation* at the exact point when the confluence of styles they'd adopted in the eighties was generating interest from the 'majors' *and* the media.

Lee Ranaldo: *Daydream Nation* put us right at the top of the whole [alternative] heap – that was number one in all the indie polls at the end of the year. That record accomplished everything we ever set out to achieve. But we also toured about nine months behind that record. Paul Smith arranged these gigs in Russia, we played Australia and Japan for the first time. That had a lot to do with the major labels getting interested, or increasing our fan base to a point where it could seem like a logical idea that a band like us could be on a major . . . the people that were [interested in] signing us were people that had come out of college radio, that grew up on this stuff, and they were all of a sudden getting jobs at record labels, and trying to bring along their tastes with them.

Where Sonic Youth superseded all other claimants – in Poneman's view – was in the way they had 'reinvest[ed] their interests and their endorsements into the various scenes across the country. They developed this influence and this clout; and they shared it.' Their contribution to the international success of Seattle's two true contenders, Mudhoney and Nirvana, cannot be underestimated. Though REM loved the music of their rawer contemporaries, and did their best to bring their fans to the fair, their own 'jangly' post-punk simply did not appeal to the same demographic. Yet even Sonic Youth were slightly taken aback to find that Mudhoney indulged in Meyers-like mayhem offstage as well as on.

Lee Ranaldo: It was almost like [Mudhoney] were on a trail of carnage. They were completely living out the life of the kind of rock & rollers they were supposed to be. They were constantly fucked up, constantly on the edge of chaos.

However, the Youth were not dissuaded from championing Sub-Pop's other contender; and next time around, it was Nirvana's turn to tag along, as the East Coasters wallowed in *Goo*, their first go on the Geffen merry-go-round. By then, Cobain was already looking beyond Sub-Pop, and was mightily interested in Geffen's treatment of the band chosen to launch their DGC subsidiary. It was only when the Youth audience responded to Cobain's swooping vocals and Nirvana's jet-dive dynamics, though, that he realized they could communicate across continents, and not just from Aberdeen to Tacoma.

Bleach, released in June 1989, had been a DIY exercise, Cobain setting out to make their debut long-player 'like it was a radio session. The key to a successful album is to get the fuck out of the studio before you're sick of the songs.' In fact, three of the cuts came from that January '88 afternoon-demo, and the songs were already well worn by the time Sub-Pop deigned to release it, having been the mainstay of every Nirvana set for two years now.

Despite its demo-like feel, *Bleach* drew a great deal of positive press, especially in the UK, where a brief tour with labelmates Tad drew favourable comparisons with the first UK shows of Dream Syndicate and Sonic Youth. In fact, Edwin Pouncey at *NME* felt: 'They manage to make labelmates Mudhoney sound like Genesis, [as they] turn up the volume and spit and claw their way to the top of the musical garbage heap.' However, when Sub-Pop issued a UK single, 'Blew', it was dismissed by Mr Post-Punk himself, Simon Reynolds, as 'dismal, muddy, thuggish trad-rock . . . These warhorse riffs are only fit for the knacker's yard.'

Perhaps feeling that they had rushed the record, Cobain decided to hang fire on that difficult second album – indeed, it would be another twenty-seven months before *Nevermind* was ready for release, by which time Nirvana were no longer a Sub-Pop act. Yet it began life as a

Sub-Pop (mini-)album, the first set of sessions taking place in April 1990, with Butch Vig producing from his Madison home-studio, at Poneman's suggestion.

Novoselic continued to check Vig out throughout Nirvana's time at Madison's Media Studio, initially unconvinced that he understood the band like Endino had. As Vig reveals, 'He asked me about a lot of punk records, asked if I could get this or that kind of sound.' But by the end of the five days' work, which proved surprisingly productive with eight tracks captured, the band were happy to let Vig get the gig. Meanwhile, Sub-Pop were considering putting these cuts out as a mini-album. The band, though, were using the tape as a demo to get *off* the label.

Jack Endino: They had actually made up these demo tapes. They gave me the tape and it said 'NIRVANA' on it with this little hand-made cover. There were six or seven songs, plus they had put 'Love Buzz' on the end of it. And they were calling it a demo. In other words, they were shopping it. And Kris said, 'Don't tell Sub-Pop I gave this to you, but this is what we're sending out to try to get a deal.'

Cobain later told his biographer, 'There [had been] this pressure from Sub-Pop and the scene to play "rock music". Strip it down and make it sound like Aerosmith.' If so, by the time Nirvana reconvened at LA's Sound City, in early May 1991, they were no longer beholden to Pavitt and Poneman, and the takes they'd cut in April 1990 were no longer shortlisted for the band's major-label debut (the sole exception was 'Polly', which they tried at Sound City, but ultimately went with the 'demo').

Nirvana had begun to suspect that the whole Sub-Pop set-up was geared to breaking Mudhoney. Like The Adverts at Stiff, Nirvana sensed they were destined to always remain an afterthought. Sub-Pop's Nils Bernstein helps put this in context: 'The first Mudhoney show was like they're the greatest band ever, no matter what . . . you just knew they were good . . . whereas Nirvana had to prove themselves – it just wasn't this automatic thing.'

Sub-Pop was an indie label, with typically precarious finances. Though it had no shortage of bands looking to ride the bandwagon, Soundgarden had already moved on to the next stepping stone, SST. Of their remaining roster, only Mudhoney and Nirvana were destined for greater things than an entry in the local good gig guide and/or inclusion on cult compilations of northwest grunge. It was too late to snap up The Melvins, The U-Men or Beat Happening, and with the Screaming Trees and Mother Love Bone already looking for dollar signs, Sub-Pop was endeavouring to sell a scene already edging past its sell-by date. They couldn't even be sure that their mainstay, Mudhoney, would stick around long enough to receive their dues. After all, Turner and Arm were veterans of the punk aesthetic and, come 1990, Turner for one was looking to apply the brakes.

Steve Turner: It was already over by 1990. I was really tired of what had become grunge. I didn't like Soundgarden's [new] records *at all*. Nirvana I loved, [but] it seemed like it had already peaked. 1989, we toured [the UK] with Sonic Youth. Maybe I had a short attention span but . . . I'd been doing this for two years now. My theory is always, 'Most bands do their best stuff in the first two or three years, and then get out.' . . . 1990 was the year I said I was stopping for a while – [I even] went back to college again. We all cut our hair – we were definitely backlashing a bit.

And even these favoured sons were starting to worry about the way that Sub-Pop was handling its unexpected critical favour. Simply put, the years 1988 through 1990 saw Seattle adopted as a happening scene by the critical fraternity, but with no sign as yet of any 'international phenomenon' percolating away at the home of Starbuck's. If Pavitt believed such a breakthrough was just around the next corner, he was draining the coffers like it had already arrived. Sub-Pop had caught a dose of SST Syndrome, the indie infection that had done for everyone from Stiff to Slash. If Pavitt knew that two bands did not make a scene, he seemed happy spending the (moderate) profits generated by this pair on finding the combos who could help him achieve critical mass.

Steve Turner: [Sub-Pop] always made good on what they owed us – eventually – but there was a point before *Nevermind* [where] I really did not think they were gonna make it, and it was like, 'Man, they owe us a lot of money, and they're friends. This is getting kinda sticky.' And they weren't listening to us, [even though] we were the primary breadwinner there. They were spending *our* money on stupid things . . . They actually took a loan from us at one point – we got the European advance, and they asked if they could have our half of the European advance for the next few months, [in order] to put out the next record. At the same time, they were flying the Afghan Whigs out [to Seattle]: 'You just borrowed $10,000 from us, and you just spent $5,000 on the Afghan Whigs' [air fares].'

... We were ready to move on. [Sub-Pop] were being distributed by Caroline at the time, and we had a meeting with them [but] the things that they were saying to us was like you'd think a major label would say: telling us we had to tour nine months out of the year, we had to sweeten up the guitar sound, and we couldn't do side projects, [i.e.] they're telling us how to record, what else we can do and how much we have to tour. [We thought,] 'Well, if this is a bigger indie, let's talk to the majors.'

Thankfully for Sub-Pop, Mudhoney decided to give their favourite label one more album, *Every Good Boy Deserves Fudge*, which was, in Turner's words, 'way more garagey, [with] Farfisa keyboards 'n' shit'. It was further proof that they were 'backlashing a bit' from the grunge bug. Unfortunately for them, it was issued a week after Geffen put out the second Nirvana album, *Nevermind*, making it a case of Never Mind Mudhoney, Here's The Dog's Bollocks.

Mark Arm barely recognized the band who'd made *Bleach*. He still suspects that 'the production on *Nevermind* was a conscious step to make a very commercial record. [In fact,] they *crashed the gates* of the mainstream.' Perhaps Nirvana hadn't envisaged making quite such a 'pop' record. Producer Butch Vig remembers that 'Kurt would come in and say, "Take all the high end off the snare." They wanted them to sound sludgy. I was trying to make them sound focused, but also to give them what they wanted.' In the end, he generally went with the former over the latter.

But Nirvana *were* looking to make an album with commercial clout. There was a reason Cobain's favourite Beatles album was *Meet The Beatles*. And though it was a long way from Abbey Road to Sound City, the audience for a pop/rock symbiosis was still alive and cursing. Quelle surprise, the demographic the band found outside the indie compound was not the one they'd envisaged being out there.

Dave Grohl: When we went to make [*Nevermind*], I had such a feeling of us versus them. All those people waving the flag and being brainwashed, I really hated them. And all of a sudden, they're all buying our record. [1992]

Whatever. The album quickly gained a life of its own. Indeed, some months before it was actually issued, it was already making jaws drop. Dream Syndicate's Steve Wynn had the same manager as the Seattle band, 'so he played me the rough mixes of *Nevermind*, and when I heard it, I thought, "This is *really* great." . . . When you heard that record, you knew it was different. It was unlike anything else – it was like this force of nature.'

Such was the effect of *Nevermind*'s September 1991 release on the hierarchy which had held since hardcore that Mark Arm remembers how on the US tour to promote *their* second Sub-Pop album, 'We were supposed to play with Nirvana in Seattle and Portland, and I think we were headlining both shows, before we left on the month-long tour. By the time we came back, we were opening.'

Though Nirvana were no longer a Sub-Pop band, they had thrown the label a lifeline. After Nirvana belatedly signed an exclusive deal, Sub-Pop were in a position to play hardball with the major but elected to take 'points' on future Nirvana product, showing Pavitt and Poneman to be a whole lot smarter than Bob Biggs or Greg Ginn. *Nevermind* outsold every eighties album on SST, Slash and Twin-Tone *combined*. And it just kept on selling, hitting the magic eight-figure mark reserved for the *Rumours* and the *Thrillers*. SST's Ray Farrell, who had joined Geffen at Sonic Youth's suggestion the previous year, was there to see it happen.

Ray Farrell: I remember predicting that [*Nevermind*] was gonna sell 350,000 records to the president of Geffen, and he said, 'You're out of your mind.' . . . [But] at their weekly meetings, there were quotes from radio stations saying, 'I hate this fucking record, but I have to play it, 'cause the phones light up when I play [it].' It was fun to watch an industry that's usually having to make bad guesses suddenly be faced with something that they couldn't do anything for after a while, you just had to get out of the way.

For one glorious moment – as Steve Turner vividly recalls – 'the major labels lost control. They had to acknowledge that they had no idea what's going on. They didn't know what was going to be popular – they were just caught blindsided.' It was just like punk's first revolution, which had sent UK A&R running around like headless chickens back in '77. There was only one problem this time around – there was almost no one worth signing.

Steve Wynn: When Nirvana [broke through], I thought, 'Wow, the music I love is now being appreciated by everybody.' What I think happened, [though], was Nirvana wasn't a movement, Nirvana was Nirvana. There was nothing else like Kurt Cobain, [whereas the Sex Pistols] led to a lot of great bands . . . Nirvana spawned a lot of bad music, ironically. When *Nevermind* came out, my first reaction was, 'This is going to change everything,' but now I look back, it was the worst thing that happened, because it was no longer Us versus Them. Us became co-opted. Until Nirvana came along, you made the choice to play this kind of music, and you were choosing – almost certainly – to *not* make a good living, to *not* drive Ferraris, [by saying] 'I am going to be underground and play shitty clubs, and get pizza for the band, but I'm gonna play the music I love.' When Nirvana came along, [some] people thought, 'Hey, I can play this underground music, with a few minor fine tunings, and make some money.' It broke the whole thing of there being an underground and an overground.

Almost all of the bands who had paved the way – making the period between 1980 and 1984 such an exciting era in American music – had given up the ghost, including Wynn's own Dream Syndicate. Even Hüsker Dü and The Replacements had made a mess of their major-label deals, and turned on each other. Excluding Sonic Youth (who *were* the reason Nirvana went to Geffen), the one band that had stuck at it through thick and thin – still making records with real resonance – was REM. And, like it or not, it was probably their influence – along with the Pixies – which had been the difference between the sludge-fest that was *Bleach* and *Nevermind*'s pop-sensibility-returns-to-punk.

Kurt Cobain: Even . . . [around] *Bleach* . . . I was heavily into pop. I really liked REM, and I was into all kinds of old sixties stuff. But there was a lot of pressure within that social scene, the underground . . . To put a jangly REM type of pop song on a grunge record, in that scene, was risky. [1994]

In fact, a surprisingly astute review of *Nevermind* in *Spin* – *Rolling Stone*'s new rival in rock monthlies – suggested that Nirvana's 'music sounds like REM married to Sonic Youth, while having an affair with the Germs'. And if, as *Nevermind* producer Butch Vig recalls, Cobain seemed constantly 'self-conscious, coming from a punk background and having these kind of gorgeously crafted rock songs', the most commercial candidate – 'Smells Like Teen Spirit' – came with a riff ripped clean from the CD of 1988's *Surfer Rosa*, the Pixies' post-powerpop classic, and an album Cobain said, 'made me finally admit, after being into punk rock for so many years, that I liked other styles of music as well'. It was a cop Cobain willingly 'fessed up to: 'I was trying to write the ultimate pop song. I was basically trying to rip off the Pixies.'

Those 'other styles of music' included that once-vibrant strain of punk which was not ashamed to display a pop sensibility. But the hardcore hammerheads had seen such musicality as a threat to their crude take on the sound. It was those reference points that had enabled REM, The Replacements and the Pixies to stop the car and get out, while Black Flag's family-convertible kept playing 'chicken' on the cliff. Leaving punk-rawk's wreckage behind, REM had responded to Warners' importuning. At the time of *Nevermind*, REM had already paid off Warners' other mistakes of judgement, *Out Of Time* and *Green* proving once and for all that a once-coveted indie status need not be the end of the rainbow, even if they'd had a long time to think about just such a move. As guitarist Buck wrote back in 1984:

We tend to bend over backwards to avoid commercial moves because we're afraid of diluting the essence of the band, but we also realize that we're part of the machine . . . now we have to decide what the difference is between doing it for its own sake and doing it because it's a potentially profitable career. [*Record*, 10/84]

Such dilemmas had always been part of the equation – even before New York and London punk bands jump-started the seventies. As Richard Hell says, looking back at all he has wrought, some thirty-something years after he first defined the _____ generation, '[The punk ideal] is so ambitious that it can't be maintained. It has such a level of intensity . . . it had to do with a kind of honesty that's so pure that it doesn't really exist; so it's going to destroy you [if] you try to [maintain] it.'

Among those who were destroyed trying to maintain it had been Peter Laughner, Sid Vicious, Darby Crash, Malcolm Owen, Ian Curtis, Stiv Bators, Will Shatter, Andrew Wood and, as recently as April 1991, Johnny Thunders, about whose death Hell wrote at the time, 'It annoys me to see cynical, exploitative, self-centred, death-drive get glamorized . . . [given that] one of the most widely felt reactions to Johnny's death was that the conclusion had been foregone for so long that there wasn't any drama left.' It seems unlikely, though, that Kurt Cobain was reading the thoughts of Chairman Richard as he lived out his own – and punk's – foregone conclusion.

EPILOGUE:
YOU GOTTA LOSE

Come out and play, make up the rules
Have lots of fun, we know we'll lose.

— lines to early draft of '(Smells Like) Teen Spirit'

All the warnings from the punk-rock 101 courses over the years. Since my first introduction to the, shall we say, ethics involved with independence and the embracement of your community has proven to be very true. I haven't felt the excitement of listening to as well as creating music along with reading and writing for too many years now. I feel guilty beyond words about these things . . . I don't have the passion any more. — Kurt Cobain's suicide note

He knew if he went [on the next tour] he'd be trapped into carrying on and on and on . . . that there would always be new 'convincing' reasons and persuasions as to why he should do just one more record, just one more tour, just one more interview, ad nauseam. Until there was nothing left of him, or the integrity of his original idea. — Genesis P. Orridge (about Ian Curtis)

On 23 August 1991, a month and a day before *Nevermind*'s release, Nirvana played the premier open-air event of that English summer, the Reading Festival, to a 100,000-strong crowd, on a bill that also included the Godfather himself, Iggy Pop; the one Mancunian survivor of punk, Mark E. Smith (and a band he liked to call The Fall); as well as their friends, Sonic Youth, who had brought along a film crew. Nirvana stole the show. A year later, they returned to the scene of that last, incandescent pre-hype triumph as the biggest band in the world, and gave of their all again. This time, though, the audience needed no persuading and Cobain's passion visibly drained away that night.

By then, the previous year's documentary had appeared, little more than a decade after Penelope Spheeris's *The Decline of Western Civilization*. *The Year That Punk Broke* — ostensibly 'about' Sonic Youth — was a celluloid version of the tipping-point when 'punk' again emerged into the light of day. Coinciding with Nirvana's remarkable success, the film seemed to suggest that there was a class of '91, just as there had been a class of '76.

Rock journalists who had also journeyed through the eighties underground predicted an avalanche of alternative sounds. Gina Arnold compiled her *Road To Nirvana* (1993) to show the arc upward. Unfortunately, she had the picture upside down. Winterland may not have been a full stop, but neither was it an authentic starting-point. As for the relationship between grunge and punk, Johnny Rotten was in no doubt, 'These bands say they were influenced by the Sex Pistols. They clearly can't be. They missed the point somewhere. You don't wear the tattered uniform of blandness – not if you're interested in the Pistols at all.'

The contradictions which commercial success must only compound had been short-circuited by the Sex Pistols. And no one after them had yet managed to hold on to the punk ideal beyond the third album Nirvana were now obliged to record (only a handful got to that landmark with the spirit intact). Quite simply, punk had always been about trying to recapture that ecstatic moment when a band plays together for the first time, in someone's bedroom or garage, a rehearsal hall, a club or a demo-studio, and the mind goes click – 'Things will never be this honest or real again.' The more tenacious held on to the lightning rod until it singed their synapses, but if punk had a moral it was that, in the end, everybody gets burned.

Cobain, though, was singularly unprepared for the consequences of all he (and those who came before) had wrought. As Steve Turner tells it, 'He never struck me as someone that knew very much about punk rock, [yet] he seemed so defensive about wanting it to be recognized as punk rock.' Hence the name-checks for all those post-Winterland bands whose musical influence on Nirvana seems barely discernible; or the time he told his biographer that in 'talk[ing] about punk rock . . . he means the do-it-yourself, be-yourself, low-tech ethos of K, Touch and Go, SST and other fiercely indie labels. It's an effort to reclaim music from the corporate realm and bring it back to the people.'

His strategy for achieving this, signing to a major label at the first opportunity, was a highly original way to 'reclaim music from the corporate realm'. But at least he now had the clout to make a keynote address to the corporate clowns, and tell it like it is. Instead, when MTV attempted a cheap act of blackmail – 'We'll boycott other alternative acts if you don't do as we ask' – to persuade him to drop 'Rape Me' from a September 1992 'MTV awards' live telecast, Cobain capitulated – and then played the opening bars of the song, before switching to 'Lithium'. What a tease!

Danny Goldberg: He hated going to awards shows, and he didn't always like being recognized; but he worked very hard to get nominated for those awards, and he worked very hard to be recognized.

Further ground went unreclaimed from the capitalist conspiracy when Cobain agreed to change the title of the same song to 'Waste Me' – an apparently more acceptable sentiment in middle America – for a special edition of Nirvana's follow-up to *Nevermind*, *In Utero*, to be sold in that cheap and cheerless chain, Wal-Mart. So much for placing integrity above the bottom line. Even Sub-Pop's Bruce Pavitt, whose label had been saved from meltdown by *Nevermind*'s success, couldn't condone such a cop-out. Sub-Pop publicist Nils Bernstein remembers asking Pavitt for a quote about Cobain's decision, and Bruce beginning to say, 'Those guys are great, they are reaching the heartland . . .' Then came the pregnant pause. Finally he said, 'There's no good excuse for that.'

Pavitt certainly knew the legend of 'God Save The Queen', and how it topped the charts despite being unavailable in every high-street chain across the land. But then he was an historian and an idealist of the punk school. Cobain was neither, and when the contradictions started coming at him, he became increasingly hard to handle. As one man who had played such an integral part in the birth of the punk aesthetic wrote, shortly after Cobain's death, 'I always saw [Cobain]'s griping as a punk-rock pose and essentially a cop-out on his part. I mean, this guy was planning on being a rock star from the age of two.' Nick Kent knew Cobain's kind, and recognized a death-knell when he heard it.

Cobain knew next to nothing about Kent's contribution, though on one occasion he did scribble in his private journal the loaded question, 'Does anyone remember Lester Bangs?' Bangs was dead before the teenager even got to see The Melvins, having ingested too much cough syrup and prescription cold-cure for one man. One of his last pieces on rock was a *Village Voice* review of a Black Flag gig, in which he lamented seeing 'a phalanx of big ugly skinhead goons imported from Washington DC . . . hurl[ing] themselves on the crowd with brutal but monotonous regularity in suddenly institutionalized slamdancing.' As a long-time closet-Sabbath fan, Bangs would probably have happily ingested his share of Nirvana's teen spirit, but hardcore appalled the man who had wanted punk to reflect the 'rambling adventurousness of . . . free jazz.'

The closest Cobain came to meeting any of the purple-prose insti-gators of punk was a 1993 interview with Jon Savage, author of *England's*

Dreaming. Savage found Cobain to be curious about the Sex Pistols. They did not, however, discuss the fate of the one man with whom Cobain had most in common, Ian Curtis, whom Savage had known personally.

Curtis was terrified at the prospect of success. Cobain was terrified by it. Curtis opted out. Cobain, as Kent baldly states, copped out. His suicide note was riddled with all the inconsistencies common in such sign-offs. It even showed that Cobain lived with the all-consuming fear of being exposed as a charlatan for 'betraying' this musical style and its attendant attitude. In *Come As You Are*, Michael Azerrad recalls a phone call from Cobain in the middle of the night, in which he pleaded with the *Rolling Stone* writer to remove a list of Kurt's favourite fifty albums from his biography. It was a list Cobain had pored over endlessly, as if second-guessing every punk's wish-list, before finally informing Azerrad, 'If you keep it in, I might as well just blow my head off.'

Of course, no one knew at the time that the idea of 'blowing my head off' increasingly occupied Cobain in his non-nodding hours. It provided an act of self-immolation that was perhaps not open to Curtis (guns being hard to acquire in leafy Cheshire, circa 1980), but like Curtis he seemed determined to punish his estranged wife, his uncomprehending child, his fellow band members and everyone who bought into the dark stuff that preoccupied him after he achieved the punk goal of making an album from the edge, and seeing it sell. As if *they* were all responsible for making him renege on everything he had espoused when integrity was easy, i.e. no one was looking. He refused to accept that when the passion's gone, one pulls the plug – on the band. And hang the commercial consequences.

Perhaps the ultimate concession to corporate thinking came when Cobain insisted on renegotiating the percentage on the publishing *retrospectively*, so that he (and his wife) received 70 per cent, instead of the even three-way split they'd agreed at the outset (à la the Pistols). When it looked like he might not get his way, he threw a tantrum and threatened to dissolve the band, the one way in which he was still tethered to this world of pain. The other two gave in, thinking they could get back to making music.

Ever the self-obsessive, Cobain had it in mind to call the next album, *I Hate Myself & I Want To Die* – which would at least have been an honest and searing statement, as well as a perfect encapsulation of where this punk's journey seemed predestined to end. But he gave in to Geffen, and called the record *In Utero* instead. Oh, and sweetened the mix on a couple of songs at their behest. By now, Cobain was truly stewing in his own contradictions. When Simon Reynolds attended a show in New York at the end of 1993, he saw a hype without hope:

Cobain seems to have taken on all the false hopes raised by rock, all the betrayals, as his own special burden, his accursed birthright. As Greil Marcus put it, 'It's as if the source of the depression is not that rock is dead but that it refuses to die' . . . In some ways, *In Utero* is his 'Public Image', a repudiation of his own iconhood. As he continues to squirm excruciatingly on all the jagged contradictions of turning-rebellion-into-$$$$, I'm sure there'll be great songs to come, but Jesus Christ, I wouldn't want to be in his shoes for all the pennyroyal tea in China. [*MM*, 27/11/93]

Reynolds was wrong in one key respect – there were no more songs to come, great or otherwise. An attempt at an *Unplugged* performance, in the same month, gave Cobain an excuse to pull out songs by the likes of The Meat Puppets (two from *II*), David Bowie, The Vaselines and Lead Belly instead. But Cobain was afraid to go the whole hog, and release such a riveting, if low-key set as the next Nirvana album. It did not appear until after his death, when some journalists tried to read a little too much into the song-selection (covers of 'Jesus Don't Want Me For A Sunbeam' and 'Lake Of Fire', in particular, receiving the full reading-between-lines treatment). *MM*'s Andrew Mueller heard it right when he described the session as being 'pitche[d] roughly halfway between REM's *Automatic For The People* and Big Star guitarist Chris Bell's *I Am The Cosmos*, bearing the resigned dignity of the former, the bereft dementia of the latter and the stark honesty of both.'

Like Chris, Kurt didn't live to see his act of acoustic apostasy appear in the shops. But *Automatic For The People* had appeared a year after *Nevermind*, consolidating REM's success in a way that surprised even their most reverent fans and going on to almost catch up with *Nevermind*. In Cobain's mind, it showed that it was possible to have a multi-million seller by turning the volume down and making an almost ambient version of alternative rock; and that refraining from the touring treadmill was not necessarily commercial suicide (REM played exactly one secret show, at the 40 Watt Club in Athens, to 'promote' *Automatic*). He also found REM singer Stipe to be just as receptive a listener as Curtis had found Genesis, when the pressures began to take their toll.

But it all seemed somehow beyond the boy from Aberdeen, who just wanted everyone to feel his pain. Whereas Stipe could conjure up something like 'Everybody Hurts', all Cobain had left to say was 'I Hate Myself & I Want To Die' (just as Curtis apparently couldn't get beyond 'I'm fucked'). And in early April 1994, after discharging himself from another treatment centre, he headed home one last time, wrote a note teeming with self-loathing, put *Automatic For The People* on the CD player, and pulled the trigger. At least this time he wouldn't have to write a note to any doctor who dared save him from self-abnegation, as he had just a month earlier in Rome. That message was curt, but heartfelt: Fuck You.

Bibliography

Periodicals

Melody Maker

16/8/75 Lake, Steve: 'Down & Out In The Bowery'
7/8/76 Coon, Caroline: 'Rotten To The Core'
       Coon, Caroline: 'Punk-Rock: Rebels Against The System'
6/11/76 Interview w/ Andrew Lauder
27/11/76 Charlesworth, Chris: 'Underground, Overground'
       Coon, Caroline: 'Punk Alphabet'
22/1/77 Interview w/ Bernie Rhodes
19/3/77 Harrigan, Brian: 'Punk Comes Of Age'
23/4/77 Harrigan, Brian: Interview w/ The Jam
30/4/77 Coon, Caroline: 'Damned Fine Gig'
       Coon, Caroline: Interview w/ Joey Ramone
7/5/77 Coon, Caroline: Interview w/ Tom Verlaine
14/5/77 'Manchester Waits For The World To Listen'
21/5/77 Doherty, Harry: 'The Best Is Yet To Come'
       Coon, Caroline: Review of 'Sheena Is A Punk Rocker'
4/6/77 Jones, Allan: Interview w/ Johnny Rotten
25/6/77 Jones, Allan: Interview w/ Elvis Costello
       Coon, Caroline: 'White Riot On The Road'
9/7/77 'The Man Who Added Sex To The Pistols'
30/7/77 Birch, Ian: 'Driving Cortinas'
       Welch, Chris: 'Fighting In The Streets'
6/8/77 Birch, Ian: 'Reading The Adverts'
       Birch, Ian: 'Rezillos: Comic Book Heroes'
       Jones, Allan: 'A Day In The Life Of A Bunch Of Stiffs'
13/8/77 Birch, Ian: 'Idol On Parade'
2/8/77 Birch, Ian: 'On Spex'
3/9/77 Jones, Allan: 'Wreckless Eric? What Kind Of Name Is That For A Rock &
       Roll Star?
       Birch, Ian: 'The Only Ones: One-Off'
17/9/77 Interview w/ The Boys
8/10/77 Review of *Blank Generation* LP
15/10/77 Feature on Bristol punk scene
22/10/77 Feature on Manchester punk scene
29/10/77 Feature on Newcastle punk scene
       Birch, Ian: 'Pere Ubu: Five Alive In Ohio'

10/12/77 Interview w/ Wire
31/12/77 Interview w/ The Fall
7/1/78 Interview w/ Tom Robinson
21/1/78 Interview w/ Howard Devoto
18/2/78 Interview w/ The Pop Group
25/2/78 Birch, Ian: Interview w/ Devo
11/3/78 Interview w/ Joe Strummer
18/3/78 Interview w/ Vic Goddard
15/4/78 Interview w/ Tom Verlaine
29/4/78 Rhodes, Bernie: Press release for Subway Sect 45
20/5/78 Letter from Joe Strummer
3/6/78 Harries, Andrew: 'Manchester – Riding The Second Wave'
8/7/78 Interview w/ Howard Devoto
5/8/78 Robinson, Tom: On The Clash
16/9/78 Headon, Topper: On Bernie Rhodes
14/10/78 Interview w/ Stiff Little Fingers
21/10/78 Interview w/ Siouxsie & the Banshees
4/11/78 Interview w/ Vivienne Westwood
11/11/78 Birch, Ian: Review of the Electric Eels 45
25/11/78 Interview w/ Joe Strummer
9/12/78 Interview w/ Wire
20/1/79 Interview w/ Paul Weller
10/2/79 Interview w/ Geoff Travis
10/3/79 Interview w/ The Undertones
24/3/79 Williams, Richard: Review of The Pop Group in Portsmouth
31/3/79 Frith, Simon: 'Afterpunk: The Different Drummer'
19/5/79 Interview w/ The Specials
26/5/79 Harron, Mary: Interview w/ Gang of Four
16/6/79 Watts, Michael: 'The Rise & Fall of Malcolm McLaren Part 1'
23/6/79 Watts, Michael: 'The Rise & Fall of Malcolm McLaren Part 2'
30/6/79 Watts, Michael: 'The Rise & Fall of Malcolm McLaren Part 3'
21/7/79 Savage, Jon: Review of *Unknown Pleasures*
28/7/79 Interview w/ Lydia Lunch
18/8/79 Interview w/ Angelic Upstarts
8/9/79 Interview w/ The Slits
22/9/79 Williams, Mark: LA Punk
6/10/79 Interview w/ the Selecter
3/11/79 Interview w/ Gang of Four
24/11/79 Bohn, Chris: Review of *Metal Box*
8/12/79 Goldman, Vivien: Interview w/ PiL
15/12/79 Interview w/ The Specials
14/3/81 Interview w/ PiL

Mojo

MJ1 Birch, Will: 'Southend & Canvey Island'
MJ2 Scabies, Rat: 'From Here, To Eternity'

MJ7 Kent, Nick: 'Kurt Cobain'

MJ8 Savage, Jon: 'Someone Take These Dreams Away: The Joy Division Story'

MJ9 Lowry, Ray: On The Clash

MJ12 Boyd, Joe: On REM

MJ19 Du Noyer, Paul: 'Maximum R&B: Paul Weller'

MJ30 Birch, Will: 'Pub-Rock'

MJ37 Black, Jonny: 'Destination Nowhere: The Anarchy Tour'

MJ47 Birch, Will: 'Stiff's Greatest Stiffs'

MJ54 Vig, Butch: On Nirvana

MJ58 Cavanagh, Dave: 'The Unchanging Man: Bob Mould'

MJ70 Cavanagh, Dave: Interview w/ Pete Shelley

MJ71 Gilbert, Pat: 'Meltdown: The Clash'

MJ76 Black, Johnny & Harris, John: 'All You Need Is Hate: The Sex Pistols '76'

MJ87 Robbins, Ira: 'Vision On: The Television Story'
Hill, Michael: 'Brat Pack: The Ramones Story'

MJ93 Dellar, Fred: 'Trashing The Pops: The Rezillos'

MJ95 Hart, Grant: 'Hello Goodbye'

MJ97 Babcock, Jay: 'America's Most Wanted: Black Flag'

MJ98 Petridis, Alexis: 'Please Look After This Band: The Specials Story'

MJ101 Wilkinson, Roy: 'The Wrong Trousers: Buzzcocks'

MJ105 Cameron, Keith: 'The Unruly Escapades Of The Stranglers'

MJ110 Cameron, Keith: 'Breathe: Nirvana'

MJ112 Perry, Andrew: 'Hell Is For The Heroes: The Damned Story'
Gilbert, Pat: 'Breakdown: The Clash 1978'

MJ122 Cameron, Keith: 'Ain't It Fun: Public Image Limited'

MJ132 Tyler, Kieron: 'It Came From Down Under'

SMJ135 Gilbert, Pat: 'I'm A Mess: The Sid Vicious Story'

MJ137 Gilbert, Pat: 'Ian Curtis: The Outsider'

New Musical Express

29/6/74 Farren, Mick: 'Dr Feelgood: A Thousand Ugly Legends'

8/11/75 Murray, Charles Shaar: 'At CBGBs'

27/12/75 Phillips, Kate: Review of All Night Ball at Queen Elizabeth College

21/2/76 Spencer, Neil: 'Don't Look Over Your Shoulder, The Sex Pistols Are Coming'

15/5/76 Kent, Nick: Review of the Ramones LP

17/7/76 Bell, Max: 'The Ramones – Waiting for World War III Blues'

11/9/76 Murray, Charles Shaar: Review of Screen on the Green All-Nighter

2/10/76 Parsons, Tony: 'Ere, Who You Screwing, John?'

6/11/76 Carr, Roy: 'On The Down Home, Dusty Flip Side Of The Record Biz'

27/11/76 Robinson, Lisa: 'Talking New York '77'
Kent, Nick: Interview w/ Malcolm McLaren

4/12/76 Review of 'Anarchy In The UK'

11/12/76 Miles, Barry: Interview w/ The Clash

15/1/77 McNeill, Phil: 'Spitting Into The Eye Of The Hurricane'

5/2/77 Feature on *Spiral Scratch* EP

19/2/77 Parsons, Tony: Review of *Damned, Damned, Damned*
19/3/77 Burchill, Julie & Parsons, Tony: 'Fear & Loathing At The Roxy'
26/3/77 McNeill, Phil: 'Rent-A-Punk Guide'
 7/5/77 Interview w/ Paul Weller
21/5/77 Carr, Roy: Interview w/ the Ramones
        Spencer, Neil: Review of the White Riot show at the Rainbow
28/5/77 Parsons, Tony: 'Get Your Chinese Rocks Off'
 2/7/77 Parsons, Tony: 'This Punkaroo Says WE'RE All Poseurs'
 9/7/77 Murray, Charles Shaar: 'Which Side Are You On?'
30/7/77 Morley, Paul: 'They Mean It Ma-a-a-a-nchester'
13/8/77 Parsons, Tony: 'They Came. They Saw. They Pogoed'
20/8/77 McNeill, Phil: 'Flush Of Success From The Roxy Toilets . . .'
27/8/77 Bell, Max: 'I Have Seen The Future Of . . . Pt 52'
        Kent, Nick: Interview w/ Elvis Costello
22/10/77 Clarke, Steve: Interview w/ Tom Robinson
29/10/77 Interview w/ Pete Shelley
 5/11/77 Murray, Charles Shaar: 'Stiffs, Drugs And Rock & Roll'
19/11/77 Farren, Mick: 'The Hollywood Binliner: LA Punk'
 3/12/77 Morley, Paul: 'School Leavers Survey Finds Prefects Jobless'
10/12/77–24/12/77 Bangs, Lester: 'Six Days On The Road With The Clash'
17/12/77 McNeill, Phil: Interview w/ Wire
 7/1/78 Bangs, Lester: 'Death By Distraction'
        Rambali, Paul: 'Pere Ubu: Weird City Robomen'
11/2/78 McNeill, Paul: 'Tom Robinson'
25/2/78 Basher, Jack: 'Grapes & Flowers For Mr Strummer'
        Murray, Charles Shaar: Interview w/ Howard Devoto
        Rambali, Paul: Interview w/ The Rezillos
 4/3/78 Morley, Paul: Interview w/ Subway Sect
11/3/78 Dowse, Stephen: 'Never Mind The Cobbers – Here's Radio Birdman'
        Kent, Nick: 'The Perversities Of Peter Perrett'
18/3/78 Heyhoe, Malcolm: 'Why The Fall Must Rise'
        Rambali, Paul: Interview w/ Devo
25/3/78 Davis, Kim: Interview w/ The Adverts
        Kent, Nick: Interview w/ Elvis Costello
 8/4/78 Salewicz, Chris: Interview w/ Generation X
22/4/78 Parsons, Tony: Review of 'The Day The World Turned Day-Glo'
13/5/78 Murray, Charles Shaar: 'Poly Styrene Is Still Strictly Roots'
        MacKinnon, Angus: Interview w/ Pere Ubu
27/5/78 Spencer, Neil: Interview w/ PiL
17/6/78 Davies, Kim: Interview w/ Buzzcocks
        Rambali, Paul: 'Suicide Is Not The Answer'
29/6/78 Morley, Paul: Interview w/ Mark Perry
 8/7/78 Parsons, Tony: Interview w/ Devo
22/7/78 Murray, Charles Shaar: Interview w/ Tommy Ramone
        Edmands, Bob: Interview w/ Throbbing Gristle
29/7/78 Edmands, Bob: Interview w/ Howard Devoto
 5/8/78 Parsons, Tony & Hamblett, John: 'Leeds – Mill City, UK'

12/8/78 Clarke, Steve: 'The Day Scarboro Turned Day-Glo'
19/8/78 Penman, Ian: Between Innocence & Forbidden Knowledge Comes The Fall'
16/9/78 Gill, Andy: Interview w/ Wire
30/9/78 Rambali, Paul: Interview w/ The Pop Group
7/10/78 Kent, Nick: 'Girl Trouble With The Slits'
21/10/78 Burchill, Julie: 'You Don't Need X-Ray Spex To See Flying Saucers'
        Elder, Bruce: 'The Last Saint Goes Under'
28/10/78 Murray, Charles Shaar: Review of *All Mod Cons*
4/11/78 Clarke, Steve: 'Rhodes to Freedom'
18/11/78 Rambali, Paul: 'Pere Ubu – Unique Ideas Lead To Prison'
2/12/78 Morley, Paul & Penman, Ian: Interview w/ Howard Devoto
9/12/78 Morley, Paul: 'War Poet Of The Modern World'
23/12/78 Salewicz, Chris: 'Johnny's Immaculate Conception'
13/1/79 Morley, Paul: 'New Stirrings On The North-West Frontier'
        Cranna, Ian: Interview w/ Bob Last
20/1/79 Thrills, Adrian: Interview w/ Gang of Four
        Lock, Graham: 'Crass By Name, Cross By Nature'
27/1/79 Kent, Nick: Watching The Defectives'
3/2/79 Thrills, Adrian: Interview w/ Essential Logic
10/2/79 Penman, Ian: 'Beat, Activity & Conversation'
17/2/79 Morley, Paul: Interview w/ Stiff Little Fingers
3/3/79 Strummer, Joe: 'A Garbled Account Of The Clash US Tour'
17/3/79 Bell, Max: Interview w/ The Only Ones
24/3/79 Thrills, Adrian: 'Ruts, Backflips & Pogoing Pakistanis'
31/3/79 Trux, John: 'America's Burning'
28/4/79 Kent, Nick: Interview w/ Howard Devoto
        Hamblett, John: Interview w/ Pete Shelley
19/5/79 Morley, Paul: 'Penetration In Five Easy Stages'
26/5/79 Morley, Paul: Interview w/ The Undertones
        Thrills, Adrian: Interview w/ The Specials
9/6/79 Thrills, Adrian: Interview w/ The Raincoats
30/6/79 Bell, Max: 'The Pop Group: Idealists In Distress'
7/7/79 Rambali, Paul: Interview w/ Wire
14/7/79 Interview w/ Mark E. Smith
18/8/79 Pearson, Deanne: 'LA Punk – Forward Into '76
1/9/79 Morley, Paul & Thrills, Adrian: 'Independent Discs'
8/9/79 Thrills, Adrian: 'Up Slit Creek'
15/9/79 Thrills, Adrian: Interview w/ The Undertones
22/9/79 Edmands, Bob: Interview w/ Stiff Little Fingers
13/10/79 Interview w/ Joe Strummer
10/11/79 Review of *Setting Sons*
24/11/79 MacKinnon, Angus: Review of *Metal Box*
5/1/80 Penman, Ian: Interview w/ Mark E. Smith
29/3/80 Martin, Gavin: 'The Suspect Devices Of Stiff Little Fingers'
5/7/80 Bohn, Chris: Interview w/ Keith Levene
9/8/80 Spencer, Neil: Interview w/ Malcolm McLaren
        Rambali, Paul: Interview w/ Bernie Rhodes

6/9/80 Bell, Max: 'My Week As A Worm In the Big Apple'

27/9/80 Salewicz, Chris: 'Stop The Tour I Want To Get Off'

11/10/80 Martin, Gavin: 'Northern Ireland: The Fantasy & The Reality'

13/12/80 Kent, Nick: Review of *Sandanista*

3/1/81 Interview w/ Joe Strummer

10/1/81 Salewicz, Chris: 'The Almost Legendary Nick Kent Story'

14/3/81 Interview w/ PiL

11/4/81 Farren, Mick: 'LA Punk'

17/10/81 Hoskyns, Barney: 'Sometimes Pleasure Heads Must Burn'

14/11/81 Hoskyns, Barney: Interview w/ Mark E. Smith

26/6/82 Cook, Richard: 'The Buzzcocks Story'

20/11/82 Hoskyns, Barney: 'Black Flag In The California Scum'

29/10/83 Rose, Cynthia: 'Life After Punk: Rank & File'

Sounds

24/4/76 Ingham, Jonh: 'The Sex Pistols Have Been Together Four Months . . .'

29/5/76 Ingham, Jonh: 'Patti Smith Is Innocent, OK?'

26/6/76 Shapiro, Susan: 'Grins & Groans With The Ramones'

10/7/76 Stilwell, Andrew: 'TV Times'

31/7/76 Ingham, Jonh: Review of Pistols Lesser Free Trade Hall gig

4/9/76 Ingham, Jonh: 'The Lost Weekend'

11/9/76 Dadomo, Giovanni: 'Pistols CAN Play, OK?'

9/10/76 Ingham, Jonh et al: Punk rock special

16/10/76 Ingham, Jonh: Review of 'I'm Stranded'

23/10/76 Ingham, Jonh: 'The Rise & Rise Of Stiff Records'

Ingham, Jonh: Review of 'New Rose'

27/11/76 Dadomo, Giovanni: 'In The Pub Across The Road With The Damned'

11/12/76 Goldman, Vivien: 'The Slits'

18/12/76 Silverton, Pete: 'What Did You Do On The Punk Tour, Daddy?'

1/1/77 Houghton, Mick: 'The Grandfathers Of Punk'

22/1/77 Fudger, Dave: Review of Wire/The Jam at the Roxy

29/1/77 Dadomo, Giovanni: Interview w/ Generation X

5/3/77 De Whalley, Chas: 'Maximum New Wave'

Dadomo, Giovanni: Interview w/ Johnny Thunders

12/3/77 Goldman, Vivien: Interview w/ Tom Verlaine

Ingham, Jonh: Review of *(I'm) Stranded*

26/3/77 Fudger, Dave: Interview w/ The Vibrators

2/4/77 'Sounds Of The New Wave'

9/4/77 Silverton, Pete: Review of *The Clash*

16/4/77 Savage, Jon: 'Running With The Ratpack'

30/4/77 De Whalley, Chas: 'Elvis Costello: Mystery Man'

Savage, Jon: Review of The Damned at the Roundhouse

14/5/77 Silverton, Pete: Interview w/ The Saints

Dadomo, Giovanni: 'On The Road With The Clash'

18/6/77 Robertson, Sandy: 'A Non-Interview With Malcolm McLaren'

Sutcliffe, Phil: 'Penetration: Anarchy In County Durham'

25/6/77 Suck, Jane: Review of Siouxsie & the Banshees
16/7/77 Mitchell, Tony: Interview w/ The Saints
         Ripper, Angela: Review of The Damned at the Marquee
23/7/77 Savage, Jon: Interview w/ Mark P.
         Gluck, Jeremy: Interview w/ The Lurkers
30/7/77 Stapleton, Ross: 'Pistols Conquer World'
 6/8/77 Lott, Tim: Interview w/ Elvis Costello
         Savage, Jon: 'Andy Czekowski – Roxy Retro'
20/8/77 Dadomo, Giovanni: 'Inside Rotten's Wardrobe'
27/8/77 Dadomo, Giovanni: Interview w/ Johnny Rotten
 3/9/77 Goldman, Vivien: 'Jah Punk'
10/9/77 Brown, David: Interview w/ Wreckless Eric
         Suck, Jane: 'Looking Through TV Smith's Eyes'
17/9/77 Rhodes, Bernie: Press release for 'Complete Control'
         Coon, Caroline: 'Whatever Happened To The Buzzcocks?'
24/9/77 Silverton, Pete: 'Up Against The Wall – Life With The Tom Robinson
         Band'
 1/10/77 Savage, Jon: Interview w/ The Heartbreakers
 8/10/77 Goldman, Vivien: 'To Hell & Back'
15/10/77 Silverton, Pete: 'Why I Quit The Damned By Rat Scabies'
         Dadomo, Giovanni: 'Why I Quit The Heartbreakers By Jerry Nolan'
22/10/77 De Whalley, Chas: 'Oh Bondage!'
29/10/77 Coon, Caroline & Dadomo, Giovanni: 'Clash In The City Of The Dead'
26/11/77 Robertson, Sandy: 'New Musick: Throbbing Gristle'
 3/12/77 'Rab': Interview w/ The Pop Group
         Goldman, Vivien: 'Siouxsie Sioux Who R U?'
10/12/77 Silverton, Pete: 'Voyage Of The Damned'
17/12/77 Savage, Jon: 'The Future Is Female'
24/12/77 Boyd, Lindsey: 'Alternative Vision'
31/12/77 Letter from Siouxie & the Banshees
28/1/78 Ingham, Jonh: Review of the Pistols at Winterland
         Wall, Mick: 'Who Loves A Lurker?'
18/2/78 Suck, Jane: 'Crossing The Irish Sea With The Adverts'
 4/3/78 Goldman, Vivien: Interview w/ John Lydon part 1
         Savage, Jon: 'People In General, Devo In Particular'
11/3/78 Goldman, Vivien: Interview w/ John Lydon part 2
18/3/78 Fudger, Dave: 'The Wire Process'
25/3/78 Suck, Jane: 'Another Movie In A Different Cinema'
 1/4/78 Confidential, Pete: 'Invasion Of The Birdmen'
 8/4/78 DeMorest, Stephen: Interview w/ Tom Verlaine
         Wood, Ian: 'The Fall Stumble Into The Void'
15/4/78 Makowski, Pete: Interview w/ Peter Perrett
22/4/78 McAllister, Ms: 'Day-Glo Goddess For A Polyvinyl World'
29/4/78 Wall, Mick: Reviews of Radio Birdman & Stiff/Chiswick Challenge
 3/6/78 Savage, Jon: Interview w/ Throbbing Gristle
         Silverton, Pete: 'Nick Lowe – This Is Your Life'
10/6/78 Interview w/ Howard Devoto

17/6/78 Silverton, Pete: 'The Music Of Greater Akron'
         Silverton, Pete: Interview w/ The Clash
24/6/78 Dadomo, Giovanni: 'The Suicide Club'
 1/7/78 Greer, Alwyn: 'Suspect Devices In The City Of The Dead'
         Savage, Jon: 'Subway Sect – Life Underground'
 8/7/78 Gill, John: Interview w/ The Pop Group
15/7/78 Herlihy, John: Interview w/ The Slits
22/7/78 Goldman, Vivien: 'If The Kids Are United'
         Coon, Caroline: 'Public Image'
16/9/78 Robertson, Sandy: Interview w/ Midge Ure
23/9/78 Bushell, Gary: Interview w/ Buzzcocks
30/9/78 McCullough, Dave: 'Teenage Kicks'
7/10/78 Silverton, Pete: Interview w/ Stiff Little Fingers
4/11/78 McCullough, Dave: 'Free Fall'
         Fielder, Hugh: 'Wire: Anything But Rock & Roll'
11/11/78 McCullough, Dave: Interview w/ Gang of Four
18/11/78 Middles, Mick: 'Joy Division: A Short Pulsating Feature'
2/12/78 McCullough, Dave: 'The Northern Soul Of Vic Goddard'
16/12/78 Fancher, Lisa: Interview w/ the Weirdos
17/2/79 Simmons, Sylvie: 'The Clash In America'
 3/3/79 Sutcliffe, Phil: 'Breakout In Newport'
24/3/79 Silverton, Pete: Interview w/ The Pop Group
16/6/79 Bushell, Gary: Interview w/ The Ruts
15/9/79 Sutcliffe, Phil: 'Miles Copeland's New Wave'
         Sutcliffe, Phil: 'In Aberdeen No-One Can Hear You Scream'
27/10/79 Sutcliffe, Phil: 'The Ruts – Tears On The Notepad'
24/11/79 McCullough, Dave: Review of *The Metal Box*
24/5/80 Simmons, Sylvie: Interview w/ John Lydon
19/7/80 Sutcliffe, Phil: 'The Making Of The Jam'
30/5/81 Sommer, Tim: 'Day Of The Locust'
29/8/81 Simmons, Sylvie: 'X . . . Communication'

Miscellaneous Articles

ZZ = *ZigZag*
RM = *Record Mirror*
TP = *Trouser Press*
NYR = *New York Rocker*
RS = *Rolling Stone*

Baker, Danny   Interview w/ The Fall, *ZZ*, 81
      Interview w/ PiL, *Smash Hits*, 6/79
Bangs, Lester   'Roots Of Punk Part III', *New Wave*
Banks, Robin   'Forty-Eight Hours (On The Road)', *ZZ*, 79
      'Vic Goddard: Down The Road On A Stick', *ZZ*, 92
Betrock, Alan   'Know Your New York Bands: The Ramones', *Soho Weekly News*, 1975
Brown, Mick   'Sex Pistols & Beyond', *Rolling Stone*, 27/1/77
Cain, Barry   Review of Damned, Damned, Damned, *RM*, 19/2/77
      'Village Of The Damned', *RM*, 5/3/77
      'Images Of Public Image', *RM*, 4/11/78
Cooper, Kim   Interview w/ Deniz Tek, *Superdope*, 2
Dalton, David   'The Sex Pistols & Other Pleasantries Of Punk', *Gadfly*, 2/98
Devo   Pass-out sheet for KIVA concert, 3/77
[Devoto, Howard]   'The Sex Pistols', *New Manchester Review*, 6/6/76
Fancher, []   Interview w/ Fear, *NYR*, 11/79
Ford, Simon   'Primal Scenes', *The Wire*, 5/02
Frith, Simon   'The Clash Rule The New Wave', *Creem*, 7/78
Garry, Mac   'The Damned: Music With No Redeeming Value', *ZZ*, 74
Gehman, Pleasant   'The Life Of The Germs', *NYR*, 3/81
Genesis P. Orridge   'TG & Punk', posted on internet, 10/4/02
Gilmore, Mikal   'John Lydon Improves His Public Image', *RS*, 1/5/80
      'Chronicling The Sex Pistols' Rise & Fall', *RS*, 1/5/80
Goldberg, Michael   'Devo: Sixties Idealists Or Nazis & Clowns?', *RS*, 10/12/81
      'Rank & File: Country Punk', *RS*, 3/2/83
      'Punk Lives', *RS*, 18/7/85
Guthrie, Brian   'The Rezillos: Fun Sculptures', *ZZ*, 86
Hell, Richard,   'Punk & History', *Discourses*, 1988
McLaren, Malcolm
  & Savage, Jon
Isler, Scott   'Fear & Loathing On The West Coast', *TP*, 51
Jaspan, Andrew   'Rocking On The New Wave', *New Manchester Review*, 2/77
      'Devo Demystified', *New Manchester Review*, 4/78
Kayky, Kex   Interview w/ Bob Biggs, *NYR*, 9/82
Kelly, Danny   Interview w/ Mick Jones, *The Word* 11/05.
Kent, Nick   'Pills and Thrills', *The Guardian*, 12/4/02
Laverty, MT   'Devo: In Search Of The Big Enema', *TP*, 27
      'X-Ray Spex Take Shot At US', *TP*, 29

Leviton, Mark	'X: Heart Of The City', *BAM*, 12/9/80
	'Black Flag', *BAM*, 12/8/83
Lewis, Sarah	Interview w/ The Only Ones, *ZZ*, 94
Marcus, Greil	Interview w/ Greil Marcus, *RS*, 2/9/82
Miles, Barry	'A Clash Of Interests', *Time Out*, 15/12/76
Morris, Teri	Interview w/ The Avengers, *ZZ*, 83
	Interview w/ The Weirdos, *ZZ*, 87
Needs, Kris	Interview w/ The Heartbreakers, *ZZ*, 71
	'Konkrete Klockwork', *ZZ*, 71
	'Silver Jubilation', *ZZ*, 73
	'Generation X: We're Not Into The Mindless Drone', *ZZ*, 74
	Interview w/ The Slits, *ZZ*, 75
	Interview w/ Wire, *ZZ*, 82
	Interview w/ Public Image Limited, *ZZ*, 96
Nemeth, Cathy	'Musings Of Magazine's Main Man' *NYR*, 9/79
Nicholls, Mike	'JR Wants You For A Sunbeam', *RM*, 28/7/79
Pierce, Jeffrey Lee	Interview w/ X, *NYR*, 9/80
	Kuepper/Younger interview, *Prehistoric Sounds*, 1/3
Pressler, Charlotte	'Those Were Different Times', *CLE*, 3
Robbins, Ira	'The New Wave Washes Out', *TP*, 21
	'The Clashmen Meet The Pearlman', *TP*, 35
Rose, Cynthia	Interview w/ Bruce Pavitt, *Dazed & Confused*, 1994
Rothwell, Nicholas	'Divine Rites: Radio Birdman Flies Again', *The Australian*, 21/4/81
Salewicz, Chris	'John Lydon At Large', *The Face*, 12/80
Savage, Jon	Interview w/ Kurt Cobain, *Guitar World*, 1997
Schulps, Dave	'Tom Verlaine: In Search Of Adventure', *TP*, 29
	Interview w/ Paul Weller, *TP*, 38
Schwartz, Andy	'Lydon In New York: The Image Goes Public', *NYR*, 5/80
Sculatti, Gene	'Everybody Needs Somebody To Hate: A History Of LA Punk Rock', *Creem*, 10/81
Shaw, Greg	Review of Sex Pistols at the 100 Club, Phonograph Record 6/76
	'New Wave Goodbye?', *NYR*, 9/78
Silverton, Pete	'The Clash: Greatness from Garageland', *TP*, 26
	'Accidents Won't Happen: The Premeditated Rise Of Elvis Costello', *TP*, 39
	'Sid Vicious Crashed My Twenty-First', *The Observer*, 1991
Simmons, Sylvie	'The Blasters: Beyond Revivalism', *Creem*, 5/82
Thompson, Dave	'The Adverts: Bored Teenagers', *Goldmine*, 9/97
Thrills, Adrian	Interview w/ Buzzcocks, *ZZ*, 77
Tobler, John	Interview w/ Suicide, *ZZ*, 75
	Interview w/ Richard Hell, *ZZ*, 82
Walsh, Steve	Interview w/ Subway Sect, *ZZ*, 76
Weingarten, Mark	'Left of the Dial', *Guitar World*, 8/95
Weizmann, Danny	'LA Punk', *Hardcore California*, 1983

Wood, Ian   'A Factory Inspection: Inside England's Intriguing Indie', *NYR*, 3/80

Wylie, Charlotte   'But Everyone Knew Him As Rotten', *TP*, 38

Additional Resources

Books Referenced

Andersen, Mark & Jenkins, Mark, *Dance of Days: Two Decades of Punk in the Nation's Capital* (Soft Skull, 2001) [quotes utilized: Ian MacKaye, Henry Rollins]

Anon *The Damned Scrapbook* (privately printed, nd)
> *Joy Division: A History In Cuttings* (privately printed, nd)
> *Siouxsie & the Banshees Scrapbook 1976–80* (privately printed, nd)

Antonia, Nina, *In Cold Blood* (Jungle, 1987) and *The One & Only Peter Perrett* (SAF, 1996) [quotes utilized: John Perry, Peter Perrett, Mike Kellie]

Arnold, Gina, *Route 666: On the Road to Nirvana* (St Martin's Press, 1993) [quotes utilized: Penelope Houston, Jello Biafra, Mike Watt, Kris Novoselic]

Azerrad, Michael, *Our Band Could Be Your Life: Scenes from the American Indie Underground 1981–91* (Little Brown, 2001) [quotes utilized: Mike Watt, Bob Mould, Bill Sullivan, Lee Ranaldo, Jonathan Poneman, Peter Prescott] and *Come As You Are: The Story of Nirvana* (Virgin, 1993) [quotes utilized: Kurt Cobain, Kris Novoselic]

Balls, Richard, *Sex & Drugs & Rock & Roll: The Life of Ian Dury* (Omnibus, 2000) [quote utilized: B. P. Fallon]

Berkenstadt, Jim & Cross, Charles, *Nevermind* (Schirmer Books, 1998), [quotes utilized: Buzz Osbourne, Butch Vig]

Bessman, Jim, *Ramones: An American Band* (St Martin's Press, 1993)

Birch, Will, *No Sleep Till Canvey Island* (Virgin, 2003) [quotes utilized: Ian Dury, Paul Riley, Dave Higgs, Dave Robinson, Graham Parker]

Blush, Steve, *American Hardcore: A Tribal History* (Feral House, 2002) [quotes utilized: Mark Stern, Joey Shithead, Joe Carducci, Tim Kerr]

Bromberg, Craig, *The Wicked Ways of Malcolm McLaren* (Harper & Row, 1989)

Burchill, Julie & Parsons, Tony *The Boy Looked At Johnny: The Obituary of Rock & Roll* (Pluto Press, 1978)

Chiesa, Guido, *Sonic Youth/Sonic Life* (Stampa Alternativa, 1992)

Coe, Jonathan, The Rotters' Club (Viking, 2001)

Colegrave, Stephen & Sullivan, Chris, *Punk: A Life Apart* (Cassell, 2004) [quotes utilized: Steve Jones, Paul Cook, Paul Simonon, Walter Lure, Boogie, Helen Wellington-Lloyd]

Coon, Caroline, *1978: The New Wave Punk Rock Explosion* (Omnibus Press, 1982)

Cope, Julian, *Head-On* (Head Heritage, 1994)

Cross, Charles, *Heavier than Heaven: The Biography of Kurt Cobain* (Hodder & Stoughton, 2001)

Dellinger, Jade & Giffels, *Are We Not Men?* (SAF, 2003)

Devoto, Howard, *It Only Looks As If It Hurts: The Complete Lyrics 1976–90* (Black Spring Press, nd)

Diggle, Steve & Rawlings, Terry, *Harmony In My Head* (Helter-Skelter, 2003)

Eden, Kevin S., *Wire . . . Everybody Loves a History* (SAF, 1991) [quotes utilized: Colin Newman, Graham Lewis]

Fitzgerald, F. Stop, *Beyond & Back: The Story of X* (Last Gasp, 1990) [quotes utilized: John Doe, Billy Zoom, D. J. Bonebrake]

Foege, Alex, *Confusion Is Next: The Sonic Youth Story* (St Martin's, 1994) [quotes utilized: Richard Edson, Paul Smith, Thurston Moore]

Ford, Simon, *Hip Priest: Mark E. Smith & The Fall* (Quartet, 2002) [quotes utilized: Martin Bramah and Una Baines] and *Wreckers of Civilization* (Black Dog, 2001)

Gilbert, Pat, *Passion is a Fashion: The Real Story of The Clash* (Aurum, 2004) [quotes utilized: Pete Townshend, Richard Dudanski, Mickey Foote, Caroline Coon, Simon Humphrey]

Gilbert, Pat (ed.), *Mojo Punk Special Edition*, 2005

Gilmore, Mikal, *Night Beat: A Shadow History of Rock & Roll* (Random House, 1999) [quotes utilized: Joe Strummer]

Gimarc, George, *Punk Diary 1970–79* (St Martin's Press, 1995) and *Post-Punk Diary 1980–82* (St Martin's Press, 1997)

Gorman, Paul, *In Their Own Write: Adventures In The Music Press* (Sanctuary, 2001) [quotes utilized: Greg Shaw, Allan Jones, Mark Perry, Tony Parsons, Jon Savage, Gary Bushell.]

Gray, Marcus, *Return of the Last Gang in Town* (Helter-Skelter, 2001) [quotes utilized: Alan Drake, Clive Timperley, Terry Chimes, Sebastian Conran, Chris Parry, Simon Humphries, Jon Moss]

Green, Johnny & Barker, Garry, *A Riot of Our Own: Night & Day with The Clash* (Orion, 1997)

Heylin, Clinton *From The Velvets To The Voidoids* (Penguin, 1993) and *Never Mind The Bollocks* (Schirmer, 1997)

Hoskyns, Barney, *Waiting For The Sun: The Story of the Los Angeles Music Scene* (Viking, 1996) [quotes utilized: Jeff Gold, Penelope Spheeris]

Johnson, Vivien, *Radio Birdman* (Sheldon Books, 1990) [quotes utilized: Deniz Tak, Warwick Gilbert, Chris Masuak]

Knox, *Twenty-One Years of Punk Mania* (privately published, nd)

Kozak, Roman, *This Ain't No Disco: The Story of CBGB* (Faber, 1988) [quotes utilized: Richard Lloyd, Roy Trakin]

Leonard, Gary & Snowden, Don, *Make the Music Go Bang!: The Early LA Punk Scene* (St Martin's, 1997)

Lydon, John, *No Irish, No Blacks, No Dogs* (St Martin's, 1994) [quotes utilized: John Lydon, Paul Cook, Steve Severin, Steve Jones, John Varnom]

Marcus, Greil, *In The Fascist Bathroom: Writings on Punk 1977–92* (Viking, 1993)

Matlock, Glen & Silverton, Pete, *I Was A Teenage Sex Pistol* (Omnibus, 1990)

Meltzer, Richard, *A Whore Just Like The Rest* (Da Capo, 2000)

Middles, Mick, *The Fall* (Omnibus, 2003) [quotes utilized: Mark E. Smith]

Miles, Barry, *The Clash* (Omnibus, 1981)

Mullen, Brendan, *Lexicon Devil: The Fast Times & Short Lives of Darby Crash & the Germs* (Feral House, 2002) [quotes utilized: Tony Kinman, Black Randy, Bob Biggs]

Mullen, Brendan & Spitz, Marc, *We Got The Neutron Bomb: The Untold Story of LA Punk* (Three Rivers Press, 2001) [quotes utilized: Black Randy, Pat Smear, Peter Case, John Denney, Tony Kinman, Lee Ving, Keith Morris, Dave Alvin, Kid Congo]

Needs, Kris, *Joe Strummer & The Legend of The Clash* (Proteus, 2005) [quote utilized: Robin Banks]

Nobakht, David, *Suicide: No Compromise* (SAF, 2005) [quotes utilized: Alan Vega, Martin Rev, Paul Smith, Phil Shoenfelt]

Nolan, David, *I Swear I Was There* (Milo, 2001) [quotes utilized: Howard Devoto, Peter Hook, Paul Morley, Jordan]

O'Neill, Sean & Trelford, Guy, *It Makes You Want to Spit: An Alternative Ulster 1977–82* (Reekus, 2003) [quotes utilized: Damian O'Neill, John O'Neill, Terri Hooley, Jake Burns]

Parker, James, *Turned On: Henry Rollins* (Phoenix Press, 1999) [quote utilized: Mugger]

Paytress, Mark, *Siouxsie & the Banshees*, (Sanctuary, 2003) [quotes utilized: Siouxsie Sioux, Steve Severin and Marco Pirroni] and *Vicious: The Art of Dying Young* (Sanctuary, 2004)

Perry, Mark, *Sniffin' Glue: The Essential Punk Accessory* (Sanctuary, 2001)

Poulsen, Henrik Bech, *'77: The Year of Punk & New Wave* (Helter-Skelter, 2005)

Reynolds, Simon, *Rip It Up & Start Again: Post-Punk 1978–84* (Faber, 2005) [quotes utilized: Keith Levene, Adele Bertei, Lydia Lunch, Mark Perry, David Byrne, Martin Atkins]

Savage, Jon, *England's Dreaming* (Faber, 1991) [quotes utilized: Malcolm McLaren, Adam Ant, Nick Kent, Sophie Richmond, Pauline Murray, Poly Styrene, John Lydon]

Stevenson, Nils, *Vacant: A Diary of the Punk Years 1976–9* (Thames & Hudson, 1999)

Sullivan, Denise, *REM Talk About The Passion: An Oral History* (Pavilion, 1995) [quote utilized: Woody Nuss]

Sutherland, Steve (ed.) *NME Originals: The Clash* (2003), *NME Originals: Punk 1975–79* (2002) and *NME Originals: Nirvana* (2002)

Thompson, Dave, *Wheels Out of Gear: Two-Tone, The Specials & A World In Flame* (Helter-Skelter, 2004) [quotes utilized: Nick Cave, Roddy Radiation, Dave Wakeling]

Thomson, Graeme, *Complicated Shadows: The Life & Music of Elvis Costello* (Canongate, 2004) [quotes utilized: Dave Robinson]

True, Everett, *Hey Ho, Let's Go: The Story of the Ramones* (Omnibus, 2002)

Valentine, Gary, *New York Rocker: My Life in the Blank Generation* (Sidgwick & Jackson, 2002)

Vermorel, Fred & Judy, *The Sex Pistols* (Star Books, 1978) [quotes utilized: Tracie, Glen Matlock, Al Clark, Johnny Rotten]

Watt, Mike, *Spiels of a Minuteman* (l'oie de cravan, 2003)

Sleeve-Notes

Alternative TV: *The Industrial Sessions 1977* – Notes by Genesis P. Orridge

Buzzcocks: *Chronology* – Notes by Pete Shelley & Steve Diggle

The Damned: *Play It At Your Sister* – Notes by Jean Encoule

Devo: *The Mongoloid Years* – Notes by Gerald V. Casale

Dream Syndicate: *Tell Me When It's Over (The Best Of)* – Quotes by Steve Wynn

Gang of Four: *100 Flowers Bloom* – Notes By Jon Savage

Green On Red: *What Were We Thinking?* – Notes by Fred Mills

The Long Ryders: *Anthology* – Notes by David Fricke

The Prefects: *Amateur Wankers* – Notes by Robert Lloyd & Helen Apperley
Rank & File: *The Slash Years* – Notes by Jimmy Guterman
Stiff Little Fingers: *The Complete John Peel Sessions* – Letter from Gordon Ogilvie to John Peel
The Undertones: *Listening In* – Notes by Mick Houghton
The Violent Femmes: *The Violent Femmes* – Notes by Michael Azerrad
X: *Make The Music Go Bang!* – Assorted quotes

Documentaries

Raw Energy (1977)
The Filth & The Fury (2000)★
Classic Albums: Never Mind The Bollocks (2002)★
Arena 'Punk' (BBC 2, 1995)
Westway To The World (1999)★
Punk In London (1977)★
Ian Dury: 'On My Life' (BBC 2, 1999)

★ = available on DVD

Websites

Perfect Sound Forever [PSF]
Interviews with Keith Levene; Andy Gill; Cosey Fanni Tutti; Tommy Ramone.
Long Ryders and the Paisley Underground (Two Parts) by Diane Roka.

Trakmarx
Interviews with Richard Hell; Johnny Strike; Colin Newman; TV Smith; Wreckless Eric; Martin Atkins.

Summer of Hate
Interview w/ Danny Furious.

The Undertones Official Website
Memoir of Mickey Bradley

Unofficial Fan Websites That Put Their Official Counterparts To Shame

Blackmarketclash
The Unofficial Fall Website
Livenirvana.com

Selected Discography

Adverts, The
One-Chord Wonders b/w Quickstep
  (45)
The Roxy, London WC2 (CD)
Crossing The Red Sea With (CD)
Cast Of Thousands/The Complete Radio
  Sessions (2-CD)

Alberto Y Lost Trios Paranoias
Snuff Rock EP (45)

Alternative TV
Live At Rat Club '77 (CD)
The Image Has Cracked: The ATV
  Collection (CD)
The Industrial Sessions 1977 (CD)

Angelic Upstarts
Murder Of Liddle Towers b/w Police
  Oppression (45)

Avengers, The
We Are The One b/w Car Crash/I
  Believe In Me (45)
The American In Me (CD)
Died For Your Sins (CD)

Birthday Party, The
Hee-Haw (CD)
Mutiny/The Bad Seed (CD)
Prayers On Fire (CD)
Junkyard (CD)

Black Flag
The First Four Years (CD)
Damaged (CD)

Blasters, The
American Music (CD)
Testament: The Complete Slash
  Recordings (2-CD)

Blondie
Blondie (CD)
The Platinum Collection (2-CD)

Blood On The Saddle
Blood On The Saddle (CD)

Boys, The
The Boys (CD)

Buzzcocks
Another Music In A Different Kitchen
  (CD)
Love Bites (CD)
The Roxy, London WC2 (CD)
Time's Up (CD)
The Peel Sessions (CD)
Chronology (CD)
Spiral Scratch (CD EP)
Midnight Special At Screen On The
  Green (Bootleg 2-CD) [w/ Sex
  Pistols/The Clash]
Never Mind The Bans (Bootleg 2-CD)
  [w/ Sex Pistols/The Clash]

Clash, The
The Clash – UK edition (CD)
The Clash – US edition (CD)
Give 'Em Enough Rope
London Calling (CD)
Super Black Market Clash (CD)
The Clash On Broadway (3-CD boxed-
  set)
Midnight Special At Screen On The Green
  (2-CD Bootleg) [w/ Pistols/Buzzcocks]
Never Mind The Bans (2-CD Bootleg)
  [w/ Pistols/Buzzcocks]
Five Go Mad In The Roundhouse
  (Bootleg CD)
I Fought The Law (Bootleg CD)

Contortions, The
Buy . . .

Cortinas, The
Fascist Dictator b/w Television Families (45)

Costello, Elvis
My Aim Is True (2-CD)
This Year's Model (2-CD)
Live At The El Mocambo (CD)
Armed Forces (2-CD)
The Singles Volume 1 (CD boxed-set)
Radio Radio (Bootleg CD)

Crass
The Feeding Of The Five Thousand (CD)

Crime
Piss On Your Turntable (CD)

Damned, The
Play It At Your Sister: The Stiff Years June 1976–September 1977 (3-CD boxed-set)

Dead Boys
Young, Loud & Snotty (CD)

Dead Kennedys
California Über Alles b/w The Man With The Dogs (45)
Holiday In Cambodia b/w Police Truck (45)
Live At The Deaf Club (CD)

Devo
Hardcore Vol. 1 (CD)
Hardcore Vol. 2 (CD)
The Mongoloid Years (CD)
Q: Are We Not Men? A: We Are Devo! (CD)
Greatest Misses (CD)
Devonia (Bootleg LP)

Dexys Midnight Runners
Searching For The Young Soul Rebels (CD)

Dils
Dils, Dils, Dils (CD)

DNA
A Taste of DNA EP

Dr Feelgood
Stupidity (CD)
Going Back Home (CD/DVD)
Down At The Doctor's (Bootleg CD)

Dream Syndicate
The Days of Wine & Roses (CD)
The Day Before Wine & Roses (Live At KPFK) (CD)

Dury, Ian & the Blockheads
New Boots & Panties (2-CD)
Do It Yourself (2-CD)

Eddie & the Hot Rods
Live At The Marquee EP
Teenage Depression (CD)

Electric Eels
God Says Fuck You! (CD)
Their Organic Majesty's Request (CD)

Essential Logic
Aerosol Burns b/w World Fiction (45)
Essential Logic EP

Fall, The
Live At The Witch Trials (2-CD)
Dragnet (2-CD)

Flip City
Our Aim Is True (Bootleg LP)

Flipper
Generic (CD)

Gang of Four
Damaged Goods EP
Entertainment (CD)

Generation X
Generation X (CD)
Wild Youth b/w Wild Dub (45)

Germs
G.I. (CD)

Green on Red
Green On Red (CD) [w/ Gas Food Lodging]

Gravity Talks (CD)
No Free Lunch (CD)
What Were We Thinking? (CD)

Green River
Come On Down (CD)
Dry As A Bone EP
Rehab Doll (CD)

Gun Club, The
The Fire Of Love (CD)
Miami (CD)

Heartbreakers
L.A.M.F. – The Lost '77 Mixes: Special
    Edition (2-CD)
D.T.K./L.A.M.F. (CD)
Live At Mother's (CD) [w/ Richard Hell]

Hell, Richard & the Voidoids
Blank Generation (CD)
Blank Generation EP
Time (2-CD)
Spurt: The Richard Hell Story (CD)

Human League, The
Being Boiled b/w Circus Of Death (45)

Hüsker Dü
Land Speed Record (CD)
Everything Falls Apart (CD)
Zen Arcade (CD)

Jam, The
Snap! (2-CD)
In The City (CD)
All Mod Cons (2-CD)
Setting Sons (CD)
At The BBC (3-CD)

Jason & the Scorchers
Reckless Country Soul (CD)
The Essential Jason & The Scorchers
    Vol. 1 (CD) [Fervour/Lost & Found]
Wildfires & Misfires (CD)

Joy Division
The Complete BBC Recordings (CD)
Still (CD)
Heart & Soul (4-CD Boxed-Set)
Substance (CD)

Kilburn & the High Roads
Handsome (CD)

Lone Justice
This World Is Not My Home (CD)

Long Ryders
The Long Ryders Anthology (2-CD)
Metallic B.O. (CD)

Lurkers, The
Fulham Fallout (CD)

Magazine
Real Life (CD)
Secondhand Daylight (CD)
The Correct Use Of Soap (CD)
Scree (Rarities 1978–81) (CD)
BBC Radio One Live In Concert (CD)

Mars
Mars EP

Meat Puppets, The
Meat Puppets I
Meat Puppets II

Mekons, The
Never Been In A Riot b/w 32 Weeks
    (45)
Where Were You? b/w I'll Have To
    Dance On My Own Then (45)
The Quality Of Mercy Is Not Strnen
    (CD)

Minor Threat
Complete (CD)

Minutemen, The
Double Nickels On The Dime (CD)

Mirrors
Hands In My Pockets (CD)

Mother Love Bone
Mother Love Bone (2-CD)

Mudhoney
Superfuzz Bigmuff/Early Singles (CD)
Every Good Boy Deserves Fudge (CD)

Nerves
Hanging On The Telephone EP

Nirvana
Bleach (CD)
Nevermind (CD)
In Utero (CD)
Incesticide (CD)
Unplugged In New York (CD)
From The Muddy Banks Of The
    Wishkah (CD)
The Complete Radio Sessions (Bootleg
    CD)

Nuns
The Nuns (Bootleg LP)

101ers
Elgin Avenue Breakdown Revisited
    (CD)

Only Ones, The
The Only Ones (CD)
Even Serpents Shine (CD)
Baby's Got A Gun (CD)
Darkness & Light: The Complete BBC
    Recordings (2-CD)
Remains (CD)
The Only Ones Live (CD)

Parker, Graham & The Rumour
Passion Is No Ordinary Word: The
    Graham Parker Anthology (2-CD)

Penetration
Moving Targets (CD)
Don't Dictate (The Best Of Penetration)
    (CD)
BBC Radio One In Concert (CD)
    [w/ The Ruts]

Pere Ubu
Datapanik In The Year Zero (5-CD
    boxed-set)
390 Degrees Of Simulated Stereo
    (CD)
One Man Drives While The Other
    Man Screams (CD)
The Shape Of Things (CD)
Terminal Tower (CD)

Pop Group, The
Y (CD)

Prefects
Amateur Wankers (CD)
Live At The Co-op Suite (CD)

Public Image Limited
Death Disco b/w Half-Mix (12" 45)
First Issue (CD)
The Metal Box (CD)
Profile (Bootleg double-LP)
Commercial Zone (LP)

Radio Birdman
Radios Appear (Domestic version) (CD)
Radios Appear (Overseas version) (CD)
Burn My Eye/More Fun EPs (CD)
Living Eyes (CD)
The Essential Radio Birdman (CD)

Rain Parade, The
Emergency Third Rail Power Trip (CD)

Ramones
The Ramones (CD)
Leave Home (CD)
Rocket To Russia (CD)
Road To Ruin (CD)
It's Alive (CD)

Rank & File
The Slash Years (CD)

REM
Eponymous (CD)
Chronic Town EP
Reckoning (CD)
Murmur (CD)
Twentieth Century Boys Vols. 1–2
    (CDs)

Replacements, The
Sorry Ma, Forgot To Take Out The
    Trash (CD)
Stink (CD)
Let It Be (CD)

Rezillos, The
Can't Stand The Rezillos: The (Almost)
    Complete Rezillos (CD)

Rich Kids
The Best Of The Rich Kids (CD)

Rocket from the Tombs
The Day The Earth Met . . . (CD)

Rudi
Big Time b/w Number One (45)

Ruts, The
The Crack/Grin & Bear It (CD)
BBC Radio One In Concert (CD)
   [w/ Penetration]
The John Peel Sessions (CD)
In A Can (CD)

Saints, The
(I'm) Stranded (CD)
Songs Of Salvation (CD)

Sex Pistols
Never Mind The Bollocks/Spunk (2-CD)
The Studio Collection (CD)
Live At Winterland 1978 (CD)
Truly Indecent Exposure (Bootleg CD)
Aggression Thru Repression (Bootleg CD)
Midnight Special At Screen On The
   Green (Bootleg 2-CD) [w/
   Buzzcocks/The Clash]
Never Mind The Bans (Bootleg 2-CD)
   [w/ Buzzcocks/The Clash]

Sham 69
I Don't Wanna b/w Ulster/Red London
   (45)
Borstal Breakout b/w Hey Little Rich
   Boy (45)

Siouxsie & the Banshees
Hong Kong Garden b/w Voices
Staircase b/w Twenty Century Boy
Playground Twist b/w Pull To Bits
Mittageisen (Metal Postcard) b/w Love
   In A Void
The Scream (2-CD)
Join Hands (CD)

Slaughter & the Dogs
Cranked Up Really High b/w The Bitch
Live At The Roxy (CD – two tracks)

Slits, The
Cut (CD)
The Peel Sessions (CD)

In The Beginning (CD)
Live At The Gibus Club (CD)

Smith, Patti
Piss Factory b/w Hey Joe
Horses (CD)
Radio Ethiopia (CD)
Free Music Store (Bootleg CD)
Let's Deodorize The Night (Bootleg CD)
Teenage Perversity & Ships In The Night
   (Bootleg LP)

Sonic Youth
Sonic Youth (CD)
Confusion Is Sex (CD)
Bad Moon Rising (CD)
EVOL (CD)
Sister (CD)
Daydream Nation (CD)
Goo (2-CD)

Soundgarden
Screaming Life/Fopp (CD)

Specials, The
The Specials (CD)
More Specials (CD)

Stiff Little Fingers
Inflammable Material (CD)
The Complete John Peel Sessions (CD)

Stooges, The
The Stooges (2-CD)
Fun House (2-CD)
Raw Power (CD)
Metallic K.O. (CD)

Stranglers, The
Rattus Norvegicus (CD)
The Singles (CD)

Subway Sect
A Retrospective (CD)

Suicide
Suicide/23 Minutes In Brussels (2-CD)

Talking Heads
'77 (CD/DVD)
More Songs About Buildings & Food
   (CD/DVD)

Teenage Jesus & the Jerks
Teenage Jesus And The Jerks EP

Television
Marquee Moon (CD)
Adventure (CD)
Live At The Old Waldorf (CD)
The Blow-Up (2-CD)
Double Exposure (Bootleg CD)
Poor Circulation (Bootleg CD)
New York Stories (Bootleg CD)

Throbbing Gristle
Second Annual Report (CD)
The Taste of T.G. (CD)

Tin Huey
Tin Huey EP

Tom Robinson Band
Power In The Darkness [U.S. Edition]
    (CD)

Undertones, The
The Undertones (CD)
Hypnotised (CD)
Listening In: Radio Sessions 1978–82 (CD)

Vibrators, The
Pure Mania (CD)

Victim
Strangers By Night b/w Mixed Up
    World
Why Are Fire Engines Red?
b/w I Need You

Violent Femmes
Violent Femmes (2-CD)
Hallowed Ground (CD)
Add It Up: 1981–93 (CD)

Weirdos
Destroy All Music EP
We Got The Neutron Bomb b/w
    Solitary Confinement (45)

Wipers, The
Is This Real?, Youth of America,
    Over the Edge (all on 3-CD
    box-set)
Is This Real? [Original Edition] (LP)

Wire
Pink Flag (CD)
Chairs Missing (CD)
154 (CD)
The Peel Sessions (CD)
Behind The Curtain (CD)
On The Box 1979 (CD/DVD)

Wreckless Eric
Wreckless Eric (CD)
The Wonderful World Of (LP)
Big Smash (CD)

X
Los Angeles (CD)
Wild Gift (CD)

X-Ray Spex
Let's Submerge: The Anthology (2-CD)

Collections

The Best Punk Album In The World
    Ever I (Virgin) (2-CD)
The Best Punk Album In The World
    Ever II (Virgin) (2-CD)
DIY– Anarchy In The UK: UK Punk I
    (all Rhino CDs)
    – The Modern World: UK Punk II
    – Teenage Kicks: UK Pop I
    – Starry Eyes: UK Pop II
    – Blank Generation: The New York
    Scene

– We're Desperate: The LA Scene
– Come Out & Play: American
    Power Pop I
– Shake It Up!: American Power
    Pop II
– Mass Ave.: The Boston Scene
Fourteen Songs From Greg Sage & The
    Wipers (T.K.) (CD)
Left Of The Dial – Dispatches From
    The 80s Underground (Rhino)
    (4-CD set)

Live From The Masque Vol. 1 (Flipside)
(CD)
Live Stiffs (Mau Mau) (CD)
The Manchester Collection (LP)
The Most Fun You Can Have With
Your Clothes On – The Beserkley
Story (Sanctuary) (2-CD)
No Thanks – The 70s Punk Rebellion
(Rhino) (4-CD set)
1–2–3–4–5 (5-CD set)
Pogo A Go-Go (NME) (CD/cassette)
Punk – Lost & Found (Shanachie) (CD)
Punk Legends: The American Roots
(Jungle) (CD)
The Roxy, London WC2 (Sanctuary)
(6-CD set)

Sleepless In Seattle – The Birth Of
Grunge (Livewire) (CD)
Sniffin' Glue: The Essential Punk
Accessory (Sanctuary) (CD)
The Stiff Records Box Set (Demon)
(4-CD)
Street To Street: A Liverpool Album
(LP)
This Are Two-Tone (Two-Tone)
(CD)
Vaultage '78 (LP)
White Dopes On Punk (Sanctuary)
(2-CD)
Winters Of Discontent – The Peel
Sessions (Strange Fruit) (CD)

A companion 4-CD box-set, compiled and annotated by the author, is to be released in February 2007 on Sanctuary Records. Called *Babylon's Burning: The Rise Of Punk-Rock 1973–78*, it features rare and unreleased tracks by the likes of The New York Dolls, Ramones, Heartbreakers, Rocket from the Tombs, Pere Ubu, Radio Birdman, The Saints, Dr Feelgood, Sex Pistols, The Damned, Buzzcocks, Subway Sect, Wire, X-Ray Spex, The Adverts, The Only Ones, The Fall, The Undertones, Stiff Little Fingers and The Ruts.

Dramatis Personae

Albertine, Viv (The Slits)
Alvin, Dave (The Blasters)
Alvin, Phil (The Blasters)
Anderson, Charlie (Selecter)
Ant, Adam (and the Ants)
Ari Up (The Slits)
Arm, Mark (Green River/Mudhoney)★
Atkins, Martin (PiL)
Bailey, Chris (The Saints)
Baines, Una (The Fall)★
Baker, Danny (Journalist)
Bangs, Lester (Journalist)
Banks, Robin (Roadie for The Clash)
Bassick, Arturo (The Lurkers)
Bayley, Roberta (Photographer)★
Bell, Max (Journalist)
Bergamo, Al (Record Executive)
Bernstein, Nils (Sub-Pop Promotions)★
Bessy, Claude (*Slash* Editor)
Betrock, Alan (*New York Rocker* Editor/
    Publisher)★
Biafra, Jello (Dead Kennedys)
Biggs, Bob (Owner of Slash Label)
Birch, Will (Kursaal Flyers/The Records/
    Record Producer)★
Black Randy (& the Metro Squad)
Boon, Richard (Buzzcocks Manager)★
Bostrom, Derrick (The Meat Puppets)
Bradley, Mickey (The Undertones)
Bradshaw, Kim (The Saints)
Bramah, Martin (The Fall)★
Branca, Glenn (Theoretical Girls)
Branson, Richard (Owner of Virgin
    Records)
Brazier, Chris (Journalist)
Brunger, Frank (EMI Label-Manager)
Buck, Peter (REM)
Burchill, Julie (Journalist)
Burnel, Jean-Jacques (The Stranglers)

Burnham, Hugo (Gang of Four)★
Burns, Jake (Stiff Little Fingers)
Bushell, Gary (Journalist)
Byrne, David (Talking Heads)
Cacavas, Chris (Green on Red)
Callis, Jo (The Rezillos)★
Carducci, Joe (SST)★
Carr, Roy (Journalist)
Carrington, Sue (Make-Up/Designer)★
Casale, Jerry (Devo)
Case, Peter (Nerves/The Plimsouls)
Cave, Nick (The Birthday Party)★
Cervenka, Exene (X)
Chance, James (Teenage Jesus & the
    Jerks/The Contortions)★
Childers, Lee (Heartbreakers' Manager)
Chimes, Terry (The Clash)
Chrome, Cheetah (Rocket from the
    Tombs/Dead Boys)
Cobain, Kurt (Nirvana)
Coley, Byron (Journalist)
Congo, Kid (The Gun Club/The
    Cramps)
Conran, Sebastian (Social Secretary/
    Scenester)
Cook, Paul (Sex Pistols)
Coon, Caroline (Journalist)★★
Cope, Julian (Teardrop Explodes)
Cornwell, Hugh (The Stranglers)
Costello, Elvis (and the Attractions)
Coulson, Glen (Stiff Publicist)
County, Wayne (& the Electric Chairs)
Crowe, Curtis (Pylon)
Crutchfield, Robin (DNA)
Curtis, Deborah (Wife to Ian)
Curtis, Ian (Joy Division)
Czekowski, Andy (Co-owner of Roxy
    Club)★
Dadomo, Giovanni (Journalist)

Dalton, David (Journalist)
Dammers, Jerry (The Specials)
Davies, Dai (The Stranglers' Manager)
Deaves, Allan (The Worst)
Dee, Dave (Atlantic A&R)
Dempsey, Michael (The Adverts' Manager)
Denney, John (Weirdos)
Devoto, Howard (Buzzcocks/Magazine)★
Diggle, Steve (Buzzcocks)
Doe, John (X)
Dromette, Johnny (Drome Records)
Dudanski, Richard (101ers/PiL)★
Dury, Ian (& the Kilburns/& the Blockheads)
Edson, Richard (Sonic Youth)
Edwards, Eddie (The Vibrators)★
Ellis, John (The Vibrators)
Elmer, Wayne (Journalist)
Endino, Jack (Record Producer)
Eno (Record Producer)
Esso, Pete (The Lurkers)★
Fallon, B. P. (Ian Dury's Manager)
Farrell, Ray (SST)★
Foster, Greg (Journalist)
Fox, Paul (The Ruts)★
Frith, Simon (Journalist)
Fudger, Dave (Journalist)
Furious, Danny (The Avengers)
Fyfe, Fay (The Rezillos)
Gano, Gordon (Violent Femmes)
Gehman, Pleasant (LA Punk)
Genesis P. Orridge (Throbbing Gristle)
Gentleman, Sir Horace (The Specials)
Geza X (LA Punk)
Gilbert, Warwick (Radio Birdman)
Gill, Andy (Gang of Four)
Gillett, Charlie (DJ/Journalist)
Gilmore, Mikal (Journalist)
Ginn, Greg (Black Flag)
Goddard, Vic (Subway Sect)★
Gold, Jeff (Rhino Records)
Goldberg, Danny (Geffen Executive)
Goldman, Vivien (Journalist)★
Goodman, Dave (Sex Pistols Soundman/ Producer)★
Goulden, Eric (aka Wreckless Eric)

Green, Derek (A&M Executive)
Green, Johnny (The Clash roadie)
Greenhalgh, Tom (The Mekons)
Griffin, Sid (Long Ryders)★
Grohl, Dave (Nirvana)
Hannett, Martin (Record Producer)
Harries, Andrew (Journalist)
Harris, Bruce (CBS A&R)
Harron, Mary (Journalist)
Hart, Grant (Hüsker Dü)
Hedgecock, Ryan (Lone Justice)
Heffington, Don (Lone Justice)
Hell, Richard (Television/Heartbreakers/ & the Voidoids)★
Higgs, Eddie (Eddie & the Hot Rods)
Hook, Peter (Joy Division)
Hooley, Terri (Good Vibrations owner)
Houston, Penelope (The Avengers)★
Hulme, Susan (Mark P's Girlfriend)★
Humphrey, Simon (Record Producer)
Hynde, Chrissie (The Pretenders)
Ingham, Jonh (Journalist)★
James, Brian (The Damned)★
James, Tony (London SS/Generation X)★
Jennings, Seggs (The Ruts)★
Jesperson, Peter (Twin-Tone Records/ Replacements Manager)★
Johnson, Wilko (Dr Feelgood)★
Jones, Allan (Journalist)
Jones, Barry (Co-owner of Roxy Club)★★
Jones, Mick (London SS/The Clash)
Jones, Steve (Sex Pistols)
Jordan (Sex Shopgirl)
Kaye, Lenny (Patti Smith Group)★
Kellie, Mike (The Only Ones)
Kent, Nick (Journalist)★
Kerr, Tim (Big Boys)
King, Jon (Gang of Four)★
Kinman, Chip (The Dils/Rank & File)
Kinman, Tony (The Dils/Rank & File)
Knox (Lipstick/The Vibrators)★
Kristal, Hilly (CBGB's Owner)
Kuepper, Ed (The Saints)★
Langford, Jon (The Mekons)
Last, Bob (Fast Product owner)★
Laughner, Peter (Rocket from the Tombs/Pere Ubu/Friction)

Lee, C. P. (Alberto Y Lost Trios Paranoias)★
Lee, Jeannette (PiL)★
Leon, Craig (Record Producer)★
Letts, Don (Roxy DJ/Filmmaker)★
Levene, Keith (The Clash/PiL)
Lewis, Graham (Wire)★
Lindsay, Arto (DNA)
Linna, Miriam (The Cramps)
Lloyd, Richard (Television)
Lloyd, Robert (Prefects)★
Logic, Lora (X-Ray Spex/Essential Logic)★
Lopez, Robert (The Zeros)
Lowe, Nick (Record Producer)
Lowry, Ray (Cartoonist)
Lunch, Lydia (Teenage Jesus & the Jerks)
Lure, Walter (Heartbreakers)
Lydon, John (Sex Pistols/PiL)
MacGowan, Shane (The Nipple Erectors)★★
MacKaye, Ian (Minor Threat)
MacMillan, Andrew (Journalist)
Marsh, Dave (Journalist)
Martin, Gavin (Journalist)
Masuak, Chris (Radio Birdman)
Matlock, Glen (Sex Pistols/The Rich Kids)★
Maylward, Michael (Tin Huey)
McCullough, Dave (Journalist)
McFadden, Owen (Protex)★
McKee, Maria (Lone Justice)
McKenna, Kristine (Journalist)
McLaren Malcolm (Sex Pistols Manager)
McNeil, Phil (Journalist)
'Mensi' (Angelic Upstarts)
Mitchell, Tony (Journalist)
Mobbs, Nick (EMI A&R)
Montesion, Tony (LA Punk)
Moore, Thurston (Sonic Youth)
Morley, Paul (Journalist)
Morris, Keith (Photographer)
Morton, John (Electric Eels)★
Moss, Jon (The Clash)
Mothersbaugh, Mark (Devo)
Mould, Bob (Hüsker Dü)
Mueller, Andrew (Journalist)

'Mugger' (Black Flag roadie)
Mullen, Brendan (Owner of The Masque/LA Punk Chronicler)★
Murray, Charles Shaar (Journalist)
Needs, Kris (ZigZag Editor)★
Newman, Colin (Wire)★
Nolan, Jerry (Heartbreakers)
Novoselic, Kris (Nirvana)
Nuss, Woody (REM soundman)
O'Neill, John (The Undertones)★
October, Gene (Chelsea)★
Ogilvie, Gordon (Stiff Little Fingers' Manager/Lyricist)
Olive, Palm (The Slits/The Raincoats)★
Orme, John (Journalist)
Osbourne, Buzz (The Melvins)
Owen, Malcolm (The Ruts)
Parker, Graham (& the Rumour)
Parry, Chris (Polydor A&R/Record Producer)
Parsons, Tony (Journalist)
Patterson, Phreddie (Back Door Man Editor)★
Pavitt, Bruce (Sub-Pop Co-owner)
Pearlman, Sandy (Record Producer)
Perez, Louis (Los Lobos)
Perrett, Peter (The Only Ones)
Perry, John (The Only Ones)★
Perry, Mark (Sniffin' Glue Editor/ Alternative TV)
Pirroni, Marco (Siouxsie & the Banshees/ Adam & the Ants)★
Poneman, Jonathan (Sub Pop Co-Owner)
Pressler, Charlotte (Peter Laughner's wife)★
Pursey, Jimmy (Sham 69)
Quine, Bob (Richard Hell & the Voidoids)★
Radiation, Roddy (The Specials)
Rambali, Paul (Journalist)
Ramone, Dee Dee (Ramones)
Ramone, Joey (Ramones)
Ramone, Tommy (Ramones)★
Ranaldo, Lee (Sonic Youth)★
Ravenstine, Allen (Pere Ubu)★
Rev, Martin (Suicide)

Reynolds, Eugene (The Rezillos)
Rhodes, Bernie (The Clash Manager)
Richmond, Sophie (Sex Pistols' Secretary)
Riley, Paul (Stiff Employee)
Ringenberg, Jason (& the Nashville Scorchers)★
Ritchie, Brian (Violent Femmes)
Rivera, Jake (Co-founder of Stiff/ Manager)
'Roadent' (Sex Pistols/The Clash roadie)
Robbins, Ira (Journalist)
Robertson, Sandy (Journalist)
Robinson, Dave (Co-founder of Stiff)
Robinson, Lisa (Journalist)
Robinson, Tom (TRB)
Rogers, Rick (The Specials' Manager)
Rollins, Henry (Black Flag)
Roman, Cliff (Weirdos)
Ruffy, Dave (The Ruts)★
Rumour, Ray (*Search & Destroy* Staff-Writer)★
Sage, Greg (The Wipers)
Sager, Gareth (The Pop Group)
Savage, Jon (Journalist)
Scabies, Rat (The Damned)★
Schneider, Michael (Journalist)
Schoenfelt, Phil (Disturbed Furniture)
Sensible, Captain (The Damned)
Severin, Steve (Siouxsie & the Banshees)★
Shapiro, Susan (Journalist)
Sharkey, Feargal (The Undertones)
Shelley, Pete (Buzzcocks)
Shithead, Joey (DOA)
Silverton, Pete (Journalist)
Simmons, Sylvie (Journalist)
Simonon, Paul (The Clash)
Siouxsie Sioux (and the Banshees)
Smear, Pat (Germs)
Smith, Bruce (The Pop Group)
Smith, Mark E. (The Fall)
Smith, Patti (NY poetess/Patti Smith Group)
Smith, Paul (Blast First/Mute)
Smith, TV (The Adverts)★
Sommers, Tim (Journalist)

Sowders, Greg (Long Ryders)★
Spector, Phil (Record Producer)
Spedding, Chris (Guitarist/Record Producer)★
Spencer, Neil (Journalist)
Spheeris, Penelope (Filmmaker)
Stein, Chris (Blondie)★
Stein, Seymour (Sire Records)
Sterling, Linder (Buzzcocks Designer)★
Stern, Mark (Youth Brigade)
Stevenson, Nils (Banshees Manager)
Stewart, Mark (The Pop Group)★
Strike, Johnny (Crime)
Strummer, Joe (The Clash)
Stuart, Dan (Green on Red)
Styrene, Poly (X Ray Spex)
Suck, Jane (Journalist)
Sullivan, Bill (The Replacements soundman)
Sumner, Bernard (Joy Division)
Symmons, Rob (Subway Sect)★
Tek, Deniz (Radio Birdman)★
Temple, Julian (Filmmaker)
Tennant, Neil (Scenester)
Thomas, Chris (Record Producer)★
Thomas, David (Rocket from the Tombs/Pere Ubu)★
Thorne, Mike (Record Producer)
Tibieri, John 'Boogie' (Sex Pistols' roadie)
Timperley, Clive (101ers)
Tish and Snooky (Blondie/The Sic Fucks)★
'Tracie' (Sex Pistols' Secretary)
Trakin, Roy (Journalist)
Travis, Geoff (Rough Trade Owner)★
Turner, Steve (Green River/Mudhoney)★
Tutti, Cosey Fanni (Throbbing Gristle)
Ure, Midge (The Rich Kids)
Valentine, Gary (Blondie)
Valentine, Jeremy (The Cortinas)
Vanian, Dave (The Damned)
Vanilla, Cherry (NY Chanteuse/Actress)★★
Varnom, John (Virgin Executive)
Vega, Alan (Suicide)★
Verlaine, Tom (Television)★
Vig, Butch (Record Producer)

Ving, Lee (Fear)
Wakeling, Dave (The Beat)
Wall, Mick (Journalist)
Wallington-Lloyd, Helen (Sex Employee)
Watt, Mike (The Minutemen)★
Watts, Ron (100 Club owner)
Weizmann, Danny (Journalist)
Weller, John (The Jam Manager)
Westerberg, Paul (The Replacements)
Westwood, Vivienne (Fashion Designer/
   Co-owner of Sex)
Weymouth, Tina (Talking Heads)
Wheldon, Michael (Mirrors)★

Williams, Richard (Journalist/Island
   A&R)★
Wilson, Chris (Flamin' Groovies)★
Wilson, Tony (Factory Records Owner)
Witts, Dick (Manchester Music
   Collective/The Passage)★
Wobble, Jah (PiL)
Wood, Andrew (Mother Love Bone)
Wood, Ian (Journalist)
Wynn, Steve (Dream Syndicate)★
Young, Brian (Rudi)★
Younger, Rob (Radio Birdman)★
Zoom, Billy (X)

★ – all asterisked names were
   interviewed by the author
★★ – double-asterisked names were
   interviewed on behalf of the
   author by Nina Antonia

Acknowledgements

Writing *Babylon's Burning* has been in many ways a case of unfinished business for myself. Having started my own version of the history of punk back in 1990, with *From the Velvets to the Voidoids*, I have sat back and watched a significant number of books misrepresent the period, written by folk with those special specs that come complete with bias bifocals. I have tried to maintain the same stance as that earlier tome, which was itself republished in 2005, and have been gratified by how many of my interviewees both knew and loved that earlier work.

So firstly, I must thank each and every interviewee for time taken to set things righter and straighter (hopefully). Their names are all given in the Dramatis Personae, so I won't bore the reader with another litany of names, but suffice to say, I have tried to quote everyone verbatim where possible. As per previous tomes, though, when earlier chroniclers have better expressed the same sense I sought, I have not shied away from giving their version priority. They are hopefully all namechecked in the bibliography but a nod of the hat must assuredly go to the likes of Jon Savage, Marcus Gray, Stephen Colegrave and Jason Gross (whose Perfect Sound Forever website continues to fan the flames).

As always with such a tangled web of a book, those who facilitated contacts and generated input from others are the unsung heroes of this venture. I'd particularly like to single out Paul Smith at Mute, who moved mountains on my behalf; Nina Antonia, who made a whole series of initial calls on my behalf, and shared her own archive of interviews into the bargain; Susan Hulme, who typed up transcripts, gave me a place to crash when interviewing New Yorkers, and tried to track yet more elusive souls down on my behalf; and finally Joe Carducci, who opened the portals on the American alternative scene of the 80s for a bemused Brit.

Others who couldn't have been more helpful in providing names and contact points were as follows: Mike Baess, Will Birch, Richard Boon, Jean Encoule, Erik Flannigan, Raymond Foye, Pat Gilbert, Colin Harper, Andrew Hasson, Nick Hill, Greil Marcus, Mick Marshall, Mick

Middles, Brandan Mullen, Phreddie Patterson, Mark Paytress, Bob Strano, Brian Swirsky, Jeremy Tepper, Pat Thomas, Steve Turner, Simon Warner and Mark Wyeth. A double shot of the author's love to y'all.

Inevitably, a little audio excavation was also an intrinsic part of the process, and the following sent a steady stream of lost tapes, recast CDs and general audio info my way: Rick Conrad at Warners, Steve Hammond and John Reed at Sanctuary, and Dave Knight and Scott Curran at their respective home-archives. Thanks must also be extended to Simon at trakMARX for providing constant reminders of the whys and wherefores of the era.

When it came to the monumental amount of printed matter, contemporary and post-punk [sic], I was once again beholden in multiple ways on many a day to my indefatigable friend Steve Shepherd, at Manchester's Henry Watson Music Library. Colin Harper and Andrew Sclanders also helped me find some of the printed oddities of the era. And the ever-obliging Sean Body at Helter Skelter kindly sent published and unpublished goodies from his archive.

The photographers Jonh Ingham, Linder Sterling and Naomi Peterson (RIP) also have my eternal thanks for having the wit to snap away at the time; and letting me have the visual counterpoint to my screed. Good vibes, too, to Jo Callis, Tony James and Tim Pittman for providing photos from their personal archives.

Finally, I'd like to thank my copy editor, Shân Morley Jones, for her thoroughness; Tad Floridis at Canongate; and my long-standing editor, Tony Lacey at Penguin, for helping make the whole thing blend. Now it's hopefully out of my system . . .

Clinton Heylin
2006

And in the End . . .

Yes, I too felt galvanized into forming a punk band, The Pits. We were. We made Mancunian contemporaries like The Worst and The Drones sound like Genesis. Aside from murdering the usual punk standards, myself and friend Alex penned a few originals, with titles like 'Sleep A Little Longer Grandma', 'Thank You God (Now Get Off)' and 'Keep It Up (But Above All Keep It)'. Though we never got to make a record, we did somehow manage to 'headline' a punk festival in Tewkesbury. As for any contribution from The Pits to a latter-day *Nuggets*, I'd want it to be this lost punk classic . . .

TERMINAL CASE

(Heylin-Salem)

Remember back to that sunny afternoon,
Or that evening when you and I stood looking at the moon,
Or that time we went bathing and you fell in the sea,
Cast your mind back and think about me.

You couldn't have known then 'bout the pain in my chest,
Or the fact that the doctor had carried out tests,
I waited six weeks, till the results came through,
And even then, baby, I couldn't tell you.

Chorus
I'm gonna die, I'm gonna die,
It's time that you and I said goodbye,
'Cause baby, I'm a terminal case.

It looks as though I've only got six months to go,
I'm not gonna make it, still you don't know,
The doctor keeps saying what an interesting case,
But I can tell my time's up by the look on his face.

The time to my funeral service is short,
I've made sure my coffin is already bought,
So when I enter into my final throes,
Start selling off my kidneys and my clothes.

Chorus

When I've given up this one-sided fight,
And the priest has given me the last rites,
And you, my babe, live here safe and sound,
Remember me six feet under the ground.
'Cause when to my Maker I am sent,
You'll find I've left you nothing in my testament.

Chorus

Index